The Acquisition of
Private Companies

The Acquisition of Private Companies

Sixth Edition

WJL Knight LLB, *Solicitor*
Partner, Simmons & Simmons

LONGMAN

© WJL Knight 1992

ISBN 0 85121 867 9

Published by
Longman Group UK Limited
21-27 Lamb's Conduit Street, London WC1N 3NJ

First published 1975
Sixth edition 1992

Associated offices

Australia, Hong Kong, Malaysia, Singapore, USA

All rights reserved. No part of this publication may be reproduced, stored in a retrieval system, or transmitted, in any form or by any means, electronic, mechanical, photocopying, recording or otherwise, without prior written permission of the copyright owner, or a licence permitting restricted copying issued by the Copyright Licensing Agency Ltd, 90 Tottenham Court Road, London W1P 9HE. Any such request to the copyright owner should be addressed in the first instance to the publishers.

A CIP catalogue record for this book is available from the British Library.

Typeset by Kerrypress Ltd, Luton.
Printed in Great Britain by Biddles of Guildford Ltd.

Contents

Contents

xi

Preface

The aim of this book remains the same, to provide a guide for the practising solicitor who is engaged in the acquisition or disposal of a private company. I hope that the book will continue to be of interest to accountants, bankers and others engaged in acquisitions.

The format of this edition has been changed and it now contains 17 chapters instead of seven. A number of the topics formerly dealt with under the head of 'general considerations' have grown to the length of chapters in their own right and the new format reflects this. The sections on financial assistance, competition law, and pensions, which now appear as separate chapters, have been recast by my partners Jane Newman, Peter Freeman and Michael Wyman respectively. Three new chapters appear, on acquisition structures, Europe and insolvency. My partner Roy Montague-Jones wrote the chapter on Europe and Jane Newman contributed the chapter on insolvency, with invaluable help from Jonathan Downey. The chapter on acquisitions by a listed company has been substantially revised to reflect changes in the *Yellow Book* and Paul Hale has reworked the chapters on taxation and has contributed much new material. I am very grateful for all this assistance.

As can be seen, it would not be possible to revise this work were it not for the help of my colleagues at Simmons & Simmons. Apart from those I acknowledge above my thanks are also due to Roger Butterworth (the agreement for sale), Stephen Coleclough (tax points on the agreement for sale), Janet Gaymer (employment), Nicholas Heald (title), Martin Smith (competition law), and Stephen Tromans (environment). Colin Mercer contributed valuable material and Richard Willoughby helped with research. I am very grateful to Kim Lyle of Ernst & Young who revised the financial information in Chapter 17 and to Jane Newman (again) who brought the documents in that chapter up to date.

The law and practice of acquisitions is a moving target and as we go to press a new version of the *Yellow Book* is due to appear for consultation. I am sorry that this could not be included.

I remain responsible for the errors and omissions. Subject thereto, the law given is that in force in England on 1 October 1992.

London,   WJL Knight
October 1992

Table of Cases

xv

Table of Statutes

xxi

Table of Statutes

Table of Statutory Instruments

EC Legislation

Chapter 1

Introduction

There are approximately 975,000 active companies registered in Great Britain and of these only about 11,500 are public companies. Although these figures give no guide to the proportion of the nation's business which is carried on through private companies, they give some indication of the popularity of the private company as a vehicle for trade and investment.

This book deals, mainly from the point of view of a purchaser, with the legal aspects of the acquisition of the share capital of a company where the selling shareholders are few enough to enable negotiations to be carried on with them individually. The company whose shares are to be acquired (called the 'target' throughout this book) in such a transaction may be a public company but is more likely to be private. Public companies are recognisable by the inclusion in their name of the words 'public limited company' or the abbreviation 'p l c' and the privilege they enjoy is the right to issue shares to the public. All other companies are private companies, and a company with a limited number of shareholders will not normally need public company status, neither will it wish to be subject to the burdens imposed on public companies by the Companies Acts.

When those who trade or invest through a private company come to dispose of their business they are faced with a choice of methods. The target can sell its assets, or the shareholders can sell their shares in the target. The latter approach is popular, not only because it is a simpler transaction, involving a transfer of ownership only of the shares in the target, but also for tax reasons. A sale of shares will normally involve individual shareholders in a charge to capital gains tax on any gain realised, but if a company sells its capital assets the company will pay corporation tax on any net gains realised and it will then be difficult to pass the consideration to individual shareholders without further taxation (eg capital gains tax on a deemed disposal of their shares in a winding-up). Vendors will, therefore, often wish to

1

sell shares rather than procure a sale of assets by the target, and a purchaser who wishes to preserve the benefit of tax losses available to the target will certainly buy shares rather than assets. These issues are considered further on p 164.

There is, however, one essential difference between purchasing the assets of a business and buying shares. A company is a person and has the capacity not only to own assets but also to incur contractual, tortious and even criminal liabilities. Therefore, when acquiring a company, it is necessary to evaluate not only the target's assets but also its liabilities. Where the shares to be acquired are the entire issued share capital of the target, the rights attaching to the shares have little or no importance and it is necessary to concentrate not upon the shares which are being bought and sold but upon the target itself.

Although investigation may go some way to establish whether or not the target owns the assets which it is said to own, the most intensive and searching enquiries cannot conclusively establish the extent of the liabilities which the target owes. It is therefore the practice for the purchaser to require warranties and indemnities from the vendors in respect of the target's affairs. These are considered in Chapter 9 and, insofar as they relate to taxation, in Chapter 13.

Regulation of acquisitions

The regulations which affect a takeover bid for a listed company are not normally applicable to the acquisition of a private company. The City Code on Takeovers and Mergers applies to listed and unlisted public companies considered by the Panel to be resident in the United Kingdom, the Channel Islands or the Isle of Man but only applies to private companies if:

  (a) their equity share capital has been listed on the London Stock Exchange at any time during the ten years prior to the relevant date; or

  (b) dealings in their equity share capital have been advertised in a newspaper on a regular basis for a continuous period of at least six months in the ten years prior to the relevant date; or

  (c) their equity share capital has been subject to a marketing arrangement as described in the Companies Act 1985, s 163(2)(b) at any time during the ten years prior to the relevant date (eg their shares have been dealt in on the Unlisted Securities Market); or

  (d) they have filed a prospectus for the issue of equity share capital at the Companies' Registry at any time during the ten years prior to the relevant date.

In each case, the relevant date is the date on which an announcement is made of a proposed or possible offer for the target or the date on which some other event occurs in relation to the target which has significance under the Code.

The City Panel appreciates that the provisions of the Code may not be appropriate to all statutory and chartered companies or to all private companies falling within the categories listed above and will, therefore, apply the Code with a degree of flexibility in suitable cases.

The Code also applies if the transaction amounts to a reverse take-over of a listed company. A reverse takeover involves the acquisition for shares by a listed company of an unlisted one in circumstances in which the number of shares issued as consideration by the listed company is so great that a change in the control of the listed company results. In those cases the Panel claims authority and expects full compliance with the Code.

Although the rules and regulations of the London Stock Exchange may affect the transaction, if the target is unlisted they will only apply if either the vendor or purchaser is a listed company (see Chapter 10).

Taxation apart, there is little legislation which has specific application to the transfer of ownership of private companies. The Stock Transfer Act 1963 prescribes a form of transfer which may be used and some sections of the Companies Act 1985 (notably s 151: see Chapter 5) place restraints upon some aspects of the transaction; but there is, for instance, no legislation which implies any term into an agreement for the sale of shares. Schemes of arrangement under the Companies Act 1985, s 425, are rarely used as a method of acquiring a private company in the circumstances with which this book deals and equally rare is the application of s 428 et seq of that Act for the purpose of acquiring the shares of dissenting minority holders.

Those who are concerned in a professional capacity with the sale and purchase of shares in private companies must consider whether they are carrying on investment business within the meaning of the Financial Services Act 1986 and therefore need to be authorised under its provisions. Activities constituting investment business are described in Sched 1 to the Act, and those which might be relevant are para 12 (dealing in investments as principal or agent), para 13 (arranging deals in investments) and para 15 (advising investors or potential investors on the merits of purchasing or selling an investment). Paragraph 21 of Sched 1, however, provides that paras 12, 13 and 15 do not apply in relation to the acquisition or disposal of shares in a body corporate other than an open-ended investment company if (in summary) more than 75 per cent of the voting share capital of the body corporate is involved in the transaction and the acquisition and disposal is between parties each of whom is a body corporate, a partnership, a single individual, or a group of connected individuals. For this purpose, a 'group of connected individuals' means people who are connected to the directors and managers of the target by being close relatives of them. 'Close relative' means a spouse, child, parent, brother or sister. If less than 75 per cent of the target is involved in the transaction, or if even one of the shareholders is not connected to a present director or manager (eg if one of them is a former director's widow) then the exemption will not apply and apparently, will not apply to those involved on either side.

Solicitors who advise on acquisitions can take some comfort from para 24 of Sched 1 which provides that para 15 (giving advice) does not apply to advice which is given in the course of a profession and the giving of which is a necessary part of other advice or services given in the course of carrying on that professional business. The paragraph goes on to provide that advice is not to be regarded as falling within the exemption if it is remunerated separately from other advice. It is to be assumed that para 15 is intended to catch advice given on the acquisition or sale of shares as an investment and not, eg, tax advice or advice about warranties and indemnities. In the case of an acquisition of a private company it is quite difficult to differentiate between the legal advice on the contract and commercial advice upon the merits of the shares as an investment. In this sense, the exception given in para 24 should be helpful. In any event, the problem does not exist for solicitors who are certified by the Law Society in its capacity as a recognised professional body as they are authorised persons. In their case, giving advice as to the merits of an investment in a private company in this context is likely to be 'incidental' within the meaning of the Solicitors Investment Business Rules 1988 and will not constitute discrete investment business.

Solicitors who contact shareholders in order to get them to join in a sale of shares will be wary of the Financial Services Act 1986, s 56 which forbids unsolicited calls 'by way of business' and unenforceable investment agreements entered into as a result of a prohibited 'cold call'. The Solicitors Investment Business Rules 1988, r 8(4) contain an exception which permits a firm to enter into an investment agreement in the course of or in consequence of a cold call in certain circumstances, but does not seem to cover investment agreements entered into with a third party. The s 56 prohibition forbids the firm from procuring or endeavouring to procure an agreement as well as from entering into one.

Section 57 of the Financial Services Act 1986 is relevant where the acquisition involves a circular to shareholders or other investment advertisement. These issues are dealt with on p 22.

Chapter 2

Acquisition Structures

Once the basic decision to buy shares rather than assets has been taken, there are a number of factors which, time and again, affect the structure of a company acquisition. They are, in no particular order:

Shareholder approval and ABI guidelines
Share premium account
Roll-over relief
Intra-group transfers
The Companies Act 1985, s 151
Preference shares in the target

Of course, these are not the only issues which can affect the structure of an acquisition, but they are factors which often have a significant impact. Most of these issues are dealt with in more detail elsewhere in this book: their treatment here is only an outline, focusing on points which often arise in practice. This chapter concludes with examples which show the interaction of some of the elements.

SHAREHOLDER APPROVAL AND ABI GUIDELINES

These issues arise where the purchaser or the vendor is a listed company. Shareholder approval can be required either because the acquisition itself requires approval or because the creation or allotment of share capital in association with the acquisition requires approval. These issues are dealt with in more detail in Chapter 10, but essentially, approval will be required under the London Stock Exchange *Yellow Book* if the transaction is Super Class 1 (more than 25 per cent of profits or assets) or Class 4 (a transaction with a director or substantial shareholder). The Companies Acts will require a shareholders' meeting if it is necessary to increase capital, or to disapply the Companies Act 1985, s 89 which requires that issues for cash must be approved by special resolution unless first offered to existing shareholders. The Companies Act 1985, s 320 provides that shareholder approval is required if the transaction is with a director or a person connected with a director. This mirrors Class 4 requirements but applies to all companies, listed or not (p 21).

Where shareholder approval of the transaction itself is required, there is little that can be done except to comply. Almost invariably, the acquisition agreement will be entered into before the notice of meeting and explanatory circular are sent to shareholders and completion of the acquisition will be conditional upon the passing of the necessary resolution (although there is a technical problem with s 320 – see p 21). The vendors will try to secure, as far as they can, that the directors of the purchaser will recommend the transaction to their shareholders. Directors should not bind themselves to act in breach of their fiduciary duties and therefore, it was generally thought that if circumstances change between contract and completion, directors must be free to change their recommendation (see *John Crowther Group v Carpets International* [1990] BCLC 460). In *Fulham Football Club v Cabra* (1992) *The Times*, 11 September the Court of Appeal made it clear, however, that directors can bind themselves as to the future exercise of their fiduciary powers, citing with approval the Australian case of *Thorby v Goldberg* (1964) 112 CLR 597 where the court said:

> If, when a contract is negotiated on behalf of a company, the directors think it in the interests of the company as a whole that the transaction should be entered into and carried into effect they may bind themselves by the contract to do whatever is necessary to effectuate it.

The *Fulham* decision should not be taken to overrule *John Crowther* which, the court said, might be justified on its own facts. Directors will seek to avoid such undertakings, where they can.

The questions of increase of capital and authority to allot raise more complicated issues. An increase of capital will normally involve an ordinary resolution, requiring 14 clear days' notice, as will authority to allot under the Companies Act 1985, s 80. A disapplication of s 89 however will require a special resolution and 21 clear days' notice and this may have adverse timetable implications. If the acquisition is a major one and, for market reasons, a rights issue is required, s 89 will fall to be considered because, of course, a rights issue is an issue for cash. However, it is probable (although not axiomatic) that the purchaser will have in place a general authority, passed at its latest annual general meeting, which will permit a rights issue of existing authorised share capital, even where the rights issue does not comply with the strict statutory requirements of s 89 *et seq.* Therefore, provided there is sufficient unissued share capital of the class required, a rights issue will not, of itself, require a shareholders' meeting. However, in practice, it is only the largest acquisitions which would be funded by a rights issue and it often happens therefore that the acquisition is Super Class 1, requiring shareholder approval of the acquisition itself.

Similarly, a vendor placing, in which the shares in the target are acquired in exchange for shares in the purchaser which are immediately placed on behalf of the vendors by the purchaser's financial advisers, will not in practice require shareholder approval unless the transaction itself requires approval (eg because it is Super Class 1). So long as the purchaser has sufficient unissued share capital it is likely that it will also, in practice, have authority to allot the capital under s 80 of the Companies Act 1985 and as the issue is technically not an issue for cash, the s 89 authority is not in point. The guidelines issued by the investment committee of the Association of British Insurers and others may, however, require an open offer to be made to shareholders.

The ABI guidelines indicate practices which its members will support. Broadly speaking, these guidelines are designed to ensure that major issues of shares do not take place at a discount unless offered to existing shareholders. The guidelines require disapplication of the Companies Act 1985, s 89 to be reviewed annually and to be limited to 5 per cent of the existing issued capital, with a cumulative limit of $7\frac{1}{2}$ per cent for non pre-emptive issues for cash in any rolling three year period. As a result, companies are not able to fund acquisitions by means of cash placings to selected shareholders but must structure issues for cash either as rights issues or accept the need for a meeting to pass a special resolution to disapply s 89, bearing in mind that institutional shareholders may well be inclined to oppose the resolution if the shares are placed at a discount of more than 5 per cent (although prior consultation with the investment committee of the ABI is always possible). The guidelines are reinforced by the *Yellow Book*, para 18, Chapter 2, Section 1 and para 37, Chapter 2, Section 5 which repeat the requirement for annual renewal of the authority. ABI guidelines also limit the amount of unissued capital over which there is s 80 authority to allot to one third of existing issued capital, but of itself this will not normally impede an acquisition, as any acquisition requiring capital in excess of that limit is likely to need an ordinary resolution of approval for some other reason.

Partly as a result of this regime, the vendor placing is a popular method of using shares to fund an acquisition. A vendor placing involves the allotment of shares in the purchaser to the vendors in exchange for shares in the target. The consideration shares are then placed on behalf of the vendors by the purchaser's bank or broker. Thus the purchaser funds the acquisition through a share issue while the vendors receive cash. A vendor placing is not a cash issue of shares and therefore does not require s 89 disapplication. However, ABI guidelines do not permit placings involving more than 10 per cent of the company's issued share capital or a discount greater than 5 per cent unless clawback is offered. Clawback is an offer to existing shareholders of the shares to be placed. The 5 per cent discount is calculated by comparing the mid-market price with the offering price net of the commission charged by the bank or broker undertaking responsibility for the placing. The London Stock Exchange will require an open offer to be open for 15 business days, but apart from that there are no prescribed formalities, unless listing particulars are required (see p 138). The offer is normally made by the bank or the broker as agent for the vendors.

SHARE PREMIUM ACCOUNT

Whether or not any particular acquisition is accounted for according to the acquisition method of accounting or the merger method of accounting is decided according to the appropriate accounting rules (to be found in the Companies Act 1985, Sched 4A, para 7 *et seq* and SSAP 23). These are summarised on p 96 and are, as usual, in debate at the time this book goes to print. It will be seen however, that whatever accounting method is chosen, the requirement to have a share premium account gives rise to problems. In the barest possible outline, the problem can be summarised by saying that merger accounting, in the limited cases where it is applicable, does not give rise to goodwill on consolidation while acquisition accounting will do so where the price paid for the target exceeds the value of the target's assets. Writing off goodwill through the profit and loss account depresses earnings and purchasers will wish to deal with the goodwill in some other way, normally by writing it off against reserves. Share premium account is not available to be written off so that creation of a large share premium account as a result of an acquisition is unwelcome because it has the indirect effect of depressing future earnings.

The Companies Act 1985, s 131 provides that it is not necessary to create a share premium account where the company issuing the consideration shares 'has secured at least a 90 per cent equity holding in another company in pursuance of an arrangement providing for the allotment of equity shares in the issuing company ...' (see p 95).

Where the equity share capital of the target is divided into different classes, s 131 does not apply unless the requirements are satisfied in relation to each of the classes taken separately. Where the arrangement involves the acquisition of non-equity shares in the target, relief extends to the issue of consideration shares in exchange for those non-equity shares.

Where it is not possible to structure the acquisition so as to avoid the need to create a share premium account, eg because it must be funded through a rights issue, it is possible to apply to the court to reduce capital by writing down the share premium account (see, for example, *Re Thorn EMI plc* (1988) 4 BCC 698). This procedure produces a reserve against which goodwill can be written off.

ROLL-OVER RELIEF

Tax can affect the structure of an acquisition in so many ways that it is difficult to pick out points that have overriding significance. Issues which affect the taxation of vendors are dealt with in Chapter 11.

In cases where the vendors accept shares or debentures as consideration for their shares, and intend to retain them, then it is clearly important to obtain roll-over relief. The conditions for roll-over relief are dealt with in detail on p 175. There is no difficulty in complying with them in a normal acquisition because as a result of the exchange the purchaser will hold more than one-quarter of the ordinary share capital of the target. One problem which sometimes causes structural difficulties however is that the shares must be issued by the purchasing company, ie the company which will hold, directly, more than one-quarter of the ordinary share capital of the target. Thus, if a listed purchaser wishes to acquire a company through one of its subsidiaries, arrangements can be made to issue shares in the parent to the vendors to satisfy the consideration, but the exchange is not eligible for roll-over relief because the consideration shares are not shares in the direct purchaser. In such a case, if relief is to be obtained, the target can be acquired by the purchaser and sold down to the subsidiary subsequently, but sometimes it may be necessary for shares in the subsidiary to be issued to the vendors and then for the parent to buy back the shares in the subsidiary by means of a subsequent exchange for shares in the parent. Shares which are issued to vendors momentarily in this way and then repurchased are sometimes called 'flip flops'.

Tax requirements can give rise to movements of assets or shares in the target within a vendor group prior to the sale. This can arise for a number of reasons, for example the requirement to sell shares in the target to a company with capital losses, before the shares are sold outside the group, thus crystallising the gain in a company which is able to offset losses against the gain arising on the sale. Where part only of the business is to be sold, tax and commercial considerations may dictate that assets are removed from the target and then the target itself sold, as opposed to the alternative option of selling to the purchaser out of the target that part of the business which is to be sold. For the corporate lawyer, these intra-group transactions raise problems of their own, and they are referred to below.

INTRA-GROUP TRANSFERS

Transferring assets inside a group before a company is sold causes more problems than are generally realised. Take a simple case in which a parent wishes to transfer the target inside the group so that it can be sold by a company which has capital losses against which the gain can be set. The price at which the target is transferred intra-group will have no effect on the taxation of the sale, and the normal reaction is to transfer the target at book value ie for a consideration equal to the value at which the shares in the target stand in the books of the vendor group, and to leave the consideration outstanding on loan account.

Suppose target T is owned by the vendor's subsidiary S, and it is proposed that the shares in T are to be transferred to be held directly by the vendor (V) before they are sold. To start with the obvious, the directors of S have a fiduciary duty to S not to dispose of the corporate assets at less than fair market value. Provided S is solvent, this does not in practice present any difficulty. In *Rolled Steel Products (Holdings) Ltd v British Steel Corporation* [1986] 1 Ch 246 it was held that the shareholders can unanimously ratify an act by directors which, although technically within the powers of the company contained in its memorandum, is done to serve a purpose other than the interests of the company. In this case, the court would probably be willing to imply the consent of V, as the sole shareholder, although for their own protection the directors of S should insist on the written instructions of V.

What gives rise to more difficulty in practice is the question of distributable profits. *Aveling Barford Ltd v Perion Ltd* (1989) 5 BCC 677 is authority for the proposition that a sale of property by a company at an undervalue to one of its shareholders or to a company controlled by one of its shareholders is a distribution of the amount of the undervalue. If, for example, the book value of T in the books of S is £750,000 but its market value is £1,000,000, then a transfer by S to V of the shares in T for £750,000 will amount to a distribution by S to V of £250,000. *Aveling Barford* was a case involving a company which had no distributable reserves and was decided on the basis of the common law rules relating to distributions. If carried to their logical conclusion and applied in the context of the statutory restrictions on distribution the principles followed in that case give rise to a number of problems for companies which are solvent but whose reserves are not sufficient to cover the distribution.

Under the Companies Act 1985, s 263 a distribution may only be made out of profits available for the purpose, and under s 270, distribution must be justified by reference to the latest annual accounts or interim accounts, if the annual accounts do not show sufficient reserves. Thus, if S has reserves of less than £250,000 a sale of the property at book value will, if considered a distribution, apparently be unlawful. Nevertheless the £250,000 represents a profit, albeit unrealised and unrecorded, of S and ordinary principles of company law ought to require that S should be free to distribute that profit by distribution of the asset itself, so long as S is solvent after the distribution so that the interests of creditors are protected. It is clear that, if S were to declare a dividend *in specie* of T, S would only need reserves of £750,000 (ie the book value of T) to cover the distribution. Thus, if V were to make a capital contribution of £750,000 to S, creating the necessary reserves, T could then be distributed back to V, creating the same economic result as a sale at £750,000. Incidentally, the capital contribution would not increase the base cost of S for capital gains tax purposes.

The Companies Act 1985, s 276 ought to help. It says that when a company makes a distribution of or including a non-cash asset and any part of the amount at which that asset is stated in the accounts relevant for the purposes of the distribution represents an unrealised profit, that profit is to be treated as a realised profit for the purpose of determining the lawfulness of the distribution. Thus, if T in fact stood in the books of S at its market value, namely £1,000,000, then S would have an additional unrealised profit of £250,000 which could be treated as realised for the purposes of determining the lawfulness of the distribution. As the amount of the distribution is only £250,000 it will be covered by the profit. To this it can be objected that it is not clear that s 276 applies to a deemed distribution of the *Aveling Barford* type, nor is it clear that the asset stated in the accounts is the asset which is distributed; it is the undervalue which is distributed, not the asset itself. The more robust view is that once transactions are treated as distributions they ought to be so treated for all purposes, including s 276 and, construing s 276 reasonably broadly, the asset in fact distributed is the property (or that part of the property which is not paid for) and that is the same asset which is stated in the accounts at an amount which includes an unrealised profit.

Unfortunately, s 276 is of no help where the asset has not been revalued but is shown at its original cost. To take advantage of s 276 a revaluation is necessary and it may be said that it seems artificial to revalue the asset to market value, draw up accounts, and then sell the asset at its original book value. However, the act of drawing up accounts does provide some safeguards. As a matter of common law, directors should not make distributions where they know that losses have been incurred which would have the effect, if accounts were prepared, of reducing reserves below the level of the distribution. The drawing of accounts is, however, of some additional protection because it forces these issues to be considered. Similarly, if a capital contribution were made to increase reserves, as suggested above, accounts would be required before the asset could be distributed. Thus the obvious ways through the *Aveling Barford* maze do involve some additional protection for creditors. On the other hand it must be said that the accounting recognition of an *Aveling Barford* distribution raises very difficult questions. Suppose S had the necessary reserves, would they be reduced by £250,000 after the transfer of T at book value?

Pending further authority it is not clear how the proposition in *Aveling Barford* interacts with the statutory restrictions on distributions. Where reserves are insufficient the safest course is to transfer the asset at market value. This will then result in a realised profit which is available to be distributed back to the parent once accounts are drawn which comply with s 270. In such a case it is better to pay cash for the asset as there can then be no doubt that the profit is 'realised'. Whether or not the profit is regarded as realised where the consideration is left outstanding on loan account will, however, depend on accounting principles (see s 262(3)) and advice from the auditors should be sought.

Where the transfer is by the target itself there is an overriding consideration. As will be seen below, the Companies Act 1985, s 151, has the practical effect of requiring the transfer of assets in these cases to be made at market value, for cash payable on completion.

THE COMPANIES ACT 1985, s 151

This section is dealt with in detail in Chapter 5. Problems arise where the target itself is a party to any transaction which is entered into for the purpose of the sale. Thus, where the purchaser is not to acquire some of the target's assets, and they are transferred out of the target to the vendors or within the vendor group prior to the sale of the target, then in addition to the points discussed above under the heading of 'Intra-group transfers', the question will arise as to whether the transfer constitutes unlawful financial assistance.

Financial assistance is defined by s 152 (p 38) and the most satisfactory method of resolving a s 151 problem is to ensure that the transaction in question is not caught by the definition. Those parts of the definition which often cause a problem in structuring transactions are subss 152(1)(a)(iii) and (iv). Subsection (iii) refers to 'financial assistance given by way of loan or any other agreement under which any of the obligations of the person giving the assistance are to be fulfilled at a time when in accordance with the agreement any obligation of any other party to the agreement remains unfulfilled'. Subsection (iv) refers to 'any other financial assistance given by a company the net assets of which are thereby reduced to a material extent or which has no net assets'.

The first point to note is that if the assistance falls within subs (iii), s 151 will be infringed whatever the amount of the assistance whereas financial assistance falling within subs (iv) only involves a breach of the section where the net assets of the target are reduced to a material extent. So where the target transfers an asset to the vendor before the sale and the price is not paid at completion, s 151 will be infringed irrespective of the amount involved, while if the price is paid in full at completion, it is only if the price is less than the market value of the asset and the difference is material in relation to the net assets of the target that financial assistance will be given. Incidentally, although the financial assistance may be said in this case to be given to the vendor rather than the purchaser, it is in breach of the section nevertheless.

For this purpose 'net assets' are defined by s 152(2) as the aggregate of the company's assets, less the aggregate of its liabilities (including provisions as liabilities). It follows that reduction in net assets is not to be calculated by reference to the book value of the net assets but to their actual value and it is not safe to assume that net assets will not be reduced by a sale at book value. Of course, selling even at 'market value' does involve risk. If, despite all precautions to ascertain fair market value, the sale is in fact at less than market value, and the difference is such as to reduce the target's net assets materially, then the section will be infringed. It seems unlikely however that in such a case, where the parties are acting bona fide, a criminal prosecution would be successful. Also, the reference to 'material' reduction gives a margin for error.

If the amount of this undervalue is a distribution on *Aveling Barford* principles, then, so long as the target has sufficient distributable reserves, it may be said to be 'a distribution of a company's assets lawfully made' within s 153(3)(a) and thus outside the ambit of s 151 altogether. Given the penal nature of the section however, there is no doubt that a sale at market value is the safer course.

However fair the price, it it is left outstanding on loan account, the transaction will fall within subs (iii) and will constitute financial assistance. The cautious view is that the issue of eg debenture stock in satisfaction of the price does not mean that the transaction falls outside subs (iii). Looking at the transaction as a whole, there is a covenant to pay which is not satisfied at the time of completion. However, there is no authority on this point and a court might well hold, for example in a case which involved the issue of a listed security, that the issue of the security did fulfil the obligations of the purchaser of the assets.

Similar considerations arise where the target is to acquire an asset which is to be included in the sale. If the target pays more than a fair market price for the asset, then the assets will have been reduced, and title to the asset must be passed to the target at the time of the payment if subs (iii) is to be avoided. Transfers into the target at less than market value can cause tax problems – see p 204.

Cases sometimes arise in which the vendor wishes to have the benefit of a future successful realisation of an asset which the purchaser is disinclined to value highly, for example, the benefit of a claim which is to be pursued by the target. To avoid s 151 problems, it is necessary that this is dealt with by adjustment to the purchase price rather than by the target accounting to the vendor for the benefit it receives. This is the obverse of the case in which the target is to be compensated by the vendor for some liability if it is brought home. For tax reasons, it is normally advantageous to deal with these problems also by way of adjustment to the purchase price – see p 229.

PREFERENCE SHARES OF THE TARGET

Where the target has preference shares, they often result from a past money-raising exercise and may be owned by a number of shareholders. The purchaser will consider whether or not these shares need to be acquired as part of the acquisition. Experience shows that there are advantages in acquiring preference shares at the same time as acquiring 100 per cent of the target's equity share capital because although the preference shares may have very limited rights they can cause problems in two respects. First, their continued existence will mean that the principle in *Rolled Steel* cannot apply so that even after the purchaser owns 100 per cent of the target, it will not be possible for the target to enter into transactions for any purpose other than for its own benefit. This may cause practical problems where the target would otherwise be expected to enter into transactions to serve the purposes of the group of which it now forms a part. Secondly, it should be borne in mind that if the target wishes to give financial assistance for the purpose of the acquisition of its shares or shares in its holding company, then holders of not less than 10 per cent in nominal value of the issued share capital of any class may apply to the court to object to the transaction. This is a risk which exists even when the shares are non-voting.

It may not be straightforward for the purchaser to acquire the preference shares by agreement with the holders. However, if the purchaser acquires 90 per cent pursuant to an offer to the whole class, then the purchaser will be able to apply the provisions of the Companies Act 1985, s 428 to acquire the minority. Even if the purchaser cannot achieve 90 per cent acceptance the target can reduce its share capital and pay off the preference shares. To do this, the purchaser will wish to ensure that following the acquisition, it can procure the passing of the necessary special resolution. The procedure involves an application to the court under the Companies Act 1985, s 165, but in *House of Fraser v ACGE Investments* [1987] AC 387 it was held, confirming earlier authorities, that a reduction of capital which involves the return of capital to preference shareholders in priority to others in accordance with the rights attaching to those shares does not amount to a variation of rights. Therefore, although it may well be that the rights attaching to the shares will allow the shareholders to vote at the meeting to pass the necessary special resolution, in the absence of any special provisions in the articles deeming the reduction to be a variation of class rights, it is not necessary to have a separate meeting of the preference shareholders and if they are outvoted at the company meeting they will be paid off whether they like it or not. Of course, this involves paying off the shares at par, and where the coupon is low, may be less advantageous than a purchase at market value.

Example 1 (Intra-group transfers)

V plc agrees to sell its wholly owned subsidiary T Limited to P plc for £5,000,000. T owns a subsidiary TS which carries on a business which P does not want and V wishes to retain. TS stands in the books of T at £500,000 and it is agreed between V and P that, before the sale of T, TS should be transferred to another subsidiary of V, VS Limited, at book value. Opinions differ as to the market value of TS. In the absence of a purchaser for TS, it is unlikely that a definitive view can be obtained. V's auditors' advice, based on experience of the industry, is that a reasonable price for TS would be around £750,000.

In order to reduce the capital gains tax on the sale, it is intended that T should pay a dividend to V of £1,000,000 being the entire amount standing to the credit of T's reserves. (See p 177 for the taxation treatment of this.) This dividend is paid and lent back by V to T. The agreement between V and P is now that on completion, P will pay £4,000,000 for shares in T and will lend £1,000,000 to enable it to discharge its indebtedness to V at the same time.

In order to comply with the Companies Act 1985, s 151, TS must be transferred to V for at least £750,000, payable in cash on completion. If this is done, then in terms of the deal with P, V will be the loser by the excess of the price paid over book value. The solution is either to persuade P to increase the price for T by the excess on the basis that T will have that amount in cash in excess of P's expectations, or if P will not do this, to pay a further dividend from T to V before the contracts are exchanged. However, the previous dividend will have exhausted T's distributable reserves and although the sale of TS will throw up a realised profit of £250,000, the latest accounts of T will not show sufficient distributable reserves to pay the additional dividend. It will therefore be necessary to draw up further interim accounts under the Companies Act 1985, s 270(4) and only the amount of distributable profit there shown can be paid by way of dividend. Drawing up accounts may of course create a number of problems, in particular verification of stock levels, and although the accounts need not be audited, the auditors should be asked to give some comfort about the level of reserves.

Example 2 (Vendor Placing)

P plc agrees to buy T Limited from a number of individual shareholders. These shareholders want cash but P wishes to finance the issue through the allotment of shares. P therefore arranges a vendor placing under which it allots new shares in P to the vendors but arranges the placing of these shares on their behalf to raise the exact amount of purchase money which they require. The transaction is Super Class 1 for P and the amount of the issue exceeds the ABI guidelines.

The elements of the transaction are that P exchanges contracts with the vendors, conditional upon a resolution of approval being passed by P shareholders. At the same time the vendors instruct P's merchant bank (MB) to place the consideration shares on their behalf, and MB agrees with P that it will do so, subject to listing. Whether the contract between P and V will provide that P is bound to produce the cash on completion, or whether the contract is capable of rescission if the placing collapses will be a matter of negotiation. Because the issue exceeds ABI guidelines, MB will offer the shares to the existing shareholders of P pro rata, before allocating them to placees. This offer will be contained in the circular to shareholders which P sends out to explain the transaction and to convene the meeting. MB will place the shares with the placees subject to claw-back. When the resolutions are passed, the consideration shares will be allotted, subject to listing, upon the 520 Notice being posted by the Stock Exchange, the transaction will be completed and the price paid by MB to the vendor. These issues are dealt with in greater detail on p 153 *et seq.*

If some of the vendors wish to retain shares in P, this is easily accommodated under this structure, but if they want some other consideration eg loan notes to enable them to roll-over their capital gains to the next financial year, then a more complicated structure is required if P wishes to finance the acquisition (including the cost of redeeming the loan notes) through a market operation (see example 3).

This transaction will not require a share premium account, because P has secured a 90 per cent equity holding in T in pursuance of an arrangement providing for the allotment of equity shares in P.

If the transaction is not conditional upon shareholder approval or on any other condition (eg OFT clearance) but it is still necessary to make the open offer to shareholders under the ABI guidelines then a number of interesting points arise. The purchaser will probably insist on being paid on completion. MB will place the shares, but as they are placed subject to clawback, the final identity of those who are to take them will not be known until the expiry of the open offer, 15 business days later. MB can effect this transaction either by acquiring the shares from the vendors as principal and selling them on, or, to save stamp duty, placing them as agent for the vendor. The key point however is that MB will have parted with the money at the beginning of the period and if something goes wrong will end up bearing the risk. Further analysis will be found on p 156.

Example 3 (Cash, shares and loan stock)

If the vendors want loan notes but the purchaser wishes to fund the acquisition wholly in shares then more complicated structures are necessary. One possibility is for MB to form a subsidiary. The subsidiary contracts to make the acquisition for cash and loan notes in the subsidiary, guaranteed by the purchaser. The purchaser agrees with MB to acquire the MB subsidiary for shares which MB then places in the market (with or without an open offer as appropriate under ABI guidelines). MB applies the proceeds of the placing to subscribe additional share capital in the MB subsidiary which is included in the sale to the purchaser. Thus, the purchaser issues shares and acquires a new company which has contracted to buy the target and owns the cash proceeds of the placing operation. The vendors have loan notes issued by the MB subsidiary and guaranteed by the purchaser, and the MB subsidiary has sufficient cash, as a result of the market operation, to pay for the target and to redeem the loan notes when they fall due.

Should the vendors want shares in the purchaser as well, then roll-over relief can be achieved by the use of flip flops. Some of the vendor shares in the target can be acquired by the MB subsidiary in exchange for shares in the MB subsidiary, which are then acquired by the purchaser from the vendors, in exchange for shares of the purchaser, at the same time as the purchaser acquires the remaining share capital of the MB subsidiary from MB.

Clearly this is a complicated structure, but it does achieve a share for share exchange for the purchaser (with merger relief and no s 89 problems) and a cash, loan note and share deal for the vendors with full roll-over relief. It is expensive in terms of stamp duty, because it involves the acquisition of the target by the MB subsidiary, the acquisition of the MB subsidiary by the purchaser, and the stamp duty costs inherent in the placing exercise (ie three lots of stamp duty). Some of the stamp duty can be avoided by incorporating the MB subsidiary as a Channel Islands company. This structure also has a certain amount of flexibility in the amount of money raised. Because all the cash (net of the bank's commissions) raised in the placing exercise goes into a company which is acquired by the purchaser, it is possible to raise rather more cash than is immediately required for the acquisition. This, however, will be subject to market reaction.

Chapter 3

Consents and Approvals

There are many cases in which it is necessary or desirable to obtain some consent or approval before shares of a private company are acquired, and those which most commonly arise in practice are outlined below.

Consents required under contracts

Contracts entered into by the vendor, purchaser or target may make it necessary to obtain prior consent for the acquisition. For example, it may be a term of loans made to the target that they become repayable if control of the target changes. If the purchaser wishes the target to continue to enjoy the benefits of these loans, the consent of the lender must be obtained. If the target is a subsidiary of the vendor, the vendor may have entered into loan agreements which contain clauses which restrict the disposal of a substantial part of the vendor's undertaking and assets and the consent of creditors or trustees for loan stockholders may be required. If the consideration for the acquisition is shares to be issued by the purchaser, the purchaser's advisers should consider whether the terms of any agreements entered into by the purchaser will be infringed by the issue of the shares. For instance, deeds constituting convertible loan stocks may restrict the issue of further share capital by the purchaser. It is not possible to give an exhaustive list of the consents which may be required under this heading because it will depend upon the previous contracts entered into by the vendor, purchaser and target. So far as the target is concerned, a warranty is often taken that no such contracts exist (see the Agreement for Sale, Sched 3, para 2 (25) on p 297).

Approval of purchaser's shareholders

If the purchaser is a company, the approval of its own shareholders may be required for the acquisition. If the consideration for the acquisition is the issue of shares in the purchaser, an ordinary resolution may be required to increase the share capital, and, unless the consideration shares can be issued under an existing general authority for the issue of share capital, an ordinary resolution will also be required to authorise the issue of the shares under the Companies Act 1985, s 80.

The statutory pre-emption rights conferred by the Companies Act 1985, s 89, which require new issues of shares first to be offered to existing shareholders, do not apply in cases where the shares are, or are to be, wholly or partly paid up otherwise than in cash (s 89(4)). It may, however, be the case that such a requirement is contained in the purchaser's articles or that there are some other relevant restrictions on the issue of share capital.

If shares in the target are sold to the purchaser by a director of the purchaser (or of the purchaser's holding company), or by a person 'connected' with such a director within the meaning of the Companies Act 1985, s 346, shareholders' approval will normally be required under the Companies Act 1985, s 320, unless the value of the shares is less than the lower of £100,000 and 10 per cent of the purchaser's relevant assets. The section forbids a company from entering into 'an arrangement' for the purchase in these circumstances unless 'the arrangement is first approved' by the company in general meeting. Thus it would seem that a conditional contract (ie conditional on shareholder approval) is forbidden and the resolution should be passed before the contract is entered into. This can have significant implications where circumstances change between the time the notice convening the meeting is despatched and the passing of the resolution. If the parties are not bound to proceed, they may change their minds. The section will also apply where a company sells shares in the target to a director or a person connected with him. Section 321 provides some exceptions, including intra-group transfers, transactions in the course of winding up (if not a member's voluntary winding up) and arrangements with persons in their characters as members.

The Companies Act 1985, s 104, imposes conditions (including the approval of shareholders) for the acquisition of 'non-cash assets' from subscribers of the memorandum of a newly incorporated public company within two years of its being issued with a certificate to do business, and from a member of a company registered or re-registered as a public company within two years from such registration or re-registration.

If the purchaser is a listed company, the approval of shareholders for the transaction may be required by the Quotations Department of The Stock Exchange if the acquisition is Super Class 1 or Class 4.

These matters are dealt with in Chapter 10. If the purchaser is a public company which is itself the subject of a takeover bid, r 21 of The City Code on Takeovers and Mergers may require shareholder approval for an acquisition.

Special qualifications of the target

The target may have some qualification which the purchaser desires to preserve; for instance, it will normally be necessary to obtain the consent of the committee of Lloyd's before shares in a Lloyd's broking company or underwriting management company can be acquired. Similar requirements can arise by statute. If the target is an insurance company the consent of the Secretary of State to a change in control may be required under the Insurance Companies Act 1982, Part II. If the target carries on investment business it will be sensible to check that its continued authorisation under the Financial Services Act 1986 will not be affected by the change of ownership.

The Financial Services Act 1986

Where the shares of the target are widely held, any circular offer to shareholders is likely to amount to an investment advertisement within the meaning of the Financial Services Act 1986, s 57 and, if that is the case, the circular may not be issued unless it is issued by an authorised person or unless its contents have been approved by an authorised person.

Article 3 of the Financial Services Act 1986 (Investment Advertisements) (Exemptions) Order 1988 (SI No 316) as amended by the Financial Services Act 1986 (Investment Advertisements) (Exemptions) Order 1992 (SI No 274) provides that s 57 does not apply to an investment advertisement 'issued or caused to be issued by a body corporate ... if the only persons to whom the advertisement is issued, other than persons to whom it may otherwise lawfully be issued are reasonably believed to be ... members of ... the body corporate ... and the advertisement contains no invitation or information which would make it an investment advertisement other than an invitation or information relating to [shares, debentures or other defined investments in that body corporate or others in the same group]'. A similar exemption was contained in s 14(3)(a)(iii) of the Prevention of Fraud (Investments) Act 1958 but the view was always taken that where a company circulated an offer on behalf of a bidder, the bidder committed an offence under the Prevention of Fraud Act by causing the document to be circulated. The exemption contained in the Order, however, is wider than the old exemption and it may be that bidders who arrange for the bid circular to be sent out by the target will obtain the benefit of the exemption, at least in the case of a cash bid. If the offer included investments as consideration, the exception would not apply, as the circular would then relate to investments other than those in the body corporate issuing the circular.

However, the cautious practitioner will note that the Financial Services Act 1986 (Investment Advertisements) (Exemptions) (No 2) Order 1988 (SI 1988 No 716) contains two exemptions which specifically address the problem of private company acquisitions and may conclude that the draftsman did not intend the exception under art 3 of the first Order to be used in these circumstances. Article 4 of the second Order allows a takeover offer if it is an offer for all the shares in, or the shares comprised in the equity or non-equity share capital of, a private company target. The conditions which must be satisfied before an offer comes within the scope of the Order are quite complicated, but the principal ones are these:

(a) the terms of the offer must be recommended by all the directors of the target (other than any director who is also a director of the offeror);

(b) if the offeror holds 50 per cent or less of the voting rights of the target and makes an offer for debentures or for non-equity share capital then the offer must include or be accompanied by an offer made by the offeror for the rest of the shares comprised in the equity share capital; and

(c) an offer for equity share capital must be conditional upon acquiring 50 per cent or more of the voting rights.

The target must be a private company and the exemption will not apply if any shares comprised in the equity share capital of the target are or have at any time within the period of ten years immediately preceding the date of the offer been:

(a) listed or quoted on an investment exchange (in the United Kingdom or elsewhere); or

(b) shares in respect of which information has, with the agreement or approval of any officer of the target, been published for the purpose of facilitating deals in them, indicating prices at which persons have dealt or were willing to deal in them other than persons who were, at the time the information was published, existing members of a relevant class; or

(c) subject to a marketing arrangement which accorded to the company the facilities referred to in s 163(2)(*b*) of the Companies Act 1985; or

(*d*) the subject of an offer (whether in the United Kingdom or elsewhere) in relation to which a copy of the prospectus was delivered to the relevant registrar of companies in accordance with s 41 of the Companies Act 1948, or s 64 of the Companies Act 1985.

For this purpose members of a relevant class are existing members or debenture holders of the target or employees or their family members.

It will be noted that if the target is resident in the United Kingdom and any of these conditions is not satisfied it is likely that the Takeover Code will apply to an offer for equity share capital (see p 2). The offer must be accompanied by advice from an independent financial adviser. The Order contains detailed requirements about the contents of the offer and these are referred to in the notes to the specimen offer in Chapter 17.

Article 5 of the Order gives a wider exemption for investment advertisements which are issued in connection with the sale or purchase of shares in a company which falls within Sched 1, para 21 to the Financial Services Act 1986 (see p 3), ie a transaction involving more than 75 per cent of the voting shares which is between parties each of whom is a body corporate, a partnership, a single individual or a group of connected individuals.

It should also be noted that under s 47 of the Financial Services Act 1986 it is a criminal offence punishable by a term of imprisonment not exceeding seven years, for any person knowingly or recklessly to make a statement, promise or forecast which is misleading, false or deceptive or dishonestly to conceal any material fact if that person makes the statement, promise or forecast or conceals the fact for the purpose of inducing another person . . . to enter or offer to enter into an investment agreement (which will include an agreement for the acquisition of shares in a private company). The section is not confined to written statements.

The Companies Act 1985, s 103

Although not strictly a question of consent or approval, this section is conveniently dealt with here.

Where the purchaser is a public company and the consideration includes an allotment of shares in the purchaser, s 103 provides that unless the transaction is exempt, the non-cash consideration must be valued by an independent person who must make a report to the purchaser, with a copy to the allottees. Failure to do this is visited with alarming consequences, namely, that the allottees become liable to pay for their shares in cash. Section 103(3) exempts an arrangement providing for the allotment of shares on terms that the whole or part of the consideration is to be provided by the transfer of all or some of the shares, or of all or some of the shares of a particular class, in another company. This exemption does not, however, operate unless it is open to all the holders of the shares in the target to take part in the arrangement. In determining whether this is the case, shares held by, or by a nominee of, the purchaser are disregarded.

In a case where some of the shareholders are to sell their shares for cash and others are to sell for shares then, unless the transaction is structured so that each shareholder of the target can participate in the arrangement providing for the allotment of shares, an expert's report must be obtained. If, however, the shares which are to be acquired for cash are acquired in one transaction and the share for share transaction is carried through subsequently, it seems that an expert's report is not required as, in considering the second transaction (which is the one providing for the allotment of shares), the shares already acquired by the purchaser can be disregarded. The cautious practitioner will not, however, separate artificially what is, in truth, a single transaction in order to avoid an expert's report. In view of the draconian consequences of failure to comply with the sections, it is safer to obtain the report.

Consents under the Taxes Acts

The purchaser will normally seek advance clearance under the Taxation of Chargeable Gains Act 1992, s 138, where the consideration for the acquisition is shares and it is expected that the vendors will thereby be enabled to 'roll over' their capital gains (see p 175). Other sections under which clearances may be sought, because of possible adverse tax consequences, are the Income and Corporation Taxes Act 1988, s 707 (see p 182), s 765 (see p 187) and s 776 (see p 186).

Chapter 4

Competition Law

Competition law plays an increasingly important role in the strategic planning of acquisitions. The carrying out of the acquisition can be affected by competition law in at least four ways: by the law controlling restrictive agreements and by the law controlling mergers, each under the United Kingdom and European Community systems respectively. These are considered in turn.

UNITED KINGDOM LAW AFFECTING AGREEMENTS

Acquisition agreements frequently contain clauses which are intended to restrict the conduct of the parties and, depending on the circumstances, their competitive activity. There may be continuing supply or purchase requirements or licences of intellectual property rights. However, the most common restrictions are covenants limiting competition. The purchaser is likely to demand a covenant from the vendor against competing with the target and may seek to extend this covenant to retiring directors or former individual shareholders of the vendor. For its part, the vendor, if it is continuing to operate in related businesses, may seek covenants from the purchaser against competing with any business retained by the vendor. Issues will arise under United Kingdom law (and EC law, considered later in this chapter) as to the scope (both in terms of subject matter and geographical extent) and duration of these covenants.

Restraint of trade

These restrictive covenants can be invalidated by the common law doctrine of restraint of trade. If the doctrine does apply (as will usually be the case in this context) then a covenant will only be

26

upheld by the courts to the extent that (i) it is necessary to protect a legitimate interest of the person wishing to enforce it, (ii) it is no more than is reasonable between the parties to protect that interest and (iii) it is reasonable in the public interest. The courts have recognised that the purchaser of a business has a legitimate interest in ensuring that the vendor does not immediately undermine the value of the transferred asset. However, the purchaser should take care to ensure that the covenants designed to achieve this are no broader – in terms of activities covered, geographical scope and duration – than necessary to provide reasonable protection. The question of what is reasonable will necessarily depend largely on the facts of each case. In practice most covenants which are acceptable under section 21(2) of the Restrictive Trade Practices Act 1976 or which are covered by the 1989 Orders (these aspects are explained in detail below) are unlikely to be invalidated by the common law, but restraint of trade remains as a trap for the unwary if covenants which are excessive in scope or duration are included. In view of this it is normal and prudent practice to draft each covenant in a form which permits it to be severed from the remainder under the usual English law rules.

The Restrictive Trade Practices Act 1976

Despite the promises of reform contained in the 1989 White Paper *Opening Markets: New Policy on Restrictive Trade Practices* (Cm 727) the Restrictive Trade Practices Act 1976 remains the principal statute controlling the legality of restrictions in agreements. It is highly formalistic and only applies where two or more persons carry on business in the manufacture or supply of goods in the United Kingdom and two or more parties to the agreement accept certain statutorily defined restrictions. Restrictions to which the Act applies include those which relate to the price to be charged for goods, the terms or conditions on which they are to be supplied and the persons to whom or from whom they are to be supplied. A non-competition covenant of the type usually contained in an acquisition agreement clearly falls within the category of defined restrictions. There is a parallel but separate system controlling agreements relating to services.

Particulars of agreements falling within the control must be furnished before the agreement takes effect to the Director General of Fair Trading on Form RTP(C), (obtainable from the Office of Fair Trading, Field House, Bream's Buildings, London EC4 1PR). The Director General places the agreement on the public register of restrictive agreements and is obliged to refer it to the Restrictive Practices Court to declare whether or not it is in the public interest.

In the meantime, although presumed to be against the public interest, an agreement registered in due time can be operated and enforced.

The Director General's duty is subject to certain exceptions and in practice acquisition agreements are either dealt with under these exceptions or exempted from the Act under the statutory instruments described below. The main exception is s 21(2) of the Act which relieves the Director General of his obligation to refer an agreement to the court if the Secretary of State for Trade and Industry gives directions to the effect that the restrictions in the agreement are too insignificant to require investigation by the court. This is an important provision and most registrable agreements are dealt with in this way. Other exceptions are s 21(1)(b)(i) where the agreement has been terminated altogether, and s 21(1)(b)(ii) where all the relevant restrictions have been removed (known as 'filleting' the agreement). In practice the Director General often applies a combination of these sections and the parties will be asked to remove objectionable or excessive restrictions while those remaining will be regarded as economically insignificant.

The 1989 Orders

In recent years, a large number of acquisition agreements have had to be furnished to the Office of Fair Trading under the Restrictive Trade Practices Act even though the restrictions they contained were innocuous. This is because of the formalistic nature of the statute. For example, an agreement under which the vendors were a husband and wife, both covenanting not to compete with the purchaser, would frequently be registrable. This situation tied up considerable resources at the Office of Fair Trading considering agreements which raised no public interest issues. Accordingly, two statutory instruments were passed in 1989 (the RTP (Sale and Purchase and Share Subscription Agreements) (Goods) Order 1989 (SI No 1081) and the RTP (Services) (Amendment) Order 1989 (SI No 1082). These sought to exclude most vendor covenants from the scope of the RTPA. Two orders were necessary because of the separate systems controlling goods and services. The orders provide that an agreement for the sale or purchase of shares in a company or the transfer of the whole of an interest in a business will be exempt from the 1976 Act if:

    (i) 50 per cent or more of the issued share capital or the whole of the vendor's interest in a business is transferred;

    (ii) no pricing restrictions are imposed;

(iii) restrictions are accepted only by vendors, their affiliates or by individual persons;
(iv) any restrictions only limit competition by those accepting them with the business which is sold; and
(v) the restrictions do not last more than five years from the date the agreement takes effect or not more than two years after the expiry of any relevant employment or services contract, whichever date is the later.

The orders apply to acquisitions of assets, as well as shares, provided that these assets comprise a business as defined in the orders. Although the need to furnish particulars is much reduced by these orders, they are, like the 1976 Act itself, highly formalistic and considerable care is needed to make sure an acquisition agreement is exempted by them. In particular the orders do not apply if any restriction is accepted by the purchaser.

In practice, it remains a painstaking task to make sure that an acquisition does not fall foul of the 1976 Act. The exercise is also rather unrewarding as no real public interest issues arise and no sale or purchase agreement has ever found its way to the Restrictive Practices Court. The problem for those involved is that covenants which may be material to the deal in question can be rendered unenforceable. Key practical points to remember are:

(i) when considering the possible application of the 1976 Act the arrangement as a whole must be considered, not only the specific contract containing the covenants;
(ii) particulars cannot validly be furnished late. It has thus become customary to include a clause in the agreement providing that, if the inclusion of any restrictions makes it subject to registration under the 1976 Act, the coming into effect of those restrictions is suspended until particulars have been duly furnished to the Director General of Fair Trading; even then, particulars must be furnished within three months of the date of signing of the agreement;
(iii) it is possible to furnish particulars of an acquisition on a 'fail-safe' basis but this practice is open to abuse. It is the job of the parties' legal advisers to form their own view on the possible application of the 1976 Act and only to furnish particulars in cases of genuine doubt, and with some explanation of the basis of that doubt. The OFT does not appreciate receiving voluminous acquisition documentation without any indication of why it may be registrable.

EC LAW AFFECTING AGREEMENTS

Restrictive covenants

The control of restrictive covenants under EC law is based on quite different principles from the United Kingdom Restrictive Trade Practices Act and is in some respects closer to the common law restraint of trade doctrine. This is not the place for an exhaustive account of EC competition law. For our purposes it is enough to be aware that the relevant principles are contained in arts 85 and 86 of the Treaty of Rome and in the 1989 Merger Regulation (see next section). Article 85 controls and (under para (1)) prohibits agreements and concerted practices which prevent, restrict or distort competition to a noticeable degree within the common market and which are liable to have an appreciable effect on trade between member states. An agreement can be exempted under para (3) of art 85 if it has beneficial effects but this power is reserved exclusively to the European Commission and normally requires an individual notification on Form A/B. Article 86 prohibits the abuse of a dominant position and can sometimes apply to acquisitions. Both articles apply directly in the United Kingdom and can be invoked in the courts; there is no system of registration and the prohibition is backed by the power of the European Commission to impose heavy fines.

Restrictive covenants in acquisition agreements can fall within art 85(1). As a general rule, however, they will fall outside the article if they are no more restrictive than is necessary to secure the successful transfer of the business in question, ie they must be limited in scope, in duration and in geographical extent. The Commission first applied this view in its *Reuter/BASF* decision in 1976 and the Court of Justice adopted a similar approach in the *Nutricia* case some ten years later. (Case 42/84 *Remia BV and Others v EC Commission* [1985] ECR 2566.) The Commission subsequently stated in the *Thirteenth Competition Policy Report* that for business transfers including knowhow and goodwill a five year restriction would be acceptable but where goodwill only was transferred, two years would usually be the maximum permissible.

These limits on duration are only rules of thumb but are not very different from the United Kingdom practice. The covenant must also be limited to the economic activity and geographical area of the business being sold. As with the United Kingdom system, the inclusion of a covenant by the purchaser will change matters considerably and will make it much more likely that the agreement will fall within art 85.

Ancillary restrictions

The Commission has confirmed its approach to restrictive covenants in the context of acquisitions in its 1990 *Notice regarding restrictions ancillary to concentrations* (OJ [1990] C203). This Notice is intended to explain the favourable attitude which the Commission will take to restrictions accepted in the context of a merger and which are directly related and necessary to the implementation of the merger. Although technically limited to acquisitions subject to the new EC Merger Regulation (dealt with in the next section), the Notice clearly applies to restrictions of the kind previously considered in the *Reuter* and *Nutricia* cases, as well as to other restrictions such as supply and purchase obligations and intellectual property licences, and to that extent indicates the Commission's attitude to restrictions in the context of acquisitions generally.

How to decide whether article 85 applies

It is often difficult to know for certain when art 85 applies to an agreement. The agreement must restrict competition to a noticeable degree and also be liable appreciably to affect trade between member states. The Commission has issued a *Notice on agreements of minor importance* (OJ [1986] C231/2) laying down turnover and market share criteria below which art 85 will not apply but many private companies have businesses big enough to fall outside this Notice. Given the growth of trade between the United Kingdom and other member states, the increasing removal of barriers to further trade and the geographical scope of covenants commonly included in acquisition agreements, the application of art 85 is becoming more likely.

If the parties feel compelled to include restrictions going beyond the limits laid down by the Commission or which cannot be regarded as ancillary to the acquisition itself, the only safe course is to notify the agreement to the Commission on Form A/B seeking exemption under art 85(3). A quick outcome is very unlikely but informal approaches to the Commission may help.

For a time the Commission tried to apply art 85 to acquisitions as such. In the so-called *Philip Morris* decision (Cases 124 and 156/84 *BAT and Reynolds v Commission* [1987] ECR 4487) it applied art 85 to an agreement for the acquisition by a tobacco undertaking of a minority interest in a competitor. Whether or not as a result of this move, the Commission was eventually given direct merger control powers, which are considered in the next section. The possibility remains of art 85 being applied in certain circumstances to an agreement between competing undertakings where one purchases a minority stake in the other with the object or effect of restricting competition between them or indeed to any acquisition agreement forming part of a wider cartel arrangement.

UK MERGER CONTROL

UK merger control is contained in the Fair Trading Act 1973 as most recently amended by the Companies Act 1989. In essence mergers which involve the taking over of assets with a gross value (worldwide) exceeding £30 million or which involve the creation or increase of a United Kingdom market share of 25 per cent or more in any given description of goods or services qualify for investigation by the Monopolies and Mergers Commission. If found by the Commission to be against the public interest qualifying mergers can be prohibited by the Secretary of State or allowed subject to conditions. If the Commission clears the merger the Secretary of State must allow it to proceed. Although the Commission must consider whether the merger is in the broadest sense against the public interest the main test is whether the merger will restrict competition to an unacceptable degree. The same concern governs decisions whether or not to refer a merger to the Commission. Private company acquisitions frequently fall within the scope of this control. Even if the assets test is not met, market shares depend on market definitions and some of these have on occasion been narrow if not arcane.

The acquisition of a controlling interest is clearly a merger but the regime also applies to the acquisition of a sufficient interest to control the policy of a company or even of one sufficient to confer the ability materially to influence the policy of a company (as a rough rule of thumb any holding over 10 per cent could, depending on the circumstances, give rise to material influence).

There is no compulsory pre-notification of mergers under the Fair Trading Act. The regime can, however, be applied to mergers 'in contemplation' as well as to completed mergers and it is usual practice to give prior notice to the Mergers Secretariat of the Office of Fair Trading of any merger where reference to the Monopolies and Mergers Commission is a serious possibility. Such notice can be a formal request for 'confidential guidance' (given by letter to the requesting party without any party outside Government being informed) or merely an informal clarification. Once the acquisition is in the public domain and particularly if it is conditional on not being referred to the Commission a formal clearance is normally requested. This leads to the Office of Fair Trading conducting a summary enquiry following which the acquisition is either cleared or referred to the Commission by the Secretary of State. The time for obtaining such clearance is not definite and can range from a few weeks to several months. The Office's enquiries lead to a recommendation by the Director General of Fair Trading which the Secretary of State normally (though not invariably) follows.

The 1989 Companies Act introduced a more formal, though still voluntary, pre-notification system. By filing a merger notice in the prescribed form, a timetable is set in train under which if no reference is made to the Commission after a given period, the merger is deemed to be cleared. The initial period is 20 working days but this can be extended by two further periods of 10 and 15 days respectively (45 working days in all). In round figures the parties are guaranteed an outcome within about nine weeks from filing. There are provisions for extending the period if false or insufficient information is provided and the period cannot start to run until the merger is in the public domain and the requisite fee has been paid (see below). The Director General can reject a merger notice in certain circumstances (for example if he believes the parties do not propose to carry out the merger) and the 'automatic clearance' procedure ceases to apply if the parties either complete the merger during the period or if either party merges with any other party (whether or not that unrelated merger restricts competition).

If the Director General recommends that a merger be referred to the Commission but considers the adverse effects could be avoided if parts of either business are disposed of, the Secretary of State now has the power to accept formal undertakings instead of making an MMC reference.

Fees, ranging from £5,000 to £15,000, depending on the value of the assets taken over, are chargeable for (i) a reference decision by the Secretary of State, (ii) a decision not to refer, and (iii) the use of the merger notice procedure. In the latter case the fee must be paid on filing, ie some time earlier than the date for payment if the informal procedure is used. In each case a controlling interest must be acquired, not a lesser interest.

There are special regimes governing the acquisition of newspapers and water companies. Newspaper mergers are subject to compulsory pre-notification to the Department of Trade and Industry under pain of criminal liability and mergers involving water companies are subject to a particularly rigorous regime requiring automatic reference to the Commission.

An unexpected reference to the Commission can be a bruising experience for the parties and prior contact with the Office of Fair

Trading will normally (but not always) limit the uncertainty. Where there is good ground for believing the authorities will wish to refer the acquisition to the Commission, there is no real alternative to making the agreement conditional on non-reference and presenting the strongest possible case to the Office of Fair Trading against a reference. Doing nothing and hoping for the best is not advisable.

EC MERGER CONTROL

The EC Merger Regulation

Since the EC Merger Regulation (*Council Regulation 4064/89* published in OJ [1990] L257) came into force on 21 September 1990 the European Community has controlled mergers ('concentrations' in Community parlance) which have a Community dimension. These are defined by reference to turnover thresholds; the definition is satisfied if:

(i) the parties' aggregate worldwide turnover exceeds 5 billion ECUs (currently about £3.9 billion); and

(ii) at least two of the parties have EC wide turnover exceeding 250 million ECUs (currently about £200 million);

but if each of the parties achieves two-thirds or more of its aggregate EC-wide turnover in one and the same member state, there is no Community dimension. Commission Regulation 2367/90 (OJ [1990] L219) gives some guidance on how to calculate these turnover figures. There are special methods of calculation for banks, other credit institutions and insurance undertakings.

Concentrations with a Community Dimension are (with a few exceptions) exclusively subject to the EC regime (ie national merger controls are disapplied). Under this regime a merger will be prohibited if it creates or strengthens a dominant position as a result of which effective competition would be significantly impeded in the Common Market or in a substantial part of it. As such the test is a stringent one and to date only one merger has been prohibited by the Commission (the *Aerospatiale/Alenia/de Havilland* decision OJ [1991] L344), although a number of others have been allowed subject to conditions.

If a merger falls within the Regulation it must be pre-notified on Form CO to the EC Commission under pain of fines. The EC Commission conducts an initial enquiry lasting four weeks. If it finds serious grounds for thinking the merger may be incompatible with the common market it initiates a more thorough investigation, which lasts up to four months. At the end it either clears or prohibits the merger by decision.

In principle, the EC regime is a 'one stop shop' and national authorities (eg the Office of Fair Trading and the Monopolies and Mergers Commission) cannot interfere. However, there is a limited right for national authorities to investigate factors other than competition and a right for national authorities to request the Commission to pass consideration of a merger back to them. This is confined to cases where there is a distinct national market and the merger's effects are confined to that market. The Commission can refuse such requests. The practical effect of this provision is to require the parties to an acquisition whose main effects are felt in the United Kingdom but which, on a turnover basis, falls within the Merger Regulation to keep both the Office of Fair Trading and the EC Commission fully informed of the details of the acquisition.

Whether private company acquisitions and disposals are subject to the EC merger control will depend on whether the relevant turnover thresholds are fulfilled. It is essential to analyse the relevant turnover figures well in advance of the date the agreement is supposed to take effect. The EC Commission's Merger Task Force (in effect a separate Directorate within Directorate General IV) makes a practice of giving informal guidance on whether the Merger Regulation applies and on more substantive issues and it is very advisable to take advantage of this openness.

The European Coal and Steel Community

Although the EC merger regime is new, control under the Treaty of Paris of mergers involving undertakings in the coal and steel sectors has applied for over 40 years. Article 66 of the ECSC Treaty subjects relevant mergers to prior authorisation by the EC Commission and the control applies even if only one of the parties is an ECSC undertaking. This can sometimes come as a surprise to the would-be purchaser of, for example, a steel stockholding subsidiary of a conglomerate group. Decision 25-67, last amended in 1991, provides reasonably generous exemption by category, depending on the tonnages of coal or steel products involved. The Commission has wide powers to order the separation of unauthorised mergers and acquisitions and to impose penalties. Unlike EC competition law, the Commission's exclusive jurisdiction does not depend on there being any effect on trade between member states or a Community dimension.

Other EC aspects

The enactment of the Merger Regulation and the confirmation by the European Commission that it will apply the doctrine of ancillary restrictions in the context of mergers have largely overtaken the previous attempts by the Commission to apply arts 85 and 86 to acquisitions, but there are still areas of uncertainty. Thus, for mergers which fall below the Merger Regulation thresholds, the Regulation disapplies the Commission's powers to investigate and act under Council Regulation 17 of 1962. This still leaves open the possibility of proceedings in a national court under art 86 based on the doctrine established in the *Continental Can* case (Case 6/72 [1973] ECR 215) which prohibits the strengthening of a dominant position by the acquisition of competitors. There is also considerable scope for difficulty in the case of joint ventures, which may or may not be concentrative in nature. If concentrative, the Merger Regulation will apply; if not, art 85 will have to be considered. However, to a significant extent, the Merger Regulation has cleared the air and assisted in removing residual uncertainty about how the Community authorities will seek to control mergers. Whether private litigants will feel similarly enlightened still remains to be seen.

Chapter 5

Financial Assistance

Any transaction proposed to be entered into by the target, whether before, at, or after its acquisition, should be examined with care in the light of the Companies Act 1985, s 151, which prohibits a target from giving financial assistance before or at the same time as an acquisition of its shares. Section 151(1) provides that:

where a person is acquiring or proposing to acquire shares in a company, it is not lawful for the company or any of its subsidiaries to give financial assistance directly or indirectly for the purpose of that acquisition before or at the same time as the acquisition takes place.

Section 151(2) further prohibits financial assistance given after the acquisition:

where a person has acquired shares in a company and any liability has been incurred (by that or any other person), for the purpose of that acquisition, it is not lawful for the company or any of its subsidiaries to give financial assistance directly or indirectly for the purpose of reducing or discharging the liability so incurred.

The section is penal, and the criminal and civil consequences of a breach are set out below (p 51).

The law as it presently stands was introduced by the Companies Act 1981. The provisions re-enact, with significant change, the Companies Act 1948, s 54. Most of the case law in this area is in respect of the old law and is of limited value in considering the application of s 151 (other than in respect of the consequences of a breach). One general point which should not be overlooked, however, is that the articles of many companies will restate s 54 of the 1948 Act (see eg reg 10 of the pre-1981 Act, Table A). It may be necessary to amend the articles by deletion of any such provision before taking advantage of the new law, which is in certain respects less restrictive than the old.

The prohibition against giving 'financial assistance'

Section 151 prohibits a target or its subsidiaries from giving 'financial assistance'. Financial assistance is defined in s 152(1)(a):

(a) 'financial assistance' means
  (i) financial assistance given by way of gift,
  (ii) financial assistance given by way of guarantee, security or indemnity, other than an indemnity in respect of the indemnifier's own neglect or default, or by way of release or waiver,
  (iii) financial assistance given by way of loan or any other agreement under which any of the obligations of the person giving the assistance are to be fulfilled at a time when in accordance with the agreement any obligation of another party to the agreement remains unfulfilled, or by way of the novation of, or the assignment of rights arising under, a loan or such other agreement, or
  (iv) any other financial assistance given by a company the net assets of which are thereby reduced to a material extent or which has no net assets.

The section provides a partial definition; a transaction proposed to be undertaken by the target company or its subsidiary which falls within one of the sub-definitions set out in s 152(1)(a)(i) – (iv) above will often be caught, but to be prohibited the transaction must also constitute 'financial assistance' since, for example, s 152(1)(a)(i) refers not simply to a 'gift', but to 'financial assistance given by way of gift'.

The expression 'financial assistance' itself has no technical meaning and it was suggested by Hoffmann J in *Charterhouse v Tempest Diesels* [1986] BCLC 1 (a case on the old law), at p 10, that the frame of reference for the expression is 'the language of ordinary commerce. One must examine the commercial realities of the transaction and decide whether it can properly be described as the giving of financial assistance by the company'. It follows that although a transaction which falls within the descriptions contained in s 152(1)(a) will often constitute the giving of financial assistance, it is also necessary to consider who is being assisted, in a financial way, by the transaction. It is established that the financial assistance may be given not only to the purchaser of the shares in the target, but also to the vendor, and, presumably, any other person (*Armour Hick*

Northern Ltd v Whitehouse [1980] 1 WLR 1520). It may not be irrelevant that the assistance may have cost the target nothing, provided some person has actually received financial assistance, since this may infer that the transaction has not been wholly in the interests of the target. So, for example, where the target purchases assets from the purchaser at their market value to put the purchaser in funds to enable it to make the acquisition, the target itself is not in a worse position, but the purchaser selling the assets to the target now has the cash funds to enable it to make the acquisition and so has been financially assisted – *Belmont Finance Corporation Ltd v Williams Furniture Ltd (No 2)* [1980] 1 All ER 393. As Buckley LJ said, in the Court of Appeal (at p 402):

If [the target] buys something from [the purchaser] without regard to its own commercial interests, the sole purpose of the transaction being to put [the purchaser] in funds to acquire shares in [the target], this would, in my opinion, clearly contravene the section, even if the price paid was a fair price for what is bought, and a fortiori that would be so if the sale to [the target] was at an inflated price.

The judge went on to say that if the transaction was in the genuine commercial interests of the target, the fact that the target entered into the transaction partly with the object of putting the purchaser in funds to acquire its own shares or with knowledge of the purchaser's intended use of the proceeds might involve no contravention of the section, but he did not wish to express a concluded opinion on that point. The law has changed since *Belmont*, and while it remains authority for the interpretation of 'financial assistance' in the non-technical sense, a court would now take a different approach. The issue would now turn on whether there was any material reduction in the company's net assets and whether (if the transaction was in the genuine commercial interests of the target) it would fall within s 153(1). See p 44 below. Interesting questions arise where a target with no assets enters into a transaction which assists a party to the share acquisition, but as a result of which the target is plainly better off. 'Any other' financial assistance is prohibited by a company with no net assets (s 152(1)(a)(iv)); however, in such case it may be possible to argue, applying the reasoning in *Tempest Diesel*, that no financial assistance has been given.

Transactions which are financial assistance within the meaning of s 152(1)(a) will be prohibited if they are 'for the purpose of' the acquisition of the shares in the target (or, in the case of s 151(2), reducing or discharging a liability incurred for that purpose). Transactions in the ordinary course of business and transactions entered into wholly for some other purpose will not be affected, but any transaction thought to be outside the scope of the section for these reasons should be examined with care. Any transaction which is entered into by a member of the target group in the course of a transaction in the target's shares or which is a step in an overall scheme or a term of the bargain between the parties is likely to be 'for the purpose' of the acquisition. Financial assistance will be prohibited if given directly for the purpose of the acquisition, or indirectly. So, for example, a loan made to a subsidiary of the purchaser, rather than to the purchaser itself, will still be prohibited if its purpose is to finance the acquisition. Section 151 will not, however, prohibit financial assistance being given to a target by its parent or 'sister' companies.

The purpose of the section has been said to be the protection of creditors and minority shareholders. With this in mind, there are some transactions which are plainly objectionable, and are clearly prohibited by s 151(1). If a purchaser does not have the cash to finance the acquisition, but the target does, creditors and minority shareholders in the target may be adversely affected if the purchaser were able to take a loan from the target, and use the proceeds of the loan to acquire the target from the vendor. This would be prohibited by s 151(1), as financial assistance within the meaning of s 152(1)(a)(iii). The loan would also be prohibited if it were made by a subsidiary of the target. While the strict wording of the section would appear also to prohibit such a loan being made by a subsidiary incorporated overseas, it is generally considered that, as the Act does not prohibit assistance by foreign-incorporated targets, it should not prohibit assistance by the foreign-incorporated subsidiary of an English target; to conclude otherwise would be to give extra-territorial effect to the Act and impose penalties on foreigners contrary to the general application of English statutes. Nevertheless, in such a case, consideration should be given as to whether the loan (or other transaction by the foreign subsidiary) involves the giving of financial assistance by the English target itself – for example where the English target permits a transaction to occur by its subsidiary for the purpose of an acquisition of its (ie the target's) shares. This acquiescence can amount to financial assistance within s 152(1)(a)(iv) and will therefore be prohibited only where the transaction gives rise to a material reduction in the assets of the target (ie the value of the shares in the foreign subsidiary is diminished), or where the target itself has no net assets.

It is often the case that a target is 'groomed' for sale – particularly where, prior to its sale, it is part of a group of companies. In that case, it is not uncommon for inter-company balances to be settled, prior to, or as part of, the sale arrangements, or for assets (for example, premises used or required for use by the target group) to be moved between group companies. Assets removed from the target group can be removed by way of pre-sale dividend which would not infringe s 151, if the target had sufficient distributable reserves (s 153(3)(a)), or might be sold to another group company. The sale of an asset intra-group may be prohibited if it results in material reduction in the net assets of the target (s 152(1)(a)(iv)) or if there are deferred payment terms (s 152(1)(a)(iii)).

For the purpose of determining whether or not there has been a material reduction in net assets in s 152(1)(a)(iv), it is necessary to look at actual values, not the book value of the asset in question. If assets are transferred at less than their actual value there will be financial assistance unless the reduction in net assets of the target is not material. There is no guidance in the Act as to what is meant by 'material', although it is generally thought to mean a reduction of between 1 and 5 per cent of total net assets. That is to say that all would agree that a reduction of less than 1 per cent is immaterial and all would agree that a reduction of more than 5 per cent is material. Some suggest that the test is not only relative but also absolute and that, for example, a reduction in net assets of more than £100,000 would always be material, irrespective of the size of the target, but that is not a view shared by the author.

If the liabilities of the target exceed its assets, all forms of financial assistance are forbidden, whether or not the net assets of the target are reduced. Applying the reasoning in *Belmont* this would appear to be the case irrespective of the fairness of the transaction to the target, and the financial assistance would be permissible only if one of the exceptions were available.

Every transaction should therefore be considered separately. It is possible, in some circumstances, that a sale at gross undervalue might, to the extent of the undervaluation, be treated as a gift (even if the undervalue is not material in the context of s 152(1)(a)(iv)), and so constitute the giving of financial assistance within the meaning of s 152(1)(a)(i), where materiality is irrelevant. Where there is an asset sale which does not give rise to a material reduction in net assets, this will not constitute the giving of financial assistance. However, this will only be the case if the terms of sale of the asset provide for all consideration to be paid at completion. If there is any deferral of consideration (and, indeed, if any part of the consideration is left outstanding to be calculated by reference to profits or some other post-completion adjustment), then the transaction is likely to fall within s 152(1)(a)(iii) and, as a result, be prohibited. Furthermore, particular care should be taken where the transfer of assets is intra-group; if there is a transfer of assets which gives rise to any reduction in net assets (even if not material) then, as described on p 11, it may be treated as a distribution by the target company, and, in the absence of adequate distributable reserves, be unlawful.

It is also an offence, under s 151(2), to give financial assistance after the acquisition of shares in the target, if the assistance is given for the purpose of reducing a liability incurred for the purpose of that acquisition. Therefore, it will be unlawful for a person who borrows to finance the acquisition of shares in the target, then to use the assets of the target to reduce his borrowings. The scope of the prohibition in s 151(2) is widened by s 152(3), which extends the definition of the reference to a person 'incurring a liability' in s 151(2), to include the case where that person '[changes] his financial position by making an agreement or arrangement (whether enforceable or unenforceable, and whether made on his own account or with any other person) or by any other means'. The section also extends the meaning of the reference in s 151(2) to financial assistance being given for the purpose of reducing or discharging a liability incurred by a person for the purpose of the acquisition to include assistance given 'for the purpose of wholly or partly restoring his financial position to what it was before the acquisition took place'.

Section 152(3) therefore has the effect of prohibiting a transaction under which a purchaser who has not borrowed (ie has not incurred a liability to finance the acquisition, but has financed it out of its own resources), then receives assets from the target, since this would wholly or partly restore the purchaser's position to what it was before the acquisition took place.

Difficulty arises in the case where third party finance is used by a purchaser and the lender requires a guarantee from the target, or security over the target's assets is to be taken to support the acquisition finance. It is not clear that, within the strict meaning of the section, a guarantee or security has the effect of 'reducing or discharging' the liability of the purchaser, or any other person who incurred that liability for the purpose of the acquisition. Nevertheless, the usual practice would be to treat the giving of any such guarantee or security of the acquisition of the target as falling within the scope of s 151(2) and, where possible, use is made of the 'whitewash' procedure under ss 155–158 to ensure that it is properly given; indeed, the well-advised lender will insist on the whitewash procedure being followed (see p 46). It will be necessary to show that the guarantee is given *bona fide* in the interests of the target, which is not easy. The principle in *Rolled Steel* may be relevant (see p 11).

A further difficulty with s 151(2) is that the prohibition on giving financial assistance after the acquisition has taken place is not limited in time. Therefore, any financial assistance given after the transaction has occurred remains prohibited if it is for the purpose of reducing or discharging a liability incurred for the purpose of the acquisition. In practice, this can cause problems with the refinancing of funds borrowed for an acquisition, where new money is borrowed partly for one purpose (the refinancing), and partly for another, lawful, purpose, (say, for group working capital purposes). It may not be safe to assume that any guarantee or security is being taken solely for the working capital purpose, rather than for the purchase of the shares. Where the original statutory declaration provides for variations to the terms of the financing this may, depending on the facts, cover a refinancing. Nevertheless, in the absence of a clear distinction between which money is being secured (eg by use of different lenders), consideration should be given to using the whitewash procedure under s 155 again.

There will be some cases where it is possible for the target to engage in transactions which will otherwise constitute financial assistance. If the transaction is properly for the company's trading purposes, or some other purpose (unrelated to its acquisition) then it may not be within s 151(2) as not being 'for the purpose' of the acquisition, or may otherwise fall within the exception set out in s 153(2), as being an incidental part of some larger purpose of the company (see below, p 45).

Exceptions to the prohibition

Transactions which are, on the face of it, prohibited by s 151 might fall within one of the exceptions, set out in s 153, or be capable of approval under the 'whitewash' procedure in ss 155–158.

Section 153(3) makes it clear that certain arrangements which might otherwise be prohibited are exempt. While this chapter only considers in detail those exceptions of relevance in the context of an acquisition, consideration should always be given to any proposal which might otherwise fall within the ambit of s 151, to see if it is exempt or whether it might be restructured so as to fall within one of the exceptions. The specific exceptions provided by s 153(3) are:

(a) a distribution of a company's assets by way of dividend lawfully made or a distribution made in the course of the company's winding up;

(b) the allotment of bonus shares;

(c) a reduction of capital confirmed by order of the court under the Companies Act 1985, s 137;

(d) a redemption or purchase of shares made in accordance with the Companies Act 1985, Part V, Chapter VII;

(*e*) anything done in pursuance of an order of the court under the Companies Act 1985, s 425 (compromises and arrangements with creditors and members);

(*f*) anything done under an arrangement made in pursuance of the Insolvency Act 1986, s 110 (acceptance of shares by liquidator in winding up as consideration for sale of property); or

(*g*) anything done under an arrangement made between a company and its creditors which is binding on the creditors by virtue of the Insolvency Act 1986, Part I (winding up imminent or in progress).

Further exceptions are contained in s 153(4), namely:

(*a*) where the lending of money is part of the ordinary business of the company, the lending of money by the company in the ordinary course of its business;

(*b*) the provision by a company, in good faith in the interests of the company, of financial assistance for the purpose of an employees' share scheme (with a further exception for the purpose of facilitating transactions in shares between a company's employees); and

(*c*) the making by a company of loans to persons (other than directors), employed in good faith by the company with a view to enabling those persons to acquire fully paid shares of the company or its holding company to be held by themselves by way of beneficial ownership.

In practice, the exception which is of particular relevance in the context of a share acquisition is that set out in s 153(3)(a) (distributions by way of dividend). Dividend restrictions contained in the Companies Act 1985, Part VII will limit the extent to which a substantial dividend may be paid. However, where there are sufficient distributable reserves, s 153(3)(a) is a useful exception. The value of the target can be reduced (so reducing the purchase price to be paid by the purchaser without actually reducing cash received by the vendor) if a cash dividend is paid to the vendor prior to sale; if assets are to be transferred to the vendor's group, this could be effected by dividend in specie. Similarly, borrowings incurred by a purchaser for the purpose of the acquisition may lawfully be repaid out of the proceeds of dividends declared after completion by the target (although it should be borne in mind that payment of an abnormal dividend following an acquisition may have adverse tax consequences — see p 182).

Section 153(4)(a) provides an exception for lending transactions where the lending of money is part of the ordinary business of the target company. The exception is of extremely limited assistance and in practice only available for banking and similar institutions, and rarely for other types of company. See *Steen v Law* [1963] 3 All ER 770 for an example of where the defence (on the old law) was raised without success.

Section 153(1) provides an exception from the prohibition on giving financial assistance (for transactions at or before the acquisition of the target company's shares) where:

(a) the company's principal purpose in giving that assistance is not to give it for the purpose of any such acquisition, or the giving of the assistance for that purpose is but an incidental part of some larger purpose of the company, and

(b) the assistance is given in good faith in the interests of the company.

Section 153(2) provides a similar exemption from s 151(2), for transactions occurring post-acquisition.

The exception set out in subss 153(1) and (2) was explained by the House of Lords in *Brady v Brady* [1988] 2 All ER 617. Subsection (a) provides two alternative exceptions. The first is where the company's principal purpose in giving the assistance is not to give it for the purpose of the acquisition of its shares, where the exception contemplates a principal and subsidiary purpose (of the type envisaged by Buckley LJ in the *Belmont* case, and upon which he was unwilling to express an opinion). The second exception contained in subsection (a) is where the assistance given 'is but an incidental part of some larger purpose' of the company. This was given a narrow construction by the House of Lords in *Brady*. It seems clear, however, that to fall within the exception, the transaction which otherwise amounts to financial assistance should be for an identifiable corporate purpose of the target, which is not the share acquisition. It is not always easy to see what a company's purpose is. Lord Oliver, delivering the judgment of the House of Lords said (at p 633):

... if [s 151] is not, effectively, to be deprived of any useful application, it is important to distinguish between a purpose and the reason why a purpose is formed. The ultimate reason for forming the purpose of financing an acquisition may, and in most cases probably will, be more important to those making the decision than the immediate transaction itself. But 'larger' is not the same thing as 'more important' nor is 'reason' the same as 'purpose'. If one postulates the case of a bidder for control of a public company financing his bid from the company's own funds, the obvious mischief at which the section is aimed, the immediate purpose which it is sought to achieve is that of completing the purchase and vesting control of the company in the bidder. The reasons why that course is considered desirable may be many and varied. The company may have fallen on hard times so that a change of management is considered necessary to avert disaster. It may merely be thought, and no doubt would be thought by the purchaser and the directors whom he nominates once he has control, that the business of the company would be more profitable under his management than it was heretofore. These may be excellent reasons but they cannot, in my judgment, constitute a 'larger purpose' of which the provision of assistance is merely an incident. The purpose and the only purpose of the financial assistance is and remains that of enabling the shares to be acquired and the financial and commercial advantages flowing from the acquisition, whilst they may form the reason for forming the purpose of providing assistance are a by-product of it rather than an independent purpose of which the assistance can properly be considered to be an incident.

As Lord Oliver said, the concept of a 'larger purpose' is not altogether easy to grasp or to apply to any particular set of facts. However, it does seem helpful if the transaction which involves the financial assistance is desirable for its own sake, from the target's point of view. Where a target purchases assets from the purchaser following completion of the acquisition, and the purchaser utilises the purchase price to reduce or discharge a loan raised for the purpose of the acquisition then financial assistance will be given in breach of s 151 if the target's net assets are thereby reduced to a material extent. If, however, there are good business reasons for acquiring these assets it may be possible to show that it was not the principal purpose of the target to reduce or discharge the liability, but rather to acquire the assets in question. This could therefore be a larger purpose, of which the giving of financial assistance could be thought to be merely an incident. In practice, it would obviously be helpful to show that there are compelling reasons to justify the target in making this purchase even though its net assets would be thereby reduced.

Except in the clearest of cases, advisers will, in view of the decision in *Brady v Brady*, often be reluctant to rely on s 153(1) or (2). It may be desirable, therefore, to sanction transactions under s 155 *et seq*, where those sections can be brought into play.

One example where s 153(1) is commonly relied upon, however, is in relation to the payment of commissions and fees, and the giving of warranties, in a typical vendor placing, This is considered in more detail at p 56.

Whitewash for private companies

A further relaxation from the prohibition on financial assistance is contained in ss 155–158, which sets out the requirements for the so-called 'whitewash' procedure.

The whitewash provisions are available only to private companies, in relation to the acquisition of shares in that company, or in that company's holding company, provided also that the holding company is itself a private company, and there is no intermediate 'plc' in the chain of ownership. Companies already incorporated as a plc can, where practicable, be re-registered as private companies under s 53 of the Companies Act 1985 so as to avail themselves of the procedure. This may be timed to coincide with the passing of any resolutions necessary to effect the whitewash, but the company must have been re-registered when the financial assistance is given. It should be borne in mind that the usual practice of the Registrar of Companies is to await the expiration of the 28 day period during which an application under s 54 of the Companies Act 1985 for cancellation of the resolution to re-register the company may be made. However, if the Registrar is satisfied that the company may be re-registered (and no person is able to bring such an action) it may be possible, by arrangement, to accelerate the re-registration.

The whitewash procedure may be adopted to enable a company to give financial assistance only if that company has net assets which are not thereby reduced, or to the extent that they are reduced, if the assistance is provided out of distributable profits (s 155(2)). Unlike s 152(1)(a)(iv), when considering whether the net assets of the private company have been reduced, and the availability of distributable reserves for the purpose of conducting a whitewash, it is the book value, and not the market value of net assets, that is relevant (s 155(2), applying s 154(2)). Difficulty can arise where the financial assistance in question is the giving of a guarantee, with the extent to which that guarantee should be recognised as a liability and whether the guarantee has the effect of reducing the company's net assets. In requiring provision to be made for certain liabilities, s 154(2)(b) adopts the wording of Companies Act 1985, Sched 4, para 89, which applies to the drawing up of statutory accounts. Amounts to be provided as liabilities, for the purpose of determining net assets, include 'any amount retained as reasonably necessary for the purpose of providing for any liability or loss which is either likely to be incurred or certain to be incurred but uncertain as to amount or as to the date on which it will arise'. Except in the case where the target is guaranteeing a liability of a company which is insolvent or whose ability to meet its obligations is in doubt, no provision will usually be necessary.

The whitewash procedure requires a special resolution of the company which is giving the financial assistance and, where the financial assistance is given for the purpose of an acquisition of shares in its holding company, a special resolution of that holding company and all intermediate holding companies is required. However, no special resolution of any wholly-owned subsidiary is required. It is possible, therefore, to eliminate the requirement for a special resolution under the whitewash in respect of assistance given immediately after the transfer of shares to the purchaser, if that company becomes the wholly-owned subsidiary of the purchaser.

The directors of the company giving the assistance and, where the assistance is being given by a subsidiary, the directors of the holding company whose shares are being acquired, and all intermediate holding companies must swear a statutory declaration in the prescribed form, and complying with the requirements of s 156. This applies whether or not there is also a requirement for a special resolution.

A statutory declaration must be given by the directors of the company giving assistance in relation to its own shares, on form 155(6)a, or if in relation to the acquisition of shares in its holding company, on form 155(6)b. It must be sworn by all the directors of the company. If one director is unavailable, therefore, arrangements must be made for him to swear his declaration, or he must have ceased to be a director at the time at which the declaration is sworn. While the form of declaration contemplates that all directors will make the declaration on the same form, it is suggested that this does not need to be the case provided separate forms are sworn at the same time, and in identical form. (See *Re NL Electrical Ltd v 3i Plc* Chancery Division, 30 April 1992 (unreported), where procedural and filing requirements in relation to the statutory declaration were not properly complied with.)

The statutory declaration to be given by the directors states that 'the directors have formed the opinion, as regards the company's initial situation immediately following the date on which the assistance is proposed to be given, that there will be no ground on which it could then be found to be unable to pay its debts; and either if – (a) it is intended to commence the winding up of the company within 12 months of that date, that the company will be able to pay its debts in full within 12 months of the commencement of the winding up, or (b) in any other case, that the company will be able to pay its debts as they fall due during the year immediately following that date' (s 156(2)). In determining whether a company is able to pay its debts, the directors are required to take into account those same liabilities as would be relevant to that question under s 122 of the Insolvency Act 1986 (s 156(3)). Serious penalties apply to a person who makes a statutory declaration without having reasonable grounds for having done so.

The directors' statutory declarations are required by s 156(4) to have annexed to them a report addressed to the directors by the auditors of the company in question, stating that the auditors have 'enquired into the state of the affairs of the company, and that they are not aware of anything to indicate that the opinion expressed by the directors in the declaration as to any of the matters mentioned in s 156(2) is unreasonable in all the circumstances'. Where it is proposed that the whitewash is to be undertaken, the auditors should be contacted in good time to ensure that they will be able to give their report under section 156(4). If it is possible to arrange that the whitewash is undertaken in conjunction with the auditors' work on the statutory audit, the costs of preparation of the report are likely to be minimised.

Careful planning of the completion procedure is necessary if, as part of the completion meeting on an acquisition, financial assistance is to be given by the target or any of its subsidiaries in relation to which the 'whitewash' procedure is to be followed. It will often be the case that the purchaser will wish to change the auditors at completion, and in such case may prefer the incoming auditors to give the report under s 156(4) supporting directors' statutory declarations. Similarly, it is very often the case that directors associated with the vendor will resign at completion, and the purchaser's directors be appointed. It will be necessary to ensure that the resignations and appointments of the new directors and auditors have taken effect, at the time that the statutory declarations are given.

The whitewash procedure is straightforward in the case of a wholly-owned subsidiary, where there is no requirement for a resolution to sanction the assistance. Where there are minority shareholders, particularly those who do not agree to the proposals, the ability to implement the financial assistance may be impeded. Section 157(2) permits an application to be made to the court for cancellation of the special resolution by (in the case of a company limited by shares) the holders of not less (in the aggregate) than 10 per cent in nominal value of the company's share capital or any class of it, unless the person proposing to make the application has consented to or voted in favour of the resolution. The application must be made within 28 days of the passing of the resolution (s 54(3), applicable by virtue of s 157(3)). One catch in s 157(2) is that 10 per cent in nominal value of 'any class' of the company's shares may bring an action for cancellation of the resolution. So where a resolution is unanimously passed by the holders of voting shares, holders of non-voting shares may nevertheless have the right to object. Wherever possible, therefore, it is advisable to ensure that, even in the case of non-voting shares, the holders of 90 per cent or more of each class of such shares consent to the resolution. It should be noted that the existence of a minority shareholder entitled to vote on a resolution, if he dissents or cannot be located, will impose a 28 day delay in completion of the transaction which constitutes financial assistance. Where third party acquisition finance has been arranged, this may be a considerable problem and in such case every effort should be made to eliminate a minority holding.

The Act imposes a strict timetable for the giving of financial assistance which has been sanctioned by the whitewash procedure, and there are various procedural requirements which affect the time at which the transaction constituting financial assistance can be entered into. In summary, the procedural and timing requirements are as follows:

(1) Convene the extraordinary general meeting for the passing of a special resolution. No special resolution for financial assistance purposes is required where the companies concerned are wholly-owned subsidiaries. Where written resolution or short notice procedures are adopted, the 21 day notice period can also be curtailed.

(2) The directors must swear the statutory declaration and the auditors give their report in support, no more than seven days before the passing of the special resolution. The statutory declaration and auditors' report is to be filed within 15 days after the declaration is made unless a special resolution is passed, when they are to be filed together (s 156(5)).

(3) On the date of the directors' statutory declaration or no more than seven days thereafter, a special resolution (if required) must be passed. Note s 157(4), which provides the draconian consequence that the resolution will not be effective unless the directors' statutory declaration was available for inspection at the meeting at which the resolution was passed.

(4) Within 28 days of passing the special resolution, application to court in respect of any objection to the passing of a resolution must be made (s 157(3)).

(5) Financial assistance may be given not earlier than the expiry of four weeks from the date on which the special resolution (if any) is passed or (where there is more than one special resolution required) the last resolution is passed and not later than the expiry of the period of eight weeks beginning with the date of the directors' statutory declaration (or where there is more than one the earliest of the declarations). Financial assistance may be given immediately where there is no requirement for any special

resolution, or where the resolution was passed unanimously by all persons entitled to vote in favour of it.

There are some peculiarities in the timing requirements of ss 157 and 158: it is necessary to have a delay of four weeks after passing of the special resolution if a single member has not voted in favour of that resolution — even where, under s 157(2) his holding is not sufficient to apply to court for the cancellation of the resolution. Conversely, if the special resolution has been passed unanimously by the holders of all voting shares, then even if there are holders of non-voting shares who could apply to court for cancellation of the resolution, there is no necessity to have a four week delay before implementing the financial assistance.

Consequences of breach

Section 151 provides substantial criminal penalties for breach. If a company acts in contravention of the section, the company is liable to a fine and every officer of the company in default is liable, upon conviction on indictment, to imprisonment for up to two years, or a fine, or both.

It is reasonable to suppose that the civil consequences of breach will be similar to the consequences of contravening s 54 of the 1948 Act. These were severe. Those who were party to a breach could be called upon to compensate the company. The action could be brought either under the head of the tort of conspiracy or as a breach of a constructive trust (*Belmont Finance Corp Ltd v Williams Furniture Ltd* [1978] 3 WLR 712). The company could sue, even though it was a party to the conspiracy, if the essence of the transaction was to deprive the company improperly of part of its assets. An individual minority shareholder could sue on behalf of the company (*Wallersteiner v Moir* [1974] 1 WLR 991).

After some judicial dispute it was settled that security given in breach of the section was invalid (see *Victor Battery Co v Curry's* [1946] 1 Ch 242; *Selanger United Rubber Estates v Craddock (a bankrupt) (No 3)* [1968] 2 All ER 1073; and *Heald v O'Connor* [1971] 2 All ER 1105). A guarantee of indebtedness incurred by the target in breach of the section was void unless it amounted to an indemnity which, on its proper construction, was intended to apply even if the loan were unenforceable (see *Yeoman Credit v Latter* [1961] 2 All ER 295 cited in *Heald v O'Connor* at p 1110).

Where an executory contract contemplated a breach of s 54 it might nevertheless have been enforceable if the transaction could be carried into effect without infringing the section (*Southwestern*

Mineral Water Ltd v Ashmore [1967] 2 All ER 953). In that case the
target was to provide security, by way of a debenture, for the
payment of the purchase price for its shares. Had the vendors been
prepared to waive the term of the agreement requiring the issue of the
debenture they would have been at liberty to enforce the contract.
They were not so prepared, however, and as the debenture was an
integral part of the arrangement it was held that the agreement was
unenforceable on either side. See also *Brady v Brady* [1988] All ER
617. For an example of where the courts were prepared to
contemplate severance of the security elements of a transaction, see
Nielson v Stewart [1991] SLT 523.

Examples

Set out below are some examples of s 151 considerations which might
arise, in the context of an acquisition of shares in a private company:
(1) *The sale of assets by the target to the vendor.* If the consideration
     for the sale of the assets is cash, paid on completion of the sale, it
     is unlikely that the transaction will be prohibited by s 151 unless
     there is a material reduction in the value of the target's net
     assets. If, however, any part of the consideration of the sale is
     left outstanding – for example as an inter-company loan — then
     the transaction will be prohibited financial assistance within the
     meaning of s 152(1)(a)(iii). If the consideration is discharged by
     the issue to the company giving the assistance of a loan note or
     other debt security it is unlikely that this will be sufficient to
     take the arrangement outside the scope of s 152(1)(a)(iii). If,
     however, the consideration issued by the purchaser is its
     marketable debt security, it seems that a court ought more
     readily to regard the indebtedness as cash equivalent and so
     outside the scope of the section, although the point has not been
     decided.
        Similar difficulties can arise where the transaction provides
     for a post-completion adjustment (for example, by reference to
     a stock-take or where a lease cannot be assigned pending
     landlord's consent). In such case if there is a deferral of the
     consideration receivable by the target, then the section may be
     infringed. It may be possible to restructure the transaction so as
     to take it outside the scope of s 152(1)(a)(iii) by ensuring that
     title does not pass from the target until the adjustable element
     has been determined, or by ensuring the only post-closing
     adjustments are obligations of the target, not the purchaser.
(2) *The acquisition of assets by the target from the purchaser.* If the

consideration for the acquisition is a cash payment by the target, and the purpose of the transaction is to put the purchaser in funds to enable it to purchase the target's shares, the transaction will be 'financial assistance', and will be prohibited by s 151 if it falls within one of the sub-definitions of s 152(1)(a). For example, if the target pays for the assets before title is transferred to it, then it will be prohibited by reason of s 152(1)(a)(iii), or if the target has no net assets or the transaction will result in a material reduction in its net assets, it will be prohibited by reason of s 152(1)(a)(iv).

(3) *Repayment of existing indebtedness.* Where the target is part of a group of companies, it may be an obligation of the target to repay intra-group indebtedness at completion. Since the repayment of the indebtedness will not give rise to a reduction in the target company's net assets, the indebtedness already being reflected as a liability in the target company's balance sheet, it is difficult to see how this will give rise to financial assistance within the meaning of s 152(1)(a). This is particularly the case where the intra-group indebtedness is 'on demand' since the group companies will be entitled at any time to make a demand and claim repayment of the debt (*Gradwell (Pty) Ltd v Rostra Printers Ltd* [1959] 4 SALR 419, cited in *Belmont*). However, where the intra-group indebtedness is not repayable until a future date, then it is possible that the acceleration of repayment might give rise to the giving of financial assistance. For example, if the target company could not readily replace the intra-group borrowing, or if the intra-group borrowing is on better terms than borrowings it could obtain elsewhere, it is possible this might result in a reduction in its net assets which, if the target has none or if material, may be prohibited as falling within s 152(1)(a)(iv).

(4) *Ex gratia payments to employees.* It is not uncommon for payment to be made to an officer or employee of the target, in connection with the sale of the target. Payments by the target will reduce its net assets and will often, directly or indirectly, affect the amount of consideration payable by the purchaser. If such a payment is made as compensation on termination of employment arising upon change of ownership, it will generally be in discharge or compromise of the target's legal liability to the employee and not constitute unlawful financial assistance under s 151. If, however, the payment is in excess of what may reasonably be regarded as the target's liability to the ex-employee, that excess payment could be prohibited if it results in a material reduction in the target's net assets (s 152(1)(a)(iv))

(and any such payments to a director should comply with s 312). It is difficult to see how such a payment might be exempt under s 153. The difficulty could readily be avoided (assuming the vendor is indirectly financing the payment by a reduction in the purchase price) if the vendor paid any excess compensation. If the vendor is to fund the ex gratia payment in circumstances where he will pay tax on the disposal proceeds,then a reduction in the price to represent the cost of the payment will give him a tax deduction for that cost. If, however, the vendor will not obtain such a deduction, or the purchaser is to fund the cost the parties may wish the payment to be made by the target so that the target obtains a tax deduction against its trading profits.

Similar considerations will apply where 'loyalty' or similar bonuses are payable to staff who are to remain in the target's employment. The vendor may wish to make payments to staff of its former subsidiary as a means of allowing them to participate in the sale proceeds or in recognition of past service. Any such payment will fall to be considered under s 151 (being a gift under s 152(1)(a)(i) or resulting in a material reduction in net assets under s 152(1)(a)(iv)). It does not seem unreasonable for some part of the employee's bonus payment to be made by a target in connection with a change of ownership, since loyalty of staff during a time of uncertainty is important. It might be arguable, in such a case, that any such payment will fall within s 153(1) or (2), although difficult issues of judgement will arise for the target directors as to what is reasonable in the circumstances. These issues will not necessarily be eliminated if the target is put in funds by the vendor so as to enable it to make the payment. The target plainly cannot borrow the funds from the vendor as this would not increase its net assets from which to make the payments, and the money must therefore be contributed by gift (capital contribution) or subscription for share capital. Section 151 problems will not be eliminated if the target is free to use the funds as it wishes, so this excludes subscription for share capital (which, when subscribed, represents funds freely available to the target). Generally, however, only a subscription for share capital will result in the payment increasing the vendor's base cost for tax purposes. It may not be possible to marry together tax considerations and the requirements of s 151 in such a situation.

(5) *Management fees.* Where the target is leaving a group of companies, management charges may be levied by other group companies. If the management charge levied on sale is at the usual rate, and is a reasonable charge for services genuinely

provided to the target, then this is unlikely to cause a problem. Where the charge is a one-off or increased charge at the time of sale, the excess payment may be prohibited by reason of s 152(1)(a)(i) or (iv). Management charges are often preferred over dividends as a means of realising an income from a subsidiary. Where the subsidiary has insufficient distributable profits, any excess management charge (ie that part unrepresented by a genuine supply of services) may be unlawful (applying *Aveling Barford v Perion* — see p 11). Where distributable reserves are adequate, however, consideration should be given to paying any doubtful management charge by way of dividend. Care must also be taken to ensure that where any 'management fee' exceeds that which would be payable on a *quantum meruit* basis, it is not a distribution for tax purposes. If it is, then the payment will not be deductible for tax purposes and in the absence of a group income election, the target will be obliged to account for ACT. Another common tax trap is to forget that, save where the payer and recipient of the management charge are in the same VAT group, management charges attract VAT.

(6) *Surrender of group relief.* Where a target leaves a group, it is usual for parties to agree arrangements in relation to past trading losses of the target, to the extent that they have not already been utilised. Losses arising in respect of any accounting period ending prior to the date of acquisition may either be carried forward and set against future trading profits of the target, or alternatively they may be surrendered to members of the vendor's group to offset the corporation tax liability of those companies. Although unutilised tax losses would not be recognised in the target's books (except to the extent that there are profits against which they may be offset), unutilised tax losses nevertheless represent an asset of the target. The surrender by the target of unutilised losses to members of the vendor's group would be prohibited by s 151 if the target had no net assets, or if it resulted in a material reduction in the target's net assets. If, therefore, substantial losses were surrendered without payment having been received by the target, it would appear that there would be a breach of s 151. It is suggested therefore that any arrangement for the surrender of losses by a target should only occur where the target receives payment for those losses. It is not necessarily the case that the target should receive an amount equal to the face value of the tax credit arising upon use of the losses; it would seem reasonable that if the losses are surrendered to the vendor

and the target receives payment on a date earlier than the date upon which the target would be able to make use of those losses then a discounted payment in respect of the losses could be made. The discount could be substantial in a case where it is not certain when, if ever, losses would be available for utilisation by the target. Furthermore, if the target is deprived of the ability to use the losses (for example where they are not able to be carried forward—see p 208) then it is suggested that any subsequent surrender to the vendor's group could be made for a nominal payment only without infringing the section. (See *Charterhouse v Tempest Diesel* for a case involving surrender of tax losses.)

(7) *Warranties and indemnities in underwriting agreements.* Where a private company is to be acquired by a public company, the public company may wish to use its shares to finance the acquisition. This could be achieved by financing the acquisition in a number of ways, for example by a vendor placing, or alternatively the acquiror could separately raise acquisition finance by way of cash placing or rights issue (see Chapter 10). The public company will arrange with its financial adviser for the issue of its shares to be underwritten and in the underwriting agreement the financial adviser will usually require warranties to be given by the public company and also an indemnity in favour of the financial adviser in relation to the underwriting. In such a case, the public company incurs a liability in connection with the issue of its shares, and consideration should be given to the application of s 151.

The giving of warranties by a public company in connection with an underwriting agreement is unlikely to amount to financial assistance, unless, at the time of giving the warranty, the company knows itself to be in breach of the warranties as a result of which there may be a material claim against the company giving rise to a material reduction in its net assets under s 152(1)(a)(iv).

Indemnities are more difficult. On the face of it, an indemnity is financial assistance within the meaning of s 152(1)(a)(ii) and it is unlikely that the indemnity will fall within the exemption provided by that section, for an indemnity limited to the indemnifier's (ie the public company's) neglect or default as this will generally be unacceptable to the financial adviser. Financial assistance by way of indemnity is not qualified by any test of materiality and in this sense, therefore, it is irrelevant that any liability under the indemnity may not be material.

Indemnities in placing agreements entered into in connection with an acquisition are generally considered to fall within the scope of the 'larger purpose' exception in s 153(1) as being an incidental part of some larger purpose of the company, and given in good faith and in the interests of the company, where the 'larger purpose' of the company is the acquisition of the target company. It seems more difficult to justify the indemnity on these grounds, however, in the case of a rights issue or cash placing. Furthermore, the extent to which a public company can rely on s 153 in the case of those types of financial assistance which are specifically prohibited, without exception, by art 23 of the Second Directive on Company Law may be in doubt. Article 23 prohibits a public company from advancing funds, making loans, or giving security 'with a view' to an acquisition of its shares, and has no exception of the type contemplated by s 153. The recent decision of the European Court of Justice in *Marleasing SA v La Comercial Internacional de Alimentación SA* [1992] 1 CMLR 305 has rendered uncertain the extent to which a company can rely on any exception from a prohibition imposed by a Directive, in a case where the Directive does not contemplate that exception. The extent to which the *Marleasing* decision will have an effect on ss 151–158 of the Companies Act 1985 will no doubt become clearer in time, but, for the present, its effect ought to be borne in mind by those seeking to rely on s 153.

Chapter 6

Employees

It is often a term of an acquisition that key employees of the target enter into service agreements with the target on completion of the acquisition. The Agreement for Sale, cl 4(D) (see p 281), takes account of this. By itself, the acquisition of the target will normally have no effect upon existing contracts of service between the target and its employees. The acquisition will not constitute a transfer of an undertaking as defined in the Transfer of Undertakings (Protection of Employment) Regulations 1981 (SI No 1794), and these will not therefore be considered. It is only in the rare case where a contract of service has a specific provision relating to a takeover of the target that the contract will be affected. However, the purchaser should have in mind that in the event of a change in employer (eg upon a transfer of employment between companies in a group, but no change in the terms of employment other than the names of the parties), there is a statutory requirement to inform employees so transferred of the nature of the change within one month (Employment Protection (Consolidation) Act 1978, s 4).

In addition to individual contracts of employment, the purchaser should also consider whether there are any collective agreements between the target and any trade union and whether any trade union is recognised. Recognition of trade unions cannot now be compelled by statute. In the event of the target proposing to dismiss employees by reason of redundancy the target is under a duty to consult independent trade unions recognised by it and to inform the Secretary of State in relation to proposed redundancies (Trade Union and Labour Relations (Consolidation) Act 1992, ss 188–198).

It is commonplace for changes in the target's employees to take place after an acquisition. Such changes may involve dismissal of the target's employees either actually or constructively, eg, where terms of employment are changed without an employee's consent and the employee resigns, accepting the breach of his contract of employment. Unlawful dismissal may be unfair (as defined in the Employment Protection (Consolidation) Act 1978, ss 54 and 55) or wrongful, that is constituting a breach of the employee's contract of employment at common law. If the target's articles provide that an executive director ceases to be an executive director upon the termination of his directorship (eg by an ordinary resolution of the target pursuant to the Companies Act 1985, s 303) it has been held that it will nevertheless be a breach of his service contract if the target removes him from office as a director (see *Shindler v Northern Raincoat Co Ltd* [1960] 1 WLR 1038).

The reasons for changes in the target's employees may include a decision to reorganise the target's management structure, prompted by economic or technical considerations, or there may be circumstances which justify dismissal by reason of redundancy as defined in the Employment Protection (Consolidation) Act 1978, s 81, as amended by the Employment Act 1982, Sched 2. Where redundancy is involved the target may become liable to make redundancy payments under the Employment Protection (Consolidation) Act 1978. As redundancy payments will be calculated by reference to the length of an employee's continuous employment and age, a purchaser contemplating redundancies will wish to have details of the employee's length of continuous employment, age and remuneration for the purpose of calculating the amount likely to be due, together with details of any collective agreements or other agreements relating to redundancy entered into by the target. In ascertaining the employee's length of continuous employment the purchaser will have in mind the provisions which deem service to have continued notwithstanding a change in employer, eg upon the change in ownership of a business or upon a transfer of employment between associated companies in a group (see the Employment Protection (Consolidation) Act 1978, ss 151 and 153(4) and Sched 13).

In order to avoid a claim of unfair dismissal, the purchaser will need to bear in mind the general provisions for fairness of dismissal contained in the Employment Protection (Consolidation) Act 1978, s 57, as amended by the Employment Act 1980, s 6. The extent to which the target, as employer of the employees concerned, has in the particular circumstances, including the size and administrative resources of the target's undertaking, acted reasonably or unreasonably in treating the reason or reasons for dismissal as sufficient reasons for dismissing the employees concerned will be particularly relevant. Where the reason for dismissal is redundancy, particular attention will need to be paid to the selection of employees who are to be made redundant, so that there is no unfair dismissal on the ground of redundancy as contemplated by the Employment Protection (Consolidation) Act 1978, s 59.

Where there has been an unlawful dismissal of an employee, such as a senior employee of the target, it will be necessary to calculate the amount which the employee would recover if he sued the target for damages for wrongful dismissal or for compensation for unfair dismissal. The following summary may be of assistance.

DAMAGES FOR WRONGFUL DISMISSAL

The calculation of damages for wrongful dismissal will be appropriate when the contract of employment of the employee concerned has been terminated unlawfully. For example, the notice required by the contract may not have been given or a fixed term of employment may have been ended prematurely without lawful cause. No damages for wrongful dismissal will be due if the employer was entitled to terminate employment without notice, as in the case of gross misconduct by the employee.

It is first necessary to ascertain the unexpired period of the contract of employment or, if the contract is not a fixed term, the length of notice which according to the contract the employee would have been entitled to receive and serve, if his employment has not been prematurely terminated.

It is then necessary to ascertain the value of the employee's entitlement (including fringe benefits which the employer is contractually bound to provide) throughout the unexpired period of employment or notice period (see *Beach v Reed Corrugated Cases Ltd* [1956] 1 WLR 807; *Bold v Brough, Nicholson & Hall Ltd* [1964] 1 WLR 201 and *Lavarack v Woods of Colchester Ltd* [1967] 1 QB 278). If the employee is entitled to commission, this must be taken into account if dismissal would result in a breach of contractual obligation to provide the employee with an opportunity to earn the commission (see eg *Newman (RS) Ltd, Re Raphael's Claim* [1916] 2 Ch 309). Where the employee has lost the use of a car provided by the target for his private purposes as well as for business the employee is entitled to be compensated. One method of assessing such a loss is to calculate the cost of purchasing and running a comparable car for the unexpired period of the contract of employment or notice period as appropriate. Loss of pension rights will need to be calculated. The terms of the employee's contract of employment and any relevant pension scheme will need to be reviewed. Loss of pension rights may be calculated in numerous ways. For example, a broker may be requested to establish the capital cost of purchasing an annuity to cover the difference between the pension receivable by the employee if he had retired at the end of the fixed term contract of employment or notice period and the pension to which he is actually entitled. Generally compensation will not be due for injury to feelings and reputation (*Addis v Gramophone Co Ltd* [1909] AC 488).

Then the employee's prospective earnings (if any) over the remaining term of the contract of employment or notice period should be calculated. There is no need to include in this calculation anticipated future salary increases unless these were provided by contract. The employee is of course under a duty to mitigate his loss and, if he takes proceedings against the target and damages are not to be reduced, he will have to show that he has made attempts to obtain suitable alternative employment. This is the most difficult of all figures to quantify in advance. Each case must be considered on its merits; for example, highly qualified technical personnel will probably find it easier to obtain alternative employment than executives of advancing age with no special qualifications. It may be that the target itself, or, where the purchaser is a company, some other company in the purchaser's group will make the employee an offer of alternative employment. It is hard to generalise, but it should be remembered that an employee is not necessarily bound to accept employment of a lower status (see *Yetton v Eastwoods Froy Ltd* [1967] 1 WLR 104). He is, however, under a duty to take reasonable steps to seek out other similar employment as quickly as possible and all benefits received from alternative employment actually obtained or which ought reasonably to have been obtained must be taken into account.

By deducting the amount which the employee can reasonably be expected to earn in alternative employment from the remuneration that he would have received under the contract of employment, a net total entitlement will be ascertained. It is then necessary to make a deduction from this amount to account for the accelerated payment. This can be done by obtaining a quotation from a suitable insurance company for the capital cost of an annuity to provide the resulting net entitlement for the remaining term of the contract of employment. This may be used as the working figure. Further amounts may be deducted from this capital sum in respect of the possibility of serious illness which would have resulted in a premature determination of the employment and the employee's national insurance contributions. Unemployment benefits will be deductible (*Westwood v Secretary of State for Employment* [1984] IRLR 209).

The incidence of taxation must be taken into account. In *British Transport Commission v Gourley* [1956] AC 185 the court ruled that the object of awarding damages should be to put the plaintiff in the same position as if the particular wrong had not occurred. Accordingly a deduction should be made for tax. The taxation of payments by way of compensation for loss of office is governed by the Income and Corporation Taxes Act 1988, ss 148 and 188. The first £30,000 of a compensatory payment is not subject to tax in the hands of the employee. Any part of a compensatory payment which exceeds £30,000 is taxable in full as earned income. Where the compensatory payment exceeds the tax-free limit, the case of *Shove v Downs Surgical plc* [1984] 1 All ER 7 suggests that an attempt should be made to estimate the net amount which would have been received by the employee after deduction of tax from gross income had he continued to be employed. The net amount would represent his actual loss. The liability to tax on the damages should be taken into account so that the actual amount received equals so far as possible the net or actual loss suffered.

COMPENSATION FOR UNFAIR DISMISSAL

Calculation of the amount which a leaving employee would recover if he presented a claim to an industrial tribunal alleging unfair dismissal by the target and claiming compensation (as opposed to re-engagement or reinstatement) will be by reference to the provisions contained in the Employment Protection (Consolidation) Act 1978, Part V, especially ss 72–76.

In the event of a finding of unfair dismissal an industrial tribunal has jurisdiction to make the following awards. The figures below are derived from the Employment Protection (Variations of Limits) Order 1992 and the Unfair Dismissal (Increase of Limits of Basic and Special Awards) Order 1992, both of which came into force on 1 April 1992. In the past these limits have been revised annually.

Basic award

This award is calculated in the same way as a redundancy payment on the basis of the employee's age, period of continuous employment and pay. The rules for calculating a week's pay are in the Employment Protection (Consolidation) Act 1978, Sched 14 as amended. The maximum week's pay which may be used for the calculation is £205 per week. The maximum entitlement under this head is £6,150.

Compensatory award

The compensatory award is such amount as the tribunal considers just and equitable having regard to the loss sustained by the employee insofar as that loss relates to the unfair dismissal. *Norton Tool Co Ltd v Tewson* [1973] 1 All ER 183 is one of the authoritative pronouncements on the calculation of such compensation. Under this head fall to be considered matters similar to, but not identical with, those already considered in relation to an amount which the employee would recover if he sued the target successfully for wrongful dismissal. The assessment of loss is calculated by reference to criteria which include: the immediate and future loss of remuneration, the loss related to the manner of the dismissal, the loss of protection in respect of unfair dismissal deriving from length of employment, expenses, pensions and loss of certain fringe benefits. The employee is under a duty to mitigate his loss and a deduction may be made accordingly. If the employee received social security benefit during a period which coincided with the period following his dismissal, then the tribunal will not deduct such benefit from the amount of its award but will warn the employer not to pay over to the employee a prescribed amount of the total award. The prescribed amount represents the tribunal's estimate of the social security benefits and other similar payments likely to have been received by the employee. The employer will subsequently receive a notice from the Secretary of State stating whether the prescribed amount is to be paid to him or to the employee (Employment Protection (Recoupment of Unemployment Benefit and Supplementary Benefit) Regulations 1977 (SI No 674) as amended by SI 1980 No 1608). The maximum sum payable in respect of a compensatory award is £10,000.

Additional award

A tribunal may make a further award where an employer has failed to comply with an order to reinstate or re-engage the employee or where there has been a finding of an unfair dismissal for certain reasons (eg trade union activities). The maximum entitlements are £5,330 and £10,660 (Employment Protection (Consolidation) Act 1978, s 71).

Special award

A special award may be made where the dismissal relates to trade union membership. The award is 104 weeks' (actual) pay or £13,400 whichever is the greater, subject to a maximum of £26,800. Where there is a failure to reinstate or re-engage and the employer cannot show that it was impracticable to comply with the award, the tribunal may award up to £20,100 or 156 weeks' (actual) pay whichever is the greater.

Since certain of the items taken into account in calculating the compensation payable following an unfair dismissal will be the same as those taken into account in calculating the amount which the employee would recover if he sued the target for wrongful dismissal, an appropriate deduction may be made from the latter calculation. There is authority for the view that redundancy payments should be deducted from damages for wrongful dismissal but the position with regard to unfair dismissal compensation is not entirely clear. (See, eg, *Stocks v Magna Merchants Ltd* [1973] 1 WLR 1505 and *Basnett v Jackson (J & A) Ltd* [1976] ICR 63.) The amount of a basic award will be reduced by the amount of any redundancy payment award made by an industrial tribunal in respect of the same dismissal or in respect of any payment made by the employer to the employee on grounds that the dismissal was by reason of redundancy (Employment Protection (Consolidation) Act 1978, s 73(9)). If the amount of any payment made by the employer to the employee on the ground that the dismissal was by reason of redundancy exceeds the amount of any basic award which would be payable but for the above provision, that excess will go to reduce the amount of any compensatory award (Employment Protection (Consolidation) Act 1978, s 74(7)).

The calculation with regard to a claim for unfair dismissal will not have to be made at all if the leaving employee belongs to one of the classes excluded by statutory provision from having a right not to be unfairly dismissed (see the Employment Protection (Consolidation) Act 1978, ss 141–146 and the Trade Union and Labour Relations (Consolidation) Act 1992, Part VII). If a claim or claims by a leaving employee of the target are settled, then certain statutory provisions should be borne in mind. If it is contemplated that a payment by way of compensation for loss of office is to be made to a director, then the provisions of the Companies Act 1985, ss 312–316, will be relevant. Section 312 provides that a payment must be approved by the target in general meeting. Where the payment is made in connection with an acquisition, s 314 provides that unless it is approved by the selling shareholders before completion the payment will be held in trust for them by the director. The sections do not apply to a bona fide payment by way of damages for a breach of contract or by way of pension (including any 'superannuation gratuity or similar payment') (s 316(3)).

In *Taupo Totara Timber Co v Rowe* [1978] AC 537 the Privy

Council held that an Australian equivalent of s 312 did not apply to payments to a director in connection with some employment held by him, nor to payments which the company was contractually bound to make. In addition it may be relevant to consider the Companies Act 1985, s 320, which provides that a company shall not enter into an arrangement whereby the company acquires one or more non-cash assets of the requisite value from a director or connected person unless the arrangement is first approved by resolution of the company in general meeting. Having reference to the definitions of 'non-cash asset' and 'the transfer or acquisition of a non-cash asset' in s 739, it is arguable that the discharge of the target's liability for damages for breach of contract could amount to the acquisition of a non-cash asset by the company. It is suggested, however, that s 320 will not apply in a normal case. If the payment and the acquisition are not independent of each other, the payment may not be deductible in calculating the taxable income of the target (see *Snook (James) & Co v Blasdale* [1952] 33 TC 244; *Peters (George) & Co v Smith* [1963] 41 TC 264; and *Smith (George J) & Co v Furlong* [1969] 45 TC 384), and may involve 'financial assistance' by the target in breach of the Companies Act 1985, s 151 (see p 53).

If it is made a provision of the settlement agreement with the leaving employee that he is precluded from presenting a complaint to or bringing any proceedings before an industrial tribunal, eg, for unfair dismissal, such a provision will be void (Employment Protection (Consolidation) Act 1978, s 140). Accordingly regard should be had to the procedures available under the Act whereby a conciliation officer may be requested to 'take action' in connection with any agreement to refrain from presenting a complaint of unfair dismissal as a result of which such an agreement may not be void (see especially ss 134(3) and 140(2)(d)).

Chapter 7

Pensions

Purchasers should pay close attention to the pension arrangements for the target employees. The purchaser will be concerned primarily with the funding of the pensions already accrued, the effect which the future pension contribution rate will have on profits and any contingent liabilities, such as for sex discrimination. The purchaser may also be concerned as to how the pension benefits compare with those provided under any existing pension scheme of the purchaser, particularly if the target's employees are to be transferred to it. The vendor will be concerned with retaining, or obtaining good value for, any surplus in the pension scheme and may also be concerned with protecting the target employees' pension expectations, at least for past service.

There are numerous different types of scheme: tax approved/non-approved; funded/unfunded; final pay/money purchase. In addition, employers may now contribute directly to a personal pension scheme taken out by the employee. In practice, however, most pension issues concern funded approved schemes and these are considered first.

FUNDED APPROVED SCHEME

A funded approved scheme may provide benefits on a final pay or a money purchase basis. If final pay, the scheme will provide for each year of pensionable service a pension from normal pension age of a sixtieth or some other fraction of final pensionable pay, being the level of pensionable pay at or near retirement. If money purchase, the scheme will provide whatever pension can be bought for the employee on retirement with the pension contributions paid by or in respect of him and the investment return on those contributions. In addition, both types of scheme will usually provide life cover and other ancillary benefits.

It is generally a requirement of the Inland Revenue that a funded approved scheme, whether final pay or money purchase, is established under irrevocable trusts (Income and Corporation Taxes Act 1988, s 592). Such a scheme is known as an 'exempt approved scheme'. As a condition of approval, benefits may not exceed certain limits (IR 12 (1991)). Approval carries with it many tax advantages: the employer is entitled to corporation tax relief on its contributions in respect of its employees and former employees; the employees are not charged to tax on any contributions made for them by their employer and are entitled to income tax relief on their own contributions; income from and capital gains on the scheme investments are also exempt from tax. However, the exemption does not extend to income derived from trading. Therefore, where the target has its own scheme, the purchaser should consider whether, having regard to the scheme investments, a warranty should be sought that the trustees have not traded.

The scheme members may be contracted-out of the state earnings related pension scheme. Lower national insurance contributions (employer and employee) are payable. If final pay, the scheme takes over the liability for part of the state pension, known as the guaranteed minimum pension (GMP). If money purchase, an amount equivalent to the reduction (the rebate) in national insurance contributions must be applied to provide money purchase benefits, known as protected rights, for the employee and the employee's benefits in the state scheme are reduced by an amount equal to the GMP. To be contracted-out the employer must hold a contracting-out certificate for the scheme in question or be named in a holding company certificate for that scheme.

CONTROL OF SCHEME

As it is established under trust, a funded approved scheme is not under the control of the sponsoring employer. This point, although obvious, is all too often forgotten by the vendors and purchasers when considering issues concerning the transfer or use of pension funds.

The scheme will be governed by its constitutory documents and by overriding legislation. The trustees' duties are quite clear, namely to administer the scheme in accordance with those documents and that legislation and, when exercising powers and discretions, to act in the interests of the members and other beneficiaries (present and future), holding the balance fairly between them. If, as is usually the case, the employer is entitled to any residual surplus on winding up the employer will also be a beneficiary but it is not thought that it should be regarded for most purposes as having a competing interest with those of the members and other beneficiaries.

The employer will have only such powers as are given to it under the scheme's governing documents. Even in relation to those powers the employer does not have uncontrolled discretion. Although often vested in the employer, the power to change trustees is a fiduciary power (*Re Skeat's Settlement* (1889) 42 ChD 522). In *Mettoy Pension Trustees Ltd v Evans* [1991] 2 All ER 513 it was found that a power vested in an employer alone over the application of surplus on winding up is also a fiduciary power. It is thought that the employer would also be under a fiduciary duty when determining a transfer amount or the funds to be applied on a partial winding-up if the power is vested in the employer alone but only under a duty of 'good faith' if the power is vested in the trustees but exercisable only with the employer's consent. However, it is also thought that even if the power is vested in the employer alone the employer will not be under a fiduciary duty when exercising an amendment power or, while the scheme is ongoing, an augmentation power but, again, the employer will be under a duty of 'good faith'.

This duty of 'good faith' has evolved from the implied term in every contract of employment:

that the employers will not, without reasonable and proper cause, conduct themselves in a manner calculated or likely to destroy or seriously damage the relationship of confidence and trust between employer and employee . . .

(see *Woods v WM Car Services (Peterborough) Ltd* [1981] ICR 666 at 670, approved by the Court of Appeal in *Lewis v Motorworld Garages Ltd* [1986] ICR 157). The duty was held to apply 'as much to the exercise of his rights and powers under a pension scheme as they do to the other rights and powers of the employer' *per* Browne-Wilkinson V-C (as he was then) in *Imperial Group Pension Trust Ltd v Imperial Tobacco Ltd* [1991] 2 All ER 597. In that case the Vice-Chancellor said it was not necessary to base a claim in contract as, construed against the background of the employment contract, the pension scheme deed and rules themselves are to be taken as being impliedly subject to the limitation that the rights and powers of the employer can only be exercised in accordance with the duty of 'good faith'. To comply with this duty an employer should exercise (or not exercise) its rights and powers under a pension scheme in such a way as will not destroy or seriously damage the relationship of trust and confidence between the employer and not only its employees but also its former employees. These rights and powers should be exercised

(a) with a view to the efficient running of the scheme and (b) not for some collateral purpose. The Vice-Chancellor added that the employer 'can have regard to its own financial interests but only to the extent that, in so doing, it does not breach the obligation of good faith . . .'. As the duty arises under the pension scheme deed and rules (and not under the employment contract) it is thought that the duty is owed by any company with rights and powers under the scheme even if it is not the employer or former employer of the member or other beneficiary concerned.

FUNDING OF FINAL PAY BENEFITS

With a final pay scheme the purchaser should ensure that the liabilities in respect of service up to completion are fully funded. To do so it is first necessary to identify those past service liabilities. It is then necessary to consider whether the available assets are sufficient to fund them. Since under a final pay scheme all pensionable service counts for pension based on final pensionable pay at retirement or earlier termination of employment, it is generally accepted that the past service liabilities should be calculated not by reference to final pensionable pay at completion but by reference to projected final pensionable pay at retirement or earlier termination of employment.

If the past service liabilities were to be based on final pensionable pay at completion the purchaser would be faced with funding not only the pension referable to service after completion but also any increase in the pension referable to service up to completion which is attributable to pay increases after completion. This would result in a significant increase in the contribution rate after completion, whereas generally the contribution rate is fixed at a level which is intended, all other things being equal, to remain reasonably stable throughout the employees' remaining working lives. Broadly, this is a requirement for accounting purposes (see SSAP 24: *Accounting for Pension Costs*).

At the time of the transaction the ultimate final pensionable pay of the employees will not, of course, be known. Likewise, the investment return which will actually be obtained on the current scheme assets will be unknown. Therefore, in order to ascertain whether the current assets are likely to be sufficient to fund the past service liabilities it is necessary to make assumptions as to the rate of future pay increases and investment return and also as to a host of other unknowns, such as mortality and the rate of withdrawals from service before retirement. In addition, the value placed on the assets may differ from the market value so as to avoid the results being distorted by short-term fluctuations in the stock market, which are not really material given the long-term nature of pension liabilities. Allowance may also be made for benefits which have historically been provided on a discretionary basis, such as periodic increases to pensions in payment and enhanced early retirement terms. If a practice, albeit discretionary, has been established, the purchaser may find it necessary to maintain it in the interests of good employee relations and, indeed, to terminate it may breach the duty of 'good faith' (see p 68).

Funding: target with own final pay scheme

If the target has its own scheme, it can be ascertained whether the past service liabilities are fully funded by comparing the respective values of the past service liabilities and the scheme assets. It may be possible to determine the position with reasonable accuracy by extrapolation from the last actuarial valuation of the scheme if that valuation is relatively recent. If reliance is to be placed on the valuation, the purchaser should obtain warranties that the valuation is accurate and that since the date as at which it was made nothing has occurred which would affect adversely the funding of the scheme. It is unlikely that the actuary owes in tort any duty of care to the purchaser unless the valuation was to the actuary's knowledge commissioned for the purpose of being made available to the purchaser (see *James McNaughton Paper Group Ltd v Hicks Anderson & Co Ltd* [1991] 2 WLR 641 and *Morgan Crucible Company Plc v Hill Samuel & Company Ltd* [1991] 2 WLR 655). Generally, however, it is preferable from the purchaser's viewpoint if the agreement for sale provides for an actuarial valuation of the scheme to be carried out after completion and for the vendor to make good any deficiency. The agreement should specify the actuarial assumptions and method to be used. Expressions such as 'reasonable assumptions' are too vague to be meaningful. A provision along these lines is better than a funding warranty as it quantifies the vendor's liability and does not come within the ambit of any provision limiting the vendor's liability for breach of warranty.

Whether the vendor agrees to such a provision is, of course, a matter for negotiation. If the scheme is in deficit the vendor may argue that the contributions have been paid as recommended by the actuary and that any part of the contributions which are being paid to fund a previously discovered deficiency should, like salaries, be regarded as part of the liabilities of the target being acquired on an 'ongoing concern' basis; furthermore, they will have been reflected in the accounts. Even if it is conceded that a valuation provision should be included, the actuarial assumptions and method are likely to be the subject of much negotiation. A small difference in the assumptions may have a very significant effect. As the financial implications are unlikely to be apparent to the principals, the actuary should be asked to quantify as well as he can on the information available any differences which may become the subject of horse-trading at the end of the day.

The vendor may also argue that any payment to be made to the purchaser in respect of a deficiency should be reduced to allow for the corporation tax relief which the target would obtain on paying a special contribution to the scheme of an amount equivalent to the deficiency. The adjustment may be made simply by reducing the amount of the payment by the percentage rate of corporation tax. However, this assumes future taxable profits against which the relief may be set and in any event results in the purchaser suffering a cash flow disadvantage. Therefore, from the purchaser's viewpoint it is preferable if the sale agreement provides for the purchaser to account to the vendor for the tax relief on the special contribution as and when it results in a deduction in taxable profits for corporation tax purposes. The vendor should ensure that account is taken of a deduction whether the deduction is in the taxable profits of the target or of any member of the group or consortium to which any loss attributable to the payment by the target of the special contribution is surrendered by way of group relief or consortium relief in accordance with the Income and Corporation Taxes Act 1988, ss 402 to 413.

In order to obtain corporation tax relief the target should pay the special contribution into the scheme. A payment by the vendor or the purchaser may not qualify for relief as it would not be in respect of its own employees or former employees. While the Income and Corporation Taxes Act 1988, s 592 generally entitles the target to relief if it pays the special contribution assuming the scheme is an exempt approved scheme (within the meaning of that section), the relief will be spread over a number of years if the total of the special contributions made by the target in the chargeable period exceeds both £25,000 and the target's aggregate ordinary annual contributions to all exempt approved schemes. The period of spread will be determined solely by the size of the special contribution in accordance with paragraph 5.6 of IR 12 (1991), viz:

£ 25,000 to £ 50,000	2 years
£ 50,001 to £100,000	3 years
£100,001 or above	4 years

In considering any adjustment it should also be borne in mind that a deficiency payment will normally be paid by way of adjustment to the consideration with the consequential capital gains tax implications.

The vendor may argue for any surplus to be reflected in the purchase price. This is probably the only way in which the vendor can obtain any benefit from it. Any attempt by the vendor to take over the target's scheme by being substituted as the principal company under the scheme and then to expel the target and its employees is likely to fail. In *Re Courage Group's Pension Schemes* [1987] 1 All ER 528, Millett J said, (at p 542):

The validity of any purported exercise of such [a power of substitution of principal company] depends on the purpose for which the substitution is made. The circumstances must be such that substitution is necessary or at least expedient in order to preserve the scheme for those for whose benefit it was established; and the substituted company must be recognisably the successor to the business and workforce of the company for which it is to be substituted. It is not enough that it is a member of the same group as, or even that it is the holding company of, the company for which it is substituted . . ..

Nevertheless, the particular circumstances of a transaction may be such that a substitution could be made (eg where a substantial part of the target's business and workforce is to be transferred to the vendor prior to completion). As the substitution would result in the target losing the benefit of the surplus (eg in the form of reduced contributions) then if the concurrence of the target is required to the substitution being made, this may amount to financial assistance by the target within the meaning of the Companies Act 1985, s 151 (see Chapter 5).

The extent of any adjustment to the purchase price on account of any surplus is a matter for negotiation. The purchaser should bear in mind (a) the tax relief available to an employer on its ordinary contributions to the scheme (Income and Corporation Taxes Act 1988, s 592); (b) the extent to which the surplus is already reflected in the target's accounts; (c) the Social Security Pensions Act 1975, s 58A, which, when implemented, will require surplus to be used to provide what is known as limited price indexation, namely increases to pensions when in payment in line with prices, up to a maximum of 5 per cent in any year; and (d) the restrictions (Inland Revenue and trust) on extracting surplus from a continuing scheme. (Broadly, the Revenue will allow only surplus in excess of 105 per cent of the liabilities (calculated on the prescribed basis) be paid to the employer. The payment will be subject to a free-standing tax (currently, 40 per cent) regardless of the profits or losses of the target

(Income and Corporation Taxes Act 1988, s 601). Unless, unusually, the employer is entitled to call for the surplus, it is, as a rule, necessary to strike a bargain with the trustees whereby, in consideration of their paying part of the surplus to the employer, certain benefit improvements are made).

Funding: group final pay scheme

If the target participates in a group final pay scheme of the vendor it will normally be necessary to make alternative pension arrangements for the target's employees and to arrange for a transfer of assets from the vendor's scheme to their new scheme. The Inland Revenue will not allow the target to continue in the vendor's scheme on an indefinite basis after the target ceases to be a subsidiary of the vendor except in exceptional circumstances (eg if the vendor is to retain a substantial, albeit minority, shareholding in the target or if the vendor and target will continue to be associated through a permanent community of interest (see IR12 (1991), para 21.1)).

On the target ceasing to participate in the vendor's scheme, there will normally be a partial winding-up of the scheme. Alternatively, the rules may just provide for leaving service benefits to be paid, although it is arguable that the exercise of any discretionary powers to provide an enhanced transfer value should at least be considered. A partial winding-up involves the segregation of a portion of the scheme assets. The scheme rules will usually provide for the portion to be determined by the trustees or the actuary but sometimes the vendor, as the principal employer under the scheme, will also be involved. The trustees' duty is to act fairly as between the target employees and the remaining members, pensioners and deferred pensioners (*Stannard v Fisons Pension Trust Ltd* [1992] IRCL 27). The actuary's duty is similar. In *Re George Newnes Group Pension Fund* [1969] 98 J Inst of Actuaries 251, it was said that the actuary should aim 'to achieve the greatest practicable degree of fairness between the various persons interested', although in the *Fisons* case Dillon LJ said he would 'not place particular emphasis on the use of the superlative'. It is thought that the principal employer will be under a fiduciary duty if the power is vested in it alone but just under a duty of 'good faith' if the power is vested in the trustees but exercisable only with the consent of the principal employer (see p 68).

In whomever the power is vested they have a duty to give properly informed consideration to the exercise of the power, and failure to do so will result in any exercise of the power being ineffective (*Kerr v British Leyland (Staff) Trustees Ltd*, unreported, 26 March 1986, CA). This duty was considered again by the Court of Appeal in the

Fisons case. Fisons plc sold its agricultural and fertilizer division. The employees continued in the Fisons scheme for a limited period (the transitional period) after completion while alternative pension arrangements were made for them. Some eight months before the end of the transitional period the trustees met and provisionally agreed upon the method of calculating the transfer, although in fact the relevant power did not become exercisable until the transitional period had ended. The method selected was the total reserve method (see below) which reflected the fact that at the time the past service liabilities were not fully funded. Between the trustees making their decision and the transitional period ending, the value of the Fisons scheme increased very greatly because of a rise in the stock market. This might have enabled the more generous past service reserve method to be used. The trustees had not been advised of the increased value of the scheme when, at the end of the transitional period and without reconsidering the matter, they authorised the payment of the transfer. Dillon LJ, upholding the decision of the trial judge that the relevant power had not been properly exercised, said:

> To give properly informed consideration to the discretion [the trustees] had to exercise, they needed also to know the relevance of the value of the fund to the problem in hand in relation to actuarial principles and the implications of their decision on future contributions. That information the actuaries could have given them (and in my opinion should have given them since it was the actuaries' duty to put the trustees in a position, so far as the actuaries could, to make a properly informed decision).

There are numerous methods which may be used to calculate the applicable portion on a partial winding-up, including:
  (*a*) the *leaving service* method, which involves valuing the past service liabilities based on current final pensionable pay;
  (*b*) the *past service reserve* method, which involves valuing the past service liabilities allowing for future pay increases;
  (*c*) the *share of fund* method, which involves dividing all the scheme assets amongst the continuing and leaving members in proportion to the respective values of their benefits; and
  (*d*) the *total service* (past and future) method, which involves assuming the members affected continue in pensionable service until retirement and contributions continue until then to be paid at the existing rate, the relevant portion being the amount by which the present net value of the benefits at retirement exceeds the present net value of the future contributions.

The past service reserve and share of fund methods were considered in *Re Imperial Foods Limited's Pension Scheme* [1986] 2 All ER 802. Under the Imperial scheme the employees' contributions were fixed and the employers' contributions varied according to what was required to meet the balance of the cost of the benefits. Two subsidiaries were sold and at the time the scheme was in surplus, the value of the scheme assets exceeding the value of the past service liabilities. The scheme rules provided for the segregation of such portion of the fund as the actuary considered appropriate. He used the past service reserve method. It was contended that he should have used the share of fund method, which would have produced a larger amount. The case was decided on the narrow point that the actuary's certificate could not be impeached, as the method used was one which could be used by a competent actuary and there had been no mistake or improper motive. In any event Walton J strongly supported the use of the past service reserve method, which he considered adequately provided for the entitlements and expectations of the outgoing employees. The judge pointed out that under a scheme where the employer pays the balance of the cost and there is no question of discontinuance the position of the members is very much the same whether the scheme is in surplus, strict balance or deficit. He considered the past service reserve method to be appropriate in all three cases (although, in the case of a deficit, it would be necessary to be satisfied as to the strength of the company's covenant to contribute). He rejected the share of fund method as it involves applying part of the surplus (which he referred to as 'temporary surplus funding by the employing company') for the benefit of the outgoing employees, whereas it does not do the same for the continuing employees. While benefits might be provided in future from the surplus, there was no certainty whatsoever that they would be and even if benefits were so provided they would have to be shared with later entrants to the scheme. The argument that, out of fairness to the subsidiaries, surplus should be made available as they had contributed towards it was rejected, as the financial position of the companies was not a relevant consideration and, even if it was, the subsidiaries' contributions had been at the ultimate expense of the parent company.

In the *Fisons* case Staughton LJ commented, *obiter dictu*, that in the *Imperial Foods* case Walton J was of the view that any surplus should be disregarded. Instead his Lordship thought the trustees should have regard to, and evaluate the likelihood that, existing employees and pensioners would receive some benefit from the surplus in the future. He also commented that it can be argued that in view of the existence of a surplus the purchaser's scheme should receive the highest figure produced by any of the four methods of calculation, namely share of fund, past service reserve, total service reserve and leaving service. In relation to share of fund his Lordship said that he imagined that there were 'a number of different ways in which a fund containing a surplus could be shared between remaining and transferring employees and there might be a good deal of argument as to which, if any, was or were just and equitable'.

It is thought that the views of Staughton LJ and Walton J may not be as far apart as it may at first seem. Walton J observed that in calculating the past service reserve 'the basis adopted was a generous one in that it certainly preserves for the transferring members not only their strict contractual rights but also a considerable surround of likely increases and additional discretionary benefits'. He also observed that benefit improvements were not being considered at the time and even if benefits were to be improved later 'there can be no conceivable reason why [the vendor] should wish to benefit persons who have already left its service'. Therefore, it may perhaps be said that an evaluation had, in fact, been made of the likelihood of the surplus being used to provide benefits in future.

SHORTFALL AND OVERAGE CLAUSES

Given the uncertainty as to the position under the vendor's scheme, the sale agreement will normally specify the method and assumptions to be used to calculate the transfer value. An obligation on the vendor to use its best endeavours to procure that the trustees of the vendor's scheme pay the prescribed transfer value probably requires the vendor to do little more than draw the trustees' attention to the sale agreement and, perhaps, ensure that they have sufficient funds with which to pay the transfer value. Therefore the purchaser should ensure that the vendor is under an obligation to make good any shortfall in the transfer value paid by the trustees. While any lesser commitment from the vendor may be commercially unacceptable to the purchaser, the vendor should bear in mind that the trustees are required to consider independently the amount to be transferred and, indeed, unless the statutory transfer right is exercised, whether to make a transfer at all. The vendor can do no more than ask the trustees to have regard to the sale agreement. Any assurance from the trustees that they will make the transfer on the proposed basis would not be binding on them as it would be given before the transfer power becomes exercisable on the target ceasing to participate in the vendor's scheme. It may, however, be possible to commit the trustees by a formal alteration to the scheme rules, although this would be unusual.

In order to reduce its exposure the vendor should require the amount payable by it to make good any shortfall in the transfer payment to be reduced to allow for any tax relief (see p 72) and also for any benefits retained in the vendor's scheme for the employees concerned.

Similarly, to cover the situation where the vendor's scheme trustees decide to pay more than the amount specified in the sale agreement, the vendor may seek an undertaking from the purchaser to pay to the vendor an amount equal to any excess payment. The undertaking would also deter the purchaser from putting the target's employees up to claiming that they are entitled to a larger transfer value under the vendor's scheme rules than that provided for in the sale agreement. The purchaser is likely to resist giving any such undertaking. The purchaser will only obtain any value from an excess payment if it will be available in the new scheme to reduce future employer contributions. It will not be available if the new scheme is to provide money purchase benefits, as the excess payment will be credited to the members immediately on transfer. Also, the requirements for limited price indexation may be pertinent (see p 72). Even if the excess payment would be available to reduce future contributions, the immediate value to the purchaser may be limited because of the requirements under SSAP 24. Tax and cash flow considerations should also be taken into account.

TRANSITIONAL PERIOD

Usually the target continues to participate in the vendor's scheme for a limited period following completion in order to give the purchaser time in which to make alternative pension arrangements for the target's employees. The Inland Revenue will, on application, normally allow the target to continue in the vendor's scheme for up to, say, a year (see IR12 (1991), para 21.6). If the vendor's scheme is contracted-out for the purposes of the state earnings related pension scheme and prior to completion the target is included in a holding company certificate of the vendor, it will be necessary for the target to obtain its own certificate. This involves issuing notices to, amongst others, the employees and any independent trade unions recognised to any extent for the purposes of collective bargaining and making formal elections to the Occupational Pensions Board (see the Board's Memorandum No 66). It is suggested that considerable care is taken in preparing these notices and that the specimens contained in that memorandum are not followed slavishly. The notices need to be reassuring to the employees but they should also preserve the target's freedom of action when making long-term alternative pension arrangements for them.

The vendor will be concerned to ensure that during any transitional period the target pays contributions and a fair share of the administrative expenses. The vendor may also seek to include in the sale agreement protective provisions against the target causing any undue increase in the liabilities under the vendor's scheme. In this respect the vendor will, for example, be vulnerable if pay increases granted during the transitional period will count for benefits under the vendor's scheme or if enhanced early retirement terms apply in the event of, eg, redundancy.

The purchaser may seek to include in the sale agreement protection against the target being called upon to make payments (other than agreed contributions and expenses) to the vendor's scheme and also against the benefits applicable to the target's employees under the vendor's scheme being changed.

If any of the target's employees leave service during the transitional period a notional profit may accrue to the vendor's scheme, the profit being the amount (if any) by which the transfer value which would have been paid in respect of the employee if he had remained in service and joined the new scheme exceeds the value of the leaving service benefits. In the *Imperial Foods* case Walton J described as 'totally absurd' a proposal that profits of that nature should be transferred to the new scheme since they relate to employees who never have anything to do with the new scheme.

EXPOSURE AFTER PARTICIPATION ENDS

The target's exposure in respect of the vendor's scheme will not necessarily end on the target ceasing to participate in it. The purchaser should ensure (whether or not there is a transitional period):

- (*a*) that the target is protected against any sex equality claims (see p 85);
- (*b*) that the target does not have any continuing liability under any indemnity under the vendor's scheme in favour of the trustees;
- (*c*) that the target does not have any obligation under the scheme rules to make good any deficiency in the vendor's scheme on ceasing to participate in it;
- (*d*) that the target does not have or is protected from any liability under the Social Security Pensions Act 1975, s 58B (as inserted by the Social Security Act 1990). This section provides that

any deficiency in the funding of a scheme on it being wound up or on any employer going into liquidation is to be treated as a debt due from the employers to the trustees. The target will continue to have any liability under this section after it ceases to participate in the scheme only if before its participation ends (i) any of the employers goes into liquidation, (ii) the scheme ceases to admit new members or (iii) the scheme commences winding up (The Occupational Pension Schemes (Deficiency on Winding Up etc) Regulations 1992 – SI No 1555);

(*e*) that no refund of surplus is made to any employer under the vendor's scheme after the target has ceased to participate in it which may prejudice Inland Revenue approval of the new scheme or result in the pensionable service of the target's employees under the two schemes not being treated as continuous for the purposes of determining Revenue maximum approvable benefits (IR12 (1991), para 13.35). Broadly, while a scheme is ongoing the Revenue will only allow surplus in excess of 105 per cent of the liabilities (when calculated on the prescribed basis) to be paid to the employer. This does not apply on a winding-up when the scheme rules may provide for any surplus in excess of the discontinuance liabilities to be paid to the employer. To prevent the restriction in relation to ongoing schemes being circumvented by the original scheme being wound up and replaced by another scheme, the Revenue will not approve the new scheme, or at least will not allow the pensionable service completed under the two schemes to be treated as continuous, unless the transfer from the original scheme is at least equal to 105 per cent of the liabilities (when calculated on the prescribed basis). The Revenue may regard any new scheme of the target as a replacement scheme for this purpose. In an open letter dated 9 April 1991 to the National Association of Pension Funds the Revenue advised that it is not their practice to apply their requirements in this respect where there is no connection between the earlier transfer and the subsequent refund but where there is a connection the length of the interval between the two events is unlikely to influence their decision.

EFFECTING TRANSFER TO NEW SCHEME

It is beyond the scope of this book to delve into the technicalities involved in effecting a transfer from the vendor's scheme to the new scheme. It is, however, worth making a few points.

Advising employees of options

As soon as practicable and, in any event, within two months of being notified by the target that the pensionable service of an employee has or is about to terminate, the trustees are required to advise the employee of the options (including the statutory transfer options) available to him under the vendor's scheme (The Occupational Pension Schemes (Disclosure of Information) Regulations 1986, reg 6(6) – SI No 1046).

Trustees' duty

Where a transfer is to be made pursuant to a discretionary power, the trustees should proceed with caution. The transfer power will be exercisable only for the purpose of providing benefits for the transferring members and other beneficiaries. It will be a fiduciary power to be exercised (or not exercised) according to what the trustees consider to be in the best interests of the members and beneficiaries concerned. The trustees will need to satisfy themselves that the transfer terms available are of sufficient overall benefit to those members and other beneficiaries to provide a better option for them than any others available. In evaluating any benefit the trustees should have regard to both quantum and security. The trustees should also consider the need for special terms and guarantees under the receiving scheme. For example, the trustees may wish to guard against any part of the transfer value being paid to the employer as surplus on winding up. This could occur where the transfer value exceeds the value of the leaving service benefits, as on a winding-up only leaving service benefits need be payable as of right, with the consequence that the excess may be payable to the employer as surplus, subject to the requirements concerning limited price indexation (see p 72).

Statutory transfer right

An employee will acquire a statutory right to a transfer value (based normally on current final pensionable pay) on the target ceasing to participate in the vendor's scheme unless he is then within one year of normal pension age (or under normal pension age if that age is below 60). The employee may elect to have the transfer value paid to any new scheme of the target or, if the employee prefers, to a personal pension scheme or an annuity policy (Social Security Pensions Act 1975, Sched 1A). If the transfer to the new scheme is made without the statutory right being exercised, that right will also be transferred and will be exercisable against the trustees of the new scheme (The Occupational Pension Schemes (Transfer Values) Regulations 1986, reg 6 – SI No 1931).

Transfers without consent

The vendor's scheme rules may authorise the trustees to effect the transfer to the new scheme without the employee's consent in certain circumstances. Under the Occupational Pension Schemes (Preservation of Benefit) Regulations 1991 (SI No 167 as amended by SI 1992 No 1531) a transfer may be made without the employee's consent only in certain prescribed circumstances. In particular, unless the transferring scheme is being wound up, it is necessary for an actuary to certify to the trustees of the new scheme that the transfer credits to be acquired under the new scheme are at least equal in value to the rights transferred based on projected final pensionable earnings. Where there is an established custom of additional benefits being awarded on a discretionary basis, the actuary is required in giving his certificate to take account of any such additional benefits as will accrue to the employees in question if the custom continues unaltered.

If the vendor's scheme is a final pay contracted-out scheme, the liability for the guaranteed minimum pension (GMP) (see p 67) may be transferred to the new scheme without the employee's consent only if the new scheme is also a final pay contracted-out scheme. If the new scheme is contracted-out on a money purchase basis the employee's consent must be obtained. If the new scheme is not contracted-out, only a transfer in respect of the liability in excess of the GMP may be made and the liability for the GMP will be retained by the vendor's scheme unless discharged by, for example, paying a transfer premium to the state scheme. (See The Contracting-out (Transfer) Regulations 1985 – SI No 1323.)

At least one month before a transfer without the consent of the employees concerned is due to take place the employees must be advised of the proposed transfer and given full information on the value of all rights to be transferred, including accrued rights, rights to survivors' benefits and rights in respect of death-in-service benefits (The Occupational Pension Schemes (Disclosure of Information) Regulations 1986, reg 6(13) – SI No 1046).

Whether it is possible to make the transfer without consent or not, the vendor's scheme trustees may wish to protect themselves by requiring consents. In any event, the employees' consents will be required to the deduction from pay of their contributions (if any) to the new scheme unless the deduction is already authorised by their employment contracts (Wages Act 1986, s 1).

Revenue requirements

The Pension Schemes Office of the Inland Revenue should be consulted in advance before a transfer is made in respect of a group of employees. Their specific authority is required if approval of the new scheme has been applied for but has not yet been granted unless the vendor's scheme is expressly named in the documents of the new scheme as one from which a transfer may be accepted. Their specific authority is always required if approval of the vendor's scheme has yet to be granted (IR12 (1991), paras 10.24 and 10.32).

Stamp duty

The transfer of shares *in specie* from the vendor's scheme to the new scheme will attract 50p fixed duty only.

Earnings cap

In making alternative arrangements care should be taken to ensure that those employees who were not previously subject to the earnings cap do not accidentally become caught by it. The earnings cap was introduced by the Finance Act 1989 and limits the earnings which may be taken into account for the purpose of determining maximum approvable benefits and member contributions. The limit is, for the tax year 1992/93, £75,000 and is increased each 6 April with prices. Broadly, employees who joined a scheme of the vendor before 1 June 1989 will not be subject to the earnings cap so long as that scheme was in existence before 14 March 1989 and since 1 June 1989 the employee has been in continuous pensionable service under one or other of the vendor's schemes apart from certain permitted breaks, such as secondment and statutory maternity leave. To avoid becoming caught by the earnings cap the employee must, upon ceasing to accrue benefits under the target scheme, become a member of the new scheme although, again, there are certain dispensations for employees then on secondment, statutory maternity leave or the like.

Whether the earnings cap applies or not is not dependent upon a transfer value being paid to the new scheme in respect of the past service benefits under the vendor's scheme. (See IR(12) 1991, Appendix III; The Retirement Benefits Schemes (Continuation of Rights of Members of Approved Schemes) Regulations 1990, SI No 2101; and The Retirement Benefits Schemes (Tax Relief on Contributions) (Disapplication of Earnings Cap) Regulations 1990, SI No 586.)

Variation of benefits

A question which sometimes arises is the extent to which pension benefits and contributions may be lawfully varied when the target ceases to participate in the vendor's scheme. The purchaser may not wish to mirror the vendor's scheme because, for example, the purchaser already has its own scheme or the target has too few employees for a final pay scheme to be a practical proposition. The flexibility available to the target depends upon the terms of the employment contract but will always be curtailed by the duty of 'good faith' (see p 68).

It is probably the intention of most employers that the employees should be entitled to no more than to be a member of the scheme subject to its rules from time to time in force. In this way the employer maintains maximum flexibility. A change in the benefits which is made without contravening any of the scheme rules would not, it is thought, constitute a variation of the employment contract. Whether an employer has been successful in maintaining such flexibility can be determined only by examining the terms of the contract and any documents which may provide evidence of those terms (eg the explanatory booklet and the written statement of the terms of employment which must be given under the Employment Protection (Consolidation) Act 1978, s 1).

If a change is to be made and it would constitute a variation of the employment contract, the employee does not have to accept it and may continue to work under protest (*Rigby v Ferodo Ltd* [1988] ICR 29 (HL)). On retirement or leaving service the employee would be able to claim for his full contractual pension. The employer should therefore terminate the existing contract and offer re-employment. Whether an industrial tribunal would regard the termination of the original contract as unfair dismissal depends upon the particular facts but it is thought that the tribunal would give considerable weight to the need for the variation from a commercial viewpoint (eg unifying employment terms with those of other employees in the purchaser's group). Procedural factors, such as prior consultation and counselling, would also be important.

Whether the employee would be entitled to leave service and claim constructive dismissal and damages is uncertain. If the scheme was a money purchase arrangement and the employer failed to pay the contractual contributions, the employee would probably be entitled to do so on the basis that failure to pay contractual remuneration is normally a fundamental and repudiatory breach (*Rigby v Ferodo Ltd*). But whether there would be such a breach by the employer simply indicating that it did not intend to provide the employee at retirement with his contractual pension is, perhaps, less certain.

MONEY PURCHASE SCHEMES

As no particular level of benefits is guaranteed under a money purchase scheme the only past service liability which can arise is for outstanding contributions and expenses. Unless there are to be completion accounts, the purchaser should obtain appropriate warranties. The purchaser should also consider whether the likely future pension contributions, when compared with those paid in the past, will have any material effect on profits because, for example, the scheme has only recently been established or contributions have not been paid on a regular basis or the target employees are to be offered membership of a final pay scheme of the purchaser. The purchaser should seek a warranty from the vendor that there is no commitment (whether legally enforceable or not) to provide any employee with a specific level of benefits. Sometimes a money purchase scheme is used simply as a funding vehicle for providing 'final pay' type benefits. This may be apparent from the scheme rules and explanatory literature but not necessarily so. If a specific level of benefits has been promised, the same funding considerations which arise in relation to final pay schemes should be addressed.

Where the target participates in a group scheme of the vendor, the purchaser should ensure that all the employees are provided with vested benefits even if they have not qualified for them under the preservation requirements of the Social Security Act 1973 because they have completed less than two years' qualifying service. Unless within one year of normal pension age (or under normal pension age if that age is below 60) the employees will have a statutory right to have their accumulated funds transferred to a new scheme (Social Security Pensions Act 1975, Sched 1A). However, it should be noted that under that schedule there is no requirement for the vendor's scheme to account for interest or investment return after the transfer option has been exercised so long as the transfer is effected within six months. Also, purchasers should be aware of the hefty penalties which some insurance companies impose when a group of members is transferred.

NON-APPROVED ARRANGEMENTS

Since the Finance Act 1989 employers may provide pension benefits through non-approved arrangements. These may be funded or unfunded. There are neither any special tax concessions nor limits on benefits. They will nevertheless give rise to similar considerations as approved schemes. One point to watch is the tax position if an employee of the vendor with an unfunded pension is to be employed after completion by the target or the purchaser. Any transfer of funds between the companies in respect of the accrued pension liability may be treated as income of the employee in the year of assessment in which the transfer is made notwithstanding that the employee has neither received nor has any entitlement to the money transferred (Income and Corporation Taxes Act 1988, s 595(1)).

The target may also be providing pensions on a discretionary basis. The amount of damages payable in the event of a breach of warranty that there are no discretionary pensions is uncertain bearing in mind that, by definition, the pensions are determinable at will. The purchaser should therefore seek to provide in the sale agreement that, in calculating the loss flowing from any breach of warranty, the target is deemed to be under a liability to continue any discretionary pensions.

PERSONAL PENSION SCHEMES

It is not thought that any particular problems should arise in relation to personal pension schemes. These are, in essence, contractual arrangements made between the employee and the insurance company or other pension provider. The schemes may be used to contract out of the state earnings related pension scheme: full national insurance contributions are payable; and an amount equivalent to the contracting-out rebate (see p 67) is remitted to the scheme by the state. The employer may contribute to the scheme and the purchaser should ensure that any such contributions have been timeously paid.

SEX DISCRIMINATION

As the law is so unclear at present, significant difficulties may be encountered concerning sex discrimination. Although it is beyond the scope of this book to consider the law in this area in detail, an outline has been included having regard, in particular, to the potential liabilities involved.

Article 119 of the Treaty of Rome established the principle that men and women should receive equal pay for equal work. 'Pay' was unequivocally held to include benefits under any kind of occupational pension scheme in a decision given on 17 May 1990 by the European Court of Justice in *Barber v Guardian Royal Exchange Assurance Group* [1990] IRLR 240. No intention to discriminate is necessary. The discrimination may be direct (eg different retirement ages) or indirect (eg a term which has a disproportionate effect on one sex or the other which cannot be objectively justified on grounds other than sex: *Bilka-Kaufhaus GmbH v Weber von Hartz* [1986] IRLR 317). Particularly likely to amount to indirect discrimination is the exclusion of part-time employees as they tend to be predominantly female.

The article may be enforced directly where the discrimination 'may be identified solely with the aid of criteria of equal work and equal pay' (*Jenkins v Kingsgate (Clothing Productions) Ltd* [1981] 1 WLR 972 at 983). Less clear is whether the article can be enforced directly if concepts of work of equal value have to be employed. Also yet to be established is whether the article can be enforced directly against the pension scheme trustees as well as the employer. If it is enforceable against the trustees the benefits under the scheme will already have been equalised by law to the extent necessary even if the scheme rules have not been formally amended.

In an attempt to limit the retrospective effect of its decision in the *Barber* case, the European Court ruled:

The direct effect of article 119 of the Treaty may not be relied on in order to claim entitlement to a pension, with effect from a date prior to that of this judgment, except in the case of workers or those claiming under them who have before that date initiated legal proceedings or raised an equivalent claim under the applicable national law.

Views differ as to the limit on retrospective claims, including the following:
- (*a*) no claim may be made by anyone in respect of any pension attributable to service before 17 May 1990, being the date of the judgment;
- (*b*) no claim may be made by anyone who left service or retired before 17 May 1990 but current employees may make a claim in respect of the whole of their pension;
- (*c*) no claim may be made by existing pensioners at 17 May 1990 but the then current employees and deferred pensioners may seek equalisation;
- (*d*) no claim may be made in respect of instalments of pension which fall due for payment before 17 May 1990 but a claim may be made by an existing pensioner in respect of future instalments as well as by current employees and deferred pensioners.

Also questionable is whether the limit applies at all to schemes which are not contracted-out of the state earnings related pension scheme. The *Barber* case was concerned mainly with whether art 119 applied to contracted-out schemes, the *Bilka-Kaufhaus* case having already established that the article was capable of applying at least to certain occupational schemes. The court justified the limitation by referring to the confusion caused by a 1986 EEC Directive which indicated that certain derogations from the principle of equal treatment were still permitted in relation to occupational social security schemes, the definition of which is wide enough to cover contracted-in as well as contracted-out schemes. On that basis, it appears that the court would, perhaps, be prepared to extend the limitation to contracted-in schemes.

In *Re Coloroll Pension Schemes* the European Court is being asked to clarify the extent of the limitation. Fearful of the huge costs which would be involved if the court ruled other than that the limit prevents any claim in respect of service before 17 May 1990 the following protocol was annexed to the Treaty on European Union as signed in February 1992 at Maastricht:

For the purposes of article 119 ... benefits under occupational social security schemes shall not be considered as remuneration if and insofar as they are attributable to periods of employment prior to 17 May 1990, except in the case of workers or those claiming under them who have before that date initiated legal proceedings or introduced an equivalent claim under the applicable national law.

Unless and until it is ratified by EC Member States, the protocol does not have the force of law. Even if it is ratified many questions remain to be answered, such as:

(*a*) whether art 119 applies directly to pension scheme trustees;

(*b*) whether unisex actuarial assumptions must be used for the purpose of calculating benefits (eg transfer values and the rate at which pension may be converted to cash);

(*c*) whether in relation to money purchase schemes unisex annuity rates must be used;

(*d*) whether 'bridging' pensions are discriminatory (these are temporary pensions payable to men up to their state pension age of 65 equivalent to the state pension payable to comparable women from their state pension age of 60); and

(*e*) whether benefits may be equalised by moving to the less favourable benefit (it is thought that they can so long as change is made before the benefit becomes payable and making the change does not involve any breach of the employment contract or pension scheme rules, which may be the case if the employment contract provides for an employee to be a member of the scheme subject to its rules from time to time and the amendment power is lawfully exercised to effect the change in benefits).

These and other questions have been raised in *Coloroll* and a number of other cases which at the time of writing are in the pipeline. Until the law has been clarified, a purchaser should seek to protect itself so far as possible. Where the target participates in a group scheme of the vendor it should be borne in mind that unless art 119 applies directly to the pension scheme trustees any claim of discrimination by any employee or former employee of the target will be against the target and not the vendor's scheme, which will not be under any obligation to equalise benefits.

PENSIONS CHECKLIST

The pensions checklist set out below will require adaptation to each particular case. It does not purport to be exhaustive but is designed to highlight some of the principal areas of potential concern to a purchaser. It is suggested that enquiries on the items listed should be made at the earliest possible stage, since the information obtained may enable the purchaser and its advisers to form a preliminary view of the state of the scheme or schemes and, in particular, to see if there are any obvious queries as to its funding. The purchaser should normally obtain actuarial advice and the checklist is not in any way suggested to be a substitute for such advice.

This checklist relates to every scheme, contract or arrangement (whether approved or non-approved and whether funded or unfunded) to which the target or any of its subsidiaries is a party and which provides 'relevant benefits' as defined by the Income and Corporation Taxes Act 1988, s 612, for any one or more present or former directors or employees or for their widows, widowers, children or dependants. The details listed below should be obtained in respect of each such scheme separately. Details of any *ex gratia* pensions should also be obtained.

1.   Name of scheme

2.   Documentation
2.1   Trust deeds and rules (including any amendments).
2.2   If a group scheme, the deed by which the target adhered to it.
2.3   Explanatory literature (including any announcements relating to benefit improvements or other amendments not yet incorporated into the formal documentation).

2.4 Latest actuarial report.
2.5 Latest scheme accounts.
2.6 Inland Revenue letter of approval.
2.7 Contracting-out certificate.
2.8 Memorandum and articles of association of any trustee company.
2.9 Insurance policies.
2.10 Registrar of Pension Schemes: form PR1 (90).

3. Scheme assets
3.1 List of scheme assets and their value.
3.2 Details of any self-investment in target or vendor's group.
3.3 Investment management agreements.
3.4 Custodian and nominee arrangements.

4. Membership data
4.1 List of members showing dates of birth, sex, pensionable service and pensionable earnings.
4.2 List of pensioners and deferred pensioners showing dates of birth, sex and pension entitlement.

5. Benefits
5.1 Discretionary increases to pensions in payment or in deferment over previous ten years.
5.2 Other discretionary practices: redundancy, early retirement, long service bonus etc.
5.3 Any credit of additional pensionable service not fully vested?
5.4 Any backdating of pensionable service on joining the scheme for pension benefits?
5.5 Any benefit augmentations or special terms?
5.6 Do benefits accrue at a uniform rate or does the rate increase with age or length of service?
5.7 Are any employees provided only with life cover?

6. Contributions
6.1 Employer's contribution rate over previous three years.
6.2 Are contributions paid in arrears?
6.3 Anticipated future contribution rate.
6.4 Is the contracting-out incentive being paid?

7. Trustees
7.1 Names of the trustees.

7.2   In whom is the power of appointment and removal vested?
7.3   Who owns the shares in any trustee company?

8.   Employers
8.1   Does any employer (other than the target and its subsidiaries) participate in the scheme?

The checklist is, it is hoped, largely self-explanatory, but questions 5 and 6 require a special mention.

In question 5 it is important to ascertain full details of the benefits and discretionary practices so that the past service liabilities can be properly quantified. If pensionable service is backdated on joining the scheme there is a contingent liability in respect of current employees who have not yet joined the scheme for which it can reasonably be argued that allowance should be made when determining the past service liabilities. Question 5.1 corresponds with the basic information which must be given to an employee on joining the scheme (Occupational Pension Schemes (Disclosure of Information) Regulations 1986, reg 5.2 and Sched 1, para 15).

In question 6 the purchaser should know how the pension contributions have varied and the likely rate payable in future so that the effect on profits can be ascertained. If currently being paid, the contracting-out incentive will be lost if the target's employees are transferred to a scheme which was contracted-out before 1 January 1986 (Social Security Act 1986, s 7). The incentive will cease to be available after 5 April 1993.

Chapter 8

Accounting for Acquisitions

The subject of accounting for acquisitions is complex and controversial. Because of the impact which acquisitions can have on reported profits and earnings, the methods of accounting for them are under continual scrutiny and review. The purpose of this chapter is to provide an introduction to the basic issues, from a purchaser's point of view. Those interested in the history of the subject should read Christopher Napier and Christopher Noke, 'Premiums and Pre-acquisition Profits: The Legal and Accountancy Professions and Business Combinations' [1991] MLR 8100. Those who would like an entertaining and colourful account of the commercial issues should try Terry Smith, 'Accounting for Growth'.

In the context of acquisitions, the problems of share premium account and pre-acquisition profits have caused difficulty for many years. They are related problems and, before considering the law, it is necessary to understand their practical significance and why they are related. Having struggled to an understanding of the law, the practitioner then has to understand the accounting rules for the treatment of mergers and acquisitions.

The Companies Act 1985, s 130, provides that where a company issues shares at a premium, whether for cash or otherwise, a sum equal to the aggregate amount or value of the premiums on those shares must be transferred to a share premium account. Once the share premium account has been set up, it cannot be used except for making bonus issues and paying certain expenses and may not be reduced without the consent of the court.

Shares are issued at a premium if they are issued for an amount in excess of their nominal value. When one company purchases the issued share capital of another in exchange for the issue of shares of the purchaser, then, on the assumption that the market value of the target's shares exceeds the nominal value of the consideration shares, the question will arise whether the consideration shares have been issued at a premium and, if so, what amount should be transferred to share premium account. Because of our accounting conventions, the question is directly related to the value at which the target's shares are brought into the purchaser's accounts. If the effect of s 130 is to oblige the purchaser to set up a share premium account of the difference between the nominal value of the consideration shares and the market value of the target's shares, it also means, in practice, that the purchaser is bound to bring the target's shares into its account at that same market value. This is called 'acquisition accounting' and is now described by the Companies Act 1985, Sched 4A, para 9.

The purchaser may not wish to account for the transaction in this way because, on the assumption that the market value of the target's share capital is greater than the book value of the underlying net assets of the target, the difference will show up as goodwill in a consolidated balance sheet. This goodwill must then be written off against reserves (and share premium account is not available for this) or quantified through the profit and loss account, thus reducing reported profits.

In addition (and this is why the problem relates to the question of pre-acquisition profits), acquisition accounting may have the effect of reducing the ability of the purchaser to pay dividends. The purchaser's share capital will be enlarged by reason of the acquisition, while its distributable reserves will remain the same. Accordingly, the amount per share which may be distributed out of reserves will be decreased. The extra reserve produced by accounting for the acquisition on a valuation basis (ie taking the target's shares into the books at a valuation) is the share premium account and is not available for dividend. The fact that the target may have reserves available for dividend will not, of itself, affect the accounts of the purchaser and, if the new subsidiary pays dividends to the purchaser out of reserves which it had at the time of the acquisition, the purchaser will normally have to apply the proceeds to reduce the value of the target's shares in its accounts. Therefore, although payment of such a dividend may provide the purchaser with cash to fund a dividend of its own, it will not increase the purchaser's distributable reserves. Acquisition accounting can also produce an increased charge for depreciation.

The rules relating to the accounting treatment of mergers and acquisitions are contained in SSAP 23. Where 'merger accounting' is permitted, the purchaser can bring the target's shares into its accounts at the nominal value of the shares which it issues in exchange. Obviously this is only possible if the law permits, but the accounting rules are generally stricter than the legal requirements and sometimes require acquisition accounting where the law would permit merger accounting. Merger accounting is never mandatory, while the share premium account is a creature of statute. These issues are dealt with below. At the time this edition goes to press it remains to be seen whether the Accounting Standards Board will permit the continuation of the practices contained in SSAP 23 or will adopt a different approach, perhaps more restrictive, in the application of merger accounting, as foreshadowed by an exposure draft (ED 48) issued by the Accounting Standards Board's predecessor, the Accounting Standards Committee.

Share premium account

The law relating to share premium account is to be found in cases decided before the introduction of merger relief under the Companies Act 1985, s 131. In *Head (Henry) Ltd v Ropner Holdings Ltd* [1952] Ch 124 a holding company was formed to acquire the shares of two other companies whose share capital was taken by the holding company into its books at a valuation corresponding to that of the assets of the targets. The court held that the excess of the valuation over the nominal value of the consideration shares had to be credited to a share premium account. Harman J said (at p 128):

Apparently, if the shares are issued for a consideration other than cash and the value of the assets acquired is more than the nominal value of the shares issued, you have issued shares at a premium.

This might be thought to be the end of the matter, but, before the decision in *Shearer (Inspector of Taxes) v Bercain Ltd* [1980] 3 All ER 295, there was a body of legal opinion which contended that it was the directors of the purchaser who placed the fetters on their own wrists. Because the existence or otherwise of the share premium account arising as a result of an acquisition is directly related to the amount at which the target's shares are brought into the holding company's books, it follows, it was said, that it is the directors' decision as to that amount which is vital in determining the question. If the target's shares are brought in at an amount in excess of the nominal amount of the consideration shares, then the excess must indeed be credited to a share premium account; but there is no statutory provision which expressly requires the directors to bring the shares in at a valuation.

In *Craddock v Zevo Finance Co Ltd* [1944] 1 All ER 566 the Court of Appeal was asked to consider, for tax purposes, whether investments acquired by a dealing company in a reconstruction in exchange for the issue of shares should be brought into the purchaser's books at 'cost' (the nominal value of the consideration shares allotted) or at their market value (which was less). It confirmed the correctness of bringing the investments in at cost. Lord Greene MR said (at p 569):

> The propriety of the course adopted is manifest when the uncertainty as to the value of the investments . . . is borne in mind. It is, I think, true as a general proposition that, where a company acquires property for fully paid shares of its own, the price paid by the company is the nominal value of the shares. It is for those who assert the contrary to establish it, as could be done, for example, in the suggested case of a deliberately inflated valuation.

If the target's shares are brought in at an amount equal to the nominal value of the consideration shares it would not be consistent with any ordinary accounting practice to have a share premium account and it was therefore said to follow (because neither s 130 nor any other provision of the Act expressly requires the target's shares to be brought in on a valuation basis) that the section could not require a share premium account where the target's shares were, in fact, brought into the books at cost.

The difficulty with s 130 in the context of acquisitions is the difficulty that lies at the root of accounting for all acquisitions in exchange for the issue of shares. The shares which the purchaser issues as consideration for the acquisition are not, in its hands, money's worth (as Lord Greene pointed out in the *Zevo* case), and in truth, there is no cost to the purchasing company at all. The purchaser suffers an addition to its balance sheet 'liabilities' of the nominal amount of the consideration shares, but this liability is not one which the company can ever be called upon to meet unless it has assets available for the purpose. In a winding up, although the rights attaching to shares may require a division of surplus assets in a certain way, the number of shares in issue does not affect the amount of the assets which are available for distribution among the members.

Shearer (Inspector of Taxes) v Bercain Ltd [1980] 3 All ER 295 placed the matter beyond doubt. In that case an investment holding company acquired shares in two other companies valued at £96,000 in exchange for 4,100 shares of a nominal value of £1 each. It created a share premium account which, after deducting expenses, amounted to £91,717. It then received dividends from the two targets of £36,000, on receipt of which it wrote down the value of its investment in its subsidiaries from £96,000 to £59,950. The Revenue contended that these dividends could have been distributed by the holding company by way of dividend and raised a shortfall assessment. The holding company pleaded that under the relevant taxation legislation, it was subject to a 'restriction imposed by law' preventing distribution, in that it was obliged to create the share premium account and therefore had no distributable reserves. Walton J agreed, following *Head (Henry) Ltd v Ropner Holdings Ltd* and said (at p 301) that the matter would appear 'as plain as a pikestaff'.

Merger relief

The Companies Act 1985, s 131, excludes the application of s 130 where the company issuing the consideration shares

> . . . has secured at least a 90 per cent equity holding in another company in pursuance of an arrangement providing for the allotment of equity shares in the issuing company on terms that the consideration for the shares allotted is to be provided—(a) by the issue or transfer to the issuing company of equity shares in that other company, or (b) by the cancellation of any such shares not held by the issuing company.

'Arrangement' is defined by s 131(7) to mean 'any arrangement, scheme or arrangement (including an arrangement sanctioned in accordance with ss 425 or 582)'. The exemption also extends to cover shares issued, under the same arrangement, by the purchaser in exchange for the issue or transfer of non-equity shares in the target.

Many share-for-share acquisitions will therefore fall outside the terms of s 130 altogether and it will not be necessary (or indeed possible) to create a share premium account. Section 133 expressly provides that a sum corresponding to any amount representing premiums which, by virtue of s 131, is not included in the company's share premium account can also be disregarded in determining the amount at which any shares or other consideration provided for the shares issued is to be included in the company's balance sheet.

The purchaser is to be regarded as having secured at least a 90 per cent equity holding in the target in pursuance of an arrangement if as a result of any acquisition or cancellation of equity shares in the target in pursuance of that arrangement it holds equity shares in the target (whether all or any of those shares were acquired in pursuance of that arrangement or not) of an aggregate nominal value equal to 90 per cent or more of the nominal value of that company's equity share capital (s 131(4)). If the equity share capital of the target is divided into different classes, the section does not apply unless the requirements are satisfied in relation to each of those classes taken separately (s 131(5)). Equity share capital is defined by s 744 as any issued share capital except any part which, neither as respects dividends nor as respects capital, carries any right to participate beyond a specified amount in a distribution, and 'equity shares' is defined by s 131(7) as meaning shares comprised in equity share capital. Relief extends to consideration shares allotted for non-equity share capital in the target as part of the same arrangement.

The accounting rules

The availability of merger relief means that merger accounting is possible, in many share-for-share acquisitions. In practice it is quite rare. The Companies Act 1985, Sched 4A, para 10 sets out the legal conditions for merger accounting. They are:

(*a*) that at least 90 per cent of the nominal value of the relevant shares in the target is held by or on behalf of the parent and its subsidiary undertakings;

(*b*) that the proportion referred to in para (*a*) was attained pursuant to an arrangement providing for the issue of equity shares by the parent company or one or more of its subsidiary undertakings;

(*c*) that the fair value of any other consideration did not exceed 10 per cent of the nominal value of the equity shares issued; and

(*d*) the adoption of merger accounting accords with generally accepted accounting principles or practice.

For this purpose, 'relevant shares' means those carrying unrestricted rights to participate in distributions and in assets upon a liquidation.

At the time of going to press, the 'generally accepted accounting principles or practice' are to be found in SSAP 23. This provides that merger accounting is only permitted if:

(*a*) the business combination results from an offer to the holders of all equity shares and the holders of all voting shares which are not already held by the purchaser;

(*b*) the purchaser has secured, as a result of the offer, a holding of
(i) at least 90 per cent of all equity shares (taking each class of equity separately) and
(ii) shares carrying at least 90 per cent of the votes of the target;

(*c*) immediately prior to the offer, the purchaser did not hold
(i) 20 per cent or more of all equity shares of the target (taking each class of the equity separately) or
(ii) shares carrying 20 per cent or more of the votes of the target; and

(*d*) not less than 90 per cent of the fair value of the total consideration given for the equity share capital (including that given for shares already held) is in the form of equity share capital; and not less than 90 per cent of the fair value of the total consideration given for voting non-equity share capital (including that given for shares already held) is in the form of equity and/or voting non-equity share capital.

To apply merger accounting the purchaser must comply with three sets of rules. He must obtain merger relief under s 131, he must meet the conditions of Sched 4A, para 10 and he must comply with SSAP 23. The purchaser who buys more than 10 per cent of the target's share capital for cash and then goes on to acquire the rest of the shares will qualify for merger relief under s 131 but will not qualify for merger accounting under para 10.

If acquisition accounting is required in a case which qualifies for merger relief then a new, non-statutory reserve will be thrown up. Because this reserve is not share premium account it is possible to use it for writing off goodwill arising on consolidation. Where acquisition accounting and share premium account are required it is possible to apply to the court to reduce share premium account. This has the effect of creating a reserve against which goodwill can be written off. See *Re Partners Group plc* (1988) 4 BCC 293, *Re Thorn EMI plc* (1988) 4 BCC 698 and *Re European Home Products plc* (1988) 4 BCC 779.

One important point to note is that, where merger accounting is permitted, the consolidated accounts for the period in which the merger took place will show profits and losses of the target for the entire period without any adjustment in respect of that part of the period prior to the merger. Although this will not affect the legal position relating to dividends, it will of course have a significant effect upon the perceived results of the purchaser for the period.

Acquisition accounting will require that on consolidation the 'fair value' of the purchase consideration must be allocated between the underlying net tangible and intangible assets of the target. See Sched 4A, para 9.

Pre-acquisition profits

The acquisition itself will not affect the ability of the target to pay dividends. If the target pays a dividend to its new holding company out of reserves arising from profits made prior to the acquisition, how is this dividend to be treated in the purchasing company's accounts? It is clearly a receipt of a capital nature and amounts to the partial realisation of a fixed asset.

Where acquisition accounting is used, pre-acquisition profits or losses of the target will be reflected in its assets at the time of the acquisition and, accordingly, distributions to the purchaser out of pre-acquisition profits will be applied in the holding company's accounts to reduce the value of the target's shares. It may not, however, be appropriate to do this where it is unnecessary to provide for a diminution in the stated value of the target. If merger accounting is used it will rarely be necessary to provide for such a diminution. To the extent that it is not necessary to provide for a diminution in value of the shares of the target it appears that the amount of the distribution received will represent a distributable profit in the hands of the purchaser.

The general rule is that any surplus accruing on the realisation of a fixed asset can be distributed by way of a dividend so long as the value of the purchaser's remaining assets is fairly represented by, or in excess of, their book value (see *Lubbock v British Bank of South America* [1892] 2 Ch 198 and *Foster v New Trinidad Lake Asphalt Co* [1901] 1 Ch 208). Whether or not non-revenue profits can be distributed in any particular case is a matter legislated for by the articles of the company concerned, and by the Companies Act 1985, Part VIII. Section 280(3) includes realised capital profits in calculating profits available for distribution, except in the case of investment companies.

The Companies Act 1948, Sched 8, para 15(5), formerly contained a provision which was held, in *Shearer (Inspector of Taxes) v Bercain Ltd* [1980] 3 All ER 295, to prevent the distribution of pre-acquisition profits in any case, by providing that such profits must not be treated as revenue profits in the accounts of the holding company for any purpose. This restriction no longer applies.

In the case where acquisition accounting is used but merger relief is available, and the holding company credits to the investment the distribution paid out of the target's pre-acquisition profits, the question will arise as to whether an equivalent amount of the non-statutory merger reserve can be regarded as realised. This is a point on which there is no authority.

Chapter 9

Investigations and Warranties

The common law rule of *caveat emptor*, although eroded beyond recognition in many fields, retains almost all its old force in relation to the acquisition of companies. Although the Financial Services Act 1986, s 47, provides that it is a criminal offence for any person to induce or attempt to induce another to enter into an agreement for the acquisition of securities by, inter alia, any dishonest concealment of material facts, it does not appear that any civil remedy based on the section (or its predecessors) has yet been awarded by the courts. In *Securities and Investments Board v Danfell SA* [1991] 4 All ER 883 Sir Nicholas Browne-Wilkinson VC said, (at p 887) '...the individual investor is given no right of action for contravention of s 47'.

No statutory provision implies into a contract for the acquisition of shares any term relating to the target's business and, although the Misrepresentation Act 1967, s 3, may have the effect of limiting the operation of clauses designed to exclude liability for misrepresentation, the provisions of the Unfair Contract Terms Act 1977 do not apply to any contract so far as it relates to the creation or transfer of securities (Sched 1, para 1 (*e*)). The ambit of this exception is not as clear as it might be, but it is generally thought that the parties to an acquisition are free to make their own bargain and the purchaser must do what he can, by investigation and contractual provision, to ensure that the target owns those assets that it is thought to possess and has no liabilities apart from those of which the purchaser is aware.

When a purchaser buys a business, as opposed to a company, it is at least theoretically possible to select the assets which he wishes to buy and the liabilities which he wishes to assume (but subject to the Transfer of Undertakings (Protection of Employment) Regulations 1981 (SI No 1794)). Although commercial considerations may require that, for the sake of maintaining the goodwill of the business, the purchaser accepts the liabilities of the business as they stand, these liabilities are taken over by contractual provisions which amount to an indemnity and which can be designed to exclude the liabilities which the purchaser does not want. A company, on the other hand, cannot so easily be fitted to the Procrustean couch. When a company is acquired, the liabilities of the target remain where they are unless creditors consent to their novation and no contractual provision between the vendor and purchaser can prevent the target being called to account for those liabilities after completion of the acquisition. Whatever warranties and indemnities the purchaser may take, the target is, and remains, liable to meet its obligations and no warranty or indemnity, however well drafted, will avoid the problem of obtaining reimbursement from a vendor who is unable or unwilling to pay. Even a retention of part of the purchase price as security for the warranties may not be adequate and will not recompense the purchaser for the loss of time involved in solving problems which he did not know he was inheriting.

Because a company is a person and has the capacity to incur contractual, tortious and criminal liabilities, the purchaser's task of ascertaining the precise nature and quality of the assets, liabilities and profit potential of the target is by no means an easy one. His twin weapons are investigation and contractual protection, and it is with these that this chapter deals. In theory at least, nothing can afford complete protection and it is certainly true that neither investigation nor contractual protection on its own is satisfactory for the cautious purchaser. In practice, a balance is struck between the two, although much will depend upon the relative strength of the vendor and purchaser. The vendor who has suffered intensive investigations of the target will be less willing to give warranties and if time does not permit exhaustive investigations the purchaser will be more ready to insist upon wide ranging contractual protection. In cases where the executives of the target are not also substantial shareholders, problems can arise because those who can be expected to know about the target's affairs are, reasonably enough, reluctant to accept liability on warranties which may go far beyond the relatively small amount which they will realise from the transaction, while those who will realise a substantial amount claim that they cannot give warranties because they are unfamiliar with the target's affairs. In these cases investigation becomes of paramount importance.

It is worth making a general comment about the search against the target which the purchaser's solicitors will make at the Companies Registration Office as a matter of course. Incidentally, they will, if cautious, also make bankruptcy searches against individual vendors at the Land Charges Registry and a search at the Companies Court to check that no winding up or administration petitions have been presented against the target and its subsidiaries or against the vendor, if a company.

The company search should show an up-to-date copy of the memorandum and articles of association and should reveal the names of the directors and secretary and the names of the shareholders shown in the last annual return, together with any details of subsequent allotments of shares and particulars of any charges given by the target over its assets. The accuracy of the information given is not, however, guaranteed, because it is compiled by the target itself. To take an example, the file may be incomplete because of failure by the target to register changes in directors. Although this technically renders the officers of the target liable to a default fine, it gives no protection to a purchaser if it discovers after completion that the target has different or more directors than were thought. Neither will the information given necessarily be up to date, even though all relevant statutory provisions have been correctly complied with. For instance, the shareholders may have changed since the last annual return and, save in the case of fresh allotments, there is no obligation to bring the file up to date between returns. The position with regard to the registration of charges is dealt with on p 117.

It follows that, although the company search may provide useful information, it is an extract from a register which may be incorrect or out of date (without any infringement of the Companies Acts) and which affords no statutory protection to the share purchaser.

This chapter deals with accountants' investigations and reports, environmental investigations, with some difficulties relating to the investigation of the target's title to its land, and, in general terms, with misrepresentation, warranty and indemnity. Taxation is a field apart and it is considered in Chapter 13.

THE ACCOUNTANTS' INVESTIGATION

Irrespective of whether the purchaser of the target is a listed company, it is quite usual to instruct a firm of accountants, often the purchaser's auditors, to carry out an investigation into the target's affairs. The objective of such an investigation is to extract financial, commercial and administrative information from the target and to subject that information to close scrutiny so that the purchaser is provided with an expert, independent assessment of the target and its activities.

The advisability of instructing a firm of accountants to carry out an independent investigation of the target's affairs is underlined by a series of recent decisions which have the effect that it is very unlikely that a purchaser will have any cause of action against those concerned in the preparation of the target's statutory accounts if they should prove to have been negligently prepared so as, for example, to overstate the target's assets.

The leading case is *Caparo Industries v Dickman* [1990] 1 All ER 568, which constitutes an important redefinition by the House of Lords of the circumstances in which professional advisers will incur tortious liability to third parties for negligently prepared information and advice. The Lords considered the test for the existence of a duty of care propounded by Lord Wilberforce in *Anns v London Borough of Merton* [1978] AC 728, which had two requirements: (1) sufficient proximity between adviser and advisee; and (2) no policy considerations which would negative or limit the existence of the duty. In *Caparo*, the Lords moved away from Lord Wilberforce's universal test and stressed instead that the correct approach was to examine whether a particular set of circumstances falls within an existing category where a duty has been imposed, with new categories being developed incrementally and by analogy with existing ones rather than by reference to a general test. With specific reference to liability for negligent misstatement, the House of Lords held that the essential elements were the same as for any other tortious liability: foreseeability of damage, proximity and whether it is 'fair, just and reasonable' to impose the duty. However, applying *Hedley Byrne and Co Ltd v Heller and Partners Ltd* [1964] AC 465, the Lords gave specific guidance on the meaning of 'proximity' in the context of liability for negligent misstatement. Lord Oliver (at p 587) identified four factors: (1) the allegedly negligent advice was required for a purpose known to the adviser at the time the advice was given; (2) the adviser knew that the advice would be communicated to the advisee, either individually or as a member of an ascertainable class, for that purpose; (3) the adviser knew that the advisee was likely to act on the advice without further enquiry; and (4) the advisee in fact acted on the advice and suffered loss by so doing.

Caparo was concerned with a takeover offer by Caparo for a public company, Fidelity PLC. Caparo claimed that it had launched its offer on the basis of Fidelity's statutory accounts, which had been prepared by Touche Ross. After the offer was successful, Caparo alleged that the accounts had been negligently prepared and that it would not have made the offer had there been an accurate disclosure of Fidelity's financial position. Caparo sued Touche Ross, claiming that the auditors owed them a duty of care, both as potential and actual investors in Fidelity. The Lords rejected Caparo's claim: the accounts had been prepared for the purpose of complying with Fidelity's statutory obligations, and even though it may have been foreseeable that they might be used as the basis for a takeover offer this was not sufficient to impose a duty of care in favour of Caparo.

A number of cases after *Caparo* have confirmed its restrictive approach to the imposition of liability to third parties for negligent misstatement: in *James McNaughton Paper Group Ltd v Hicks Anderson and Co* [1991] 1 All ER 134 (CA), an accountant who had been asked by a company which was the target of a takeover offer to prepare draft accounts was held to owe no duty of care to the offeror in respect of the accounts, and in *Al-Nakib Investments (Jersey) Ltd v Longcroft* [1990] 3 All ER 321 an allegedly negligent statement in a rights issue prospectus could not be relied on by investors who subsequently acquired the shares which were the subject of the rights issue in the market and not by way of rights. The one limited exception to this trend came in *Morgan Crucible Co plc v Hill Samuel Bank Ltd* [1991] 1 All ER 148 (CA), in which, in an interlocutory decision, the Court of Appeal held that it was arguable that an offeror for a public company might have a cause of action in respect of negligent misstatements in the target's defence circulars.

In the light of these decisions a purchaser should not rely on the target's statutory accounts for financial information in the absence of a specific assumption of liability to the purchaser by the target's auditors. Of course, the same considerations should not arise in relation to an investigation of the target carried out by the purchaser's own accountants who will owe their client a duty of care.

A full acquisition report is not dissimilar to the type of report required by an issuing house which is sponsoring a company seeking a listing for its securities for the first time. In such a case, the issuing house requires a considerable amount of information regarding the company's affairs, both because it may be taking the risk of underwriting the issue and because of the need to preserve its reputation. However, these two types of report differ both from the accountants' report included in an acquisition circular issued to shareholders in accordance with the rules of the London Stock Exchange and from that included in a prospectus. Both these latter reports are brief and are required to contain only a summary of the target's accounts covering a specified period, together with the accounting policies on which they have been based and the associated notes. They do not, for example, nor are they required to, include any commentary on how the company's profits were earned, whether it is sufficiently profitable, or what its future prospects might be.

The requirements for circulars relating to acquisitions are

contained in the Stock Exchange's *Admission of Securities to Listing* (the *Yellow Book*), Section 6, Chapter 1. It should be noted that certain of the information required by the regulations relates to the acquiring company. In classifying an acquisition, and so determining which requirements have to be met, no distinction is generally made between acquisitions for cash and acquisitions for shares or other securities. Where, however, the acquisition would increase the shares of a class already listed by 10 per cent or more or debt securities of any amount are issued, then full listing particulars are required (see also Section 3, Chapter 1 and Section 6, Chapter 2).

The requirements of the Stock Exchange concerning accountants' reports are set out in Section 4 of the *Yellow Book*. In their report the accountants are required to express an opinion whether or not the financial information given shows a true and fair view of the state of affairs of the target at the end of the period and of the results and cash flows for each of the periods reported upon.

An example of a short form accountants' report on a target which could be included in a Super Class 1 acquisition circular is shown on p 525. The short form report is designed to inform the purchaser's shareholders solely about the trading record and asset position of the target. By contrast, the acquisition report is designed to inform the purchaser's management about the target, so that management is in a position to decide whether the proposed acquisition represents a sound commercial investment.

Because the scope of an acquisition investigation is wide and can cover the whole range of a target's business, the accountants will usually hold an early meeting with the purchaser in order to discuss the scope of the report. At this time the accountants should learn of any particular aspects of the target's business about which the purchaser has already been satisfied, and they should be forewarned of any areas which merit special attention.

If other professional advisers are involved at this stage, it is advisable that they too should be engaged in these discussions so that they can liaise and thus prevent unnecessary duplication of work. For instance, the accountants and the solicitors would both normally expect to enquire into the terms of any leases held by the target, and it is obviously not in the purchaser's interest to retain both these professional advisers to carry out such an examination. On the other hand, the accountants can often assist the solicitors by gathering for them information from the target's premises. Liaison between professional advisers should also ensure that all relevant areas are covered within the limitations imposed by the purchaser's timetable. The implications of this latter factor are too often overlooked but are most important because time constraints, imposed for one reason or another, undoubtedly limit the depth to which the accountants will be able to probe.

Before the accountants start their investigation they should be given clear instructions, in writing, from the purchaser. These instructions should refer specifically to any areas which they are required to examine in depth, such as the impact on the target of the wide-ranging legislation contained in the Financial Services Act 1986, and also to any areas specifically to be excluded from their investigation. The accountants should then seek access to the target. Usually this will have been agreed to by the target during the course of the negotiations and the accountants should make detailed arrangements with the management of the target accordingly. Confidentiality is an important factor and the accountants should be fully aware of the need to respect the wishes of the management of the target, not only because there may be other potential acquiring companies, but also because it may be harmful to the target's business if staff, customers and suppliers become aware of a possible change in ownership.

In general terms, the acquisition report should be designed to present the information which the purchaser requires (within the cost and time scale limitations imposed) at a time when it is of most use to the purchaser in influencing the course which the negotiations will take prior to their finalisation. The accountants should be mindful that a well presented report may be of little use if it is delivered to the purchaser late.

The report will include much financial information which will be historical and will have been audited by the target's auditors. At an early stage, the accountants will require access to the auditors' working papers, both to obtain an insight into the target's business and to establish the degree of reliance that can be placed upon the figures which depict the target's historical performance. Of course, the most recent financial information available may not, and probably will not, be audited and the accountants will have to make an assessment of the reliability of the unaudited management accounts. Generally they will do this through an examination of previous trends and by a comparison of previous management accounts with the audited accounts for the corresponding periods. It is important to appreciate that the accountants will not themselves conduct an audit of the target's affairs unless the purchaser's instructions, unusually, require them to do so. The accountants will perform an appraisal of the target's accounts, but will not necessarily verify the target's assets and liabilities independently or make an in-depth examination of the target's systems of internal control.

Much of the information required by the accountants should be readily available in one form or another at the target's principal place of business and can be obtained most easily by the management of the target. Accountants therefore often find it convenient to leave with management a list of the basic information they require for the purpose of their report. This enables them to spend more of their time appraising and interpreting the information obtained than in finding it.

Accountants' acquisition reports can, of course, take a number of different forms, but a report should be tailor-made to suit the particular requirements of the purchaser and the business environment in which the target operates. It may be useful to consider the outline of an acquisition report, an example of which is set out below, in order to provide an indication of the content of a typical report on a small manufacturing target company.

ACCOUNTANTS' ACQUISITION REPORT

1   Introduction
This will normally recite the terms of reference under which the report is written; it should set out the scope of the work undertaken and refer to any general caveats relevant to the report as a whole. The prime sources of information should be identified and the reader's attention drawn to material areas not covered by the accountants' examination and to the reasons why these areas have been excluded.

2   History and business
2.1   *History*. A brief history of the target should be set out.
2.2   *Business*. Details of the target's present business with a description of its products, its principal operations and an assessment of its general position within the market in which it operates, within the context of the national economic situation, should be included.
2.3   *Growth*. An indication of the recent growth of the target and of its present size should be given, normally by reference to a brief summary of the net assets and profitability shown in its most recent audited accounts.
2.4   *Premises and locations*. The amount of work done will depend upon the division of work agreed with the solicitors. Certainly brief details of each property, its location and of any professional valuation should be included.

3   Corporate structure
3.1   *Capital structure*. Details of the target's present capital structure and of its present shareholders should be given.
3.2   *Group structure*. If the target comprises more than one company, information about the structure of the target group should be set out

together with a description of the relationship between the subsidiaries and the parent company. Minority interests in subsidiaries should also be identified.

3.3 *Memorandum and articles of association.* This section should contain details of any unusual (but relevant) clauses in the target's memorandum and articles of association and details of share rights if relevant to the offer.

4 Management and personnel

4.1 *Directors and senior executives.* Details of the remuneration, including pensions and commissions, of the target's executives should be given, together with information on the terms of any service contracts and on any facilities granted to executives which may form part of their contracts of employment. The executives' qualifications should also be set out, and the accountants should make an assessment of the competence of the management if this is a part of their brief.

4.2 *Other employees.* The number of other employees should be analysed by department and location, and the basis on which they are remunerated should be shown. The facilities available to employees should be described and information given as to any known employee turnover statistics.

4.3 *Pension arrangements.* Details of pension arrangements for employees should be given and an assessment made of any unfunded liabilities.

4.4 *Succession and training.* The target's policy for management succession should be set out and an assessment made of any problems which the reporting accountants anticipate may arise. Details of the target's policies for staff and trade training schemes and the cost of such schemes should be included.

4.5 *Labour relations.* An assessment of the target's labour relations should be made, and any negotiating rights given to unions representing employees should be identified. The reporting accountant may also comment on the likely reaction of executives and employees to a change in ownership of the business.

5 Operations and systems

5.1 *Research and development.* The level of, and need for, research and development in the target's business should be discussed together with any future plans for the commitment of manpower to research.

5.2 *Purchasing and sources of supply.* A description of the purchasing procedure should be given with an assessment of the effectiveness of the buying department. The principal suppliers to the target should be identified and the dependence upon individual suppliers for goods or services disclosed.

5.3 *Production.* The scale of production and the approach of management to present and future production problems should be discussed. The current manufacturing capacity and any bottlenecks should be referred to, as should the age of the plant, its serviceability, and the plans for its renewal and replacement. The degree of dependence on assembly or manufacturing at more than one location and on sub-contractors should be considered.

5.4   *Warehousing.* The procedures for receiving, storing and issuing stock should be assessed, and the adequacy and suitability of the warehousing facilities should be commented upon.

5.5   *Marketing, competition and selling.* In this section the target's major customers and competitors (which may often include the purchaser) should be mentioned. Details of any significant contracts with customers, of the selling prices and discounts offered by the target, of the sales force (or any appointed agents), of the dependence on export sales and the approach to exports, and of the advertising policy of the target should all be set out.

5.6   *Distribution.* A description should be given of the methods of distribution used, including the use of the target's own vehicle fleet, and whether the fleet is owned or leased. If a number of different transport facilities is used, the extent of the target's dependence on any one facility should be noted.

5.7   *Accounting.* This section should comprise a description and appraisal of the target's accounting systems and management accounting information.

6   **Taxation and indemnities**

The purpose of this section is to inform the purchaser of the target's outstanding corporation tax liabilities, when its corporation tax liabilities were last agreed with the Inland Revenue, compliance with VAT and PAYE legislation, and whether there are any close company or other tax problems associated with a change in ownership. Reference should be made to any indemnities recommended by the accountants which should be sought from the vendor of the target.

7   **Accounting policies**

This section should set out the accounting policies of the target in considerable detail so that the accounts can be properly understood. Any unusual accounting policies or any variations from best accounting practice should be highlighted.

8   **Turnover and profits**

This section should include not only the statutory published profit and loss account information but also a detailed breakdown of overhead expenses. An analysis of margins, variances and ratios covering the previous four- or five-year period should be included with a report on the performance of the target during that period.

9   **Assets and liabilities**

This section should consist of a complete description of each item in the target's balance sheet. A commentary on contingent liabilities and capital commitments should also be included.

10   Cash flows

A table showing the target's sources and application of funds during the period covered by the report should be summarised in this section.

11   Future prospects

According to the quantity and quality of information prepared by the target, the contents of this section may vary from a general discussion on the target's future, such as the effects of technological changes and trends in customer demand, to a detailed analysis of profit forecasts, cash flow projections and long term forecasts, and an assessment of their probable reliability.

12   Miscellaneous

12.1   *Borrowing facilities.* Details of the target's existing facilities should be shown; the security given and the further security available should also be set out as should a summary of principal banking covenants and compliance by the target with such covenants.

12.2   *Leasing commitments.* A summary of the target's commitments under leasing and hire-purchase agreements should be provided together with the nature and terms of the agreements.

12.3   *Insurance.* Details of the target's major insurance policies and of any deficiencies in insurance cover should be brought to the purchaser's attention.

12.4   *Government legislation.* An assessment of any relevant government enactments or guidelines affecting the target's operations should be included, whether or not the target has contravened such regulations, and whether a change in ownership would affect either the purchaser's or the target's position in relation to these regulations.

13   Summary and conclusions

This section should set out the main points included in the report, especially the matters of which the purchaser should be wary in its negotiations with the target.

The report, without summary and conclusions, should be discussed at an early draft stage with the target's management to ensure that all the facts presented in it are correct. This will give the target's management the opportunity to make representations to the accountants if it believes there are serious omissions or misplaced emphases in the report. The reporting accountants can then consider, but may not necessarily agree with, these representations before signing their report and presenting it to the purchaser. On reading the report the purchaser might ask for further work to be carried out; it is more likely that he will accept the report and find it an invaluable aid during the final stages of negotiations with the target's owners or management. A well constructed report also acts as a permanent record of the state of the target's affairs at the time of the purchase.

ENVIRONMENTAL INVESTIGATIONS

Environmental regulation is at present increasing considerably both in width and stringency: such regulation can impose considerable costs and operational constraints upon businesses and may have a substantial effect on the value of assets. It is therefore essential that those dealing with company transactions are alert to potential environmental problems and that environmental risks are taken into account within the context of the particular transaction. Environmental problems may arise not only in respect of a company's existing operations, but also as a result of contamination from past, even historic, operations carried out by previous occupiers of a site. With stringent environmental quality standards being imposed by the European Community, and with political and public awareness of environmental problems being heightened, expectations as to what constitutes responsible corporate behaviour have changed dramatically in recent years. Activities relating to the storage and use of common chemical products or wastes, which may have been thought unexceptionable relatively recently, may now present very serious or even irreversible effects on the environment, for example, by contaminating ground water resources (*see Cambridge Water Company Limited v Eastern Counties Leather plc and Hutchings and Hardings Limited* (1991) *The Times*, 23 October, QBD.

A much wider range of operations of processes are now controlled by environmental legislation than was previously the case, particularly under the systems of integrated pollution control and and air pollution control introduced by Part I of the Environmental Protection Act 1990, and the widened range of activities requiring a waste management licence under Part II of the Environmental Protection Act. Failure to obtain the necessary licence or other authorisation may fundamentally affect the ability of a company to carry on its business, as may the modification, suspension or revocation of an authorisation under statutory powers. No less important are the conditions attached to authorisations, which may present significant operational constraints on a company's business, or may require heavy current and capital expenditure.

A number of the most significant types of consents and

authorisations required under environmental legislation are listed below:

NATURE OF THE CONSENT	LEGISLATION
Authorisation to carry on processes prescribed for integrated pollution control or for air pollution control by local authorities	Environmental Protection Act 1990, Part I.
Waste Disposal Licences for the disposal and deposit of controlled waste, or for the use of plant and equipment for dealing with waste in a specified manner to be replaced as from 1 April 1993 by	Control of Pollution Act 1974, Part I.
Waste Management Licences for the keeping, treatment, disposal and deposit of controlled waste	Environmental Protection Act 1990, Part II.
Transportation of controlled waste in the course of a business	Control of Pollution (Amendment) Act 1989.
Consents for activities involving genetically modified organisms	Environmental Protection Act 1990, Part VI.
Storage and disposal of radioactive waste	Radioactive Substances Act 1992.
Discharge of effluent into controlled waters	Water Resources Act 1991.
Abstraction and impounding of water	Water Resources Act 1991.
Discharge of trade effluent into sewers	Water Industry Act 1991.
Disposal of substances at sea	Food and Environment Protection Act 1985.

Keeping of specified hazardous substances in prescribed quantities in, on or over land	Planning (Hazardous Substances) Act 1990.

In addition to those activities requiring authorisation or consent, there are other potentially harmful activities which are regulated by alternative means. For example, the Environmental Protection Act 1990, s 34 imposes a statutory duty of care on all persons importing, producing, carrying, keeping or disposing of controlled waste; breach of this duty of care may result in a criminal prosecution. Similarly, activities giving rise to a statutory nuisance may be the subject of an abatement notice under Part III of the Environmental Protection Act, as well as criminal penalties. The entry of poisonous, noxious or polluting matter into controlled waters (including groundwater) may likewise result in a criminal prosecution.

A particularly worrying feature of environmental legislation for many companies is the growing threat of actions to force the 'polluter' to carry out or to fund operations to remedy the consequences of environmental pollution. The possibility of common law actions for nuisance or strict liability under the rule in *Rylands v Fletcher* have been supplemented by a range of statutory provisions which may result in such liability. Examples are the powers of the National Rivers Authority to carry out 'anti pollution works' under the Water Resources Act 1991, s 61 and the duties of waste regulation authorities, under the Environmental Protection Act 1990, s 61, to remedy sites where controlled waste may have been deposited in the past in order to prevent risks to human health and the environment. In the former case, costs may be recovered from the person causing or knowingly permitting the pollution, or potential pollution, of controlled waters. In the second case, all or part of the costs may be recovered from the 'owner for the time being' of the relevant land. Proposals from within the European Commission for a directive on strict civil liability for damage or impairment of the environment caused by waste have also given rise to much concern, raising the possibility of companies being strictly liable for environmental problems caused by their waste whilst being stored on site and even, in certain circumstances, after it has left the site.

The scale and unpredictability of such environmental liabilities means that acquisition of a company, or its assets, may present a dangerous trap for the unwary. It is therefore important to be aware of the means by which the position of the purchaser may, so far as possible within the context of the particular transaction, be protected.

Considerable information can be gleaned about a company's environmental performance and about possible problems from public sources of information, without that company's consent or knowledge. This means that in some cases problems may be identified even before negotiations start. In most cases where a process or operation requires an authorisation or consent, such as those listed above, information relating to the authorisation will be contained on a public register. Such information may include the initial application for the authorisation (which may of itself give considerable information as to the nature of the process in question, the raw materials used, wastes generated and pollution reduction measures), the outcome of such applications, conditions attached to authorisations, sampling records and monitoring data, and details of any prosecutions and statutory notices served by the relevant authorities. In addition, the Environmental Protection Act 1990, s 143 makes provision for registers of land which may be subject to contamination, by reference to a prescribed list of uses. The fact that a site has been, or is being, put to a particular use may be indicative of the possibility of chemical contamination of the soil. Such registers will also contain details of any investigative or remedial measures carried out in relation to the particular site. The amount of environmental information available to the public seems likely to increase, both under the EC directive on Freedom of Access to Environmental Information which is given effect in the UK by the Environmental Information Regulations 1992 and under the proposed EC regulation on 'eco-auditing' (at least for those companies participating within the scheme).

Going beyond these public sources of information, a purchaser may well wish to elicit further information from the vendor, either by way of enquiries, or by seeking warranties (which is likely to result in disclosure). For example, the purchaser should seek confirmation from the vendor that all requisite information has been made available to the statutory authorities and that so far as the vendor is aware the contents of the public registers are correct. The vendor should also be asked to disclose any complaints or any actual or threatened proceedings, whether by statutory authorities or by third parties. Whether it is necessary for a given process to obtain authorisation or consent may depend upon the detailed nature of that process and, accordingly, on facts within the particular knowledge of the vendor. The vendor should therefore be asked to warrant that all necessary authorisations have been obtained, and also possibly to give sufficient detail as to the nature of processes and operations to allow the purchaser to form for itself a view on whether any further authorisations are needed. Examples of environmental warranties are included in the Agreement for Sale in Chapter 16.

Increasingly, many companies will carry out for their own internal purposes some form of environmental investigation or audit, either for use by the management, or possibly for presentation to a third party, such as an insurer. The purchaser should ask whether any such reports have been produced and, if so, may wish to ask for sight of copies. However, the purchaser should bear in mind that any such reports may have been produced for an entirely different purpose from the proposed acquisition: consequently, their usefulness may be limited and it will be imprudent to rely on statements in the report without the report being re-issued in favour of the purchaser, or some form of collateral warranty being given.

All of the previous sources of information have their limitations, and ultimately the purchaser and its advisers will need to take a view on whether an independent environmental investigation should be commissioned. If so, an environmental consultant will need to be instructed and the scope of the investigation defined. Most investigations will begin with some form of desk study, assembling and collating existing documentary sources of information about site history and the company's current operations. Public sources of information will be consulted, and additional informal enquiries may be addressed to the relevant regulatory officers. Other sources of information, such as old maps, trade directories, deeds, county and other archives, and aerial photographs, may be consulted. Background information will be obtained on other factors such as the underlying geology of the site, nearby sources of potable water abstraction, watercourses and other vulnerable environmental features. Such investigations will enable a picture to be built up of the nature and degree of likely environmental risks. In the light of these preliminary investigations, it may be necessary to go further and carry out a visual inspection of the site, and possibly interview site managers or operatives. This will enable obvious signs of trouble, such as bad practices in materials handling, or areas of soil discolouration or staining, to be observed; it will, however, require the consent and co-operation of the vendor. Going even further, physical investigations may be undertaken, involving the sampling of discharges to the various environmental media and the inspection and chemical analysis of soil. Such investigations are both time consuming and costly and are potentially highly disruptive of a continuing business. They are, however, becoming increasingly common in cases where the site or operations have obvious potential for environmental problems (for example, heavy manufacturing industry or waste disposal), or where the purchaser is particularly sensitive to the potential problems (for example, a North American company).

Having carried out such investigations as the purchaser sees fit, a number of problems, of varying seriousness, may well have been identified. How these are to be reflected in the transaction, and the risk allocated between vendor and purchaser, is a matter for negotiation. The purchaser may, for example, argue that a reduction in price or a retention should be made to deal with obvious problems requiring attention, or to reflect the risk of future problems occurring.

Many acquisition agreements now contain relatively detailed warranties as to environmental matters; these may give a degree of comfort to the purchaser. However, there are a number of potential limitations to the effectiveness of warranties, in respect of which environmental claims may pose particular problems. The purchaser may therefore seek specific indemnities against costs, claims, liabilities or diminution in value of assets resulting from environmental problems, such as past spillages or escapes of hazardous materials into the environment. The vendor will wish to ensure that such indemnities are not of a general nature, and are as narrowly confined as possible. In particular, in the case of an on-going business, there may be difficulties, when a claim arises, in determining to what extent it is the result of activities carried out prior to completion, and to what extent it is due to subsequent activities of the purchaser. It is here that the detailed acquisition audit may be helpful in determining a 'base line' against which such claims are to be assessed. The vendor will, in any event, wish to be protected by the normal provisions as to prompt notification of claims, rights to investigate claims and to take over the defence of third party proceedings, time limitations and upper limits on the value of claims.

Another common source of controversy relates to warranties as to compliance with applicable laws, or indemnities against non-compliance with such laws. Not unreasonably, both vendor and purchaser will have in mind the possibility of environmental laws becoming considerably stricter within a relatively short time scale, and the vendor will not wish to be fixed with liability by reference to legal standards stricter than those applicable at the date of completion. General interpretation provisions which extend the definition of applicable laws to modifications or re-enactments of existing legislation should therefore be considered carefully by the vendor. Even in the case of existing environmental legislation, there may be considerable doubt as to how strictly this will be applied, and how provisions such as the requirement to use 'best available techniques not entailing excessive cost' (Environmental Protection Act 1990, s 7) may be applied in specific cases. Ultimately, this is something which the purchaser will have to take a commercial view on, assisted by its professional advisers.

DIFFICULTIES WITH INVESTIGATION OF TITLE

If the target has significant interests in property or has properties which, although they have little or no market value, are crucial to the continuance of the target's business, the purchaser's solicitors will either investigate title or ask for a certificate of title from the vendor's solicitors in addition to seeking the usual property warranties (see Agreement for Sale—Warranties p 302). In order to give a certificate of title the vendor's solicitors will themselves first have to carry out a full up-to-date investigation of title. There may be insufficient time for this. For reasons of confidentiality the vendor's solicitors may not be able to approach those employees of the target with the greatest knowledge of the target's property interests. Other factors may lead to restrictions in the scope of the certificate. In addition, there may be difficulty in persuading the vendor's solicitors to give a certificate in a form which the purchaser's solicitors consider sufficiently comprehensive to be of value to the purchaser and its financiers. For these reasons and since an investigation of title carried out by the purchaser's solicitors will often reveal matters affecting the value of the property interests, or matters relevant to the running of the target's business which, not being matters of title, may not be disclosed in a title certificate, it is usually helpful to a purchaser to have an investigation carried out by the purchaser's solicitors.

As no change in the ownership of the target's properties is involved in the acquisition, any such investigation (and, consequently, the giving of any such certificate) is considerably hampered. How far do these difficulties affect reliance upon such an investigation or certificate? A complete account of title investigation is beyond the scope of this book, but the following notes may be of interest. The tools of the title investigator are searches and inspection of title documents, and these will be considered separately. In addition to inspection by the purchaser's surveyor, inspection of the property itself by the title investigator is always desirable but rarely feasible either because it is simply impractical or for reasons of confidentiality. In addition, the title investigator will raise enquiries and requisitions of the vendor's solicitors. The replies to these should be annexed to the disclosure letter or incorporated by reference, and the accuracy of those replies warranted (see Warranty 40(f) on p 304). The purchaser's solicitors should resist attempts by the vendor's solicitors to circumvent this warranty by giving replies to the enquiries and requisitions which are qualified, eg 'Not so far as the vendor is aware, but no warranty is given', or 'The purchaser should rely on inspection and survey', where in the latter case for reasons of confidentiality this is impractical.

An investigation of title depends to a large extent on the quality and quantity of information supplied by the vendors, and the target and their directors and solicitors by way of copies of title deeds (and inspection of the originals) and in replies to enquiries and requisitions. The purchaser requires protection against non-disclosure or inadequate disclosure of relevant property matters in that investigation and should require the normal property warranties (see Agreement for Sale, Warranties 39 to 41 on pp 302–304). The vendor should have nothing to fear from this if he has made full and proper disclosure of property matters since such disclosure will override the property warranties to the extent of that disclosure.

Searches

The intending purchaser or mortgagee of land who searches a statutory register is usually protected by his search. This protection, however, is not afforded if the ownership of the land remains unchanged.

Companies Registration Office

The Companies Act 1985, s 395 *et seq*, requires registration within twenty-one days of certain types of charges created by companies, but the list of charges required to be registered is by no means exhaustive and does not include, for instance, incumbrances such as leases or contracts for sale. In any event, a clear mortgage register gives no protection to the purchaser of shares. A registrable charge which is not registered is void only against a liquidator or creditor of the company and not against the company itself or its shareholders (see *Independent Automatic Sales Ltd v Knowles & Foster* [1962] 3 All ER 27). When a charge is rendered void against a liquidator or creditor the moneys secured thereby become automatically repayable so that non-registration may even affect the target (and thus the purchaser) adversely. It is also possible that a registrable charge has been granted, but has not yet been registered. Prior to the expiry of the statutory period, it seems that charge would be valid (see *Burston Finance Ltd v Speirway Ltd* [1974] 3 All ER 735).

Local authority searches including Local Land Charges Registry

Non-registration does not affect the enforceability of local land charges, but, if a local land charge is not revealed by a search because of non-registration or because of an error by the local authority, compensation may be payable under the Local Land Charges Act 1975. It is, however, only payable to a 'purchaser' which is defined by s 10(3) of the Act as any person who 'for valuable consideration . . . acquires any interest in land or the proceeds of sale of land . . .'. Although lessees and mortgagees are specifically included, a purchaser of shares does not fall within the definition and any person searching in this capacity will not obtain a right to compensation.

Land Registry

Under the Land Registration Act 1925, s 20, failure to register a registrable incumbrance will render it void, but only in the case of a disposition of the land in favour of a purchaser for value (including a mortgagee or lessee but, again, not including a purchaser of shares). A search by a person other than a purchaser for value of the land confers no priority period (see the Land Registration (Official Searches) Rules 1990 (SI No 1361), r 10).

Land Charges Department

Again, official searches only protect purchasers of the land itself (Land Charges Act 1972, ss 4 and 11) and compensation for loss arising out of charges registered against estate owners prior to a good root of title will be payable only to such a person (Law of Property Act 1969, s 25). Failure to register such a charge created by the target will not affect its validity as against the target.

Other searches

Although no protection will be conferred on a purchaser of shares, it will usually be prudent for other searches to be made. Two examples are mining searches with British Coal for land in past or present mining areas, and searches of the relevant county council or London borough under the Commons Registrations Act 1965 for land in all areas.

Inspection of title documents

The title investigator should inspect the title documents in the target's or mortgagee's possession and will require their production upon completion of the acquisition (see the Agreement for Sale, cl 4(C)(6) on p 281). How much protection does this afford?

Registered land

Inspection of a land or charge certificate held by the target or its mortgagee will show that the target is the registered proprietor of the land described. It is worth making a careful check that the target's name corresponds with that entered in the register when the entry was made. Although the Land Registry will accept the inclusion of a company number in the proprietorship register it is not obliged to do so, and name swaps between companies can have the effect of confusing the investigator. Although inspection of the land or charge certificate will yield that much information, and coupled with the Land Registry search on form 94C mentioned below will also assure the purchaser of shares that the Land Registry is not, at that moment, registering a disposition in favour of some other person (as the Registry normally requires land certificates to be deposited with it for that purpose—Land Registration Act 1925, s 64), the mere fact that there are no other encumbrances noted on the register does not mean that they do not exist. For example, overriding interests (see the Land Registration Act 1925, s 3(xvi)) cannot be registered in any event and the purchaser's solicitors should enquire as to the existence of these in their enquiries and requisitions of the vendor's solicitors. Also, the registration of a caution, to protect a contract for sale or an option, does not require the production of the certificate at the Land Registry. In certain circumstances the Land Registry may dispense with production of the certificate (eg registration of a general vesting declaration—Land Registration Rules 1925 (SI No 1093), r 13). The safest course is to obtain from the target, or direct from the Land Registry (the Land Registration (Open Register) Rules 1991 (SI No 122)) up-to-date office copy entries of the register together with a search in form 94C obtained immediately prior to completion which, while it confers no priority, will cover any adverse dealings affecting the title which have been lodged for registration at the Land Registry. Because the statutory search procedure does not give any priority, even unregistered incumbrances which should have been registered will continue to subsist after the completion of the share acquisition.

Unregistered land

Inspection of title deeds to unregistered land will not reveal oral leases, estate contracts or the unregistered land equivalent of overriding interests, neither will it give any protection against the existence of puisne mortgages (registered at the Land Charges Registry or not) or even against previous sales of the property or part not protected by endorsement of a memorandum on the retained title deeds (see *Claridge v Tingey, Re Sea View Gardens, Warden* [1967] 1 WLR 134).

As in the case of registered land, a check should be made that the target's present name corresponds with that applying at the date of the conveyance, lease or assignment of the land.

In practice, the conveyancing investigator to a large extent relies upon the efficiency of mortgagees or other incumbrancers. They will, the investigator hopes, have effected the necessary registrations or secured possession of the title deeds, in order to guard against subsequent dealings with the land by the target which would render their security or incumbrance void. The share purchaser should remember, however, that he is merely hoping that incumbrancers have donned some visible armour to protect themselves against weapons which are more powerful than those available to him.

MISREPRESENTATION, WARRANTY AND INDEMNITY

If a false statement of fact is made by the vendor to the purchaser about the target, what remedies does the purchaser have? Of all the questions with which this book deals, none is more difficult to answer, particularly in a brief space. Although there are few decided cases which specifically relate to company acquisitions, the basic problem—a false statement followed by a sale—has been one which has occupied the courts for centuries and it is surrounded by such a web of rules and classifications, many of which are only of historical interest, that any exposition of the modern law, however brief, is bound to reflect its complexity.

Until the decision in *Hedley Byrne & Co Ltd v Heller & Partners Ltd* [1964] AC 465 the law gave no damages for a non-fraudulent misrepresentation which was not a term of the contract between the parties. Not until *Esso Petroleum Co Ltd v Mardon* [1976] 2 WLR 583 (considered on p 129) did it become clear that the rule in *Hedley Byrne*, which gives damages for a negligent misstatement, can apply if the parties to the statement subsequently proceed to contract. The problem, therefore, was to distinguish between 'mere' representations giving no right to damages and representations which did form part of the contract between the parties. In this search the characterisation and classification of the offending statement was all important. Was it a mere recommendation of the object to be sold, a statement of opinion or a statement of fact? If it was a misrepresentation of fact, was it made innocently or fraudulently? Was it part of the contract between the parties (ie a warranty) or was it a collateral contract? It was necessary to answer these questions to determine whether the representee had a remedy at all and, if so, what his remedy was: was it rescission, an indemnity or damages? If damages, were they to be assessed on the tortious or contractual basis? Since the passing of the Misrepresentation Act 1967 many of these classifications have become less significant in terms of the net result to the representee. Nevertheless, the Act is grafted on to the law as it stood before 1967 and the classifications are with us still.

Non-contractual misrepresentation

The contract for the acquisition of a private company is a unique type of contract. Its operative terms are often straightforward, simply providing for a sale and purchase of shares. However, for the reasons noted on p 100, this simple contract is often accompanied by a long string of representations and warranties relating to the target. Because such contracts are normally negotiated between solicitors and are complex and carefully thought-out documents, it is perhaps less likely than in other fields that representations made by the vendor to the purchaser which do not appear in the written contract will be held to have induced the contract, thus giving rise to remedies.

If a false statement of fact does induce the contract then, whether the misrepresentation was made fraudulently, negligently, or innocently, the purchaser will have the right to rescind the contract even if the misrepresentation has become a term of the contract or the contract has been performed (Misrepresentation Act 1967, s 1). If the representation is true when made, but becomes untrue to the knowledge of the representor and he dishonestly fails to correct it before the conclusion of the contract, the other party can rescind (*British and Commonwealth Holdings v Quadrex Holdings Inc* [1989] QB 842). Rescission will not be possible if the contract has been affirmed by the purchaser; if the purchaser has taken some action since the contract which makes it impossible to put the parties back as they were before (eg if the target's business has ceased or changed substantially); or if any innocent third party would be prejudiced. If the misrepresentation is fraudulent, damages can be claimed in the tort of deceit, and if it is negligent within the meaning of the Misrepresentation Act 1967 (ie if the representor cannot prove that he had reasonable ground to believe and did believe up to the time the contract was made that the facts represented were true—s 2(1)), damages can be claimed under the provisions of s 2(1) of the Act. Section 2(2) of the Act provides that upon an action for rescission the court may declare the contract subsisting and award damages in lieu. The purchaser who is victim of an innocent misrepresentation may therefore, if the court thinks fit, be awarded damages instead of, but not as well as, rescission. The question of damages is considered on p 126.

It is the object of the Agreement for Sale (Chapter 16) to restrict liability to those representations given as warranties in the agreement or contained in the disclosure letter which qualifies the warranties. Clause 8(B) provides that the written agreement is the sole agreement between the parties and by Sched 7, para 1, the purchaser acknowledges that it has not entered into the agreement in reliance on any representations other than those contained in the agreement or the disclosure letter. It is the latter provision which is directly relevant to the question of representations. In *Alman and Benson v Associated Newspapers Group Ltd* [1980] Ch D (an unreported case available on *Lexis*), Browne-Wilkinson J held that a clause similar to cl 8(B) which provided that the written contract constituted 'the entire agreement and understanding between the parties with respect to all matters therein referred to' was not apt to exclude liability for representations. He said that:

If [the clause] were designed to exclude liability for misrepresentation it would, I think, have to be couched in different terms, for example a clause acknowledging that the parties had not relied on any representations in entering into the contract.

This, of course, is the effect of Sched 7, para 1. In deciding how far such provisions are effective it is necessary to refer to the Misrepresentation Act 1967, s 3 (as amended by the Unfair Contract Terms Act 1977). This section provides that:

If a contract contains a term which would exclude or restrict—
(a) any liability to which a party to a contract may be subject by reason of any misrepresentation made by him before the contract was made; or
(b) any remedy available to another party to the contract by reason of such misrepresentation,
that term shall be of no effect except in so far as it satisfies the requirement of reasonableness as stated in section 11(1) of the Unfair Contract Terms Act 1977; and it is for those claiming that the term satisfies that requirement to show that it does.

The Unfair Contract Terms Act 1977, s 11(1), provides that the requirement of reasonableness is that the term should have been a fair and reasonable one to be included, having regard to the circumstances which were, or ought reasonably to have been, known to, or in the contemplation of, the parties when the contract was made.

The result of the operation of s 11(1) was illustrated (although in the context of a conveyancing transaction) in *Goff v Gauthier* 62 P & CR 388. In that case, a contract for the sale of land contained an 'entire agreement' clause stating that the written contract contained all of the terms of the agreement between the parties and that the purchaser was not relying on any other warranty or representation. In order to induce the purchaser to exchange contracts, the vendor orally represented to the purchaser that the vendor would withdraw from negotiations with the purchaser unless contracts were exchanged forthwith. The court found as a fact that the vendor had no such intention and his statement to the purchaser was therefore a misrepresentation. As a result, the purchaser (whose financial arrangements fell through) was permitted to rescind the contract and recover his deposit notwithstanding the entire agreement clause, which was held not to be reasonable within the meaning of s 11(1).

It is suggested that in a normal company acquisition, the inclusion in the contract of an acknowledgment by the purchaser that he has not entered into the contract on the basis of any representation other than those contained in the contract should be effective. If a representation has been made by the vendor, and the purchaser is relying upon it, then he has this opportunity to include it as an express warranty in the contract. If he does not do so, then in subsequent proceedings it will be difficult to show, having regard to the acknowledgment, that the contract was entered into in reliance upon the representation. It can be said that a provision of this nature is not subject at all to the Misrepresentation Act 1967, s 3, and that it is not the case that liability is excluded or restricted by the contractual provision, but that no liability arises because of the state of affairs of which the acknowledgment is a record. It is unlikely, however, that this argument will find sympathy with the court. In *Cremdean Properties v Nash* (1977) 244 EG 547, at p 551, Bridge LJ indicated that, in his view, exclusion clauses which purported to deny the very existence of a representation did not avoid the effect of s 3. Nevertheless, in a commercial transaction such as an acquisition, when the parties on each side are businessmen who take advice, it is difficult to see why the provision should not be regarded by the court as fair and reasonable in a normal case. In *Alman and Benson v Associated Newspapers Group Ltd* (see above) it was found as a fact that clauses similar to cl 8(B) of the Agreement for Sale (although not excluding liabilities for misrepresentation) are commonly included by skilful and reputable solicitors in share purchase agreements. It is suggested that a similar finding would have been made in relation to a provision such as Sched 7, para 1.

Vendors are well advised to seek to include an acknowledgment of this type in the contract. The acquisition of shares in the target will probably have been preceded by discussion and correspondence and it is reasonable to ask the purchaser to specify in the contract those representations upon which reliance is placed.

The purchaser may also have a remedy, in tort, if he enters into the contract in reliance upon a negligent misstatement. The rule in *Hedley Byrne & Co Ltd v Heller & Partners Ltd* [1964] AC 465 has been stated thus (Lord Denning MR in *Esso Petroleum Co Ltd v Mardon* [1976] 2 WLR 583, at p 595):

> If a man, who has or professes to have special knowledge or skill, makes a representation by virtue thereof to another—be it advice, information or opinion—with the intention of inducing him to enter into a contract with him, he is under a duty to use reasonable care to see that the representation is correct and that the advice, information or opinion is reliable. If he negligently gives unsound advice or misleading information or expresses an erroneous opinion and thereby induces the other side to enter a contract with him, he is liable in damages.

Liability under the rule in *Hedley Byrne* is not restricted to professional advisers (see dicta of Ormrod LJ in *Esso Petroleum Co Ltd v Mardon*, above, at p 601) and the above formulation seems wide enough to embrace a misstatement by a vendor whose knowledge of the target will of course be more extensive than the purchaser's. As a practical matter, however, the damages remedy for negligent representation given by the Misrepresentation Act 1967 probably renders this cause of action redundant (ibid, at p 602). For an analysis of the difference, see *Howard Marine and Dredging Co Ltd v Ogden (A) & Sons (Excavations) Ltd* [1978] 2 All ER 1134 at p 1144.

Contractual misrepresentation

A warranty is a subsidiary contractual term, breach of which will not entitle the innocent party to treat the contract as discharged but which will give rise to a claim for damages.

The warranties included in a contract for the acquisition of a private company are, for the most part, statements of fact and, as such, can be classed as representations. If a representation is made during negotiations and then appears in the written agreement, the party relying on it can still claim rescission of the contract if it proves to be false. The Misrepresentation Act 1967, s 1, provides that:

> Where a person has entered into a contract after a misrepresentation has been made to him and—
>   (a) the misrepresentation has become a term of the contract;
>   . . . . then, if otherwise he would be entitled to rescind the contract without alleging fraud, he shall be so entitled . . . .

To enable the contract to be rescinded for misrepresentation, however, it seems on the face of the section that the misrepresentation must have been made to the purchaser before the contract was entered into. It can be said that if the representation appears only once in the history of the transaction, and is included in the written contract as a term of it, then the Act does not apply. Although the courts may be reluctant to draw this distinction, it is common practice to safeguard the purchaser by expressly including the right of rescission in the contract, at least for any breach discovered before completion (see the Agreement for Sale, cl 7(f), on p 284).

The drafting of warranties in an acquisition agreement will depend, in many respects, upon the type of business in which the target is engaged. The purchaser's solicitors will, after consultation with their client and their study of any accountants' report, attempt to obtain assurances with regard to those aspects of the target's business which are important to the purchaser. There are, however, many warranties which are standard for almost any type of acquisition. These general warranties will be aimed, in more or less detail, at ensuring that the latest audited accounts of the target are accurate and that the target has carried on its business in the normal course since the date of the last accounts without incurring any extraordinary liabilities. In addition, the purchaser will want details of other matters such as significant contracts, litigation etc. A full set of these 'standard' warranties is contained in the Agreement for Sale, Sched 3, para 2 (see p 290), which is drafted with a trading company in mind. It is unlikely that all these warranties will be appropriate to any individual transaction. Taxation is dealt with in Chapter 13.

It is the scheme of the Agreement for Sale to oblige the vendors to make disclosures which qualify the warranties by means of one specific disclosure letter, so that it will be possible to say, after completion, what was disclosed and what was not. For an example of the argument that can otherwise result, see *Levison v Farin* [1978] 2 All ER 1149. In that case Gibson J said, at p 1157:

A protection by disclosure will not normally be achieved by merely making known the means of knowledge which may or do enable the other party to work out certain facts and conclusions.

Purchasers will resist general disclosures, eg relating to board minutes over a period of years, unless they have had an ample opportunity of considering them.

It must be doubted, however, whether clauses such as cl 7(A) of the Agreement for Sale are completely effective. Where a purchaser has actual knowledge of facts relating to the target it is difficult for him to deny them simply because they were not referred to in the disclosure letter. *Eurocopy plc v Teesdale* CA, 10 April 1991 (unreported) was an interlocutory decision in an action arising out of a company acquisition in which the agreement for sale contained a clause which sought to preserve the purchaser's rights where he had information relating to the breach of warranty which was not disclosed in the disclosure letter, Eurocopy, the purchaser, alleged an undisclosed breach of warranty, but, despite the terms of the agreement for sale the defence alleged, among other things, that Eurocopy could have no claim because it was aware of the relevant facts, albeit other than through the disclosure letter. Eurocopy applied to have this part of the defence struck out, but was unsuccessful both at first instance and in the Court of Appeal.

If an accountants' report has been obtained, the vendors will often wish to refer to it in the disclosure letter so as to ensure that all the matters of which they have informed the accountants, and which appear in the report, are regarded as disclosed. This can cause difficulty in practice, because the purchaser may wish to resist showing the vendors the report in its final form. It may be possible to resolve the problem by agreeing that the report is regarded as disclosed even though not seen by the vendors.

One difficulty which sometimes arises is the problem of representations made to the vendors in connection with the warranties. The vendors may ask the directors of the target to check the warranties and to confirm their accuracy. Such a confirmation, if incorrect, could give rise to a claim for negligent representation which might fall on the target, either because the representation was given on behalf of the target or because the directors are entitled to be indemnified by the target. The purchaser will obviously not wish the target to be liable in this way, and Sched 3, para 2(2) to the Agreement for Sale (p 291) contains a disclaimer.

Damages for misrepresentation

The measure of damages is different in contract and tort. The contractual measure aims to place the plaintiff in the position which he would have enjoyed had the contract not been broken. The plaintiff is therefore entitled to the loss of his bargain. The tortious measure aims to place the successful plaintiff in the position in which he would have been if the tort had not been committed (ie in the case of a misrepresentation inducing a contract, as if he had not entered into the contract at all).

If damages are calculated according to the contractual measure, the purchaser is entitled to the difference between the market value of the target's shares as they are and their value as it would have been if the warranty had been true. Under the tortious measure, on the other hand, the purchaser is entitled to the difference between the market value of the target's shares as they are and the price paid. The practical difference between the two approaches can be simply illustrated. Suppose a balance sheet warranty is given and the target has a liability which was not, but which should have been, disclosed in the balance sheet; then the purchaser of the whole of the target's capital would, under the contractual measure, normally be entitled to recover the amount necessary to discharge the liability. It would not affect the position if the target possessed an unrelated asset, not taken into account in the calculation of the purchase price, which was worth as much as, or more than, the undisclosed liability. However, on the tortious basis, the existence of such an asset would affect the calculation and there would be no damage, if, despite the misrepresentation, the target was worth the price paid.

The foregoing is subject to one very important qualification. The measure of damages is calculated according to the value of the shares of the target and while the amount of the assets and liabilities of the target will certainly affect the value of those shares, the relationship may be neither simple nor direct. In a case where undisclosed liabilities, or a shortfall in assets, is small in relation to the target's business it may well be that the value of the target's shares is not affected at all. Where the target is bought for its profit earning capacity, and it can be demonstrated that the value of its shares was calculated by reference to earnings, then a shortfall in assets will normally only affect the value of the shares if the profit earning capacity of the target is affected. The purchaser will, however, normally expect to be reimbursed for undisclosed liabilities and shortfalls in assets, except when they arise within negotiated limits, and it is for this reason that the so-called 'pound for pound' clause is frequently found in the agreement for sale. See the Agreement for Sale, cl 7(c) on p 284. This clause purports to say that, without affecting the purchaser's ability to claim damages on any appropriate basis, the vendors will pay to the purchaser an amount equal to any deficiency or liability of the target which arises from any breach of any of the warranties or which would not have existed or arisen if the warranties had been true. It should always be borne in mind that, in a case where the value of the shares is calculated by reference to profits and profits have been misstated, the purchaser's damages claim may well be a multiple of the shortfall.

Most of the litigation which has come before the courts relating to contracts for the sale of shares has been concerned not with breach of contract but with the tort of deceit following a fraudulent misrepresentation or under statutes which impose liability on company directors for misstatements or omissions in company prospectuses. In these cases the tortious measure applies and the plaintiff is entitled to the difference between the price paid and the value of the shares received and is not entitled to be compensated for the loss of his bargain (see eg *McConnel v Wright* [1903] 1 Ch 546, CA; *Doyle v Olby (Ironmongers) Ltd* [1969] 2 QB 158; and *Siametis v Trojan Horse (Burlington) Inc* (1979) 25 OR (2d) 120 (High Court of Ontario)). For a recent case see *Smith New Court Securities v Scrimgeour Vickers (Asset Management)* (1992) *The Times*, 7 April. Damages for non-contractual negligent misrepresentation awarded under the Misrepresentation Act 1967, s 2(1), will be ascertained according to the tortious rules, *F & H Entertainments Ltd v Leisure Enterprises Ltd* (1976) 120 SJ 331, *Alman and Benson v Associated Newspapers Group Ltd* (1980) (an unreported case available on *Lexis*) and *Cenup Properties (UK) v Dentsply Research and Development Corp.* [1991] 34 EG 62, although damages for innocent misrepresentation awarded in lieu of rescission under s 2(2) may perhaps be limited to an indemnity on the principles laid down in *Whittington v Seale-Hayne* (1900) 82 LT 49.

What measure will the courts apply when assessing damages for breach of a contractual representation? In *JEB Fasteners Ltd v Marks Bloom & Co* [1983] 1 All ER 583 the plaintiffs bought a manufacturing company without obtaining warranties. The accounts of the target for its first year of operations were inaccurate and the disappointed plaintiffs sued the accountants. It was held that the defendants had been negligent in the preparation of the accounts, but because the plaintiffs' motive for the acquisition was to obtain the services of the target's two directors the court held that the accounts had not affected the purchaser's judgment to any material degree in deciding to proceed with the acquisition and their claim was therefore dismissed (the case should now be understood in the light of *Caparo Industries v Dickman* — see p 102). At p 587 Donaldson LJ said:

The plaintiffs did not take the usual precaution of requiring the directors of [the target] to warranty the accuracy of the audited accounts and the fact that there had been no material change in the profitability of the company since the end of the period covered by those accounts. Accordingly they cannot sue the directors for breach of warranty but must rely on a claim against the defendant auditors for negligent misstatement. Furthermore, the measure of damage is different. It is not the difference between the value of the company if the facts had been as stated in the accounts and its actual value, but the loss which the plaintiffs have sustained as a result of acting in reliance on the accuracy of the accounts.

These remarks are, of course, obiter dicta but they are a very helpful clarification of a question which had been rendered obscure by the difficult case of *Esso Petroleum Co Ltd v Mardon* [1976] 2 WLR 583. In that case Esso let Mr Mardon a petrol station, representing to him that the potential throughput was likely to reach 200,000 gallons by the third year of operation. That estimate had been made before the requirements of the planning authority were known. In fact, the planning authority had required that the petrol station be built backing on the main road and not facing it so that the gallonage actually achieved was far less. Although the actual configuration of the site was known to Esso at the time they let the site to Mr Mardon, already having made their representation, they did not revise their figure. The representation was made before the Misrepresentation Act 1967 came into force, but the Court of Appeal held that Esso were liable in damages both on the basis of the rule in *Hedley Byrne* and also because what they had said amounted to a contractual warranty. Although they had not guaranteed the throughput, the court held that Esso had by implication warranted that on a careful assessment they had estimated the throughput of the service station at 200,000 gallons in the third year. This warranty was broken because there was no such careful assessment based on the site as finally constructed. The court decided that the measure of damages was the same whether Mr Mardon's claim was founded on *Hedley Byrne* or breach of warranty. In a crucial passage Lord Denning said (at p 595):

Mr Mardon is not to be compensated here for 'loss of a bargain'. He was given no bargain that the throughput would amount to 200,000 gallons a year. He is only to be compensated for having been induced to enter into a contract which turned out to be disastrous for him. Whether it be called breach of warranty or negligent misrepresentation, its effect was not to warrant the throughput, but only to induce him to enter the contract. So the damages in either case are to be measured by the loss he suffered.

The key to *Esso Petroleum Co Ltd v Mardon* seems to be that the warranty found was that reasonable care had been used in making the representation as to the throughput. If this warranty had been true then the representation would not have been made at all and accordingly the plaintiff would not have been induced to enter into the contract. Since the tortious measure would also seek to put the purchaser into the position which he would have enjoyed had he not entered into the contract, it can be seen that in this case the two measures produce the same result.

It is not always the contractual measure which produces the highest damages for the purchaser. Suppose the purchaser buys a company in circumstances where only limited warranties are given. An example might be a management buy-out, where the existing management team purchases the shares of the target and the vendors refuse to give substantial warranties because, as they claim, the purchasers know more of the business than they do themselves. However, it might be that, in such a case, a warranty would be given as to, for example, the operation of a group pension scheme. If that warranty were misleading, damages on the contractual basis would compensate the purchaser for any corresponding diminution in the value of his shares. Suppose, however, that the purchase was a disastrous one and that there were very substantial undisclosed liabilities. The purchaser does not have the protection of the normal warranties and so therefore cannot claim against the vendors unless he can say that the existence of the warranty about the pension scheme induced him to enter into the contract and that he is therefore liable to be compensated for the damage he has suffered as a result, ie the difference between the price paid and the value received. If the purchaser could show that the statement in question amounted to a tortious misrepresentation (whether a negligent misstatement at common law or a negligent misrepresentation within the 1967 Act) which induced the contract then he could claim damages on the tortious basis; but what if the representation is not negligent, but nevertheless amounts to a contractual warranty as in the example above? Unfortunately there does not appear to be any clear authority and the cautious practitioner acting for a vendor on these occasions will do his best to limit the vendor's liability to the contractual measure. In the United States the law clearly restricts the plaintiff, in these circumstances, from recovering any loss which the defendant can prove with reasonable certainty the plaintiff would have suffered had the contract been performed. (See the Second Restatement of Contracts, s 349.) For English authorities on the subject see *Cullinane v British 'Rema' Manufacturing Co Ltd* [1954] 1 QB 292, *Lloyd v Stanbury* [1971] 1 WLR 535; *Anglia Television Ltd v Reed* [1972] 1 QB 60 and *C & P Haulage v Middleton* [1983] 3 All ER 94.

Although the above discussion has tended to emphasise the differences between the consequences of assessing damages on the contractual and tortious basis, in most cases the price paid is likely to be equal to the value of the shares as warranted; so the result of applying either measure to any particular breach of warranty is the same and argument does not focus on the practical effect of the difference. In *Levison v Farin* [1978] 2 All ER 1149 the target had made losses in the period between the date of the warranted balance sheet and the date of completion, and the vendors had given a warranty that between the balance sheet date and the completion date there would have been no material adverse change in the overall value of the net assets of the company on the basis of a valuation adopted in the balance sheet allowing for normal trade fluctuations. It was found that the disclosures which the vendors had made were not sufficient to avoid their liability under the warranty and damages were assessed in the amount of the diminution of the net assets of the target in the period between the accounts and completion, less the tax benefit which subsequently accrued to the target, and therefore to the purchaser, from the losses in the period (for which see p 208). Gibson J formulated the measure of damages in contractual language, saying (at p 1159) that it was true that the purchaser was entitled to receive the company with the warranty as to net asset value performed as at the date of completion. Given that the purchase price actually paid (the make up of which the judge investigated) was the same as the value of the target as it would have been had the warranty been performed, the application of either the tortious or the contractual basis would have produced the same result. In deducting the tax benefits from the damages Gibson J followed Viscount Haldane LC in *British Westinghouse Electric & Manufacturing Co Ltd v Underground Electric Railways & Co of London Ltd* [1912] AC 673, at p 689:

When in the course of his business [the plaintiff] has taken action arising out of the transaction, which action has diminished the loss, the effect in actual diminution of the loss he has suffered may be taken into account even though there was no duty on him to act.

In other words, although it was not suggested that the purchaser was under a duty to earn profits against which the tax losses could have been offset, the fact that he had received a benefit was taken into account and was not regarded as too remote.

Limiting clauses

Those who sell the share capital of the company with limited liability should not be confident that damages recoverable as a result of a misrepresentation breach of warranty cannot exceed the purchase price, even if the tortious basis of assessing damages is applicable. Although the purchaser cannot recover in respect of damage which could have been avoided if he had taken reasonable steps to minimise the loss caused by the breach of warranty, it is suggested that there is no reason to suppose that the purchaser must allow the target to be placed in liquidation. If the target owes a liability in circumstances in which the vendor should have disclosed this liability to the purchaser, so that he is in breach of, for example, a balance sheet warranty in not doing so, then, even if this liability exceeds the purchase price of the target's shares, the purchaser may have excellent reasons for providing the target with funds to meet the liability (and claiming reimbursement from the vendors) rather than allowing the target to be placed in insolvent liquidation. For example, abandoning the target might cause severe damage to the purchaser's commercial reputation or involve the purchaser in loss in respect of guarantees which he had given after completion. Indeed, by the time the liability comes to light the purchaser may well have provided further funds to the target by way of share or loan capital and these will now be required towards meeting the liability. All these matters may involve the vendor in a claim for consequential loss and vendors who wish to limit their liability to the amount of the purchase price should insist upon an express stipulation to this effect in the sale agreement.

Apart from clauses which place a limit on the vendor's liability, vendors often stipulate that no claim is to be made for breach of warranty unless the purchaser has given notice of the claim before the expiry of a specified period (see the Agreement for Sale, Sched 7, para 4(3), on p 351). Such an attempt to shorten the limitation period can be particularly useful if the vendor is old, as the existence of a potential liability for breach of warranty can cause difficulties in the administration of an estate. It is not always sensible for vendors to stipulate that proceedings must be commenced within a specified period, as this can force a purchaser who considers that he may wish to make a claim to issue a writ before the expiry of the period, exacerbating a situation which could perhaps otherwise have been resolved by negotiation. Other provisions which vendors commonly insist upon are clauses which limit the individual liability of a number of vendors who are each giving warranties and clauses which provide that no claims are to be made until the total liability under the agreement has exceeded a certain amount, thus sparing the vendors claims for small sums.

How far are limiting clauses of this type affected by the Misrepresentation Act 1967, s 3? The section only refers to misrepresentations made before contract. In the peculiar circumstances of an acquisition it is often the purchaser who prepares the draft contract which contains the warranties and it is, in practice, often difficult to say that vendors have given the representations until they actually sign the contract. If the limiting clauses are restricted only to the contractual terms it would seem, therefore, that they should not be affected by s 3, but recent trends in the courts to assimilate the law as it relates to contractual and non-contractual misrepresentation have yet to be fully worked out and the position may not be as clear as it appears. As noted on p 123, in the normal acquisition both parties are advised and it is difficult to see why these limiting clauses should not be regarded as reasonable by the courts in a normal case.

Joint and several liability

Warranties may be given for all the selling shareholders in the sale agreement, by those who are substantial shareholders, or by the directors of the target (or by any combination). When more than one person is liable on the warranties, the purchaser normally requires the liability to be joint and several. The purchaser is then able to bring proceedings against all or any of the warrantors as he wishes and to bring separate actions against each. For further detail about joint and several liability see Glanville Williams, *Joint Obligations* and *The Law Commission Report on Contribution* (1977 Law Com No 79).

Recovery of judgment against one of a number of joint or joint and several warrantors will not prevent proceedings against the others in respect of the same claim, although of course satisfaction of the judgment will discharge the whole liability. The plaintiff who brings successive actions will not, however, be able to recover costs in any action other than the first unless the court is of the opinion that there are reasonable grounds for bringing the action (Civil Liability (Contribution) Act 1978, s 3). If any of the warrantors should die, his personal representatives will be liable jointly and severally with the surviving warrantors. If the purchaser wishes to discharge one joint and several warrantor from his liability, he will take care to preserve his rights against the others. If one joint and several warrantor is effectively discharged (ie by release under seal or by accord and satisfaction), the other warrantors will also be released (*North v Wakefield* (1849) 13 QB 536). If the purchaser wishes to release one warrantor without the others, then unless all agree, the best that can be done is a covenant not to sue the warrantor who is to be released. A release which reserves rights against other warrantors will take effect as covenant not to sue.

If one joint and several warrantor is called upon to pay damages he may claim a contribution from the other warrantors who are liable in respect of the same damage. The right to contribution is governed by the Civil Liability (Contribution) Act 1978. The amount recoverable will be such as may be found by the court to be just and equitable having regard to the extent of the defendant's responsibility for the damage in question and may extend from nothing to a complete indemnity, but if the defendant's liability was limited by contract, he will not be liable to pay a contribution in excess of that limit (s 2). The joint and several warrantor who has made a bona fide settlement of the warranty claim can still claim a contribution (s 1(4)). The limitation period is two years from the date of judgment or the date when the compromise was agreed (Limitation Act 1980, s 10).

If vendors accept joint liability on warranties it may be sensible for them to stipulate between themselves that in the event of liability arising they will make payments to ensure that any liability (including costs) is borne in proportion to the number of shares sold by each of them. Agreements to contribution are not affected by the Act (s 7(3)).

Warranties by the purchaser

Cases arise in which the vendors seek warranties from the purchaser. The normal example is a case where the purchaser is issuing shares as consideration for the acquisition and the vendors intend to retain those shares. Because the acquisition of the purchaser's shares will represent a substantial investment by the vendors, they will seek warranties about the purchaser's affairs. Where the purchaser is listed or the subject of dealings on the Unlisted Securities Market, the warranties can normally be in a much shorter form than those which the purchaser will seek in relation to the target.

The rule in *Houldsworth v City of Glasgow Bank* (1880) 5 App Cas 317 formerly made such warranties ineffective. In that case the plaintiff sought to avoid his liability to make a contribution in the winding up of a company by claiming that he had been induced to take his shares by misrepresentation and, accordingly, that he had a claim as a creditor equivalent to the amount which he was obliged to pay as a contributory. The court held that he could not claim as a creditor in respect of the transaction under which he had become a member. The rule is now set aside by the Companies Act 1985, s 111A which provides that a person is not debarred from obtaining damages or other compensation from a company by reason only of his holding or having held shares in the company.

Indemnity

Liability in respect of misrepresentation arises because of breach of a duty imposed by law or by contract, but liability under an indemnity arises not because of breach but because the parties have stipulated that one shall save another from loss in specified circumstances. Contractual provisions relating to tax are considered in Chapter 13. Indemnities are useful when the vendors have disclosed matters to the purchaser (so that the warranties are thereby robbed of their force) but the purchaser still demands contractual protection against the consequences of the matter in question, but see p 229 for a comment on the tax-effectiveness of indemnities.

Indemnities are normally strictly construed and liability under them will not go beyond that expressly stipulated. It is therefore common expressly to include liability for interest and costs incurred. Where indemnities are given by more than one person in the agreement for sale the liabilities are normally assumed jointly and severally. It may be sensible to provide that those giving the indemnity contribute between themselves to ensure that each vendor bears the liability in proportion to any benefit enjoyed by him.

Insurance

Insurance against liability under warranties and indemnities is quite often sought. Insurers will seek to exclude liability under warranties which look to the future (eg as to recoverability of debts) and, because they are insurers, will be extremely wary in accepting liability under a warranty which relates to the adequacy of other insurance policies (see eg the Agreement for Sale, Sched 3, para 2(27) on p 298). They will also seek to exclude liability relating to any matter within the warrantors' knowledge at the date of the agreement or, of course, liability arising from fraud or dishonesty on the part of the insured. Tax avoidance schemes are also unpopular in this connection.

Although insurers should be consulted at an early stage, they may be wary of committing themselves to provide cover until after contracts have been exchanged. They require a report on the contract from their own solicitors (for which the proposers have to pay) before agreeing to cover. The following is a list of points which may be relevant in connection with such a report and serves as a useful checklist for vendors generally (even when not insured).

(1) Is there any 'pound for pound' clause? (see p 127). The effect of such a clause may be that damages might be claimed by the purchaser in circumstances where the value of the target as a whole is not diminished by the circumstances giving rise to the breach of warranty.

(2) Some of the warranties may be qualified with statements such as 'so far as the vendors are aware'. Does the contract provide

that this implies due and careful enquiry by the vendors? (see p 278). This could mean that the vendors become liable under warranties so qualified, even though they are honestly ignorant of the circumstances giving rise to the liability.

(3) If accounts are warranted as 'accurate' the warranty is unlikely to be true, but it is unlikely that any claim would be made unless the deficiency is material. On the other hand, if accounts are warranted as making 'full' provision for all liabilities (including perhaps contingent or unquantified liabilities) then the warranty does not reflect accounting practice. Accounts normally only make provisions for material contingent losses which can be estimated with reasonable accuracy. (See Statement of Standard Accounting Practice 18.)

(4) A warranty that no liability has been incurred since a balance sheet date 'otherwise than in the normal course of trading' is quite restrictive as it would not cover, for example, replacement or repair of fixed assets or redundancy claims.

(5) Warranties under which plant or equipment is warranted as being in any particular condition or having any particular value are dangerous.

(6) A warranty that debts are recoverable is in the nature of a guarantee.

(7) Warranties relating to management accounts or profit forecasts are dangerous and should be carefully considered. The vendors should be alert to spot whether or not management accounts are warranted in a roundabout way, for example by being annexed to the disclosure letter which is itself warranted as true.

(8) Any warranty which says that a pension scheme is adequately funded is dangerous.

(9) A warranty under which insurance is said to be adequate causes underwriters (who are insurers themselves) to be on their guard.

(10) Any warranty which warrants the truth of written or oral information other than information contained in the disclosure letter is worrying.

(11) 'Sweeper' warranties under which the vendors warrant that all material facts have been disclosed are obviously wide-ranging.

(12) So far as tax warranties are concerned, official shortfall clearances are rare; capital allowances are often claimed; intra-group transactions are quite common and book values are not normally equal to base costs. If warranties covering

these points are given without qualification or disclosure, it is likely that insufficient work has been done by the vendors on tax disclosures.

(13) The sale agreement will contain a deed of tax indemnity or the more modern provisions relating to adjustment of the purchase price for tax claims Chapter 13. Insurers will wish to check that the indemnity is limited to taxation arising before completion; that it is limited to claims falling on the target and does not cover claims against the purchaser arising otherwise than in respect of the target or the shares to be sold; that it excludes claims arising from transactions in the ordinary course of business since the accounts, claims in respect of which provisions have been made which are insufficient only by reason of any increase of rates of taxation or retrospective changes of the law, and claims which would not have arisen but for a voluntary act or transaction of the purchaser.

Is credit allowed for other provisions relating to taxation? Does the indemnity include requirements that notice be given of claims and that the indemnifiers be entitled to require that the target takes steps to minimise the loss? Is there a grossing up clause? (see Chapter 13).

(14) The agreement should contain limitations on liability. Is there a minimum claim level (whether in the aggregate or in respect of any particular claim)? Is there a limit on total liability? (see p 131). Are there time limits within which claims are to be made? Are there provisions which limit liability to representations contained in the agreement and the disclosure letter? Does the payment of a claim under the indemnity provisions pro tanto satisfy a claim under the warranties?

(15) In preparing the disclosure letter, has care been taken to ensure that all items of the disclosure letter are not warranted 'correct', eg management accounts? Is it clear from the agreement that the disclosure letter does actually qualify the warranties? Surprisingly, it sometimes is not.

Chapter 10

Acquisitions by a Listed Company

The requirements of The International Stock Exchange of the United Kingdom and the Republic of Ireland Limited (now called the 'London Stock Exchange') are set out in *The Admission of Securities to Listing* (the *Yellow Book*). The *Yellow Book* contains the listing rules made under Part IV of the Financial Services Act 1986, and reflects three EC directives: the Admission Directive, the Listing Particulars Directive and the Interim Reports Directive. These lay down minimum requirements for the admission of securities to listing; the content, scrutiny and publication of listing particulars as a condition of admission to listing; and the continuing obligations of issuers after admission. Listing particulars will be required if shares are to be issued which will increase shares of a class already listed by 10 per cent or more, or if listed debt securities of any amount are to be issued.

The directives make provision for the competent authority in each member state to impose additional requirements for these purposes. The London Stock Exchange is the competent authority appointed under the Financial Services Act 1986. The Exchange has delegated most of its functions as competent authority to the Committee on Quotations and the Quotations Department.

The requirements concerning acquisitions or realisations of assets by listed companies and their subsidiaries arise from the continuing obligations which a listed company owes to its shareholders and which are set out in the *Yellow Book*, Section 5, Chapter 2. The requirements relating to acquisitions and realisations are set out in Section 6, Chapter 1. The summary given in this chapter concentrates on the requirements in relation to the purchaser. The regulations apply to the acquisition and disposal of assets of all kinds, but, in the context of this book, the comment in this chapter is limited to the acquisition of companies.

Classes of acquisition

Transactions are divided into five classes for the purpose of the regulations—'Super Class 1' and Classes 1 to 4. If the acquisition is Super Class 1 it will be necessary for the purchaser to make an announcement to the Company's Announcements Office of the London Stock Exchange, to send a circular to shareholders, and to obtain approval of the transaction by the passing of an ordinary resolution in general meeting. A Class 1 acquisition requires an announcement and a circular, but no meeting. A Class 2 transaction requires an announcement, but no circular, and a Class 3 transaction does not require announcement or circular unless all or part of the consideration is to be satisfied by the issue of securities for which listing is being sought, in which case an announcement must be made. Class 4 transactions are those which involve a past or present director or a substantial shareholder and in these cases it is often necessary to obtain shareholder approval. If the transaction is so large as to amount to a reverse takeover, the purchaser will normally be treated as a new applicant for listing.

The basis used to decide into which class the acquisition falls is a comparison between the purchaser and the target.

Super Class 1

The transaction will be Super Class 1 where the book value of the net assets of the target is in excess of 25 per cent of the book value of the net assets of the purchaser. The figures used for comparison will be taken from the latest published consolidated accounts, adjusted, in the case of the purchaser, to take account of subsequent transactions in respect of which adequate information has already been issued to shareholders. The Exchange reserves the right to disregard assets on which the auditors are unable to report without qualification. The transaction will also fall within Super Class 1 if the net profits (after deducting all charges except taxation and excluding extraordinary items) of the target exceed 25 per cent of the net profits of the purchaser or if the value of the consideration for the acquisition exceeds 25 per cent of the purchaser's net assets or, if the consideration is equity share capital, it exceeds 25 per cent of the equity capital of the purchaser previously in issue. Where the consideration is in the form of equity share capital, the department may determine the value of the consideration by reference either to the market value of the share capital or the book value of the net assets represented by such share capital.

There is an additional test based on the respective 'gross' capitals of each party. 'Gross' capital for this purpose is calculated by aggregating the equity capital of the purchaser at its market value immediately prior to the announcement, its preference capital and debt securities (also at market value if listed), all other liabilities (other than current liabilities) including for this purpose minority interests and deferred taxation, and the excess of current liabilities over current assets. This is compared with the gross capital of the target, which is calculated similarly, save that the value of the consideration payable is taken instead of the equity capital at market value. The aggregation should be made on the basis that 100 per cent of the equity capital is to be acquired, whether or not such is the case. If the gross capital of the target exceeds 25 per cent of the gross capital of the purchaser the acquisition will be Super Class 1.

Where the transaction falls within the Super Class 1 definition only because the value of the consideration for the acquisition exceeds 25 per cent of the assets of the purchaser, then special dispensations apply. In a case where the consideration is calculated by reference to the market value of equity capital the Exchange will be prepared to deem a Super Class 1 acquisition to fall into Class 1 if the other comparative figures are less than 25 per cent. Where the consideration takes another form, if the other comparatives and a comparison of the consideration to the market value of the purchaser's equity share capital are all materially less than 25 per cent, the Exchange will treat the transaction as Class 1.

There are special rules for property companies.

Class 1

A Class 1 transaction is one where the relevant figures amount to 15 per cent or more, but which does not fall within Super Class 1.

Class 2

A Class 2 transaction is one where the relevant figures amount to 5 per cent or more but which does not fall within Class 1 or Super Class 1.

Class 3

A Class 3 transaction is one where all the comparisons on the bases described above are less than 5 per cent.

Class 4

An acquisition may be Class 4 if shares of the target are held by a director or substantial shareholder of the purchaser (or of any company in a group of which the purchaser forms part) or by any associate of such a director or substantial shareholder. This may apply even if the director or substantial shareholder is retaining his holding. The expressions 'director' and 'substantial shareholder' are defined to include persons who ceased to be directors or substantial shareholders within the last 12 months, and 'associate' is also defined (Section 6, Chapter 1, para 1.2). Whether or not the acquisition falls within Class 4 will depend on the extent of the interest involved. The department should be consulted (through the brokers acting for the listed company) as early as possible.

An acquisition may also be Class 4 if any part of the equity share capital of the target has recently been, or is to be, acquired (whether by subscription or otherwise) by a director, or an associate of the director.

Announcements

It will be seen that an announcement to the Company Announcements Office and the press will be required in any case where all or part of the consideration for the acquisition is satisfied by the issue of securities of the purchaser for which listing is being sought. Otherwise, an announcement will only be required if the transaction is Super Class 1, Class 1, Class 2 or (in practice) Class 4.

Six copies of the announcement should be given to the Company Announcements Office for release to the market giving the following information:

(*a*) particulars of the target, including its name;

(*b*) a description of the trade carried on;

(*c*) the aggregate value of the consideration, explaining how this is being satisfied, including the terms of any arrangements for payment on a deferred basis;

(*d*) the value of the target;

(*e*) the net profits applicable to the target;

(*f*) the benefits which are expected to accrue to the purchaser as a result of the transaction;

(*g*) details of any service contracts of proposed directors of the purchaser.

When an announcement is not required but the purchaser wishes to make one, the announcement should include either details of the consideration or the value of the assets being acquired. Any announcement about the transaction, however small, which does not state the value of the consideration or indicate the size of the transaction may mislead shareholders.

An announcement should be made as soon as possible after terms have been agreed (usually directly upon exchange of contracts).

Circulars

A circular to shareholders will be required if the transaction is Super Class 1 or falls within Classes 1 or 4. The content requirements differ depending on the class within which the transaction falls, and, so far as they relate to acquisition circulars, are set out below. An important point to note is that a Super Class 1 circular requires a borrowings statement and a working capital letter. These take time to produce and the timetable for the transaction must take them into account. In addition to the *Yellow Book* contents requirements, Super Class 1 and Class 4 circulars will contain a notice of meeting and Super Class 1 circulars will often contain an open offer to shareholders where the consideration for the acquisition is shares (see p 154). A specimen Super Class 1 circular will be found on p 523.

Exceptionally, the Exchange may aggregate transactions that have taken place since the date of the last audited balance sheet, listing particulars or circular, whichever is the later. Such transactions may then be treated as if they were one transaction and therefore the latest transaction may be treated as falling within Super Class 1 or Class 1 even though, alone, it may not do so.

The Department's approval of a Super Class 1 circular is required in advance, and drafts of the circular should be submitted as soon as possible through the company's brokers. The same applies to Class 4, but Class 1 circulars are not required to be submitted to the Department for approval before they are published unless listing particulars are also required. Where securities are being issued as consideration for an acquisition, listing will not normally be granted until the circular has been published.

CONTENTS OF SUPER CLASS 1 CIRCULAR

1   Information about the acquisition

1.1   *Particulars of the target's business.*   Particulars of the assets being acquired, including the name of the target, a description of the trade carried on, the value of the assets being acquired, and the net profits attributable to the assets being acquired (Section 6, Chapter 1, paras 3.4, 4.3 and 5.2).

1.2   *Consideration.*   The aggregate value of the consideration, explaining how this is being satisfied, including the terms of any arrangements for payment on a deferred basis (Section 6, Chapter 1, para 5.2 and Section 3, Chapter 2, para 4.14). A statement that an application has been or will be made to the London Stock Exchange for any consideration shares to be admitted to the Official List (Section 3,

Chapter 2, para 2.1). Confirmation that the directors consider the value to the purchaser justifies the price paid (Section 6, Chapter 1, paras 3.4 and 4.3).

1.3 *Accountants' report.* Where the target is not listed an accountants' report on the target must be included covering the last three audited financial years. The requirements of the Committee concerning accountants' reports are set out in Section 4, and particular requirements relating to property companies are set out in Chapter 1 of Section 10. Summarised details of the last audited balance sheet and of the last three years profit and loss accounts must be included together with details of the basis of preparation and of any non-compliance with United Kingdom (or US or International) Accounting Standards and of any audit qualifications (Section 6, Chapter 1, paras 3 and 4.3).

1.4 *Effect of the acquisition.* The benefits which are expected to accrue to the purchaser as a result of the transaction and the effect of the acquisition on earnings or assets and liabilities of the purchaser should also be stated (Section 6, Chapter 1, paras 3.4 and 5.2).

1.5 *Taxation.* In the absence of a statement that income tax and apportionment clearances as appropriate have been obtained, a statement that appropriate indemnities have been given and, in the absence of a statement that capital transfer or inheritance tax indemnities have been given, a statement that the directors have been advised that no material liability for capital transfer or inheritance tax would be likely to fall on the group (Section 3, Chapter 2, paras 3.13 and 3.14).

2 Information about the group

2.1 *Name and office.* Name of the purchaser, registered office and head office if different from the registered office (Section 3, Chapter 2, para 1.1).

2.2 *Changes since latest accounts.* Statement of any significant change in the financial or trading position of the purchaser group which has occurred since either the end of the last financial year for which annual accounts have been published or the publication of the latest interim financial statement, or an appropriate negative statement (Section 3, Chapter 2, para 5.10).

2.3 *Significant litigation.* Information on any legal or arbitration proceedings pending or threatened against any member of the purchaser group which may have or have had during the previous twelve months a significant effect on the group's financial position or an appropriate negative statement (Section 3, Chapter 2, para 3.15).

2.4 *Borrowings.* Indication as at the most recent practicable date (which must be stated) of the following, on a consolidated basis if material:
  (a) the total amount of any loan capital outstanding in any member of the purchaser group and loan capital created but unissued,

and term loans, distinguishing between loans guaranteed, unguaranteed, secured (whether the security is provided by the issuer or by third parties) and unsecured;

(b) the total amount of all other borrowings and indebtedness in the nature of borrowing of the group, distinguishing between guaranteed, unguaranteed, secured and unsecured borrowings and debts, including bank overdrafts and liabilities under acceptances (other than normal trade bills) or acceptance credits or hire purchase commitments;

(c) all mortgages and charges of the group; and

(d) total amount of any contingent liabilities or guarantees of the group.

An appropriate negative statement must be given, where relevant, in the absence of any such loan capital, borrowings and indebtedness and contingent liabilities. As a general rule, no account should be taken of liabilities between undertakings within the same group, a statement of that effect being made if necessary (Section 3, Chapter 2, para 5.16).

2.5 *Working capital.* A statement (which will relate to the purchasing group as enlarged by the acquisition) that in the opinion of the directors of the purchaser the working capital available to the group is sufficient, or, if not, how it is proposed to provide the additional working capital thought by the directors to be necessary. Where cash forms a substantial part of the consideration for a transaction falling within Super Class 1, the Department will require a letter from the purchaser's brokers to the effect that they have received confirmation from the directors of the purchaser that the working capital available to this group is sufficient and they are satisfied that the confirmation has been made by the directors after due and careful enquiry and that persons or institutions providing finance have stated in writing that such facilities exist (Section 6, Chapter 1, para 3.6 and Section 3, Chapter 2, para 2.19).

2.6 *Material contracts.* A summary of the principal contents of each material contract (not being a contract entered into in the ordinary course of business) entered into by any member of the group within the two years immediately preceding the publication of the circular, including particulars of dates, parties, terms and conditions, any consideration passing to or from the purchaser or any member of the group, unless they have been on view in the last two years, in which case it will be sufficient to refer to them collectively as being on view (Section 3, Chapter 2, para 3.16).

2.7 *Prospects.* Information on the group's prospects for at least the current financial year including special trade factors and risks (Section 3, Chapter 2, para 7.1(b)).

2.8 *Profit forecasts.* Where a profit forecast appears in the circular the principal assumptions, including commercial assumptions, upon which the directors have based their profit forecast, must be stated. The accounting policies and calculations for the forecast must be examined and reported on by accountants and their report must be set out. The company's broker must report in addition whether or not they have satisfied themselves that the forecast has been stated by the directors after due and careful enquiry, and such report must be set out (Section 3, Chapter 2, para 7.2).

2.9 *Substantial interests in shares.* The name of any person other than a director, so far as known by the purchaser, who, directly or indirectly, is interested in 3 per cent or more of the purchaser's capital, together with the amount of each such person's interest or, if there are no such persons, an appropriate negative statement (Section 3, Chapter 2, para 3.9).

3 Directors' interests

3.1 *Interests in share capital.* Interests (distinguishing between beneficial and non-beneficial interests) of each director relating to listed securities and which:

(*a*) have been notified to the purchaser pursuant to the Companies Act 1985, ss 324 or 328; or

(*b*) are required pursuant to s 325 of that Act to be entered in the register referred to therein; or

(*c*) are interests of a person connected with a director within the meaning of s 346

or an appropriate negative statement.

In the case of companies not subject to the Companies Act, the interest of each director, including his spouse and children under 18, whether or not held through another party, in the share capital of the company, together with any options in respect of such capital (Section 3, Chapter 2, para 6.6). The Exchange has issued guidance on para (c).

3.2 *Interests in transactions.* All relevant particulars, including the consideration passing to or from any member of the group, about the nature and extent of any interest of directors of the purchaser in transactions which are or were unusual in their nature or conditions or significant to the business of the group, and which:

(*a*) were effected by the purchaser during the current or immediately preceding financial year; or

(*b*) were effected by the purchaser during an earlier financial year and remain in any respect outstanding or unperformed;

or an appropriate negative statement (Section 3, Chapter 2, para 6.5).

3.3 *Service contracts.* Details of directors (including proposed directors), existing or proposed service contracts with any member of the group, excluding contracts expiring or determinable by the employing company without payment of compensation (other than statutory compensation) within one year, except contracts previously made available for inspection in accordance with Section 5 and not subsequently varied, or an appropriate negative statement (Section 6, Chapter 1, para 5.2 and Section 3, Chapter 2, para 6.4).

3.4   *Emoluments.* If the total emoluments receivable by the directors of the purchaser will be varied in consequence of the transaction, all particulars of the variations; if there will be no variation, a statement to that effect (Section 3, Chapter 2, para 4.14).

4   Experts' consents

In the case of a statement or report attributed to an expert, a statement in that the expert has given and has not withdrawn his written consent to the issue of the circular with the statement included in the form or context in which it is included (Section 3, Chapter 2, para 1.8).

5   Documents for inspection

A statement that for a period (being not less than fourteen days) at a named place in the City of London (or such other centre as the Committee may determine) as well as at the registered office of the purchaser, the following documents (or copies thereof) where applicable may be inspected:

(1) the memorandum and articles of association of the purchaser;
(2) any trust deed or other document constituting debt securities which are to be issued as consideration for the acquisition;
(3) material contracts;
(4) directors' service contracts;
(5) the acquisition agreement;
(6) all reports, letters or other documents, balance sheets, valuations and statements by any expert any part of which is extracted or referred to in the circular;
(7) a written statement signed by the auditors or accountants setting out the adjustments made by them in arriving at the figures shown in any reports and giving the reasons therefor; and
(8) the accounts of the purchaser or, in the case of a group, the consolidated audited accounts of the purchaser and its subsidiaries for each of the two financial years preceding the publication of the circular together with, in the case of a United Kingdom company, all notes, reports or information required by the Companies Act.

Where any of these documents are not in the English language, there must be available for inspection translations either notarially certified or made by a person certified by a solicitor qualified to practise in any part of the United Kingdom to be in his opinion competent to make such translations (Section 3, Chapter 2, para 3.17).

CONTENTS OF CLASS 1 CIRCULAR

1   Information about the acquisition

1.1   *Particulars of the target's business.* Particulars of the assets being
acquired, including the name of the target, a description of the trade
carried on, the value of the assets being acquired, and the net profits
attributable to the assets being acquired (Section 6, Chapter 1, paras
4.3 and 5.2).
1.2   *Consideration.* The aggregate value of the consideration, explaining
how this is being satisfied, including the terms of any arrangements for
payment on a deferred basis (Section 6, Chapter 1, para 5.2 and
Section 3, Chapter 2, para 4.14). A statement that an application has
been or will be made to the London Stock Exchange for any
consideration shares to be admitted to the Official List (Section 3,
Chapter 2, para 2.1). Confirmation that the directors consider the
value to the purchaser justifies the price paid (Section 6, Chapter 1,
para 4.3).
1.3   *Accounting information.* Summarised details of the last audited
balance sheet and of the last three years profit and loss accounts
together with details of the basis of preparation and of any non-
compliance with United Kingdom (or US or International) Accounts
Standards and of any audit qualifications (Section 6, Chapter 1, para
4.3).
1.4   *Effect of the acquisition.* The benefits which are expected to accrue to
the purchaser as a result of the transaction should be stated (Section 6,
Chapter 1, paras 3.4 and 5.2).
1.5   *Taxation.* In the absence of a statement that income tax and
apportionment clearances as appropriate have been obtained, a
statement that appropriate indemnities have been given and, in the
absence of a statement that capital transfer or inheritance tax
indemnities have been given, a statement that the directors have been
advised that no material liability for capital transfer or inheritance tax
would be likely to fall on the group (Section 3, Chapter 2, paras 3.13
and 3.14).

2   Information about the group

2.1   *Name and office.* Name of the purchaser, registered office and head
office if different from the registered office (Section 3, Chapter 2, para
1.1).
2.2   *Changes since latest accounts.* Statement of any significant change in
the financial or trading position of the purchaser group which has
occurred since either the end of the last financial year for which annual
accounts have been published or the publication of the latest interim
financial statement, or an appropriate negative statement (Section 3,
Chapter 2, para 5.10).

2.3 *Significant litigation.* In relation to the acquisition only, information on any legal or arbitration proceedings pending or threatened against any member of the purchaser group which may have or have had during the previous twelve months a significant effect on the group's financial position or an appropriate negative statement (Section 3, Chapter 2, para 3.15).

2.4 *Working capital.* A statement (which will relate to the purchasing group as enlarged by the acquisition) that in the opinion of the directors of the purchaser the working capital available to the group is sufficient, or, if not, how it is proposed to provide the additional working capital thought by the directors to be necessary (Section 6, Chapter 1, para 3.6 and Section 3, Chapter 2, para 2.19).

2.5 *Prospects.* Any changes since the last published accounts or circular, in the group's prospects for the current financial year including special trade factors and risks (Section 3, Chapter 2, para 7.1(b)).

2.6 *Profit forecasts.* Any changes since the last published accounts or circular, in profit forecast information (Section 3, Chapter 2, para 7.2).

3 Directors' interests

3.1 *Interests in share capital.* Any changes since the last published accounts or circular, in interests (distinguishing between beneficial and non-beneficial interests) of each director relating to listed securities and which:

    (*a*) have been notified to the purchaser pursuant to the Companies Act 1985, ss 324 or 328; or

    (*b*) are required pursuant to s 325 of that Act to be entered in the register referred to therein; or

    (*c*) are interests of a person connected with a director within the meaning of s 346

or an appropriate negative statement.

In the case of companies not subject to the Companies Act, the interest of each director, including his spouse and children under 18, whether or not held through another party, in the share capital of the company, together with any options in respect of such capital (Section 3, Chapter 2, para 6.6). The Exchange has issued guidance on para (c).

3.2 *Interests in transactions.* Any changes since the last accounts or circular in relevant particulars, including the consideration passing to or from any member of the group, about the nature and extent of any interest of directors of the purchaser in transactions which are or were unusual in their nature or conditions or significant to the business of the group, and which:

    (*a*) were effected by the purchaser during the current or immediately preceding financial year; or

    (*b*) were effected by the purchaser during an earlier financial year and remain in any respect outstanding or unperformed;

or an appropriate negative statement (Section 3, Chapter 2, para 6.5).

3.3 *Service contracts.* Any changes since the last accounts or circular in details of directors' (including proposed directors') existing or proposed service contracts with any member of the group, excluding contracts expiring or determinable by the employing company without payment of compensation (other than statutory compensation) within one year, except contracts previously made available for inspection in accordance with Section 5 and not subsequently varied, or an appropriate negative statement (Section 6, Chapter 1, para 5.2 and Section 3, Chapter 2, para 6.4).

3.4 *Emoluments.* If the total emoluments receivable by the directors of the purchaser will be varied in consequence of the transaction, all particulars of the variations; if there will be no variation, a statement to that effect (Section 3, Chapter 2, para 4.14).

4 Experts' consents

In the case of a statement or report attributed to an expert, a statement in that the expert has given and has not withdrawn his written consent to the issue of the circular with the statement included in the form or context in which it is included (Section 3, Chapter 2, para 1.8).

CONTENTS OF CLASS 4 CIRCULAR

1 Information about the acquisition

1.1 *Fairness of the transaction.* The primary objective is that the circular should demonstrate the reasonableness and fairness of the proposed transaction. The balance of advantage or disadvantage to the purchaser must be readily apparent to enable a shareholder to reach his own conclusions on the proposal. While the ideal approach would generally involve an arithmetical valuation being set out in the circular, this may not be practical in the case of a complex transaction. It is however essential that sufficient information is provided to enable any recipient of the circular to evaluate the effects on the purchaser (Section 6, Chapter 1, para 7.3).

1.2 *Valuations and opinions.* In the case of an acquisition of an asset the primary significance of which is in terms of capital value (such as property) an independent valuation is required. Notwithstanding the inclusion of an independent valuation, the circular must contain sufficient information, and an explanation to satisfy the objectives referred to in 1.1 above. An opinion by an independent expert acceptable to the Exchange as to whether the transaction is fair and reasonable so far as the shareholders in the company are concerned must be included (Section 6, Chapter 1, para 7.3).

1.3   *Interests in the transaction.* The name of the director or substantial shareholder concerned and also, where applicable, of the relative associate must be given as must the nature and extent of the interest of such person in the transaction (Section 6, Chapter 1, para 7.3).

1.4   *Accountants' report.* Where appropriate an accountants' report may be required in relation to the target (Section 6, Chapter 1, para 7.3).

1.5   *Taxation.* In the absence of a statement that income tax and apportionment clearances as appropriate have been obtained, a statement that appropriate indemnities have been given and, in the absence of a statement that capital transfer or inheritance tax indemnities have been given, a statement that the directors have been advised that no material liability for capital transfer or inheritance tax would be likely to fall on the group (Section 3, Chapter 2, paras 3.13 and 3.14).

2   **Information about the group**

2.1   *Name and office.* Name of the purchaser, registered office and head office if different from the registered office (Section 3, Chapter 2, para 1.1).

2.2   *Changes since latest accounts.* Statement of any significant change in the financial or trading position of the purchaser group which has occurred since either the end of the last financial year for which annual accounts have been published or the publication of the latest interim financial statement, or an appropriate negative statement (Section 3, Chapter 2, para 5.10).

2.3   *Material contracts.* A summary of the principal contents of each material contract (not being a contract entered into in the ordinary course of business) entered into by any member of the group within the two years immediately preceding the publication of the circular, including particulars of dates, parties, terms and conditions, any consideration passing to or from the purchaser or any member of the group, unless they have been on view in the last two years, in which case it will be sufficient to refer to them collectively as being on view (Section 3, Chapter 2, para 3.16).

2.4   *Substantive interests in shares.* The name of any person other than a director, so far as known by the purchaser, who, directly or indirectly, is interested in 3 per cent or more of the purchaser's capital, together with the amount of each such person's interest or, if there are no such persons, an appropriate negative statement (Section 3, Chapter 2, para 3.9).

3   **Directors' interests**

3.1   *Interests in share capital.* Interests (distinguishing between beneficial and non-beneficial interests) of each director relating to listed securities and which:

    (*a*) have been notified to the purchaser pursuant to the Companies Act 1985, ss 324 or 328; or

    (*b*) are required pursuant to s 325 of that Act to be entered in the register referred to therein; or

    (*c*) are interests of a person connected with a director within the meaning of s 346

or an appropriate negative statement. In the case of companies not subject to the Companies Act, the interest of each director, including his spouse and children under 18, whether or not held through another party, in the share capital of the company, together with any options in respect of such capital (Section 3, Chapter 2, para 6.6). The Exchange has issued guidance on para (c).

3.2   *Interests in transactions.* All relevant particulars, including the consideration passing to or from any member of the group, about the nature and extent of any interest of directors of the purchaser in transactions which are or were unusual in their nature or conditions or significant to the business of the group, and which:

    (*a*) were effected by the purchaser during the current or immediately preceding financial year; or

    (*b*) were effected by the purchaser during an earlier financial year and remain in any respect outstanding or unperformed;

or an appropriate negative statement (Section 3, Chapter 2, para 6.5).

3.3   *Service contracts.* Details of directors' (including proposed directors') existing or proposed service contracts with any member of the group, excluding contracts expiring or determinable by the employing company without payment of compensation (other than statutory compensation) within one year, except contracts previously made available for inspection in accordance with Section 5 and not subsequently varied, or an appropriate negative statement (Section 6, Chapter 1, para 5.2 and Section 3, Chapter 2, para 6.4).

3.4   *Emoluments.* If the total emoluments receivable by the directors of the purchaser will be varied in consequence of the transaction, all particulars of the variations; if there will be no variation, a statement to that effect (Section 3, Chapter 2, para 4.14).

4   **Experts' consents**

In the case of a statement or report attributed to an expert, a statement in that the expert has given and has not withdrawn his written consent to the issue of the circular with the statement included in the form or context in which it is included (Section 3, Chapter 2, para 1.8).

5   **Documents for inspection**

A statement that for a period (being not less than 14 days) at a named place in the City of London (or such other centre as the

Committee may determine) as well as at the registered office of the purchaser, the following documents (or copies thereof) where applicable may be inspected:

(1) the memorandum and articles of association of the purchaser;
(2) any trust deed or other document constituting debt securities which are to be issued as consideration for the acquisition;
(3) material contracts;
(4) directors' service contracts;
(5) the acquisition agreement;
(6) all reports, letters or other documents, balance sheets, valuations and statements by any expert any part of which is extracted or referred to in the circular;
(7) a written statement signed by the auditors or accountants setting out the adjustments made by them in arriving at the figures shown in any reports and giving the reasons therefor; and
(8) the accounts of the purchaser or, in the case of a group, the consolidated audited accounts of the purchaser and its subsidiaries for each of the two financial years preceding the publication of the circular together with, in the case of a United Kingdom company, all notes, reports or information required by the Companies Act.

Where any of these documents are not in the English language, there must be available for inspection translations either notarially certified or made by a person certified by a solicitor qualified to practise in any part of the United Kingdom to be in his opinion competent to make such translations (Section 3, Chapter 2, para 3.17).

Indemnities

Section 6, Chapter 1, para 3.3 contains a provision which requires shareholders' approval to be obtained to any agreement or arrangement, not being in the ordinary course of business, whether or not in connection with an acquisition, under which a listed company agrees to accept liability for costs, expenses, commissions or losses, whether in whole or in part, incurred by a third party or parties unless the actual or potential liability is less than 25 per cent of the average of the published audited net profits of the listed company. Where there is no limit the arrangement must also be subject to shareholders' prior approval.

On the face of it this provision is extremely wide and catches indemnities in, for example, underwriting or placing agreements. It is understood, however, that the Exchange takes the view that such transactions are 'in the ordinary course of business' ie indemnities in such agreements are 'normal'. This prohibition remains a trap for the unwary, however, and in cases of doubt the Exchange should be consulted.

Shareholders' approval

The approval of shareholders to the transaction will normally be required if the transaction is Super Class 1 or Class 1.

The Committee will require that a very substantial acquisition or reverse takeover be subject to the approval of shareholders in general meeting. The acquiring company will normally be treated as a new applicant for listing. Listing for the company's securities will be suspended until after the shareholders' approval has been obtained. Listing will then be cancelled prior to the publication of listed particulars, following which the company's securities will normally be restored to listing.

When the following conditions are satisfied, the company will not be treated as a new applicant, and listing will normally be restored before shareholders' approval has been obtained but only after full information has been published:

(*a*) the target is of a similar size to the purchaser;

(*b*) the two companies are in a similar line of business;

(*c*) the enlarged group is suitable for listing; and

(*d*) there will be no material change in the board or voting control or in the management.

If there is a possibility that shareholders' approval should be obtained by virtue of the Department's rules, the Department should be approached before exchange of contracts as it will be necessary to determine whether completion of the acquisition should be made expressly subject to shareholders' approval in the contract. In these cases the circular giving the required information will be sent to shareholders before completion of the acquisition and will include a notice of meeting and a proxy card complying with the Department's requirements.

Shareholders' approval will also be required if it is necessary to increase the authorised share capital of the purchaser to make the acquisition. In these cases the Department will require a statement that no issue will be made which will effectively alter the control of the purchaser without prior approval of shareholders if 10 per cent or more of the voting capital will remain unissued after completion of the acquisition. In calculating the 10 per cent, shares reserved for options or the exercise of conversion rights are disregarded.

Using shares to fund an acquisition

When a listed company makes an acquisition it frequently wishes to use its own shares to fund the price. The vendors may be willing to accept some shares in the purchaser as consideration, but more often than not they require cash. There are essentially two methods of using shares in the London market to raise cash for an acquisition: the rights issue and the placing. Which method is used will depend upon a number of considerations, and market reaction will often be the most important, but the following part of this chapter deals with a number of points which arise under the heads of timing, accounting, stamp duty, and the r 520 notice.

As used in this chapter, a 'rights issue' means an offer to existing shareholders of new shares for cash on renounceable provisional letters of allotment, while a placing means a sale of new shares to selected persons. A placing may be a 'vendor placing' in which the new shares are allotted to the vendors as consideration for the acquisition and then sold by them to the placees, or it may be a 'cash placing' in which the new shares are placed for cash which is used to pay the price. Although the legal and accounting results are different, the net economic effect to the vendors of these two types of placing is the same. It is common practice, at least in the case of a large placing, to offer some or all of the shares to be placed to existing shareholders, with the placees taking those shares which the existing shareholders do not want. This type of offering does not, however, turn the issue into a rights issue. The Association of British Insurers has said that its members will expect an offer to existing shareholders where the issue amounts to more than 10 per cent of the purchaser's existing capital or involves a discount of more than 5 per cent on the market price of the consideration shares (see Chapter 2).

It is obvious that a rights issue and a cash placing can be used to raise more money than is needed for the acquisition, while the vendor placing will only raise the purchase price. On the other hand the rights issue is not suitable solely to fund a small acquisition involving, as it does, a fairly major market operation. There are a number of variants on the basic theme of rights issue or placing, including the so-called 'vendor rights issue' where the consideration shares are allotted to the vendors and then offered to the purchaser's shareholders on an underwritten basis. This chapter, however, deals only with the basic types of transaction.

Timing

Timing is important for a number of reasons and in a number of ways. The vendors will want the cash consideration at completion, and, normally, as quickly as possible. The timing of the announcement of the issue is no longer subject to official control, following the general consent issued under the Control of Borrowing Order 1958 (SI No 1208) on 14 March 1989 which exempts any transaction from the order, except transactions by local authorities. In practice, the London Stock Exchange is consulted.

Issues in the London market to fund acquisitions are invariably underwritten. That is to say they are not announced until a securities house has entered into a commitment to take the securities. In the case of a rights issue, the underwriting will be in the classic form and underwriters will agree to take rights shares not taken up, which cannot be sold in the market at or above the offer price. In the case of a placing the bank (or broker) involved will agree to find purchasers of the new shares from the vendors or, in the case of a cash placing, subscribers for the new shares to be allotted by the company direct to the placees. The period from the entering into of this commitment, normally on the announcement of the issue, and the date when the shares are finally taken up is the underwriting period and underwriters will receive a fee according to its length. A typical fee structure might be 2 per cent of the amount of the issue for the first thirty days of the underwriting period and one-eighth of 1 per cent for every week or part of a week thereafter. With this in mind, the purchaser will wish to keep the underwriting period as short as possible.

Where the sole or main purpose of a rights issue is to fund an acquisition, it is likely in practice that a meeting of the purchaser's shareholders will be required to approve the acquisition (if it is Super Class 1—see p 139) or to increase share capital and grant the directors authority to allot under s 80 of the Companies Act 1985—see p 20. The resolutions to carry these matters into effect are ordinary resolutions and fourteen clear days' notice will be required (although the articles of the purchaser should be checked). The acquisition agreement will be conditional on these matters and on the admission of the new shares to the official list. Because the provisional allotment letters are negotiable documents they cannot in practice be issued until the conditions of the issue have been satisfied, so the steps are: sign the acquisition agreement, announce and post circular to shareholders, wait fourteen days, hold shareholders' meeting, complete acquisition (having borrowed the money to do so), post provisional allotment letters, wait twenty-one days, collect proceeds, repay borrowings.

In the case of a placing the underwriting period is shorter, even where some or all of the new shares are offered to existing shareholders. Such an offer need not be made on renounceable documents and can therefore take place during the notice period for the meeting, although the London Stock Exchange requires the offer to be kept open for 15 *business* days. The steps are: sign the acquisition agreement, announce and post circular to shareholders containing offer, wait 15 business days, hold a shareholders' meeting, complete the acquisition and placing simultaneously.

If the acquisition is not conditional upon shareholder approval or on any other condition (eg OFT clearance) but it is still necessary to make the open offer to shareholders under the ABI guidelines then a number of interesting points arise. The purchaser will probably insist on being paid on completion. The bank will place the shares, but as they are placed subject to clawback, the final identity of those who are to take them will not be known until the expiry of the open offer, 15 business days later. The bank can effect this transaction either by acquiring the shares from the vendors as principal and selling them on, or, to save stamp duty, placing them as agent for the vendor. The key point however is that the bank will have parted with the money at the beginning of the period and, if something goes wrong, will end up bearing the risk.

In the case of a conditional acquisition contract the bank can protect itself in the placing agreement against unexpected events occurring prior to completion but once the money has passed the risks clearly become greater. Thus, for example, if one of the vendors becomes bankrupt or enters into liquidation during the period between the date on which the money is paid and the date on which the shares are finally allocated, the bank will wish to ensure that the agency arrangements remain binding and incorporate appropriate powers of attorney to permit it to allocate the shares to the purchasing shareholders or placees. Subject to the rules about voidable transactions (see Chapter 15), which are unlikely to apply, there will be no problem here if the bank has purchased the shares as principal, but the agency relationship does require careful study if it is to withstand a liquidation. Quite where the beneficial interest in the consideration shares has gone during this period following *Sainsbury v O'Connor* (see p 194) is an interesting academic question. So long as the arrangements are such that the beneficial interest in the shares either never was in the vendors, or has left them before the bankruptcy or liquidation, it is unlikely that the transaction will be upset.

Interesting questions also arise if a placee defaults. If the contract is entered into with the vendors (with the bank acting as agent) can the bank then sue the placee? If it does so in the name of the vendor, what loss has the vendor suffered, as he has already been paid? The answer is to impose a direct collateral obligation by the placee to the bank that it will pay the price on time and include provisions in the agency agreement which, in the event of default, permit the bank to sell the shares in the market and to claim against the defaulting placee under its direct obligation, and keep the proceeds.

What if the placees claim rescission on the grounds of some misrepresentation in the circular or listing particulars? In the case where the contract is conditional the bank will not be at risk because it will have the right to rescind the placing agreement if there is such a misstatement, and it will never become liable to pay the vendors. Where it has already paid however, it will be unable to recover from the vendors and will be exposed because it cannot recover from the placees either. The purchaser will give warranties and indemnities in the placing agreement which, subject to the operation of the Companies Act 1985, s 151 (see p 56) will give the Bank a right of recovery against the purchaser if it is unable to recover from its placees. Whether or not it takes security for the warranties and indemnities in these circumstances will be a matter of negotiation between the bank and the purchaser.

In the case of a cash placing it may be necessary to pass a special resolution to disapply pre-emption rights under s 89 of the Companies Act 1985, s 89 (see p 21). This requirement will extend the notice period to twenty-one clear days and therefore increase the underwriting period. Most listed companies pass a general disapplication of s 89 at their annual general meetings, but this will only normally cover new shares up to 5 per cent of their issued capital, in accordance with the guidelines published by the Association of British Insurers, and is unlikely to be sufficient to fund a major acquisition. This is one of the reasons for the popularity of the vendor placing.

It is obviously important, in order to keep the underwriting period to a minimum, to ensure that a rights issue does not require a s 89 disapplication. The scheme of s 89 *et seq* is not to require a disapplication if there is an offer to existing shareholders which complies with the statutory procedure, but there are a number of points to watch. First, a statutory offer must remain open for twenty-one clear days which does not start until the offer is made. Where the offer is sent by post it is deemed to be made at the time at which the letter would be delivered in the ordinary course of post (s 90(2)). This poses obvious difficulties in the case of foreign shareholders, and indeed the impossibility of knowing when a letter would be delivered to them in the ordinary course of post makes it imperative to find another way of communicating the offer to them. This problem is compounded by the fact that certain jurisdictions, notably the United States and Canada, have securities laws which prohibit the making of offers in those jurisdictions without regulatory filings. Luckily s 90(5) provides that where a holder has no registered address in the United Kingdom, the offer may be made by publishing it in the *London Gazette*. It is the practice therefore to make the offer by these means but, in addition, to send the documents for convenience to foreign shareholders unless prohibited from doing so by the local law.

Another point to watch in the statutory procedure is the treatment of fractions. It is the normal practice to aggregate fractions and sell them in the market, but s 89 provides that the offer must be made to shareholders in proportions which are 'as nearly as practicable' equal to the shares held by them. Where the computer will do it, this seems to require allocations to be rounded up and down as appropriate. The sale in the market of the shares resulting from the aggregation of fractions amounts to a cash issue, but this will normally be covered by the general disapplication obtained at the purchaser's latest annual general meeting.

In practice, almost all listed companies will have disapplied s 89 at their last annual general meeting for a 'rights issue' thus permitting an issue of ordinary shares which does not accord strictly with the statutory requirements. Where a new class of shares (eg convertible preference shares) is used to fund the issue, however, existing authorities will not apply.

Accounting

An issue of shares for cash, whether as a rights issue or as a placing will involve a share premium account of the difference between the net price and the nominal value of the shares. These matters are discussed in Chapter 8. The acquisition will be accounted for on an acquisition basis and, if the price paid exceeds the fair value of the assets of the target, goodwill will arise on consolidation, which cannot be written off against share premium account. It will normally be possible, however, to reduce capital by writing down the share premium account (see p 97). This will involve a special resolution which must be sanctioned by the court. The purchaser will not wish to extend the underwriting period by including the special resolution as one of the matters to be dealt with at the extraordinary general meeting convened to approve the acquisition, but it is possible to convene a separate extraordinary general meeting by notice included in the same circular.

In a vendor placing it will normally be possible to obtain merger relief under the Companies Act 1985, s 131. If the acquisition is accounted for on a merger basis no goodwill will arise, and if it is accounted for on an acquisition basis the difference between the nominal value and the fair value of the consideration shares will show up as a non-statutory reserve against which goodwill arising on consolidation can be written off.

Stamp duty

The stamp duty costs of the acquisition itself will not be increased by a rights issue or a cash placing. However, in the case of a vendor placing, a further transaction in securities is involved, namely a sale of the shares from vendors to placees, and this will be subject to stamp duty reserve tax (see p 190). In a case where the bank arranging the placing acts as a principal, and agrees to buy the shares from the vendor and sell them on to the placees there will be a double charge to stamp duty reserve tax unless the transaction is within the Finance Act 1986, s 89A. Section 89A will exempt the agreement to sell to the issuing house if:

(*a*) the agreement is part of an arrangement, entered into as part of its business, under which it is to offer the securities for sale to the public;

(*b*) the agreement is conditional on admission of the securities to listing;

(*c*) the consideration under the agreement is the same as the price at which the issuing house is to offer the security for sale; and

(*d*) the issuing house sells the securities in accordance with the arrangement referred to in (*a*).

There can be doubts about the applicability of s 89A in many cases, either because the securities are not offered to 'the public' but to a small class of persons or because part of the placing takes place after the listing has become effective, so that the agreement to place is not in fact conditional upon listing. These problems can be avoided if the bank acts as agent for the vendors in placing the shares rather than as principal, and the vendor placing agreement on p 489 is prepared on this basis.

A vendor placing may also add to the stamp duty costs of the acquisition itself. Many cases arise in which the target owes substantial sums to the vendor. Such a debt may exist before the acquisition or may be created as a result of the payment of a substantial pre-sale dividend (see p 177). In this case the purchaser is normally required to pay for the shares and to put the target in funds to repay the indebtedness resulting from the payment of the dividend and its lending back. In order to raise the money to repay the indebtedness by means of a vendor placing and to obtain merger relief under the Companies Act 1985, s 131, it will be necessary to capitalise the debt owing from target to vendor in the form of equity share capital. Procuring the repayment of indebtedness by the target does not involve a stamp duty charge (see p 189), but purchasing share capital does. A vendor placing will therefore increase the cost of the acquisition to the purchaser by 0.5 per cent of the value of the debt which has to be capitalised.

The rule 520 notice

Even after the London Stock Exchange has granted permission for the admission of the new shares to the Official List, the listing will not become fully effective until a notice is posted (or, these days, screened) under rule 520 of the rules of the London Stock Exchange (see *Yellow Book*, Section 1, Chapter 1, para 8). The notice will not be posted until after the shares have been allotted. There has only been one case in which, after the permission had been granted, the notice was not posted, but underwriters will invariably insist that their commitment is conditional upon the posting of the notice.

This gives rise to practical difficulties. In the case of a vendor placing the purchaser cannot allot the consideration shares until completion of the acquisition, but the vendors will not complete until they get their cash and the placees will not pay until the listing is fully effective. The normal procedure is for the Exchange to post the notice after they have been notified of the allotment, but vendors are understandably reluctant to part with the target and then wait until they are paid. In that case they bear the risk of something happening which means that the notice is not posted. Such an event is almost inconceivable, but the consequences are severe, and a vendor who has stipulated for cash will not run any risk, however slight, of ending up with unlisted shares in a purchaser with a problem.

The normal way out of this conundrum is to go through all the completion procedures but for the parties' solicitors to hold the completion documents in escrow subject to the posting of the rule 520 notice. The consideration shares are allotted subject to completion, the Exchange is informed of the allotment and posts the notice, whereupon the acquisition automatically completes simultaneously. In a case where there is a delay between contract and completion it is necessary for the acquisition agreement (as well as the placing agreement) to provide that completion is conditional not merely on the grant of permission for the admission of the consideration shares to the Official List, but upon the listing becoming fully effective. The escrow is often informal, but is sometimes evidenced by an escrow letter.

Much the same procedures can be applied in the case of a cash placing, but the considerations in a rights issue are somewhat different. The underwriters will still insist on their commitment being subject to the posting of the rule 520 notice, but the notice will not be posted until after the provisional letters of allotment have been despatched. It will not normally be desirable for the letters of allotment to be expressed as being subject to completion of the acquisition, as the rights letters are negotiable and of value, but on the other hand, where the purpose of the issue is to raise the purchase price, shareholders are entitled to be assured that the acquisition has been completed. In such a case it would create a major problem if the issue went ahead without the acquisition. On the other hand there is clearly a major problem for the purchaser if the acquisition were to go ahead without the issue. As the rights issue proceeds will not be available for some weeks after all the conditions of the acquisition have been satisfied the acquisition will normally be completed with borrowed funds. If something goes wrong between completion of the acquisition and the posting of the rule 520 notice the purchaser could be left with a new subsidiary and a large overdraft.

There used to be a useful section in the Companies Act 1985 and its predecessors (s 86) which provided that where a prospectus stated that an application had been made for listing and the listing was not granted the allotment was void. This section has now been repealed and not replaced by anything in the Financial Services Act 1986. The result is that, in the event of a failure to post the rule 520 notice, the allotment is still valid. As the notice has not been posted when the rights letters are despatched, it is good practice to include a statement in the provisional letters of allotment, that they will lapse if the rule 520 notice is not posted. This degree of conditionality does not cause a problem because the condition will normally have been satisfied by the time the letters have been received. It is possible to take advantage of this by completing the acquisition in escrow, in the same way as described above for a vendor placing, mailing the letters, and releasing the documents from escrow when the rule 520 notice is posted. Then, if the notice is not posted, the allotment letters lapse, the underwriters are off the hook and the acquisition does not complete. In this case, of course, it is necessary for the acquisition agreement to be conditional upon the listing becoming fully effective.

The Unlisted Securities Market

Where the purchaser has securities traded in the Unlisted Securities Market then it must refer to the terms and conditions of entry to the Unlisted Securities Market in connection with the acquisition. The purchaser's obligations arise under paragraph 5 of the general undertaking which such companies are required to give to the London Stock Exchange. In general terms, the requirements are similar to those of the *Yellow Book*, but are less onerous.

Reference should be made to the following tests in order to classify transactions:

(a) the value of the assets acquired compared with the assets of the purchaser;

(b) net profits (after deducting all charges for taxation and excluding extraordinary items) attributable to the assets acquired, compared with the profits of the acquiring or disposing company;

(c) the aggregate value of the consideration given or received, compared with the assets of the purchaser;

(d) equity capital issued by the purchaser as consideration for the acquisition compared with the equity capital already in issue.

The classification of transactions is similar to the *Yellow Book* rules. Notification to the Department is required when comparison in any of the above cases gives a result of 5 per cent or more. The notification should be in the form of an announcement including details of the assets acquired, how the consideration was satisfied, the value of the assets and the profits attributable to those assets.

If comparison in one or more of the above cases shows results of 35 per cent or more, the transaction is 'Class 1' ie sufficiently material to call for not only an announcement but also a circular to be sent to shareholders. The requirements and the contents of such circulars are contained in Section D of the document *The Stock Exchange Unlisted Securities Market*. Circulars are required irrespective of whether the consideration was in cash or securities. If the comparison shows results of 75 per cent or more shareholder approval will be required. The Department must be consulted in advance where the relative tests amount to 100 per cent or more, or where a change of control might result, when the company will be treated as a new applicant.

Transactions which involve a director, substantial shareholder or past substantial shareholder of the company (or any other company being its subsidiary, holding company or a subsidiary of its holding company) should be subject to prior approval of the company in general meeting and the issue of an explanatory circular. This also includes transactions with associates of any of the foregoing. Where it is proposed to enter into such a transaction, the Department must be consulted as soon as possible, and prior to any contract being entered into.

Accountants' reports covering a three year period (or since commencement of business if less than three years) will be required for all 'Class 1' acquisitions and may be required for 'Class 4'. Rights issues and the offering of shares to existing holders in a placing will be excluded from the operation of Part III of the Companies Act

1985 where the shares are listed—see Sched 4 to the Financial Services Act 1986 (Commencement No 3) Order 1986 (SI No 2246), but at the time of publication, Part III will apply to such offers by a USM company and it will therefore be necessary to file a prospectus. Part III will be replaced when the Public Offers Directive is fully implemented.

Chapter 11

Taxation of the Transaction

Almost every aspect of taxation can apply, in some way, to the acquisition of a private company. Detailed discussion of all possible revenue considerations is outside the scope of this book, and the purpose of this chapter and Chapter 12, which deals with the taxation position of the target is to mention (in more or less detail) matters which often arise in practice.

STRUCTURING THE TRANSACTION

One of the initial decisions the purchaser and the vendors will have to take is whether it is the shares in the target company or its assets which are to be sold. There are a number of advantages and disadvantages to each course of action, and what benefits one party may, of course, be unattractive to the other.

The main taxation issues which arise are:

(1) On an asset sale, the purchaser may be able to obtain capital allowances for certain of the assets acquired. The vendor (that is, the target), however, may suffer claw-back or balancing charges in respect of any capital allowances it has previously claimed itself. Where the target is sold, its capital allowance position is unaffected.

(2) An asset sale provides opportunities for capital gains tax roll over relief under the Taxation of Chargeable Gains Act 1992, s 152. The target may be able to roll over its gains on the disposal of qualifying assets into other assets bought by it or another company in its group within the relevant period, while the purchaser may be able to use its acquisition to shelter gains realised by it or another company in its group. On a share sale relief will be available only to vendors who receive shares or loan stock in the circumstances set out in the Taxation of Chargeable Gains Act 1992, s 135.

(3) On a share sale, the base cost for capital gains tax purposes to

164

the target of its assets is unaffected (unless the Taxation of Chargeable Gains Act 1992, s 178 applies). A purchaser who acquires assets may obtain a higher base cost. This will also increase the amount of indexation allowance available on a future disposal of the assets. However, the tax liability of the target may be greater on an asset sale than the vendors would suffer on a share sale, and the vendors may incur further taxation in extracting the proceeds of sale from the target.

(4) On an asset sale, the purchaser may obtain a deduction as a trading expense for corporation tax purposes for the cost of any trading stock acquired. The target will include such amount as part of its trading income.

(5) In some instances, an asset sale may produce a stamp duty saving, perhaps if the assets consist mainly of chattels which pass by delivery. On the other hand ad valorem stamp duty on a transfer of shares is charged on the consideration at the rate of 50p per £100 or part, while the rate of stamp duty on the consideration for other property is £1 per £100 or part. The amount of any liabilities of the target which are assumed by the purchaser on an asset sale form part of the consideration (Stamp Act 1891, s 57). Thus the stampable consideration may be much greater, and subject to stamp duty at a higher rate, on an asset purchase than on a share purchase.

(6) Value added tax will not be chargeable on a sale of assets (except perhaps in respect of certain property interests) provided the acquisition amounts to a transfer of a going concern within the Value Added Tax (Special Provisions) Order 1981, SI No 1741, article 12. If the target is required to charge value added tax, the purchaser will have to consider the extent to which it will be able to recover this as input tax. The transfer of shares, on the other hand, is exempt from value added tax.

The considerations to be taken into account are by no means limited to taxation matters. For instance, an asset sale may be preferred by a purchaser who wishes to acquire part only of the target's business. However, the target will be left with the remainder of the business which may not be saleable by itself. On an asset sale the purchaser will not automatically assume all the continuing liabilities of the target or its business. This can reduce the need for investigation by the purchaser and limit the warranties sought from the vendors (see p 99). Equally, however, the target would remain party to its business contracts. While the benefit of these may in some cases be assignable to the purchaser, the obligations under the contracts will remain with the target unless the parties to the contracts agree to novate them to the purchaser. Some of the target's assets, essential to its business, may not be freely transferable by it.

Consideration also has to be given to the possible application of the Transfer of Undertakings (Protection of Employment) Regulations 1981 (SI No 1794) which may treat the company's employees as continuing to be employed by the purchaser.

More often than not, it proves desirable for shares rather than assets to be sold, and that, of course, is the situation which this book considers.

TAXATION OF THE VENDORS

This part of the chapter is concerned with tax payable by the vendors. It does not deal with the taxation treatment of any reconstruction or reorganisation which may be undertaken as a preparatory step to any sale. Nor is there any detailed examination of the tax planning opportunities available to the vendors. Readers should, however, note that the unification of income tax and capital gains tax rates and March 1982 rebasing for capital gains tax purposes introduced by the Finance Act 1988 have overturned much conventional wisdom as to the optimum method of structuring a transaction and every transaction should be approached afresh. Consideration is now commonly given to proposals which formerly would have seemed heretical, such as constituting part of the consideration as dividends or remuneration. Indeed, it can be easier to shelter income, through pension scheme payments or investments in business expansion scheme companies and enterprise zone properties, than it is to shelter capital gains from tax in the absence of retirement relief or a share-for-share exchange. The Finance Act 1988 changes have had an equally dramatic effect on anti-avoidance legislation, most of which is framed with a view to preventing the conversion of income into capital. Nevertheless, sections on those provisions are retained in this chapter as they are still of concern in some cases and will, of course, be of renewed importance if the differential between income and capital gains tax rates is re-introduced.

Tax will normally be payable on any gain made by the vendors on the sale of their shares in the target. Where the gain is not part of a trade an individual will, subject to any exemption or special charge which may be applicable, pay capital gains tax on the gain. Corporations will pay corporation tax on the gain whether or not it forms part of their trade, but, if it does not form part of their trade, the tax will normally be assessed under the same rules as apply to capital gains tax. Corporation tax on capital gains is currently payable at the rate of 33 per cent (unless the small companies rate of 25 per cent is available), while capital gains tax is payable at the individual's marginal rate of income tax (currently the lower rate of 20 per cent, the basic rate of 25 per cent or the higher rate of 40 per cent) but under the Taxation of Chargeable Gains Act 1992, s 3 exemption is granted, to individuals only, on the first £5,800 of total chargeable gains (less allowable losses) in the year of assessment. For the purposes of computing the gain an indexation allowance is granted for both individuals and companies by the Taxation of Chargeable Gains Act 1992, ss 53–57.

The indexation allowance is calculated from March 1982, or the date of acquisition if later, on the acquisition cost (subject to any rebasing election under the Taxation of Chargeable Gains Act 1992, s 35(5)) or, if greater, the market value of the asset on 31 March 1982 if held at that date. Expenditure allowable under the Taxation of Chargeable Gains Act 1992, s 38 also qualifies for indexation. Acquisition costs have generally been rebased to 31 March 1982, although special provisions apply to ensure that neither chargeable gains nor allowable losses are thereby increased (see Taxation of Chargeable Gains Act 1992, s 35). While the rate of tax applied will be the same, an individual vendor will generally, because of the availability of the indexation allowance and rebasing to 31 March 1982 (and, in appropriate cases, retirement relief), be concerned to obtain a capital gains tax rather than an income tax treatment (but see pre-sale dividends below).

Several matters which should be considered when advising vendors are outlined below, classified as follows:

(*a*) the non-resident vendor;
(*b*) the use of trusts;
(*c*) transfer of assets on retirement;
(*d*) consideration payable by instalments;
(*e*) share-for-share exchanges;
(*f*) pre-sale dividends;
(*g*) sale of debts;
(*h*) the Income and Corporation Taxes Act 1988, s 703;
(*i*) the Income and Corporation Taxes Act 1988, s 776;
(*j*) the Income and Corporation Taxes Act 1988, ss 765 and 765A.

The non-resident vendor

An individual is chargeable to capital gains tax if he is resident or ordinarily resident in the United Kingdom. It is beyond the scope of this book to examine in detail what constitutes 'residence' or 'ordinary residence' or to deal with the complicated cases which arise in connection with visitors to the United Kingdom. It is worth, however, making a few points.

(1) In order to escape liability for capital gains tax it is normally necessary to be neither resident nor ordinarily resident in the United Kingdom, nor carrying on a trade, profession or vocation through a branch or agency in the United Kingdom with which the shareholding is connected, for the whole of the year of assessment in which the disposal is made. In the case of the sale of shares in a private company, the disposal will be made when an unconditional contract is entered into for the disposal, or, if there is no unconditional contract, on the date of completion. If an individual is ordinarily resident in the United Kingdom, he will not escape capital gains tax simply by departing for the whole of the year of assessment in which the gain is made and then subsequently returning. If he has an intention to return, even if he is physically absent through the whole of the year, he will still be 'ordinarily resident'.

(2) Where a vendor intends to live abroad permanently, it can be worth ensuring that the gain does not arise in a year of assessment for any part of which he has been resident in the United Kingdom. There are, however, valuable extra-statutory concessions. If a person claims that he has ceased to be resident and ordinarily resident in the United Kingdom, and can produce some evidence of this (eg that he has sold his house here and set up a permanent home abroad), his claim is usually admitted provisionally with effect from the date following his departure. Normally, this provisional ruling is confirmed after he has remained abroad for a period which includes a complete tax year and during which any visits to this country have not exceeded three months in aggregate. If, however, he cannot produce sufficient evidence, the decision on his claim will be postponed for three years and will then be made by reference to what actually happened in that period. During the three intervening years, his tax liability is computed provisionally on the basis that he remains resident in the United Kingdom. His liability is adjusted, if necessary, when the final decision is made at the end of three years. When a person leaves the United Kingdom and is treated on his departure as not resident and not ordinarily resident in the United Kingdom he is not charged to capital gains tax on gains accruing to him on disposals made after the date of his departure. (See Extra-Statutory Concession D2 and the Inland Revenue booklet IR20(1992) *Residents and Non-residents Liability to Tax in the United Kingdom*, paras 16 and 17.) The Revenue is not obliged to apply the Extra-Statutory Concession if there is any tax avoidance motive and, particularly where the intention to dispose of the shares is formed while the vendor is still resident in the United Kingdom, its use should be approached with care. (See *R v IRC, ex p Fulford-Dobson* [1987] STC 344.)

(3) Special provisions may apply to non-residents who carry on a trade, profession or vocation in the United Kingdom through a branch or agency or who are dual resident companies. (See, for instance, Taxation of Chargeable Gains Act 1992, ss 10, 25, 185 and 186.)

(4) The non-resident vendor may, of course, have a liability to tax in his own country of residence. However, under a number of the double taxation conventions to which the United Kingdom is party, a gain realised by a resident of the other party to the convention is exempted from tax by that party if, under the convention, the United Kingdom is entitled to charge the gain to taxation, notwithstanding that, under the United Kingdom's domestic law, the gain is not chargeable because the person who realised it is neither resident nor ordinarily resident in the United Kingdom, nor carrying on a trade, profession or vocation through a branch or agency. It is therefore possible to escape tax entirely.

The use of trusts

As capital gains tax is charged at the vendor's income tax rate, the proceeds of a disposal of shares in a private company may well be subject to capital gains tax at the rate of 40 per cent. This liability can be mitigated by, prior to the disposal, transferring the shares to a United Kingdom resident settlement which, although entitled to an annual exemption equivalent to only one-half of the exempt amount available to an individual, will be liable to tax at the basic rate only, or, in the case of discretionary and accumulation and maintenance settlements, at the rate of 35 per cent. Gifting shares to a settlement will not, provided the requirements of the Taxation of Chargeable Gains Act 1992, s 165 are met, crystallise a chargeable gain if the shares in question are unquoted shares in a 'trading company' or in the 'holding company' of a 'trading group' or if the company is the transferor's 'family company' (see page 171). In these circumstances, the transferor on making an appropriate claim will avoid the liability to tax. On the subsequent sale of the shares by the trustees of the settlement, the gain arising will be calculated using the acquisition cost of the shares to the transferor. Advantage can only be taken of the settlement's lower rate of tax if the transferor and his spouse are excluded from benefiting under the settlement. If they are not so excluded then gains realised by the trustees will be taxed as the gains of the transferor (see Taxation of Chargeable Gains Act 1992, s 77).

Non-resident trusts have for many years provided United Kingdom resident vendors with a means of mitigating capital gains tax. Because the holdover relief under the Taxation of Chargeable

Gains Act 1992, s 165 described above is not available on a gift to a person resident outside the United Kingdom or to a company controlled by persons resident outside the United Kingdom, to be most effective forward planning has been essential, in order to transfer shares into a non-resident trust before any significant increase in value accrues. Nevertheless, the use of a non-resident trust and holdover relief under s 165 can be combined by gifting the shares in the target company to a company in which up to 49 per cent of the share capital is held by non-resident trustees. The transferee company is subsequently sold to the purchaser, so that a significant proportion of the proceeds of sale accrue to the non-resident trustees.

The advantages afforded by non-resident trusts have been much restricted by recent legislation, particularly the new regime for taxation of settlors and beneficiaries introduced by the Finance Act 1991 (now Taxation of Chargeable Gains Act 1992, ss 80–98 and Sched 5) but their use remains a possible option, in particular where the settlor is domiciled outside the United Kingdom or does not retain an interest in the property of the trust. It is worth noting that 'professional trustees' resident in the United Kingdom are treated as non-resident where the settlor was not resident, ordinarily resident or domiciled in the United Kingdom at the time of the settlement (Taxation of Chargeable Gains Act 1992, s 69).

Transfer of assets on retirement

The Taxation of Chargeable Gains Act 1992, s 163 and Sched 6, grants valuable relief from capital gains tax to the owner of a family business selling after reaching 'retirement age' (now 55) or who has been forced to retire through ill health. The first £150,000 of gains and half the next £450,000 of gains will be free of capital gains tax if they arise on a 'material disposal of business assets' by a person who has reached the age of 55 or who has retired through ill health before that age (s 163(1)). A 'disposal of business assets' includes a sale of shares (s 163(2)(c)).

The provisions are complex and will need to be reviewed in each case. The qualifying conditions applying to the company and applying to the disposal are summarised below.

Conditions applying to the company

A disposal of business assets is 'material' if throughout a period of one year ending with the 'operative date' the vendor *either* owns the business then owned by the company *or* the company is a 'family company' of which the vendor is a full time working director and the company is either a trading company or the holding company of a trading group (s 163(5)).

A 'family company' is a company in respect of which the vendor can exercise 25 per cent of the voting rights or, if not less than 51 per cent of the voting rights are exercisable by him or a member of his family, not less than 5 per cent are exercisable by the vendor himself. 'Family' means husband or wife of the vendor and relatives of the vendor or the vendor's husband or wife; 'relative' means brother, sister, ancestor or lineal descendant. Uncles, aunts and cousins do not count. A 'trading company' is defined as any company whose business consists wholly or mainly of the carrying on of a trade or trades. The holding company of a trading group also qualifies for relief; a 'trading group' is defined to mean a group of companies (being the parent and its 51 per cent subsidiaries) the business of whose members taken together consists wholly or mainly of the carrying on of a trade or trades.

A 'full time working director' is defined as a director who is required to devote substantially the whole of his time in a managerial or technical capacity to the service of the company or, as the case may be, the companies in the group taken together.

Qualifying conditions for disposal

The conditions relating to the company need to be fulfilled in relation to each vendor who seeks relief and if the period ending with the 'operative date' on which they are fulfilled exceeds ten years the full relief is obtained. For the purposes of calculating this period separate periods during which the vendor carried on a business may be aggregated provided that not more than two years elapse between any two qualifying periods. If the conditions are fulfilled over a shorter period than ten years (with a minimum of one year) relief is reduced pro rata.

For the purposes of the relief the 'operative date' is the date of the disposal or, if earlier, either the date on which the company ceased trading (provided the vendor had reached the age of 55 or retired through ill health prior to such cessation) or the date on which the vendor retired from a full time working directorship. If the operative date is the date of retirement the company must continue to qualify as a family company carrying on a trade and the vendor must continue as a director of the company to devote at least ten hours per week to the service of the company (or of the group) in a technical or managerial capacity until the date of sale or cessation of trade.

The amount of the gain available for relief will be restricted by reference to the chargeable business assets of the company (or the group) at the time of the disposal. Relief is given on that part of the gain which bears the same proportion to the total gain as the value of the 'chargeable business assets' bears to the value of the 'chargeable assets' of the target (or the group). Every asset is a chargeable asset except those on the disposal of which no chargeable gain would arise (Sched 6, para 7(3)). Examples of a non-chargeable asset would be tangible moveable property of less than £6,000 and debts (not being debts on securities) on which the company is the original creditor. 'Chargeable business assets' means assets (including goodwill but not including investments) which are assets used for the purposes of a trade carried on by the company or by a member of the group. Special rules apply in the case of groups to exclude investments in subsidiaries from the definition of chargeable assets and to apportion the value of assets in subsidiaries which are not wholly owned.

A number of detailed rules exist making provision for disposals by trustees, for aggregating several disposals and in relation to assets which have been owned by the vendor's spouse.

A vendor who has obtained relief under the Taxation of Chargeable Gains Act 1992, s 135, on an exchange of shares in the target for shares in the purchaser will not be entitled to retirement relief on a disposal of the consideration shares (unless they qualify for relief in their own right) even though a disposal of shares in the target would have been eligible for relief. The Taxation of Chargeable Gains Act 1992, Sched 6, para 2, allows such a vendor to elect within two years of a share for share exchange (or of any reorganisation of capital falling within the Taxation of Chargeable Gains Act 1992, s 126) for the provisions of s 127 not to apply to the exchange. The exchange will therefore be treated as a disposal for capital gains tax purposes and retirement relief will be available if the other conditions for relief are fulfilled.

Consideration payable by instalments

It is often the case that some part of the consideration payable for the acquisition of a private company will be payable after completion. Examples include where part of the consideration is retained as security for warranties or where the consideration is based on profits yet to be earned. In these cases it is necessary to consider the impact of capital gains tax upon the arrangements which are proposed.

It is the normal rule (Taxation of Chargeable Gains Act 1992, s 48) that capital gains tax is payable on the disposal by reference to the total consideration receivable. Consideration is brought into account without a discount for postponement of the right to receive any part of it and, in the first instance, without regard to a risk of any part being irrecoverable or to the right to receive it being contingent. The Taxation of Chargeable Gains Act 1992, s 49(1)(*c*) specifically provides that no allowance will be made for any contingent liability in respect of a warranty or representation made on the disposal by way of sale of any property other than land, although, if the contingent liability becomes enforceable, adjustments are made. A retention as security for warranties will not therefore normally affect the capital gains tax computation.

The Taxation of Chargeable Gains Act 1992, s 280 applies where consideration is payable by instalments over a period exceeding eighteen months beginning not earlier than the time when the disposal is made. Liability to tax may be deferred if the vendor satisfies the Board of Inland Revenue that he would otherwise suffer undue hardship. The Board may allow the tax to be paid by instalments over a period not exceeding eight years and ending not later than the time at which the last of the instalments of consideration is payable. The vendor has to show hardship and it seems that this will normally be shown if he cannot pay the tax out of the resources made available to him by the transaction. The section only applies where the consideration is truly payable by instalments. For instance, if the consideration is paid by means of a 'vendor placing' and the vendor then deposits part of the consideration with the purchaser, even though that part of the consideration might only be returnable at some future date, the consideration does not appear to be payable by instalments within the meaning of the section.

Where consideration is calculated by reference to profits earned after completion (sometimes called an 'earnout'), or is otherwise indeterminate in amount, the computation is more difficult. In these cases the practice of the Revenue is to value the contingent right to receive the consideration and to charge tax by reference to the aggregate of the consideration actually received and the value of the contingent right. The contingent right is itself a chargeable asset and in *Marren (Inspector of Taxes) v Ingles* (1980) 54 TC 76 it was held that this right was disposed of when the vendor received the future consideration, thus giving rise (in that case) to a further chargeable gain. The Taxation of Chargeable Gains Act 1992, s 22(1), provides that there is a disposal of assets by their owner where any capital sum is derived from assets, even though no asset is acquired by the person paying the capital sum. It was argued on behalf of the taxpayer that this subsection was confined to cases where no asset was acquired by the person paying the capital sum and, of course, in cases relating to deferred consideration an asset (ie the shares in the target) is so acquired even though it is acquired before the final consideration is paid. The House of Lords rejected this argument, holding that the section applies whether or not assets are acquired by the person paying the capital sum. See also *Marson (Inspector of Taxes) v Marriage* (1979) 54 TC 59. It has been suggested that, if there is a limit on the total consideration payable, or if the amount to be paid is definite although payable at an indeterminate time, it may be that *Marren v Ingles* does not apply, and s 48 does, so that tax is to be calculated by reference to the full amount, not the value of the contingent right. This area is one of some uncertainty and although some clarification has been given where the deferred consideration consists solely of shares or debentures (see below), in many cases the treatment will depend on the view taken by the vendor's Inspector of Taxes.

A further consequence of *Marren v Ingles* is that deferral of the charge to capital gains tax by means of roll-over relief (see share for share exchanges below) will, in strict law, not be available to the extent that the consideration shares are to be issued at some future date, since the contingent right to an allotment of shares does not amount to an issue of shares within the Taxation of Chargeable Gains Act 1992, s 135.

In order to avoid the problems arising from *Marren v Ingles*, it became common to issue shares or other securities of the purchaser to which special rights attached, in place of a simple covenant to pay. These securities were issued to the vendors at completion and carried rights to ensure that their value fell to be determined by reference to the earn-out formula. Similar arrangements involving the retention by or issue to the vendors of special shares in the target carrying a right to a dividend or to be repurchased by the target on the basis of the earnout formula have also been used.

The Revenue have now agreed (see Extra-Statutory Concession D27) that where, under the sale agreement, a right is created to an unascertainable amount (whether or not subject to a maximum) which is to be satisfied wholly by the issue of shares or debentures, the Revenue will, if the vendor so elects, treat that right as a security for capital gains tax purposes, so that roll-over relief will be available. In those circumstances, therefore, there is no longer any need for such special shares or securities. If, however, the deferred consideration is to be satisfied or may be satisfied in cash, then the value of the right to the deferred consideration will be brought into the capital gains tax computation. Since many purchasers will require to retain the right to satisfy the deferred consideration in cash, the scope of this concession may be limited in practice.

Share for share exchanges

Where the consideration for the acquisition is the issue of shares or debentures by a purchaser company, capital gains tax otherwise payable on the sale of shares in the target may be deferred. The relevant provisions are contained in the Taxation of Chargeable Gains Act, ss 126–138.

If the provisions apply, no disposal is treated as occurring. Consequently no tax is payable on the exchange and the new shares or debentures are treated in the hands of the vendors as if they had been acquired at the time when, and for the consideration for which, the shares in the target were acquired; in other words the gain (or loss) accrued at the time of the exchange is 'rolled over' into the consideration shares or debentures.

This treatment is modified where the consideration debentures are 'qualifying corporate bonds' within the meaning of the Taxation of Chargeable Gains Act 1992, s 117, broadly, any sterling denominated, non-convertible company debenture, whether or not it is quoted on a stock exchange. Instead the consideration debentures are treated as acquired at the date of the exchange for a consideration equal to the market value of the shares in the target. The gain (or loss) on the shares in the target is calculated but is 'held over' and does not accrue until a subsequent disposal of the consideration debentures (Taxation of Chargeable Gains Act 1992, s 116(10)). Any gain or loss on a qualifying corporate bond is outside the scope of capital gains tax (Taxation of Chargeable Gains Act 1992, s 115(1)), including any loss attributable to the indexation allowance. Accordingly, if the purchaser subsequently proves unable to redeem the consideration debentures, the vendor not only has a non-allowable capital loss but the held-over gain will be brought into charge in full. Provisions now contained in the Taxation of Chargeable Gains Act 1992, s 254 were introduced in 1990 to give loss relief on the same basis as is available on a qualifying loans to traders (Taxation of Chargeable Gains Act 1992, s 253). However, it is not clear that s 254 will be available in the circumstances of all exchanges because of the restrictions on relief in s 253(1) which require the borrower (ie the purchaser) to use the money lent (ie the nominal amount of the consideration debentures) for the purposes of its trade or to lend it to another group company which so uses it. This requirement is obviously not met in every case. The vendors may therefore wish the terms of the consideration debentures to be such that they are not qualifying corporate bonds. This is possible in a number of ways, eg by providing an option for redemption in a foreign currency other than at the rate of exchange prevailing at redemption (see s 117(2)). Care must be taken that the consideration debentures are not 'deep gain securities' for the purposes of the Finance Act 1989, Sched 11 as these are automatically qualifying corporate bonds (s 117(3)).

In order to obtain roll-over relief it is necessary that at least one of the following circumstances exists:

(a) the purchaser holds, or in consequence of the exchange will hold, more than one quarter of the ordinary share capital of the target. 'Ordinary share capital' is defined for this purpose (by the Income and Corporation Taxes Act 1988, s 832(1)) as 'all the issued share capital (by whatever name called) of the company, other than capital the holders of which have a right to a dividend at a fixed rate but have no other right to share in the profits of the company'; or

(b) the exchange takes place as the result of a general offer made to members of the target or any class of them (with or without exceptions for persons connected with the purchaser), the offer being made in the first instance on a condition such that if it were satisfied the purchaser would have control of the target; or

(c) the purchaser holds, or in consequence of the exchange will hold, the greater part of the voting power in the target.

Circumstance (c) was introduced by the Finance (No 2) Act 1992, s 35 in order to bring the provisions of the Taxation of Chargeable Gains Act 1992, s 135 into compliance with the EC Directive on Cross-Border Mergers (90/434/EEC). However, it applies also to purely domestic transactions. It has effect in relation to exchanges made on or after 1 January 1992.

The consideration shares or debentures must be issued to the vendors. For the purposes of the Taxation of Chargeable Gains Act 1992, s 135 'issue' includes 'allot' (Taxation of Chargeable Gains Act 1992, s 288(5)) and consideration shares or debentures may therefore be issued on renounceable letters of allotment without prejudicing the availability of relief although, of course, any subsequent renunciation will result in a disposal of the shares for capital gains tax purposes.

The Taxation of Chargeable Gains Act 1992, s 137 imposes an overriding condition on the application of roll-over or hold-over relief in these circumstances. The condition is that the exchange is effected for bona fide commercial reasons and does not form part of a scheme or arrangements of which the main purpose, or one of the main purposes, is avoidance of liability to capital gains tax or corporation tax. This condition, however, does not affect relief available to any vendor who (together with persons connected with him) does not hold more than 5 per cent of, or of any class of, the shares in or debentures of the target. It is open either to the purchaser or to the target to apply for clearance and, if the Board of Inland Revenue notifies the applicant that it is satisfied that the exchange will be effected for bona fide commercial reasons and will not form part of any such scheme or arrangements, the condition is deemed satisfied. If the overriding condition imposed by s 137 operates to defeat roll-over relief, the section provides that tax assessed on vendors and not paid within six months from the date when it is payable is recoverable within two years from any other person who holds all or any part of the consideration shares or debentures that were issued to the vendor and who acquired them without there having been a chargeable disposal for capital gains tax purposes or who acquired them from the vendor in the circumstances referred to in the Taxation of Chargeable Gains Act 1992, s 58(1) (disposals between spouses), or s 171(1) (disposals between members of a group of companies).

On a subsequent disposal of the new holding the calculation of the tax payable can be complex, particularly where only part of the new holding is disposed of and the shares in the target were originally acquired at different dates and at different prices. The basic rules are to be found in the Taxation of Chargeable Gains Act 1992, ss 104–109 and (in relation to shares held on 6 April 1965) Sched 2, para 4.

Vendors who have reached retirement age and who wish to avail themselves of the reliefs conferred by the Taxation of Chargeable Gains Act 1992, s 163 should consider carefully before they sell the shares in their family business in exchange for shares in the purchaser so as to obtain roll-over relief, as the retirement relief will not be applicable to the sale (as there is no disposal) and may not be available on a subsequent disposal of the consideration shares, if these do not themselves qualify for relief. In these circumstances, the vendor may elect that roll-over relief should not apply.

Pre-sale dividends

If the target has significant distributable reserves, a United Kingdom resident corporate vendor will be able to reduce its capital gain on the sale of the target by procuring the payment of a dividend by the target prior to the sale. In the hands of a United Kingdom resident company such a dividend is free of corporation tax (Income and Corporation Taxes Act 1988, s 208) and such a payment allows the purchase price of the target to be reduced while the vendor still receives the same total consideration, including the dividend. Because the purchase price of the target's shares is reduced, the capital gain is, of course, lower. The Taxation of Chargeable Gains

Act 1992, ss 30–34 reduce the scope for avoidance of tax on capital gains by companies on disposal of subsidiaries by treating the consideration for the disposal as increased by such amount as may be just and reasonable where the value of the shares are materially reduced and a tax-free benefit is conferred, unless it is shown that avoidance of tax was not the main purpose or one of the main purposes of the scheme or arrangements in question. A payment of a dividend to a company in the same group is not caught by these provisions save to the extent that it is attributable to profits realised by the target as a result of certain tax free disposals of assets. A pre-sale dividend paid out of the target's 'normal' profits and reserves remains effective. A pre-sale dividend cannot be used to create a capital loss (Taxation of Chargeable Gains Act 1992, s 177).

A pre-sale dividend will normally be paid under the terms of a group election under the Income and Corporation Taxes Act 1988, s 247 (see p 195) and so no liability to advance corporation tax (ACT) will arise. Both purchaser and vendor will wish to satisfy themselves that a valid group election is in force at the date of payment of the dividend. The group election ceases to apply when the purchaser ceases to be the beneficial owner of the target (s 248(4)) so that where the parties wish to make the payment under a group election it will be necessary to pay the dividend prior to exchange of contracts. For group relief purposes, 'arrangements' for the transfer of beneficial ownership can affect the ability of purchaser and target to surrender group relief (Income and Corporation Taxes Act 1988, s 410: see p 199), but these provisions do not apply to group elections and accordingly the election will remain in force while the beneficial ownership of the target is with the purchaser notwithstanding that arrangements exist for its sale, unless these amount to 'option arrangements' within the Income and Corporation Taxes Act 1988, Sched 18, para 5B such that, by application of the provisions of Sched 18, the target is no longer a 51 per cent subsidiary of the vendor. The vendor should not enter into an exclusivity agreement with the purchaser. The agreement not to seek another purchaser while negotiations proceed could amount to a fetter on the vendor's beneficial ownership of the target within *Wood Preservation Ltd v Prior* [1969] 1 WLR 1077, although see also *O'Connor (Inspector of Taxes) v J Sainsbury plc* [1991] STC 318 where the existence of options granted to a third party over shares in a subsidiary did not cause the taxpayer company to cease to be their beneficial owner.

The purchaser who agrees to a pre-sale dividend will wish to be sure that the target is not going to become liable to pay ACT in respect of the dividend and will, for safety's sake, also wish to ensure that the terms of the sale agreement give the target an effective indemnity against that liability if it should arise.

In some circumstances however it may be desirable to make the dividend payment outside the group election. This will be the case where the vendor can use the ACT to frank its own dividend (Income and Corporation Taxes Act 1988, s 239) and if the purchase price is adjusted to allow for the interest cost of the ACT payment over the period prior to its recovery by the target the result can be satisfactory for both parties. However, the provisions of the Income and Corporation Taxes Act 1988, ss 245–245B, which prevent the set-off of ACT where there is a change in ownership of the company and certain other circumstances exist, must be borne in mind (see p 212). Section 247 provides that it is for the target to choose whether or not to pay the dividend within the group election and on the face of the section it seems that the choice must be made while the group election remains in force.

In practice, the target may not have sufficient funds to pay the dividend and therefore it will be necessary for the vendor to lend an equivalent amount to fund the payment. The sale agreement will provide that, at completion, the purchaser must put the target in funds to repay this loan. Because the purchase price will have been reduced by the amount of the dividend, this will not involve any additional cash outlay on the purchaser's part (and may indeed reduce his liability to stamp duty on the acquisition). Where the parties wish to make the payment under a group election then of course it is necessary that the dividend is 'received' while the election remains in force, and if no money is to pass (because the dividend is immediately to be re-lent) then the question will arise whether the mere crediting of accounts is a sufficient receipt. On the authority of *Garforth (Inspector of Taxes) v Newsmith Stainless Ltd* (1978) 52 TC 522, the crediting of an account is probably sufficient, but it is prudent to ensure that cheques are passed from target to vendor and vice versa, and cashed. The Companies Act 1985, s 153(3), specifically provides that a distribution by way of dividend is not prohibited by s 151 which prohibits financial assistance by the target in connection with the sale of its own shares (see p 43).

A pre-sale dividend may also prove beneficial for individual vendors, for whom the ACT paid in respect of the dividend represents a basic rate income tax credit. As a £75 dividend carries with it a £25 tax credit (at current rates of tax), further tax of only £15 need be paid to satisfy liability to higher rate income tax at 40 per cent, thus giving an effective tax rate of 20 per cent (£15 out of £75) on the cash dividend. Of course, no group election is available for individual vendors so this route will only be of use if the target can utilise any ACT payable on the dividend. This may well be the case as privately owned companies tend not to have paid significant dividends so that mainstream corporation tax paid by the target in past years will be available against which ACT can be recovered (Income and Corporation Taxes Act 1988, s 239(3)).

Because these transactions involve the payment of an abnormal dividend in connection with a transaction in securities the practitioner will consider whether or not the Income and Corporation Taxes Act 1988, s 703, is in point. If time permits the parties may well seek a clearance under s 707 but it is suggested that the section ought not to apply. A pre-sale dividend has the effect of turning capital into income rather than the reverse, and represents an extraction of profit from the target which could have taken place at any time while the target belonged to the vendor. It is a curious effect of the structural changes to income and capital gains taxation introduced by the Finance Act 1988 that it is now in certain circumstances less tax efficient to receive capital rather than income—the mischief that s 703 was designed to prevent!

As a matter of company law, it will be necessary to consider the provisions of the Companies Act 1985, Part VIII, to ascertain the distributable reserves of the target. Under s 270, the distribution must be justified by reference to the company's accounts and in some cases it may be necessary to prepare interim accounts. Last, but not least, the duties of the directors of the target must be considered. It is, of course, their duty to act in the interests of the target and in some cases it may be appropriate for them to seek assurances from the vendors or the purchaser that the target will have sufficient working capital following payment of the dividend.

Sale of debts

It is not uncommon for the target to owe debts to the vendors. Normally, these can be dealt with by the purchaser placing the target, at completion, in funds to repay the debt, but, if the debts are too substantial for the target to bear the cost of repaying or refinancing them, the only practical solution may be for the vendors to assign the debts to the purchaser. In such a case, it is likely that the target's business has not been successful and such assignments commonly occur as part of a transaction which realises a capital gains tax loss for the vendors. In this case, any loss which the vendors realise on a sale of the debt will not normally be allowable for tax purposes, since a debt, unless it is a debt on a security, is not a chargeable asset. The relief in respect of loans to traders contained in the Taxation of Chargeable Gains Act 1992, s 253 may be of assistance, but it is quite limited in scope. In particular, it does not apply where the borrower and lender are companies in the same group (s 253(3)(c)) or where the lender assigns the loan (s 253(3)(b)). Can the vendors convert the debts, before the sale, into securities, so as to realise a capital gains tax loss when they sell? At least part of the answer is given by *Harrison v Nairn Williamson Ltd* (1977) 51 TC 135.

In that case the taxpayer company received a holding of preferred shares in a subsidiary company in replacement of a holding of loan stock worth considerably less than its nominal value. In computing its allowable loss arising on a subsequent sale of the preferred shares, the taxpayer company claimed to bring into account the full amount paid for the subscription of the loan stock. It was held, however, that the predecessor provision to what is now the Taxation of Chargeable Gains Act 1992, s 17 applied to the acquisition of the loan stock by the taxpayer company because it was acquired 'otherwise than by way of a bargain made at arm's length'. Accordingly, the acquisition cost of the loan stock (and hence the preferred shares) was its market value at the date of its subscription and the allowable loss was restricted to the difference between the market value and the sale consideration.

It was argued for the taxpayer company that the provision did not apply, because there was no 'disposal' of the loan stock by the target, only an acquisition by the taxpayer company, but the Court of Appeal did not agree. In any event s 17 as it now stands clearly applies in such a case unless the consideration is of an amount or value lower than the market value of the asset. This last condition stops the market value rule applying to give a higher base cost than the actual consideration in these cases.

It follows that debt reconstructions of this nature made shortly before a sale are unlikely to have the effect of making losses on debts allowable in full for capital gains tax purposes. The same will apply if new shares were issued as a rights issue, providing funds to repay the debt (see *IRC v Burmah Oil Co Ltd* (1981) 54 TC 200 and the Taxation of Chargeable Gains Act 1992, s 128(2)). The question of what is or is not a reorganisation of share capital within the Taxation of Chargeable Gains Act 1992, s 127 was considered in *Dunstan (Inspector of Taxes) v Young Austen and Young Ltd* [1989] STC 69.

If the vendor waives debts due from the target he should take care to apportion part of the sale consideration to the waiver. If all the consideration is attributed to the shares, the vendor may find he has translated what should be a capital loss into a capital gain. In *Aberdeen Construction Group Ltd v IRC* (1978) 52 TC 281 the taxpayer company narrowly avoided such a fate. See also *Booth (EV) (Holdings) Ltd v Buckwell (Inspector of Taxes)* (1980) 53 TC 425 where the vendor was bound by the allocation of consideration stipulated in the sale agreement although a different allocation would have produced a more favourable result.

The Income and Corporation Taxes Act 1988, s 703

The Income and Corporation Taxes Act 1988, s 703 and succeeding sections are concerned, as the headnote to Part XVII of the Act states, with 'tax avoidance'. The sections provide the Revenue with powers enabling them to serve notices cancelling income tax advantages arising from a very wide range of transactions involving securities, although it appears that s 703, when originally enacted as the Finance Act 1960, s 28, was intended only to provide the Revenue with power to counteract 'dividend stripping'.

It is instructive to remember what dividend stripping was. If a company had large revenue reserves and the owner of shares in the company was in a position to have these paid out by way of dividend, he would wish to avoid income tax on the dividend. He would therefore sell the shares 'cum dividend', receiving a purchase price equal to the value of the securities including the potential dividend. The purchase price would not be subject to income tax but would only be chargeable to any relevant capital gains tax in his hands (before 1965, of course, there was no capital gains tax). The purchaser would be a person or company who would not suffer the same rate of tax on the dividend and, once the dividend had been declared to the purchaser, the purchaser would then sell the shares back to the original owner at their 'ex dividend' price. If the purchaser of shares was, for instance, a dealer in securities, the loss which the purchaser made on selling the shares back to the original owner at a low price would be allowable for income tax purposes and be available to offset the tax chargeable on the large dividend he had received in the meantime. Payment of the dividend therefore caused the purchaser no tax disadvantage, whereas the original owner had converted the dividend into capital and obtained a tax advantage.

The powers conferred on the Revenue by s 703 to counteract dividend stripping have been used to counteract a wide range of tax advantages deriving from the sale of private companies. In order for the Revenue to be able to serve a s 703 notice the following conditions have to be satisfied (s 703(1)):

(a) one of the circumstances mentioned in s 704 must have occurred;

(b) there must be a transaction in securities;

(c) in consequence of the transaction the taxpayer must be in a position to obtain, or have obtained, a tax advantage;

(*d*) the taxpayer must be unable to show that the transaction or transactions were carried out either for bona fide commercial reasons or in the ordinary course of making or managing investments and that none of them had as their main object, or one of their main objects, to enable tax advantages to be obtained.

Two cases in point which illustrate the potential application of the section to private company acquisitions are those of *IRC v Cleary* (1967) 44 TC 399 and *IRC v Brown* (1971) 47 TC 217. The facts in the *Cleary* and *Brown* cases were broadly the same. In each case, the taxpayer had arranged for the sale of the shares owned by him or her in one company to another company controlled by the taxpayer and his or her associates. Were it not for the section, the taxpayer would have been charged only to any applicable capital gains tax on the sale. In both cases, however, the taxpayer paid income tax on the consideration received. (For the quantum of the tax advantage see *Bird v IRC* [1988] 2 WLR 1237, HL.)

In order to understand the cases, it is necessary to analyse them in the light of the conditions for the application of the section given above.

Condition (a)

Had any of the circumstances mentioned in s 704 occurred? In both cases the part of s 704 which was relevant was s 704D which states the relevant circumstances in effect as follows:

(1) That in connection with the *distribution* of *profits* of a company to which this paragraph applies, the person in question . . . receives [a consideration which either—
  (i) is, or represents the value of, assets which are (or apart from anything done by the company in question would have been) available for distribution by way of dividend, or
  (ii) is received in respect of future receipts of the company, or
  (iii) is, or represents the value of, trading stock of the company and the said person so receives the consideration that he does not pay or bear tax on it as income].
(2) The companies to which this paragraph applies are—
  (*a*) any company under the control of not more than five persons; and
  (*b*) any other company which does not satisfy the condition that its shares or stocks or some class thereof (disregarding debenture stock, preferred shares or preferred stock), are authorised to be dealt in on a stock exchange in the United Kingdom, and are so dealt in (regularly or from time to time),
so, however, that this paragraph does not apply to a company under the control of one or more companies to which this paragraph does not apply.

Reading s 704D in the light of nature it is impossible to conceive that it applies to the circumstances of the *Brown* and *Cleary* cases, but the words shown in (author's) italics are given extended and artificial meanings by s 709(3) which provides that, in s 704:

(*a*) references to profits include references to income reserves or other assets,

(*b*) references to distribution include references to transfer or realisation (including application in discharge of liabilities).

It is therefore possible to render the opening words of s 704D so that they read: 'That in connection with the *transfer* of *assets* of a company to which this paragraph applies'.

In both the *Brown* and *Cleary* cases the purchaser company was one to which the paragraph applied and it had transferred assets (ie it had paid cash) to the taxpayer.

In the *Cleary* case the purchaser company had sufficient reserves and cash to pay a dividend of an amount equal to the purchase price and it was therefore held that the consideration was 'assets which are (or apart from anything done by the company in question would have been) available for distribution by way of dividend'. In the *Brown* case the company had sufficient standing to the credit of its profit and loss account to pay a dividend equal to the cash element of the consideration, but its current liabilities exceeded its current assets by £3,000. It therefore had to borrow the amount of the cash consideration from a bank. Megarry J took the view, affirmed on appeal, that as the company had reserves available for distribution there was no legal impropriety in its borrowing the money to effect that distribution. The money once borrowed was, therefore, 'assets available for distribution'. Even though a prudent or cautious financier might not have paid a dividend in such circumstances, it was legally possible and that was sufficient.

Condition (b)

In neither case was there any difficulty on this point. The sale of shares in a company is obviously a transaction in securities (which in any event is defined to include a sale by s 709).

Condition (c)

Did the taxpayer obtain a tax advantage? In *IRC v Parker* (1966) 43 TC 396 Lord Wilberforce indicated that a taxpayer obtains a tax advantage if he receives something which is not subject to income tax but which, if he had received it in another way, would have been. In both the *Brown* and *Cleary* cases, if the purchaser company had declared a dividend, the taxpayer would have received it. It did not declare a dividend but used its assets to pay the consideration for the shares acquired from the taxpayer. In both cases, therefore, the taxpayer received cash as consideration for shares when, if it had been received by way of dividend, it would have been subject to income tax. The tax advantage was therefore obtained. (See also *Anysz v IRC* and *Manolescue v IRC* (1977) 53 TC 601 and *Williams v IRC* (1980) 54 TC 257.)

Condition (d)

In neither case was the taxpayer able to show that the transactions were carried out for bona fide commercial reasons and that none of them had, as their main objects, to enable tax advantages to be obtained. In the *Brown* case Russell LJ said (on appeal—(1971) 47 TC 217, at p 239) that:

[The] evidence amounts to no more than saying that the taxpayer and his wife wanted some money and entered into the transaction to get it. Now it seems to me that you do not show that a transaction of sale of securities for full consideration to a company already owned by yourself is a transaction to be entered into for bona fide commercial reasons merely by saying that it is such a sale transaction and that you wanted the money.

In considering the application of s 703 to acquisitions, the potential application of s 704C should not be overlooked. This section applies if the taxpayer receives a consideration which represents the value of assets which are (or would have been) available for distribution as dividend, 'in consequence of a transaction whereby any other person . . . receives . . . an abnormal amount by way of dividend'. In *Emery v IRC* [1981] STC 150 the target owned valuable properties which it sold for a profit of £244,000. The taxpayer then sold his shares in the target to an investment company for £223,409 payable by instalments and subsequently sold his right to receive those instalments to a wholly owned subsidiary of the purchaser for the same price. The target then paid a dividend of £260,500 to the purchaser. It was held that the vendor had received the consideration in consequence of an operation whereby the purchaser received an abnormal dividend and accordingly the consideration was treated as income.

In *IRC v Garvin* [1981] STC 344 the facts were similar but there the House of Lords held that there was no sufficient connecting link between the sale of the shares in the target and the declaration of the dividend. The fact that the purchaser acquired the whole of the share capital of a target with substantial undistributed profit did not by itself form sufficient ground for holding that such acquisition was the cause of the subsequent distribution of those profits by the target.

The court held that the word 'whereby' in s 704 imported some causal connection between the transactions and the subsequent receipt of the abnormal dividend. In that case the Revenue attempted also to bring s 704D into play, by contending that the consideration was received 'in connection with the distribution of the profits' of a company to which s 704D applied. The targets were under the control of five or fewer persons at the time they were sold, but there was no evidence that they were so controlled at the date of the distribution. The court held that the relevant date was the day of the distribution of profits and accordingly that s 704D did not apply.

It is fair to say that in both these and the *Brown* and *Cleary* cases there was an element of tax avoidance. In each case the vendors entered into a series of transactions with a view to obtaining as capital that which could more easily have been obtained as dividend. If an acquisition has this result then it must be prudent to utilise the clearance procedure given in s 707. In the *Brown* case Megarry J said:

Having provided reasonable safeguards for the bona fide or ordinary transaction, I do not think that the legislature has given any indication of intending to use kid gloves in these cases.

In the light of the Finance Act 1988 changes to the taxation of income and capital gains, the potential for obtaining a tax advantage (condition *(c)*) is reduced and so the importance of this section has been diminished. However, the rebasing to 1982, the indexation allowance, the individual's annual exemption and the possibility of deferral of the charge to tax through roll-over or other reliefs may make a capital gains tax treatment preferable, so that the prudent practitioner will continue to give consideration to the section.

The Income and Corporation Taxes Act 1988, s 776

This section attempts to counter tax avoidance by the realisation of gains in a capital form on a disposal of land which, if realised in another way, might be assessed as trading income. The section can have the effect of taxing as income under Case VI of Schedule D capital gains realised on the sale of shares in a company.

The section applies (s 776(2)):

(*a*) if land or any property deriving its value from land has been acquired for the sole or main object of realising a gain from disposing of the land; or

(*b*) if land is held as trading stock; or

(*c*) if land is developed with the sole or main object of realising a gain from disposing of the land when developed.

It is necessary that the land should be situated in the United Kingdom (s 776(14)).

If a gain of a capital nature is obtained from the disposal of the land either by the person holding or developing the land or by any connected person (as defined by the Income and Corporation Taxes Act 1988, s 839) or, indirectly, by any person who is a party to any arrangement as respects the land which enables a gain to be realised, the gain may be taxed as income. The section does not require that there should be any tax avoidance motive for the transaction (*Page v Lowther* [1983] 61 Ch D).

The section is very widely drafted. In particular s 776(4) provides that land is disposed of if, by any one or more transactions or by any arrangement or scheme, whether concerning the land or property deriving its value from land, the property in the land or control over the land is effectually disposed of. Accordingly, the sale of a land owning company or a company which controls a land owning company could fall within the section.

Under s 776(10) there is an exemption in respect of a disposal of shares in a company which holds land as trading stock or a company which owns directly or indirectly 90 per cent or more of the ordinary share capital of another company which holds land as trading stock, provided all the land so held is disposed of in the normal course of its trade by the company which held it and so as to procure that all opportunity of profit in respect of the land arises to that company. This exemption does not extend to 'arrangements' or 'schemes' for realising gains by indirect methods or by a series of transactions, which are caught by s 776(2)(ii).

Although there is a procedure under s 776(11) for obtaining a clearance, this is rarely used, since the Revenue have proved reluctant to confirm such clearance, so that application merely serves to put the Revenue on notice. For recent cases see *Chilcott v IRC* (1982) 57 TC 446, and *Sugarwhite v Budd (Inspector of Taxes)* [1988] STC 533.

The Income and Corporation Taxes Act 1988, ss 765 and 765A

The origins of the Income and Corporation Taxes Act 1988, s 765 lie in foreign exchange control. It has proved a useful anti-avoidance measure in addition and so survived the 1979 abolition of foreign exchange control. Section 765 makes unlawful without prior consent of HM Treasury certain transactions undertaken or permitted by a company resident in the United Kingdom in relation to a non-resident company over which it has control. The United Kingdom resident company may not cause or permit the non-resident company to create or issue any shares or debentures nor (except for the purposes of enabling a person to be qualified to act as a director) may it transfer to any person, or cause or permit to be transferred to any person, any shares or debentures of the non-resident company, being shares or debentures which it owns or in which it has an interest. Contravention of the section is a criminal offence, and consideration must accordingly be given by a corporate vendor to its possible application where the target company is a non-resident company or, where the target is resident in the United Kingdom, debt owed by non-resident subsidiaries of the target company to the vendor or other companies in the vendor's group is to be assigned to the purchaser.

Provided that the purchaser and the vendor are not connected persons within the meaning of the Income and Corporation Taxes Act 1988, s 839, a sale of shares or debentures of a non-resident company will normally fall within one of the published general consents (contained in The Treasury General Consents 1988). The transfer must be for full consideration paid to the vendor and no arrangements must exist as a consequence of which the vendor or a person connected with the vendor might become entitled to, or to any interest in, any of the shares or debentures transferred.

If there is no relevant general consent, special consent must be sought from HM Treasury (who are advised by the Inland Revenue) unless the transaction is exempted from s 765 by the Income and Corporation Taxes Act 1988, s 765A.

The Directive of the Council of the European Communities dated 24 June 1988 (88/361/EEC) which took effect from 1 July 1990 requires there to be free movement of capital between residents of Member States. Accordingly, the Income and Corporation Taxes Act 1988, s 765A prevents s 765 from applying to all such transactions carried out on or after that date. Transactions will be within the scope of the Directive only if they involve the transfer of capital between persons resident in different Member States. However, if the transaction, were it to be subject to s 765, would require special consent of HM Treasury, s 765A requires the United Kingdom resident company to report it to the Inland Revenue within six months of the transaction being carried out. The information specified under the Movements of Capital (Required Information) Regulations 1990 (SI No 1671) must be provided. This is substantially the same information as would be required in an application for special consent.

No complete definition of 'movement of capital' is given in the Directive, but it is clear that this must be widely construed. The Directive also requires residence to be determined by reference to exchange control regulations. A number of Member States including the United Kingdom no longer have such regulations, and the United Kingdom will adopt the test of residence for tax purposes in those cases. The views of HM Treasury and the Inland Revenue on the operation of the Directive and s 765A are set out in the Inland Revenue Statement of Practice SP2/92.

STAMP DUTY AND STAMP DUTY RESERVE TAX

Part III of the Finance Act 1990 made provision for the abolition of stamp duty and stamp duty reserve tax on transactions in securities. The scope of the proposed abolition was extended by the Finance Act 1991, s 110 to all property other than land. However, the appointed day for these provisions to come into effect has been linked with the introduction of the London Stock Exchange's TAURUS system (even though the abolition is not confined to quoted securities). TAURUS has been postponed at least until mid-1993 and accordingly stamp duty and stamp duty reserve tax remain for the time being at least relevant on an acquisition of shares. Liabilities to these taxes may also arise where the cash consideration for the purchase is raised through a vendor placing (see p 159).

Stamp duty is chargeable under the head 'conveyance or transfer on sale' on transfers of registered shares from vendor to purchaser. Unless stock transfer forms are presented for stamping within 30 days a penalty is payable, and the company secretary will be liable to a £25 fine under the Stamp Act 1891, s 17, if he registers a transfer which is not duly stamped. The exemptions which apply to transfers of property certified at £30,000 or less do not apply to share transfers. Duty is payable by the purchaser and is chargeable at the rate of 50p per £100 (or part) of the consideration.

Loan capital is generally exempt from stamp duties. However, where the purchaser agrees to pay to the vendor the amount of any indebtedness which is due from the target to the vendor, the amount of the indebtedness repaid may be treated as consideration for the shares in the target (see Stamp Act 1891, s 57). An undertaking by the purchaser instead to procure repayment by the target will not be regarded by the Stamp Office as falling within s 57, unless it is plain that the target does not have sufficient resources to make payment. In such circumstances, the indebtedness could be reconstituted as loan capital and assigned to the purchaser against payment of the amount involved.

Duty is charged on so much of the consideration as is ascertainable at the date the transfer is stamped. The consideration is ascertainable if the information exists from which it may be calculated. Thus, where the consideration is, for example, to be determined following the preparation of completion accounts, the transfer should be presented for stamping within the thirty day period and the duty paid subsequently, once the amount of the consideration has been determined. Where the consideration is unascertainable, the 'contingency principle' may operate, whereby all contingencies are ignored. Accordingly, if there is a specified maximum amount of consideration or, in the absence of a maximum, a minimum amount, this will be treated as the consideration payable and the duty calculated accordingly.

The contingency principle applies in 'earnout deals' where part of the consideration given for the purchase of shares is deferred and becomes payable only if profit targets are met. The level of future profits is unascertainable, and so this consideration should not be liable to duty, but if it is subject to a maximum (or minimum) amount stamp duty will become payable on the transfer of the shares to the purchaser by reference to that maximum (or minimum). Should the profit targets not be met, so that the full consideration does not become payable, the stamp duty cannot be reclaimed.

Where the deferred consideration is to be satisfied in shares, it is possible to argue that part of the consideration received by the vendors is the right to the future allotment. This right is a chose in action (see *Marren (Inspector of Taxes) v Ingles* (1980) 54 TC 76) and as such is not dutiable consideration at all. However, in many cases the purchaser will retain the option to satisfy the deferred consideration in cash, and this may be regarded by the Stamp Office as sufficient to make the transfer stampable in respect of the deferred consideration as well.

Part IV of the Finance Act 1986 introduced a new tax, the stamp duty reserve tax, which is chargeable where there is an agreement to transfer 'chargeable securities' which is not completed within two months by a duly stamped instrument. Where the agreement is completed later, but within six years, repayment of the stamp duty reserve tax may be obtained if the duly stamped instrument of transfer is presented to the Stamp Office. Despite its name, stamp duty reserve tax is a tax distinct from stamp duty, and unlike stamp duty it is directly assessable. 'Chargeable securities' are defined by the Finance Act 1986, s 99(3) to include stocks, shares, loan capital and units under a unit trust scheme, but the definition does not include shares in companies incorporated outside the United Kingdom (unless recorded in a register kept in the United Kingdom), bearer shares or most forms of loan capital. Renounceable letters of allotment are, however, subject to the tax (Finance Act 1986, s 88(2)).

Although the charge to stamp duty reserve tax is potentially of very wide scope, it will not, in practice, usually be of concern in relation to the acquisition of shares in a private company because the purchaser will wish to complete the purchase and registration of the shares in its name. An exception may occur where a purchaser company intends that on completion the shares in the target should be transferred into the beneficial ownership of another company within the purchaser's group. Unless the acquisition agreement contains provision for the purchaser to substitute the other company to complete the agreement, a direct transfer of the shares from the vendor to the purchaser's subsidiary must not be taken, as there is no relief from stamp duty reserve tax equivalent to that from stamp duty afforded by the Finance Act 1930, s 42 (see below). Instead, in order to avoid stamp duty reserve tax on the acquisition agreement, it is necessary for there to be two transfers, first, from the vendor to the purchaser and, secondly, from the purchaser to its associated company. Relief under the Finance Act 1930, s 42 may then be claimed in respect of the latter transfer, and the acquisition agreement will not be subject to stamp duty reserve tax, as it will have been duly completed by a stamped instrument.

Although bearer shares are subject neither to stamp duty on sale (since ownership passes by renunciation or delivery and no instrument of transfer is created) nor to stamp duty reserve tax on the agreement to sell, bearer shares have not come to replace registered shares since, on issue, duty is payable under the head 'bearer instrument' of an amount equal to three times the transfer duty (ie £1.50 per £100 (or part) of the consideration given for the issue). Under the Finance Act 1963, s 60(4) the company issuing the bearer shares is liable to pay the duty. The proposed abolition of stamp duty extends to bearer instrument duty and the issue of such shares may therefore become more common once stamp duty is abolished.

Capital duty was formerly payable upon certain increases in the capital of a company and was therefore relevant to company acquisitions where the consideration took the form of an issue of shares in the purchasing company. Capital duty was introduced by Part V of the Finance Act 1973 on the entry of the United Kingdom into the European Community in compliance with Council Directive 69/335/EEC of 17 July 1969, the provisions of which ceased to be mandatory from 1985. Capital duty was repealed in the United Kingdom by the Finance Act 1988, s 141 with effect from midnight on 15 March 1988. Where exemption from capital duty under the provisions of the Finance Act 1973, Sched 19, para 10 had been provisionally obtained prior to that date, the relief will be confirmed provided that the circumstances in which the relief may be lost had not arisen at that date. Despite the repeal of capital duty, it remains necessary to comply with the requirements of the Companies Act 1985, s 88 and to make returns of allotments to the Registrar of Companies together, where appropriate, with the duly stamped contract or written particulars where the contract is not reduced to writing.

As part of the reform of stamp duties in 1986 which included the introduction of stamp duty reserve tax and the reduction of the rate of stamp duty chargeable on transfers of registered shares, various reliefs from stamp duty, as well as from capital duty, available where the consideration for the acquisition was or included the issue of shares in the purchasing company were repealed. It will now usually be impossible to avoid a charge either to stamp duty or else to stamp duty reserve tax.

Exemption from stamp duty may be available if the vendor and the purchaser are companies associated within the meaning of the Finance Act 1930, s 42. To meet this requirement, the vendor or the purchaser must be directly or indirectly the beneficial owner of not less than 90 per cent of the issued share capital of the other, or not less than 90 per cent of the issued share capital of each of the vendor and the purchaser must be directly or indirectly in the beneficial ownership of a third company. It is apparent that this exemption may be available in the case of the reorganisation of a group of companies, but is unlikely to apply to an acquisition of a company at arm's length.

Relief from stamp duty is also available for certain reconstructions or reorganisations falling within the provisions of the Finance Act 1986, ss 75, 76 and 77 and in respect of transfers by way of gift (see Finance Act 1985, s 82 and the Stamp Duty (Exempt Instruments) Regulations 1987 (SI No 516)), but consideration of these lies outside the scope of this book.

Chapter 12

Taxation of the Target

This chapter deals in outline with some of the aspects of the target's affairs which, in practice, often arise in connection with acquisitions, namely:
- (*a*) the target in a group;
- (*b*) tax losses;
- (*c*) advance corporation tax carry forward;
- (*d*) the close company target;
- (*e*) value added tax;
- (*f*) inheritance tax.
- (*g*) *Ramsay* and *Furniss v Dawson*

It will be seen that tax problems and considerations can arise not only because of the target's past transactions but also because of the acquisition itself, which can give rise to tax charges on the target or loss of reliefs or allowances.

The target in a group

The target may be a member of a group for tax purposes if it has subsidiaries or if it is itself a subsidiary of another company. It may be, of course, that the target has subsidiaries and is itself a subsidiary. In such a case the acquisition will carve a sub-group out of a larger group. Different provisions of the Tax Acts apply to different types of subsidiary. The statutes describe subsidiaries as '51 per cent subsidiaries', '75 per cent subsidiaries' or, occasionally, '90 per cent subsidiaries'. The relevant definitions are contained in the Income and Corporation Taxes Act 1988, s 838, and in the sections referred to below. The basic rules are that a company is a 51 per cent subsidiary of another if and so long as more than 50 per cent of its 'ordinary share capital' is owned directly or indirectly by that other, and a company is a 75 per cent subsidiary of another if and so long as not less than 75 per cent of its ordinary share capital is owned directly or indirectly by that other; however, it will only be a 90 per cent subsidiary if the other company owns not less than 90 per cent of its ordinary share capital *directly*. It is obvious from this that a company which is a 75 per cent subsidiary will always be a 51 per cent subsidiary and a company which is a 90 per cent subsidiary will be both a 75 per cent subsidiary and a 51 per cent subsidiary. However, if company A owns 100 per cent of the ordinary share capital of company B which in turn owns 100 per cent of the ordinary share capital of company C, company C will not be a 90 per cent subsidiary of company A (although it will be both a 75 per cent and a 51 per cent subsidiary of company A and a 90 per cent subsidiary of company B).

References to ownership are to beneficial ownership. There are circumstances short of an outright disposal in which beneficial ownership of an asset may be lost. Beneficial ownership is a wider concept than equitable ownership. It is possible for a person to cease to have beneficial ownership of an asset without it passing to another person, eg on entering into a conditional contract for sale (see *Wood Preservation Ltd v Prior* [1969] 1 WLR 1077). This question was most recently examined in *J Sainsbury plc v O'Connor (Inspector of Taxes)* [1991] STC 318, itself a group relief case although the decision is of much wider application. Sainsburys held 75 per cent of the issued share capital of a joint venture company but of this holding 5 per cent was the subject of put and call options on terms such that any increase or decrease in value of the 5 per cent holding would not accrue to Sainsburys but to its joint venture partner. The Court of Appeals applied (as it was bound to do) its earlier decision in *Wood Preservation Ltd* but provided some further explanation of that case's ratio. It held that the test to be applied was whether the nature and extent of the rights retained by Sainsburys left it with more than the bare legal shell of ownership. On the facts, despite the commercial effect of the option arrangements, this was so.

References to indirect ownership are to ownership through another body corporate. Where all subsidiaries in a chain are wholly owned the top company indirectly owns all the share capital of the bottom company, but where some companies in the chain are only partially owned s 838 contains provisions for ascertaining the percentage owned by one company of another. The provisions are complex but they work out as might be expected. The definition of 'ordinary share capital' in the Income and Corporation Taxes Act 1988, s 832(1) is not, however, quite as might be expected. It means 'all the share capital (by whatever name called) of the company, other than capital the holders of which have a right to a dividend at a fixed rate but have no other right to share in the profits of the company'.

In addition to the rules in s 838, the tests in the Income and Corporation Taxes Act 1988, Sched 18 will generally have to be applied. These apportion the profits of a company available for distribution and its assets available for distribution on a notional winding up among 'equity holders' in the company. An equity holder is any person who holds 'ordinary shares' (any shares other than fixed rate preference shares) or who is a loan creditor of the company in respect of a loan which is not a 'normal commercial loan' (see Sched 18, para 1(5)). A company will not be treated as a subsidiary of another company unless the latter is entitled under these tests to the appropriate percentage of the first company's income and assets. These provisions, whose purpose is to ensure that the company is a subsidiary in commercial and economic terms and not merely in legal form, were also considered in *Sainsbury v O'Connor*. It was held that the put and call options did not amount to 'arrangements' in respect of shares or securities for the purposes of Sched 18, para 5(3) by virtue of which the equity holder's entitlement to profits on the profit distribution or to assets on the notional winding up could be changed. Thus the joint venture company was not prevented from being a 75 per cent subsidiary of Sainsburys. This part of the decision has been reversed by the Finance (No 2) Act 1992, s 24 and Sched 6 in respect of option arrangements made on or after 15 November 1991.

If the target is a member of a group many tax consequences ensue. The main points which may be significant in the context of an acquisition are dealt with below and these relate to: group income; group relief; surrender of advance corporation tax (ACT); and tax on capital gains.

Group income

Under the Income and Corporation Taxes Act 1988, s 247, a United Kingdom resident company which is a 51 per cent subsidiary of another United Kingdom resident company may pay dividends, annual payments or interest to that other or to that other's 51 per cent subsidiaries without paying ACT in respect of the dividends or deducting tax at source from the annual payments or interest under the Income and Corporation Taxes Act 1988, s 349(1) or (2). Payments so made are called 'group income'. In order that a company may avail itself of this privilege the paying company and the receiving company must make a joint election to the inspector. The election comes into force three months after it is made (or earlier if the inspector is satisfied that it is validly made) but ceases to have effect if the companies become no longer entitled to make it. It follows from this that any purchaser will wish to ensure that any dividends or other group-income paid or received by the target before completion and which were paid gross because of an election under the section were validly so paid. Under s 247(6) the inspector is empowered to make assessments or adjustments in the event that a company purports to make a payment gross under an election but the election is invalid.

If a target is a 51 per cent subsidiary of another company before the acquisition and proposes to pay a dividend before it is acquired, the dividend should be paid before any arrangements are entered into which might fetter the vendor's beneficial ownership (see *Wood Preservation Ltd v Prior* [1969] 1 WLR 1077 and *O'Connor (Inspector of Taxes) v J Sainsbury plc* [1991] STC 318) and certainly before contracts are exchanged, as references to ownership of share capital in the context of subsidiaries are to beneficial ownership and the target will therefore cease to be a 51 per cent subsidiary of the vendor at the latest when contracts are exchanged for the sale of the target's share capital. If there is an interval between contract and completion, the vendor will probably remain the registered shareholder and thus remain entitled to receive any dividend paid during that period (subject to the terms of the acquisition agreement), but the vendor will have ceased to be the beneficial owner of the target's share capital even if the contract is conditional, and in that case, for tax purposes, the target will have ceased to be a 51 per cent subsidiary of the vendor so that under the Income and Corporation Taxes Act 1988, s 248(4) its former group election will have become invalid on exchange of contracts.

For group income purposes a company is not a 51 per cent subsidiary of another ('the parent company') if, in tracing a chain of indirect ownership, one of the owners in the chain is not resident in the United Kingdom or holds the shares as trading stock (see s 247(8)). Additionally, the parent company must be beneficially entitled to more than 50 per cent of any profits available for distribution to equity holders of the subsidiary company and to more than 50 per cent of any assets of the subsidiary company available for distribution to its equity holders on a winding-up, applying for these purposes the tests in the Income and Corporation Taxes Act 1988, Sched 18.

The group income provisions also apply where a company is a trading company or a holding company owned by a consortium (see s 247(9)).

Group relief

Under the Income and Corporation Taxes Act 1988, s 402 group relief applies between companies resident in the United Kingdom if one is a 75 per cent subsidiary of another or if both are 75 per cent subsidiaries of a third. The ownership chain is broken if it passes through a company not resident in the United Kingdom or if shares are held as trading stock (see the Income and Corporation Taxes Act 1988, s 413(3) and (5)). Section 413(7)–(10) strikes at certain artificial arrangements.

If a company which is a member of such a group has incurred trading losses in an accounting period or has certain other amounts eligible for relief from corporation tax arising in that period, it may surrender the amounts to another company within the group which can utilise them to relieve its own tax liability in respect of a 'corresponding accounting period'. Group relief can also be surrendered by companies owned by a consortium to the members of the consortium (and members of the same group as those consortium members) and vice versa (s 402(3)). A claim for group relief must be made by the company receiving the benefit of the relief (called the claimant company by the legislation), requires the consent of the company surrendering the relief (the surrendering company), and must be made within two years after the end of the surrendering company's accounting period. A very general form of claim will suffice, provided (in the case of claims received by the Inland Revenue on or after 1 September 1992) it contains the minimum information required by the Inland Revenue pursuant to the Taxes Management Act 1970, s 42(5) (see Inland Revenue Press Release, 31 July 1992 and *Gallic Leasing Ltd v Coburn (Inspector of Taxes)* [1991] STC 699). Different arrangements will apply following the introduction of 'pay and file' from October 1993. The claimant company may pay the surrendering company for the relief. It is provided by s 402(6) that payments for group relief are not to be taken into account for corporation tax purposes, either in respect of the claimant company or the surrendering company. Any payments for group relief have to be made 'in pursuance of an agreement' between the claimant company and the surrendering company and must not exceed the relief surrendered. The amount paid is usually approximately equal to, the corporation tax which would otherwise be paid, so that, in effect, instead of paying tax to the Inland Revenue the claimant company pays it to the surrendering company.

If the target itself is a company owning 75 per cent subsidiaries, it may well have been the claimant company or surrendering company in respect of group relief, but when it is sold still owning its subsidiaries then, so long as the target is not itself a subsidiary of any other company or is not owned by, or by a member of, a consortium, the purchaser in effect buys the complete group and all the group relief arrangements will pass under the purchaser's control. The purchaser will be concerned to see, or to take a warranty to the effect, that all group relief surrenders and payments within the target group have been properly made, but at least the group relief arrangements will not have to be disentangled.

More difficult problems arise when the target is itself a 75 per cent subsidiary of another company or is owned by a consortium. In a case where the target has been surrendering or claiming group relief from companies which are not to be acquired at the same time as the acquisition of the target, it is necessary, at the time of the acquisition, to give some thought to the group relief arrangements. It is necessary to consider accounting periods completed before the acquisition and the accounting period current at the date of acquisition.

It is probable that the group relief arrangements in respect of some accounting periods completed before acquisition will not have been finalised because the tax computations remain to be agreed. If the target is a loss maker, it may well be necessary or desirable, after the acquisition has been completed, for the vendor to receive and pay for group relief in respect of accounting periods completed before the acquisition. In such a case the vendor will be anxious to ensure that it is able to obtain the benefit of the target's losses and the purchaser will wish to ensure that the target will be paid for them (and vice versa if the target is a profit maker obtaining the benefit of group relief surrendered to it by companies in the vendor group). In either case it will be necessary to have a written group relief agreement and to make arrangements for liaison between vendor and purchaser with regard to the corporation tax computations. It was settled by *Chapman (AW) Ltd v Hennessey* (1981) 55 TC 516 that it is possible to make surrenders of group relief after the target has left the group.

Group relief in respect of the accounting period current at the time of the acquisition tends to be complicated. There is provision in the Income and Corporation Taxes Act 1988, s 409 for apportionment of group relief when companies join or leave a group during an accounting period but the Income and Corporation Taxes Act 1988, s 410 provides that if in any accounting period arrangements are in existence by virtue of which, at some time during or after the expiry of that accounting period, a company could leave a group, there can be no group relief between the company and the members of the group which it proposes to leave. It should be noted that the section applies whether the company is a surrendering company or a claimant company. The section (certainly in its form prior to consolidation) could be interpreted as providing that, if any such arrangements exist, the company shall be deemed never to have been a member of the previous group for group relief purposes, but this was confirmed as incorrect in *Shepherd (Inspector of Taxes) v Law Land plc* [1990] STC 795). Prior to that decision, the Inland

Revenue's practice had been to apply the section back to the beginning of the accounting period during which the 'arrangements' came into existence but the taxpayer successfully argued that relief is only deprived from the actual date on which 'arrangements' came into existence.

'Arrangements' is a deliberately loose term and arrangements can come into existence before contracts are in fact exchanged. Previously, it was often advantageous to the vendor if the target changed its accounting date so that an accounting period ended just before the arrangements arose (although pinning down the date when the arrangements arose can be difficult). In the light of the *Law Land plc* decision, this is no longer strictly necessary but may afford certainty. Under s 409, the purchaser group will only have the benefit of group relief involving the target on and after the date upon which the beneficial ownership of the target's share capital passes (profits and losses are apportioned on a time basis unless this would be unreasonable or unjust). An accounting period should not, however, be changed too lightly as there may well be many tax consequences that flow from such a change, beside the need to prepare audited accounts for the shortened period. The object of s 410 seems to be to prevent companies with large losses arising or due to arise in an accounting period (caused perhaps by capital allowances) joining an unconnected group or acquiring an unconnected company, surrendering their losses and separating again under pre-existing 'arrangements'. It should also be noted that the provisions apply to a company remaining within the selling group if the company which is sold has succeeded to its trade. Packaging a trade in a company for subsequent sale may therefore affect group relief between the company to which the trade formerly belonged and the other members of the group.

For a discussion of the meaning of the word 'arrangements' in this context and the wide meaning given to it see *Pilkington Bros Ltd v IRC* [1981] STC 705 and also Inland Revenue Statement of Practice SP5/80, although this has been withdrawn pending issue of a revised Statement of Practice.

For a note on group relief and financial assistance under the Companies Act 1985, s 151, see p 55.

Surrender of advance corporation tax

Under the Income and Corporation Taxes Act 1988, s 240, a resident company can surrender ACT paid in respect of dividends to its resident 51 per cent subsidiaries provided they are 51 per cent subsidiaries throughout the accounting period in which the dividends were paid. The rules about following the ownership chain are the same as for group relief (see p 196) and the provisions of the Income and Corporation Taxes Act 1988, Sched 18 are also applied by s 240(11)(*b*) to determine whether a company is a 51 per cent subsidiary.

A claim to surrender ACT must be made within six years after the end of the accounting period to which it relates and requires the consent of the subsidiaries concerned.

A company may wish to surrender ACT if it cannot use it for set-off against its own liability to mainstream corporation tax. Under the Income and Corporation Taxes Act 1988, s 239(2), the amount of ACT which can be set against a company's liability for mainstream corporation tax in any accounting period is limited to ACT which would have been payable on a distribution made at the end of that period, being a distribution which, together with the ACT payable in respect of it, is equal to the company's income and capital gains charged to corporation tax for that period. If a company has paid distributions in an accounting period which, when grossed up, exceed its chargeable profits, the excess is called surplus ACT and can be set off against tax in other accounting periods. Under s 239(3) surplus ACT can be carried back to accounting periods beginning in the previous six years if a claim is made to that effect within two years after the end of the accounting period (*see Procter & Gamble Limited v Taylerson (Inspector of Taxes)* [1988] STC 854) and under s 239(4) it can be carried forward indefinitely, but surrendering ACT under s 240 can enable it to be used by a subsidiary in a current accounting period. It should be noted that a surrender under s 240 can be made in respect of any ACT and not just surplus ACT.

ACT surrendered to a subsidiary is treated as if it were ACT paid by that subsidiary subject to certain limitations. If it is surplus to the subsidiary's own requirements it cannot be carried back (although it is treated as the first amount to be set off against mainstream corporation tax, leaving the subsidiary's own ACT free to be carried back) and s 240(5) provides that ACT surrendered to a subsidiary may not be set off against that subsidiary's mainstream corporation tax for any accounting period in which, or in any part of which, it was not a subsidiary of the surrendering company.

Section 240(1) prevents ACT surrenders between the target and the selling group in an accounting period during which arrangements are in existence for the target to leave the group. The section also strikes at certain artificial arrangements and is the ACT equivalent of the group relief anti-avoidance provisions contained in the Income and Corporation Taxes Act 1988, ss 410 and 413.

It is common for payments to be made by subsidiaries to surrendering companies in return for ACT surrendered. Such payments are treated in the same way as payments for group relief, and are not taken into account for tax purposes in calculating the profits or losses of the paying or receiving company (s 240(8)).

Where the target is a parent company and is not itself a subsidiary, the purchaser will be concerned to see that any ACT surrenders have been properly made, so that the target group's corporation tax computations have been correctly prepared. If the target is a subsidiary and has received the benefit of surrender of ACT from a parent which is not being purchased, the purchaser will wish to ensure that the target has not paid for, and will not become liable to pay for, any ACT which becomes irrecoverable under s 240(5) when the target leaves the vendor group. It should be noted that there is no provision for surrendering back any unusable ACT.

A number of anti-avoidance measures directed at the sale of subsidiaries with surplus ACT were introduced into the Income and Corporation Taxes Act 1988 by the Finance Act 1989. These are considered on p 213.

Surrender of tax refunds under 'pay and file'

A detailed description of 'pay and file' which comes into operation in respect of accounting periods ending on or after 1 October 1993 is beyond the scope of this book. Briefly, the new system will require companies to pay their corporation tax liabilities on or before the due date for payment (ie nine months after the end of the relevant accounting period). This may result in additional amounts becoming due (together with interest) or an entitlement arising to a tax refund (attracting interest at a lesser rate). The Finance Act 1989, s 102 will permit a company in a group to surrender its right to a refund to another company which has a liability to additional tax, thus reducing the interest charge. The companies must be members of the same group throughout the relevant accounting period and remain so at the date the claim is made. Any payment made between the companies in respect of the surrender will, like payments for group relief and ACT, be outside the scope of corporation tax.

For the purposes of determining whether two companies are members of the same group the provisions relating to group relief are applied. It is not clear that this is sufficient to import s 410, since one of the conditions of that section operating is that one company should have amounts which it would be entitled to surrender by way of group relief. Section 413(7) and Sched 18 will apply for the purposes of determining whether the relevant company is a 75 per cent subsidiary.

Tax on capital gains

Groups for the purposes of corporation tax on chargeable gains are defined under the Taxation of Chargeable Gains Act 1992, s 170. A company ('the principal company of the group') and all its 75 per cent subsidiaries form a group. If any of those subsidiaries have 75 per cent subsidiaries, the group includes them and their 75 per cent subsidiaries, and so on, but a group does not include any company (other than the principal company of the group) that is not an 'effective 51 per cent subsidiary' of the principal company of the group. A company is an effective 51 per cent subsidiary of another company if that other company is beneficially entitled to more than 50 per cent of any profits available for distribution to equity holders of the subsidiary and to more than 50 per cent of any assets available for distribution to equity holders on a winding up. For this purpose, the tests in Sched 18 apply, with slight modifications (see the Taxation of Chargeable Gains Act 1992, s 170(8)).

A company cannot be the principal company of a group if it is itelf a 75 per cent subsidiary of another company, unless it is prevented from being a member of the same group as the other company because it is not an effective 51 per cent subsidiary of the principal company of the group to which the other company belongs. A company cannot be a member of more than one group, and s 170(6) contains rules for determining to which of two or more potential groups a company belongs.

The rules for determining a capital gains tax group are less restrictive than those for other corporation tax purposes, because a member of a group is not required to be a 75 per cent subsidiary of the principal company of the group, provided it is an effective 51 per cent subsidiary of it and is a 75 per cent subsidiary of that company. Further, although all the members of the group must be United Kingdom resident companies, it is permitted to trace ownership through companies resident outside the United Kingdom and to take account of shares held as trading stock.

As a general point, the provisions now considered will not cause great difficulty where the target is a parent company (sold with its subsidiaries intact) but is not and has not been a 75 per cent subsidiary of any other company. If, however, the target is or has been a 75 per cent subsidiary (whether or not it has subsidiaries itself) the provisions may give rise to unexpected liabilities.

Tax recoverable from other group members. Under the Taxation of Chargeable Gains Act 1992, s 190, if a chargeable gain accrues to a company which at the time is a member of the group and the company fails to pay its corporation tax assessed for that accounting period within six months of the due date, if the tax so assessed included any amount in respect of chargeable gains, an amount of that tax not exceeding corporation tax on the amount of that gain may be recovered from a company which was at the time when the gain accrued the principal company of the group and any other company which, within the two year period preceding the gain, was a member of the group and owned the asset disposed of or any part of it (or, where the asset in question was an interest or right in or over another asset, owned either asset or any part of either asset).

It should be noted that what can be recovered is corporation tax on the amount of the gain, so it seems that any allowable capital losses available to the company which should have paid the tax and which might have reduced the tax payable need not be brought into account when assessing the other group company.

It will be seen, therefore, that if the target is the principal company of a group, it may be made liable for its subsidiary's chargeable gains even if the subsidiary in question is not a subsidiary of the target at the time of the acquisition. Moreover, if the target owned an asset which was disposed of before the acquisition of the target to another member of the group (perhaps the vendor), the target can be made liable after the acquisition to account for tax on chargeable gains payable by a company with which it has then no relationship. Section 190(3) provides that the company paying tax assessed under s 190(1) can recover an equal amount from other group companies, but the purchaser is likely to want an express indemnity from the vendor.

A number of other provisions, notably those relating to the migration of companies and the taxation of gains of non-resident or dual resident companies, also allow tax to be recovered from other companies in the same group.

Intra-group transfers. Under the Taxation of Chargeable Gains Act 1992, s 171 transfers of chargeable assets within a group do not give rise to any immediate charge to tax. The section provides that both parties to the transfer are treated as if the asset were acquired for a consideration of such amount as would secure that on the transferor's disposal, neither a gain nor a loss would accrue. In other words, the consideration is assumed to be the disposing company's base value including any indexation allowance (Taxation of Chargeable Gains Act 1992, s 56(2)). To take a simple example, suppose that company B acquires an asset at a cost of £10,000 which subsequently increases in value to £20,000. Company B is then acquired by company A and becomes its 75 per cent subsidiary. A transfer of that asset from company B to company A will be deemed to be made at the price (ignoring indexation allowance) of £10,000 irrespective of the asset's worth and of what company A actually pays company B for it. Suppose company A pays the market value, ie £20,000. When company A sells the asset to a third party at a price of £30,000 the chargeable gain would be £20,000 (ie £30,000 less £10,000) even though company A has actually paid £20,000 for the asset.

By s 171(2) certain disposals fall outside the terms of the section. Examples are the disposal of a debt and the disposal of an interest in shares in a company in consideration for a capital distribution. This means that the liquidation of a subsidiary will involve a chargeable disposal of its shares by the parent (see the Taxation of Chargeable Gains Act 1992, s 122).

Section 171 also does not apply where the transaction is treated by the Taxation of Chargeable Gains Act 1992, ss 127 and 135 as not involving a disposal (s 171(3)). This is an important provision and ensures that where, for example, shares in a subsidiary are hived down to a second subsidiary on a share-for-share basis that second subsidiary acquires those shares at current market value while the consideration shares received by the parent in the share-for-share exchange will have the original base cost of the shares transferred. These statutory provisions reverse the decision in *Westcott (Inspector of Taxes) v Woolcombers Ltd* [1987] STC 600.

Section 171 is obviously useful, as assets can be transferred within a group of companies without incurring an immediate liability to tax on any chargeable gains, but in the context of an acquisition it can cause problems. The section may mean, for instance, that an asset owned by the target has a lower base value for tax purposes than its actual cost. If the target has acquired that asset from a company which was in the same group at the time of the acquisition, on any subsequent disposal of that asset outside the group the purchaser may be aggrieved to find that the target's tax bill is higher than he thought (see the example given above). A general warranty is therefore taken to cover this point (the Agreement for Sale, Sched 4, warranty (p 22)).

The section may also in conjunction with the 'value shifting' provisions of the Taxation of Chargeable Gains Act 1992, ss 30 to 34) affect the liability to capital gains tax arising on the disposal of shares in a subsidiary from which assets have been transferred.

Companies leaving a group. In the early days of capital gains tax it was possible to make use of what is now s 171 to avoid the charge to corporation tax on capital gains by means of what became known as 'the envelope trick'. If company Y owned an asset which had grown substantially in value it could transfer that asset to a new 75 per cent subsidiary, X, formed for the purpose in exchange for the issue of shares by X. The shares of X were deemed acquired by Y at their current market value (ie the actual value of the asset at the time of the transfer), but s 171 applied to the transfer of the asset. Y could then sell the shares of X to a purchaser so that dominion over the asset passed without any charge to tax on capital gains. X was the 'envelope' in which the asset was placed before it was sold.

To prevent this form of tax avoidance what is now the Taxation of Chargeable Gains Act 1992, s 178 was enacted. (Equivalent provisions in the Taxation of Chargeable Gains Act 1992, s 179 will apply instead on the introduction of 'pay and file'.) This provides that if company X, called 'the chargeable company' by the section, leaves a group owning an asset which it has acquired within the last six years from company Y which was at the time of the acquisition a member of the group which X is leaving, X is treated as if, at the time of the acquisition from Y, it had sold and immediately reacquired the asset at its market value. Under s 178(10) X's assessment to corporation tax for the accounting period in which it acquired the asset from Y is reopened and recomputed. It should be noted that the provisions of the Taxation of Chargeable Gains Act 1992, s 35 and Sched 3 which allow for the rebasing of acquisition costs to the market value as at 31 March 1982, will not apply where X acquired the asset from Y prior to 6 April 1988. Instead, where the asset was acquired by the group on or before 31 March 1982, the gain that would otherwise be chargeable under s 178 is to be reduced by one-half (Taxation of Chargeable Gains Act 1992, s 36 and Sched 4).

The section also applies if, at the time when X leaves the group, it does not itself own the asset in question, but the asset is owned by an 'associated company' of X which is also leaving the group. For the purposes of the section, two or more companies are associated companies if, by themselves, they would form a group (s 178(8)). The section does not apply, however, if X and Y both leave the group together and are associated companies (s 178(2)).

The section applies not only to the original asset which X acquired but also to any replacement asset if any gain on the asset has been rolled over into that replacement asset under the Taxation of Chargeable Gains Act 1992, ss 152 to 158.

References to companies ceasing to be a member of a group are construed in accordance with the Taxation of Chargeable Gains Act 1992, s 170(10) which provides that a group remains the same group so long as the same company remains the principal company of the group and, if at any time the principal company of a group becomes a member of another group, the group of which it was the principal company before that time is regarded as the same as that other group. However, it would be possible for a member of the first group not to become a member of the other group if, although a 75 per cent subsidiary, it is not an effective 51 per cent subsidiary of the principal company of the other group. In those circumstances, s 178 will not apply, unless during the following six years the company ceases to be a 75 per cent subsidiary and an effective 51 per cent subsidiary of one or more members of the other group and it or another company at that time in the same group as it holds the asset or a replacement asset (s 178(4) to (6)). A company does not cease to be a member of a group for the purposes of s 178 if it ceases to be a member of a group in consequence of another member of the group ceasing to exist (s 178(1) as amended by the Finance (No 2) Act 1992, s 25).

Section 178 is difficult to construe. Assume a group which looks like this:

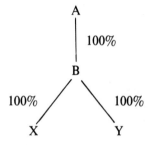

The following permutations (among others) are possible.

(1) If X is the target, X will leave the A group (all the companies) and the section will therefore apply to any asset which X owns at the time of the acquisition and which was acquired from any of the other companies within the six year period. If Y sold the asset to X, it will not help if Y is bought by the same purchaser at the same time. X and Y are not associated companies because, by themselves, they do not form a group.

(2) If B is the target and is sold with its subsidiaries intact, B, X and Y will leave the A group. Prima facie the section will apply, again, to any asset which X owns and has acquired within the six year period from any of the other companies, but if the asset has been acquired by X from B or Y it seems that the section will not in fact apply, because of s 178(2). Two or more associated companies (B, X and Y) are ceasing to be members of a group (the A group) at the same time and the section does not have effect as respects an acquisition by one from another of those associated companies. B, X

and Y are associated because, by themselves, they form a group. If X has acquired the asset from A then, of course, the section will apply.

(3) If B is the target and X owns the asset which it has acquired from B, which in turn acquired it from A within the six year period, although the acquisition by X from B is not in point (because of s 178(2)) the section will still apply to B as the chargeable company because B is leaving the group having acquired the asset from A and 'an associated company' (X) is also leaving the group owning the asset. B and X are associated because by themselves they form a group. However, if A sold the asset to Y rather than B and Y sold it to X, will the section still apply when B, X and Y leave the group? It will not apply to X because its acquisition from Y is taken outside the charge by s 178(2). Y no longer owns the asset, so the section will only apply to Y if the asset is now owned by a company which is Y's 'associated company' and which is also leaving the group. It is possible to argue that X is not associated with Y because *by themselves* they do not form a group, although they do if B is added. This is an odd result and one that presumably was not intended by the draftsman. Where a sub-group leaves a larger group it is clear for the purposes of the exemption in s 178(2) that each of the members of the sub-group is associated with each other member, but it is not clear that the same result is obtained from construing the reference to 'associated company' in s 178(3).

(4) If A is the target, no company will leave any group and the section will not apply.

(5) It should be noted that the section applies if X leaves a group owning an asset which it acquired from another company which was a member of that group at the time of the acquisition of the asset. The section does not in fact say that X has to be a member of the same group at the time the asset was acquired, although this is clearly the intention. Suppose that X and Y were quite unrelated at the time of the acquisition of the asset by X from Y but subsequently B acquired X's share capital so that X became a member of the B group. If X is the target and is sold by B within the period of six years from the date of X's acquisition of the asset from Y, the section appears to apply because X is ceasing to be a member of the B group and, at the time of the acquisition of the asset, Y was a member of the B group. Normally, of course, this will not matter because the section only supposes the asset to have been sold and reacquired at market value at the time of the acquisition, and if X and Y were unrelated the sale was probably at market value, so that X's base value will be high and no further tax will be payable. It is possible, however, that X acquired the asset at an undervalue (eg pursuant to an option granted some time before) and in that case the section would appear to

produce a charge to tax even though s 171 had never applied to the asset in question.

Under s 178(9) tax assessed on the chargeable company can be recovered, if it is not paid within six months, from any company which was the principal company of the group which the chargeable company left (or which is the principal company at the date on which the tax became payable) and also from any company which owned the asset in question on the date for payment of the tax or when the chargeable company ceased to be a member of the group. It is difficult to believe that this provision is as wide as it appears. If X leaves the group owning the asset and then sells it at arm's length to an unrelated third party and X is subsequently assessed for tax under s 178, it seems from the section that if the third party is a company it can be charged to tax. Innocent purchasers will hardly regard as sufficient the right to indemnity from X which is conferred by s 178(9).

Tax losses

If a company has incurred a loss in carrying on a trade, it may claim to have the loss set off for tax purposes against profits, of whatever description (including chargeable gains), made in the accounting period in which the loss is sustained or, if the company was then carrying on the trade, of preceding accounting periods falling wholly or partly within the three years previous to that accounting period (Income and Corporation Taxes Act 1988, s 393A). In respect of a loss incurred in accounting periods ended before 1 April 1991, the loss may be carried back to accounting periods falling wholly or partly within a period equal to the length of the accounting period in which the loss is incurred (Income and Corporation Taxes Act 1988, s 393(2)). Alternatively, the company may carry forward the loss against any trading income from the trade in succeeding accounting periods until the loss is exhausted (Income and Corporation Taxes Act 1988, s 393). If a target has trading losses otherwise eligible for carry forward, the purchaser will wish to know whether the change in ownership of the target's shares will affect the availability of these losses for set-off against future profits made by the target. The Income and Corporation Taxes Act 1988, s 768, which is considered below, has the effect of preventing such a carry forward in many cases. In relation to changes of ownership occurring on or after 14 June 1991, the Income and Corporation Taxes Act 1988, s 768A will in the same circumstances prevent a carry back of losses under s 393A. Sections 768 and 768A are in addition to, and not in substitution for, a considerable body of authority on this question.

Although the acquisition of shares in the target will not itself affect the target's trade, the target's business may change following the acquisition as its affairs come under new control. In each case it is a question of fact whether or not the old trade has been discontinued and a new trade has been commenced. If this has occurred, any losses incurred in the old trade are not available for carry forward against the profits of the new, because the new trade is not 'the trade' within the meaning of s 393.

Before the enactment (originally in the Finance Act 1969) of what is now s 768, many cases came before the courts which concerned changes in a target's business at the same time as the acquisition of its shares.

In *Ingram (JG) & Son Ltd v Callaghan (Inspector of Taxes)* (1968) 45 TC 151 the target's trade consisted of manufacturing rubber goods. For a period of nine months the company ceased to manufacture rubber goods but sold similar products made of plastic which had been made by another company. At the end of this nine month period the target was acquired by the purchaser and thereafter manufactured and sold similar products but now made of plastic. It was held on appeal that the target's trade had been permanently discontinued and a new trade set up. Losses made in the manufacture of rubber goods were therefore not available to be carried forward to be set off against the profits of the manufacture of the plastic goods.

In *Gordon and Blair Ltd v IRC* (1962) 40 TC 358 the target was a brewer. Shortly before the acquisition it had ceased to brew its own beer and entered into arrangements with the eventual purchaser to the effect that the purchaser would brew the beer which was then sold by the target under the target's brand name. It was held that the target's former trade had ceased when it ceased to brew beer and a new trade had been commenced. Similar cases relating to changes in a trade prior to or following an acquisition are *Tryka Ltd v Newall (Inspector of Taxes)* (1963) 41 TC 146 and *Seaman (Inspector of Taxes) v Tucketts Ltd* (1963) 41 TC 422.

In all the cases cited above it was held, on the facts, that the changes in the target's trade had amounted to a discontinuance, but it is not every change in the nature of a trade which amounts to a discontinuance and therefore means that losses cannot be carried forward. The expansion of an existing trade is not necessarily regarded as a new trade and a trade may be suspended for some time and then revived. In *Robroyston Brickworks Ltd v IRC* (1976) 51 TC 230 the target manufactured and sold bricks and had been making losses for a number of years. In March 1968 the target ceased brick production and by August 1968, when the purchaser acquired it, had sold off its entire stock of bricks and its plant and machinery, paid off its creditors and gradually dispensed with the services of the remaining employees. Following the acquisition the target commenced manufacturing bricks at the purchaser's brickworks. The Court of Session held that the target's trade had only been suspended and that accordingly losses accrued prior to the transfer of the trade from one works to another were available to be set off against future profits. Cases such as this are now likely to be caught by s 768.

Section 768(1) has the effect of disallowing carry forward if:

(a) within any period of three years there is both a change in the ownership of the company and (either earlier or later in that period, or at the same time) a major change in the nature or conduct of a trade carried on by the company, or

(b) at any time after the scale of the activities in a trade carried on by a company has become small or negligible, and before any considerable revival of the trade, there is a change in the ownership of the company.

By s 768(4) 'major change in the nature or conduct of a trade' includes:

(a) a major change in the type of property dealt in, or services or facilities provided, in the trade; or

(b) a major change in customers, outlets or markets of the trade.

Section 768 applies even if the change is the result of a gradual process which began outside the period of three years referred to in s 768(1).

As a result, events which might not formerly have been held to amount to the discontinuance of one trade and the setting up of another will, if coupled with a change of ownership, prevent losses being carried forward. In *Willis (Inspector of Taxes) v Peeters Picture Frames Ltd* (1983) 56 TC 436, it was held that whether a change is 'major' is a question of fact and degree for the Commissioners and it seems that the word will not be construed literally, ie as relating to more than one half of the type of property dealt in or of the customers, outlets or markets. It is also necessary to consider whether the events amount to a change in the trade (*Purchase (Inspector of Taxes) v Tesco Stores Ltd* (1984) 58 TC 46).

The Inland Revenue have given some guidance, in Statement of Practice SP10/91, on the circumstances in which a 'major change in the nature or conduct of a trade' may occur. Generally, a major change will not be regarded as having occurred when a company makes changes to increase its efficiency or keep pace with developing technology or management techniques. Likewise, rationalisation of a product range by withdrawing unprofitable items and, perhaps, replacing them with new products of a kind related to those already being produced will not cause the section to have effect.

Section 768(1)(*b*) deals with cases (such as the *Robroyston* case cited above) in which the target's trade has been suspended and its shares acquired during the period when the trade was suspended. Although suspension of a trade does not necessarily amount to a discontinuance, losses will not be available for carry forward in cases caught by the section.

The section contains machinery for enabling the inspector to ascertain the beneficial ownership of shares in the company for the purposes of ascertaining whether or not a change in the ownership of the company has taken place.

Section 769 defines a 'change of ownership'. The definition is wide and certainly includes an acquisition of a controlling interest by a single purchaser. When the purchaser is already a shareholder in the target, however, it is worth checking the rules carefully, because not every sale and purchase of shares between shareholders results in a change of ownership. If the target is a 75 per cent subsidiary of another company (applying for this purpose the tests in the Income and Corporation Taxes Act 1988, Sched 18) and continues to be so after a change in the direct ownership of the target, that change of ownership is disregarded (s 769(5)). In other words, the transfer within a group of shares in a subsidiary will not normally trigger the section. However, the sale of the parent company will mean a change of ownership of all of its 75 per cent subsidiaries (s 769(6)).

Capital allowances available to a trading company are treated as trading expenses (Capital Allowances Act 1990, s 144). If they go to increase the trading loss, ss 768 and 768A will apply to prevent their carry forward in the same way as the sections apply to other trading losses. Neither s 393 nor s 768 restrict the purchaser taking advantage of any capital allowances unclaimed at the date of sale. It may therefore be advantageous to disclaim such allowances for periods prior to completion and to claim them in later periods when they can be used to reduce profits of the target or, by way of group relief, of the purchaser or other companies in the purchaser's group.

'Losses' which do not form part of a trade, eg an investment company's excess management expenses and charges on income (plus unused capital allowances), can be carried forward but not back (Income and Corporation Taxes Act 1988, s 75) and the carry forward is not restricted by s 768; neither are losses for the purposes of tax on capital gains subject to the restrictions (although see p 222 below for the possible application of *Ramsay* principles to restrict the utilisation of such losses). As noted above, trading losses may to a limited extent be set off against chargeable gains, but there is no reciprocal treatment, so that allowable capital losses may only be carried forward to be set off against chargeable gains.

As a general point it should be noted that trading losses, management expenses, charges on income and capital allowances are only capable of being surrendered under group relief arrangements in respect of the accounting period in which they are incurred (Income and Corporation Taxes Act 1988, s 403). The purchaser acquiring a target with losses accrued in completed accounting periods can therefore only utilise these losses against profits or gains made in the target itself. Only losses accruing in future accounting periods will be available for group relief within the purchaser group. The Income and Corporation Taxes Act 1988, s 409 deals with the treatment of the accounting period current at the date of acquisition (see p 198). Capital losses are not available for group relief at all.

Advance corporation tax carry forward

Surplus ACT can, under the Income and Corporation Taxes Act 1988, s 239(4), be carried forward indefinitely to be set off against a company's liability to mainstream corporation tax (see p 200). A target which was once profitable but has ceased to be so, or which has significant foreign source income received subject to foreign withholding taxes so that its mainstream corporation tax liability is reduced, may therefore have a large amount of surplus ACT capable of being carried forward and set off against its mainstream corporation tax in future accounting periods. This can be attractive for a purchaser if the purchaser expects to be able to arrange for the target to increase its United Kingdom taxable profits (eg by diverting business from another member of the purchaser group) as he will then have the benefit of the target's surplus ACT. The Income and Corporation Taxes Act 1988, s 245, however, prevents the carry forward of surplus ACT in similar circumstances as the Income and Corporation Taxes Act 1988, s 768 prevents the carry forward of tax losses (ie change of ownership coupled with a major change in the trade or a revival of the trade).

If s 245 applies, the date of the change of ownership is deemed to start a new accounting period and there is no carry forward into that and subsequent accounting periods. Section 768 only applies to trading companies, but, as surplus ACT can arise in investment companies, s 245 applies to them as well and defines 'major change in the nature or conduct of a trade or business' as including a change whereby the company ceases to be a trading company and becomes an investment company or vice versa and, if the company is an investment company, a major change in the nature of the investments held by the company. The Inland Revenue Statement of Practice SP10/91 (see p 210) is relevant to s 245 as well as to s 768. Section 245 applies to ACT which the company is treated as having paid by virtue of the Income and Corporation Taxes Act 1988, s 240 (surrender of ACT to a subsidiary) as it applies to ACT which it has actually paid. Further, the Income and Corporation Taxes Act 1988, s 245A prevents the carry forward of surrendered ACT where there is a major change in the nature or conduct of a trade or business of the company which surrendered the ACT within the period commencing three years before the change of ownership and ending three years after the change of ownership.

It used also to be possible for the purchaser to turn the target company's surplus ACT to advantage by transferring prior to their disposal to a third party purchaser assets intended for sale to the target company. As a consequence of the Taxation of Chargeable Gains Act 1992, s 171 the gain on disposal would be realised by the target and the tax on the gain could be off set by the surplus ACT. The Income and Corporation Taxes Act 1988, s 245B now restricts the carried forward ACT available to the target company where such an intra-group transfer followed by a disposal occurs within three years after the change in ownership of the target company.

The close company target

A company controlled by a few individuals has the potential to become a tax avoidance vehicle. A number of provisions have been enacted to counter this, of which the most notorious were those relating to shortfall apportionment, now repealed by the Finance Act 1989 and replaced by a simpler regime which applies to close companies whose income consists mainly of passive investment income ('close investment-holding companies'). What follows is intended as a brief summary of the close company legislation. It includes the shortfall apportionment rules (which apply to accounting periods commencing before 1 April 1989), as these will continue to be relevant since apportionments can be made up to six years (and in some cases longer) after the end of the accounting period.

Close companies

Most resident targets will be close unless they are part of a listed group. Close companies are defined by the Income and Corporation Taxes Act 1988, s 414, and the target will be close if it is United Kingdom resident and satisfies either the 'control test' in s 414(1) or the 'apportionment test' in s 414(2). By virtue of s 414(5), however, the target will not be close if it is controlled by a United Kingdom resident 'open' company (ie a company which is not close).

Under the control test, the target is close if it is under the control of five or fewer participators or of any number of participators who are directors. The words 'control', 'participator' and 'director' are given extended meanings by ss 416 and 417 which prevent most attempts to 'open' a company which would otherwise be close.

A person is taken to have 'control' of a company if he 'exercises or is able to exercise or is entitled to acquire' control, whether direct or indirect, over the company's affairs, and in particular a person is taken to have control if he possesses or is entitled to acquire:

(a) the majority of the share capital or issued share capital of the company or of the voting power in the company; or

(b) such part of the issued share capital as would entitle him to the greater part of the income if it were distributed; or

(c) rights which entitle him to receive the greater part of the assets of the company on a winding up.

Where two or more persons together satisfy any of the conditions of control they are taken to have control of the target, so that if it is possible to point to any five or fewer participators (or any number of participators who are directors) who together have control, the target will be close. For this purpose rights or powers of nominees or 'associates' (relatives, partners, co-trustees and co-beneficiaries) are attributed to participators. 'Participator' is so defined that almost any person who could have control over or an interest in a company's affairs (alone or together with others) falls within the definition. In particular it includes those who possess or are entitled to acquire share capital or voting rights in the target; any loan creditor of the target (widely defined but excluding banks lending in the ordinary course of business—s 417(9)); any person who possesses or is entitled to acquire a right to receive or participate in distributions etc; and any person who is entitled to secure that income or assets will be applied directly or indirectly for his benefit (s 417(1)).

'Director' includes any person occupying the position of director by whatever name called, any person in accordance with whose directions or instructions the directors are accustomed to act and any person who is a manager and owns or controls alone or with associates 20 per cent or more of the ordinary share capital of the target (s 417(5)).

The target satisfies the apportionment test if five or fewer participators or any number of participators who are directors would, in the event of the winding-up of the company, be entitled to receive the greater part of the assets of the company which would then be available for distribution to participators, or would be so entitled if the rights of any loan creditor were disregarded. For the purpose of this test, any participator which is a company is itself assumed to be wound up.

This book deals with companies whose controllers are few enough to enable negotiations for an acquisition to be carried on with them individually. In such a case, if the target is resident, the definitions are cast so widely that it is almost bound to be close unless it is controlled by a company which is not a close company. If a parent company of a group is close, all its subsidiaries will normally be close, but if the parent company of a group is open (otherwise than by reason of foreign residence), the companies which it controls (directly or indirectly) will escape closeness via s 414(5). In practice, if the target is open, it is most likely to be open because the ultimate holding company of the group of which it forms part has shares listed on the London Stock Exchange and falls within s 415, which takes most listed companies out of the net of closeness.

In deciding whether or not a target is close, the trail does not stop at these shores. If the target is controlled directly or indirectly by non-residents, it is necessary to look at their structure to decide whether or not they would be close if they were resident, as under s 414(6) foreign companies which would be close if resident here are treated as close in determining the status of resident companies which they control.

Close investment-holding companies

A close company is a close investment-holding company in any accounting period unless throughout that period it exists wholly or mainly for the purpose of carrying on a trade or trades on a commercial basis or one or more of the other activities listed in the Income and Corporation Taxes Act 1988, s 13A(2). Broadly, only a company which makes portfolio investments will be a close investment-holding company.

A close investment-holding company is not eligible for the small companies' rate of corporation tax (Income and Corporation Taxes Act 1988, s 13). A shareholder may have his entitlement to be paid the amount of the tax credit attaching to distributions made by the company restricted, if it appears to the Inspector that arrangements exist (such as a dividend waiver) whereby he is enabled to claim such an amount, or a greater amount than would otherwise have been the case, unless the company's ordinary share capital consists of only one class of shares and no person waived his entitlement to any dividend or failed to receive any dividend in the relevant accounting period (Income and Corporation Taxes Act 1988, s 231(3A) and (3B)).

Shortfall apportionment

The rules relating to shortfall apportionment apply for accounting periods beginning before 1 April 1989. If a company is close on the last day of its accounting period it can be treated by the Revenue as having distributed its income for that period when it has not in fact done so. The object of the legislation is to prevent the accumulation of income by individuals in companies which they control, thus avoiding the higher rates of taxation.

The relevant provisions are contained in the Income and Corporation Taxes Act 1988, ss 423–430 and Sched 19 which oblige the inspector to 'apportion' the income of a close company among the participators. If an apportionment is made, ACT (subject to the rules in s 430) falls to be paid by the target and higher rate tax by the participators by reference to the amount apportioned. Section 429 provides that, if the tax assessed on the participators is not paid, the tax may be assessed on the target. A purchaser of the target's share capital will therefore wish to know that there is no likelihood of a shortfall apportionment in respect of accounting periods ended before completion, because any such apportionment could result in a tax charge falling on the target after completion.

The amount of income which would normally fall to be apportioned is the excess of 'relevant income' for the accounting period over distributions made in respect of the accounting period. In the case of non-trading companies and in other special cases, however, wider powers are given to the Revenue (ss 423 and 424).

'Relevant income' is defined by Sched 19, para 1, and, in the case of a company which is a trading company or a member of a trading group (defined by Sched 19, para 7), is so much of its 'distributable income' for that period as can be distributed without prejudice to the requirements of the company's business (including such requirements as may be necessary or advisable for the acquisition of a trade). The trading income of such a company is exempt from apportionment. Higher standards apply in the case of companies which are not trading companies. For any company the limit of 'relevant income' is its 'distributable investment income' plus 50 per cent of its 'estate or trading income' (Sched 19, para 2).

The rules relating to the computation of relevant income are contained in Sched 19, paras 1–6. Distributable investment income is subject to apportionment except in the case of a trading company or member of a trading group which can show that distribution would prejudice the requirements of its business. A number of allowances are available to other companies. Schedule 19, para 8(1) provides that certain expenditure is to be regarded as available for distribution and is not to be regarded as applicable to the requirements of the companys business. Among the expenditure so regarded are amounts expended in connection with 'first business loans', ie bans incurred in connection with the original acquisition of the company's business.

In the case of a group of companies all of which are close, shortfall apportionment can apply throughout the group, income being apportioned and sub-apportioned until it reaches the individual participators in the holding company.

Under Sched 19, para 3, the distributions of a company for an accounting period are taken to consist of any dividends declared in respect of the period and paid during the period or within a reasonable time thereafter. If there is danger of a shortfall apportionment and if the purchaser is an open company, it will therefore be possible to declare a dividend within a reasonable time after completion (payable to the new owner) which will avoid a shortfall apportionment in respect of an accounting period ended before completion. 'Reasonable time', for once, is not defined, but the limit used to be eighteen months after the end of the accounting period (Income and Corporation Taxes Act 1970, s 291) and it is understood that a dividend paid within this period will be regarded as paid within a reasonable time. Any such dividend can often be paid without incurring liability for advance corporation tax because of a group income election made pursuant to the Income and Corporation Taxes Act 1988, s 247.

Schedule 19, para 16 provides for shortfall clearances. A trading company, a member of a trading group or a company with estate or trading income may at any time after the general meeting at which accounts are adopted forward to the inspector a copy of the accounts and the directors' report. The inspector may, having received the accounts, call for further information and, once he is satisfied, he must intimate within three months whether or not he proposes to make an apportionment in respect of the company for the accounting period covered by the accounts. In all cases, whether clearances have been obtained or not, it is normal for the purchaser to take an indemnity from the vendor in respect of apportionments made by reference to income in accounting periods ended before completion.

Loans to participators

Under the Income and Corporation Taxes Act 1988, s 419, a loan by a close company to an individual participator (including 'associates', certain companies and participators in any company controlling the lender) can give rise to a liability on the lender to make a payment equivalent to advance corporation tax on the amount of the loan. The payment is not in fact ACT and does not, therefore, fall to be set off in computing the lender's liability to mainstream corporation tax.

The section extends to cover cases where the participator incurs a debt to the close company or a debt due from the participator to a third party is assigned to the close company. Debts which participators incur for the supply by the close company of goods or services in the ordinary course of trade are not included unless the credit given exceeds six months or is longer than that normally given to the company's customers. The section does not apply to loans made in the ordinary course of a business carried on by the close company which includes the lending of money, and there are limited exemptions for full time employees or directors who do not have a 'material interest' in the close company (5 per cent: see Income and Corporation Taxes Act 1988, s 168(11)). Outright misappropriation of the company's funds cannot be regarded as an act of the company and is therefore not a loan or advance for this purpose (*Stephens (Inspector of Taxes) v Pittas (T) Ltd* [1983] STC 576).

By s 419(4) relief is given where the loan is subsequently repaid, although if payment of tax has not been made under s 419 the Revenue will normally seek payment of interest on any such amount for the period from the date on which payment should have been made to the date relief becomes available. Under s 421 an individual can incur a charge to higher rate tax if the company releases or writes off the loan. Section 422 applies the provisions to loans made by companies which are controlled by close companies but which are not themselves close, eg because they are non-resident. Section 419 will then apply as if the loan had been made by the close company itself.

Where the participator is a director or employee of the target the provisions of the Income and Corporation Taxes Act 1988, s 160 (beneficial loan arrangements) may also be relevant.

If the target is close, the purchaser will require a warranty to the effect that no such loans have been made by the target or by companies controlled by the target.

Payments treated as distributions

Under the Income and Corporation Taxes Act 1988, s 418(2), expenditure incurred by a close company in providing for a participator's living or other accommodation, entertainment, domestic or other services or 'other benefits or facilities of whatever nature' is treated as a distribution by the company. Unlike s 419, this does not apply to benefits provided for individuals who are taxed on benefits in kind in any event (directors or employees earning more than £8,500) and does not apply to provision for relatives of any pension or gratuity given on death or retirement of a director or employee.

If the target is close the purchaser will require a warranty to the effect that the target is not liable to be treated as having made a distribution within this section as a result of any event prior to completion, as otherwise ACT on the deemed distribution can become payable by the target.

Inheritance tax apportionment

Under the Inheritance Tax Act 1984, ss 94 and 202, a close company is liable to pay inheritance tax in respect of transfers of value made by it. The section provides for apportionment among the participators according to their respective rights and interests in the company immediately before the transfer and if the company does not pay the tax, the persons to whom amounts are apportioned are liable to pay. If the target is itself a participator in a close company it can become liable to apportioned inheritance tax under s 202(2) even though its liability may (if the target is close) be sub-apportioned among the target's own participators by virtue of s 94(2). Purchasers will therefore normally require a warranty or indemnity covering liability under s 202.

Value added tax

In most cases the target will be liable to register for VAT and either will have a VAT registration in its own name or benefit from a group registration under the Value Added Tax Act 1983, s 29. If a group registration is not in force the purchaser's main concern will be that the accounts show full provision for any VAT liability and that in respect of transactions in the current accounting period all VAT has been properly accounted for. It is also prudent to take specific warranties against certain VAT matters. For instance, the purchaser will wish to know if the target has made any election to waive exemption under the Value Added Tax Act 1983, Sched 6A, para 2, or is authorised to use any special method for attribution of input tax. If the target has received a default surcharge liability notice under the Finance Act 1985, s 19 or a serious misdeclaration penalty under the Finance Act 1985, s 14, it may indicate poor accounting systems. Such matters are provided for in the Agreement for Sale, Sched 4, warranty (p 44).

If a group registration is in force additional considerations arise. The effect of a group registration is to enable all companies within the scope of that registration (and not all the companies in a group need be included) to make supplies from one to the other without accounting for VAT (Value Added Tax Act 1983, s 29(1)). The representative member is liable to account to or recover from Customs and Excise all VAT payable by or due to the group, but all the members of the group will be liable jointly and severally for any VAT due from the representative member. If the target and its subsidiaries include all the companies within the group registration then the purchaser will probably wish to continue with that registration and may in due course wish to include the acquired companies within its own group registration. If, on the other hand, the group registration includes companies in the vendor's group which the purchaser is not acquiring, the terms of the group registration will need to be amended. Whether the purchaser takes over the group registration will depend in part upon whether the representative member is included in the target and its subsidiaries or whether it is a company retained by the vendor. Agreement will have to be reached between the parties and arrangements made either to separate out the group members and apply for a new group registration for the target and its subsidiaries or for inclusion of the target and its subsidiaries in the purchaser's group registration. The tax indemnity in the Agreement for Sale, Sched 4 will cover any liability falling on the target or its subsidiaries for VAT attributable to any other member of the vendor's group registration.

Inheritance tax

Under the Inheritance Tax Act 1984, s 1, inheritance tax is charged on the value transferred by a 'chargeable transfer'. Section 3 of that Act defines a 'transfer of value' as (subject to certain exceptions) any disposition made by 'a person' which brings about a reduction in the value of that person's 'estate'. Section 2(1) defines a chargeable transfer as 'any transfer of value which is made by an *individual* [other than] an exempt transfer'. Consequently, although a company, being a person and having an estate, can make a transfer of value, no company can make a chargeable transfer. It follows that inheritance tax problems relating to the acquisition of companies at arm's length are mercifully few. However, a company can be liable to pay inheritance tax in the following exceptional circumstances:

(1) Under the Inheritance Tax Act 1984, s 202 (apportionment in the case of close companies: see p 219).

(2) Any company (whether open or close) may, like any other person, be liable to inheritance tax in respect of a chargeable transfer by virtue of the Inheritance Tax Act 1984, ss 199 to 201, in any of the capacities listed in those sections (other than those of transferor and settlor). Generally speaking, it is unlikely that any liability will arise unless the target has been involved in tax avoidance schemes. The liability may arise:

(*a*) if the target is a transferee of value;

(*b*) if at any time after the transfer in question there is vested in the target (beneficially or not) property to the value of which any inheritance tax is attributable or if the target is beneficially entitled to an interest in possession in such property (the liability will not arise if the target has obtained the property as purchaser or derives title from a purchaser, unless the property is subject to an Inland Revenue charge);

(*c*) if property (or income from it) which has become comprised in a settlement as a result of a chargeable transfer is applied for the benefit of the target;

(*d*) if a transfer has been made under the settled property provisions, and:

  (i) if the target is trustee of a settlement;

  (ii) if the target is entitled (whether beneficially or not) to an interest in possession in settled property; or

  (iii) if any settled property is applied for the benefit of the target at or after the time of the transfer in question; or

(*e*) in the case of a transfer on death:

  (i) if the target is a personal representative of a deceased person;

  (ii) if the target is trustee of a settlement in which was comprised property to the value of which inheritance tax is attributable; or

  (iii) if property (or income from it) which was comprised in a settlement at the time of the transfer in question, is applied for the benefit of the target.

The terms 'trustee' and 'personal representative' include anyone who has acted in relation to the property so as to become liable as executor or trustee.

It may be noted that, where a close company is entitled to an interest in possession in settled property, the participators in the company are treated by the Inheritance Tax Act 1984, s 101 as the persons beneficially entitled to that interest according to their respective rights and interests in the company. This is illustrated by *Powell-Cotton v IRC* [1992] STC 625.

In addition to an indemnity against liability under ss 199 to 201 the purchaser should also seek protection against diminution in the value of the target's assets through the imposition of the Inland Revenue charge for unpaid tax under the Inheritance Tax Act 1984, s 237.

There is also the question of any adjustment to the burden of inheritance tax. There is, of course, nothing to prevent the parties to any transaction agreeing how the burden of tax is to be borne. Moreover, ss 211 and 212 may give other persons rights against the target in this respect. In particular:

(a) under s 211(3) where personal representatives have paid inheritance tax arising on a death and an Inland Revenue charge is imposed on any property, the personal representatives may in certain circumstances require repayment to them of the tax by the person in whom the property is vested; and

(b) by virtue of s 212(1) and subject to certain exceptions, where a person is liable for inheritance tax attributable to the value of any property, he has the power, whether or not the property is vested in him, to raise the amount of the tax (either for payment or recoupment) by a sale or mortgage of, or terminable charge on, the property.

A purchaser may therefore wish to seek protection against any diminution of the assets of the target through any claims against the target in respect of adjustment of the burden of inheritance tax and in particular against any claims arising under ss 211 and 212.

Ramsay and Furnisss v Dawson

The 'emerging principle' or 'new approach' in *Ramsay (WT) Ltd v IRC* (1981) 54 TC 101 and *Furniss (Inspector of Taxes) v Dawson* (1984) 55 TC 324 has created uncertainty in a number of areas which affect the purchase of private companies. It is a principle of statutory construction which requires an intervening transaction with no commercial purpose inserted for tax avoidance reasons into a composite transaction to be disregarded so that the same tax consequences are to be taken to follow from the composite transaction as would follow in the absence of the intervening transaction. It cannot create a liability simply because of the existence of a tax avoidance motive where that liability would not otherwise exist (*Countess Fitzwilliam v IRC* [1992] STC 185). It is not a general anti-avoidance measure. The principle may affect the transaction itself and the taxation of the target both before and after the acquisition.

The limits of the principle have to some degree been resolved through the further cases which have now been decided by the House of Lords (notably *Craven v White, IRC v Bowater Property Developments Ltd, Baylis v Gregory* [1988] 3 WLR 423 and *Ensign Tankers (Leasing) Limited v Stokes (Inspector of Taxes)* [1992] STC 226), but the extent to which the principle applies to stamp duty and to value added tax remains uncertain (*Ingram v IRC* [1985] STC 848 and *Raceshire Ltd v Commissioners & Customs & Excise* MAN/91/1135, respectively). Some practical guidance to the circumstances in which the Revenue had indicated the principle would be sought to be applied prior to these decisions can be found in the correspondence with the Revenue in 1985 published by the Institute of Chartered Accountants in England and Wales (TR588). This must now be considered out of date in some respects, particularly in the light of *Shepherd (Inspector of Taxes) v Lyntress Ltd, News International plc v Shepherd (Inspector of Taxes)* [1989] STC 617, considered below.

Furniss v *Dawson* was, of course, itself a case relating to the acquisition of a private company. In cases where the parties are seeking to avoid tax the principle may apply to disregard steps inserted into the transaction for no commercial purpose other than the avoidance of tax. Purchasers will be concerned to know whether the target has been involved in any transactions to which the principle might apply and a warranty should be sought (see the Agreement for Sale, Sched 4, warranty (p 17). Vendors may wish to give this warranty 'to the best of their knowledge and belief' rather than accepting absolute liability.

If the target has accrued capital losses, the purchaser may wish, after the acquisition, to transfer assets to the target before they are disposed of, so as to ensure that gains are realised in the target against which the losses can be off set. This was the situation which fell to be considered in *News International plc v Shepherd (Inspector of Taxes)*. News International plc transferred holdings of quoted shares to its wholly-owned subsidiary, Lyntress Limited. By reason of what is now the Taxation of Chargeable Gains Act 1992, s 171, no chargeable gain accrued on the transfer. Lyntress Limited subsequently sold the shares on the London Stock Exchange, realising chargeable gains against which it claimed to set carried forward capital losses. The related appeal in *Shepherd (Inspector of Taxes) v Lyntress Ltd* concerned the artificial manner in which the company had acquired the capital losses. The taxpayer was successful in each case. The High Court rejected the Revenue's contention that there were composite transactions including steps whose purpose was not commercial but the avoidance of tax, but held that the statutory provisions for the transfer of capital asseis between members of the same group of companies contemplaced that 'group relief' for capital losses should thereby be available. It is important, however, that beneficial ownership of the asset should not have been lost at the time of its transfer to the capital loss company (see *Wood Preservation Ltd v Prior* [1969] 1 WLR 1077 and *O'Connor (Inspector of Taxes) v J Sainsbury plc* [1991] STC 318). In the correspondence with the Institute of Chartered Accountants referred to above, the Revenue stated it would be unlikely that the *Ramsay* principle would be invoked where the losses were a 'relatively insubstantial element in the acquisition, as evidenced by the circumstances in which they were utilised and the commerciality of the circumstances surrounding the acquisition'. This is clearly too narrow a statement of the law. Nevertheless, while a warranty as to the existence of capital losses may be given, the prudent vendor will not give any warranty as to their availability to off-set any particular gain. Similar considerations will apply to the use of excess management expenses in investment companies.

Chapter 13

Taxation Warranties and Indemnities

No consistent and logical treatment of tax in agreements for the sale of private companies has yet evolved. Given the complexity and arbitrary nature of the legislation concerned, it is doubtful if it ever will.

Even though an accountants' investigation may have been commissioned, the purchaser is likely to require assurances in one form or another:

(*a*) that the target has complied with all appropriate tax legislation;

(*b*) that the latest accounts contain proper provision for taxation;

(*c*) that there are no surprises (perhaps in the form of disguised base values);

(*d*) that the target has not been involved in any of the transactions which anti-avoidance legislation or case law has rendered dangerous;

(*e*) that the target has all the reliefs and allowances which should be available to it; and

(*f*) that the target is not going to be visited with liability to pay tax assessed on others (eg liability under the Taxation of Chargeable Gains Act 1992, ss 190 and 191 to pay tax in respect of chargeable gains incurred by other group members).

The purchaser's advisers will therefore wish to obtain warranties and indemnities from the vendors to cover all these eventualities. Faced with the bewildering array of potential liabilities it is possible to overreact. In a famous phrase Lord Davey remarked that 'every grocer's shop takes power to bridge the mighty Zambezi'. Those acquiring grocer's shops today are more inclined to suspect the proprietor of having issued quoted Eurobonds or having dual resident status. It is a foolhardy purchaser, however, who does not seek to obtain as much information and protection as he reasonably can in respect of the taxation of the target. What form should this protection take? In relation to some taxation matters, warranties are clearly appropriate and in relation to others an indemnity is more suitable, but in many cases the selection of warranty or indemnity (or both) to cover a potential liability is largely a matter of taste.

Warranties should be taken with regard to the taxation attributes of the target's assets as indemnities will not normally be appropriate. The accounts will show the assets at a valuation. Is this valuation the same as the base value for the purpose of corporation tax on chargeable gains? There may be many reasons why it is not so and a simple example arises in connection with the replacement of business assets. Suppose the target has at some time in the past disposed of a branch office for £200,000 realising a capital gain of £100,000. It has not become chargeable to tax on this gain, because the whole of the consideration has been used to purchase a new office for £200,000. Under the provisions of the Taxation of Chargeable Gains Act 1992, s 152 the gain is 'rolled over' and the acquisition cost of the new offices is deemed to be not £200,000 but £100,000 so that upon the sale of the new offices for £300,000 a chargeable gain of £200,000 (not £100,000) will arise. This fact is not disclosed in negotiations and when the target comes to dispose of the office in due course the purchaser is aggrieved. He looks to his indemnities but finds they do not relate to gains made by the target after completion. Why indeed should the vendors indemnify the target against tax on gains made after completion when they will not have the benefit of these gains? The purchaser is, however, objecting to the fact that he was not aware of the amount of the contingent liability to tax which was inherent in the asset in question. A warranty that the base cost was the same as the value attributed to the office in the accounts would have given him a remedy against the vendors.

Warranties are also appropriate where the purchaser wishes to be assured that the target has or has not taken any particular action. A warranty that all taxation returns have been made accurately and on time and that all taxation has been properly and punctually paid is of obvious value. The purchaser will not wish to be involved with back duty claims with the Inland Revenue or with PAYE or VAT audits, even in relation to quite small sums. The loss of management time can be substantial, particularly if key employees of the target leave as a result of the acquisition so that the facts have to be mastered by incoming staff. It may be said that the purchaser is adequately protected if the target is indemnified by the vendors against the tax due and against penalties, costs and interest relating to taxation, but in practice this is not the case. A more satisfactory result may well be achieved by asking for a warranty; if the vendors have knowledge of a dispute they are unlikely to deceive the purchaser by giving a false warranty (indeed if they do, they may consider their liability under the Financial Services Act 1986, s 47) and it is usually better for the purchaser to force a disclosure so that he knows the worst before the acquisition and can make appropriate arrangements (including perhaps a specific indemnity) to enable him to deal with the problem.

An indemnity is appropriate where the target is liable to pay tax arising from the income or gains of others. As explained above, under the Taxation of Chargeable Gains Act 1992, s 190 the target may be made liable for chargeable gains realised by other members of the same group. A warranty that no such chargeable gains had occurred would not normally be acceptable by itself. The purchaser is not, in fact, concerned to see that the primary liability has not arisen; he is concerned to ensure that the target is properly indemnified against the liability. Indemnities are also useful when obtaining protection against liability under anti-avoidance sections. It is often simpler to take an indemnity rather than to attempt to draft a warranty. Of course, if it is likely that the target has entered into tax avoidance transactions then warranties may be more appropriate, as they may bring out disclosures.

In many cases, however, it will be a matter of taste whether a warranty or an indemnity is taken and the choice of warranties (in addition to the general indemnity) included in the Agreement for Sale (Chapter 16) is to that extent arbitrary. Neither does the selection pretend to be exhaustive or mandatory in all cases. The choice of what protection to demand must be left to the individual practitioner in the circumstances of the particular transaction with which he or she is concerned. For example, no specialised type of company (eg an insurance company) is considered.

Tax warranties

Examples of tax warranties are given in the Agreement for Sale, Sched 4. One basic warranty is that the provisions in the latest audited accounts are adequate. The warranties relate to general taxation matters ((1) to (5)); distributions and payments ((6) to (11)); losses ((12) to (13)); close companies ((14)); anti-avoidance clearances and elections ((15) to (17)); capital assets ((18) to (28)); claims, elections and clearances ((29) to (31)); miscellaneous matters ((32) to (34)); taxation of employees and agents ((35) to (39)/(40)); stamp duty ((40) to (42)); VAT ((43)) and inheritance tax ((44) to (45)). It is unlikely that all the warranties will be appropriate in any particular transaction.

One problem in formulating suggestions is the question of how specific to make the warranties. Is it, for instance, satisfactory to take a simple warranty that the target has properly operated the PAYE system? Or is it desirable to go further and ask for a warranty that tax has been properly deducted from, for example, all payments as compensation for loss of office (Income and Corporation Taxes Act 1988, s 148) and in respect of all benefits in kind (Income and Corporation Taxes Act 1988, s 143)? Apart from the comfort of seeing the likely problem areas written down in the agreement, the advantage of being specific is that it focuses the minds of the vendors on the point in question and may lead to a disclosure. Most practitioners acting for purchasers will yield to the temptation to use general words and then go to the specific 'without prejudice to the generality of the foregoing'.

The drafting problem of general and specific wording also arises because one warranty tends to overlap with another. For instance, it is normal to take a warranty that the latest audited accounts contain full provision for all tax liability. This general warranty will overlap with many other specific warranties (eg that all claims for group relief have been properly made) but the advantage of the specific warranty remains. An element of repetition is inevitable.

Tax indemnity

The established method of giving tax indemnities has been for the vendor to indemnify the target itself by a deed given at completion containing perhaps both a general indemnity and specific indemnities, although specific indemnities are now less commonly required. Some practitioners preferred to include the indemnities in the sale contract and to indemnify the purchaser against any depletion or diminution in the assets of the target. However, for the reasons discussed below in the final section of this chapter, it has become usual for the benefit of a deed of indemnity to include the purchaser, so that payments made by the vendor to the purchaser in respect of tax liabilities of the target may fall to be treated for tax purposes as adjustments to the purchase price. The Agreement for Sale adopts this method and extends it. The Agreement contains, in Sched 4, paras 1 and 2 the vendor's agreement to make to the purchaser payments by way of reduction in the consideration in respect of 'relevant taxation claims' falling on the target (see p 313). The Agreement takes the process to its logical conclusion by excluding the target altogether from the benefit of the indemnity.

Schedule 4, para 2(A) contains a general indemnity designed to cover any liability incurred before completion which is not reflected in the audited accounts of the target, excluding only liabilities incurred in the ordinary course of business since the date of the last accounts (see the definition of 'relevant taxation claim' in para 1(6)). The vendor will seek to add further exclusions as appropriate to the circumstances of the particular transaction.

Tax treatment of payments under warranties and indemnities

If the vendor is called upon to make any payment to the purchaser or the target under the warranties or indemnities he will wish to be satisfied that any payment goes to reduce the consideration which he is treated as having received for the purposes of computing any capital gain. In respect of payments under the warranties statutory provision is made in the Taxation of Chargeable Gains Act 1992, s 49(1)(c) which provides that:

In the first instance no allowance shall be made . . . for any contingent liability in respect of a warranty or representation made on a disposal by way of sale or lease of any property other than land.

The section goes on to provide that if any contingency subsequently becomes enforceable the capital gains tax computation will be adjusted accordingly. Where the disposal is for cash this will result in a repayment of tax or a discharge of any outstanding liability. The application of the section is, however, not clear where the consideration is one to which the Taxation of Chargeable Gains Act 1992, s 138 applies as no actual tax will have become payable as a result of the sale. In these circumstances it is understood that any payment under the warranties will serve to increase the base cost of the consideration shares on any ultimate disposal. In either event the purchaser's position, ie his overall acquisition cost of the target, will be adjusted correspondingly.

In the case of indemnities the position is less clear. Indemnities may be given to the target although provision may be made for the sums so indemnified to be paid to the purchaser (particularly in the case of a sale of less than a 100 per cent interest in the target). In the past the Revenue seem to have allowed any payments under the indemnities made to the target as a deduction against the vendor's consideration for the purposes of calculating the capital gain. The position is far from clear and it may nevertheless be open to the purchaser to argue that the fact that the company has received indemnities against specific matters cannot affect the position or reduce the amount which is treated as having been paid for the acquisition of the shares in the target.

Whatever the position of the vendor, it is, however, generally accepted that a right of indemnity enforceable by the target against the vendor is an asset for capital gains tax purposes falling within the

Taxation of Chargeable Gains Act 1992, s 22 so that any amount received by the target will be subject to tax. This results from the decision in *Zim Properties Ltd v Procter* (1984) 58 TC 371 (and see also Inland Revenue Extra Statutory Concession D33) that a right to bring an action to seek to enforce a claim that was neither frivolous nor vexatious, where the right could be turned to account by negotiating a compromise yielding a capital sum, constituted an asset for the purposes of capital gains tax. Where the right of action is acquired on or after 10 March 1981 (when what is now the Taxation of Chargeable Gains Act 1992, s 17 came into effect), and its holder (as will generally be the case) gave no consideration to acquire it, it will be treated as acquired without cost. The result of this is that the target's net of tax receipt from an indemnity payment would be reduced and in order to provide a full indemnity the payment would need to be increased. A vendor will, not unnaturally, be unwilling to gross up for tax any payment made to the target under an indemnity and the prudent vendor should, indeed, refuse to give any indemnity which has that effect. Since any payment made to the purchaser in respect of a tax liability of the target would seem not to be subject to tax in the purchaser's hands (although it would correspondingly reduce the purchaser's acquisition cost for the target's shares) the Agreement for Sale, Sched 4, paras 1 and 2 provides for the vendor instead to make payments to the purchaser by way of reduction in the consideration in respect of relevant taxation claims. If such payments are subject to tax in the purchaser's hands (which it is not thought to be the case) then it is submitted that it is appropriate for these to be grossed up and para 1(5)(ii) has this effect.

Cases arise in which provision must be made for a non-tax liability which is expected to fall on the target but which is unquantified at the time of the sale. As a condition of the sale the purchaser may insist that the target receives an indemnity against this payment, but if this liability is itself deductible in calculating the target's liability to tax, then it may be more satisfactory for the vendor to agree to make payment, as in respect of tax liabilities, direct to the purchaser. Not only will this have the effect of ensuring that this amount is deducted for the purposes of calculating the vendor's capital gains tax bill, but, because the target retains the benefit of the tax deduction, the payment from vendor to purchaser can be calculated by reference to the net, after tax, diminution in the target's assets.

Chapter 14

Europe

Cross-border acquisitions have assumed growing prominence in Europe in recent years. The approach of the deadline for completion of the European Community single internal market has provided a strong stimulus for takeover activity. Cross-border activity has been increasing, with EC companies venturing abroad to secure competitive advantages in preparation for the single market. Although the level of acquisitions by United Kingdom companies in Europe has recently fallen, the United Kingdom remains among the leading countries whose companies are making European acquisitions.

Notwithstanding this increase in activity, European acquisitions continue to be the subject of a number of legal difficulties and there are significant differences in the laws and regulations applicable to acquisitions in different European countries. These differences are being reduced to a certain extent, in the case of EC Member States at least, as a result of the EC harmonisation programme. However, the harmonisation of company law and the regulations governing takeovers is unlikely to be the panacea it might appear to be. The principal legislative instruments employed by the EC in this area are Directives. These are binding on Member States as to the result to be achieved within a stated period, but it is left to national governments to decide on the method by which they are transformed into national law. As a result, there are often significant differences between the measures enacted to implement Directives in individual Member States. In addition, the measures proposed by the EC Commission to level the playing field for takeovers across the European Community would apply only to public companies or, in the case of the proposed 13th Directive on takeovers and other general bids, only to listed companies, and not to the acquisition of private companies. Furthermore, the field of acquisitions, especially those involving public takeovers, is one in which national business culture and practices play a role which is at least as important as the strict legal

231

requirements. The differences between the regimes governing acquisitions in the various countries of Europe, in many cases, have more to do with differing attitudes towards ownership and control of companies, than differences in technical legal requirements.

This chapter gives an outline of some of the most significant considerations which are likely to be relevant in the case of an acquisition by a United Kingdom company of a target incorporated in another European jurisdiction. It is not a substitute for local advice in relation to any particular transaction or its implementation, but it may be helpful in drawing attention to potential problem areas in order that they can be considered and, if necessary, taken into account in the planning of the acquisition at an early stage.

The considerations mentioned in this chapter will in general be applicable to the acquisition of a target which is legally the equivalent, in the jurisdiction concerned, of an unquoted public company, as well as a target which is the local equivalent of a private company in the United Kingdom. In addition to the direct acquisition of a target incorporated in another European jurisdiction, the acquisition by a United Kingdom company of a United Kingdom target with European subsidiaries or shareholders may require compliance with the laws and regulations of the jurisdiction in which those subsidiaries or shareholders are located.

The conduct of acquisitions of unquoted companies (whether the equivalent of a private company in the United Kingdom or a plc) is not generally the subject of specific regulation in Europe, in contrast to the United Kingdom, where the rules of the City Code apply to acquisitions of all public companies resident in the United Kingdom, the Channel Islands or the Isle of Man (whether listed or not) and to some private companies. There are, however, some exceptions. For example, in Belgium, the Banking Commission regulates all acquisitions of companies whose shares are regarded as being in public hands, in Germany, the non-statutory Takeover Recommendations of the Advisory Committee of Stock Exchange Experts apply to all public offers for AGs, and in Portugal, public offers for all companies whose shares have at any time been held by the general public are subject to special rules.

GENERAL CONSIDERATIONS

Share acquisitions are, in general, much more common than acquisitions of business assets in Europe. Share acquisitions tend to be simpler transactions than transactions involving the transfer of individual assets and liabilities. A share acquisition is less likely to involve the need to obtain consents from third parties (although changes of control may require consents, for example, under financing or joint venture agreements), whereas third parties who have contracts with the target are likely to need to consent to the transfer of assets and liabilities by the target in order for the transfer to be effective. However, there may in some cases be tax advantages in structuring the transaction as an acquisition of business assets. In addition, in the case of a share acquisition, whereas the purchaser will acquire the target with all its liabilities in addition to its assets, if the purchaser buys assets, it will be able to choose which assets it acquires and will normally be able to avoid assuming the target's liabilities, which it may be difficult to quantify. This rule is not universal, however. In the case of assets acquisitions in Germany, if the purchaser acquires all or substantially all the business assets of the vendor company, it will also acquire joint and several liability for all the vendor company's debts and obligations, by operation of law.

A further method by which an acquisition can be effected is by way of statutory or legal merger. To effect a legal merger, the purchaser must use a company incorporated in the jurisdiction of incorporation of the target. The detailed formalities of legal mergers vary from country to country but, in general, legal mergers are normally achieved either by the absorption of the target, or the contribution of its assets and liabilities, into the acquisition vehicle, with shareholders in the target receiving shares in the acquisition vehicle, or the merger of the target with the acquisition vehicle into a new company set up for the purpose, with the shareholders in each of the merged companies receiving shares in the new company. In each case, the assets of the companies involved must be valued by an accountant, who may be required to be independent, and the terms of the merger must be set out in a formal merger agreement which must be put to shareholders and approved by resolution requiring (depending on the jurisdiction and the type of company concerned) a majority of two-thirds or 75 per cent in favour. However, acquisition by legal merger is relatively rare. In some countries, such as France and the Netherlands, this is due to the tax treatment of the operation and, in others, it is due to the degree of the formalities involved and to the time required to complete the merger. For example, in Italy, Norway, Portugal and Spain, a waiting period, ranging from one to three months, must normally elapse after the passing of the necessary shareholders' resolutions, before completion. In some countries, creditors have rights to require that their debts are either guaranteed or secured prior to the merger becoming effective.

In the case of a share acquisition, the contract will be made between the purchaser and the shareholders of the target. Most companies in Europe are privately held and, in many cases, will be held by a limited number of members of the same family. Alternatively, the target may be a subsidiary of another company. In most cases, therefore, the number of shareholders will be small and it will be possible for the purchaser to acquire the target by means of a private contract between itself and each of the selling shareholders. This contract will normally contain warranties, indemnities and other protections concerning the target, its assets and liabilities and its business, in favour of the purchaser, and is likely to afford the purchaser the greatest level of protection. However, traditionally, acquisition agreements in European jurisdictions have been a great deal shorter and simpler than would be normal in the United Kingdom. While this is changing, and longer Anglo-Saxon forms are now being adopted, presenting the vendors with a standard United Kingdom style draft acquisition agreement could be counterproductive, especially in the case of an acquisition of a small family held target.

If the number of selling shareholders is large, it may be logistically impracticable to arrange for all the selling shareholders to become parties to a single agreement, particularly if this is to contain extensive warranties and other protections in favour of the purchaser. It may therefore be necessary to send out a circular to the target's shareholders. In this case, it will be necessary to investigate the relevant local regulations for the distribution of circulars. The rules governing the information to be made available to prospective investors, and imposing liability if that information is incomplete or misleading, will be relevant. Additional rules may be applicable if the consideration payable by the purchaser includes shares or other securities. As mentioned in Chapter 3 (p 22), under English law, a circular offer to shareholders of a target is likely to constitute an investment advertisement within the meaning of the Financial Services Act 1986, s 57 and, if so, subject to certain exceptions, may not be issued unless it is issued by an authorised person, or unless its contents have been approved by an authorised person.

The governing law of the acquisition agreement is a matter of major importance which should be decided at an early stage. It may be thought that the law of the jurisdiction of incorporation of the target will be the most suitable. However, the legal rules affecting the validity and enforceability of the provisions of the acquisition agreement, the remedies available for breaches of warranty and the limitation periods within which claims may be brought vary in each jurisdiction. It is not safe to proceed on the basis that these rules will be more or less the same as those applicable under English law. For example, in Germany, in the absence of express agreement to the contrary, a limitation period for warranty claims of six months will be applicable. By contrast, in Italy, in the absence of an express provision on time limits, warranties will last for ten years under Italian law. It may be the case that, in the absence of specific provision, damages for breach of warranty will not be payable after completion of the acquisition. The implications of the choice of law will need to be carefully reviewed. Even if English law is chosen to govern the acquisition agreement, where the target is incorporated in another European jurisdiction, local law will remain relevant to the target's constitution, business and tax position and will still need to be investigated and, if possible, warranted by the vendors.

HEADS OF AGREEMENT

Once agreement in principle has been reached between the vendors and the purchaser on the basic terms and structure of the acquisition, the parties may wish to record these terms in writing, as an intermediate step, before the conclusion of the formal acquisition agreement. It may be felt that heads of agreement will serve to reinforce the commitment of the parties to the transaction and to identify and avoid any possible misunderstandings between the parties as to the major terms. In the United Kingdom, heads of agreement (which may also be called a letter of intent or memorandum of understanding) are normally non-binding. One reason is that settling heads of agreement which create legal rights and obligations would be time consuming and the time is generally better spent in negotiating the definitive acquisition agreement. Furthermore, one party may find particular terms in heads of agreement invoked against it by the other party insisting at a later stage in the negotiations that those terms, which may have been only briefly described in the heads, be included in the definitive agreement in a form which accords with the other party's interpretation.

When contemplating heads of agreement in connection with the acquisition of a target in Europe, however, United Kingdom purchasers should proceed with caution. The laws of a number of countries in Europe (for example, Belgium, France, Germany and Luxembourg) impose on parties to negotiations the obligation to negotiate in good faith and not to break off negotiations except for good reason. This is directly contrary to the position under English law, as set forth by Lord Ackner in the case of *Walford v Miles* [1992] 2 WLR 174, when he said:

The concept of a duty to carry on negotiations in good faith is inherently repugnant to the adversarial position of the parties when involved in negotiations. Each party to the negotiations is entitled to pursue his (or her) own interest, so long as he avoids making misrepresentations ... A duty to negotiate in good faith is as unworkable in practice as it is inherently inconsistent with the position of a negotiating party.

In a number of European jurisdictions, a party that breaks off negotiations, after having reached agreement in principle with another party, may find itself liable to pay damages to that other party. In some jurisdictions, actions for specific performance may be possible. This can be the case even if heads of agreement are expressed to be 'subject to contract', which should be sufficient to avoid the creation of legal relations under English law, or are qualified in some other similar manner. While, in these jurisdictions, the obligation to negotiate in good faith is not dependent on the conclusion of heads of agreement, the signature of heads of agreement will be evidence that agreement in principle has in fact been reached.

INVESTIGATION OF THE TARGET

The scope of the investigation to be carried out by the purchaser and its advisers will need to be agreed with the vendors. Although the First EC Company Law Directive, which has been implemented by all Member States, sets basic standards for information to be publicly filed by companies with commercial registries, most of the information which a purchaser will wish to review before proceeding formally with the acquisition will not be available from public sources. Such information as is publicly filed may well be out of date. However, vendors and particularly the owners of small and medium-sized family controlled companies may be unwilling to disclose details of the target's business until they are certain that the purchaser will buy the company. This is especially so if the purchaser could be regarded as a competitor.

A balance has to be struck between these competing interests. For example, it is normal practice for a purchaser or its accountants and lawyers to be allowed access to information on the target's business, provided that the purchaser and its advisers sign an agreement to keep the information thus disclosed strictly confidential. The smaller the amount of information made available to the purchaser, the greater the protection the purchaser should seek from the vendors by means of warranties. The purchaser may also seek to defer payment of part of the consideration in these circumstances. As regards accounts of the target which the purchaser may obtain, while the Fourth EC Company Law Directive, which includes rules as to the format and content of company accounts (including a requirement that such accounts must be audited and show a 'true and fair view of the company's assets, liabilities, profits, losses and financial position'), has now been implemented in all EC Member States, the Directive does not deal with accounting standards and practices. These vary substantially between the countries of Europe and, in a number of countries, the content of a company's published accounts is influenced by the objective of producing information for tax authorities. Such information will therefore need to be interpreted with particular care.

EXCHANGE CONTROL, FOREIGN INVESTMENT CONTROL AND INDUSTRY CONTROLS

Exchange control

Exchange control restrictions on acquisitions by purchasers from EC Member States have largely been abolished by EC countries, as a result of a number of Directives on Capital Movements, and have been replaced by requirements for notification of the transactions concerned to appropriate regulatory authorities. However, permission is still required for some direct investments in certain countries. These include Ireland, Portugal and Greece.

In Norway, no exchange control permission is required where the shares are acquired through a Norwegian broker (but the broker must report changes in ownership to the Central Bank) and, in Sweden, no permission is required for direct investments, but any cash payment must be made through a Swedish exchange bank.

Once the acquisition itself has been completed, the purchaser will need to ensure that dividends and profits declared or earned by the target can be remitted to the acquiror in its home country. Local rules in the jurisdiction of incorporation of the target, and any other jurisdictions where the target carries on business, will need to be checked to establish the extent of any consents that may be required.

Foreign investment control and industry controls

An overseas acquisition may be restricted by rules on foreign ownership which apply generally, or which are applicable to the particular industry in which the target operates. In addition, in some countries, there are special rules applicable to the ownership of particular types of asset eg land. For example, in Switzerland, a law, known as the 'lex Friedrich', regulates the acquisition of certain companies holding Swiss land and also restricts the direct foreign acquisition of Swiss land. Foreigners are not permitted to acquire any interest in a company the objects of which are directly related to real estate business. Where Swiss real estate accounts for more than one-third of the market value of a company's assets, an acquisition by a foreign purchaser of more than one-third of the shares or voting rights in the company will require prior authorisation from the relevant cantonal authority.

Furthermore, certain types of industry are often subject to close regulation which affects acquisitions by any purchaser, whether local or foreign. Examples include banking, financial services and insurance, defence, the media and utilities (water, gas, electricity etc). The precise forms of these regulations vary widely, and may require the purchaser to obtain prior consent before the acquisition will be permitted, or may allow the acquisition to be made without specific consent, but leave the target open to having its authorisation or licence to operate in the relevant sector revoked as a result of the change of control. It will also be important to review the target's corporate constitution to establish whether it contains restrictions on the acquisition of shares by foreigners (these are common in Sweden, for example, although in the course of being phased out) or the percentage of voting rights that may be exercised by foreigners.

The manner in which the controls on acquisitions by foreigners and industry controls are implemented in practice is generally much more important than their mere existence and may be dependent on the political climate in the country concerned at the time. In the United Kingdom, for example, the Government could have effectively blocked the takeover of Jaguar plc by Ford in 1989 through the exercise of the powers attached to the 'golden share' issued to the Secretary of State at the time of Jaguar's privatisation. However, in keeping with the Government's free market approach, these powers were not invoked.

In many countries, approval or exemption is readily available in relation to most industries. In other cases (eg banking and the media), in several countries, it is unlikely that a cross-border acquisition of a major company would be permitted in normal circumstances, even where legislation does not specifically restrict acquisitions by foreigners. Indeed, in the case of some industries (eg defence), governmental and municipal contracts, or the licences which are required to carry on specific operations or to sell certain products, are so important that the authorities have considerable influence even if they lack specific legal powers to regulate a particular transaction. The EC has recognised that some activities are so sensitive that Member States should be permitted to exercise controls, even as regards acquisitions by EC resident investors, on the grounds of ensuring public security, plurality of the media, prudential rules for financial institutions and any other 'legitimate interest' accepted by the EC Commission.

MERGER CONTROL AND COMPETITION LAW

As described in Chapter 4, the largest acquisitions are subject to control at European Community level. Under the EC Merger Regulation, mergers and joint ventures involving participants whose aggregate turnover (both worldwide and within the EC) meets the specified thresholds must be pre-notified to the EC Commission. Where these thresholds are met (and the transaction therefore deemed to have a 'Community dimension'), the EC Commission will in principle have exclusive jurisdiction, and the transaction will not be subject to control at the national level. The most important exception to this is the ability of the Commission to permit a Member State to exercise jurisdiction where the transaction threatens to create or strengthen a dominant position in that State. Conversely, transactions which are not regarded as having a Community dimension will remain subject to national control, subject to the right of a Member State to request the EC Commission to intervene. The Merger Regulation can also have an extraterritorial effect: acquisitions made outside the EC can be subject to review by the EC Commission if the turnover of the parties involved within the EC is sufficient to meet the relevant threshold specified in the Merger Regulation.

Where the transaction does not fall within the jurisdiction of the EC Commission (and the turnover thresholds in the Merger Regulation are high), national merger controls may be relevant. The approach of European countries to merger control varies enormously. Outside the United Kingdom, merger control is highly developed in Germany, but is limited in Denmark, the Netherlands, Norway and Switzerland and did not exist at all in Italy (except in relation to newspaper mergers) until 1990.

The legislation comes in various forms, and may provide for the control of acquisitions and mergers on competition grounds alone, or may provide for other factors, such as considerations of industrial or social policy or wider public interest, to be taken into account by the national authorities. The new Belgian competition law, which will come into force on 1 April 1993, provides that the Competition Council may allow a transaction to proceed if the likely improvements to production or distribution, the promotion of technological or economic progress or improvements to the competitive structure of the market outweigh the drawbacks arising from the restriction of competition. By contrast, in the Netherlands, only competition issues will be relevant.

In some countries, such as Germany, if certain criteria specified in the legislation are fulfilled, prior notification to the national authorities is mandatory. The legislation may provide that, if no notice is issued by the local competition authority that the transaction is prohibited within a specified waiting period, it may then proceed. In other cases, there is no requirement for prior notification to the competition authority, but the authority concerned has power to prohibit, or require the parties to modify, any transaction which it considers, for example, would result in the creation of a dominant position in the local market, or the infringement of other applicable principles laid down in the national legislation.

The effect of merger control legislation on the proposed acquisition in each country where the target carries on business should be considered, not only in the jurisdiction of incorporation of the target. For example, German merger control law may apply to the acquisition by one foreign company of another, if one has a German subsidiary and the combined worldwide sales of the participants satisfy the tests in the Act against Restraints on Competition, regardless of the size of the German subsidiary. Where it is anticipated that a proposed transaction will give rise to difficulties with national merger control authorities, it may be possible to enter into negotiations with the authorities in advance of the acquisition and agree on the giving of undertakings by the purchaser as to the future conduct of the business of the purchaser and the target in the country concerned, or on a post-acquisition disposal programme, and thus avoid the authorities exercising their powers.

EMPLOYEE CONSIDERATIONS

Although, in the case of a share acquisition, there will be no change in the identity of the employer of the employees of the target, and therefore no effect on the contracts of employment of the target's employees, employment legislation in the countries in which the target carries on business will be relevant to the ongoing business of the target. Employment legislation should be investigated, particularly if the purchaser intends to reorganise the business of the target

and implement redundancies following completion of the acquisition. Minimum wage and maximum working hours legislation is in
force in most EC Member States. Collective agreements with trade
unions may be relevant, and may impose duties to inform and
consult with recognised trade unions or works councils in relation to
proposed reductions in manning levels. In a number of countries,
employees of companies beyond a certain size have the right to board
representation or to be consulted on the appointment of board
members.

Immigration rules and work permit requirements should also be
considered if the purchaser may wish to transfer key personnel to run
the target's business after completion of the acquisition. In some
countries, legislation requires that a certain proportion of the
directors of local companies must be local residents or nationals.

TAXATION

Tax rates vary among the countries of Europe to such an extent that
they may exercise a considerable influence on the price at which a
purchaser is prepared to proceed with an acquisition. Although the
EC Commission has from time to time expressed the desire to co-
ordinate and approximate national policies on all aspects of direct
corporate taxation, it is generally recognised that the goal of
harmonisation of the bases and rates of taxation across the Member
States to provide overall tax neutrality will be difficult to achieve.
The EC has, however, adopted a number of Directives which will
have consequences for cross-border acquisitions, two of which are
referred to below. The level of pre-tax return from investment in one
country which is required to produce the same post-tax return for a
parent company in another country will vary according to the
country of incorporation of the purchaser and of the target, and the
discrepancies can be surprisingly large.

Any acquisition raises significant tax considerations. In relation to
the acquisition by a United Kingdom purchaser of a United Kingdom resident target, these are dealt with in Chapter 11. Where the
target is resident in another country, the problems are compounded
by the interaction of different tax regimes. Tax considerations will
influence the choice of the entity which legally acquires the shares in
the target (eg the purchaser itself, a domestic vehicle resident in the
purchaser's own jurisdiction, or a special acquisition vehicle incorporated in the target's jurisdiction). These will relate primarily to the
method of funding, but there may be other factors, such as the desire
to accumulate dividends from the target in the foreign jurisdiction to

avoid withholding tax (although in the EC, as a result of the Parent/ Subsidiary Companies Directive (90/435/EEC), profits of a subsidiary resident in one Member State distributed to a parent company resident in another are exempt from withholding tax), and the ability to benefit from reliefs which may apply in the target's jurisdiction. The vendor's tax position may now be assisted by the EC Directive on Cross-Border Mergers (90/434/EEC) which requires Member States to permit deferral of any tax charge on a disposal in particular circumstances, even where the purchaser is incorporated in another Member State.

If a special locally incorporated acquisition vehicle is used, this can be funded either by capital from the parent or by debt, either from third parties or from the parent. Consideration will need to be given to the treatment of dividend flows on any capital and the treatment of any interest paid, including its deductibility. An advantage of a locally incorporated acquisition vehicle is that, very often, interest expenses can be offset against the profits of the target, thus reducing the overall rate of tax in the target's jurisdiction. However, thin capitalisation rules may apply to restrict the amount of interest for which tax relief can be obtained.

An acquisition of a company in Europe will almost certainly involve foreign currency and, for a United Kingdom purchaser, there is therefore the possibility of a foreign currency exposure against sterling. To the extent that the acquisition in foreign currency is funded by borrowings in that currency, any currency gain or loss can be matched commercially. However, the hedging may not be effective for tax purposes. The treatment of exchange gains and losses varies from jurisdiction to jurisdiction, and there is no internationally recognised way of treating them. Any number of anomalies can arise resulting, for instance, in the taxability of exchange gains which were not recognised in a company's accounts and the non-deductibility of exchange losses which were so recognised. The United Kingdom tax regime is particularly notorious. Two Inland Revenue consultative documents, issued in 1989 and 1991, have produced proposals for reform, but it is not clear when, or indeed whether, legislation will be introduced. The taxation of exchange gains and losses is a difficult area and should be approached with particular care.

Where there is an immediate intention to dispose of a significant part of the target's assets in order to repay borrowings, care will need to be taken to ensure that any proceeds of sale from the local jurisdiction can be remitted without tax penalty back to the entity that incurred the borrowing. In addition to tax charges, there may be company law, exchange control and other regulatory constraints on the remittance of profits.

Where the purchaser wishes to pay for the acquisition with an issue of shares to the vendors, there may be tax advantages for the target's shareholders in being issued with shares in a company incorporated in the target's jurisdiction, in addition to shares in the purchaser, which are then paired with the shares in the purchaser. The paired shares are sometimes known as 'stapled stock'. In simple terms, paired shares are a method by which the shareholders in the target in another jurisdiction can receive shares in the purchaser, but be treated for tax purposes largely as if the purchaser was resident for tax purposes in their own country, and so avoid the possibility of a withholding tax on dividends or other tax charge in the purchaser's jurisdiction.

CONCLUSION

The legal and regulatory systems of the countries of Europe which impinge on the planning and execution of acquisitions differ substantially. They can constitute a major trap for an unwary purchaser who assumes that the rules that will apply will be the same as those in the United Kingdom. Any prospective purchaser contemplating an acquisition in Europe should seek advice on the local law and practice applicable to the particular transaction in question at the outset. Legal issues in the jurisdiction of the target and local practices may well affect the basic structure of the acquisition, as well as the conduct of the negotiations and the form of the final agreement itself.

Chapter 15

Insolvency

Special considerations apply where the vendor is insolvent. For the purpose of this chapter, a distinction is drawn between the case where an insolvency procedure (whether receivership, administration, liquidation or bankruptcy) has commenced, and that where such a procedure has not yet begun but is, or may be, imminent. In the first case, where shares in the target are one of the assets to be realised in the vendor's receivership or liquidation, the primary considerations for the purchaser are the validity of the transaction, the ability of the vendor to deliver good title to the shares in the target and the warranty and other protections he is able to achieve. In the second case, the sale of the target may be liable to avoidance or adjustment under the provisions of the Insolvency Act 1986 and the ability to recover in full for any breaches of warranty will be cast into doubt. This chapter deals mainly with the insolvency of a corporate vendor.

SHARES OR ASSETS?

The fundamental question where the vendor is in financial difficulties is whether to purchase the target's shares or its assets. In a corporate acquisition, the purchaser will protect itself from hidden liabilities by investigation and by taking warranties and indemnities from the vendor. Where a receiver, administrator or liquidator has already been appointed it is very unlikely, in practice, that warranties will be given as the well-advised office-holder will wish to minimise any personal liability in respect of the sale. Where the vendor's group is in financial difficulties but no appointment of a receiver, administrator or liquidator has yet occurred, the position will seem better since warranties will be available in the normal way, but the purchaser should bear in mind that his ability to recover his loss in the event of the vendor's subsequent insolvency is likely to be limited.

If warranties are unavailable or of questionable value, a share acquisition will be a risky transaction to a purchaser. He will not be protected from liabilities which have not been revealed by his own investigations and even if the target's business is sound he will have no way of knowing whether the target has been effectively ring-fenced from liabilities of other members of the vendor's group.

If the receivership, administration or liquidation has already commenced against the vendor, the purchaser will almost invariably try to purchase assets, rather than shares. He is then less dependent on warranties, since he will not inherit liabilities other than those he agrees to assume, and his primary concern will be to verify the value of the assets and to ensure that he will receive good title to them, free from any charges or other rights in favour of any other person. These are matters which, to a large extent, he will be able to verify by his own investigation and his need for warranties will be much diminished. The principal exception to the rule that on the acquisition of assets, a purchaser will not inherit liabilities, will arise where the business is sold as a going concern. In such a case its employees, with their accrued rights, will generally transfer automatically to the purchaser by virtue of the Transfer of Undertakings (Protection of Employment) Regulations 1981 (SI No 1794).

On instance in which it will be possible for a purchaser to reduce the risk associated with the purchase of shares is where the business of a company in receivership has been hived down to a new subsidiary with a view to its sale. The hive down of a business to a new subsidiary is commonly chosen to make more saleable those parts of a company in receivership which are capable of continuing as a going concern (see p 246). Even where there has been no hive down there may be occasions, nevertheless, when a purchaser decides to proceed with a share acquisition despite the lack of warranty protection. One situation might be where there is value in the target itself which cannot be transferred on an asset sale. For example, the target may have valuable licences under which the rights are not transferable (and will not terminate on change of control).

If a share acquisition is to proceed, the purchaser will place particular emphasis on conducting a detailed investigation of the target to satisfy himself, as far as possible, that there are no problems. The purchaser should ensure he has access to key management and is able to satisfy himself as to the extent of their knowledge. He may consider seeking formal representations from management, if it seems appropriate. It is highly desirable that he is able to approach third parties, such as customers, suppliers, bankers, and others with whom the target has important relationships.

Another practical precaution for the purchaser is in the negotiation of the acquisition agreement, where the best protection he may be able to achieve is a retention, either in an escrow account or as deferred consideration, of as much of the consideration as possible. However, since the receiver, liquidator or administrator will wish to realise assets as rapidly as possible, such a proposal may well be unwelcome. If consideration can be withheld, it will be necessary to negotiate an appropriate basis upon which the escrow is released or the deferred consideration payable, which will often be by reference to a closing balance sheet or post-acquisition profits. Alternatively, it may be appropriate to provide that the money is released if no claims relating to the period prior to the purchaser's ownership are made within an agreed period after completion. Such an arrangement can be structured to be similar in effect to a warranty. Where an escrow arrangement is established the purchaser should ensure that express rights of set-off for any claim by the purchaser against the deferred consideration are set out in the agreement to minimise reliance on any implied right, which will be less clear. While the statutory rights of set-off on liquidation are fairly wide it should be noted that to the extent that contractual rights of set-off exceed the statutory rules they will be invalid in the event of the vendor's liquidation (Insolvency Rules 1986, r 4.90). Difficulties may arise when seeking to establish the applicability of statutory set-off under r 4.90 and it may be preferable to express the vendor's entitlement to receive money from the escrow fund as a condition, rather than an asset against which the purchaser has a right of set-off. See Wood, *English and International Set-Off* (Sweet & Maxwell) (1989) and also the commentary to the Insolvency Act 1986, s 323 (the equivalent provision in personal bankruptcy) in *Muir Hunter on Personal Insolvency* (Sweet & Maxwell) (1988).

HIVE DOWN

In a hive down, the company in receivership (the parent) will transfer those parts of its business to be sold to one or more newly incorporated subsidiaries (a newco) in consideration either for the issue of shares in newco, or for a debt left outstanding from newco to the parent which is discharged by the purchaser on the subsequent sale of newco. A key feature is that newco will not inherit the liabilities of the parent except to the extent specifically assumed in the transfer, and so a purchaser will acquire the newco shares free of such liabilities. However, the receiver will only transfer to newco such title to the assets as the parent has; if the assets transferred to newco are subject to encumbrances or other charges, the purchaser will need to make arrangements, in its subsequent purchase of newco, for release of those encumbrances or must otherwise satisfy himself as to the burden they represent. It will be usual for the receiver to exclude personal liability on the sale, and also to exclude liability of the parent under any implied warranties (for instance, he will not sell as beneficial owner, and will seek to exclude implied terms under the Sale of Goods Act 1979).

A particular attraction of a hive down to a newco, rather than the direct purchase of the assets themselves, is the ability to transfer past trading losses of the parent with the business, to offset against newco's future profits. The transfer of losses to newco arises by virtue of the Income and Corporation Taxes Act 1988, s 343, which treats newco as succeeding to the parent's trade without any discontinuance of the trade occurring, provided that at any time within two years after the hive down at least a 75 per cent interest in the trade is owned by the same persons as such an interest belonged to at some time within a year before the hive down. This condition will be met provided that at least 75 per cent of the issued share capital of newco is beneficially owned by the parent when the hive down occurs. It will not be met if the parent has gone into liquidation, since a company in liquidation ceases to be the beneficial owner of its assets. Making arrangements for sale of newco prior to the hive down may also result in the parent ceasing to be the beneficial owner of its assets and deprive the parties of relief under s 343; the possible effect of any such arrangements on beneficial ownership should thus be considered (*Wood Preservation Ltd v Prior* [1969] 1 WLR 1077 and *O'Connor (Inspector of Taxes) v J Sainsbury plc* [1991] STC 318 — see p 194). After liquidation has commenced, since relief under s 343 is not available, there will be no tax advantage of a hive down over selling the assets themselves.

Even where s 343 relief applies, the parent's trading losses are not automatically available in full to newco; they will be reduced under s 343(4) by the excess of 'relevant liabilities' retained by the parent over the market value of its 'relevant assets' (see Income and Corporation Taxes Act 1988, s 344(5)–(12)). Section 343 also requires newco to assume the capital allowance position of the parent, which may not be to newco's advantage. Further, relief from stamp duty under the Finance Act 1930, s 42 on the transfer of dutiable assets to newco will generally not be available by reason of the Finance Act 1967, s 27(3). Therefore, stamp duty is likely to be a further cost of hive down as well as being payable on the sale of newco shares. On the sale of newco, a charge to corporation tax on chargeable gains in respect of capital assets transferred to it from the parent may be incurred by newco under the Taxation of Chargeable Gains Act 1992, s 178 (see p 204). A prospective purchaser of the parent's business must therefore consider carefully whether the availability of tax losses afforded by a hive down will be outweighed by any tax disadvantages.

The purchaser will wish to see how the employees of the business have been dealt with. Generally speaking, on the sale of a business as a going concern, the Transfer of Undertakings (Protection of Employment) Regulations 1981, reg 5 will operate to transfer automatically to the purchaser contracts of employment of all employees employed immediately before the transfer. Regulation 4, however, was designed to permit a receiver or administrator to hive down an undertaking or part of an undertaking to newco which can then be sold to the purchaser free of employees. Regulation 4 operated by postponing the date of the first transfer (the hiving down to newco of the undertaking or part) to the date of the second transfer (the disposal of newco or newco's business). If employees were dismissed between the first transfer and the second transfer by the receiver or the administrator they were not employed immediately before the date of the second transfer and so liability did not pass to newco or the purchaser. In *Litster v Forth Dry Dock and Engineering Company Ltd* [1990] 1 AC 546, however, the House of Lords decided that liability for the claims of employees employed immediately before a transfer, or who would have been so employed had they not been dismissed prior to the transfer for a reason connected with the transfer, is transferred to the transferee in the absence of an economic, technical or organisational reason involving a change in the workforce. While reg 4 was not discussed in *Litster* the effect of that decision appears to be to make reg 4 ineffective because employees dismissed between the hiving down and the disposal of newco are considered still to be employed immediately before the second transfer if their dismissals were not for an economic, technical or organisational reason involving a change in the workforce.

The economic need to dismiss the workforce in order to achieve a sale of the business is not an economic, technical or organisational reason for these purposes (*Wheeler v Patel and J Goulding Group of Companies* [1987] IRLR 211). Regulation 8 provides that a dismissal for a reason connected with the transfer is automatically unfair unless it is for an economic, organisational or technical reason involving a change in the workforce. The remedies available to unfairly dismissed employees are described in Chapter 6.

In other respects, the hivedown to newco is no more than a particular type of asset sale and all the usual difficulties common to such a transaction can arise; if the business depends on contractual arrangements, those contracts will need to be assigned, novated or sub-contracted to newco and it will be necessary to check that the contractual terms permit this. If the parent is in receivership, novation will be the preferred approach although where there are a large number of contracts, this can be a practical problem. Similarly, trademark, patent, software and other licences will need to be transferred and their transferability will be a matter which the purchaser must investigate. It will also be necessary to deal specifically with the different assets comprised in the hive down; in common with any business transfer, difficulties may be experienced in the assignment of leasehold premises, where any necessary landlord's consent to the assignment is withheld or delayed. The purchaser of newco will also wish to review the hive-down documentation to see what has been transferred to newco, and what arrangements the receiver has put in place for the collection of book debts, and transfer or use of any assets he will need to enable newco to carry on business. These may include freehold premises, plant and machinery, or property held under finance or hire purchase contracts. Furthermore, whilst the terms of hive down may exclude any liability to creditors, if these include important suppliers, the purchaser will wish to know that any delay in payment will not affect continuity of supply since he might otherwise find himself paying the creditor to preserve the business.

PRACTICAL POINTS — WHERE AN INSOLVENCY PROCEDURE HAS ALREADY COMMENCED AGAINST THE VENDOR

It is normal practice when embarking upon a company acquisition to conduct a search against the target at the Companies Registry (see p 100). A company search and searches of the central register of winding-up and administration petitions at the Companies Court should also be conducted against the vendor (tel: 071–936 6000/ 7328). Although in practice the purchaser will usually know whether he is dealing with a company against which some insolvency procedure has commenced, the results of these searches may alert the purchaser to the presentation of a petition for winding-up or administration of the vendor, the appointment of a receiver or other matters (such as charges over the assets of the vendor) where special considerations will be relevant.

Equally, where the vendors include private individuals, a search of the Land Charges Registry should be made to determine whether any bankruptcy petition or order has been registered against any vendor.

There are different types of insolvency procedure which may affect the vendor and each has slightly different implications for the purchaser. The law in this area is extensive and the following is intended as a summary only.

Receivers

A receiver may be appointed under a fixed charge given by the company over some or all of its assets. The receiver may be appointed either by the chargeholders under the charge, or by the court, or may be appointed by a mortgagee in exercise of his powers under the Law of Property Act 1925, s 101.

The receiver's appointment, authority and powers will vary depending upon whichever of the foregoing is the basis of his appointment. This section concentrates on the considerations for a purchaser dealing with a receiver appointed in respect of a corporate vendor under powers contained in a debenture secured by a fixed charge. Such a receiver is generally appointed in respect of specific assets and where there is no floating charge, unlike an administrative receiver who will be appointed under a floating charge, the latter is appointed in respect of the whole of the company's property and has power to carry on the company's business in the exercise of his functions. The considerations relevant to receivers appointed under a fixed charge are also applicable to administrative receivers, although the additional statutory provisions applicable to administrative receivers are considered below (p 255).

A receiver appointed by the court is an officer of the court and his powers are derived from the order appointing him, He is personally liable on contracts entered into by him and while he is entitled to an indemnity out of the assets of the company, to the extent they are sufficient, for liabilities incurred in the proper performance of his duties, he will be most unwilling to incur any such liability under warranties given on the sale of any assets (such as shares in the target). The appointment takes effect from the date of the order appointing him, and upon his appointment the powers of the company and its directors are entirely in abeyance in respect of the property put in his possession or under his control.

The appointment of a receiver in respect of a company, whether pursuant to a court order or the exercise of powers in a debenture, must be notified to the Registrar of Companies within seven days of the appointment (Companies Act 1985, s 405; after implementation of relevant changes by the Companies Act 1989, this will be s 408). All invoices, orders or business letters on which the company's name appears issued by or on behalf of the company or the receiver must state a statement that the receiver has been appointed (Insolvency Act 1986, s 39). A receiver appointed under the terms of a debenture must be appointed in the manner set out in the debenture; if he is to execute any deed (such as a transfer of shares in the target where the target's articles require transfers to be by deed) as agent of the company then he must be appointed by deed.

Much more common than a court-appointed receiver is the receiver appointed by the debenture holder under the terms of the debenture held by him with security over the company's assets. In such case, the receiver's powers will be derived from the terms of the debenture, which will generally be extensive. The debenture will usually appoint the receiver as the agent of the company in respect of the assets which are the subject of the charge, although the relationship of a receiver with his principal, the company, does not accord with all the usual rules of agency; the principal cannot terminate the agency, and while he owes certain duties to the company, he has a primary responsibility to the debenture holder who appointed him for collection and realisation of the assets in respect of which he is appointed. The receiver's appointment by the debenture holder suspends, during the period of receivership, the powers of the directors over the assets in respect of which the receiver has been appointed so far as is requisite to enable the receiver to discharge his functions. Where a receiver is appointed, any person wishing to deal with the company in receivership in relation to those assets should expect, therefore, to deal with the receiver and not with the directors, although he will need to satisfy himself as to the authority of the receiver to act, and his powers (see below). A receiver appointed by a debenture holder under the terms of the debenture takes office from the time at which the instrument appointing the receiver is received by him, provided he accepts the appointment by the end of the next business day (Insolvency Act 1986, s 33). The Insolvency Rules 1986, Pt 3, Chap 1 set out the requirements for confirmation of the fact and time of his acceptance, and its publication.

Where the shares in the target are one of the assets to be sold in the receivership, the purchaser will wish to satisfy himself that he will receive good title to the assets. The power of a court-appointed receiver to sell will be derived from his appointment, and the court order should be checked to ensure that he is duly empowered to make such a sale. If he is not or if it is a requirement that the court sanctions such a transaction, any agreement must be conditional upon such sanction.

The authority of the receiver to act is more difficult where he is appointed under the powers contained in the debenture and it will be necessary to make careful checks to ensure that he is properly authorised. It will be necessary to check the instrument setting out his powers, and whether any formalities for his appointment have been complied with; if he is expressed to act as agent of the company, his powers will be subject to the same limitations as those of the company. There are a number of circumstances which could render invalid the appointment of a receiver or the exercise of his powers. These will include:

(*a*) where the debenture pursuant to which he is appointed is illegal or unenforceable (if, for example, it constituted the giving of unlawful financial assistance by the company (see Chapter 5), or had not been duly executed, or had not been duly registered under the Companies Act 1985, s 395);

(*b*) where the conditions under the debenture enabling the debenture holder to appoint him have not arisen, or been duly complied with;

(*c*) where any formalities for his appointment set out in the debenture have not been complied with. If joint receivers are appointed, does the debenture permit this, and are they able to act severally?

(*d*) where the powers conferred on him by the debenture do not extend to the act or acts he purports to take. Unlike an administrative receiver, a receiver appointed under a fixed charge does not by virtue of his office have any powers expressly conferred on him (except to the extent that the Law of Property 1925, s 109 applies); and

(*e*) where winding-up has commenced against the company (this will terminate his agency on behalf of the company, but not his appointment—see p 259).

It will not be possible for a purchaser dealing with such a receiver to investigate all these matters fully. However, it should be possible to make the following checks:

(*a*) conduct a company search against the vendor to check for registration of the charge and any winding-up or administration petition or order;

(*b*) obtain a copy of the debenture and seek evidence of compliance with any unusual requirements; and

(*c*) obtain copies of the receiver's appointment and his acceptance under s 33.

Where there is any apparent irregularity, the purchaser should satisfy himself that it will not invalidate the appointment. Indeed, since a receiver who purports to act in the absence of proper authority may incur significant liability both to the company, and to persons with whom he deals, the well-advised receiver can be expected to have satisfied himself as to these matters.

Despite these checks, it is possible that the appointment might not be valid. If the charge is void *ab initio* (for example, improperly executed), then it would seem that the receiver will never have had the requisite authority to act. While any want of authority will generally be capable of ratification by the company, in the absence of such ratification the remedy of a purchaser acting in good faith and without notice of such defect will be rather unsatisfactory, being a claim for damages in an action against the receiver for breach of warranty of authority (see *Bowstead on the law Agency*, 15th edn (1985) (Sweet & Maxwell).

A receiver appointed under powers contained in an instrument is personally liable on contracts entered into by him in the performance of his functions, except so far as the contract otherwise provides (s 37). It is normal practice for a receiver to exclude his personal liability in a contract for disposal of the shares or other assets in the target. While this will not affect the liability of the company on whose behalf he is acting as agent, he will be reluctant for the company to give warranties on the sale since he will not wish to expose the company and possibly himself to claims in damages.

In addition to checking the authority of the receiver, the purchaser will wish to ensure that any transfer of the target's shares to him will be free of any other security. If the vendor's assets, including the target's shares, are subject to other charges, then it will be necessary to examine whether the receiver is able to deliver title to the shares free of such security. If the receiver's appointment is under a debenture secured by mortgage made by deed, with security ranking in priority to all other security, then it will be possible for the shares to be delivered to the purchaser free from other charges ranking behind that charge, by the debenture holder selling as mortgagee and exercising his power of sale under the Law of Property Act 1925, s 101(1). In such a case, it will be the debenture holder, not the receiver acting as agent for the company, who will execute the transfer (if the company or its agent, the receiver, executes the transfer, releases from subsequent charges must be obtained). However, if there exists security ranking in priority to the security of the debenture under which the receiver has been appointed, statute cannot be invoked to overreach such interests (unlike an administrative receiver who may apply to court for such purpose).

Where prior charges cannot be overreached, it will be necessary to obtain a release of the shares from such charges by the chargeholder.

In all cases, the purchaser will also need to give consideration as to the manner in which the shares are to be transferred; a legal charge of the shares will have been effected by registering the shares in the name of the chargee, who must transfer the shares; alternatively, a chargee's interest may be protected by deposit of the share certificate and a stock transfer executed in blank (as to the transferee). Simple completion of the executed transfer will usually suffice to effect the transfer.

Apart from the provisions of the Insolvency Act dealing with transactions at an undervalue and preferences (see p 263), a purchaser will generally be concerned only as to the authority of the receiver to act, and not any neglect by the receiver in the exercise of his powers. A receiver appointed by debenture holders owes a duty of care to the company in respect of whose assets he has been appointed, and if he fails to exercise reasonable care in the circumstances to obtain the true market value of the assets on a sale, he will be liable for any loss suffered by the company or any guarantor of the relevant debt (see *Standard Chartered Bank Ltd v Walker* [1982] 1 WLR 1410, and *American Express International Banking Corp v Hurley* [1985] 3 All ER 564). Breach of this duty of care will, therefore, give rise to a right to damages against the receiver, but will not affect the purchaser whose transaction will not, for this reason alone, be invalidated.

Somewhat different considerations apply where the receiver or debenture holder has an interest in the purchaser. It is clear that a sale by the receiver of the company's assets to himself is liable to be set aside irrespective of the merits of sale. Where the sale is to a company in which the receiver has an interest, however, it seems that a 'fair dealing' rule applies. In their judgment in *Tse Kwong Lam v Wong Chit Sen* [1983] 1 WLR 1394 (concerning sale by a mortgagee), the view of the Privy Council was expressed by Lord Templeman as follows:

In the view of this Board on authority and on principle there is no hard and fast rule that a mortgagee may not sell to a company in which he is interested. The mortgagee and the company seeking to uphold the transaction must show that the sale was in good faith and that the mortgagee took reasonable precautions to obtain the best price reasonably obtainable at the time.

This approach appears to have been accepted by the court in the case of a sale by a receiver (*Watts v Midland Bank plc* [1986] BCLC 15, concerning an application for interlocutory relief). It should be apparent, therefore, that particular care should be taken to ensure that the requirements of 'fair dealing' are satisfied, where the receiver or debenture holder has an interest in the purchasing company. The burden of proof seems to fall on the receiver to show that there was no conflict between his duty and interest. The nature of the receiver's conflict of interest and duty may take a number of forms; the transaction might involve a sale to persons connected with the receiver, to the debenture holder who appointed him, or to a company in which the debenture holder has an interest. The burden of showing tnat the receiver acted fairly will vary depending on the nature and extent of the conflict, and the extent, if any, to which the debenture holder sought to influence his acts. In the *Watts* case, it was suggested (at p 23) that such a fair dealing rule would apply where the sale by the receiver to a purchaser in which the solicitor acting for the receiver was financially interested.'Financially interested' is presumably not limited to a shareholding, and it would be prudent to infer that the principle will apply if the debenture holder under whose debenture the receiver was appointed is also a significant provider of finance to the purchaser.

Administrative receivers

An administrative receiver is a special category of receiver with powers and obligations defined by statute (Insolvency Act 1986, s 42 *et seq*). A very broad distinction between an administrative receiver and other receivers is that the administrative receiver will have been appointed under a floating charge over substantially the whole of a company's assets, whereas other receivers will be appointed under a fixed charge for the purpose of realising specific assets only, or by the court. Unlike a receiver appointed under a fixed charge, however, an administrative receiver must be a licensed insolvency practitioner.

Generally speaking, therefore, receivers appointed under a floating charge will be administrative receivers, and provisions of the Insolvency Act discussed below will apply in addition to those provisions of general application (under 'Receivers' above, p 250).

A receiver will be an administrative receiver if he is 'a receiver or manager of the whole (or substantially the whole) of a company's property appointed by or on behalf of the holders of debentures of the company secured by a charge which, as created, was a floating charge, or by such a charge and one or more other securities' (s 29(2)). An administrative receiver may therefore be appointed if the floating charge has crystallised, or where the charge comprises both floating and fixed security. Appointment of an administrative receiver does not prevent another receiver being appointed in respect of specific assets, or any liquidation of the company. It will, however, be a bar to the appointment of an administrator, unless the security by virtue of which he is appointed can be challenged (s 9(3)).

The administrative receiver is deemed to be the company's agent unless and until the company goes into liquidation. However, he is personally liable in any contract entered into by him in the carrying out of his function, unless the contract otherwise provides (s 44). This mirrors the position of a receiver appointed under a fixed charge. An administrative receiver, therefore, will also be unwilling to give warranties on sale, both in his own capacity and as agent for the company.

A purchaser dealing with an administrative receiver will need to make the same enquiries as to the validity of his appointment and his powers to act as he would if dealing with a receiver appointed under a fixed charge (see p 252), although the Insolvency Act will provide additional protection. Section 232 provides that the acts of an administrator, administrative receiver, liquidator or provisional liquidator of a company are valid notwithstanding any defect in his appointment, nomination or qualifications. Although s 232 will prevent defects in formalities associated with his appointment from invalidating his acts, it is thought that it will not validate his acts if the debenture under which he was appointed is void (see *Morris v Kanssen* [1946] AC 459, concerning a predecessor to the section). A purchaser should therefore satisfy himself of the administrative receiver's appointment, where there is any apparent reason to doubt the validity of the debenture under which he has been appointed.

An administrative receiver, in addition to the powers contained in the debenture appointing him, has wide powers conferred on him by statute: the debenture by virtue of which he was appointed is deemed, by s 42(1), to include (except in so far as they are inconsistent with any of the provisions of the debenture) the powers set out in Sched 1 to the Act. These powers are extensive and include a power of sale (para 2). Although it is unlikely, it would be prudent for the purchaser dealing with an administrative receiver to check the debenture to ensure that it does not limit the exercise of his powers; however, a purchaser will derive considerable assistance from s 42(3), which provides that a person dealing with the administrative receiver in good faith and for value is not concerned to inquire whether the receiver is acting within his powers.

An administrative receiver is able to transfer the target's shares to the purchaser free from any other security interests: as with a receiver appointed under a fixed charge, any charges whose security ranks after the charge securing the debenture under which the administrative receiver was appointed may be overreached by the debenture holder exercising his power of sale under the Law of Property Act 1925, s 101(1). It is also possible, however, for an administrative receiver to dispose of assets free of charges which rank ahead of his charge, since the Insolvency Act 1986, s 43(1) permits the court, on an application by the administrative receiver, to authorise him to dispose of the property as if it were not subject to the security. For such an order to be made, the section provides that the court is to be satisfied that 'the disposal . . . would be likely to promote a more advantageous realisation of the company's assets than would otherwise be effected'. The section may be only invoked to enable disposal of assets free from prior security (see s 43(2)); if holders of subsequent security refuse to give a release of their charge, the sale may have to be made by the Mortgagee under his Statutory power.

Administrators

The purpose of an administrator's appointment is to achieve one of the objectives set out in the Insolvency Act, including the survival of the company, in whole or in part, as a going concern or a more advantageous realisation of the company's assets than would be effected on winding-up (s 8(3)). An administrator is appointed by the court, following a petition by the company, its directors or creditors. Generally speaking, where an administrative receiver has already been appointed, an administrator may not be appointed by the court (s 9(3)). The appointment of administrator and administrative receiver are mutually exclusive and any appointment of an administrator, being made with the consent of the administrative receiver's appointor, will require the administrative receiver to vacate office. If the administrator requires it, any receiver appointed in respect of specific assets must also vacate office (s 11(2)). Similarly, administration is inconsistent with liquidation, and after presentation of a petition for administration, any winding-up order may not be made or resolution passed until the petition is heard or dismissed. An administration order will result in dismissal of a winding-up petition.

Administration has far-reaching consequences for a company and its creditors; while the administration order is in force no steps may be taken to enforce security over the company's property, nor may other proceedings be commenced or continued against the company, in either case without the consent of the administrator or the leave of the court (s 11(3)). A purchaser would thus be prevented from bringing proceedings for warranty or other claims arising on a previous acquisition during the period of the administration.

The appointment of an administrator must be advertised immediately in the *Gazette* and in an appropriate newspaper, and, within 14 days of the order appointing the administrator, be notified to the Registrar of Companies (s 21(2)). All invoices, orders for goods or business letters issued by or on behalf of the company or administrator at any time when the administration order is in force in relation to the company must contain the administrator's name and a statement that the affairs of the company are being managed by the administrator (s 12(1)). Since the application for the appointment of an administrator is by order of the court, a search of the central index of administration petitions at the Companies Court may reveal the existence of his appointment at an earlier date than a search of the Companies Registry.

Section 232 applies in respect of the appointment of an administrator, and a person dealing with an administrator need not enquire into the validity of his appointment. The administrator, following his appointment, has very wide powers to do all such things as may be necessary for the management of the affairs, business and property of the company, and including the powers set out in Sched 1 to the Act (s 14) which are also conferred on an administrative receiver. The administrator is deemed to act as the company's agent (s 14(5)), and powers of the company or its directors are limited during the period of the administration. The purchaser dealing with the administrator in relation to the target's shares is protected by s 14(6), which provides that a person dealing with an administrator in good faith for value is not concerned to enquire whether the administrator is acting within his powers.

The administrator must draw up proposals for achieving the purpose of the administration and put these before the company's creditors at a meeting to be held within three months of his appointment (s 23); he is obliged to act in accordance with such proposals, as modified with creditors' approval from time to time. This does not mean he cannot act prior to the creditors' meeting; he has a general power to act (s 14(1)) and he may apply to court for directions to act prior to the meeting (ss 14(3) and 17(2)). Notwithstanding the protection afforded him by s 14(6), the purchaser should consider whether the administrator is acting within his powers and, where the sale is to occur prior to the creditors' meeting, whether the sale should be made with, or conditional upon, court approval.

An administrator is able to dispose of the company's property free from the security of any person in that property. Where the property of the company is subject to security which, as created, was a floating charge, he may dispose of the property free from the security without consent (s 15(1)) (notwithstanding crystallisation of the security). In the case of any other security, the administrator must seek an order of the court to sell the property to the purchaser free from the security (s 15(2)). Where such an order is sought on the sale of shares in the target which are subject to a legal charge, it will be necessary to ensure that shares registered in the name of the chargee can be transferred (which may entail an appropriate direction to that effect in the court order).

Liquidators

A liquidator is appointed for the winding-up of a company. Winding-up may either be voluntary or compulsory. A voluntary winding-up commences when the resolution to wind up the company is passed, and a compulsory winding-up is deemed to commence when the petition is presented. This section principally addresses compulsory winding-up.

A resolution or order for winding-up cannot be passed or made while the vendor is in administration (s 11(3)). However, an existing appointment of a receiver or administrative receiver will not prevent the winding-up of the company nor does winding-up prevent the appointment of a receiver or administrative receiver. The making of a winding-up order will terminate any such receiver's agency on behalf of the company, but termination of the receiver's agency to bind the company does not, however, affect the exercise of powers given by the debenture to hold and dispose of the property charged (*Sowman v David Samuel Trust Ltd* [1978] 1 WLR 22). Commencement of winding-up in respect of the vendor, therefore, will not prevent a receiver or administrative receiver from delivering good title to shares which are charged by the debenture under which he was appointed. Winding-up will, however, usually terminate any power of attorney granted to the receiver under the debenture, unless the power granted to him (and not merely the appointor) is irrevocable in accordance with the Powers of Attorney Act 1974, s 4.

A compulsory winding-up will occur following an order of the court. If a winding-up order is granted, then (provided no resolution for winding-up has previously been passed) the winding-up is deemed to commence on the date upon which the winding-up petition was presented, not the date upon which the order was made (s 129). A purchaser who is dealing with a vendor against whom a winding-up petition has been presented should be aware of the effect of s 127 which provides that any disposition of the company's property after the commencement of the winding-up is, unless the court otherwise orders, void. This will be the case even if the disposition is unarguably to the benefit of the company, although in such a case a court would no doubt validate the transaction. The backdating effect of s 129 in relation to the commencement of a winding-up will therefore mean that, in the absence of any court approval, a purchaser should not contract to purchase the target's shares after presentation of the petition. Problems could arise under s 127 where contracts for the purchase of the target shares have been exchanged, but not completed. If the contract is conditional or voidable by the company, waiver of conditions or confirmation of the contract might constitute a disposition of property under s 127, and similarly if the terms of the contract are varied. In practice it may be prudent to seek the court's approval for completion (which will be obtained in advance of the winding-up), although where the contract is plainly specifically enforceable and there is no possible defence, this would seem to be unnecessary (see *Re French's Wine Bar Ltd* [1987] BCLC 499). Section 127 does not apply to invalidate a disposition of the company's property by a receiver (*Sowman v David Samuel Trust*). Of course, the above assumes that the purchaser wishes to proceed notwithstanding the vendor's insolvency. If he does not, then he must look to his contract to see if he may rescind. There is no general rule that the insolvency of one party renders the contract unenforceable or offers grounds for rescission.

Upon the appointment of a liquidator, the control of the company's affairs passes out of the hands of the directors, who cease to have authority. The powers of the liquidator will depend on whether the liquidation is voluntary or compulsory. In a compulsory winding-up, the liquidator has the powers set out in the Insolvency Act, Sched 4 which may be exercised with the sanction of the court (if they fall within Pt I or II) or without it (if within Pt III). So far as the sale of any subsidiary or business by the vendor in liquidation is concerned, para 6, Sched 4 empowers the liquidator, without sanction, to sell any of the company's property by public auction or private contract. Para 7 confers authority for the execution of documents and use of the company's seal. The court's sanction will be required if the sale also involves, say, a compromise with creditors.

A purchaser dealing with the liquidator of a vendor does not need to enquire into the formal validity of the liquidator's appointment (s 232). It is nevertheless important to distinguish between a voluntary or compulsory liquidation. If the liquidation is a creditors' voluntary liquidation, the liquidator may only exercise his powers prior to the creditors' meeting required to be held as part of the insolvency procedure, with the sanction of the court (s 166). Therefore, although it is unlikely that any sale of a subsidiary would take place prior to that meeting, it will be important to check that procedural requirements have been complied with or, where appropriate, any variation in the procedure has been properly sanctioned by the court. If the liquidation is compulsory or a members' voluntary liquidation, the liquidator is under no such restriction (although it should be noted that a provisional liquidator's ability to act is likely to be limited by the court order appointing him (s 135(5))).

Bankruptcy of individual vendors

The bankruptcy of an individual commences on the date on which the bankruptcy order is made, and continues until it is discharged (s 278). Following the bankruptcy order, a trustee in bankruptcy will be appointed, although this may take place several weeks after the bankruptcy order is made. Upon the trustee's appointment, the bankrupt's estate vests in the trustee. In the case of shares in a company owned by the bankrupt, s 306(2) provides that this vesting will occur without any transfer, although the target's articles may contain provisions for the registration of shares in the name of the trustee, and for transfers by the bankrupt or his trustee. The trustee's powers derive from s 314 and Sched 5 to the Act. Paragraph 9, Sched 5 confers on the trustee the power to sell any part of the property for the time being comprised in the bankrupt's estate, without requiring any permission from the bankrupt's creditors or the court. If the sale involves payment in deferred consideration, however, it will require the permission of the court or creditors' committee (being a power falling within Pt I of Sched 5 (para 3)) and it may be prudent to make the contract for the acquisition conditional upon that permission; although s 314(3) provides protection for a person dealing in good faith and for value and where such court or creditors' permission is required, he is not concerned to enquire whether any such permission is given.

Where the vendor is an individual who has a bankruptcy petition outstanding against him, the purchaser should be aware that if a bankruptcy order is subsequently made, any disposition of property by the bankrupt in the period commencing on the date on which the petition was presented, and ending on the vesting of the bankrupt's estate in his trustee (on the trustee's appointment) is void, except where it is made with the consent of the court or is subsequently ratified by the court (s 284). The retrospective effect of s 284 is similar to that applicable to the compulsory winding-up of a company, under s 127 (see p 259). Unlike s 127, however, s 284(4) provides relief for persons dealing with an individual against whom a bankruptcy petition is pending 'in respect of any property or payment which he received before the bankruptcy in good faith, for value and without notice that the petition had been presented'. Unlike a petition for winding-up of a company, a petition in bankruptcy need not be advertised prior to the hearing, although notice of the petition must be sent for registration as a land charge. In consequence, a purchaser is likely in practice to have the benefit of the section, where his land charges search does not reveal the petition, and he is not otherwise aware of it.

VENDOR'S SUBSEQUENT INSOLVENCY

Where the purchaser becomes aware that the vendor from whom he has acquired a target has gone into liquidation, he should review the acquisition document, and decide whether or not he has grounds for claims against the vendor. Any claims should be submitted to the liquidator and, so far as possible, quantified, although the amount he is ultimately able to prove in the liquidation will be governed by the Insolvency Act and the Insolvency Rules. Unless he has taken security, a purchaser would be an unsecured creditor of the vendor in respect of any claims, and for this reason any losses may not be paid in full if indeed there is any amount available for distribution to unsecured creditors.

However, where the vendor has claims against the purchaser, for instance in respect of the purchaser's failure to pay any deferred consideration, the purchaser will wish, so far as possible, to be able to offset his liability against any claim he has against the vendor. After the commencement of liquidation the purchaser's right to exercise set-off will be governed by the Insolvency Rules 1986, r 4.90. In summary, this provides that set-off will operate where, before the company goes into liquidation, there have been mutual credits, mutual debts or other mutual dealings between the company and creditor in proving the liquidation.

While this provision is wide, if the contractual set-off exceeds this principle of mutuality, then to that extent it cannot be exercised. Even if the contract does not provide for set-off, a purchaser may be able to assert set-off upon liquidation if there exists the mutuality required by the rule; in a normal case, warranty claims should be capable of being set off against deferred consideration. Insolvency set-off may only operate for a provable debt; to the extent the purchaser's claim exceeds the amount for which set-off may operate, he must prove in the liquidation in the usual way.

Where the vendor has gone into administration or liquidation after the target has been acquired by the purchaser, the acquisition of the target by the purchaser may be liable to adjustment — for example, if the acquisition of the target was a transaction at an undervalue or was a preference given by the insolvent party under the Insolvency Act, ss 238–41 (or, in the case of bankruptcy of an individual vendor, ss 339–42).

In a corporate acquisition, any transaction which has been entered into in good faith and on an arm's length basis between unconnected parties is unlikely to be the subject of attack under these provisions.

Transactions at an undervalue (s 238)

Where a company goes into administration or liquidation, the administrator or liquidator is able to apply to the court for the adjustment of certain prior transactions at an undervalue.

Section 238 is concerned with transactions which occurred in the period of two years prior to the date on which the petition for the administration order was presented, or the date of commencement of the winding-up (being, in the case of compulsory winding-up, the date of presentation of the winding-up petition). Transactions at risk under the section are those which, in summary, involved a gift by the company or where it received no consideration, or consideration having a monetary value significantly less than that given by the company (s 238(4)). If, however, it can be shown that at the time of entering into the transaction in question, the company was able to pay its debts (within the meaning of s 123) and did not become unable to pay its debts in consequence of the transaction, then the transaction will not be liable to adjustment as a transaction at an undervalue (s 240(2)). Where, however, there is a 'connection' between the vendor and purchaser, an inability to pay debts is presumed, and it will be for the parties to show otherwise. 'Transaction' includes a gift, agreement or arrangement (s 436).

There is a distinction to be drawn between cases of poor judgement by the vendor or where, with hindsight, the price paid by a purchaser proved to be a bargain, and cases where there has been an improper transfer of assets. This is recognised by s 238(5) which provides a defence where the conditions for a transaction at an undervalue otherwise apply and the court is 'satisfied that (a) the company which entered into the transaction did so in good faith and for the purpose of carrying on its business, and (b) that at the time it did so there were reasonable grounds for believing that the transaction would benefit the company'. It should be noted that for the defence under s 238 to be available, the company must have acted in good faith. The fact that the purchaser alone acted in good faith will not prevent any adjustment of the transaction nor will it prevent an order being made against the purchaser (although s 241(2) places limits on the orders to be made against innocent third parties, it seems that a purchaser, since he is party to the transaction, cannot benefit from them).

Provided, however, there is good faith on the part of the vendor, the defence will be available if it can be shown, objectively, that there were reasonable grounds for believing the transaction would benefit the company. In cases of doubt, and particularly where there is a presumption of insolvency by reason of a connection between vendor and purchaser, it would be prudent for the purchaser to insist that the vendor provides him with a comprehensive board minute evidencing, so far as is possible, satisfaction of the criteria in s 238(5). ('Connection' between vendor and purchaser is discussed below (p 266).)

If the grounds are established to the court's satisfaction, then it may make such order as it may think fit to restore the position of the company to that which it would have been if the company had not entered into the transaction. The court has a very wide discretion in the type of order it may make for this purpose, and s 241 gives specific authority to the court to order that the property be restored to the vendor, that money be paid or repaid or security be given or released, not only against the immediate parties to the transaction, but also by third parties (subject to s 241(2)).

In addition to the s 238 provisions, where it can be shown that the company entered into a transaction at an undervalue for the purpose of putting assets beyond the reach of his creditors, s 423 permits a court to make orders which may result in the transaction being unwound. Unlike s 239, the provisions relating to transactions defrauding creditors can apply irrespective of insolvency and are not limited to transactions within the two-year period prior to administration or liquidation; in principle, therefore, a purchaser proposing an acquisition from any vendor, irrespective of his solvency, should be alert to the section, although it will generally be where there is an impending insolvency that the matter will fall to be considered. An arm's length transaction should not, of course, fall within the section. In addition to an administrator or liquidator, the person who is, or is capable of being, prejudiced by the transaction may bring an application under s 423 to adjust or unwind it.

Preferences (s 239)

An administrator or liquidator may apply to the court for an order to adjust a transaction if the company has by that transaction given a preference within the period of six months prior to the commencement of its winding-up or date of presentation of the petition for administration. Where the preference is given to a person who is connected with the company, however, this period is extended to two years (see below).

A preference is given by a company to a person if that person is one of the company's creditors, or a surety or guarantor for any of the company's debts or liabilities, and the company does or permits to be done anything which has the effect of putting that person into a position which, in the event of the company going into insolvent liquidation, will be better than the position he would have been in if that thing had not been done (s 239(4)). A transaction may not be attacked as a preference unless at the time, or in consequence of the transaction, the company was unable to pay its debts (s 240(2)). For a preference to be attacked, the administrator or liquidator must show that the company was influenced in deciding to give it by a desire to improve the position in an insolvent liquidation of the person to whom it has given the preference. This is a significant change from the old law concerning voidable preferences, where it was necessary to show a dominant intention to prefer. In *Re M C Bacon Ltd* [1990] BCLC 324, Millet J makes it plain that s 239(5) contains a completely different test. He says (at p 336) '[sub-section (5)] ... requires only that the desire should have influenced the decision. That requirement is satisfied if it was one of the factors which operated on the minds of those who made the decision. It need not have been the only factor or even the decisive one'. Where there is a connection between the parties (other than by reason of the person preferred being an employee), it is presumed that the company giving the preference was influenced in doing so by a desire to improve the recipient's position in an insolvent liquidation (s 239(6)).

As noted above, in an arm's length transaction between unconnected parties the giving of preferences will not usually arise. It will be prudent to examine questions of preference, however, when there are (apart from the acquisition of the target) dealings between the vendor and purchaser or where the purchaser is 'connected' with the vendor. A simple example of where a preference might arise in the context of an acquisition of the target is where the vendor is indebted to the purchaser, and the target is transferred to the purchaser as part of an arrangement for the reduction of that indebtedness.

The application of s 239 is significantly extended where the vendor and purchaser are connected. Where there is a connection (other than by reason of the person preferred being an employee) the period prior to administration or liquidation during which preferences can be attacked is extended from six months to two years and the company's intent to give the preference is presumed. It should be noted that the inability of a company to pay its debts, which is a precondition to adjustment of a transaction at an undervalue under s 238, is presumed under that section where the parties are connected.

'Connected' is defined by s 249, and a person is connected with a company for the purpose of giving a preference if he is a director or shadow director of the company, or an associate of any such person, or if he is an associate of the company. 'Associate' is widely defined by s 435 and includes, as may be expected, husbands, wives, relatives, partners, directors and companies under such a person's control. In addition, however, by s 435(4), employees and employers are included as associates — significantly extending the scope of the section. Under ss 238 and 239, any connection between vendor and purchaser will have a significant impact on any transaction which may be at risk of attack under these sections, placing the burden of proof as to insolvency on the parties (where a transaction at an undervalue) or, in the case of a preference (other than where the connection arises solely by reason of the person preferred being an employee), extending the period prior to administration or winding up during which transactions are at risk and presuming, under s 239(5) a desire to prefer. Careful consideration should be given as to whether any such a connection exists, and if it is possible to eliminate such a connection, it will be helpful to do so.

In a management buy-out, the 'connected person' test will often be satisfied if the purchasing management group includes directors of the vendor (but will not be a problem if the group comprises exclusively the vendor's employees, or directors of the target only). For example, a release of directors' loan accounts could be liable to attack as a preference.

Individual vendors

Where the vendor is an individual the Insolvency Act 1986, ss 339–42, contain similar provisions enabling transactions at an undervalue and preferences prior to a personal bankruptcy to be adjusted. One significant difference in the case of an individual, however, is that the relevant time at which a transaction at an undervalue may be attacked is five years prior to presentation of the bankruptcy petition, provided he was insolvent at the time (if he was solvent, it may still be attacked, but the period is reduced to two years).

PRESERVATION OF COMPANY NAME

Taking on directors of companies in the vendor's group which have gone into insolvent liquidation could adversely affect the continued use of the target's name. The Insolvency Act 1986, s 216, contains, a restriction designed to prevent directors whose company goes into insolvent liquidation from thereafter setting up in business under a similar name. The section will only be of concern to a purchaser where it acquires, with the target, individuals who were also formerly directors of any vendor company which has gone into insolvent liquidation within 12 months after such an individual ceased to be a director. It should be noted that the subsequent insolvent liquidation of such a company, after the purchaser has acquired the target, may result in the application of the section. Where s 216 applies, such individuals cannot be directors of or involved in the promotion, formation or management of any company known by a name by which the liquidated company in liquidation was known in the 12 months prior to its liquidation, or a name so similar to such a name so as to suggest an association with that company (s 216(2)). There are exceptions to the prohibition on re-use of such a company name. If the purchaser acquires a target with a name which, though suggesting an association with the name of the insolvent company, has been the target's name throughout the relevant period, then the prohibition resulting from employment of the ex-directors will not apply (Insolvency Rules 1986, r 4.230).

Section 216 will be of particular relevance in the case where a management group, comprising directors of the company in liquidation, is formed to purchase the target. Where directors of vendor group companies are part of the management group, the parties should also be alert to the provisions of the Companies Act 1985, s 320, requiring shareholder approval (see p 21).

Chapter 16

The Agreement for Sale

Two forms of agreement are set out in this chapter: a form for use when purchasing from individual vendors and a form for use when purchasing from a corporate vendor. Although the two forms are very similar, the differences are such as to make it convenient for the reader to set out both forms in full, rather than to include a note of the differences. These agreements are not so much agreements as collections of useful clauses. It would be rare indeed to find all the provisions of these agreements incorporated in a contract for the sale of a private company.

With each edition of this work these agreements grow longer, mainly because of additional warranties. Unfortunately it does not seem possible to prevent this. The fact is that a specific warranty forces the vendor to address the issue and, perhaps, to produce a disclosure while more general wording (which would produce a shorter agreement) does not. It is hoped, however, that practitioners will regard these precedents as a library of provisions from which to select rather than agreements to be used as they stand.

The agreements contemplate a target with subsidiaries, and will therefore require amendment if there are none. Amendments will also be required if the consideration is paid wholly in cash. Where the consideration is shares in the purchaser, an additional engrossment should be signed for filing at the Companies Registration Office (Companies Act 1985, s 88).

The notes to both agreements appear on p 462.

AGREEMENT FOR SALE — INDIVIDUAL VENDORS

CONTENTS

THIS   AGREEMENT is made the   day of 19

BETWEEN:

(1)   THE PERSONS whose names and addresses are set out in the first
      column of Part I of the first schedule (hereinafter together called
      'the Vendors'); and
(2)   PLC ('the Purchaser') a company registered in
      England under number [   ] whose registered office is at
      [   ]

WHEREAS:

The Purchaser wishes to acquire the entire issued share capital of
[   ] Limited from the Vendors on the terms of this
Agreement.

NOW IT IS HEREBY AGREED as follows:

1   INTERPRETATION

(A)   Definitions
In this Agreement where the context admits:
(1)   'Company' means [   ] Limited a company registered
      in England under number [   ] and incorporated on
      [19   ] as a private company limited by shares
      under the Companies Act(s) [   ];
(2)   'Completion' means completion of the sale and purchase of the
      Sale Shares;[1]
(3)   'Consideration Shares' means ordinary shares of [   ] each
      in the Purchaser credited as fully paid;
(4)   'Directors' means the persons named in Part II of the first
      schedule and 'the Continuing Directors' means the persons
      named in Part III of that schedule;
(5)   'Disclosure Letter' means the letter dated the date hereof
      written by or on behalf of the Vendors to the Purchaser in
      agreed terms;[2]
(6)   'Placing Agreement' means an agreement in agreed terms
      proposed to be entered into simultaneously with this

Agreement between the Purchaser and [   ] providing for the placing of the Consideration Shares;[3]

(7) 'Properties' means the properties particulars of which are set out in the list annexed to the Disclosure Letter;

(8) 'Sale Shares' means the shares to be bought and sold pursuant to clause 2;

(9) 'Subsidiaries' means the companies listed in Part II of the second schedule; and

(10) 'Warranties' means the warranties and representations set out in paragraph 2 of the third schedule, in paragraph 3 of the fourth schedule and in paragraph [   ] of the sixth schedule.

(B)   Construction of Certain References
In this Agreement where the context admits:

(1) words and phrases the definitions of which are contained or referred to in Part XXVI Companies Act 1985 shall be construed as having the meanings thereby attributed to them;

(2) references to statutory provisions shall be construed as references to those provisions as amended or re-enacted or as their application is modified by other provisions from time to time and shall include references to any provisions of which they are re-enactments (whether with or without modification);

(3) where any statement is qualified by the expression 'so far as the Vendors are aware' or 'to the best of the Vendors' knowledge and belief' or any similar expression, that statement shall be deemed to include an additional statement that it has been made after due and careful enquiry;[4]

(4) references to clauses and schedules are references to clauses hereof and schedules hereto, references to sub-clauses or paragraphs are, unless otherwise stated, references to sub-clauses of the clause or paragraphs of the schedule in which the reference appears, and references to this Agreement include the schedules;

(5) references to any document being in agreed terms are to that document in the form signed on behalf of the parties for identification; and

(6) references to the Vendors include a reference to each of them.

(C)   Joint and Several Liabilities
All warranties, representations, indemnities, covenants, agreements and obligations given or entered into by more than one person in this Agreement are given or entered into jointly and severally.[5]

(D)   Headings
The headings and sub-headings are inserted for convenience only and shall not affect the construction of this Agreement.

(E) Schedules
Each of the schedules shall have effect as if set out herein.

2   SALE OF SHARES

(A) Sale and Purchase
Subject to the terms of this Agreement, each of the Vendors shall sell
and the Purchaser shall purchase, free from all liens, charges, equities
and encumbrances and together with all rights now or hereafter
attaching thereto the number of [   ] ordinary shares of
[   ] each set opposite his name in the second column of Part I
of the first schedule which shares together comprise the entire issued
share capital of the Company.

(B) Simultaneous Completion
Neither the Purchaser nor the Vendors shall be obliged to complete
the purchase of any of the Sale Shares unless the purchase of all the
Sale Shares is completed simultaneously.

(C) Waiver of Pre-emption Rights
Each of the Vendors hereby waives any pre-emption rights he may
have relating to the Sale Shares, whether conferred by the
Company's Articles of Association or otherwise.

3   CONSIDERATION

(A) Amount [Consideration Shares]
The total consideration for the Sale Shares shall be the sum of
£[   ], but subject to adjustment as provided in the fourth,
fifth and sixth schedules. [The total consideration for the Sale Shares
shall be the allotment to the Vendors of [   ] Consideration
Shares].

(B) Placing[1]
The total consideration for the Sale Shares shall be the allotment to the
Vendors of the number of Consideration Shares which, when placed
with placees nominated by the Purchaser, shall produce payment to
the Vendors of aggregate net proceeds of £[   ]. The Purchaser
shall arrange a placing to produce such aggregate net proceeds and
shall procure the payment of that amount to the Vendors at
Completion against the renunciation by the Vendors of the allotment
of such Consideration Shares as directed by the Purchaser.

(C) Dividends etc
The Consideration Shares shall rank *pari passu* and as a single class
with the ordinary shares of [   ] each in the Purchaser in issue at the
date of this Agreement, and shall carry the right to receive in full all
dividends and other distributions declared, made or paid after the

date of this Agreement [save that they shall not carry the right to participate in the [interim] [final] dividend of the Purchaser for the year ending [19   ] [declared on   ].[2]

4   CONDITIONS AND COMPLETION

(A)   Conditions[1]

Completion is conditional upon:

(1)   the passing at a general meeting of the Purchaser duly convened and held of a resolution to:

  (*a*)   approve the acquisition by the Purchaser of the Sale Shares;

  (*b*)   increase the authorised share capital of the Purchaser to not less than £[   ]; and

  (*c*)   to authorise the directors of the Purchaser to allot the Consideration Shares;[2]

(2)   the admission by the Council of the London Stock Exchange of the Consideration Shares to the Official List, and such listing having become fully effective by the making of the appropriate announcement under Rule 520 of the London Stock Exchange Rules; and[3]

(3)   the Placing Agreement being entered into and becoming, in accordance with its terms, unconditional in all respects;[4]

and in the event that the above conditions[5] are not satisfied on or before [19   ] this Agreement shall lapse and no party shall make any claim against any other in respect hereof, save for any antecedent breach.[6]

(B)   Date of Completion

Subject to the provisions of this clause, Completion shall take place on [19   ] at the offices of [   ].

(C)   Vendors' Obligations[7]

On Completion the Vendors shall:

(1)   deliver to the Purchaser:

  (*a*)   duly executed transfers of the Sale Shares by the registered holders thereof in favour of the Purchaser or its nominees together with the relative share certificates;

  (*b*)   such waivers or consents as the Purchaser may require to[8] enable the Purchaser or its nominees to be registered as holders of the Sale Shares; and

  (*c*)   [powers of attorney in agreed terms].[9]

(2)   procure the passing of a resolution of the board of directors of the Company resolving to register the transfers referred to in item (1)(*a*) [subject only to due stamping];[10]

(3)   cause such persons as the Purchaser may nominate to be validly

appointed as additional directors of the Company and the Subsidiaries and, upon such appointment, forthwith cause the Directors (other than the Continuing Directors) and the secretary or secretaries of the Company and the Subsidiaries to retire from all their offices and employments with the Company or the Subsidiaries, each delivering to the Purchaser a deed acknowledging that he has no claim outstanding for compensation or otherwise and without any payment under the Employment Protection (Consolidation) Act 1978;[11]

(4) procure revocation of all authorities to the bankers of the Company and the Subsidiaries relating to bank accounts, giving authority to such persons as the Purchaser may nominate to operate the same;

(5) procure the resignation of the auditors of the Company and the Subsidiaries in accordance with s 392 of the Companies Act 1985, accompanied by a statement pursuant to s 394 of that Act that there are no circumstances connected with their resignation which should be brought to the notice of the members or creditors of each such company and that no fees are due to them and procure the appointment of [   ] as the new auditors of the Company;[12]

(6) deliver to the Purchaser as agent for the Company and the Subsidiaries:

 (a) a certificate from [   ] in agreed terms as to the title of the Company or the Subsidiaries to the Properties;[13]

 (b) the title deeds to the Properties;[14]

 (c) all the statutory and other books (duly written up to date) of the Company and each of the Subsidiaries and its/their certificate(s) of incorporation and common seal(s); and[15]

 (d) certificates in respect of all issued shares in the capital of each of the Subsidiaries and transfer of all shares in any Subsidiary held by any nominee in favour of such persons as the Purchaser shall direct; [and][16]

(7) deposit the sum of £[   ] with the Purchaser on the terms of clause 7; [and]

(8) comply with clause 3( ); [and]

(9) procure the discharge of the guarantees and other obligations stipulated in the Disclosure Letter to be discharged at completion.

(D) Service Agreements

On Completion the Company and [   ] shall enter into service agreements in the form of the draft(s) in agreed terms.[17]

(E)   Purchaser's Obligations

On Completion the Purchaser shall [pay] [satisfy] the consideration for the Sale Shares as provided by clause 3 [and comply with the provisions of paragraph 3 of the seventh schedule] [any payment in cash to be made] by way of town clearing banker's draft made payable to [   ].

(F)   Failure to Complete[18]

If in any respect the preceding provisions of this clause (other than sub-clause (A)) are not complied with on the date for Completion set by sub-clause (B) the party not in default (or, in the case of non-compliance with sub-clause (D), the Purchaser) may:

(1)   defer Completion to a date not more than 28 days after the date set by sub-clause (B) (and so that the provisions of this sub-clause (F), apart from this item (1), shall apply to Completion as so deferred); or

(2)   proceed to Completion so far as practicable (without prejudice to its rights hereunder); or

(3)   rescind this Agreement.

5   PURCHASER'S RIGHT OF ACCESS[1]

From the date hereof the Purchaser and its accountants and agents shall be allowed access to all the premises and books of account of the Company and the Subsidiaries, and the Vendors shall supply any information reasonably required by the Purchaser relating to the Company and the Subsidiaries.

6   RESTRICTION OF VENDORS

(A)   Restricted Business

In this clause, 'Restricted Business' means [   ].

(B)   Covenants

Each of the Vendors undertakes with the Purchaser that he will not:

(1)   for the period of [   ] after Completion, either on his own account or in conjunction with or on behalf of any person, firm or company, carry on, or be engaged, concerned or interested (directly or indirectly) in carrying on Restricted Business (other than as a holder of less than 5 per cent of any class of shares or debentures listed on the London Stock Exchange) within [   ];

(2)   for the period of [   ] after Completion, either on his own account or in conjunction with or on behalf of any other person, firm or company, solicit or entice away from the Company or any of the Subsidiaries any person who at the date hereof is an officer, manager, servant or customer of the Company or any of

the Subsidiaries whether or not such person would commit a breach of contract by reason of leaving service or transferring business; and

(3)   directly or indirectly use or attempt to use in the course of any business, at any time hereafter, on his own account or in conjunction with or on behalf of any person, firm or company any trade or service mark or logo (including the Listed Intellectual Property referred to in the third schedule) used in the business of the Company and the Subsidiaries or any other name, logo, trade or service mark which is or might be confusingly similar thereto.

(C)   Reasonableness[1]
The restrictions contained in sub-clause (B) are considered reasonable by the parties, but in the event that any such restriction shall be found to be void but would be valid if some part thereof were deleted, or the period or area of application reduced, such restriction shall apply with such modification as may be necessary to make it valid and effective.

(D)   Registration
[Any provision of this Agreement, or of any agreement or arrangement of which it forms part, by virtue of which such agreement or arrangement is subject to registration under the Restrictive Trade Practices Act 1976 shall only take effect the day after particulars of such agreement or arrangement have been furnished to the Director General of Fair Trading pursuant to s 24 of that Act].[2]

(E)   Confidentiality
The Vendors shall not divulge to any third party (other than to the Vendors' professional advisers for the purpose of this Agreement in which case the Vendors shall use all reasonable endeavours to procure that such advisers keep such information confidential on terms equivalent to this clause) any confidential information relating to the Company and the Subsidiaries save only insofar as the same has lawfully become a matter of public knowledge otherwise than by reason of a breach of this clause or its unlawful disclosure by any person or to the extent required by law.

7   WARRANTIES AND DEPOSIT

(A)   Purchaser's Knowledge
The Warranties are given subject to matters fairly disclosed in this Agreement or in the Disclosure Letter, but no other information relating to the Company or the Subsidiaries of which the Purchaser

has knowledge (actual or constructive) shall prejudice any claim made by the Purchaser under the Warranties or operate to reduce any amount recoverable.[1]

(B)   Warranties to be Independent
Each of the Warranties shall be separate and independent and, save as expressly provided, shall not be limited by reference to any other Warranty or anything in this Agreement.

(C)   Damages[2]
Without restricting the rights of the Purchaser or the ability of the Purchaser to claim damages on any basis in the event that any of the Warranties is broken or proves to be untrue or misleading, the Vendors shall, on demand, pay to the Purchaser:
(1)   the amount necessary to put the Company and each of the Subsidiaries into the position which would have existed if the Warranties had not been broken and had been true and not misleading; and
(2)   all costs and expenses incurred by the Purchaser, the Company or the Subsidiaries, directly or indirectly, as a result of such breach.

(D)   Pending Completion[3]
The Vendors shall procure that (save only as may be necessary to give effect to this Agreement) neither the Vendors nor the Company nor any of the Subsidiaries shall do, allow or procure any act or omission before Completion which would constitute a breach of any of the Warranties if they were given at any and all times from the date hereof down to Completion or which would make any of the Warranties inaccurate or misleading if they were so given. In particular, without prejudice to the generality of the foregoing, the Vendors shall procure that items (a) to (g) of paragraph 2(22) of the third schedule shall be complied with at all times from the date hereof down to Completion.

(E)   Further Disclosure by Vendors
The Vendors shall forthwith disclose in writing to the Purchaser any matter or thing which may arise or become known to the Vendors after due and careful enquiry, which the Vendors are hereby required to make, after the date hereof and before Completion which is inconsistent with any of the Warranties or which might make any of them inaccurate or misleading if they were given at any and all times from the date hereof down to Completion or which is material to be known to a purchaser for value of the Sale Shares.

(F)   Right of Rescission[4]
In the event of any such matter or thing as is mentioned in sub-clause

(E) becoming known to the Purchaser before Completion or in the event of its becoming apparent on or before Completion that the Vendors are at any time in breach of any of the Warranties or any other term of this Agreement the Purchaser may rescind this Agreement by notice in writing to the Vendors.

(G)   Application of Deposit[5]
Subject to sub-clauses (H) and (I), the Purchaser may apply all or part of the deposit referred to in sub-clause 4(C)(7) ('the Deposit') in recouping any amount lawfully due to it under or by reason of any breach of the terms of this Agreement and any amount so applied shall *pro tanto* satisfy the liability concerned.

(H)   Interest
The Deposit shall be deposited by the Purchaser with bankers selected by it and any interest earned thereon shall accrue to and form part of the Deposit and shall, accordingly, belong to the Vendors subject to the provisions of this Agreement.

(I)   Release
In the event that the Purchaser shall not have notified the Vendors in writing of any claim hereunder before [   ] 19[   ] the Deposit shall be released to the Vendors' solicitors [   ] whose receipt shall be an absolute discharge. In the event that the Purchaser shall have so notified any such claim, it shall use its best endeavours to quantify the amount claimed and any balance shall be so released on that date. Upon final determination of the total amount (if any) falling to be applied by the Purchaser under this clause, any balance of the Deposit shall be released to the Vendors' solicitors provided that no amount shall be released before the said [   ] 19[   ].

8   PROVISIONS RELATING TO THIS AGREEMENT

(A)   Assignment
This Agreement shall be binding upon and enure for the benefit of the successors of the parties but shall not be assignable, save that the Purchaser may assign the benefit of the Warranties to any transferee of the share capital of the Company or any of the Subsidiaries.

(B)   Whole Agreement
This Agreement (together with any documents referred to herein) constitutes the whole agreement between the parties hereto relating to its subject matter and no variations hereof shall be effective unless made in writing. This Agreement supersedes [   ].[1]

(C)   Agreement Survives Completion
The Warranties and all other provisions of this Agreement, in so far

as the same shall not have been performed at Completion, shall remain in full force and effect notwithstanding Completion.

(D)   Rights of Rescission
Any right of rescission conferred upon the Purchaser hereby shall be in addition to and without prejudice to all other rights and remedies available to it and no exercise or failure to exercise such a right of rescission shall constitute a waiver by the Purchaser of any such other right or remedy. Completion shall not constitute a waiver by the Purchaser of any breach of any provision of this Agreement whether or not known to the Purchaser at the date of Completion.

(E)   Release of one Vendor
The Purchaser may release or compromise the liability of any Vendor hereunder without affecting the liability of any other Vendor.[2]

(F)   Further Assurance
At any time after the date hereof the Vendors shall, at the request and cost of the Purchaser, execute such documents and do such acts and things as the Purchaser may reasonably require for the purpose of vesting the Sale Shares in the Purchaser or its nominees and giving to the Purchaser the full benefit of all the provisions of this Agreement.

(G)   Invalidity
If any provision of this Agreement shall be held to be illegal or unenforceable, the enforceability of the remainder of this Agreement shall not be affected.

(H)   Payment to the Vendors
[Subject to clause 4(E)] any payment falling to be made to the Vendors under any provision of this Agreement may be made to the Vendors' solicitors Messrs [   ] whose receipt shall be an absolute discharge.

(I)   Counterparts
This Agreement may be executed in any number of counterparts, which shall together constitute one Agreement.

(J)   Notices
Any notice required to be given hereunder shall be in writing in the English language and shall be served by sending the same by pre-paid first class post, telex or telecopy or by delivering the same by hand, in the case of the Purchaser to its registered office and in the case of the Vendors to [   ]. Any notice sent by post, as provided in this sub-clause, shall be deemed to have been served 48 hours after despatch and any notice sent by telex or telecopy, as

provided in this sub-clause, shall be deemed to have been served at
the time of despatch and in proving the service of the same it will be
sufficient to prove, in the case of a letter, that such letter was properly
pre-paid, addressed and placed in the post and, in the case of a telex
or telecopy, that such telex or telecopy was duly despatched to a
current telex or telecopy number of the addressee.

(K)   English Law
This Agreement shall be governed by, and construed in accordance
with, English law.[3]

9   ANNOUNCEMENTS

The Vendors and the Purchaser shall consult in respect of any
announcement to be made by them or by the Company or the
Subsidiaries concerning the transaction referred to in this
Agreement, other than announcements required to be made by the
Purchaser by the London Stock Exchange in respect of the
Consideration Shares. No such announcement shall be made, save as
aforesaid, without the prior written consent of the other unless such
announcement is required by the London Stock Exchange, by a
court of competent jurisdiction or by any other competent authority
or constitutes an announcement by the Purchaser concerning the
affairs of the Purchaser's group generally.

10   COSTS

Each party to this Agreement shall pay its own costs of and
incidental to this Agreement and the sale and purchase hereby agreed
to be made, provided that if the Purchaser shall exercise any right
hereby conferred to rescind this Agreement the Vendors shall
indemnify the Purchaser against expenses and costs incurred in
investigating the affairs of the Company and the Subsidiaries and in
the preparation of this Agreement.

AS WITNESS the hands of the parties or their duly authorised
representatives the day and year first before written.

FIRST SCHEDULE

Vendors and Directors

(1)   Part I — Vendors   (2)

Name and Address   *Sale Shares*

Part II — Directors

Name of Director   *Company/Companies of which (s)he is a director*

Part III (Continuing Directors)

Name of Director   *Company/Companies of which (s)he is a director*

Part IV (Secretary)

Name of Secretary   *Company/Companies of which (s)he is the secretary*

SECOND SCHEDULE

Company and Subsidiaries

Part I — the Company

Name and Number of Company	*Authorised Capital*	*Issued Capital*	*Held by*	*Beneficially owned by*

Part II — the Subsidiaries

Name and Number of Subsidiary	*Authorised Capital*	*Issued Capital*	*Held by*	*Beneficially owned by*

THIRD SCHEDULE
Warranties and Representations[1]

1 INTERPRETATION

In this schedule where the context admits:

(1) 'Audited Accounts' means the audited consolidated balance sheet of the Company and the Subsidiaries made up as at the Balance Sheet Date and the audited consolidated profit and loss account of the Company and the Subsidiaries for the year ended on the Balance Sheet Date, true copies of which are annexed to the Disclosure Letter, including the notes thereto;

(2) 'Balance Sheet Date' means [19   ];

(3) 'Computer Svstems' means all computer systems used by or for the benefit of the Company at any time, including computer processors, associated and peripheral equipment, computer programs, technlcal and other documentation, and data entered into or created by the foregoing from time to time;

(4) 'Companies Acts' means statutes from time to time in force concerning companies;

(5) 'encumbrance' includes any interest or equity of any person (including, without prejudice to the generality of the foregoing, any right to acquire, option or right of pre-emption) or any mortgage, charge, pledge, lien, assignment, hypothecation, security interest, title retention or any other security agreement or arrangement;

(6) 'environmental liability' includes liability for any form of damage to the environment and for any of the following: damage to living organisms or persons (including impairment of health and interference with amenity); damage to land or personal property; interference with riparian or other proprietory or possessory rights; and public or private nuisance;

(7) 'intellectual property' means patents, trade marks, service marks, rights (whether registered or unregistered) in any designs, applications for any of the foregoing, trade or business names and copyright;

(8) 'intellectual property agreements' means agreements or arrangements relating (wholly or partly) to intellectual property or to the disclosure, use, assignment or patenting of any inventions, discovery, improvements, processes, formulae or other knowhow;

(9) 'Listed Intellectual Property' means the Intellectual Property listed in the list annexed to the Disclosure Letter;

(10) 'Listed Intellectual Property Agreements' means the Intellectual Property Agreements listed in the list annexed to the Disclosure Letter;

(11) 'Management Accounts' means the management accounts for the period ended on [19   ] true copies of which are annexed to the Disclosure Letter;

(12) 'SSAP' means Statement of Standard Accounting Practice in force at the date hereof;

(13) any question whether a person is connected with another shall be determined in accordance with the Income and Corporation Taxes Act 1988, s 839 which shall apply in relation to this schedule as it applies in relation to that Act;[2]

(14) references to 'the Company' include each of the Subsidiaries; and

(15) reference to any Act, statutory instrument, regulation, bye-law or other requirement of English law and to any English legal term for any action, remedy, method of judicial proceeding, legal document, legal status, court, official or any legal concept or thing shall in respect of any jurisdiction other than England be deemed to include that which most nearly approximates in that jurisdiction to the English legal term.

2 WARRANTIES AND REPRESENTATIONS

The Vendors hereby warrant and represent to and for the benefit of the Purchaser in the following terms.

THE COMPANY AND THE VENDORS

(1) Capacity
Each Vendor has full power to enter into and perform this Agreement and this Agreement constitutes binding obligations on the Vendors in accordance with its terms.

(2) Liabilities owing to or by Vendors
There is not outstanding any indebtedness or other liability (actual or contingent) owing by the Company to any Vendor or any Director or any person connected with any of them, nor is there any indebtedness owing to the Company by any such person, and no promise or representation has been made to any Vendor in connection with the Warranties or the Disclosure Letter in respect of which the Company or any of the Subsidiaries might be liable.

(3) Vendors' other interests
No Vendor nor any person connected with any Vendor has any interest, direct or indirect, in any business other than that now carried on by the Company which is or is likely to be or become

competitive with the business or any proposed business of the Company.

THE COMPANY'S CONSTITUTION

(4)   Share Capital
Part I of the second schedule contains true particulars of the authorised and issued share capital of the Company and all the shares there shown as issued are in issue fully paid and are beneficially owned and registered as set out therein free from any encumbrance.

(5)   Memorandum and Articles
The copy of the memorandum and articles of association of the Company annexed to the Disclosure Letter is true and complete and has embodied therein or annexed thereto a copy of every such resolution or agreement as is referred to in the Companies Act 1985, s 380[3].

(6)   Company Resolutions
Neither the Company nor any class of its members has passed any resolution (other than resolutions relating to business at annual general meetings which was not special business).

(7)   Options etc
No person has the right (whether exercisable now or in the future and whether contingent or not) to call for the allotment, issue, sale, transfer or conversion of any share or loan capital of the Company under any option or other agreement (including conversion rights and rights of pre-emption).

THE COMPANY AND THE LAW

(8)   Compliance with Laws
The Company has conducted its business in all material respects in accordance with all applicable laws and regulations of the United Kingdom and any relevant foreign country and there is no order, decree or judgment of any Court or any governmental agency of the United Kingdom or any foreign country outstanding against the Company or which may have a material adverse effect upon the assets or business of the Company.

(9)   Licences etc
All necessary licences, consents, permits and authorities (public and private) have been obtained by the Company to enable the Company to carry on its business effectively in the places and in the manner in which such business is now carried on and all such licences, consents, permits and authorities are valid and subsisting and the Vendors know of no reason why any of them should be suspended, cancelled or revoked.

(10)   Breach of Statutory Provisions
Neither the Company, nor any of its officers, agents or employees
(during the course of their duties in relation to the Company) have
committed, or omitted to do, any act or thing the commission or
omission of which is, or could be, in contravention of any Act, Order,
Regulation or the like in the United Kingdom or elsewhere which is
punishable by fine or other penalty.
(11)   Litigation
The Company is not engaged in any litigation or arbitration
proceedings and so far as the Vendors are aware no litigation or
arbitration proceedings are pending or threatened by or against the
Company and there are no facts likely to give rise to any litigation or
arbitration and the Company has not been a party to any
undertaking or assurance given to any Court or governmental
agency which is still in force.
(12)   Insolvency[4]
   (a)   No order has been made or petition presented or
         resolution passed for the winding up of the Company, nor
         has any distress, execution or other process been levied
         against the Company or action taken to repossess goods in
         the Company's possession.
   (b)   No steps have been taken for the appointment of an
         administrator or receiver of any part of the Company's
         property.
   (c)   No floating charge created by the Company has
         crystallised and, so far as the Vendors are aware, there are
         no circumstances likely to cause such a floating charge to
         crystallise.
   (d)   The Company has not been a party to any transaction
         which could be avoided in a winding up.
   (e)   The Company has not made or proposed any arrangement
         or composition with its creditors or any class of its
         creditors.
(13)   Fair Trading
   (a)   No agreement, practice or arrangement carried on by the
         Company or to which the Company is a party:
         (i)   is or ought to be or ought to have been registered in
               accordance with the provisions of the Restrictive
               Trade Practices Acts 1976 and 1977 or contravenes
               the provisions of the Resale Prices Act 1976 or is or
               has been the subject of any enquiry, investigation or
               proceeding under any of those Acts; or
         (ii) is or has been the subject of an enquiry, investigation,
               reference or report under the Fair Trading Act 1973

(or any previous legislation relating to monopolies or mergers) or the Competition Act 1980; or

(iii) infringes Article 85 of the Treaty establishing the European Economic Community or constitutes an abuse of dominant position contrary to Article 86 of the said Treaty or infringes any Regulation or other enactment made under Article 87 of the said Treaty or is or has been the subject of any enquiry, investigation or proceeding in respect thereof; or

(iv) has been notified to the Directorate General of Competition of the Commission of the European Communities; or

(v) is by virtue of its terms or by virtue of any practice for the time being carried on in connection therewith a 'Consumer Trade Practice' within the meaning of section 13 of the Fair Trading Act 1973 and susceptible to or under reference to the Consumer Protection Advisory Committee or the subject matter of a report to the Secretary of State or the subject matter of an Order by the Secretary of State under the provisions of Part II of that Act; or

(vi) infringes any other competition, anti-restrictive trade practice, anti-trust or consumer protection law or legislation applicable in the United Kingdom or elsewhere and not specifically mentioned in this sub-paragraph.

(*b*) The Company has not given any assurance or undertaking to the Restrictive Practices Court or the Director General of Fair Trading or the Secretary of State for Trade and Industry or the Commission or Court of Justice of the European Communities or to any other court, person or body and is not subject to any Act, decision, regulation, order or other instrument made by any of them relating to any matter referred to in this sub-paragraph (13).

(*c*) The Company is not in default or in contravention of any Article, Act, decision, regulation, order or other instrument or of any undertaking relating to any matter referred to in this sub-paragraph.

(14) Defective Products

The Company has not manufactured, sold or supplied products which are, or were, or will become, in any material respect faulty or defective or which do not comply in any material respect with any warranties or representations expressly or impliedly made by the

Company or with all applicable regulations, standards and requirements in respect thereof.

(15) Inducements

So far as the Vendors are aware no officer, agent or employee of the Company has paid any bribe or used any of the Company's assets unlawfully to obtain an advantage for any person.

THE COMPANY'S ACCOUNTS AND RECORDS

(16) Books and Records

All accounts, books, ledgers, financial and other records of whatsoever kind ('records') of the Company:

  (a) have been fully, properly and accurately maintained, are in the possession of the Company and contain true and accurate records of all matters required by law to be entered therein;

  (b) do not contain or reflect any material inaccuracies or discrepancies; and

and no notice or allegation that any of the records is incorrect or should be rectified has been received. Where any of the records of the Company are kept on Computer Systems, the Company is the owner of all hardware and all software licences necessary to enable it to keep, copy, maintain and use the records in the course of its business and does not share any hardware or software relating to the records with any person.

(17) Accounts Warranty[5]

The Audited Accounts have been prepared in accordance with the requirements of all relevant statutes and generally accepted accounting principles and show a true and fair view of the assets and liabilities of the Company and the Subsidiaries at the Balance Sheet Date and the profits of the Company and the Subsidiaries for the year ended on the Balance Sheet Date and apply bases and policies of accounting which have been consistently applied in the audited balance sheet and profit and loss accounts for the three financial years prior to the Balance Sheet Date.

(18) Provision for Liabilities

Full provision has been made in the Audited Accounts for all actual liabilities of the Company outstanding at the Balance Sheet Date and proper provision (or note) in accordance with generally accepted accounting principles has been made therein for all other liabilities of the Company then outstanding whether contingent, quantified, disputed or not including (without limitation) the cost of any work or material for which payment has been received or credit taken, any future loss which may arise in connection with uncompleted contracts and any claims against the Company in respect of completed contracts.

(19) Stock Valuation and Accounting Policies[6]

For the purposes of the Audited Accounts, the Company's stock in trade and work in progress has been valued in accordance with SSAP 9 and on a basis in all material respects consistent with that adopted for the purpose of the Company's audited accounts in respect of the beginning and end of each of the last three preceding accounting periods and the value of redundant or obsolete materials and materials below standard has been written down to realisable market value or adequate provision has been made therefor.

(20) Management Accounts[7]

The Management Accounts have been prepared in accordance with the Company's normal practices and the Vendors do not consider them misleading.

(21) Returns

The Company has complied with the provisions of the Companies Acts and all returns, particulars, resolutions and other documents required under any legislation to be delivered on behalf of the Company to the Registrar of Companies or to any other authority whatsoever have been properly made and delivered. All such documents delivered to the Registrar of Companies or to any other authority whatsoever, whether or not required by law, were true and accurate when so delivered.

THE COMPANY'S BUSINESS

(22) Business since the Balance Sheet Date[8]

Since the Balance Sheet Date:

    (*a*) the Company has carried on its business in the ordinary and usual course and without entering into any transaction, assuming any liability or making any payment which is not in the ordinary course of its business and without any interruption or alteration in the nature, scope or manner of its business;

    (*b*) the Company has not borrowed or raised any money or taken any financial facility;

    (*c*) the Company has paid its creditors within the times agreed with such creditors and so that there are no debts outstanding by the Company which have been due for more than four weeks;

    (*d*) there has been no unusual change in the Company's stock levels;

    (*e*) the Company has not entered into, or agreed to enter into, any capital commitments;

(*f*) no share or loan capital has been issued or agreed to be issued by the Company;

(*g*) no distribution of capital or income has been declared, made or paid in respect of any share capital of the Company and (excluding fluctuations in overdrawn current accounts with bankers) no loan or share capital of the Company has been repaid in whole or part or has become liable to be repaid; and

(*h*) there has been no material deterioration in the financial position, prospects or turnover of the Company.[9]

(23) Working Capital

Having regard to existing bank and other facilities, the Company has sufficient working capital for the purposes of continuing to carry on its business in its present form and at its present level of turnover for the foreseeable future and for the purposes of executing, carrying out and fulfilling in accordance with their terms all orders, projects and contractual obligations which have been placed with, or undertaken by the Company.

(24) Commission

No one is entitled to receive from the Company any finder's fee, brokerage or other commission in connection with this Agreement or the sale and purchase of shares in the Company.

(25) Consequence of Share Acquisition by the Purchaser

The acquisition of the Sale Shares by the Purchaser or compliance with the terms of this Agreement:

(*a*) will not cause the Company to lose the benefit of any right or privilege it presently enjoys or so far as the Vendors are aware, cause any person who normally does business with the Company not to continue to do so on the same basis as previously;

(*b*) will not relieve any person of any obligation to the Company or enable any person to determine any such obligation or any right or benefit enjoyed by the Company or to exercise any right whether under an agreement with or otherwise in respect of the Company;

(*c*) will not result in any present or future indebtedness of the Company becoming due or capable of being declared due and payable prior to its stated maturity; and

(*d*) will not give rise to or cause to become exercisable any right of pre-emption;

and, to the best of the knowledge and belief of the Vendors, the Company's relationships with clients, customers, suppliers and employees will not be adversely affected thereby.[10]

(26)   Grants

[The Company has not applied for or received any financial assistance from any supranational, national or local authority or government agency.] [Full particulars of all grants received from any supranational, national or local authority or government agency (and all applications for any such) are contained in the Disclosure Letter and there are no circumstances which might lead to any such grant being refunded or forfeited in whole or in part].

(27)   Insurances[11]

    (*a*)   Full particulars of all the Company's insurances are given in the Disclosure Letter and the insurances which are maintained by the Company afford the Company adequate cover against such risks as companies carrying on the same type of business as the Company commonly cover by insurance and in particular:

        (i)   the assets of the Company are insured against fire in their full replacement value;

        (ii) the Computer Systems are insured for all foreseeable risks to their full replacement value, together with incidental expenses, including, without limitation, costs and expenses of data recovery and reconstruction; and

        (iii) the Company is now, and has at all material times been, adequately covered against accident, damage, injury, third party loss (including product liability), loss of profits and other risks normally covered by insurance.

    (*b*)   All the Company's insurances referred to in the Disclosure Letter are in full force and effect, there are no circumstances which might lead to any liability under any of the Company's insurances being avoided by the insurers or the premiums being increased, there are no special or unusual terms, restrictions or rates of premium, all premiums have been paid on time and there is no claim outstanding under any such insurance nor are the Vendors aware of any circumstances likely to give rise to a claim.

(28)   Trading Name

The Company does not trade under any name other than as set out in the Disclosure Letter.

(29)   Trade Associations

True and complete details of all trade or business associations of which the Company is a member are set out in the Disclosure Letter, and the Company is and has at all material times complied in all material respects with the regulations or guidelines laid down by any such trade association and all reports, comments and recommendations made by any such association are annexed to the Disclosure Letter.

(30) Terms of Business

True and complete copies of the standard terms upon which the Company carries on business or provides services to any person are annexed to the Disclosure Letter and the Company does not provide and has not provided any service to any person on terms which differ from its standard terms as annexed.

THE COMPANY'S ASSETS

(31) Net Asset Value

The value of the net tangible assets of the Company at Completion determined in accordance with the same accounting policies as those applied in the Audited Accounts (and on the basis that each fixed asset is valued at a figure no greater than the value attributed to it in the Audited Accounts or, in the case of any fixed asset acquired by the Company after the Balance Sheet Date, at a figure no greater than cost) will not be less than the value of the net tangible assets of the Company at the Balance Sheet Date as shown in the Audited Accounts.[12]

(32) Assets and Charges

(*a*) Except for current assets disposed of by the Company in the ordinary course of its business, the Company is the owner of and has good marketable title to all assets included in the Audited Accounts and all assets which have been acquired by the Company since the Balance Sheet Date and no such asset, nor any of the undertaking, goodwill or uncalled capital of the Company is subject to any encumbrance or any agreement or commitment to give or create any encumbrance.

(*b*) Since the Balance Sheet Date, save for disposals in the ordinary course of its business, the assets of the Company have been in the possession of, or under the control of, the Company.

(*c*) No asset is shared by the Company with any other person and the Company does not depend for its business upon any assets, facilities or services owned or supplied by any Vendor or any person connected with any Vendor.

(*d*) No charge in favour of the Company is void or voidable for want of registration.

(33) Debts[13]

Any debts owed to the Company as recorded in the Company's books and records will realise their full face value and be good and collectable in the ordinary course of business and not subject to any dispute, right of set-off or counter-claim of any kind arising from an act or omission occurring prior to the date of this Agreement and no amount included in the Audited Accounts as owing to the Company at the Balance Sheet Date has been released for an amount less than the value at which it was included in the Audited Accounts or is now regarded by the Vendors as irrecoverable in whole or in part. The Company has not factored or discounted any of its debts or agreed to do so.

(34)   Title Retention

The Company has not acquired or agreed to acquire any material asset on terms that property therein does not pass until full payment is made.

(35)   Intellectual Property Rights

    (*a*)   The Company is the sole beneficial owner of the Listed Intellectual Property and (where such property is capable of registration) the registered proprietor thereof and (save for copyrights) owns no other intellectual property. Save as may appear from the Listed Intellectual Property Agreements no person has been authorised to make any use whatsoever of any intellectual property owned by the Company and the Company has not disclosed (except in the ordinary course of its business) any of its knowhow, trade secrets or list of customers to any other person.

    (*b*)   All the intellectual property used by the Company is owned by it and it does not use any intellectual property in respect of which any third party has any right, title or interest.

    (*c*)   So far as the Vendors are aware, none of the processes or products of the Company infringes any right of any other person relating to intellectual property or involves the unlicensed use of confidential information disclosed to the Company by any person in circumstances which might entitle that person to a claim against the Company and none of the Listed Intellectual Property is being used, claimed, opposed or attacked by any person.

    (*d*)   The Vendors are not aware of any infringement of the Listed Intellectual Property by any third party.

    (*e*)   There are no outstanding claims against the Company for infringement of any intellectual property used (or which has been used) by it and no such claims have been settled by the giving of any undertakings which remain in force.

    (*f*)   Confidential information and knowhow used by the

Company is kept strictly confidential and the Company operates and fully complies with procedures which maintain such confidentiality. The Vendors are not aware of any such confidentiality having been breached.

(*g*) All application and renewal fees, costs and charges relating to the Listed Intellectual Property have been duly paid on time.

(*h*) The Listed Intellectual Property Agreements are all the intellectual property agreements to which the Company is a party and each of them is valid and binding.

(36) Condition of Stock

The Company's stock in trade is in good condition, meets all relevant statutory, regulatory and industry accepted standards and is capable of being sold by the Company in the ordinary course of its business in accordance with its current price list without rebate or allowance to a purchaser.

(37) Plant

The machinery and plant, including fixed plant and machinery, and all vehicles and the Computer Systems and other office and other equipment used in connection with the business of the Company:

(*a*) is in good repair and condition and in satisfactory working order;

(*b*) is capable, and will (subject to fair wear and tear) be capable, over the period of time during which it will be written down to a nil value in the accounts of the Company, of doing the work for which it was designed or purchased;

(*c*) is not surplus to the Company's requirements; and

(*d*) is in the possession and control of, and is the absolute property free from any encumbrance of, the Company save for those items held under hire purchase or rental agreements the value of which items in the aggregate does not exceed [£   ].

(38) Computer Systems

(*a*) The Computer Systems have been satisfactorily maintained and supported and have the benefit of an appropriate maintenance and support agreement terminable by the contractor by not less than 24 months notice.

(*b*) The Computer Systems have adequate capability and capacity for the projected requirements of the Company for not less than four years following Completion for the processing and other functions required to be performed for the purposes of the business of the Company.

(c) Disaster recovery plans are in effect and are adequate to ensure that the Computer Systems can be replaced or substituted without material disruption to the business of the Company.

(d) In the event that any person providing maintenance or support services for the Computer Systems ceases or is unable to do so, the Company has all necessary rights to obtain the source code and all related technical and other information free of charge and to procure the carrying out of such services by employees or by a third party.

(e) The Company has sufficient technically competent and trained employees to ensure proper handling, operation, monitoring and use of the Computer Systems.

(f) The Company has adequate procedures to ensure internal and external security of the Computer Systems, including procedures for taking and storing on-site and off-site back-up copies of computer programs and data.

(39) Title to Properties

The particulars of the Properties shown in the list annexed to the Disclosure Letter are true and correct and the owner shown therein has good and marketable title to and exclusive occupation of each Property which it is said to own free from any encumbrance, sub-lease, tenancy or right of occupation, reservation, easement, quasi-easement or privilege in favour of any third party and there are appurtenant to each Property all rights and easements necessary for its use and enjoyment and except as shown the Company has no other interest in land and does not occupy any other property.

(40) Matters affecting Properties

(a) No Property or any part thereof is affected by any of the following matters or is to the knowledge of the Vendors likely to become so affected:

(i) any outstanding dispute, notice or complaint or any exception, reservation, right, covenant, restriction or condition which is of an unusual nature or which affects or might in the future affect the use of any of the Properties for the purpose for which it is now used or which affects or might in the future affect the value of the Properties; or

(ii) any notice, order, demand, requirement or proposal of which the owner has notice or of which the Vendors are aware made or issued by or on behalf of any government or statutory authority, department or body for acquisition, clearance, demolition or closing, the carrying out of any work upon any building, the modification of any planning permission, the discontinuance of any use or the imposition of any building or improvement line; or

(iii) any compensation received as a result of any refusal of any application for planning consent or the imposition of any restrictions in relation to any planning consent; or

(iv) any commutation or agreement for the commutation of rent or payment of rent in advance of the due dates of payment thereof.

(*b*) Each of the Properties is in a good and substantial state of repair and condition and fit for the purposes for which it is at present used and no high alumina cement, woodwool, calcium chloride, sea dredged aggregates or asbestos material was used in the construction thereof or of any of them and there are no development works, redevelopment works or fitting out works outstanding in respect of any of the Properties.

(*c*) All restrictions, conditions and covenants (including any imposed by or pursuant to any lease) affecting any of the Properties have been observed and performed and no notice of any breach of any of the same has been received or is to the Vendors' knowledge likely to be received.

(*d*) The use of the Properties and all machinery and equipment therein and the conduct of any business therein complies in all respects with all relevant statutes and regulations including without prejudice to the generality of the foregoing the Factories Act 1961, the Offices Shops and Railway Premises Act 1963, the Fire Precautions Act 1971, the Health and Safety at Work etc Act 1974 and with all rules, regulations and delegated legislation thereunder and all necessary licences and consents required thereunder have been obtained.

(*e*) There are no restrictive covenants or provisions, legislation or orders, charges, restrictions, agreements, conditions or other matters which preclude the use of any of the Properties for the purposes for which the Properties are now used and each such user is the permitted user under the provisions of the Town and Country Planning Act 1990 and regulations made thereunder and is in accordance with the requirements of the Local Authorities and all restrictions, conditions and covenants imposed by or pursuant to the said Town and Country Planning Acts have been observed and performed and no agreements have been entered into under the Town and Country Planning Act 1971, s 52 in respect of any of the Properties.

(*f*) All replies by or on behalf of the Vendors or the Company to enquiries relating to any of the Properties made by or on behalf of the Purchaser were when given and are now true and correct.

(41)   Properties Previously Owned

The Company has no existing or contingent liabilities in respect of any properties previously occupied by it or in which it owned or held any interest, including, without limitation, leasehold premises assigned or otherwise disposed of.

THE COMPANY AND THE ENVIRONMENT[14]

(42)   Authorisations

(*a*) Full particulars are given in the Disclosure Letter of all material authorisations, permissions, consents, licences and agreements ('authorisations') held by the Company:

(i) to abstract water;

(ii) to hold raw materials, products or wastes;

(iii) to carry on processes;

(iv) to construct and maintain buildings, plant and equipment; and

(v) to keep, treat, carry, consign and dispose of waste materials, gases and effluents.

All the authorisations have been lawfully obtained and are in full force and effect.

(*b*) The Company has complied with all conditions attaching to the authorisations, and the Vendors are not aware of any circumstances which would make it impossible or difficult for the Company to comply with such conditions in the future.

(*c*) The Company has received no communication revoking, suspending, modifying or varying any of the authorisations and is not aware of any circumstances which might give rise to any such communication being received.

(43)   Compliance with Environmental Protection Laws

(*a*) The Company has not committed any breach of statutory requirements for the protection of the environment or of human health or amenity, and has acted at all times in conformity with all relevant codes of practice, guidance, notes, standards and other advisory material issued by any competent authority.

(b) The Company has not received any communication from any competent authority in respect of the Company's business, failure to comply with which would constitute breach of any statutory requirements or compliance with which could be secured by further proceedings. The Vendors are not aware of any circumstances which might give rise to any such communication being received.

(44) Environmental Liability

The Vendors are not aware of any actual or potential environmental liability on the part of the Company arising from any activities or operations of the Company from wastes or other substances used, kept or produced by the Company or from the condition of any properties now or formerly owned or occupied by the Company or facilities now or formerly used by the Company.

(45) Wastes and other Substances

(a) The Company has at all times taken all necessary steps to ensure proper keeping, treatment, consignment, carriage and disposal of wastes produced in the course of the Company's business so as to comply with all statutory requirements and duties and in accordance with all codes of practice, notes, standards and other advisory material issued by any competent authority. For the purposes of this warranty 'wastes' includes substances which are wastes to the Company notwithstanding that they may be of value or utility to some other person.

(b) Without prejudice to the generality of sub-paragraph (a) the Company has taken all necessary steps to ensure:

(i) that all such wastes are consigned only to a properly authorised disposer or carrier for disposal at a facility licensed to receive such wastes;

(ii) that all such wastes have been properly described, and

(iii) that adequate contractual rights exist so as to enable the Company to obtain indemnity for any claim arising against the Company in respect of such wastes by reason of breach of statutory duty, lack of due care, or malpractice on the part of the disposer or carrier.

Particulars of all relevant contracts are given in the Disclosure Letter.

(c) No dispute, claim or proceedings exists between the Company and any disposer or carrier with regard to the Company's wastes, whether or not yet consigned to such disposer or carrier, and the Vendors are not aware of any circumstances which are likely to give rise to such dispute, claim or proceedings.

(*d*) All other substances used or kept by the Company are stored, handled and used in such a way as to minimise the risk of environmental liability and there have been no unintended discharges or escapes of such substances so as to present the risk of environmental liability.

(46) Condition of Sites

(*a*) All sites owned or occupied by the Company are free from any contamination which could give rise (whether on the relevant site or elsewhere) to environmental liability.

(*b*) The Vendors are not aware of any circumstances which may require expenditure (whether by the Company or by any other person or authority) on cleaning up or decontaminating any sites now owned or occupied by the Company so as to avoid or reduce the risk of environmental liability or which may require expenditure on investigatory, monitoring, precautionary or remedial engineering measures in relation to any such site, nor are the Vendors aware of circumstances which may give rise to a claim against the Company in respect of such expenditure on any site formerly owned or occupied by the Company.

(*c*) No communication has been received from any competent authority relating to the condition of any site now or formerly owned or occupied by the Company or relating to a proposal for the inclusion of any such site in any register of potentially contaminated land nor are the Vendors aware of any circumstances likely to give rise to the service of such a communication.

(47) Environmental Information

The Company has at all times supplied to the competent authorities such information and assessments as to the Company's processes, substances, discharges, wastes and effluents as are required by law to be supplied. All such information given (whether under a legal obligation or otherwise) was correct at the time the information was supplied and so far as the Vendors are aware all information contained on public registers relating to such matters is correct.

(48) Internal Environmental Policy and Audits

(*a*) The Company has complied with any internal or published statements of corporate environmental policy and operating procedures.

(*b*) All environmental investigations, audits or appraisals undertaken or commissioned by the Company as to the Company's operations, plant, equipment or sites ('audits') are particularised in the Disclosure Letter, including details of the date and nature of the audit, by whom the audit was undertaken and of any report prepared as a result of the audit. So far as the Vendors are aware the audits were carried out competently and the contents of any reports are correct.

THE COMPANY'S CONTRACTS

(49) Documents
All title deeds and agreements to which the Company is a party and other documents owned by or which ought to be in the possession of the Company are in the possession of the Company and are properly stamped and are free from any encumbrance.

(50) Material Contracts
The Company is not a party to or subject to any agreement, transaction, obligation, commitment, understanding, arrangement or liability which:

(*a*) is incapable of complete performance in accordance with its terms within six months after the date on which it was entered into or undertaken; or

(*b*) is known by the Vendors or by the Company to be likely to result in a loss to the Company on completion of performance; or

(*c*) cannot readily be fulfilled or performed by the Company on time and without undue or unusual expenditure of money and effort; or

(*d*) involves or is likely to involve obligations, restrictions, expenditure or receipts of an unusual, onerous or exceptional nature and not in the ordinary course of the Company's business; or

(*e*) is a lease or a contract for hire or rent, hire purchase or purchase by way of credit sale or periodical payment; or

(*f*) is with any trade union or body or organisation representing its employees; or

(*g*) requires an aggregate consideration payable by the Company in excess of [£   ]; or

(*h*) involves or is likely to involve the supply of goods by or to the Company the aggregate sales value of which will represent in excess of [ten] per cent of the turnover of the Company for its last financial year; or (*i*)   is a contract for services (other than contracts for the supply of electricity or normal office services); or

(*j*)   requires the Company to pay any commission, finder's fee, royalty or the like; or

(*k*)   in any way restricts the Company's freedom to carry on the whole or any part of its business in any part of the world in such manner as it thinks fit; or

(*l*)   involves liabilities which may fluctuate in accordance with an index or rate of currency exchange; or

(*m*)   is a contract for the sale of shares or assets which contains warranties or indemnities; or

(*n*)   is in any way otherwise than in the ordinary course of the Company's business.

(51)   Defaults

Neither the Company nor any other party to any agreement with the Company is in default thereunder, being a default which would be material in the context of the financial or trading position of the Company nor (so far as the Vendors are aware) are there any circumstances likely to give rise to such a default.

(52)   Sureties

No person other than the Company or a Subsidiary has given any guarantee of or security for any overdraft loan or loan facility granted to the Company.

(53)   Powers of Attorney

No powers of attorney given by the Company (other than to the holder of an encumbrance solely to facilitate its enforcement) are now in force. No person, as agent or otherwise, is entitled or authorised to bind or commit the Company to any obligation not in the ordinary course of the Company's business, and the Vendors are not aware of any person purporting to do so.

(54)   Insider Contracts

(*a*)   There is not outstanding, and there has not at any time during the last six years been outstanding, any agreement or arrangement to which the Company is a party and in which any Vendor, any person beneficially interested in the Company's share capital or any Director or any person connected with any of them is or has been interested, whether directly or indirectly.

(*b*)   The Company is not a party to, nor have its profits or financial position during such period been affected by, any agreement or arrangement which is not entirely of an arm's length nature.

(*c*)   All costs incurred by the Company have been charged to the Company and not borne by any other person.

(55) Debts
There are no debts owing by or to the Company other than debts which have arisen in the ordinary course of business, nor has the Company lent any money which has not been repaid.

(56) Options and Guarantees
The Company is not a party to any option or pre-emption right, or a party to any guarantee, suretyship, comfort letter or any other obligation (whatever called) to pay, provide funds or take action in the event of default in the payment of any indebtedness of any other person or default in the performance of any obligation of any other person.

(57) Tenders etc
No offer, tender or the like is outstanding which is capable of being converted into an obligation of the Company by an acceptance or other act of some other person.

THE COMPANY AND ITS BANKERS

(58) Borrowings
The total amount borrowed by the Company from its bankers does not exceed its facilities and the total amount borrowed by the Company from whatsoever source does not exceed any limitation on its borrowing contained in its articles of association, or in any debenture or loan stock deed or other instrument.

(59) Continuance of Facilities
Full and accurate details of all overdrafts, loans or other financial facilities outstanding or available to the Company are contained in the Disclosure Letter and true and correct copies of all documents relating thereto are annexed to the Disclosure Letter and neither the Vendors nor the Company have done anything whereby the continuance of any such facilities in full force and effect might be affected or prejudiced.

(60) Off-balance Sheet Financing
The Company has not engaged in any borrowing or financing not required to be reflected in the Audited Accounts.

(61) Bank Accounts
A statement of all the bank accounts of the Company and of the credit or debit balances on such accounts as at a date not more than seven days before the date hereof is annexed to the Disclosure Letter. The Company has no other bank or deposit accounts (whether in credit or overdrawn) and since such statement there have been no payments out of any such accounts except for routine payments and the balances on current account are not now substantially different from the balances shown on such statements.

THE COMPANY AND ITS EMPLOYEES

(62) Directors

The particulars shown in the first schedule are true and complete and no person not named therein as such is a director or shadow director of the Company.

(63) Particulars of Employees[15]

    (*a*) The particulars shown in the schedule of employees annexed to the Disclosure Letter show all remuneration payable and other benefits provided or which the Company is bound to provide (whether now or in the future) to each officer, employee or consultant of the Company or any person connected with any such person and are true and complete and include particulars of all profit sharing, incentive and bonus arrangements to which the Company is a party whether legally binding on the Company or not.

    (*b*) Since the Balance Sheet Date no change has been made in the rate of remuneration, or the emoluments or pension benefits of any officer, ex-officer or employee of the Company and no change has been made in the terms of engagement of any such officer or employee, and no additional officer or employee has been appointed.

    (*c*) No present officer or employee of the Company has given or received notice terminating his employment except as expressly contemplated under this Agreement.

    (*d*) The Company has not given notice of any redundancies to any employee or government department or started consultations with any trade union pursuant to any statute or regulation.

(64) Service Contracts

There is not outstanding any contract of service between the Company and any of its directors, officers or employees which is not terminable by the Company without compensation (other than any compensation payable by statute) on not more than three months' notice given at any time.

(65) Disputes with Employees

The Vendors are not aware of any outstanding claim against the Company by any person who is now or has been an officer or employee of the Company or any dispute between the Company and a material number or class of its employees and no payments are due by the Company under the provisions of the Employment Protection (Consolidation) Act 1978.

THE COMPANY AND ITS SUBSIDIARIES

(66) Particulars of Subsidiaries
The particulars of the Subsidiaries set out in part II of the second schedule are true and complete and the Company has no other subsidiary.

(67) Investments Associations and Branches
The Company:

(*a*) is not the holder or beneficial owner of, and has not agreed to acquire, any class of the share or other capital of any other company or corporation (whether incorporated in the United Kingdom or elsewhere) other than the Subsidiaries;

(*b*) is not and has not agreed to become a member of any partnership, joint venture, consortium or other unincorporated association or arrangement for sharing commissions or income; and

(*c*) has no branch, agency or place of business outside England and no permanent establishment (as that expression is defined in the relevant double taxation relief orders current at the date hereof) outside the United Kingdom.

MISCELLANEOUS

(68) Circular
The information contained in the proof circular to shareholders of the Purchaser in agreed terms (incorporating listing particulars) and the draft Press Announcement in agreed terms, insofar as it relates to the Company and the Vendors, is true and accurate in all material respects, is in accordance with the facts and is not misleading.

(69) Sale Memorandum
All information contained or referred to in the sale memorandum (including any annexure thereto) ('the Sale Memorandum') attached to the Disclosure Letter is accurate in all respects and the Vendors are not aware of any other fact or matter which renders any such information misleading or which might reasonably affect the willingness of a purchaser to acquire the Sale Shares on the terms, including price, of this Agreement. All forecasts, estimates and expressions of opinion, intention or expectation expressed in the Sale Memorandum are reasonably based and are fair and honest in all respects and have been made after due and careful enquiry.

(70) All Material Matters Disclosed[15]
All information contained or referred to in the Disclosure Letter or in any annexure thereto is accurate in all respects and the Vendors

are not aware of any other fact or matter which renders any such information misleading or which might reasonably affect the willingness of a purchaser to acquire the Sale Shares on the terms, including price, of this Agreement.

FOURTH SCHEDULE

Taxation[1]

1 INTERPRETATION

In this schedule, where the context admits:

(1) 'Audited Accounts'[2] and 'Balance Sheet Date' have the same meanings as in the third schedule;

(2) 'event' includes (without limitation):

(a) any omission, transaction or distribution whether or not the Company is a party thereto;[3]

(b) the death of any person;[4]

(c) the failure to avoid an apportionment or deemed distribution of income (whether or not it is or was possible, by taking action after Completion, to avoid such apportionment or deemed distribution)[5];

(d) the Company ceasing to be a member of any group or associated with any person on or before Completion[6];

(e) Completion[6]; and

(f) any event which is treated as having occurred for the purposes of any legislation;[6]

and references to the result of events on or before the date of Completion shall include the combined result of two or more events the first of which shall have taken place on or before the date of Completion;[7]

[(3) 'group relief' has the meaning given to that expression by the Taxes Act 1988, s 402];[37]

(4) 'relief' means any relief, allowance or credit in respect of taxation or any deduction in computing income, profits or gains for the purpose of taxation;[8]

(5) 'taxation claim' means a claim for taxation against the Company or the Purchaser[9] or any member of the Purchaser's Group, whether made before or after the date hereof, whether satisfied[10] or unsatisfied at the date hereof and whether or not the taxation in question is also chargeable against or attributable to any other person, and includes any assessment, notice, demand or other communication from or action taken by any person, authority or body responsible for the assessment, collection or recovery of taxation in any country which claims:

(a) payment of taxation;

(b) to deprive the Company or the Purchaser of any relief whether arising before or after the date hereof[11]; or (*c*) to nullify or cancel any right to the repayment of taxation whether arising before or after the date hereof;[12]

and which arises from or by reference to:

    (i) any income, profits or gains earned, accrued[13] or received on or before the date of Completion or any event on or before the date of Completion, whether alone or in conjunction with other circumstances; or

    (ii) a payment under paragraph 2(A)[14];

(6) 'relevant taxation claim' means any taxation claim save to the extent that:

    (*a*) provision or reserve in respect thereof has been made in the Audited Accounts or to the extent that payment or discharge of such claim has been taken into account in the Audited Accounts;[15]

    (*b*) provision or reserve in respect thereof has been made in the Audited Accounts which is insufficient only by reason of any increase in rates of taxation or change in law[16] after the date hereof having retrospective effect;

    (*c*) it is a claim for which the Company is or may become liable as a result of transactions (not including distributions) entered into by the Company in the ordinary course of trading[17] after the Balance Sheet Date and for the purposes of this sub-paragraph the following shall not be regarded as arising in the ordinary course of trading:

    (i) any liability under Part VIII of the Taxes Management Act 1970 (charges on non-residents);

    (ii) any liability under Part XVII of the Taxes Act 1988 (anti-avoidance);

    (iii) any liability in respect of any distribution (as defined in Part VI of the Taxes Act 1988) or deemed distribution; and

    (iv) any liability arising from the disposal of or acquisition or deemed disposal or acquisition of any asset other than trading stock;

    (*d*) it is a claim against the Purchaser or any member of the Purchaser's Group which does not relate to the Sale Shares or the Company or a payment under paragraph 2(A) or which is for stamp duty or stamp duty reserve tax arising out of this Agreement or Completion; or (*e*) it is a claim which would not have arisen but for a voluntary act or transaction, which could reasonably have been avoided, carried out by the Purchaser (or persons deriving title from it) or the Company after the date of completion otherwise than in the ordinary course of business and which the Purchaser was aware could give rise to a claim, but so that this exclusion shall not extend to any voluntary act carried out with the approval, concurrence or assistance of the Vendors[18];

(7) 'taxation' includes (without limitation) corporation tax, advance corporation tax, income tax, capital gains tax, the charge under s 601(2) Taxes Act 1988, value added tax, customs and other import duties, capital transfer tax, inheritance tax, stamp duty[19], stamp duty reserve tax, capital duty, national insurance contributions, foreign taxation and any payment whatsoever which the Company may be or become bound to make to any person as a result of the operation of any enactment relating to taxation and all penalties, charges and interest relating to any claim for taxation or resulting from a failure to comply with the provisions of any enactment relating to taxation;

(8) 'Taxes Act 1988' means the Income and Corporation Taxes Act 1988;

(9) 'TCGA 1992' means the Taxation of Chargeable Gains Act 1992;

(10) references to income or profits or gains earned, accrued or received shall include income or profits or gains treated as earned, accrued or received for the purposes of any legislation;

(11) references to 'the Company' include each of the Subsidiaries; and

(12) any taxation claim arising out of any of the following shall be treated as a relevant taxation claim for all the purposes of this schedule notwithstanding any other provision hereof[20]:

[   ]

2   TAXATION PAYMENTS

(A) Payments

(1) Subject to and in accordance with the terms of this schedule the Vendors shall make payments to the Purchaser[21] equal to the amount of each relevant taxation claim and all costs properly incurred by the Purchaser or

the Company in connection therewith and in enforcing the Purchaser's rights thereunder.

(2) For this purpose the amount of any relevant taxation claim shall depend upon whether the claim is of the type described in item (*a*), (*b*) or (*c*) of paragraph 1[(5)]. In the case of a claim of the type described in item (*a*), the amount is the payment claimed; in the case of a claim of the type described in item (*b*), the amount is the amount of taxation (on the basis of rates current at the date of the loss of the relief)[22] which would have been relieved, allowed or credited by the relief of which it is claimed to deprive the Company or the Purchaser, and in the case of a claim of the type described in item (*c*), the amount is the repayment which it is claimed to nullify or cancel.

(3) Where any relevant taxation claim has been reduced or eliminated by (or where a relevant taxation claim would have arisen but for) some relief available to the Company then such relief shall be disregarded for the purposes of determining whether, in what amount, and on what date any payment should be made by the Vendors hereunder, and accordingly the relevant taxation claim shall be treated as not being reduced or eliminated (or, as the case may be, shall be treated as having arisen).[23]

(B)   Date for Payment

The Vendors shall be bound to make payments in respect of relevant taxation claims on the following dates:

(1) in so far as a relevant taxation claim represents taxation to be borne by the Company but which has not yet become due, the Vendors shall make the payment in respect of that claim (or so much thereof as represents that taxation) on the date on which that taxation becomes due;

(2) in so far as a relevant taxation claim consists of the nullification or cancellation of a right to repayment of taxation the Vendors shall make the payment in respect of that claim (or so much thereof as represents that nullification or cancellation) on the date on which that repayment would otherwise have become due; and

(3) in any other case the Vendors shall make the payment 14 days after the date on which a notice setting out details of the relevant taxation claim is delivered to the Vendors[24];

and for this purpose references to a date on which taxation becomes due include a reference to the date on which it would have become due were it not for the availability of some relief. Any payment which becomes due on a day which is not a business day shall be paid on the next following business day, and any payment which is made after noon on any day before shall, for the purposes of calculating interest, be deemed to have been paid on the next following business day. No payment shall be treated as made until cleared funds in respect thereof are available to the Purchaser.

(C) Reduction in Consideration

Insofar as the payments made by the Vendors to the Purchaser pursuant to sub-paragraph (A) are less than the consideration for the Sale Shares, they shall constitute a repayment of and a reduction in such consideration, but nothing in this paragraph shall limit the liability of the Vendors to make payments under sub-paragraph (A).[25]

(D) Disclosure not Relevant

The Vendors' obligations to make payments under sub-paragraph (A) shall not be affected by the disclosure, in the Disclosure Letter or otherwise, of the relevant taxation claim giving rise to the payment, or the circumstances giving rise to that relevant taxation claim.[26]

(E) Credits and Reductions

If any relevant taxation claim is disputed by the Company or by either party or represents taxation for which credit is or may become due to the Company at a later date or in respect of which it is subsequently found that there arises a corresponding credit or right to repayment of taxation, the amount of the relevant taxation claim shall nevertheless be payable in full by the Vendors on the due date ascertained in accordance with sub-paragraph (B)[27] but if subsequently any reduction is made in the claim or it is found that the liability in respect thereof falls short of the amount claimed or such credit or repayment is received by the Company the Purchaser shall promptly repay to the Vendors an amount equal to such reduction, shortfall, credit or repayment up to the amount previously paid by the Vendors in respect of that relevant taxation claim and without interest[28], save to the extent that interest is included (or allowed) in such credit, repayment, reduction or shortfall. For this purpose, no credit shall be taken to have been received by the Company unless it shall have relieved the Company of a present obligation to pay taxation.

(F) Over-Provisions

If, at the request and cost of the Vendors, the Company's auditors shall certify that any provision for taxation (not being a provision for deferred taxation)[29] contained in the Audited Accounts is an over-provision, the value of such over-provision shall be set against the liability of the Vendors under sub-paragraph (A), except in so far as such over-provision is attributable to the effect of a change in rates of taxation after the date hereof, but no deduction shall be made from any payment which the Vendors shall be obliged to make hereunder unless such certificate is in existence on the due date for that payment. In the event that such a certificate is given after the Vendors have made a payment hereunder, the Purchaser shall refund to the Vendors (without interest) any payment made by the Vendors to the Vendors (without interest) any payment made by the Vendors to the extent that such over-provision could have been set against such payment if the certificate had been in existence on the due date of payment. The Purchaser shall procure that the Company shall co-operate in obtaining any such certificate if the Vendors shall so request.

(G)   Notice and Mitigation

    (1)   If the Purchaser shall become aware of any relevant taxation claim it shall forthwith give written notice thereof to the Vendors setting out reasonable particulars thereof, including the amount and the date on which the Vendors are bound to make a payment in respect of that relevant taxation claim, ascertained in accordance with sub-paragraph (B), but no failure by the Purchaser to comply with this sub-clause shall affect the Vendors' obligations under sub-paragraph (A)[30].

    (2)   Except in a case where fraud or negligent misconduct is alleged the Purchaser shall take such action and give such information and assistance in connection with the affairs of the Company as the Vendors may reasonably and promptly by notice request to avoid, resist, appeal or compromise a relevant taxation claim provided that:

        (*a*)   the Company shall not be obliged to appeal against any assessment, notice, demand or decision if, having given the Vendors written notice of the receipt thereof, the Purchaser has not within 7[31] days thereafter received instructions in writing from the Vendors to do so; and

        (*b*)   the Company shall not in any circumstances be obliged to pursue any appeal beyond the General Commissioners of Inland Revenue, the Special Commissioners of Inland Revenue, or Value Added Tax Tribunal or any equivalent forum in the United Kingdom or any other jurisdiction[32].

    (3)   The action which the Vendors may request under sub-paragraph (2) shall include (without limitation) the

Company applying to postpone (so far as legally possible)[33] the payment of any taxation and allowing the Vendors to take on or take over at their own expense the conduct of all proceedings of whatsoever nature arising in connection with the relevant taxation claim in question. If the Vendors take on or take over the conduct of proceedings, the Purchaser shall, and shall procure that the Company shall, provide such information and assistance as the Vendors may reasonably require in connection with the preparation for and conduct of such proceedings.

(4) Where the Company is entitled to recover from some other person (including any taxing[34] or other authority) any sum in respect of any relevant taxation claim the Purchaser shall take such action as the Vendors may reasonably and promptly by notice request to enforce such recovery by the Company and shall account to the Vendors for any amount so recovered by the Company not exceeding the amount paid by the Vendors hereunder in respect of that relevant taxation claim together with any interest or repayment supplement included in such recovery less any taxation payable thereon.

(5) Notwithstanding anything in this Agreement, neither the Purchaser nor the Company shall be obliged to take any steps to reduce the amount of any relevant taxation claim or to recover any amount from any other person unless the Vendors shall first indemnify and secure the Company and the Purchaser to their satisfaction against all losses, costs, interest, damages and expenses which may be incurred thereby.

(H) Interest
The Vendors shall make all payments under this schedule in immediately available funds before noon on the due date for payment without deduction or withholding on any account (save as expressly provided in this schedule) and if any amount is not paid when due the Vendors shall pay to the Purchaser interest on such amount at the rate of [   ][35] per cent per annum above the base rate of [   ] Bank plc from time to time from the due date until the date of actual payment (as well after judgment as before).

(I) Deductions and Withholdings
(1) Any amount payable pursuant to sub-paragraphs (A) or (H) shall be paid free and clear of all deductions,

withholdings or set-offs whatsoever, save only as may be required by law[36].

(2) If any deductions or withholdings are required by law to be made from any sums, the Vendors shall be obliged to pay the Purchaser such amount as will after the deduction or withholding has been made, leave the Purchaser with the same amount as it would have been entitled to receive in the absence of such requirement to make a deduction or withholding provided that if the Purchaser subsequently receives a credit for such deduction or withholding then such credit shall be applied in accordance with the provision of sub-paragraph (E).

3 TAXATION WARRANTIES AND REPRESENTATIONS

The Vendors hereby warrant and represent to and for the benefit of the Purchaser in the following terms[37].

GENERAL TAXATION MATTERS

(1) Residence
The Company is and always has been resident for taxation purposes only in the jurisdiction in which it is incorporated.

(2) Tax Provisions
Full provision or reserve has been made in the Audited Accounts for all taxation liable to be assessed on the Company or for which it is accountable in respect of income, profits or gains earned, accrued or received on or before the Balance Sheet Date or any event on or before the Balance Sheet Date including distributions made down to such date or provided for in the Audited Accounts and full provision has been made in the Audited Accounts for deferred taxation calculated in accordance with generally accepted accounting principles.

(3) Returns
The Company has properly and punctually made all returns and provided all information required for taxation purposes and none of such returns is disputed by the Inland Revenue or any other authority concerned (in the United Kingdom or elsewhere) and the Vendors are not aware that any dispute is likely, or that any event has occurred which would or might give rise to a payment under paragraph 2(A).

(4) Payment of Tax
The Company has duly and punctually paid all taxation which it has become liable to pay and is under no liability to pay any penalty or interest in connection with any claim for taxation and has not paid any tax which it was and is not properly due to pay.

(5)   Audits
The Company has not in the last six years received any visit or inspection from any taxation authority.

DISTRIBUTIONS AND PAYMENTS

(6)   Distributions
  (*a*)   No distribution within the meaning of ss 209, 210 and 212 of the Taxes Act 1988 has been made by the Company except dividends shown in its audited accounts nor is the Company bound to make any such distribution.
  (*b*)   No securities (within the meaning of the Taxes Act 1988, s 254(1)) issued by the Company and remaining in issue at the date hereof were issued in such circumstances that the interest payable thereon falls to be treated as a distribution under the Taxes Act 1988, s 209(2)(*e*)(iii).
  (*c*)   The Company has not made or received any distribution which is an exempt distribution within the Taxes Act 1988, s 213.
  (*d*)   The Company has not received any capital distribution to which the provisions of the Taxes Act 1988, s 346 could apply.
  (*e*)   The Company has not used any credit, relief or set-off that may be disallowed pursuant to TCGA 1992, s 189.
  (*f*)   The Company has not issued any share capital, nor granted options or rights to any person which entitles that person to require the issue of any share capital to which the provision of the Taxes Act 1988, s 249 could apply.

[(7)   Group Income [Membership of Group]³⁷
[The Disclosure Letter contains particulars of all elections made by the Company under the Taxes Act 1988, s 247 and the Company has not paid any dividend without paying advance corporation tax or made any payment without deduction of income tax in the circumstances specified in sub-section (6) of that section. In respect of each such election the conditions of the Taxes Act 1988, s 247 have at all times and continue to be satisfied.] [The Company is not and never has been a member of a group of companies for the purposes of any taxation.]

[(8)   Surrender of Advance Corporation Tax³⁷
The Disclosure Letter contains particulars of all arrangements and agreements to which the Company is or has been a party relating to the surrender of advance corporation tax made or received by the Company under the Taxes Act 1988, s 240 and:
  (*a*)   the Company has not paid nor is liable to pay any amount in excess of the advance corporation tax surrendered to it

nor for the benefit of any advance corporation tax which is or may become incapable of set-off against the Company's liability to corporation tax;

(*b*)   the Company has received all payments due to it under any such arrangement or agreement for all surrenders of advance corporation tax made by it; and

(*c*)   save in respect of this Agreement, there have not been in existence in relation to the Company any such arrangements as are referred to in the Taxes Act 1988, s 240(11).]

(9)   ACT Carry Forward

There has been no major change in the business of the Company within the meaning of the Taxes Act 1988, s 245.

(10)   Payments under Deduction

All payments by the Company to any person which ought to have been made under deduction of tax have been so made and the Company has (if required by law to do so) provided certificates of deduction to such person and accounted to the Inland Revenue for the tax so deducted.

(11)   Payments and Disallowances

No rents, interest, annual payments or other sums of an income nature paid or payable by the Company or which the Company is under an obligation to pay in the future are wholly or partially disallowable as deductions or charges in computing profits for the purposes of corporation tax by reason of the provisions of ss 74, 125, 338, 577, 779 to 784, and 787 of the Taxes Act 1988 or otherwise.

Losses

[(12)   Group Relief

The Disclosure Letter contains particulars of all arrangements and agreements relating to group relief to which the Company is or has been a party and:

(*a*)   all claims by the Company for group relief were when made and are now valid and have been or will be allowed by way of relief from corporation tax;

(*b*)   the Company has not made nor is liable to make any payment under any such arrangement or agreement save in consideration for the surrender of group relief allowable to the Company by way of relief from corporation tax and equivalent to the taxation for which the Company would have been liable had it not been for the surrender;

(*c*)   the Company has received all payments due to it under any such arrangement or agreement for surrender of group relief made by it and no such payment is liable to be repaid;

(*d*) the Company is not a dual resident investing company within the meaning of the Taxes Act 1988, s 404; and

(*e*) save in respect of this Agreement, there have not been in existence in relation to the Company any such arrangements as are referred to in the Taxes Act 1988, s 410.]

(13) <u>Tax Losses</u>

There has not within the three years preceding the date hereof been a major change in the business of the Company within the meaning of the Taxes Act 1988, s 768.

CLOSE COMPANIES

(14) <u>Close Company</u>

(*a*) [The Company is] [The Company is not and has not been within the last six years] a close company[38].

(*b*) No distribution within s 418 of the Taxes Act 1988 has been made by the Company.

(*c*) The Company has not made (and will not be deemed to have made) any loan or advance to a participator or an associate of a participator so as to become liable to make any payment under the Taxes Act 1988, s 419.

(*d*) The Company has in respect of accounting periods beginning on or before 31 March 1989 supplied to the inspector such information and particulars as are necessary to make full and accurate disclosure of all facts and considerations material to be known by him to enable him to make intimations pursuant to the Taxes Act 1988, Sched 19, para 16 that he does not intend to make apportionments in respect of the Company for any accounting period ending on or before the Balance Sheet Date and the Company has received such intimations.

(*e*) No apportionment pursuant to the Taxes Act 1988, s 423 and Sched 19 has ever been made or could be made against the Company.

(*f*) In respect of accounting periods beginning on or before 31 March 1989 the Company has at all times been a 'trading company' or a 'member of a trading group' as defined in the Taxes Act 1988, Sched 19, para 7.

(*g*) The Company is not, and has not since 31 March 1989 been, a close investment holding company within the meaning of the Taxes Act 1988, s 13A.

(*h*) The Company has not expended or applied any sum liable to be regarded as income available for distribution pursuant to the Taxes Act 1988, Sched 19, para 8 (first business loans) and is not bound (contingently or otherwise) to expend or apply any such sum.

ANTI-AVOIDANCE

(15)   Income and Corporation Taxes Act 1988, s 765
The Company has not without the prior consent of the Treasury been a party to any transaction for which consent under the Taxes Act 1988, s 765 was required. Where such consent would have been required but for the provisions of the Taxes Act 1988, s 765A(1) the Company has complied in full with the requirements of The Movements of Capital (Required Information) Regulations 1990 and a copy of the notification required pursuant thereto is annexed to the Disclosure Letter.

(16)   Controlled Foreign Companies
   (*a*)   [The Disclosure Letter contains full details of the Company's] [The Company has no] interest in the share capital of any company not resident in the United Kingdom for taxation purposes (or which is treated for the purposes of any double taxation convention as not being so resident) which is controlled by persons resident in the United Kingdom for taxation purposes and in which the Company has 10 per cent or more of the voting rights (a 'controlled foreign company')[39].
   [(*b*)   No enquiries have been made or intimated by the Inland Revenue in respect of any controlled foreign company.
   (*c*)   No direction has been made by the Board of Inland Revenue under the Taxes Act 1988, s 747 in respect of each controlled foreign company.
   (*d*)   Section 748(1) of the Taxes Act 1988 applies to each controlled foreign company.]

(17)   Anti-avoidance
   (*a*)   The Company has not at any time entered into or been a party to a transaction or series of transactions either (i) containing steps inserted without any commercial or business purpose or (ii) being transactions to which any of the following provisions could apply: ss 703, 729, 730, 737, 739, 770, 774, 776, 779, 780, 781 or 786 of the Taxes Act 1988 without, in the appropriate cases, having received clearance in respect thereof from the Inland Revenue.
   (*b*)   The Company has never been requested to furnish information pursuant to notices served under ss 745 or 778 of the Taxes Act 1988.

CAPITAL ASSETS

(18)   Base Values
    (*a*) The Disclosure Letter contains full and accurate particulars of:
        (i) the extent to which the book value of an asset or a particular class of assets as shown in the Audited Accounts is in excess of either (*aa*) the amount falling to be deducted under TCGA 1992, s 38 from the consideration receivable on a disposal of that asset, or (*bb*) the balance of the qualifying expenditure attributable to that asset or pool of assets, as the case may be, brought forward into the accounting period in which Completion will occur and save to the extent disclosed, no such excess exists; and
        (ii) the extent to which provision for taxation in respect of such excess has been made in the Audited Accounts.
    (*b*) No election under TCGA 1992, s 35 is in effect in relation to the Company and full particulars are given in the Disclosure Letter of the first relevant disposal for the purposes of the said s 35.
    (*c*) The Disclosure Letter contains full and accurate particulars of all assets held by the Company on or after 6 April 1988 in respect of which relief is or would be available under TCGA 1992, Sched 4 upon disposal.

(19)   Roll-over Relief
The Disclosure Letter contains full and accurate particulars of all claims made by the Company under TCGA 1992, ss 152 to 156, s 158, ss 242 to 244, s 247 or s 248 and no such claim or other claim has been made by any other person (in particular pursuant to TCGA 1992, s 165 [or s 175]) which affects or could affect the amount or value of the consideration for the acquisition of any asset by the Company taken into account in calculating liability to corporation tax on chargeable gains on a subsequent disposal.

(20)   Depreciatory Transactions
No loss which might accrue on the disposal by the Company of any share in or security of any company is liable to be reduced by virtue of any depreciatory transaction within the meaning of TCGA 1992, s 176 and s 177 nor is any expenditure on any share or security liable to be reduced under TCGA 1992, s 125.

(21)   Value Shifting
The Company does not hold, and has not held, any shares upon the disposal of which TCGA 1992, ss 31 or 32 could apply.

(22)   Connected Party and Intra-Group Transactions
    (*a*)   The Company has not disposed of or acquired any asset to or from any person connected with it within the Taxes Act 1988, s 839 or in circumstances such that the provision of TCGA 1992, s 17 could apply to such disposal or acquisition.
    [(*b*)   The Company has not acquired any asset (past or present) from any other company then belonging to the same group of companies as the Company within the meaning of TCGA 1992, s 170(2) to (14).][37]
    (*c*)   The Company has not made and is not entitled to make a claim pursuant to TCGA 1992, s 172.

(23)   Group Reconstructions
The Company has not been party to any scheme of reconstruction or reorganisation to which the provisions of TCGA 1992, s 139, the Taxes Act 1988, s 703 or to which the Taxes Act 1988, s 343 could apply.

(24)   Chargeable Debts
No gain chargeable to corporation tax will accrue to the Company on the disposal of any debt owing to the Company not being a debt on a security or on the disposal of any corporate bond not being a qualifying corporate bond.

(25)   Chargeable Policies
The Company has not acquired benefits under any policy of assurance otherwise than as original beneficial owner.

(26)   Gains Accruing to Non-resident Companies or Trusts
There has not accrued any gain in respect of which the Company may be liable to corporation tax on chargeable gains by virtue of the provisions of TCGA 1992, s 13 or s 87.

[(27)   Indexation: Groups and Associated Companies
The Company does not own any debts or shares to which the provision of TCGA 1992, ss 182 to 184 could apply.][37]

(28)   Company Migration[37]
    (*a*)   The Company is not a dual resident company for the purposes of TCGA 1992, s 139(3) or s 160 or s 188.
    (*b*)   There are no circumstances pursuant to which the Company may become liable to tax pursuant to TCGA 1992, s 185 (Deemed disposal of assets on company ceasing to be resident in UK), s 186 (Deemed disposal of assets on company ceasing to be liable to UK tax), s 187 (Postponement of charge on deemed disposal) [or Finance Act 1988, s 132 (Liability of other persons for unpaid tax) or TCGA 1992, s 191 (Non-payment of tax by non-resident companies)].

CLAIMS, ELECTIONS AND CLEARANCES

(29)   Claims by the Company
The Company has made no claim under any of the following:

(*a*)   TCGA 1992, s 279 (assets situated outside the United Kingdom);

(*b*)   TCGA 1992, s 24(2) (assets of negligible value);

(*c*)   TCGA 1992, s 280 (tax on chargeable gains payable by instalments);

(*d*)   Taxes Act 1988, ss 242 and 243 (surplus franked investment income); or

(*e*)   Taxes Act 1988, s 584 (unremittable income arising outside the United Kingdom).

(30)   Elections
The Disclosure Letter contains full particulars of all elections made by the Company under the following provisions:

(*a*)   Taxes Act 1988, ss 524, 527 and 534 (lump sum receipts for patents and copyright);

(*b*)   Capital Allowances Act 1990, s 37 (short life assets); and

(*c*)   Capital Allowances Act 1990, s 11 (leasehold interests).

(31)   Clearances
There are annexed to the Disclosure Letter copies of all correspondence relating to applications for clearance under any enactment relating to taxation. All facts and circumstances material to such applications for clearance were disclosed in such applications.

MISCELLANEOUS

(32)   Assessment of Tax on Lessees
No notice pursuant to the Taxes Act 1988, s 23 has been served on the Company.

(33)   Leaseholds
The Company is not liable to taxation under the provisions of ss 34, 35 and 36 of the Taxes Act 1988 nor does it own any leasehold interest to which the said s 35 may apply.

[(34)   Incorporation of Partnership/Acquisition of Unincorporated Business
In respect of the [Agreement]:

(*a*)   the Vendors and the Company have jointly made elections pursuant to the Capital Allowances Act 1990, ss 77 or 158;

(*b*)   all capital assets were transferred at market value and no claim for relief under TCGA 1992, s 165 has been or will be made;

  (*c*) stock and work in progress were transferred at the lower of cost or net realisable value;

  (*d*) for the purposes of value added tax, the transfer of assets was neither a supply of goods nor services;

  (*e*) stamp duty has been properly paid on the [agreement] and on all documents executed pursuant thereto; and

  (*f*) all capital duty due on the allotment of shares in consideration (in whole or in part) for the acquisition of the assets of [   ] has been paid and the appropriate return filed pursuant to the Companies Act 1985, s 88(2)].

TAXATION OF EMPLOYEES AND AGENTS

(35) PAYE
The Company has properly operated the Pay As You Earn system deducting tax as required by law from all payments to or treated as made to employees and ex-employees of the Company and punctually accounted to the Inland Revenue for all tax so deducted and all returns required pursuant to the Taxes Act 1988, s 203 and regulations made thereunder have been punctually made and are accurate and complete in all respects.

(36) Dispensations and PAYE Audits
The Disclosure Letter contains full details of all dispensations obtained by the Company and all details of any visit from the Audit Office of the Inland Revenue within the last six years including full details of any settlement made pursuant thereto.

(37) Benefits for Employees

  (*a*) The Company has not made any payment to or provided any benefit for any officer or employee or ex-officer or ex-employee of the Company which is not allowable as a deduction in calculating the profits of the Company for taxation purposes.

  (*b*) The Company has not issued any shares in the circumstances described in the Taxes Act 1988, s 138(1) and has complied with the Taxes Act 1988, s 139(5).

  (*c*) The Company has not issued any shares in the circumstances described in the Finance Act 1988, s 77(1) and has complied with s 85 of that Act.

  (*d*) The Company has not made any payment to which the Taxes Act 1988, s 313 applies.

(38) Slave Companies
Any payment made to or for the direct or indirect benefit of any person who is or might be regarded by any taxation authority as an

employee of the Company is made to such person direct and is not made to any company or other entity associated with that person.

(39)   Sub-Contractors

[The Company is not and never has been either a contractor or a sub-contractor for the purposes of the Taxes Act 1988, Chapter IV, Part XIII.]

[The Company has properly operated the sub-contractors' scheme deducting tax as required by law from all payments made to sub-contractors of the Company and punctually accounted to the Inland Revenue for all tax so deducted.]

(40)   National Insurance

The Company has paid all national insurance contributions for which it is liable and has kept proper books and records relating to the same and has not been a party to any scheme or arrangement to avoid any liability to account for primary or secondary national insurance contributions.

STAMP DUTIES

(41)   Stamp Duty

The Company has duly paid or has procured to be paid all stamp duty on documents to which it is a party or in which it is interested and which are liable to stamp duty.

(42)   Stamp Duty Reserve Tax

The Company has made all returns and paid all stamp duty reserve tax in respect of any transaction in securities to which it has been a party or in respect of which it is liable to account for stamp duty reserve tax.

(43)   Capital Duty

The Company has complied with the provisions of the Finance Act 1973 relating to capital duty and has duly paid all capital duty which it is liable to pay.

VALUE ADDED TAX

(44) (*a*)   The Company has complied with all statutory provisions and regulations relating to value added tax and has duly paid or provided for all amounts of value added tax for which the Company is liable.

(*b*)   All supplies made by the Company are taxable supplies and the Company is not and will not be denied credit for any input tax by reason of the operation of the Value Added Tax Act 1983, s 15 and regulations made thereunder.

(*c*)   All input tax for which the Company has claimed credit has been paid by the Company in respect of supplies made to it relating to goods or services used or to be used for the purpose of the Company's business.

[(*d*) The Company is not and has not been, for value added tax purposes, a member of any group of companies (other than that comprising the Company and the Subsidiaries alone) and no act or transaction has been effected in consequence whereof the Company is or may be held liable for any value added tax chargeable against some other company except where that other company is a Subsidiary.][37]

(*e*) No supplies have been made to the Company to which the provisions of the Value Added Tax Act 1983, s 7 might apply.

(*f*) The Company has not committed any offence contrary to the Finance Act 1985, ss 12 or 13, nor has it received any penalty liability notice pursuant to s 14A(3), surcharge liability notice pursuant to s 19, or written warning issued pursuant to s 21(1A) of that Act.

(*g*) The Company has not been and is not liable to be registered for value added tax otherwise than pursuant to the provisions of the Value Added Tax Act 1983, Sched 1, para 1.

(*h*) The Company has not been required to give security under the Value Added Tax Act 1983, Sched 7, para 5.

(*i*) The Disclosure Letter contains details and copies of all elections, together with the relevant notification, made by the Company pursuant to the Value Added Tax Act 1983, Sched 6A, para 2.

(*j*) The Company is not and has not since 1 August 1989 been in relation to any land, building or civil engineering work a developer within the meaning of the Value Added Tax Act 1983, Sched 6A, para 5(5).

(*k*) The Disclosure Letter contains copies of all certificates issued by the Company pursuant to the Finance Act 1989, Sched 3, para 13(4)(*f*).

(*l*) The Company has not paid and is not liable to pay any interest pursuant to the Finance Act 1985, s 18.

(*m*) The Disclosure Letter contains full details of any assets of the Company to which the provisions of Part VA of the Value Added Tax (General) Regulations 1985 (the Capital Goods Scheme) apply and in particular:

　　(i) the identity (including in the case of leasehold property, the terms of years), date of acquisition and cost of the asset; and

(ii) the proportion of input tax for which credit has been claimed (either provisionally or finally in a tax year and stating which).

INHERITANCE TAX AND GIFTS

(45) Powers of Sale for Inheritance Tax Purposes

There are not in existence any circumstances whereby any such power as is mentioned in the Inheritance Tax Act 1984, s 212 could be exercised in relation to any shares in, securities of, or assets of, the Company.

(46) Gifts

(*a*) The Company is not liable to be assessed to corporation tax on chargeable gains or to inheritance tax as donor or donee of any gift or transferor or transferee of value.

(*b*) The Company has not been a party to associated operations in relation to a transfer of value within the meaning of the Inheritance Tax Act 1984, s 268.

(*c*) No Inland Revenue Charge (as defined in the Inheritance Tax Act 1984, s 237) is outstanding over any asset of the Company or in relation to any shares in the capital of the Company.

(*d*) The Company has not received any asset as mentioned in TCGA 1992, s 282.

FIFTH SCHEDULE
Adjustment of Consideration

1 INTERPRETATION

In this schedule where the context admits:

    (1) 'Audited Accounts' 'Balance Sheet Date' [and any other term defined in the third schedule] have the same meanings as in the third schedule;

    (2) 'Completion Accounts' means the accounts prepared in accordance with paragraph 2;

    (3) 'net tangible assets' means the aggregate value of all fixed and current assets (excluding goodwill, patents, trademarks and other intangible assets) minus the aggregate value of all liabilities and provisions (including provisions in accordance with SSAP 18 in respect of contingent liabilities) and excluding any reserves or capital created by the upward revaluation of assets subsequent to the Balance Sheet Date;

    (4) 'Provisional Consideration' means the consideration for the Sale Shares of £[   ] stated in clause 3(A);

    (5) 'Purchaser's Accountants' means [   ]; and

    (6) 'Vendors' Accountants' means [   ].

2 COMPLETION ACCOUNTS

(A) Preparation

The parties shall procure that, forthwith after Completion, accounts for the Company and the Subsidiaries shall be prepared and reported on in accordance with this schedule and the parties shall use their best endeavours to secure compliance with this schedule by their respective accountants.

(B) Description

The Completion Accounts shall consist of a consolidated balance sheet of the Company and the Subsidiaries as at the close of business on the date of Completion and a consolidated profit and loss account of the Company and the Subsidiaries in respect of the period from the day following the Balance Sheet Date to the date of Completion (both dates inclusive).

(C) General Requirements

Subject to sub-paragraph (D), the Completion Accounts shall:

    (1) be prepared as if the period from the day following the

Balance Sheet Date to the date of Completion were a
financial year of the Company;

(2) make full provision for all actual, future and contingent
liabilities of the Company and the Subsidiaries as at the
date of Completion;

(3) be prepared in accordance with the requirements of all
relevant statutes and generally accepted accounting
principles;

(4) show a true and fair view of the assets and liabilities of the
Company and the Subsidiaries at the date of Completion
and the profits of the Company and the Subsidiaries for
the period from the Balance Sheet Date to the date of
Completion; and

(5) adopt bases and policies of accounting applied for the
purposes of the Audited Accounts.

(D) Specific Requirements[1]
In preparing the Completion Accounts:

(1) no value shall be attributed to goodwill or any other
intangible asset;

(2) other fixed assets shall be included at the value at which
they were included in the Audited Accounts (or, if
acquired after the Balance Sheet Date, their cost), less
depreciation on the written down value, calculated at the
following annual rates:

Plant and machinery	: [	] per cent
Fixtures and fittings	: [	] per cent
Motor vehicles	: [	] per cent
Immovable assets and improvements thereto	: [	] per cent

(3) no value shall be attributed to any assets (including in
particular any prepayment or debt) except to the extent
that (following Completion) the Company or a Subsidiary
will have the benefit of the same;

(4) full provision shall be made for rebates or discounts that
will fall due and fees and commissions that will become
payable after Completion in either case in respect of sales
or other transactions that took place before Completion;

(5) full provision shall be made for any liability arising as a
result of the change of control of the Company on
Completion; and

(6) [to the extent that it is not capable of being set off against
the liability of the Company for corporation tax for the
current financial year or any previous financial year, full

provision shall be made for the advance corporation tax payable on any distribution declared or paid before Completion];

(7) full provision shall be made in respect of the cost of making good dilapidations or wants of repair on or to the Properties; and

(8) [full provision shall be made in respect of all payments in favour of [   ] and [   ] in their capacity as directors or employees or former directors or employees.]

(9) [   ]

3 PROCEDURE

(A) Submission of Draft

Within 60 days after the date of Completion, the Purchaser's Accountants shall deliver a final draft of the Completion Accounts to the Vendors' Accountants and, unless the Vendors' Accountants shall notify the Purchaser's Accountants in writing within 21 days after receipt of such draft that they do not accept that such draft complies with paragraph 2, the Vendors shall be deemed to have accepted such draft as complying with paragraph 2.

(B) Agreement of Draft

If, within the period of 21 days referred to in sub-paragraph (A), the Vendors' Accountants shall notify the Purchaser's Accountants in writing that they do not accept that the said draft complies with paragraph 2 then the Purchaser's Accountants and the Vendors' Accountants shall use their best endeavours to reach agreement upon adjustments to the draft to meet the objections of the Vendors' Accountants.

(C) Independent Accountant[2]

In the event that the Vendors' Accountants and the Purchaser's Accountants are unable to reach agreement as aforesaid, any matter in dispute shall be referred to the decision of a single independent chartered accountant or an independent firm of chartered accountants to be agreed upon between them or, or in default of such agreement, to be selected (at the instance of either party) by the President for the time being of the Institute of Chartered Accountants in England and Wales, and any such chartered accountant or firm of chartered accountants (whose costs shall be paid as he or they shall direct) shall act as expert (and not as arbitrator) in connection with the giving of such decision which shall, save in the event of manifest error, be binding. In giving such decision, the accountant or firm shall state what adjustments (if any) are to be made to the said draft in order that it shall comply with paragraph 2.

(D) Report
If the Vendors' Accountants accept, or are deemed to accept, that the said draft complies with paragraph 2 the Purchaser's Accountants shall sign a report to the effect that the Completion Accounts comply with paragraph 2 and any Completion Accounts so reported on, or (if sub-paragraph (C) shall apply) the final draft of the Completion Accounts, as adjusted by the independent accountant, shall be the Completion Accounts for the purposes of this Agreement and shall be final and binding on the parties.

(E) Information and Explanations
The Purchaser's Accountants shall provide such information and explanations relating to the draft Completion Accounts and their preparation as the Vendors' Accountants, or any independent chartered accountant appointed pursuant to sub-paragraph (C), shall reasonably require.

4 ADJUSTMENT OF CONSIDERATION

(A) Increase or Reduction
When the Completion Accounts have become binding, the Provisional Consideration shall forthwith:
    (1) be increased by the amount (if any) by which the net tangible assets of the Company and the Subsidiaries as at the date of Completion as shown by the Completion Accounts are greater than the net tangible assets of the Company and the Subsidiaries as at the Balance Sheet Date as shown by the Audited Accounts; or (as the case may be)
    (2) be reduced by the amount (if any) by which the net tangible assets of the Company and the Subsidiaries as at the date of Completion as shown by the Completion Accounts are less than the net tangible assets of the Company and the Subsidiaries as at the Balance Sheet Date as shown by the Audited Accounts.

(B) Payment
Any increase or reduction in the Provisional Consideration shall be paid by the Purchaser or the Vendors (as appropriate) within 14 days after the Completion Accounts have become binding as aforesaid and any amount not paid when due shall carry interest (accrued daily and compounded monthly) at the rate of [   ] per cent per annum above the base rate of [   ] Bank PLC from time to time from

the due date until the date of actual payment (as well after judgment as before).

5   INTERACTION WITH OTHER PROVISIONS[3]

[Subject to the due performance of paragraph 4, if the Purchaser shall have any claim against the Vendors under this Agreement in respect of any liability or deficiency which is taken into account in the Completion Accounts the amount of such liability or deficiency so taken into account shall be deducted from the amount of the Purchaser's claim but, save as aforesaid, preparation and acceptance of the Completion Accounts by the Purchaser shall be without prejudice to any claim which the Purchaser may have against the Vendors under or in respect of any breach of this Agreement.]

SIXTH SCHEDULE
Pensions [Company has own final salary scheme]

1 INTERPRETATION

[(A) Definitions]
In this schedule, where the context admits:
   (1) 'Actuarial Assumptions' means the actuarial assumptions
        and method set out in a letter in agreed terms dated
        [   ] from the Vendors' Actuary to the Purchaser's
        Actuary;
   (2) 'Actuary' means a Fellow of The Institute of Actuaries or
        of The Faculty of Actuaries in Scotland;
   (3) 'Company' means the Company and the Subsidiaries or
        such one or more of them, as the context requires;
   (4) 'Pension Scheme' means [the retirement benefits scheme
        known as [   ] which was established by a
        deed dated [   ] (or the trustees from time to time
        of that scheme, as the context requires);] [Scheme A [,
        Scheme B] and Scheme C (or such one or [other] [more] of
        them as the context requires;]
   (5) 'Purchaser's Actuary' means [   ] (or such other
        Actuary as the Purchaser may appoint for the purposes of
        this schedule);
   (6) 'Relevant Employee' means any past or present employee
        or officer of the Company or of any predecessor to all or
        part of its business;
  [(7) 'Scheme A' means the retirement benefits scheme known
        as [   ] which was established by a trust deed dated
        [   ] (or the trustees from time to time of that
        scheme, as the context requires);]
  [(8) 'Scheme B' means the retirement benefits scheme known
        as [   ] which was established by a trust deed dated
        [   ] (or the trustees from time to time of that
        scheme, as the context requires);]
  [(9) 'Scheme C' means the retirement benefits scheme known
        as [   ] which was established by a trust deed dated
        [   ] (or the trustees from time to time of that
        scheme, as the context requires);]
  (10) 'Shortfall' means an amount, calculated in accordance
        with the Actuarial Assumptions, equal to the amount (if
        any) by which the capital value at Completion of the
        benefits which are then payable, or prospectively or
        contingently payable, under the Pension Scheme exceeds

the value at Completion of the then net assets of the Pension Scheme. For the purposes of this definition:

[(*a*) assets shall be valued by reference to their mid-market price at the close of business on the date upon which Completion occurs unless that date is not a business day in which event at the close of business on the last business day preceding that date (where 'business day' means a day upon which the London Stock Exchange is open for business);][1]

(*b*) when calculating the value of the net assets of the Pension Scheme no account shall be taken of:

(i) any debts of the Company to the Pension Scheme;[2] or

(ii) any contributions payable to the Pension Scheme after Completion;

(*c*) when calculating the liabilities of the Pension Scheme no account shall be taken of any benefits in respect of service after the date upon which Completion occurs but allowance shall be made in accordance with the Actuarial Assumptions for:

(i) projected increases in earnings up to the assumed date of cessation of pensionable service;[3] and

(ii) increases to pensions in payment or in deferment;

(*d*) when calculating the liabilities of the Pension Scheme allowance shall also be made in accordance with the Actuarial Assumptions for any refund of contributions and any benefits in pension form payable in the event of death whilst in service but, save where death occurs before Completion, no account shall be taken of any other lump sum death-in-service benefits;

(*e*) any improvement to the benefits under the Pension Scheme which has been announced before Completion shall be deemed to have been duly effected under the Pension Scheme and to have come into force before Completion; and

(*f*) the Pension Scheme shall be deemed to be under an overriding obligation to provide benefits on a basis which does not discriminate between men and women and without reducing the benefits of either sex;[4]

(11) 'Vendors' Actuary' means [   ] (or such other

Actuary as may be appointed by the Vendors for the purposes of this schedule).

[(B)   Schedule applies separately to each Pension Scheme
Paragraphs 2 and 3 of this schedule apply separately to each Pension Scheme.][5]

2   CALCULATION OF SHORTFALL

(A)   Data
The Vendors and the Purchaser shall use all their respective reasonable endeavours to procure that all such information as the Vendors' Actuary or the Purchaser's Actuary or any independent Actuary appointed under paragraph 2(C) may reasonably request for the purposes of this schedule is supplied promptly to such Actuary and that all such information is complete and accurate in all respects.

(B)   Agreement of Shortfall
The Purchaser's Actuary shall determine the amount of the Shortfall and shall submit his findings in writing to the Vendors' Actuary for agreement. If the Vendors' Actuary and the Purchaser's Actuary agree the amount (if any) of the Shortfall, the Vendors shall procure that the Vendors' Actuary and the Purchaser shall procure that the Purchaser's Actuary jointly certify that amount as the Shortfall.

(C)   Dispute
If the Vendors' Actuary and the Purchaser's Actuary fail to agree the amount (if any) of the Shortfall within two months from the date upon which the Purchaser's Actuary first submits his findings to the Vendors' Actuary in accordance with paragraph 2(B), the matter may, at the option of either the Vendors or the Purchaser, be referred to an independent Actuary to be agreed between the Vendors and the Purchaser or, in default of agreement within 14 days from the first nomination of an Actuary by one party to the other, to be appointed by the President for the time being of The Institute of Actuaries on the application of either the Vendors or the Purchaser. The certificate of the independent Actuary as to the amount (if any) of the Shortfall shall, save in the event of manifest error, be final and binding on the parties and, in so certifying, the independent Actuary shall be deemed to be acting as an expert and not as an arbitrator.[6] His costs shall be paid as he directs.

3   PAYMENT OF SHORTFALL

The Vendors shall within a period of 14 days commencing on and

including the date upon which the amount (if any) of the Shortfall is
certified as aforesaid pay, by way of adjustment to the consideration
for the Sale Shares,[7] to the Purchaser (or to a third party, as the
Purchaser may direct) a sum in cash equal to the amount shown in
the certificate as being the Shortfall together with interest thereon
(accruing daily and compounded monthly) from and including the
date upon which Completion occurs to but excluding the date upon
which final payment is made in accordance with this paragraph, such
interest to be at the Agreed Rate up to and including the last day in
the aforesaid 14-day period and thereafter shall be at the Agreed
Rate plus [   ] per cent. In this paragraph 'Agreed Rate' means the
base rate from time to time of [   ] Bank PLC plus [   ]
per cent.

4   WARRANTIES AND REPRESENTATIONS[8]
The Vendors hereby warrant and represent to and for the benefit of
the Purchaser in the following terms:
(1)   No Other Pension Arrangements
Save for the Pension Scheme the Company is not a party to nor
participates in nor contributes to any scheme, arrangement or
agreement (whether legally enforceable or not) for the provision of
any pension, retirement, death, incapacity, sickness, disability,
accident or other like benefits (including the payment of medical
expenses) for any Relevant Employee or for the widow, widower,
child or dependant of any Relevant Employee.
(2)   No Assurances etc
Neither the Company nor any of the Vendors:
  (*a*)   has given any undertaking or assurance (whether legally
        enforceable or not) to any Relevant Employee or to any
        widow, widower, child or dependant of any Relevant
        Employee as to the continuance, introduction,
        improvement or increase of any benefit of a kind described
        in (1) above; or
  (*b*)   is paying or has in the last two years paid any benefit of a
        kind described in (1) above to any Relevant Employee or to
        any widow, widower, child or dependant of any Relevant
        Employee.
(3)   All Details Disclosed
All material details relating to the Pension Scheme are contained in
or annexed to the Disclosure Letter including (without limitation)
the following:
  (*a*)   a true and complete copy of the deed or other instrument
        by which the Pension Scheme was established and all deeds
        and other instruments supplemental thereto;

(*b*)   a true and complete copy of all announcements, explanatory literature and the like of current effect which have been issued to any Relevant Employee in connection with the Pension Scheme;

(*c*)   a true and complete copy of the report on the last actuarial valuation of the Pension Scheme to be completed prior to the date of this Agreement and of any subsequent written recommendations of an actuarial nature;

(*d*)   a true and complete copy of the last audited accounts of the Pension Scheme to be completed prior to the date of this Agreement and details of any material change in the investment policy of the Pension Scheme since the date as at which those accounts were made up;

(*e*)   a true and complete copy of all investment management, nominee and custodian agreements (if any) of current effect to which the Pension Scheme is a party;

(*f*)   a true and complete copy of all insurance policies (if any) and annuity contracts (if any) held for the purposes of the Pension Scheme and details of any such policies and contracts which the Pension Scheme has agreed to effect;

(*g*)   a true and complete copy of the memorandum and articles of association of any company which is a trustee of the Pension Scheme and the names and addresses of the directors and secretary of that company;

(*h*)   the names and addresses of the trustees of the Pension Scheme;

(*i*)   details of all amendments (if any) to the Pension Scheme which have been announced or are proposed but which have not yet been formally made;

(*j*)   details of all discretionary increases (if any) to pensions in payment or in deferment under the Pension Scheme which have been granted in the ten years prior to the date of this Agreement or which are under consideration;

(*k*)   details of all discretionary practices (if any) which may have led any person to expect additional benefits in a given set of circumstances (by way of example, but without limitation, on retirement at the behest of the Company or in the event of redundancy); and

(*l*)   details of the rate at which and basis upon which the Company currently contributes to the Pension Scheme, any change to that rate and/or basis which is proposed or which is under consideration and all contributions paid to the Pension Scheme by the Company in the three years prior to the date of this Agreement.

(4)   Augmentation

No power under the Pension Scheme has been exercised in relation to any employee or officer of the Company or, since the date as at which the last actuarial valuation of the Pension Scheme to be completed prior to the date of this Agreement was undertaken, in respect of any other person:

  (*a*)   to provide terms of membership of the Pension Scheme (whether as to benefits or contributions) which are different from those generally applicable to the members of the Pension Scheme; or

  (*b*)   to provide any benefits which would not but for the exercise of that power have been payable under the Pension Scheme; or

  (*c*)   to augment any benefits under the Pension Scheme.

(5)   Death Denefits Insured

All benefits (other than any refund of members' contributions with interest where appropriate) payable under the Pension Scheme on the death of any person while in employment to which the Pension Scheme relates are insured fully under a policy with an insurance company of good repute and there are no grounds on which that company might avoid liability under that policy.

(6)   Contributions and Expenses

Contributions to the Pension Scheme are not paid in arrear and all contributions and other amounts which have fallen due for payment have been paid. No fee, charge or expense relating to or in connection with the Pension Scheme has been incurred but not paid. If any such fee, charge or expense has been paid by any person other than the Pension Scheme the Pension Scheme has reimbursed that person if and to the extent that the Pension Scheme is or may become liable so to do.

(7)   Company's Obligations

The Company:

  (*a*)   has observed and performed those provisions of the Pension Scheme which apply to it; [and]

  (*b*)   may (without the consent of any person or further payment) terminate its liability to contribute to the Pension Scheme at any time subject only to giving such notice (if any) as is expressly provided for in the documentation containing the current provisions governing the Pension Scheme[9] [.] [; and

  (*c*)   has at all material times held or been named in a contracting-out certificate (within the meaning of the Social Security Pensions Act 1975) referable to the Pension Scheme.]

(8) No Other Employer

The Company is the only employer for the time being participating in the Pension Scheme. No employer which has previously participated in the Pension Scheme has any claim under the Pension Scheme and in respect of any such employer the period of participation has been terminated and benefits have been provided in accordance with the provisions of the Pension Scheme.

(9) Administration

All documentation and records in respect of the Pension Scheme are up to date and so far as the Vendors are aware complete and accurate in all material respects.

(10) Investments

None of the assets of the Pension Scheme:

(*a*) is invested in or in any description of employer-related investments (within the meaning of s 57A of the Social Security Pensions Act 1975); or

(*b*) save for deposits with banks, building societies and other financial institutions and save for any instrument creating or acknowledging an indebtedness listed on any recognised stock exchange of repute, is loaned to any person; or

(*c*) is subject to any encumbrance or agreement or commitment to give or create any encumbrance.

(11) No Payment to Employer

No payment to which the Income and Corporation Taxes Act 1988, s 601 applies has been made out of the funds which are or have been held for the purposes of the Pension Scheme.

(12) Compliance

The Pension Scheme:

(*a*) is an exempt approved scheme (within the meaning of the Income and Corporation Taxes Act 1988, s 592);

(*b*) has properly and punctually accounted to the Inland Revenue for all and any tax for which the Pension Scheme is liable or accountable;

(*c*) is not liable to taxation on any income from or capital gains on any of the funds which are or have been held for the purposes of the Pension Scheme;[10] and

(*d*) complies with and has at all times been administered in accordance with all applicable laws, regulations and requirements (including those of the Board of Inland Revenue and of trust law).

(13) Actuarial[11]

[The report dated [   ] of [   ] on the actuarial valuation of the Pension Scheme as at [   ] (the 'Valuation

Date') (a true copy of the report being annexed to the Disclosure Letter) shows a true and fair view of the respective actuarial values of the assets and liabilities of the Pension Scheme at the Valuation Date on the basis of the actuarial assumptions and method detailed in that report. Since the Valuation Date nothing has occurred, been done or been omitted to be done which may affect materially the level of funding of the benefits under the Pension Scheme.]

[The data used for the purposes of the last actuarial valuation of the Pension Scheme to be completed prior to the date of this Agreement was complete and accurate in all material respects and since the date as at which that valuation was undertaken nothing has occurred, been done or been omitted to be done which may affect materially the level of funding of the benefits under the Pension Scheme.]

(14)   Litigation

Neither the Pension Scheme nor the Company is engaged or involved in any proceedings which relate to or are in connection with the Pension Scheme or the benefits thereunder and no such proceedings are pending or threatened and so far as the Vendors are aware there are no facts likely to give rise to any such proceedings. In this sub-paragraph 'proceedings' includes any litigation or arbitration and also includes any investigation or determination by the Pensions Ombudsman.

(15)   Indemnities

In relation to the Pension Scheme or funds which are or have been held for the purposes thereof neither the Company nor the trustees or administrator of the Pension Scheme has given an indemnity or guarantee to any person (other than in the case of the Company any general indemnity in favour of the trustees or administrator under the documentation governing the Pension Scheme).

5   DAMAGES FOR BREACH OF PENSION WARRANTIES

In determining the damages flowing from any breach of Warranties contained in paragraph 4, the Company shall be deemed to be under a liability:

(1)   to provide and to continue to provide any benefit of a kind referred to in that paragraph which is now provided or has been announced or is proposed; and

(2)   to maintain and to continue to maintain (without benefits being reduced) the Pension Scheme and any other arrangements of a kind described in that paragraph which are now in existence or are proposed and any discretionary practices of a kind referred to in that paragraph which have hitherto been carried on.[12]

[6   SEX EQUALITY

The Vendors undertake to the Purchaser, for its own benefit and as trustee and agent for the Company and for the Pension Scheme, to indemnify and to keep indemnified and held harmless on a continuing basis the Company and the Pension Scheme against all and any liabilities, actions, claims and costs (including legal expenses) which may be brought or made against or incurred by the Company and/or the Pension Scheme of any nature relating to discrimination on grounds of sex as to the provision under the Pension Scheme for or in respect of all or any of the Relevant Employees of benefits referable to any period prior to Completion and/or the terms of their employment or former employment with the Company relating to relevant benefits (within the meaning of the Income and Corporation Taxes Act 1988, s 612).][13]

SIXTH SCHEDULE

Pensions [Company has own money purchase scheme]

1 INTERPRETATION

In this schedule, where the context admits:

(1) 'Company' means the Company and the Subsidiaries or such one or more of them as the context requires;

(2) 'Pension Scheme' means [the retirement benefits scheme known as [   ] which was established by a deed dated [   ] (or the trustees from time to time of that scheme, as the context requires);] [Scheme A [, Scheme B] and Scheme C (or such one or [other] [more] of them, as the context requires;]

(3) 'Relevant Employee' means any past or present employee or officer of the Company or of any predecessor to all or part of its business [.] [;

[(4) 'Scheme A' means the retirement benefits scheme known as [   ] which was established by a trust deed dated [   ] (or the trustees from time to time of that scheme, as the context requires);] [and]

(5) 'Scheme B' means the retirement benefits scheme known as [   ] which was established by a trust deed dated [   ] (or the trustees from time to time of that scheme, as the context requires) [.] [; and

(6) 'Scheme C' means the retirement benefits scheme known as [   ] which was established by a trust deed dated [   ] (or the trustees from time to time of that scheme, as the context requires).]

2 WARRANTIES AND REPRESENTATIONS[38]

The Vendors hereby warrant and represent to and for the benefit of the Purchaser in the following terms:

(1) No Other Pension Arrangements

Save for the Pension Scheme the Company is not a party to nor participates in nor contributes to any scheme, arrangement or agreement (whether legally enforceable or not) for the provision of any pension, retirement, death, incapacity, sickness, disability, accident or other like benefits (including the payment of medical expenses) for any Relevant Employee or for the widow, widower, child or dependant of any Relevant Employee.

(2) No Assurances etc

Neither the Company nor any of the Vendors:

(*a*) has given any undertaking or assurance (whether legally enforceable or not) to any Relevant Employee or to any widow, widower, child or dependant of any Relevant Employee as to the continuance, introduction, improvement or increase of any benefit of a kind described in (1) above; or

(b) is paying or has in the last two years paid any benefit of a kind described in (1) above to any Relevant Employee or to any widow, widower, child or dependant of any Relevant Employee.

(3) All Details Disclosed

All material details relating to the Pension Scheme are contained in or annexed to the Disclosure Letter including (without limitation) the following:

(a) a true and complete copy of the deed or other instrument by which the Pension Scheme was established and all deeds and other instruments supplemental thereto;

(b) a true and complete copy of all announcements, explanatory literature and the like of current effect which have been issued to any Relevant Employee in connection with the Pension Scheme;

(c) a true and complete copy of the report on the last actuarial valuation of the Pension Scheme to be completed prior to the date of this Agreement and of any subsequent written recommendations of an actuarial nature;[39]

(d) a true and complete copy of the last audited accounts of the Pension Scheme to be completed prior to the date of this Agreement and details of any material change in the investment policy of the Pension Scheme since the date as at which those accounts were made up;

(e) a true and complete copy of all insurance policies (if any) and annuity contracts (if any) held for the purposes of the Pension Scheme and details of any such policies and contracts which the Pension Scheme has agreed to effect;

(f) a true and complete copy of the memorandum and articles of association of any company which is a trustee of the Pension Scheme and the names and addresses of the directors and secretary of that company;

(g) the names and addresses of the trustees of the Pension Scheme;

(h) details of all amendments (if any) to the Pension Scheme which have been announced or are proposed but which have not yet been formally made;

(i) details of all discretionary increases (if any) to pensions in payment or in deferment under the Pension Scheme which have been granted in the five years prior to the date of this Agreement or which are under consideration;

(*j*)   details of all discretionary practices (if any) which may have led any person to expect additional benefits in a given set of circumstances (by way of example, but without limitation, on retirement at the behest of the Company or in the event of redundancy); and

(*k*)   details of the rate at which and basis upon which the Company currently contributes to the Pension Scheme, any change to that rate and/or basis which is proposed or which is under consideration and all contributions paid to the Pension Scheme by the Company in the three years prior to the date of this Agreement.

(4)   Benefits

All benefits which are not money purchase benefits and which are payable under the Pension Scheme on the death of any person while in employment to which the Pension Scheme relates are insured fully under a policy with an insurance company of good repute and there are no grounds on which that company might avoid liability under that policy. All other benefits payable under the Pension Scheme are money purchase benefits. In this sub-paragraph 'money purchase benefits' has the same meaning as in s 84(1) of the Social Security Act 1986.

(5)   Contributions and Expenses

Contributions to the Pension Scheme are not paid in arrear and all contributions and other amounts which have fallen due for payment have been paid punctually. No fee, charge or expense relating to or in connection with the Pension Scheme has been incurred but not paid. If any such fee, charge or expense has been paid by any person other than the Pension Scheme the Pension Scheme has reimbursed that person if and to the extent that the Pension Scheme is or may become liable so to do.

(6)   Company's Obligations

The Company:

(*a*)   has observed and performed those provisions of the Pension Scheme which apply to it; [and]

(*b*)   may (without the consent of any person or further payment) terminate its liability to contribute to the Pension Scheme at any time subject only to giving such notice (if any) as is expressly provided for in the documentation containing the current provisions governing the Pension Scheme[40] [.] [; and

(*c*)   has at all material times held or been named in a contracting-out certificate (within the meaning of the

Social Security Pensions Act 1975) referable to the Pension Scheme.]

(7) No Other Employer

The Company is the only employer for the time being participating in the Pension Scheme. No employer which has previously participated in the Pension Scheme has any claim under the Pension Scheme and in respect of any such employer the period of participation has been terminated and benefits have been provided in accordance with the provisions of the Pension Scheme.

(8) Administration

All documentation and records in respect of the Pension Scheme are up to date and so far as the Vendors are aware complete and accurate in all respects.

(9) Investments

Save for any deposit with a bank or building society the only assets which the Pension Scheme has held are insurance policies and annuity contracts with insurance companies of good repute.

(10) Compliance

The Pension Scheme:

    (*a*) is an exempt approved scheme (within the meaning of the Income and Corporation Taxes Act 1988, s 592);

    (*b*) has properly and punctually accounted to the Inland Revenue for all and any tax for which the Pension Scheme is liable or accountable[40]; and

    (*c*) complies with and has at all times been administered in accordance with all applicable laws, regulations and requirements (including those of the Board of Inland Revenue and of trust law).

(11) Litigation

Neither the Pension Scheme nor the Company is engaged or involved in any proceedings which relate to or are in connection with the Pension Scheme or the benefits thereunder and no such proceedings are pending or threatened and so far as the Vendors are aware there are no facts likely to give rise to any such proceedings. In this sub-paragraph 'proceedings' includes any litigation or arbitration and also includes any investigation or determination by the Pensions Ombudsman.

3　Damages for Breach of Pension Warranties

In determining the damages flowing from any breach of Warranties contained in paragraph 2, the Company shall be deemed to be under a liability:

    (1) to provide and to continue to provide any benefit of a kind

referred to in that paragraph which is now provided or has been announced or is proposed; and

(2)   to maintain and to continue to maintain (without benefits being reduced) the Pension Scheme and any other arrangements of a kind described in that paragraph which are now in existence or are proposed and any discretionary practices of a kind referred to in that paragraph which have hitherto been carried on.[41]

[4   SEX EQUALITY

The Vendors undertake to the Purchaser, for its own benefit and as trustee and agent for the Company and for the Pension Scheme, to indemnify and to keep indemnified and held harmless on a continuing basis the Company and the Pension Scheme against all and any liabilities, actions, claims and costs (including legal expenses) which may be brought or made against or incurred by the Company and/or the Pension Scheme of any nature relating to discrimination on grounds of sex arising out of or in connection with the provisions or former provisions of the Pension Scheme applicable to all or any of the Relevant Employees and/or the terms of their employment or former employment with the Company relating to relevant benefits (within the meaning of the Income and Corporation Taxes Act 1988, s 612).][42]

SEVENTH SCHEDULE
Vendors' Protection

1 No Other Representations

The Purchaser admits that it has not entered into this Agreement in reliance upon any representation or promise other than those incorporated in the Disclosure Letter or this Agreement.[1]

2 Guarantees

The Purchaser shall use its best endeavours to secure the release of the Vendors from the guarantees and other contingent liabilities listed in the Disclosure Letter for the purpose of this paragraph (offering its own covenant in substitution if requested by the Vendors) and shall in the meantime indemnify the Vendors and keep the Vendors indemnified against any liability (including costs, damages and expenses) thereunder or which may be incurred in relation thereto.

3 Loan Accounts

At Completion the Purchaser shall procure that the Company and the Subsidiaries shall repay to the Vendors the amounts owing to them as specified in the Disclosure Letter.

4 Limitation of Liability

The provisions of this paragraph shall operate to limit the liability of the Vendors under or in connection with the Warranties and the Disclosure Letter and references to 'such liabilities' shall be construed accordingly. The parties agree as follows:

(1) no such liabilities shall attach to the Vendors unless the aggregate amount of such liabilities shall exceed the total sum of £[   ] but if such liabilities shall exceed that sum the Vendors shall (subject to the other provisions hereof) be liable for the whole of such liabilities and not merely for the excess;

(2) the aggregate amount of such liabilities shall not exceed £[   ];

(3) claims against the Vendors shall be wholly barred and unenforceable unless written particulars thereof (giving reasonable details of the specific matter or claim in respect of which such claim is made so far as then known to the Purchaser) shall have been given to the Vendors:

(*a*) in relation to the Warranties (other than those

contained in the fourth schedule) within a period of
[   ] years from the date hereof; and

(b) in relation to paragraph 2 of the fourth schedule and
the Warranties contained in the fourth schedule,
within a period of [   ] years from the date
hereof,

but this item (3) shall not apply to claims which (or delay in
the discovery of which) are the consequence of fraud,
wilful misconduct or wilful concealment by the Vendors;

(4) if the Vendors make any payment by way of damages for
breach of the Warranties and within twelve months of the
making of the relevant payment the Company, the
Subsidiaries or the Purchaser receives any benefit
otherwise than from the Vendors which would not have
been received but for the circumstances giving rise to the
claim in respect of which the damages payment was made
the Purchaser shall, once it or the relevant company has
received such benefit, forthwith repay to the Vendors an
amount equal to the lesser of (a) the amount of such benefit
and (b) the damages payment in question.

5 Avoidance of Double Claims

In the event that the Purchaser is entitled to claim under paragraph
2(A) of the fourth schedule or under the Warranties in respect of the
same subject matter the Purchaser may choose to claim under either
or both but payments under paragraph 2(A) of the fourth schedule
shall *pro tanto* satisfy and discharge any claim which is capable of
being made under the Warranties in respect of the same subject
matter and *vice versa*.

SIGNED by the said   )
[   )
                        ]   )

SIGNED by the said   )
[   )
                        ]   )

SIGNED by the said   )
[   )
                        ]   )

```
SIGNED by                    )
[                    ]        )
duly authorised for          )
and on behalf of             )
[              ] PLC         )
```

AGREEMENT FOR SALE — CORPORATE VENDOR

CONTENTS

THIS AGREEMENT is made the   day of 19

BETWEEN:

(1)   PLC ('the Vendor') a company registered in England under number [   ] whose registered office is at [   ]; and

(2)   PLC ('the Purchaser') a company registered in England under number [   ] whose registered office is at [   ]

WHEREAS:

The Purchaser wishes to acquire the entire issued share capital of [   ] Limited from the Vendor on the terms of this Agreement.

NOW IT IS HEREBY AGREED as follows:

1 INTERPRETATION

(A) Definitions
In this Agreement where the context admits:
(1) 'Company' means [   ] Limited a company registered in England under number [   ] and incorporated on [19] as a private company limited by shares under the Companies Act(s) [   ];
(2) 'Completion' means completion of the sale and purchase of the Sale Shares;[1]
(3) 'Consideration Shares' means ordinary shares of [   ] each in the Purchaser credited as fully paid;
(4) 'Directors' means the persons named in Part I of the first schedule and 'the Continuing Directors' means the persons named in Part II of that schedule;
(5) 'Disclosure Letter' means the letter dated the date hereof written by or on behalf of the Vendor to the Purchaser in agreed terms;[2]
(6) 'Placing Agreement' means an agreement in agreed terms proposed to be entered into simultaneously with this

Agreement between the Purchaser and [　　　] providing for the placing of the Consideration Shares;[3]

(7) 'Properties' means the properties particulars of which are set out in the list annexed to the Disclosure Letter;

(8) 'Sale Shares' means the shares to be bought and sold pursuant to clause 2;

(9) 'Subsidiaries' means the companies listed in Part II of the second schedule;

(10) 'Vendor's Group' means the Vendor and each of its subsidiaries other than the Company and the Subsidiaries; and

(11) 'Warranties' means the warranties and representations set out in paragraph 2 of the third schedule, in paragraph 4 of the fourth schedule and in paragraph [　] of the sixth schedule.

(B)　Construction of Certain References
In this Agreement where the context admits:

(1) words and phrases the definitions of which are contained or referred to in Part XXVI Companies Act 1985 shall be construed as having the meanings thereby attributed to them;

(2) references to statutory provisions shall be construed as references to those provisions as amended or re-enacted or as their application is modified by other provisions from time to time and shall include references to any provisions of which they are re-enactments (whether with or without modification);

(3) where any statement is qualified by the expression 'so far as the Vendor is aware' or 'to the best of the Vendor's knowledge and belief' or any similar expression, that statement shall be deemed to include an additional statement that it has been made after due and careful enquiry;[4]

(4) references to clauses and schedules are references to clauses hereof and schedules hereto, references to sub-clauses or paragraphs are, unless otherwise stated, references to sub-clauses of the clause or paragraphs of the schedule in which the reference appears, and references to this Agreement include the schedules; and

(5) references to any document being in agreed terms are to that document in the form signed on behalf of the parties for identification.

(C)　Headings
The headings and sub-headings are inserted for convenience only and shall not affect the construction of this Agreement.

(D)　Schedules
Each of the schedules shall have effect as if set out herein.

2 SALE OF SHARES

(A) Sale and Purchase
Subject to the terms of this Agreement, the Vendor shall sell and the Purchaser shall purchase, free from all liens, charges, equities and encumbrances and together with all rights now or hereafter attaching thereto the entire issued share capital of the Company [comprising [   ] [ordinary] shares of [   ] each].

(B) Simultaneous Completion
Neither the Purchaser nor the Vendor shall be obliged to complete the purchase of any of the Sale Shares unless the purchase of all the Sale Shares is completed simultaneously.

3 CONSIDERATION

(A) Amount [Consideration Shares]
The total consideration for the Sale Shares shall be the sum of £[   ], but subject to adjustment as provided in the fourth, fifth and sixth schedules. [The total consideration for the Sale Shares shall be the allotment to the Vendor of [   ] Consideration Shares.]

(B) Placing[1]
The total consideration for the Sale Shares shall be the allotment to the Vendor of the number of Consideration Shares which, when placed with placees nominated by the Purchaser, shall produce payment to the Vendor of aggregate net proceeds of £[   ]. The Purchaser shall arrange a placing to produce such aggregate net proceeds and shall procure the payment of that amount to the Vendor at Completion against the renunciation by the Vendor of the allotment of such Consideration Shares as directed by the Purchaser.

(C) Dividends etc
The Consideration Shares shall rank *pari passu* and as a single class with the ordinary shares of [   ] each in the Purchaser in issue at the date of this Agreement, and shall carry the right to receive in full all dividends and other distributions declared, made or paid after the date of this Agreement [save that they shall not carry the right to participate in the [interim] [final] dividend of the Purchaser for the year ending [19   ] [declared on   ][2].

4 CONDITIONS AND COMPLETION

(A) Conditions[1]
Completion is conditional upon:

(1)   the passing at a general meeting of the Purchaser duly convened and held of a resolution to:

    (*a*)   approve the acquisition by the Purchaser of the Sale Shares;

    (*b*)   increase the authorised share capital of the Purchaser to not less than £[   ]; and

    (*c*)   to authorise the directors of the Purchaser to allot the Consideration Shares;[2]

(2)   the admission by the Council of the London Stock Exchange of the Consideration Shares to the Official List, and such listing having become fully effective by the making of the appropriate announcement under Rule 520 of the London Stock Exchange Rules; and[3]

(3)   the Placing Agreement being entered into and becoming, in accordance with its terms, unconditional in all respects;[4]

and in the event that the above conditions[5] shall not have been satisfied on or before [19] this Agreement shall lapse and no party shall make any claim against any other in respect hereof, save for any antecedent breach.[6]

(B)   Date of Completion

Subject to the provisions of this clause, Completion shall take place on [19] at the offices of [   ].

(C)   Vendor's Obligations[7]

On Completion the Vendor shall:

(1)   deliver to the Purchaser:

    (*a*)   duly executed transfers of the Sale Shares by the registered holders thereof in favour of the Purchaser or its nominees together with the relative share certificates;

    (*b*)   such waivers or consents[8] as the Purchaser may require to enable the Purchaser or its nominees to be registered as holders of the Sale Shares; and

    (*c*)   [powers of attorney in agreed terms.[9]

(2)   procure the passing of a resolution of the board of directors of the Company resolving to register the transfers referred to in item (1)(a) [subject only to due stamping;[10]

(3)   cause such persons as the Purchaser may nominate to be validly appointed as additional directors of the Company and the Subsidiaries and, upon such appointment, forthwith cause the Directors (other than the Continuing Directors) and the secretary or secretaries of the Company and the Subsidiaries to retire from all their offices and employments with the Company or the Subsidiaries, each delivering to the Purchaser a deed acknowledging that he has no claim outstanding for

compensation or otherwise and without any payment under the Employment Protection (Consolidation) Act 1978;[11]

(4) procure revocation of all authorities to the bankers of the Company and the Subsidiaries relating to bank accounts, giving authority to such persons as the Purchaser may nominate to operate the same;

(5) procure the resignation of the auditors of the Company and the Subsidiaries in accordance with s 392 of the Companies Act 1985, accompanied by a statement pursuant to s 394 of that Act that there are no circumstances connected with their resignation which should be brought to the notice of the members or creditors of each such company and that no fees are due to them and procure the appointment of [   ] as the new auditors of the Company;[12]

(6) deliver to the Purchaser as agent for the Company and the Subsidiaries:

    (*a*) a certificate from [   ] in agreed terms as to the title of the Company or the Subsidiaries to the Properties;[13]

    (*b*) the title deeds to the Properties;[14]

    (*c*) all the statutory and other books (duly written up to date) of the Company and each of the Subsidiaries and its/their certificate(s) of incorporation and common seal(s); and[15]

    (*d*) certificates in respect of all issued shares in the capital of each of the Subsidiaries and transfer of all shares in any Subsidiary held by any nominee in favour of such persons as the Purchaser shall direct; [and][16]

(7) deposit the sum of £[   ] with the Purchaser on the terms of clause 7; [and]

(8) comply with clause 3(B); [and]

(9) procure the discharge of the guarantees and other obligations stipulated in the Disclosure Letter to be discharged at Completion.

(D) Service Agreements
On Completion the Company and [   ] shall enter into service agreements in the form of the draft(s) in agreed terms.[17]

(E) Purchaser's Obligations
On Completion the Purchaser shall [pay] [satisfy] the consideration for the Sale Shares as provided by clause 3 [and comply with the provisions of paragraph 3 of the seventh schedule] [any payment in cash to be made] by way of town clearing banker's draft made payable to the Vendor.[18]

(F) Failure to Complete[19]
If in any respect the preceding provisions of this clause (other than sub-clause (A)) are not complied with on the date for Completion set by sub-clause (B) the party not in default (or, in the case of non-compliance with sub-clause (D), the Purchaser) may:

(1) defer Completion to a date not more than 28 days after the date set by sub-clause (B) (and so that the provisions of this sub-clause (F), apart from this item (1), shall apply to Completion as so deferred); or

(2) proceed to Completion so far as practicable (without prejudice to its rights hereunder); or

(3) rescind this Agreement.

5 PURCHASER'S RIGHT OF ACCESS[1]

From the date hereof the Purchaser and its accountants and agents shall be allowed access to all the premises and books of account of the Company and the Subsidiaries, and the Vendor shall supply any information reasonably required by the Purchaser relating to the Company and the Subsidiaries.

6 RESTRICTION OF VENDOR

(A) Restricted Business
In this clause, 'Restricted Business' means [   ].

(B) Covenants
The Vendor undertakes with the Purchaser that it will not and that none of its subsidiaries will:

(1) for the period of [   ] after Completion, either on its own account or in conjunction with or on behalf of any person, firm or company, carry on, or be engaged, concerned or interested (directly or indirectly) in carrying on Restricted Business (other than as a holder of less than 5 per cent of any class of shares or debentures listed on the London Stock Exchange) within [   ];

(2) for the period of [   ] after Completion, either on its own account or in conjunction with or on behalf of any other person, firm or company, solicit or entice away from the Company or any of the Subsidiaries any person who at the date hereof is an officer, manager, servant or customer of the Company or any of the Subsidiaries whether or not such person would commit a breach of contract by reason of leaving service or transferring business; and

(3) directly or indirectly use or attempt to use in the course of any business, at any time hereafter, on its own account or in

conjunction with or on behalf of any person, firm or company any trade or service mark or logo (including the Listed Intellectual Property referred to in the third schedule) used in the business of the Company and the Subsidiaries or any other name, logo, trade or service mark which is or might be confusingly similar thereto [exceptions for group logos etc].

(C) Reasonableness[1]
The restrictions contained in sub-clause (B) are considered reasonable by the parties, but in the event that any such restriction shall be found to be void but would be valid if some part thereof were deleted, or the period or area of application reduced, such restriction shall apply with such modification as may be necessary to make it valid and effective.

(D) Registration
[Any provision of this Agreement, or of any agreement or arrangement of which it forms part, by virtue of which such agreement or arrangement is subject to registration under the Restrictive Trade Practices Act 1976 shall only take effect the day after particulars of such agreement or arrangement have been furnished to the Director General of Fair Trading pursuant to s 24 of that Act.][2]

(E) Confidentiality
The Vendor shall not and shall procure that no other member of the Vendor's Group nor any officer or employee of any member of the Vendor's Group shall divulge to any third party (other than to the Vendor's professional advisers for the purpose of this Agreement in which case the Vendor shall use all reasonable endeavours to procure that such advisers keep such information confidential on terms equivalent to this clause) any confidential information relating to the Company and the Subsidiaries save only insofar as the same has lawfully become a matter of public knowledge otherwise than by reason of a breach of this clause or its unlawful disclosure by any person or to the extent required by law.

7 WARRANTIES AND DEPOSIT

(A) Purchaser's Knowledge
The Warranties are given subject to matters fairly disclosed in this Agreement or in the Disclosure Letter, but no other information relating to the Company or the Subsidiaries of which the Purchaser has knowledge (actual or constructive) shall prejudice any claim made by the Purchaser under the Warranties or operate to reduce any amount recoverable.[1]

(B)   Warranties to be Independent
Each of the Warranties shall be separate and independent and, save as expressly provided, shall not be limited by reference to any other Warranty or anything in this Agreement.

(C)   Damages[2]
Without restricting the rights of the Purchaser or the ability of the Purchaser to claim damages on any basis in the event that any of the Warranties is broken or proves to be untrue or misleading, the Vendor shall, on demand, pay to the Purchaser:
(1)   the amount necessary to put the Company and each of the Subsidiaries into the position which would have existed if the Warranties had not been broken and had been true and not misleading; and
(2)   all costs and expenses incurred by the Purchaser, the Company or the Subsidiaries, directly or indirectly, as a result of such breach.

(D)   Pending Completion[3]
The Vendor shall procure that (save only as may be necessary to give effect to this Agreement) no member of the Vendor's Group nor the Company nor any of the Subsidiaries shall do, allow or procure any act or omission before Completion which would constitute a breach of any of the Warranties if they were given at any and all times from the date hereof down to Completion or which would make any of the Warranties inaccurate or misleading if they were so given. In particular, without prejudice to the generality of the foregoing, the Vendor shall procure that items (*a*) to (*g*) of paragraph 2(22) of the third schedule shall be complied with at all times from the date hereof down to Completion.

(E)   Further Disclosure by Vendor
The Vendor shall forthwith disclose in writing to the Purchaser any matter or thing which may arise or become known to the Vendor after due and careful enquiry, which the Vendor is hereby required to make, after the date hereof and before Completion which is inconsistent with any of the Warranties or which might make any of them inaccurate or misleading if they were given at any and all times from the date hereof down to Completion or which is material to be known to a purchaser for value of the Sale Shares.

(F)   Right of Rescission[4]
In the event of any such matter or thing as is mentioned in sub-clause (E) becoming known to the Purchaser before Completion or in the event of its becoming apparent on or before Completion that the Vendor is at any time in breach of any of the Warranties or any other

term of this Agreement the Purchaser may rescind this Agreement by notice in writing to the Vendor.

(G) Application of Deposit[5]

Subject to sub-clauses (H) and (I), the Purchaser may apply all or part of the deposit referred to in sub-clause 4(C)(7) ('the Deposit') in recouping any amount lawfully due to it under or by reason of any breach of the terms of this Agreement and any amount so applied shall *pro tanto* satisfy the liability concerned.

(H) Interest

The Deposit shall be deposited by the Purchaser with bankers selected by it and any interest earned thereon shall accrue to and form part of the Deposit and shall, accordingly, belong to the Vendor subject to the provisions of this Agreement.

(I) Release

In the event that the Purchaser shall not have notified the Vendor in writing of any claim hereunder before [   ] 19[   ] the Deposit shall be released to the Vendor's solicitors [   ] whose receipt shall be an absolute discharge. In the event that the Purchaser shall have so notified any such claim, it shall use its best endeavours to quantify the amount claimed and any balance shall be so released on that date. Upon final determination of the total amount (if any) falling to be applied by the Purchaser under this clause, any balance of the Deposit shall be released to the Vendor's solicitors provided that no amount shall be released before the said [   ] 19[   ].

8 PROVISIONS RELATING TO THIS AGREEMENT

(A) Assignment

This Agreement shall be binding upon and enure for the benefit of the successors of the parties but shall not be assignable, save that the Purchaser may assign the benefit of the Warranties to any transferee of the share capital of the Company or any of the Subsidiaries.

(B) Whole Agreement

This Agreement (together with any documents referred to herein) constitutes the whole agreement between the parties hereto relating to its subject matter and no variations hereof shall be effective unless made in writing. This Agreement supersedes [   ].[1]

(C) Agreement Survives Completion

The Warranties and all other provisions of this Agreement, in so far as the same shall not have been performed at Completion, shall remain in full force and effect notwithstanding Completion.

(D) Rights of Rescission
Any right of rescission conferred upon the Purchaser hereby shall be in addition to and without prejudice to all other rights and remedies available to it and no exercise or failure to exercise such a right of rescission shall constitute a waiver by the Purchaser of any such other right or remedy. Completion shall not constitute a waiver by the Purchaser of any breach of any provision of this Agreement whether or not known to the Purchaser at the date of Completion.

(E) Further Assurance
At any time after the date hereof the Vendor shall, at the request and cost of the Purchaser, execute such documents and do such acts and things as the Purchaser may reasonably require for the purpose of vesting the Sale Shares in the Purchaser or its nominees and giving to the Purchaser the full benefit of all the provisions of this Agreement.

(F) Invalidity
If any provision of this Agreement shall be held to be illegal or unenforceable, the enforceability of the remainder of this Agreement shall not be affected.

(G) Counterparts
This Agreement may be executed in any number of counterparts, which shall together constitute one Agreement.

(H) Notices
Any notice required to be given hereunder shall be in writing in the English language and shall be served by sending the same by pre-paid first class post, telex or telecopy or by delivering the same by hand to the registered office for the time being of the addressee. Any notice sent by post, as provided in this sub-clause, shall be deemed to have been served 48 hours after despatch and any notice sent by telex or telecopy, as provided in this sub-clause, shall be deemed to have been served at the time of despatch and in proving the service of the same it will be sufficient to prove, in the case of a letter, that such letter was properly pre-paid, addressed and placed in the post and, in the case of a telex or telecopy, that such telex or telecopy was duly despatched to a current telex or telecopy number of the addressee.

(I) English Law
This Agreement shall be governed by, and construed in accordance with, English law.[3]

9 ANNOUNCEMENTS

The Vendor and the Purchaser shall consult in respect of any announcement to be made by them or by the Company or the

Subsidiaries concerning the transaction referred to in this Agreement. No such announcement shall be made by either party without the prior written consent of the other unless such announcement is required by the London Stock Exchange, by a court of competent jurisdiction or by any other competent authority or constitutes an announcement concerning the affairs of the Vendor's group or Purchaser's group generally.

10 COSTS

Each party to this Agreement shall pay its own costs of and incidental to this Agreement and the sale and purchase hereby agreed to be made, provided that if the Purchaser shall exercise any right hereby conferred to rescind this Agreement the Vendor shall indemnify the Purchaser against expenses and costs incurred in investigating the affairs of the Company and the Subsidiaries and in the preparation of this Agreement.

AS WITNESS the hands of duly authorised representatives of the parties the day and year first before written.

FIRST SCHEDULE

Directors

Part I — Directors

Name of Director

*Company/Companies
of which (s)he is
a director*

Part II — Continuing Directors

Name of Director

*Company/Companies
of which (s)he is
a director*

Part III — Secretary

Name of Secretary

*Company/Companies of
which (s)he is the
secretary*

SECOND SCHEDULE

Company and Subsidiaries

Part I — the Company

Name and Number of Company	*Authorised Capital*	*Issued Capital*	*Held by*	*Beneficially owned by*

Part II — the Subsidiaries

Name and Number of Subsidiary	*Authorised Capital*	*Issued Capital*	*Held by*	*Beneficially owned by*

THIRD SCHEDULE
Warranties and Representations[1]

1 INTERPRETATION

In this schedule where the context admits:
(1) 'Audited Accounts' means the audited consolidated balance sheet of the Company and the Subsidiaries made up as at the Balance Sheet Date and the audited consolidated profit and loss account of the Company and the Subsidiaries for the year ended on the Balance Sheet Date, true copies of which are annexed to the Disclosure Letter, including the notes thereto;
(2) 'Balance Sheet Date' means [19   ];
(3) 'Computer Systems' means all computer systems used by or for the benefit of the Company at any time, including computer processors, associated and peripheral equipment, computer programs, technical and other documentation, and data entered into or created by the foregoing from time to time;
(4) 'Companies Acts' means statutes from time to time in force concerning companies;
(5) 'encumbrance' includes any interest or equity of any person (including, without prejudice to the generality of the foregoing, any right to acquire, option or right of pre-emption) or any mortgage, charge, pledge, lien, assignment, hypothecation, security interest, title retention or any other security agreement or arrangement;
(6) 'environmental liability' includes liability for any form of damage to the environment and for any of the following: damage to living organisms or persons (including impairment of health and interference with amenity); damage to land or personal property; interference with riparian or other proprietory or possessory rights; and public or private nuisance;
(7) 'intellectual property' means patents, trade marks, service marks, rights (whether registered or unregistered) in any designs, applications for any of the foregoing, trade or business names and copyright;
(8) 'intellectual property agreements' means agreements or arrangements relating (wholly or partly) to intellectual property or to the disclosure, use, assignment or patenting of any inventions, discovery, improvements, processes, formulae or other knowhow;

(9) 'Listed Intellectual Property' means the Intellectual Property listed in the list annexed to the Disclosure Letter;

(10) 'Listed Intellectual Property Agreements' means the Intellectual Property Agreements listed in the list annexed to the Disclosure Letter;

(11) 'Management Accounts' means the management accounts for the period ended on [19   ] true copies of which are annexed to the Disclosure Letter;

(12) 'SSAP' means Statement of Standard Accounting Practice in force at the date hereof;

(13) any question whether a person is connected with another shall be determined in accordance with the Income and Corporation Taxes Act 1988, s 839 which shall apply in relation to this schedule as it applies in relation to that Act;[2]

(14) references to 'the Company' include each of the Subsidiaries; and

(15) reference to any Act, statutory instrument, regulation, bye-law or other requirement of English law and to any English legal term for any action, remedy, method of judicial proceeding, legal document, legal status, court, official or any legal concept or thing shall in respect of any jurisdiction other than England be deemed to include that which most nearly approximates in that jurisdiction to the English legal term.

2   WARRANTIES AND REPRESENTATIONS

The Vendor hereby warrants and represents to and for the benefit of the Purchaser in the following terms.

THE COMPANY AND THE VENDOR

(1)   Capacity

The Vendor has full power to enter into and perform this Agreement and this Agreement constitutes binding obligations on the Vendor in accordance with its terms.

(2)   Liabilities Owing to or by Vendor

There is not outstanding any indebtedness or other liability (actual or contingent) owing by the Company to any member of the Vendor's Group or any Director or any person connected with any of them, nor is there any indebtedness owing to the Company by any such person, and no promise or representation has been made to the Vendor in connection with the Warranties or the Disclosure Letter in respect of which the Company or any of the Subsidiaries might be liable.

(3)   Vendor's Other Interests

No member of the Vendor's Group nor any person connected with any such member has any interest, direct or indirect, in any business other than that now carried on by the Company which is or is likely to be or become competitive with the business or any proposed business of the Company.

THE COMPANY'S CONSTITUTION

(4)   Share Capital
Part I of the second schedule contains true particulars of the authorised and issued share capital of the Company and all the shares there shown as issued are in issue fully paid and are beneficially owned and registered as set out therein free from any encumbrance.

(5)   Memorandum and Articles
The copy of the memorandum and articles of association of the Company annexed to the Disclosure Letter is true and complete and has embodied therein or annexed thereto a copy of every such resolution or agreement as is referred to in the Companies Act 1985, s 380[3].

(6)   Company Resolutions
Neither the Company nor any class of its members has passed any resolution (other than resolutions relating to business at annual general meetings which was not special business).

(7)   Options etc
No person has the right (whether exercisable now or in the future and whether contingent or not) to call for the allotment, issue, sale, transfer or conversion of any share or loan capital of the Company under any option or other agreement (including conversion rights and rights of pre-emption).

THE COMPANY AND THE LAW

(8)   Compliance with Laws
The Company has conducted its business in all material respects in accordance with all applicable laws and regulations of the United Kingdom and any relevant foreign country and there is no order, decree or judgment of any court or any governmental agency of the United Kingdom or any foreign country outstanding against the Company or which may have a material adverse effect upon the assets or business of the Company.

(9)   Licences etc
All necessary licences, consents, permits and authorities (public and private) have been obtained by the Company to enable the Company to carry on its business effectively in the places and in the manner in which such business is now carried on and all such licences, consents, permits and authorities are valid and subsisting and the Vendor

knows of no reason why any of them should be suspended, cancelled or revoked.

(10) Breach of Statutory Provisions

Neither the Company, nor any of its officers, agents or employees (during the course of their duties in relation to the Company) have committed, or omitted to do, any act or thing the commission or omission of which is, or could be, in contravention of any Act, Order, Regulation or the like in the United Kingdom or elsewhere which is punishable by fine or other penalty.

(11) Litigation

The Company is not engaged in any litigation or arbitration proceedings and so far as the Vendor is aware no litigation or arbitration proceedings are pending or threatened by or against the Company and there are no facts likely to give rise to any litigation or arbitration and the Company has not been a party to any undertaking or assurance given to any court or governmental agency or the subject of any injunction which is still in force.

(12) Insolvency[4]

    (*a*) No order has been made or petition presented or resolution passed for the winding up of the Company, nor has any distress, execution or other process been levied against the Company or action taken to repossess goods in the Company's possession.

    (*b*) No steps have been taken for the appointment of an administrator or receiver of any part of the Company's property.

    (*c*) No floating charge created by the Company has crystallised and, so far as the Vendor is aware, there are no circumstances likely to cause such a floating charge to crystallise.

    (*d*) The Company has not been a party to any transaction which could be avoided in a winding up.

    (*e*) The Company has not made or proposed any arrangement or composition with its creditors or any class of its creditors.

(13) Fair Trading

    (*a*) No agreement, practice or arrangement carried on by the Company or to which the Company is a party:

        (i) is or ought to be or ought to have been registered in accordance with the provisions of the Restrictive Trade Practices Acts 1976 and 1977 or contravenes the provisions of the Resale Prices Act 1976 or is or has been the subject of any enquiry, investigation or proceeding under any of those Acts; or

      (ii) is or has been the subject of an enquiry, investigation, reference or report under the Fair Trading Act 1973 (or any previous legislation relating to monopolies or mergers) or the Competition Act 1980; or

     (iii) infringes art 85 of the Treaty establishing the European Economic Community or constitutes an abuse of dominant position contrary to art 86 of the said Treaty or infringes any Regulation or other enactment made under art 87 of the said Treaty or is or has been the subject of any enquiry, investigation or proceeding in respect thereof; or

     (iv) has been notified to the Directorate General of Competition of the Commission of the European Communities; or

     (v) is by virtue of its terms or by virtue of any practice for the time being carried on in connection therewith a 'Consumer Trade Practice' within the meaning of the Fair Trading Act 1973, s 13 and susceptible to or under reference to the Consumer Protection Advisory Committee or the subject matter of a report to the Secretary of State or the subject matter of an Order by the Secretary of State under the provisions of Part II of that Act; or

     (vi) infringes any other competition, anti-restrictive trade practice, anti-trust or consumer protection law or legislation applicable in the United Kingdom or elsewhere and not specifically mentioned in this sub-paragraph.

    (*b*)   The Company has not given any assurance or undertaking to the Restrictive Practices Court or the Director General of Fair Trading or the Secretary of State for Trade and Industry or the Commission or Court of Justice of the European Communities or to any other court, person or body and is not subject to any Act, decision, regulation, order or other instrument made by any of them relating to any matter referred to in this sub-paragraph (13).

    (*c*)   The Company is not in default or in contravention of any Article, Act, decision, regulation, order or other instrument or of any undertaking relating to any matter referred to in this sub-paragraph.

(14) <u>Defective Products</u>

The Company has not manufactured, sold or supplied products which are, or were, or will become, in any material respect faulty or defective or which do not comply in any material respect with any warranties or representations expressly or impliedly made by the Company or with all applicable regulations, standards and requirements in respect thereof.

(15) Inducements

So far as the Vendor is aware no officer, agent or employee of the Company has paid any bribe or used any of the Company's assets unlawfully to obtain an advantage for any person.

THE COMPANY'S ACCOUNTS AND RECORDS

(16) Books and Records

All accounts, books, ledgers, financial and other records of whatsoever kind ('records') of the Company:

(a) have been fully, properly and accurately maintained, are in the possession of the Company and contain true and accurate records of all matters required by law to be entered therein; and

(b) do not contain or reflect any material inaccuracies or discrepancies; and

and no notice or allegation that any of the records is incorrect or should be rectified has been received. Where any of the records of the Company are kept on Computer Systems, the Company is the owner of all hardware and all software licences necessary to enable it to keep, copy, maintain and use the records in the course of its business and does not share any hardware or software relating to the records with any person.

(17) Accounts Warranty[5]

The Audited Accounts have been prepared in accordance with the requirements of all relevant statutes and generally accepted accounting principles and show a true and fair view of the assets and liabilities of the Company and the Subsidiaries at the Balance Sheet Date and the profits of the Company and the Subsidiaries for the year ended on the Balance Sheet Date and apply bases and policies of accounting which have been consistently applied in the audited balance sheet and profit and loss accounts for the three financial years prior to the Balance Sheet Date.

(18) Provision for Liabilities

Full provision has been made in the Audited Accounts for all actual liabilities of the Company outstanding at the Balance Sheet Date and proper provision (or note) in accordance with generally accepted accounting principles has been made therein for all other liabilities of the Company then outstanding whether contingent, quantified, disputed or not including (without limitation) the cost of any work or material for which payment has been received or credit taken, any future loss which may arise in connection with uncompleted contracts and any claims against the Company in respect of completed contracts.

(19)   Stock Valuation and Accounting Policies[6]

For the purposes of the Audited Accounts, the Company's stock in trade and work in progress has been valued in accordance with SSAP 9 and on a basis in all material respects consistent with that adopted for the purpose of the Company's audited accounts in respect of the beginning and end of each of the last three preceding accounting periods and the value of redundant or obsolete materials and materials below standard has been written down to realisable market value or adequate provision has been made therefor.

(20)   Management Accounts[7]

The Management Accounts have been prepared in accordance with the Company's normal practices and the Vendor does not consider them misleading.

(21)   Returns

The Company has complied with the provisions of the Companies Acts and all returns, particulars, resolutions and other documents required under any legislation to be delivered on behalf of the Company to the Registrar of Companies or to any other authority whatsoever have been properly made and delivered. All such documents delivered to the Registrar of Companies or to any other authority whatsoever, whether or not required by law, were true and accurate when so delivered.

THE COMPANY'S BUSINESS

(22)   Business since the Balance Sheet Date[8]

Since the Balance Sheet Date:

    (*a*)   the Company has carried on its business in the ordinary and usual course and without entering into any transaction, assuming any liability or making any payment which is not in the ordinary course of its business and without any interruption or alteration in the nature, scope or manner of its business;

    (*b*)   the Company has not borrowed or raised any money or taken any financial facility;

    (*c*)   the Company has paid its creditors within the times agreed with such creditors and so that there are no debts outstanding by the Company which have been due for more than four weeks;

    (*d*)   there has been no unusual change in the Company's stock levels;

    (*e*)   the Company has not entered into, or agreed to enter into, any capital commitments;

(*f*)   no share or loan capital has been issued or agreed to be issued by the Company;

(*g*)   no distribution of capital or income has been declared, made or paid in respect of any share capital of the Company and (excluding fluctuations in overdrawn current accounts with bankers) no loan or share capital of the Company has been repaid in whole or part or has become liable to be repaid; and

(*h*)   there has been no material deterioration in the financial position, prospects or turnover of the Company.[9]

(23)   Working Capital

Having regard to existing bank and other facilities, the Company has sufficient working capital for the purposes of continuing to carry on its business in its present form and at its present level of turnover for the foreseeable future and for the purposes of executing, carrying out and fulfilling in accordance with their terms all orders, projects and contractual obligations which have been placed with, or undertaken by, the Company.

(24)   Commission

No one is entitled to receive from the Company any finder's fee, brokerage or other commission in connection with this Agreement or the sale and purchase of shares in the Company.

(25)   Consequence of Share Acquisition by the Purchaser

The acquisition of the Sale Shares by the Purchaser or compliance with the terms of this Agreement:

(*a*)   will not cause the Company to lose the benefit of any right or privilege it presently enjoys or so far as the Vendor is aware, cause any person who normally does business with the Company not to continue to do so on the same basis as previously;

(*b*)   will not relieve any person of any obligation to the Company or enable any person to determine any such obligation or any right or benefit enjoyed by the Company or to exercise any right whether under an agreement with or otherwise in respect of the Company;

(*c*)   will not result in any present or future indebtedness of the Company becoming due or capable of being declared due and payable prior to its stated maturity; and

(*d*)   will not give rise to or cause to become exercisable any right of pre-emption;

and, to the best of the knowledge and belief of the Vendor, the Company's relationships with clients, customers, suppliers and employees will not be adversely affected thereby.[10]

(26)   Grants
[The Company has not applied for or received any financial assistance from any supranational, national or local authority or government agency.] [Full particulars of all grants received from any supranational, national or local authority or government agency (and all applications for any such) are contained in the Disclosure Letter and there are no circumstances which might lead to any such grant being refunded or forfeited in whole or in part.]

(27)   Insurances[11]

    (*a*)   Full particulars of all the Company's insurances are given in the Disclosure Letter and the insurances which are maintained by the Company afford the Company adequate cover against such risks as companies carrying on the same type of business as the Company commonly cover by insurance and in particular:

        (i) the assets of the Company are insured against fire in their full replacement value;

        (ii) the Computer Systems are insured for all foreseeable risks to their full replacement value, together with incidental expenses, including, without limitation, costs and expenses of data recovery and reconstruction; and

        (iii) the Company is now, and has at all material times been, adequately covered against accident, damage, injury, third party loss (including product liability), loss of profits and other risks normally covered by insurance.

    (*b*)   All the Company's insurances referred to in the Disclosure Letter are in full force and effect, there are no circumstances which might lead to any liability under any of the Company's insurances being avoided by the insurers or the premiums being increased, there are no special or unusual terms, restrictions or rates of premium, all premiums have been paid on time and there is no claim outstanding under any such insurance nor is the Vendor aware of any circumstances likely to give rise to a claim.

(28)   Trading Name
The Company does not trade under any name other than as set out in the Disclosure Letter.

(29)   Trade Associations
True and complete details of all trade or business associations of which the Company is a member are set out in the Disclosure Letter, and the Company is and has at all material times complied in all material respects with the regulations or guidelines laid down by any

such trade association and all reports, comments and recommendations made by any such association are annexed to the Disclosure Letter.

(30) Terms of Business
True and complete copies of the standard terms upon which the Company carries on business or provides services to any person are annexed to the Disclosure Letter and the Company does not provide and has not provided any service to any person on terms which differ from its standard terms as annexed.

THE COMPANY'S ASSETS

(31) Net Asset Value
The value of the net tangible assets of the Company at Completion determined in accordance with the same accounting policies as those applied in the Audited Accounts (and on the basis that each fixed asset is valued at a figure no greater than the value attributed to it in the Audited Accounts or, in the case of any fixed asset acquired by the Company after the Balance Sheet Date, at a figure no greater than cost) will not be less than the value of the net tangible assets of the Company at the Balance Sheet Date as shown in the Audited Accounts.[12]

(32) Assets and Charges
  (*a*) Except for current assets disposed of by the Company in the ordinary course of its business, the Company is the owner of and has good marketable title to all assets included in the Audited Accounts and all assets which have been acquired by the Company since the Balance Sheet Date and no such asset, nor any of the undertaking, goodwill or uncalled capital of the Company is subject to any encumbrance or any agreement or commitment to give or create any encumbrance.
  (*b*) Since the Balance Sheet Date, save for disposals in the ordinary course of its business, the assets of the Company have been in the possession of, or under the control of, the Company.
  (*c*) No asset is shared by the Company with any other person and the Company does not depend for its business upon any assets, facilities or services owned or supplied by other members of the Vendor's group.
  (*d*) No charge in favour of the Company is void or voidable for want of registration.

(33) Debts[13]
Any debts owed to the Company as recorded in the Company's books and records will realise their full face value and be good and

collectable in the ordinary course of business and not subject to any defence, right of set-off or counter-claim of any kind arising from an act or omission occurring prior to the date of this Agreement and no amount included in the Audited Accounts as owing to the Company at the Balance Sheet Date has been released for an amount less than the value at which it was included in the Audited Accounts or is now regarded by the Vendor as irrecoverable in whole or in part. The Company has not factored or discounted any of its debts or agreed to do so.

(34)   Title Retention

The Company has not acquired or agreed to acquire any material asset on terms that property therein does not pass until full payment is made.

(35)   Intellectual Property Rights

    (*a*)   The Company is the sole beneficial owner of the Listed Intellectual Property and (where such property is capable of registration) the registered proprietor thereof and (save for copyrights) owns no other intellectual property. Save as may appear from the Listed Intellectual Property Agreements no person has been authorised to make any use whatsoever of any intellectual property owned by the Company and the Company has not disclosed (except in the ordinary course of its business) any of its knowhow, trade secrets or list of customers to any other person.

    (*b*)   All the intellectual property used by the Company is owned by it and it does not use any intellectual property in respect of which any third party has any right, title or interest.

    (*c*)   So far as the Vendor is aware, none of the processes or products of the Company infringes any right of any other person relating to intellectual property or involves the unlicensed use of confidential information disclosed to the Company by any person in circumstances which might entitle that person to a claim against the Company and none of the Listed Intellectual Property is being used, claimed, opposed or attacked by any person.

    (*d*)   The Vendor is not aware of any infringement of the Listed Intellectual Property by any third party.

    (*e*)   There are no outstanding claims against the Company for infringement of any intellectual property used (or which has been used) by it and no such claims have been settled by the giving of any undertakings which remain in force.

    (*f*)   Confidential information and knowhow used by the Company is kept strictly confidential and the Company operates and fully complies with procedures which maintain such confidentiality. The Vendor is not aware of any such confidentiality having been breached.

(*g*) All application and renewal fees, costs and charges relating to the Listed Intellectual Property have been duly paid on time.

(*h*) The Listed Intellectual Property Agreements are all the intellectual property agreements to which the Company is a party and each of them is valid and binding.

(36) Condition of Stock

The Company's stock in trade is in good condition, meets all relevant statutory, regulatory and industry accepted standards and is capable of being sold by the Company in the ordinary course of its business in accordance with its current price list without rebate or allowance to a purchaser.

(37) Plant

The machinery and plant, including fixed plant and machinery, and all vehicles and the Computer Systems and other office and other equipment used in connection with the business of the Company:

(*a*) is in good repair and condition and in satisfactory working order;

(*b*) is capable, and will (subject to fair wear and tear) be capable, over the period of time during which it will be written down to a nil value in the accounts of the Company, of doing the work for which it was designed or purchased;

(*c*) is not surplus to the Company's requirements; and

(*d*) is in the possession and control of, and is the absolute property free from any encumbrance of, the Company save for those items held under hire purchase or rental agreements the value of which items in the aggregate does not exceed [£   ].

(38) Computer Systems

(*a*) The Computer Systems have been satisfactorily maintained and supported and have the benefit of an appropriate maintenance and support agreement terminable by the contractor by not less than 24 months notice.

(*b*) The Computer Systems have adequate capability and capacity for the projected requirements of the Company for not less than four years following Completion for the processing and other functions required to be performed for the purposes of the business of the Company.

(*c*) Disaster recovery plans are in effect and are adequate to ensure that the Computer Systems can be replaced or substituted without material disruption to the business of the Company.

(*d*)   In the event that any person providing maintenance or support services for the Computer Systems ceases or is unable to do so, the Company has all necessary rights to obtain the source code and all related technical and other information free of charge and to procure the carrying out of such services by employees or by a third party.

(*e*)   The Company has sufficient technically competent and trained employees to ensure proper handling, operation, monitoring and use of the Computer Systems.

(*f*)   The Company has adequate procedures to ensure internal and external security of the Computer Systems, including procedures for taking and storing on-site and off-site back-up copies of computer programs and data.

(39)   Title to Properties

The particulars of the Properties shown in the list annexed to the Disclosure Letter are true and correct and the owner shown therein has good and marketable title to and exclusive occupation of each Property which it is said to own free from any encumbrance, sublease, tenancy or right of occupation, reservation, easement, quasi-easement or privilege in favour of any third party and there are appurtenant to each Property all rights and easements necessary for its use and enjoyment and except as shown the Company has no other interest in land and does not occupy any other property.

(40)   Matters Affecting Properties

(*a*)   No Property or any part thereof is affected by any of the following matters or is to the knowledge of the Vendor likely to become so affected:

(i)   any outstanding dispute, notice or complaint or any exception, reservation, right, covenant, restriction or condition which is of an unusual nature or which affects or might in the future affect the use of any of the Properties for the purpose for which it is now used or which affects or might in the future affect the value of the Properties; or

(ii)   any notice, order, demand, requirement or proposal of which the owner has notice or of which the Vendor is aware made or issued by or on behalf of any government or statutory authority, department or body for acquisition, clearance, demolition or closing, the carrying out of any work upon any building, the modification of any planning permission, the discontinuance of any use or the imposition of any building or improvement line; or

(iii) any compensation received as a result of any refusal of any application for planning consent or the imposition of any restrictions in relation to any planning consent; or

(iv) any commutation or agreement for the commutation of rent or payment of rent in advance of the due dates of payment thereof.

(*b*) Each of the Properties is in a good and substantial state of repair and condition and fit for the purposes for which it is at present used and no high alumina cement, woodwool, calcium chloride, sea dredged aggregates or asbestos material was used in the construction thereof or of any of them and there are no development works, redevelopment works or fitting out works outstanding in respect of any of the Properties.

(*c*) All restrictions, conditions and covenants (including any imposed by or pursuant to any lease) affecting any of the Properties have been observed and performed and no notice of any breach of any of the same has been received or is to the Vendor's knowledge likely to be received.

(*d*) The use of the Properties and all machinery and equipment therein and the conduct of any business therein complies in all respects with all relevant statutes and regulations including without prejudice to the generality of the foregoing the Factories Act 1961, the Offices Shops and Railway Premises Act 1963, the Fire Precautions Act 1971 the Health and Safety at Work etc, Act 1974 and with all rules, regulations and delegated legislation thereunder and all necessary licences and consents required thereunder have been obtained.

(*e*) There are no restrictive covenants or provisions, legislation or orders, charges, restrictions, agreements, conditions or other matters which preclude the use of any of the Properties for the purposes for which the Properties are now used and each such user is the permitted user under the provisions of the Town and Country Planning Act 1990 and regulations made thereunder and is in accordance with the requirements of the Local Authorities and all restrictions, conditions and covenants imposed by or pursuant to the said Town and Country Planning Acts have been observed and performed and no agreements have been entered into under the Town and Country Planning Act 1971, s 52 in respect of any of the Properties.

(*f*)   All replies by or on behalf of the Vendor or the Company to enquiries relating to any of the Properties made by or on behalf of the Purchaser were when given and are now true and correct.

(41)   Properties Previously Owned

The Company has no existing or contingent liabilities in respect of any properties previously occupied by it or in which it owned or held any interest, including, without limitation, leasehold premises assigned or otherwise disposed of.

THE COMPANY AND THE ENVIRONMENT[14]

(42)   Authorisations

(*a*)   Full particulars are given in the Disclosure Letter of all material authorisations, permissions, consents, licences and agreements ('authorisations') held by the Company:

    (i)   to abstract water;

    (ii)   to hold raw materials, products or wastes;

    (iii)   to carry on processes;

    (iv)   to construct and maintain buildings, plant and equipment; and

    (v)   to keep, treat, carry, consign and dispose of waste materials, gases and effluents.

All the authorisations have been lawfully obtained and are in full force and effect.

(*b*)   The Company has complied with all conditions attaching to the authorisations, and the Vendor is not aware of any circumstances which would make it impossible or difficult for the Company to comply with such conditions in the future.

(*c*)   The Company has received no communication revoking, suspending, modifying or varying any of the authorisations and is not aware of any circumstances which might give rise to any such communication being received.

(43)   Compliance with Environmental Protection Laws

(*a*)   The Company has not committed any breach of statutory requirements for the protection of the environment or of human health or amenity, and has acted at all times in conformity with all relevant codes or practice, guidance, notes, standards and other advisory material issued by any competent authority.

(*b*)   The Company has not received any communication from any competent authority in respect of the Company's business, failure to comply with which would constitute breach of any statutory requirements or compliance with which could be secured by further proceedings. The Vendor is not aware of any circumstances which might give rise to any such communication being received.

(44) Environmental Liability

The Vendor is not aware of any actual or potential environmental liability on the part of the Company arising from any activities or operations of the Company from wastes or other substances used, kept or produced by the Company or from the condition of any properties now or formerly owned or occupied by the Company or facilities now or formerly used by the Company.

(45) Wastes and Other Substances

    (*a*) The Company has at all times taken all necessary steps to ensure proper keeping, treatment, consignment, carriage and disposal of wastes produced in the course of the Company's business so as to comply with all statutory requirements and duties and in accordance with all codes of practice, notes, standards and other advisory material issued by any competent authority. For the purposes of this warranty 'wastes' includes substances which are wastes to the Company notwithstanding that they may be of value or utility to some other person.

    (*b*) Without prejudice to the generality of sub-paragraph (*a*) the Company has taken all necessary steps to ensure:

        (i) that all such wastes are consigned only to a properly authorised disposer or carrier for disposal at a facility licensed to receive such wastes;

        (ii) that all such wastes have been properly described, and

        (iii) that adequate contractual rights exist so as to enable the Company to obtain indemnity for any claim arising against the Company in respect of such wastes by reason of breach of statutory duty, lack of due care, or malpractice on the part of the disposer or carrier.

    Particulars of all relevant contracts are given in the Disclosure Letter.

    (*c*) No dispute, claim or proceedings exist between the Company and any disposer or carrier with regard to the Company's wastes, whether or not yet consigned to such disposer or carrier, and the Vendor is not aware of any circumstances which are likely to give rise to such dispute, claim or proceedings.

(*d*) All other substances used or kept by the Company are stored, handled and used in such a way as to minimise the risk of environmental liability and there have been no unintended discharges or escapes of such substances so as to present the risk of environmental liability.

(46) Condition of Sites

(*a*) All sites owned or occupied by the Company are free from any contamination which could give rise (whether on the relevant site or elsewhere) to environmental liability.

(*b*) The Vendor is not aware of any circumstances which may require expenditure (whether by the Company or by any other person or authority) on cleaning up or decontaminating any sites now owned or occupied by the Company so as to avoid or reduce the risk of environmental liability or which may require expenditure on investigatory, monitoring, precautionary or remedial engineering measures in relation to any such site, nor is the Vendor aware of circumstances which may give rise to a claim against the Company in respect of such expenditure on any site formerly owned or occupied by the Company.

(*c*) No communication has been received from any competent authority relating to the condition of any site now or formerly owned or occupied by the Company or relating to a proposal for the inclusion of any such site in any register of potentially contaminated land nor is the Vendor aware of any circumstances likely to give rise to the service of such a communication.

(47) Environmental Information

The Company has at all times supplied to the competent authorities such information and assessments as to the Company's processes, substances, discharges, wastes and effluents as are required by law to be supplied. All such information given (whether under a legal obligation or otherwise) was correct at the time the information was supplied and so far as the Vendor is aware all information contained on public registers relating to such matters is correct.

(48) Internal Environmental Policy and Audits

(*a*) The Company has complied with any internal or published statements of corporate environmental policy and operating procedures.

(*b*) All environmental investigations, audits or appraisals undertaken or commissioned by the Company as to the Company's operations, plant, equipment or sites ('audits') are particularised in the Disclosure Letter, including details of the date and nature of the audit, by whom the audit was undertaken and of any report prepared as a result of the audit. So far as the Vendor is aware the audits were carried out competently and the contents of any reports are correct.

THE COMPANY'S CONTRACTS

(49) Documents
All title deeds and agreements to which the Company is a party and other documents owned by or which ought to be in the possession of the Company are in the possession of the Company and are properly stamped and are free from any encumbrance.

(50) Material Contracts
The Company is not a party to or subject to any agreement, transaction, obligation, commitment, understanding, arrangement or liability which:

(*a*) is incapable of complete performance in accordance with its terms within six months after the date on which it was entered into or undertaken; or

(*b*) is known by the Vendor or by the Company to be likely to result in a loss to the Company on completion of performance; or

(*c*) cannot readily be fulfilled or performed by the Company on time and without undue or unusual expenditure of money and effort; or

(*d*) involves or is likely to involve obligations, restrictions, expenditure or receipts of an unusual, onerous or exceptional nature and not in the ordinary course of the Company's business; or

(*e*) is a lease or a contract for hire or rent, hire purchase or purchase by way of credit sale or periodical payment; or

(*f*) is with any trade union or body or organisation representing its employees; or

(*g*) requires an aggregate consideration payable by the Company in excess of [£   ]; or

(*h*) involves or is likely to involve the supply of goods by or to the Company the aggregate sales value of which will represent in excess of [ten] per cent of the turnover of the Company for its last financial year; or

- (*i*)   is a contract for services (other than contracts for the supply of electricity or normal office services); or
- (*j*)   requires the Company to pay any commission, finder's fee, royalty or the like; or
- (*k*)   in any way restricts the Company's freedom to carry on the whole or any part of its business in any part of the world in such manner as it thinks fit; or
- (*l*)   involves liabilities which may fluctuate in accordance with an index or rate of currency exchange; or
- (*m*)   is a contract for the sale of shares or assets which contains warranties or indemnities; or
- (*n*)   is in any way otherwise than in the ordinary course of the Company's business.

(51)   <u>Defaults</u>

Neither the Company nor any other party to any agreement with the Company is in default thereunder, being a default which would be material in the context of the financial or trading position of the Company nor (so far as the Vendor is aware) are there any circumstances likely to give rise to such a default.

(52)   <u>Sureties</u>

No person other than the Company or a Subsidiary has given any guarantee of or security for any overdraft loan or loan facility granted to the Company.

(53)   <u>Powers of Attorney</u>

No powers of attorney given by the Company (other than to the holder of an encumbrance solely to facilitate its enforcement) are now in force. No person, as agent or otherwise, is entitled or authorised to bind or commit the Company to any obligation not in the ordinary course of the Company's business, and the Vendor is not aware of any person purporting to do so.

(54)   <u>Insider Contracts</u>

- (*a*)   There is not outstanding, and there has not at any time during the last six years been outstanding, any agreement or arrangement to which the Company is a party and in which the Vendor, any member of the Vendor's Group, any person beneficially interested in the Company's share capital or any Director or any person connected with any of them is or has been interested, whether directly or indirectly.
- (*b*)   The Company is not a party to, nor have its profits or financial position during such period been affected by, any agreement or arrangement which is not entirely of an arm's length nature.
- (*c*)   All costs incurred by the Company have been charged to

the Company and not borne by any other member of the Vendor's Group.

(55) Debts

There are no debts owing by or to the Company other than debts which have arisen in the ordinary course of business, nor has the Company lent any money which has not been repaid.

(56) Options and Guarantees

The Company is not a party to any option or pre-emption right, or a party to any guarantee, suretyship, comfort letter or any other obligation (whatever called) to pay, provide funds or take action in the event of default in the payment of any indebtedness of any other person or default in the performance of any obligation of any other person.

(57) Tenders etc

No offer, tender or the like is outstanding which is capable of being converted into an obligation of the Company by an acceptance or other act of some other person.

THE COMPANY AND ITS BANKERS

(58) Borrowings

The total amount borrowed by the Company from its bankers does not exceed its facilities and the total amount borrowed by the Company from whatsoever source does not exceed any limitation on its borrowing contained in its articles of association, or in any debenture or loan stock deed or other instrument.

(59) Continuance of Facilities

Full and accurate details of all overdrafts, loans or other financial facilities outstanding or available to the Company are contained in the Disclosure Letter and true and correct copies of all documents relating thereto are annexed to the Disclosure Letter and neither the Vendor nor the Company has done anything whereby the continuance of any such facilities in full force and effect might be affected or prejudiced.

(60) Off-balance Sheet Financing

The Company has not engaged in any borrowing or financing not required to be reflected in the Audited Accounts.

(61) Bank Accounts

A statement of all the bank accounts of the Company and of the credit or debit balances on such accounts as at a date not more than seven days before the date hereof is annexed to the Disclosure Letter. The Company has no other bank or deposit accounts (whether in credit or overdrawn) and since such statement there have been no payments out of any such accounts except for routine payments and the balances on current account are not now substantially different from the balances shown on such statements.

THE COMPANY AND ITS EMPLOYEES

(62)   Directors
The particulars shown in the first schedule are true and complete and no person not named therein as such is a director or shadow director of the Company.

(63)   Particulars of Employees[15]

    (*a*)   The particulars shown in the schedule of employees annexed to the Disclosure Letter show all remuneration payable and other benefits provided or which the Company is bound to provide (whether now or in the future) to each officer, employee or consultant of the Company or any person connected with any such person and are true and complete and include particulars of all profit sharing, incentive and bonus arrangements to which the Company is a party whether legally binding on the Company or not.

    (*b*)   Since the Balance Sheet Date no change has been made in the rate of remuneration, or the emoluments or pension benefits of any officer, ex-officer or employee of the Company and no change has been made in the terms of engagement of any such officer or employee, and no additional officer or employee has been appointed.

    (*c*)   No present officer or employee of the Company has given or received notice terminating his employment except as expressly contemplated under this Agreement.

    (*d*)   The Company has not given notice of any redundancies to any employee or government department or started consultations with any trade union pursuant to any statute or regulation.

(64)   Service Contracts
There is not outstanding any contract of service between the Company and any of its directors, officers or employees which is not terminable by the Company without compensation (other than any compensation payable by statute) on not more than three months' notice given at any time.

(65)   Disputes with Employees
The Vendor is not aware of any outstanding claim against the Company by any person who is now or has been an officer or employee of the Company or any dispute between the Company and a material number or class of its employees and no payments are due

by the Company under the provisions of the Employment Protection (Consolidation) Act 1978.

THE COMPANY AND ITS SUBSIDIARIES

(66) Particulars of Subsidiaries
The particulars of the Subsidiaries set out in part II of the second schedule are true and complete and the Company has no other subsidiary.

(67) Investments Associations and Branches
The Company:
    (*a*) is not the holder or beneficial owner of, and has not agreed to acquire, any class of the share or other capital of any other company or corporation (whether incorporated in the United Kingdom or elsewhere) other than the Subsidiaries;

    (*b*) is not and has not agreed to become a member of any partnership, joint venture, consortium or other unincorporated association or arrangement for sharing commissions or income; and

    (*c*) has no branch, agency or place of business outside England and no permanent establishment (as that expression is defined in the relevant double taxation relief orders current at the date hereof) outside the United Kingdom.

MISCELLANEOUS

(68) Circular
The information contained in the proof circular to shareholders of the Purchaser in agreed terms (incorporating listing particulars) and the draft Press Announcement in agreed terms, insofar as it relates to the Company and the Vendor, is true and accurate in all material respects, is in accordance with the facts and is not misleading.

(69) Sale Memorandum
All information contained or referred to in the sale memorandum (including any annexure thereto) ('the Sale Memorandum') attached to the Disclosure Letter is accurate in all respects and the Vendor is not aware of any other fact or matter which renders any such information misleading or which might reasonably affect the willingness of a purchaser to acquire the Sale Shares on the terms, including price, of this Agreement. All forecasts, estimates and expressions of opinion, intention or expectation expressed in the Sale Memorandum are reasonably based and are fair and honest in all respects and have been made after due and careful enquiry.

(70)   <u>All Material Matters Disclosed</u>[15]

All information contained or referred to in the Disclosure Letter or in any annexure thereto is accurate in all respects and the Vendor is not aware of any other fact or matter which renders any such information misleading or which might reasonably affect the willingness of a purchaser to acquire the Sale Shares on the terms, including price, of this Agreement.

FOURTH SCHEDULE

Taxation[1]

1 INTERPRETATION

In this schedule, where the context admits:
  (1) 'Audited Accounts'[2] and 'Balance Sheet Date' have the same meanings as in the third schedule;
  (2) 'event' includes (without limitation):
    (*a*) any omission, transaction or distribution whether or not the Company is a party thereto[3];
    (*b*) the death of any person[4];
    (*c*) the failure to avoid an apportionment or deemed distribution of income (whether or not it is or was possible, by taking action after Completion, to avoid such apportionment or deemed distribution)[5];
    (*d*) the Company ceasing to be a member of any group or associated with any person on or before Completion[6];
    (*e*) Completion[6]; and
    (*f*) any event which is treated as having occurred for the purposes of any legislation[6];
    and references to the result of events on or before the date of Completion shall include the combined result of two or more events the first of which shall have taken place on or before the date of Completion[7];
  [(3) 'group relief' has the meaning given to that expression by the Income and Corporation Taxes Act 1988, s 402][37];
  (4) 'relief' means any relief, allowance or credit in respect of taxation or any deduction in computing income, profits or gains for the purpose of taxation[8];
  (5) 'taxation claim' means a claim for taxation against the Company or the Purchaser[9] or any member of the Purchaser's Group, whether made before or after the date hereof, whether satisfied[10] or unsatisfied at the date hereof and whether or not the taxation in question is also chargeable against or attributable to any other person, and includes any assessment, notice, demand or other communication from or action taken by any person, authority or body responsible for the assessment, collection or recovery of taxation in any country which claims:
    (*a*) payment of taxation;
    (*b*) to deprive the Company or the Purchaser of any relief whether arising before or after the date hereof[11]; or

    (*c*) to nullify or cancel any right to the repayment of taxation whether arising before or after the date hereof[12];

and which arises from or by reference to:

    (i) any income, profits or gains earned, accrued[13] or received on or before the date of Completion or any event on or before the date of Completion, whether alone or in conjunction with other circumstances; or

    (ii) a payment under paragraph 2(A)[14];

(6) 'relevant taxation claim' means any taxation claim save to the extent that:

    (*a*) provision or reserve in respect thereof has been made in the Audited Accounts or to the extent that payment or discharge of such claim has been taken into account in the Audited Accounts[15];

    (*b*) provision or reserve in respect thereof has been made in the Audited Accounts which is insufficient only by reason of any increase in rates of taxation or change in law[16] after the date hereof having retrospective effect;

    (*c*) it is a claim for which the Company is or may become liable as a result of transactions (not including distributions) entered into by the Company in the ordinary course of trading[17] after the Balance Sheet Date and for the purposes of this sub-paragraph the following shall not be regarded as arising in the ordinary course of trading:

    (i) any liability under Part VIII of the Taxes Management Act 1970 (charges on non-residents);

    (ii) any liability under Part XVII of the Taxes Act 1988 (anti-avoidance);

    (iii) any liability in respect of any distribution (as defined in Part VI of the Taxes Act 1988) or deemed distribution; and

    (iv) any liability arising from the disposal of or acquisition or deemed disposal or acquisition of any asset other than trading stock;

    (*d*) it is a claim against the Purchaser or any member of the Purchaser's Group which does not relate to the Sale Shares or the Company or a payment made under paragraph 2(A) or which is for stamp duty or stamp duty reserve tax arising out of this Agreement or Completion; or (*e*) it is a claim which would not have arisen but for a voluntary act or transaction, which could reasonably have been avoided, carried out by the Purchaser (or persons deriving title from it) or the Company after the date of completion otherwise than in the ordinary course of business and which the Purchaser was aware could give rise to a claim, but so that this exclusion shall not extend to any voluntary act carried out with the approval, concurrence or assistance of the Vendor[18];

(7) 'taxation' includes (without limitation) corporation tax, advance corporation tax, income tax, capital gains tax, the charge under the Taxes Act 1988, s 601(2), value added tax, customs and other import duties, capital transfer tax, inheritance tax, stamp duty[19], stamp duty reserve tax, capital duty, national insurance contributions, foreign taxation and any payment whatsoever which the Company may be or become bound to make to any person as a result of the operation of any enactment relating to taxation and all penalties, charges and interest relating to any claim for taxation or resulting from a failure to comply with the provisions of any enactment relating to taxation;

(8) 'Taxes Act 1988' means the Income and Corporation Taxes Act 1988;

(9) 'TCGA 1992' means the Taxation of Chargeable Gains Act 1992;

(10) references to income or profits or gains earned, accrued or received shall include income or profits or gains treated as earned, accrued or received for the purposes of any legislation;

[(11) references to 'the Company' include each of the Subsidiaries;][37] and

(12) any taxation claim arising out of any of the following shall be treated as a relevant taxation claim for all the purposes of this schedule notwithstanding any other provision hereof[20]:

[   ]

2 TAXATION PAYMENTS

(A) Payments

(1) Subject to and in accordance with the terms of this schedule the Vendor shall make payments to the Purchaser[21] equal to the amount of each relevant taxation claim and all costs properly incurred by the Purchaser or

the Company in connection therewith and in enforcing the Purchaser's rights thereunder.

(2) For this purpose the amount of any relevant taxation claim shall depend upon whether the claim is of the type described in item (*a*), (*b*) or (*c*) of paragraph 1[(5)]. In the case of a claim of the type described in item (*a*), the amount is the payment claimed; in the case of a claim of the type described in item (*b*), the amount is the amount of taxation (on the basis of rates current at the date of the loss of the relief)[22] which would have been relieved, allowed or credited by the relief of which it is claimed to deprive the Company or the Purchaser, and in the case of a claim of the type described in item (*c*), the amount is the repayment which it is claimed to nullify or cancel.

(3) Where any relevant taxation claim has been reduced or eliminated by (or where a relevant taxation claim would have arisen but for) some relief available to the Company then such relief shall be disregarded for the purposes of determining whether, in what amount, and on what date any payment should be made by the Vendor hereunder, and accordingly the relevant taxation claim shall be treated as not being reduced or eliminated (or, as the case may be, shall be treated as having arisen).[23]

(B) Date for Payment

The Vendor shall be bound to make payments in respect of relevant taxation claims on the following dates:

(1) in so far as a relevant taxation claim represents taxation to be borne by the Company but which has not yet become due, the Vendor shall make the payment in respect of that claim (or so much thereof as represents that taxation) on the date on which that taxation becomes due;

(2) in so far as a relevant taxation claim consists of the nullification or cancellation of a right to repayment of taxation the Vendor shall make the payment in respect of that claim (or so much thereof as represents that nullification or cancellation) on the date on which that repayment would otherwise have become due; and

(3) in any other case the Vendor shall make the payment 14 days after the date on which a notice setting out details of the relevant taxation claim is delivered to the Vendor[24];

and for this purpose references to a date on which taxation becomes due include a reference to the date on which it would have become due were it not for the availability of some relief. Any payment which becomes due on a day which is not a business day shall be paid on the next following business day, and any payment which is made after noon on any day before shall, for the purposes of calculating interest, be deemed to have been paid on the next following business day. No payment shall be treated as made until cleared funds in respect thereof are available to the Purchaser.

(C) Reduction in Consideration
Insofar as the payments made by the Vendor to the Purchaser pursuant to sub-paragraph (A) are less than the consideration for the Sale Shares, they shall constitute a repayment of and a reduction in such consideration, but nothing in this paragraph shall limit the liability of the Vendor to make payments under sub-paragraph (A).[25]

(D) Disclosure not Relevant
The Vendor's obligation to make payments under sub-paragraph (A) shall not be affected by the disclosure, in the Disclosure Letter or otherwise, of the relevant taxation claim giving rise to the payment, or the circumstances giving rise to that relevant taxation claim.[26]

(E) Credits and Reductions
If any relevant taxation claim is disputed by the Company or by either party or represents taxation for which credit is or may become due to the Company at a later date or in respect of which it is subsequently found that there arises a corresponding credit or right to repayment of taxation, the amount of the relevant taxation claim shall nevertheless be payable in full by the Vendor on the due date ascertained in accordance with sub-paragraph (B)[27] but if subsequently any reduction is made in the claim or it is found that the liability in respect thereof falls short of the amount claimed or such credit or repayment is received by the Company the Purchaser shall promptly repay to the Vendor an amount equal to such reduction, shortfall, credit or repayment up to the amount previously paid by the Vendor in respect of that relevant taxation claim and without interest[28], save to the extent that interest is included (or allowed) in such credit, repayment, reduction or shortfall. For this purpose, no credit shall be taken to have been received by the Company unless it shall have relieved the Company of a present obligation to pay taxation.

(F) Over-provisions
If, at the request and cost of the Vendor, the Company's auditors shall certify that any provision for taxation (not being a provision for deferred taxation)[29] contained in the Audited Accounts is an over-provision, the value of such over-provision shall be set against the liability of the Vendor under sub-paragraph (A), except in so far as

such over-provision is attributable to the effect of a change in rates of taxation after the date hereof, but no deduction shall be made from any payment which the Vendor shall be obliged to make hereunder unless such certificate is in existence on the due date for that payment. In the event that such a certificate is given after the Vendor has made a payment hereunder, the Purchaser shall refund to the Vendor (without interest) any payment made by the Vendor to the extent that such over-provision could have been set against such payment if the certificate had been in existence on the due date of payment. The Purchaser shall procure that the Company shall co-operate in obtaining any such certificate if the Vendor shall so request.

(G) Notice and Mitigation

    (1) If the Purchaser shall become aware of any relevant taxation claim it shall forthwith give written notice thereof to the Vendor setting out reasonable particulars thereof, including the amount and the date on which the Vendor is bound to make a payment in respect of that relevant taxation claim, ascertained in accordance with sub-paragraph (B), but no failure by the Purchaser to comply with this sub-clause shall affect the Vendor's obligations under sub-paragraph (A).[30]

    (2) Except in a case where fraud or negligent misconduct is alleged the Purchaser shall take such action and give such information and assistance in connection with the affairs of the Company as the Vendor may reasonably and promptly by notice request to avoid, resist, appeal or compromise a relevant taxation claim provided that:

        (*a*) the Company shall not be obliged to appeal against any assessment, notice, demand or decision if, having given the Vendor written notice of the receipt thereof, the Purchaser has not within 7 days[31] thereafter received instructions in writing from the Vendor to do so; and

        (*b*) the Company shall not in any circumstances be obliged to pursue any appeal beyond the General Commissioners of Inland Revenue, the Special Commissioners of Inland Revenue, or Value Added Tax Tribunal or any equivalent forum in the United Kingdom or any other jurisdiction.[32]

    (3) The action which the Vendor may request under sub-paragraph (2) shall include (without limitation) the Company applying to postpone (so far as legally

possible)[33] the payment of any taxation and allowing the Vendor to take on or take over at its own expense the conduct of all proceedings of whatsoever nature arising in connection with the relevant taxation claim in question. If the Vendor takes on or takes over the conduct of proceedings, the Purchaser shall, and shall procure that the Company shall, provide such information and assistance as the Vendor may reasonably require in connection with the preparation for and conduct of such proceedings.

(4) Where the Company is entitled to recover from some other person (including any taxing[34] or other authority) any sum in respect of any relevant taxation claim the Purchaser shall take such action as the Vendor may reasonably and promptly by notice request to enforce such recovery by the Company and shall account to the Vendor for any amount so recovered by the Company not exceeding the amount paid by the Vendor hereunder in respect of that relevant taxation claim together with any interest or repayment supplement included in such recovery less any taxation payable thereon.

(5) Notwithstanding anything in this Agreement, neither the Purchaser nor the Company shall be obliged to take any steps to reduce the amount of any relevant taxation claim or to recover any amount from any other person unless the Vendor shall first indemnify and secure the Company and the Purchaser to their satisfaction against all losses, costs, interest, damages and expenses which may be incurred thereby.

(H) Interest

The Vendor shall make all payments under this schedule in immediately available funds before noon on the due date for payment without deduction or withholding on any account (save as expressly provided in this schedule) and if any amount is not paid when due the Vendor shall pay to the Purchaser interest (accruing daily and compounded monthly) on such amount at the rate of [ ] per cent per annum above the base rate of [ ] Bank PLC from time to time from the due date until the date of actual payment (as well after judgment as before).

(I) Deductions and Withholdings

(1) Any amount payable pursuant to sub-paragraphs (A) or (H) shall be paid free and clear of all deductions,

withholdings or set-offs whatsoever, save only as may be required by law[36].

(2)   If any deductions or withholdings are required by law to be made from any sums, the Vendor shall be obliged to pay the Purchaser such amount as will after the deduction or withholding has been made, leave the Purchaser with the same amount as it would have been entitled to receive in the absence of such requirement to make a deduction or withholding provided that if the Purchaser subsequently receives a credit for such deduction or withholding then such credit shall be applied in accordance with the provision of sub-paragraph (E).

3   GROUP ARRANGEMENTS AND NEGOTIATIONS

(A)   Group Relief and ACT

(1)   In respect of the accounting period ended on [199] the [Vendor] and its subsidiaries ('surrendering companies') shall surrender group relief or Advance Corporation Tax ('ACT') to such of [the Company and the Subsidiaries] as can utilise the same ('claimant companies') and the [Purchaser] shall procure that [   ] per cent of the amount so surrendered (in the case of group relief) and 100 per cent of the amount surrendered (in the case of ACT) shall be paid by each relevant claimant company to the relevant surrendering company on or before [199].

(2)   The amount of group relief and ACT surrendered shall be determined by the surrendering companies but shall not exceed the maximum amount which can be utilised by the claimant companies by way of relief from liability to corporation tax after utilising all other reliefs (including other group relief available to them).

(3)   If any part of the amounts so surrendered shall not be allowed to the claimant company by way of a relief from corporation tax the surrendering company shall refund to the claimant company forthwith the amount paid by the claimant company in respect of that part of the amount so surrendered.

(4)   The parties shall co-operate to secure the agreement with the Inland Revenue of the accounts relating to the accounting period referred to above and shall take all necessary action to procure the surrenders as aforesaid.

(B) Value Added Tax Group Registration

   (1) On the date of Completion, the Vendor shall procure that an application is made to HM Customs and Excise pursuant to the Value Added Tax Act 1983, s 29(5) for the exclusion from the [Vendor's] group registration of [such of the Company and the Subsidiaries as are presently within that group registration] and for such exclusion to take effect at the earliest date permitted by the said section.

   (2) Until such application has taken effect, the parties shall furnish or procure to be so furnished such information as may be required to enable the continuing representative member of the group in question to make the returns required in respect of the group and the [Vendor] [Purchaser] shall arrange for such returns to be made accordingly.

   (3) Such payments shall be made as may be appropriate to ensure that the resulting position between all the companies and bodies concerned is the same as it would have been if such applications had been granted with effect from the date of [Completion].

(C) Conduct of Negotiations

   (1) The Vendor (which may act through a duly authorised agent for the purposes of this sub-paragraph) shall prepare the Company's tax returns for accounting periods ended on or prior to Completion. The Purchaser shall procure that such returns are authorised, signed and submitted by the Company to the appropriate authority without amendment or with such amendments as the Vendor shall agree (such agreement not to be unreasonably withheld) and that the Vendor is given all such assistance as may be required to agree the said returns with the appropriate authorities. The Vendor shall prepare all documentation and deal with all matters (including correspondence) relating to the said returns and the Purchaser shall procure that such access to the books, accounts and records of the Company is afforded as may be required to enable the Vendor to prepare the said returns and conduct matters relating thereto in accordance with the Vendor's rights under this sub-paragraph.

   (2) Without the prior written approval of the Purchaser the Vendor shall take no action the effect of which is likely to increase the amount of taxation payable by the Company in respect of accounting periods after the Balance Sheet

Date or likely to prejudice the business or tax affairs of the Company.

4 TAXATION WARRANTIES AND REPRESENTATIONS

The Vendor hereby warrants and represents to and for the benefit of the Purchaser in the following terms.[37]

GENERAL TAXATION MATTERS

(1) Residence
The Company is and always has been resident for taxation purposes only in the jurisdiction in which it is incorporated.

(2) Tax Provisions
Full provision or reserve has been made in the Audited Accounts for all taxation liable to be assessed on the Company or for which it is accountable in respect of income, profits or gains earned, accrued or received on or before the Balance Sheet Date or any event on or before the Balance Sheet Date including distributions made down to such date or provided for in the Audited Accounts and full provision has been made in the Audited Accounts for deferred taxation calculated in accordance with generally accepted accounting principles.

(3) Returns
The Company has properly and punctually made all returns and provided all information required for taxation purposes and none of such returns is disputed by the Inland Revenue or any other authority concerned (in the United Kingdom or elsewhere) and the Vendor is not aware that any dispute is likely, or that any event has occurred which would or might give rise to a payment under paragraph 2(A).

(4) Payment of Tax
The Company has duly and punctually paid all taxation which it has become liable to pay and is under no liability to pay any penalty or interest in connection with any claim for taxation and has not paid any tax which it was and is not properly due to pay.

(5) Audits
The Company has not in the last six years received any visit or inspection from any taxation authority.

DISTRIBUTIONS AND PAYMENTS

(6) Distributions
　　　(*a*) No distribution within the meaning of the Taxes Act 1988, ss 209, 210 and 212 has been made by the Company except dividends shown in its audited accounts nor is the Company bound to make any such distribution.

(*b*) No securities (within the meaning of the Taxes Act 1988, s 254(1)) issued by the Company and remaining in issue at the date hereof were issued in such circumstances that the interest payable thereon falls to be treated as a distribution under the Taxes Act 1988, s 209(2)(*e*)(iii).

(*c*) The Company has not made or received any distribution which is an exempt distribution within the Taxes Act 1988, s 213.

(*d*) The Company has not received any capital distribution to which the provisions of TCGA 1992, s 189 could apply.

(*e*) The Company has not used any credit, relief or set-off that may be disallowed pursuant to the Taxes Act 1988, s 237.

(*f*) The Company has not issued any share capital, nor granted options or rights to any person which entitles that person to require the issue of any share capital to which the provision of the Taxes Act 1988, s 249 could apply.

[(7) Group Income[37]

The Disclosure Letter contains particulars of all elections made by the Company under the Taxes Act 1988, s 247 and the Company has not paid any dividend without paying advance corporation tax or made any payment without deduction of income tax in the circumstances specified in sub-section (6) of that section. In respect of each such election the conditions of the Taxes Act 1988, s 247 have been at all times and continue to be satisfied.]

[(8) Surrender of Advance Corporation Tax[37]

The Disclosure Letter contains particulars of all arrangements and agreements to which the Company is or has been a party relating to the surrender of advance corporation tax made or received by the Company under the Taxes Act 1988, s 240 and:

(*a*) the Company has not paid nor is liable to pay any amount in excess of the advance corporation tax surrendered to it nor for the benefit of any advance corporation tax which is or may become incapable of set-off against the Company's liability to corporation tax;

(*b*) the Company has received all payments due to it under any such arrangement or agreement for all surrenders of advance corporation tax made by it; and

(*c*) save in respect of this Agreement, there have not been in existence in relation to the Company any such arrangements as are referred to in the Taxes Act 1988, s 240(11).]

(9) ACT Carry Forward

There has been no major change in the business of the Company within the meaning of the Taxes Act 1988, s 245.

(10)   Payments under Deduction

All payments by the Company to any person which ought to have been made under deduction of tax have been so made and the Company has (if required by law to do so) provided certificates of deduction to such person and accounted to the Inland Revenue for the tax so deducted.

(11)   Payments and Disallowances

No rents, interest, annual payments or other sums of an income nature paid or payable by the Company or which the Company is under an obligation to pay in the future are wholly or partially disallowable as deductions or charges in computing profits for the purposes of corporation tax by reason of the provisions of the Taxes Act 1988, ss 74, 125, 338, 577, 779 to 784 and 787, or otherwise.

Losses

(12)   Group Relief[37]

The Disclosure Letter contains particulars of all arrangements and agreements relating to group relief to which the Company is or has been a party and:

- (*a*)   all claims by the Company for group relief were when made and are now valid and have been or will be allowed by way of relief from corporation tax;
- (*b*)   the Company has not made nor is liable to make any payment under any such arrangement or agreement save in consideration for the surrender of group relief allowable to the Company by way of relief from corporation tax and equivalent to the taxation for which the Company would have been liable had it not been for the surrender;
- (*c*)   the Company has received all payments due to it under any such arrangement or agreement for surrender of group relief made by it and no such payment is liable to be repaid;
- (*d*)   the Company is not a dual resident investing company within the meaning of the Taxes Act 1988, s 404; and
- (*e*)   save in respect of this Agreement, there have not been in existence in relation to the Company any such arrangements as are referred to in the Taxes Act 1988, s 410.

(13)   Tax Losses

There has not within the three years preceding the date hereof been a major change in the business of the Company within the meaning of the Taxes Act 1988, s 768.

CLOSE COMPANIES

(14) Close Company
  (*a*) [The Company is] [The Company is not and has not been within the last six years] a close company[38].
  (*b*) No distribution within the Taxes Act 1988, s 418 has been made by the Company.
  (*c*) The Company has not made (and will not be deemed to have made) any loan or advance to a participator or an associate of a participator so as to become liable to make any payment under the Taxes Act 1988, s 419.
  (*d*) The Company has in respect of accounting periods beginning on or before 31 March 1989 supplied to the inspector such information and particulars as are necessary to make full and accurate disclosure of all facts and considerations material to be known by him to enable him to make intimations pursuant to the Taxes Act 1988, Sched 19, para 16 that he does not intend to make apportionments in respect of the Company for any accounting period ending on or before the Balance Sheet Date and the Company has received such intimations.
  (*e*) No apportionment pursuant to the Taxes Act 1988, s 423 and Sched 19 has ever been made or could be made against the Company.
  (*f*) In respect of accounting periods beginning on or before 31 March 1989 the Company has at all times been a 'trading company' or a 'member of a trading group' as defined in the Taxes Act 1988, Sched 19, para 7.
  (*g*) The Company is not, and has not since 31 March 1989 been, a close investment holding company within the meaning of the Taxes Act 1988, s 13A.
  (*h*) The Company has not expended or applied any sum liable to be regarded as income available for distribution pursuant to the Taxes Act 1988, Sched 19, para 8 (first business loans) and is not bound (contingently or otherwise) to expend or apply any such sum.

ANTI-AVOIDANCE

(15) Taxes Act 1988, s 765
The Company has not without the prior consent of the Treasury been a party to any transaction for which consent under the Taxes Act 1988, s 765 was required. Where such consent would have been required but for the provisions of the Taxes Act 1988, s 765A, the Company has complied in full with the requirements of The

Movements of Capital (Required Information) Regulations 1990 and a copy of the notification required pursuant thereto is annexed to the Disclosure Letter.

(16) Controlled Foreign Companies

  (*a*) [The Disclosure Letter contains full details of the Company's] [The Company has no] interest in the share capital of any company not resident in the United Kingdom for taxation purposes (or which is treated for the purposes of any double taxation convention as not being so resident) which is controlled by persons resident in the United Kingdom for taxation purposes and in which the Company has 10 per cent or more of the voting rights (a 'controlled foreign company')[39].

  [(*b*) No enquiries have been made or intimated by the Inland Revenue in respect of any controlled foreign company.

  (*c*) No direction has been made by the Board of Inland Revenue under the Taxes Act 1988, s 747 in respect of any controlled foreign company.

  (*d*) Section 748(1) of the Taxes Act 1988 applies to each controlled foreign company.]

(17) Anti-avoidance

  (*a*) The Company has not at any time entered into or been a party to a transaction or series of transactions either (i) containing steps inserted without any commercial or business purpose or (ii) being transactions to which any of the following provisions could apply: Taxes Act 1988, ss 703, 729, 730, 737, 739, 770, 774, 776, 779, 780, 781 or 786 without, in the appropriate cases, having received clearance in respect thereof from the Inland Revenue.

  (*b*) The Company has never been requested to furnish information pursuant to notices served under ss 745 or 778 of the Taxes Act 1988.

CAPITAL ASSETS

(18) Base Values

  (*a*) The Disclosure Letter contains full and accurate particulars of:

    (i) the extent to which the book value of an asset or a particular class of assets as shown in the Audited Accounts is in excess of either (*aa*) the amount falling to be deducted under TCGA 1992, s 38 from the consideration receivable on a disposal of that asset, or (*bb*) the balance of the qualifying expenditure attributable to that asset or pool of assets, as the case may be, brought forward into the accounting period in which Completion will occur and save to the extent disclosed, no such excess exists; and

    (ii) the extent to which provision for taxation in respect of such excess has been made in the Audited Accounts.

(*b*) No election under TCGA 1992, s 35 is in effect in relation to the Company and full particulars are given in the Disclosure Letter of the first relevant disposal for the purposes of the said s 35.

(*c*) The Disclosure Letter contains full and accurate particulars of all assets held by the Company on or after 6 April 1988 in respect of which relief is or would be available under TCGA 1992, Sched 4 upon disposal.

(19) Roll-over Relief

The Disclosure Letter contains full and accurate particulars of all claims made by the Company under TCGA 1992, ss 152 to 156, s 158, ss 242 to 244, s 247 or s 248 and no such claim or other claim has been made by any other person (in particular pursuant to TCGA 1992, s 165 or s 175) which affects or could affect the amount or value of the consideration for the acquisition of any asset by the Company taken into account in calculating liability to corporation tax on chargeable gains on a subsequent disposal.

(20) Depreciatory Transactions

No loss which might accrue on the disposal by the Company of any share in or security of any company is liable to be reduced by virtue of any depreciatory transaction within the meaning of TCGA 1992, s 176 and s 177 nor is any expenditure on any share or security liable to be reduced under TCGA 1992, s 125.

(21) Value Shifting

The Company does not hold, and has not held, any shares upon the disposal of which TCGA 1992, ss 31 or 32 could apply.

(22) Connected Party and Intra Group Transactions

(*a*) The Company has not disposed of or acquired any asset to or from any person connected with it within the Taxes Act 1988, s 839 or in circumstances such that the provision of TCGA 1992, s 17 could apply to such disposal or acquisition.

(*b*) The Company has not acquired any asset (past or present) from any other company then belonging to the same group of companies as the Company within the meaning of TCGA 1992, s 170(2) to (14).[37]

(*c*) The Company has not made, and is not entitled to make, a claim pursuant to TCGA 1992, s 172.

(23)   Group Reconstructions

The Company has not been party to any scheme of reconstruction or reorganisation to which the provisions of TCGA 1992, s 139, the Taxes Act 1988, s 703 or to which the Taxes Act 1988, s 343 could apply.

(24)   Chargeable Debts

No gain chargeable to corporation tax will accrue to the Company on the disposal of any debt owing to the Company not being a debt on a security or on the disposal of any corporate bond not being a qualifying corporate bond.

(25)   Chargeable Policies

The Company has not acquired benefits under any policy of assurance otherwise than as original beneficial owner.

(26)   Gains Accruing to Non-resident Companies or Trusts

There has not accrued any gain in respect of which the Company may be liable to corporation tax on chargeable gains by virtue of the provisions of TCGA 1992, s 13 or s 87.

(27)   Indexation: Groups and Associated Companies[37]

The Company does not own any debts or shares to which the provisions of TCGA 1992, ss 182 to 184 could apply.

(28)   Company Migration

    (a)   The Company is not a dual resident company for the purposes of TCGA 1992, s 139(3) or s 160 or s 188.

    (b)   There are no circumstances pursuant to which the Company may become liable to tax pursuant to TCGA 1992, s 185 (Deemed disposal of assets on company ceasing to be resident in UK), s 186 (Deemed disposal of assets on company ceasing to be liable to UK tax), s 187 (Postponement of charge on deemed disposal) or Finance Act 1988, s 132 (Liability of other persons for unpaid tax) or TCGA 1992, s 191 (Non-payment of tax by non-resident companies).

CLAIMS, ELECTIONS AND CLEARANCES

(29)   Claims by the Company

The Company has made no claim under any of the following:

    (a)   TCGA 1992, s 279 (assets situated outside the United Kingdom);

    (b)   TCGA 1992, s 24(2) (assets of negligible value);

    (c)   TCGA 1992, s 280 (tax on chargeable gains payable by instalments);

    (d)   Taxes Act 1988, ss 242 and 243 (surplus franked investment income); or

(e)   Taxes Act 1988, s 584 (unremittable income arising outside the United Kingdom).

(30)   Elections

The Disclosure Letter contains full particulars of all elections made by the Company under the following provisions:

(a)   Taxes Act 1988, ss 524, 527 and 534 (lump sum receipts for patents and copyright);

(b)   Capital Allowances Act 1990, s 37 (short life assets); and

(c)   Capital Allowances Act 1990, s 11 (leasehold interests).

(31)   Clearances

There are annexed to the Disclosure Letter copies of all correspondence relating to applications for clearance under any enactment relating to taxation. All facts and circumstances material to such applications for clearance were disclosed in such applications.

MISCELLANEOUS

(32)   Assessment of Tax on Lessees

No notice pursuant to the Taxes Act 1988, s 23 has been served on the Company.

(33)   Leaseholds

The Company is not liable to taxation under the provisions of the Taxes Act 1988, ss 34, 35 and 36 nor does it own any leasehold interest to which the said s 35 may apply.

TAXATION OF EMPLOYEES AND AGENTS

(34)   PAYE

The Company has properly operated the Pay As You Earn system deducting tax as required by law from all payments to or treated as made to employees and ex-employees of the Company and punctually accounted to the Inland Revenue for all tax so deducted and all returns required pursuant to the Taxes Act 1988, s 203 and regulations made thereunder have been punctually made and are accurate and complete in all respects.

(35)   Dispensations and PAYE Audits

The Disclosure Letter contains full details of all dispensations obtained by the Company and all details of any visit from the Audit Office of the Inland Revenue within the last six years including full details of any settlement made pursuant thereto.

(36)   Benefits for Employees

(a)   The Company has not made any payment to or provided any benefit for any officer or employee or ex-officer or ex-employee of the Company which is not allowable as a deduction in calculating the profits of the Company for taxation purposes.

(*b*) The Company has not issued any shares in the circumstances described in the Taxes Act 1988, s 138(1) and has complied with the Taxes Act 1988, s 139(5).

(*c*) The Company has not issued any shares in the circumstances described in the Finance Act 1988, s 77(1) and has complied with s 85 of the Finance Act 1988.

(*d*) The Company has not made any payment to which the Taxes Act 1988, s 313 applies.

(37)   Slave Companies

Any payment made to or for the direct or indirect benefit of any person who is or might be regarded by any taxation authority as an employee of the Company is made to such person direct and is not made to any company or other entity associated with that person.

(38)   Sub-Contractors

[The Company is not and never has been either a contractor or a sub-contractor for the purposes of the Taxes Act 1988, Chapter IV, Part XIII.]

[The Company has properly operated the sub-contractors' scheme deducting tax as required by law from all payments made to sub-contractors of the Company and punctually accounted to the Inland Revenue for all tax so deducted.]

(39)   National Insurance

The Company has paid all national insurance contributions for which it is liable and has kept proper books and records relating to the same and has not been a party to any scheme or arrangement to avoid any liability to account for primary or secondary national insurance contributions.

STAMP DUTIES

(40)   Stamp Duty

The Company has duly paid or has procured to be paid all stamp duty on documents to which it is a party or in which it is interested and which are liable to stamp duty.

(41)   Stamp Duty Reserve Tax

The Company has made all returns and paid all stamp duty reserve tax in respect of any transaction in securities to which it has been a party or in respect of which it is liable to account for stamp duty reserve tax.

(42)   Capital Duty

The Company has complied with the provisions of the Finance Act 1973 relating to capital duty and has duly paid all capital duty which it is liable to pay.

VALUE ADDED TAX

(43) (*a*) The Company has complied with all statutory provisions and regulations relating to value added tax and has duly paid or provided for all amounts of value added tax for which the Company is liable.

(*b*) All supplies made by the Company are taxable supplies and the Company is not and will not be denied credit for any input tax by reason of the operation of the Value Added Tax Act 1983, s 15 and regulations made thereunder.

(*c*) All input tax for which the Company has claimed credit has been paid by the Company in respect of supplies made to it relating to goods or services used or to be used for the purpose of the Company's business.

[(*d*) The Company is not and has not been, for value added tax purposes, a member of any group of companies (other than that comprising the Company and the Subsidiaries alone) and no act or transaction has been effected in consequence whereof the Company is or may be held liable for any value added tax chargeable against some other company except where that other company is a Subsidiary.][37]

(*e*) No supplies have been made to the Company to which the provisions of the Value Added Tax Act 1983, s 7 might apply.

(*f*) The Company has not committed any offence contrary to the Finance Act 1985, ss 12 or 13, nor has it received any penalty liability notice pursuant to s 14A(3), surcharge liability notice pursuant to s 19, or written warning issued pursuant to s 21(1A) of that Act.

(*g*) The Company has not been and is not liable to be registered for value added tax otherwise than pursuant to the provisions of the Value Added Tax Act 1983, Sched 1, para 1.

(*h*) The Company has not been required to give security under the Value Added Tax Act 1983, Sched 7, para 5.

(*i*) The Disclosure Letter contains details and copies of all elections, together with the relevant notification, made by the Company pursuant to the Value Added Tax Act 1983, Sched 6A, para 2.

(*j*) The Company is not and has not since 1 August 1989 been in relation to any land, building or civil engineering work a developer within the meaning of the Value Added Tax Act 1983, Sched 6A, para 5(5).

(*k*) The Disclosure Letter contains copies of all certificates issued by the Company pursuant to the Finance Act 1989, Sched 3, para 13(4)(*f*).

(*l*) The Company has not paid and is not liable to pay any interest pursuant to the Finance Act 1985, s 18.

(*m*) The Disclosure Letter contains full details of any assets of the Company to which the provisions of Part VA of the Value Added Tax (General) Regulations 1985 (the Capital Goods Scheme) apply and in particular:

(i) the identity (including in the case of leasehold property, the terms of years), date of acquisition and cost of the asset; and

(ii) the proportion of input tax for which credit has been claimed (either provisionally or finally in a tax year and stating which).

INHERITANCE TAX AND GIFTS

(44) Powers of Sale for Inheritance Tax Purposes

There are not in existence any circumstances whereby any such power as is mentioned in the Inheritance Tax Act 1984, s 212 could be exercised in relation to any shares in, securities of, or assets of, the Company.

(45) Gifts

(*a*) The Company is not liable to be assessed to corporation tax on chargeable gains or to inheritance tax as donor or donee of any gift or transferor or transferee of value.

(*b*) The Company has not been a party to associated operations in relation to a transfer of value within the meaning of the Inheritance Tax Act 1984, s 268.

(*c*) No Inland Revenue Charge (as defined in the Inheritance Tax Act 1984, s 237) is outstanding over any asset of the Company or in relation to any shares in the capital of the Company.

(*d*) The Company has not received any asset as mentioned in TCGA 1992, s 282.

FIFTH SCHEDULE
Adjustment of Consideration

1 INTERPRETATION

In this schedule where the context admits:

(1) 'the Audited Accounts' 'the Balance Sheet Date' [and any other term defined in the third schedule] have the same meanings as in the third schedule;

(2) 'the Completion Accounts' means the accounts prepared in accordance with paragraph 2;

(3) 'net tangible assets' means the aggregate value of all fixed and current assets (excluding goodwill, patents, trademarks and other intangible assets) minus the aggregate value of all liabilities and provisions (including provisions in accordance with SSAP 18 in respect of contingent liabilities) and excluding any reserves or capital created by the upward revaluation of assets subsequent to the Balance Sheet Date;

(4) 'the Provisional Consideration' means the consideration for the Sale Shares of £[   ] stated in clause 3(A);

(5) 'the Purchaser's Accountants' means [
                              ]; and

(6) 'the Vendor's Accountants' means [
                              ].

2 COMPLETION ACCOUNTS

(A) Preparation

The parties shall procure that, forthwith after Completion, accounts for the Company and the Subsidiaries shall be prepared and reported on in accordance with this schedule and the parties shall use their best endeavours to secure compliance with this schedule by their respective accountants.

(B) Description

The Completion Accounts shall consist of a consolidated balance sheet of the Company and the Subsidiaries as at the close of business on the date of Completion and a consolidated profit and loss account of the Company and the Subsidiaries in respect of the period from the day following the Balance Sheet Date to the date of Completion (both dates inclusive).

(C) General Requirements

Subject to sub-paragraph (D), the Completion Accounts shall:

(1) be prepared as if the period from the day following the

Balance Sheet Date to the date of Completion were a
financial year of the Company;
(2)   make full provision for all actual, future and contingent
liabilities of the Company and the Subsidiaries as at the
date of Completion;
(3)   be prepared in accordance with the requirements of all
relevant statutes and generally accepted accounting
principles;
(4)   show a true and fair view of the assets and liabilities of the
Company and the Subsidiaries at the date of Completion
and the profits of the Company and the Subsidiaries for
the period from the Balance Sheet Date to the date of
Completion; and
(5)   adopt bases and policies of accounting applied for the
purposes of the Audited Accounts.

(D)   Specific Requirements[1]
In preparing the Completion Accounts:
(1)   no value shall be attributed to goodwill or any other
intangible asset;
(2)   other fixed assets shall be included at the value at which
they were included in the Audited Accounts (or, if
acquired after the Balance Sheet Date, their cost), less
depreciation on the written down value, calculated at the
following annual rates:

Plant and machinery	: [ ] per cent
Fixtures and fittings	: [ ] per cent
Motor vehicles	: [ ] per cent
Immovable assets and improvements thereto	: [ ] per cent

(3)   no value shall be attributed to any assets (including in
particular any prepayment or debt) except to the extent
that (following Completion) the Company or a Subsidiary
will have the benefit of the same;
(4)   full provision shall be made for rebates or discounts that
will fall due and fees and commissions that will become
payable after Completion in either case in respect of sales
or other transactions that took place before Completion;
(5)   full provision shall be made for any liability arising as a
result of the change of control of the Company on
Completion; and
(6)   [to the extent that it is not capable of being set off against
the liability of the Company for corporation tax for the
current financial year or any previous financial year, full

provision shall be made for the advance corporation tax payable on any distribution declared or paid before Completion];

(7) full provision shall be made in respect of the cost of making good dilapidations or wants of repair on or to the Properties; and

(8) [full provision shall be made in respect of all payments in favour of [   ] and [   ] in their capacity as directors or employees or former directors or employees.]

(9) [   ]

3 PROCEDURE

(A) Submission of Draft

Within 60 days after the date of Completion, the Purchaser's Accountants shall deliver a final draft of the Completion Accounts to the Vendor's Accountants and, unless the Vendor's Accountants shall notify the Purchaser's Accountants in writing within 21 days after receipt of such draft that they do not accept that such draft complies with paragraph 2, the Vendor shall be deemed to have accepted such draft as complying with paragraph 2.

(B) Agreement of Draft

If, within the period of 21 days referred to in sub-paragraph (A), the Vendor's Accountants shall notify the Purchaser's Accountants in writing that they do not accept that the said draft complies with paragraph 2 then the Purchaser's Accountants and the Vendor's Accountants shall use their best endeavours to reach agreement upon adjustments to the draft to meet the objections of the Vendor's Accountants.

(C) Independent Accountant[2]

In the event that the Vendor's Accountants and the Purchaser's Accountants are unable to reach agreement as aforesaid, any matter in dispute shall be referred to the decision of a single independent chartered accountant or an independent firm of chartered accountants to be agreed upon between them or, or in default of such agreement, to be selected (at the instance of either party) by the President for the time being of the Institute of Chartered Accountants in England and Wales, and any such chartered accountant or firm of chartered accountants (whose costs shall be paid as he or they shall direct) shall act as expert (and not as arbitrator) in connection with the giving of such decision which shall, save in the event of manifest error, be binding. In giving such decision, the accountant or firm shall state what adjustments (if any) are to be made to the said draft in order that it shall comply with paragraph 2.

(D)   Report
If the Vendor's Accountants accept, or are deemed to accept, that the said draft complies with paragraph 2 the Purchaser's Accountants shall sign a report to the effect that the Completion Accounts comply with paragraph 2 and any Completion Accounts so reported on, or (if sub-paragraph (C) shall apply) the final draft of the Completion Accounts as adjusted by the independent accountant, shall be the Completion Accounts for the purposes of this Agreement and shall be final and binding on the parties.

(E)   Information and Explanations
The Purchaser's Accountants shall provide such information and explanations relating to the draft Completion Accounts and their preparation as the Vendor's Accountants, or any independent chartered accountant appointed pursuant to sub-paragraph (C), shall reasonably require.

4   ADJUSTMENT OF CONSIDERATION

(A)   Increase or Reduction
When the Completion Accounts have become binding, the Provisional Consideration shall forthwith:
>   (1)   be increased by the amount (if any) by which the net tangible assets of the Company and the Subsidiaries as at the date of Completion as shown by the Completion Accounts are greater than the net tangible assets of the Company and the Subsidiaries as at the Balance Sheet Date as shown by the Audited Accounts; or (as the case may be)
>   (2)   be reduced by the amount (if any) by which the net tangible assets of the Company and the Subsidiaries as at the date of Completion as shown by the Completion Accounts are less than the net tangible assets of the Company and the Subsidiaries as at the Balance Sheet Date as shown by the Audited Accounts.

(B)   Payment
Any increase or reduction in the Provisional Consideration shall be paid by the Purchaser or the Vendor (as appropriate) within 14 days after the Completion Accounts have become binding as aforesaid and any amount not paid when due shall carry interest (accrued daily and compounded monthly) at the rate of [   ] per cent per annum above the base rate of [   ] Bank PLC from time to time from

the due date until the date of actual payment (as well after judgment as before).

5 INTERACTION WITH OTHER PROVISIONS[3]

[Subject to the due performance of paragraph 4, if the Purchaser shall have any claim against the Vendor under this Agreement in respect of any liability or deficiency which is taken into account in the Completion Accounts the amount of such liability or deficiency so taken into account shall be deducted from the amount of the Purchaser's claim but, save as aforesaid, preparation and acceptance of the Completion Accounts by the Purchaser shall be without prejudice to any claim which the Purchaser may have against the Vendor under or in respect of any breach of this Agreement.]

SIXTH SCHEDULE

Pensions [Company has own final salary scheme]

1 INTERPRETATION

[(A) Definitions]

In this schedule, where the context admits:

(1) 'Actuarial Assumptions' means the actuarial assumptions and method set out in a letter in agreed terms dated [   ] from the Vendor's Actuary to the Purchaser's Actuary;

(2) 'Actuary' means a Fellow of The Institute of Actuaries or of The Faculty of Actuaries in Scotland;

(3) 'Company' means the Company and the Subsidiaries or such one or more of them as the context requires;

(4) 'Pension Scheme' means [the retirement benefits scheme known as [   ] which was established by a deed dated [   ] (or the trustees from time to time of that scheme, as the context requires);] [Scheme A [, Scheme B] and Scheme C (or such one or [other] [more] of them as the context requires;]

(5) 'Purchaser's Actuary' means [   ] (or such other Actuary as the Purchaser may appoint for the purposes of this schedule);

(6) 'Relevant Employee' means any past or present employee or officer of the Company or of any predecessor to all or part of its business;

[(7) 'Scheme A' means the retirement benefits scheme known as [   ] which was established by a trust deed dated [   ] (or the trustees from time to time of that scheme, as the context requires);]

[(8) 'Scheme B' means the retirement benefits scheme known as [   ] which was established by a trust deed dated [   ] (or the trustees from time to time of that scheme, as the context requires);]

[(9) 'Scheme C' means the retirement benefits scheme known as [   ] which was established by a trust deed dated [   ] (or the trustees from time to time of that scheme, as the context requires);]

(10) 'Shortfall' means an amount, calculated in accordance with the Actuarial Assumptions, equal to the amount (if any) by which the capital value at Completion of the benefits which are then payable, or prospectively or contingently payable, under the Pension Scheme exceeds

the value at Completion of the then net assets of the Pension Scheme. For the purposes of this definition:

[(*a*) assets shall be valued by reference to their mid-market price at the close of business on the date upon which Completion occurs unless that date is not a business day in which event at the close of business on the last business day preceding that date (where 'business day' means a day upon which the London Stock Exchange is open for business);][1]

(*b*) when calculating the value of the net assets of the Pension Scheme no account shall be taken of:

    (i) any debts of the Company to the Pension Scheme;[2] or

    (ii) any contributions payable to the Pension Scheme after Completion;

(*c*) when calculating the liabilities of the Pension Scheme no account shall be taken of any benefits in respect of service after the date upon which Completion occurs but allowance shall be made in accordance with the Actuarial Assumptions for:

    (i) projected increases in earnings up to the assumed date of cessation of pensionable service;[3] and

    (ii) increases to pensions in payment or in deferment;

(*d*) when calculating the liabilities of the Pension Scheme allowance shall also be made in accordance with the Actuarial Assumptions for any refund of contributions and any benefits in pension form payable in the event of death whilst in service but, save where death occurs before Completion, no account shall be taken of any other lump sum death-in-service benefits;

(*e*) any improvement to the benefits under the Pension Scheme which has been announced before Completion shall be deemed to have been duly effected under the Pension Scheme and to have come into force before Completion; and

(*f*) the Pension Scheme shall be deemed to be under an overriding obligation to provide benefits on a basis which does not discriminate between men and women and without reducing the benefits of either sex;[4]

(11) 'Vendor's Actuary' means [   ] (or such other Actuary as may be appointed by the Vendor for the purposes of this schedule).

[(B)   Schedule applies separately to each Pension Scheme
Paragraphs 2 and 3 of this schedule apply separately to each Pension Scheme.][5]

2   CALCULATION OF SHORTFALL

(A)   Data

The Vendor and the Purchaser shall each use all reasonable endeavours to procure that all such information as the Vendor's Actuary or the Purchaser's Actuary or any independent Actuary appointed under paragraph 2(C) may reasonably request for the purposes of this schedule is supplied promptly to such Actuary and that all such information is complete and accurate in all respects.

(B)   Agreement of Shortfall

The Purchaser's Actuary shall determine the amount of the Shortfall and shall submit his findings in writing to the Vendor's Actuary for agreement. If the Vendor's Actuary and the Purchaser's Actuary agree the amount (if any) of the Shortfall, the Vendor shall procure that the Vendor's Actuary and the Purchaser shall procure that the Purchaser's Actuary jointly certify that amount as the Shortfall.

(C)   Dispute

If the Vendor's Actuary and the Purchaser's Actuary fail to agree the amount (if any) of the Shortfall within two months from the date upon which the Purchaser's Actuary first submits his findings to the Vendor's Actuary in accordance with paragraph 2(B), the matter may, at the option of either the Vendor or the Purchaser, be referred to an independent Actuary to be agreed between the Vendor and the Purchaser or, in default of agreement within 14 days from the first nomination of an Actuary by one party to the other, to be appointed by the President for the time being of The Institute of Actuaries on the application of either the Vendor or the Purchaser. The certificate of the independent Actuary as to the amount (if any) of the Shortfall shall, save in the event of manifest error, be final and binding on the parties and, in so certifying, the independent Actuary shall be deemed to be acting as an expert and not as an arbitrator.[6] His costs shall be paid as he directs.

3   PAYMENT OF SHORTFALL

The Vendor shall within a period of 14 days commencing on and including the date upon which the amount (if any) of the Shortfall is certified as aforesaid pay, by way of adjustment to the consideration for the Sale Shares,[7] to the Purchaser (or to a third party, as the Purchaser may direct) a sum in cash equal to the amount shown in the certificate as being the Shortfall together with interest thereon (accruing daily and compounded monthly) from and including the date upon which Completion occurs to but excluding the date upon which final payment is made in accordance with this paragraph, such interest to be at the Agreed Rate up to and including the last day in the aforesaid 14-day period and thereafter shall be at the Agreed Rate plus [ ] per cent. In this paragraph 'Agreed Rate' means the base rate from time to time of [   ] Bank PLC plus [ ] per cent.

4 WARRANTIES AND REPRESENTATIONS[8]

The Vendor hereby warrants and represents to and for the benefit of the Purchaser in the following terms:

(1) No Other Pension Arrangements

Save for the Pension Scheme the Company is not a party to nor participates in nor contributes to any scheme, arrangement or agreement (whether legally enforceable or not) for the provision of any pension, retirement, death, incapacity, sickness, disability, accident or other like benefits (including the payment of medical expenses) for any Relevant Employee or for the widow, widower, child or dependant of any Relevant Employee.

(2) No Assurances etc

Neither the Company nor any member of the Vendor's Group:

(*a*) has given any undertaking or assurance (whether legally enforceable or not) to any Relevant Employee or to any widow, widower, child or dependant of any Relevant Employee as to the continuance, introduction, improvement or increase of any benefit of a kind described in (1) above; or

(*b*) is paying or has in the last two years paid any benefit of a kind described in (1) above to any Relevant Employee or to any widow, widower, child or dependant of any Relevant Employee.

(3) All Details Disclosed

All material details relating to the Pension Scheme are contained in or annexed to the Disclosure Letter including (without limitation) the following:

(*a*) a true and complete copy of the deed or other instrument by which the Pension Scheme was established and all deeds and other instruments supplemental thereto;

(*b*) a true and complete copy of all announcements, explanatory literature and the like of current effect which have been issued to any Relevant Employee in connection with the Pension Scheme;

(*c*)   a true and complete copy of the report on the last actuarial valuation of the Pension Scheme to be completed prior to the date of this Agreement and of any subsequent written recommendations of an actuarial nature;

(*d*)   a true and complete copy of the last audited accounts of the Pension Scheme to be completed prior to the date of this Agreement and details of any material change in the investment policy of the Pension Scheme since the date as at which those accounts were made up;

(*e*)   a true and complete copy of all investment management, nominee and custodian agreements (if any) of current effect to which the Pension Scheme is a party;

(*f*)   a true and complete copy of all insurance policies (if any) and annuity contracts (if any) held for the purposes of the assets of the Pension Scheme and details of any such policies and contracts (if any) which the Pension Scheme has agreed to effect;

(*g*)   a true and complete copy of the memorandum and articles of association of any company which is a trustee of the Pension Scheme and the names and addresses of the directors and secretary of that company;

(*h*)   the names and addresses of the trustees of the Pension Scheme;

(*i*)   details of all amendments (if any) to the Pension Scheme which have been announced or are proposed but which have not yet been formally made;

(*j*)   details of all discretionary increases (if any) to pensions in payment or in deferment under the Pension Scheme which have been granted in the ten years prior to the date of this Agreement or which are under consideration;

(*k*)   details of all discretionary practices (if any) which may have led any person to expect additional benefits in a given set of circumstances (by way of example, but without limitation, on retirement at the behest of the Company or in the event of redundancy); and

(*l*)   details of the rate at which and basis upon which the Company currently contributes to the Pension Scheme, any change to that rate and/or basis which is proposed or which is under consideration and all contributions paid to the Pension Scheme by the Company in the three years prior to the date of this Agreement.

(4)   Augmentation

No power under the Pension Scheme has been exercised in relation to any employee or officer of the Company or, since the date as at which the last actuarial valuation of the Pension Scheme to be completed prior to the date of this Agreement was undertaken, in respect of any other person:

(*a*) to provide terms of membership of the Pension Scheme (whether as to benefits or contributions) which are different from those generally applicable to the members of the Pension Scheme; or

(*b*) to provide any benefits which would not but for the exercise of that power have been payable under the Pension Scheme; or

(*c*) to augment any benefits under the Pension Scheme.

(5) Death Benefits Insured

All benefits (other than any refund of members' contributions with interest where appropriate) payable under the Pension Scheme on the death of any person while in employment to which the Pension Scheme relates are insured fully under a policy with an insurance company of good repute and there are no grounds on which that company might avoid liability under that policy.

(6) Contributions and Expenses

Contributions to the Pension Scheme are not paid in arrear and all contributions and other amounts which have fallen due for payment have been paid. No fee, charge or expense relating to or in connection with the Pension Scheme has been incurred but not paid. If any such fee, charge or expense has been paid by any person other than the Pension Scheme the Pension Scheme has reimbursed that person if and to the extent that the Pension Scheme is or may become liable so to do.

(7) Company's Obligations

The Company:

(*a*) has observed and performed those provisions of the Pension Scheme which apply to it; [and]

(*b*) may (without the consent of any person or further payment) terminate its liability to contribute to the Pension Scheme at any time subject only to giving such notice (if any) as is expressly provided for in the documentation containing the current provisions governing the Pension Scheme[9] [.] [; and

(*c*) has at all material times held or been named in a contracting-out certificate (within the meaning of the Social Security Pensions Act 1975) referable to the Pension Scheme].

(8) No Other Employer

The Company is the only employer for the time being participating in the Pension Scheme. No employer which has previously participated in the Pension Scheme has any claim under the Pension Scheme and in respect of any such employer the period of participation has been terminated and benefits have been provided in accordance with the provisions of the Pension Scheme.

(9)   Administration

All documentation and records in respect of the Pension Scheme are up to date and so far as the Vendor is aware complete and accurate in all material respects.

(10)   Investments

None of the assets of the Pension Scheme:

    (*a*)   is invested in or in any description of employer-related investments (within the meaning of the Social Security Pensions Act 1975, s 57A); or

    (*b*)   save for deposits with banks, building societies and other financial institutions and save for any instrument creating or acknowledging an indebtedness listed on any recognised stock exchange of repute, is loaned to any person; or

    (*c*)   is subject to any encumbrance or agreement or commitment to give or create any encumbrance.

(11)   No Payment to Employer

No payment to which the Income and Corporation Taxes Act 1988, s 601 applies has been made out of the funds which are or have been held for the purposes of the Pension Scheme.

(12)   Compliance

The Pension Scheme:

    (*a*)   is an exempt approved scheme (within the meaning of the Income and Corporation Taxes Act 1988, s 592);

    (*b*)   has properly and punctually accounted to the Inland Revenue for all and any tax for which the Pension Scheme is liable or accountable;

    (*c*)   is not liable to taxation on any income from or capital gains on any of the funds which are or have been held for the purposes of the Pension Scheme;[10] and

    (*d*)   complies with and has at all times been administered in accordance with all applicable laws, regulations and requirements (including those of the Board of Inland Revenue and of trust law).

(13)   Actuarial[11]

[The report dated [   ] of [   ] on the actuarial valuation of the Pension Scheme as at [   ] (the 'Valuation Date') (a true copy of the report being annexed to the Disclosure Letter) shows a true and fair view of the respective actuarial values of the assets and liabilities of the Pension Scheme at the Valuation Date on the basis of the actuarial assumptions and method detailed in that report. Since the Valuation Date nothing has occurred, been done or been omitted to be done which may affect materially the level of funding of the benefits under the Pension Scheme.]

[The data used for the purposes of the last actuarial valuation of the Pension Scheme to be completed prior to the date of this Agreement was complete and accurate in all material respects and since the date as at which that valuation was undertaken nothing has occurred, been done or been omitted to be done which may affect materially the level of funding of the benefits under the Pension Scheme.]

(14) Litigation

None of the Pension Scheme, the Company or any member of the Vendor's group is engaged or involved in any proceedings which relate to or are in connection with the Pension Scheme or the benefits thereunder and no such proceedings are pending or threatened and so far as the Vendor is aware there are no facts likely to give rise to any such proceedings. In this Sub-paragraph 'proceedings' includes any litigation or arbitration and also includes any investigation or determination by the Pensions Ombudsman.

(15) Indemnities

In relation to the Pension Scheme or funds which are or have been held for the purposes thereof neither the Company nor the trustees or administrator of the Pension Scheme has given an indemnity or guarantee to any person (other than in the case of the Company any general indemnity in favour of the trustees or administrator under the documentation governing the Pension Scheme).

5 DAMAGES FOR BREACH OF PENSION WARRANTIES

In determining the damages flowing from any breach of Warranties contained in paragraph 4, the Company shall be deemed to be under a liability:

(1) to provide and to continue to provide any benefit of a kind referred to in that paragraph which is now provided or has been announced or is proposed; and

(2) to maintain and to continue to maintain (without benefits being reduced) the Pension Scheme and any other arrangements of a kind described in that paragraph which are now in existence or are proposed and any discretionary practices of a kind referred to in that paragraph which have hitherto been carried on.[12]

[6 SEX EQUALITY

The Vendor undertakes to the Purchaser, for its own benefit and as trustee and agent for the Company and for the Pension Scheme, to indemnify and to keep indemnified and held harmless on a continuing basis the Company and the Pension Scheme against all and any liabilities, actions, claims and costs (including legal expenses) which may be brought or made against or incurred by the Company and/or the Pension Scheme of any nature relating to discrimination on grounds of sex as to the provision under the Pension Scheme for or in respect of all or any of the Relevant Employees of benefits referable to any period prior to Completion and/or the terms of their employment or former employment with the Company and/or any member of the Vendor's Group relating to relevant benefits (within the meaning of the Income and Corporation Taxes Act 1988, s 612).][13]

SIXTH SCHEDULE

Pensions [Company participates in group final salary scheme]

1 INTERPRETATION

(A) Definitions

In this schedule, where the context admits:

(1) 'Actuarial Assumptions' means the actuarial assumptions and method set out in a letter in agreed terms dated [   ] from the Vendor's Actuary to the Purchaser's Actuary;

(2) 'Actuary' means a Fellow of The Institute of Actuaries or of The Faculty of Actuaries in Scotland;

(3) 'Adjusted Transfer Value' means an amount equal to [the Transfer Value multiplied by the Investment Adjustment from and including the Membership Transfer Date to and including the Payment Date;]

(4) 'Basic Amount' means an amount, calculated in accordance with the Actuarial Assumptions, equal to [the greater of:

(a) an amount equal to] the capital value at Completion of the benefits which are then payable under the Pension Scheme to or in respect of the Transferring Employees [.] [; and

(b) an amount which bears the same proportion to the Relevant Assets (as defined below) as the amount referred to at (a) bears to the capital value at Completion of the benefits which are then payable to or in respect of all members of the Pension Scheme who are, or but for being absent from work would have been, in pensionable service under the Pension Scheme at Completion, where 'Relevant Assets' means the amount by which the aggregate value at Completion of the then net assets of the Pension Scheme exceeds the capital value at Completion of the benefits which are then payable to or in respect of the pensioners and deferred pensioners.[14]

For the purposes of this definition:

[(i) assets shall be valued by reference to their mid-market price at the close of business on the date upon which Completion occurs unless that date is not a business day in which event at the close of business on the last business day preceding that date (where 'business day' means a day upon which the London Stock Exchange is open for business);][15]

(ii) benefits include any benefits which are contingently or prospectively payable;

(iii) when calculating the value of the net assets of the Pension Scheme no account shall be taken of:

(*aa*)   any debts of the Company to the Pension Scheme; or

(*bb*)   any contributions payable to the Pension Scheme after the Calculation Date;

(iv) when calculating the value of the benefits payable under the Pension Scheme no account shall be taken of any benefits in respect of service after the date upon which Completion occurs but allowance shall be made in accordance with the Actuarial Assumptions for:

(*aa*)   projected increases in earnings up to the assumed date of cessation of pensionable service;[17] and

(*bb*)   increases to pensions in payment or in deferment;

(v) when calculating the value of the benefits payable under the Pension Scheme allowance shall also be made in accordance with the Actuarial Assumptions for any refund of contributions and any benefits in pension form payable in the event of death whilst in service but, save where death occurs before Completion, no account shall be taken of any other lump sum death-in-service benefits;

(vi) any improvement to the benefits under the Pension Scheme which has been announced before Completion shall be deemed to have been duly effected under the Pension Scheme and to have come into force before Completion; and

(vii) the Pension Scheme shall be deemed to be under an overriding obligation in respect of members who are, or but for being absent from work would have been, in pensionable service at Completion to provide benefits on a basis which does not discriminate between men and women and without reducing the benefits of either sex;[18]

(5) 'Company' means the Company and the Subsidiaries or such one or more of them as the context requires;

(6) 'Interest' means, in respect of any period and any principal sum, an amount of interest (accruing daily and

compounded monthly) at a rate equal to the base rate from time to time of [   ] Bank PLC plus [   ] per cent;

(7) 'Interim Period' means the period from Completion to but excluding the Membership Transfer Date;

[(8) 'Investment Adjustment' means, in relation to any period, one plus, when expressed as a fraction, the rate of investment return (whether positive or negative) during that period on a notional portfolio comprising [ ] per cent in the FT-Actuaries All Share Index and [ ] per cent in the FT-Actuaries British Government Fixed Interest Over 15 Year Index (as published in the Financial Times) with allowance for income to be reinvested at monthly intervals. For the purposes of this definition the notional return shall be measured by taking the respective figures on the indices published for the close of business on the last business day preceding the commencement of the relevant period and for the close of business on the last business day preceding the day upon which that period ends;][19]

(9) 'Membership Transfer Date' means [   ] (or such earlier date as the Purchaser may by not less than one month's notice in writing to the Vendor specify or such later date as the Vendor and the Purchaser may agree in writing) except that if for any reason the Company is unable to participate in the Pension Scheme in accordance with paragraph 3(A) until the date which would (apart from this exception) be the Membership Transfer Date then the 'Membership Transfer Date' means the day next following the date upon which the Company ceases so to participate in the Pension Scheme;[20]

[(10)'Life Assurance Employee' at any time means a person who at that time is both an employee or officer of the Company and covered by the Pension Scheme for certain death-in-service benefits but is not a Pensionable Employee;]

(11) 'Payment Date' means the date which falls seven days after the later of:

    (a)   the date upon which the amount of the Transfer Value is certified in accordance with paragraph 5(A) or 7, as the case may be; and

    (b)   the date upon which the Purchaser notifies the Vendor in writing that the Purchaser's Scheme is an exempt approved scheme (within the meaning of s 592 of the Income and Corporation Taxes Act 1988) or that the Board of Inland Revenue has confirmed that the Purchaser's Scheme may accept a transfer payment from the Pension Scheme and (in either case) that if the employment of the Transferring Employees is to be contracted-out by reference to the Purchaser's Scheme the Company holds or is named in a contracting-out certificate in respect of the Purchaser's Scheme;

unless before the date first referred to in this definition the Adjusted Transfer Value is paid in full in accordance with paragraph 5(B), in which event the date on which that payment is made;[21]

(12) 'Pension Scheme' means [the retirement benefits scheme known as [   ] which was established by a deed dated [   ] (or the trustees from time to time of that scheme, as the context requires);] [Scheme A [, Scheme B] and Scheme C (or such one or [other] [more] of them as the context requires;]

(13) 'Pensionable Employee' at any time means a person who at that time is both an employee or officer of the Company and is, or but for being absent from work would be, in pensionable service under the Pension Scheme;

(14) 'Purchaser's Actuary' means [   ] (or such other Actuary as the Purchaser may appoint for the purposes of this schedule);

(15) 'Purchaser's Scheme' means the retirement benefits scheme or schemes nominated by or at the instance of the Purchaser pursuant to paragraph 4(A);

(16) 'Relevant Employee' means any present or past employee or officer of the Company or of any predecessor to all or any part of its business;

[(17) 'Scheme A' means the retirement benefits scheme known as [   ] which was established by a trust deed dated [   ] (or the trustees from time to time of that scheme, as the context requires);]

[(18) 'Scheme B' means the retirement benefits scheme known as [   ] which was established by a trust deed dated [   ] (or the trustees from time to time of that scheme, as the context requires);]

[(19) 'Scheme C' means the retirement benefits scheme known as [   ] which was established by a trust deed dated [   ] (or the trustees from time to time of that scheme, as the context requires);]

(20) 'Transferring Employee' means a person who immediately prior to the Membership Transfer Date is a Pensionable Employee and who:

(a) accepts the offer of membership of the Purchaser's Scheme to be made pursuant to paragraph 4(B) and joins the Purchaser's Scheme with effect from the Membership Transfer Date; and

(b) consents in writing to a transfer payment being made in respect of him to the Purchaser's Scheme from the Pension Scheme;[22]

(21) 'Transfer Value' means an amount equal to the sum of:

(a) the Basic Amount multiplied by the Investment Adjustment for the period from and including the day next following the date of Completion to and including the Membership Transfer Date; plus

(b) the aggregate contributions paid in respect of the Interim Period to the Pension Scheme by or in respect of the Transferring Employees [(other than, in relation to any Transferring Employee, any such contributions paid whilst he was a Life Assurance Employee)] less [   ] in respect of the cost of insuring the death-in-service benefits in respect of the Transferring Employees together with Interest on the balance from the date of payment of each such contribution to the Membership Transfer Date;

reduced, but only if the employment of the Transferring Employees is not to be contracted-out by reference to the Purchaser's Scheme, by an amount equal to the capital value at the Membership Transfer Date of the accrued rights under the Pension Scheme of the Transferring Employees to guaranteed minimum pensions, such value being determined in accordance with the Actuarial Assumptions;

(22) 'Vendor's Actuary' means [   ] (or such other Actuary as the Vendor may appoint for the purposes of this schedule).

[(B) Contracting-out Terms

In this schedule, where the context admits, 'contracted-out', 'contracted-out scheme', 'contracting-out certificate', 'guaranteed minimum' and 'guaranteed minimum pension' shall have the same meanings as in the Social Security Pensions Act 1975.]

[(C) Schedule applies separately to each Pension Scheme

Paragraphs 2 to 7 of this schedule shall apply separately to each Pension Scheme.][23]

2   DATA

The Vendor and the Purchaser shall each use all reasonable endeavours to procure that all such information as the Vendor's Actuary or the Purchaser's Actuary or any independent Actuary appointed under paragraph 7 may reasonably request for the purposes of this schedule is supplied promptly to such Actuary and that all such information is complete and accurate in all respects.

3   THE PENSION SCHEME

(A)   Vendor's Undertakings

The Vendor undertakes to the Purchaser for its own benefit and as trustee and agent for the Company:

(1)   to procure that subject to the consent of the Board of Inland Revenue being obtained (which consent the Vendor shall use all reasonable endeavours to procure) the Company is permitted to participate in the Pension Scheme throughout the period which would (apart from the exception to the definition of 'Membership Transfer Date') be the Interim Period;

(2)   to procure that until after payment has been made in full in accordance with paragraph 5 no power or discretion under the Pension Scheme is exercised in a way which would or might affect the Company and/or all or any of its employees or officers save with the consent of the Purchaser;

(3)   to use all reasonable endeavours to procure that none of the employees or officers or former employees or officers of the Company is discriminated against in the exercise of any discretionary power (including, without limitation, the grant of discretionary pension increases) under the Pension Scheme;

(4)   to procure that no payment is made by the Pension Scheme which would or might result in the Purchaser's Scheme not obtaining approval under or, as the case may be, ceasing to be approved under the Income and Corporation Taxes Act 1988, s 591 or in the pensionable service completed by a Transferring Employee under the Pension Scheme not being treated as continuous with the pensionable service completed by him under the Purchaser's Scheme for the purpose of determining the maximum benefits which may be paid under the Purchaser's Scheme without prejudicing the obtaining of approval of or, as the case may be, the approval of the Purchaser's Scheme as aforesaid;[24]

(5) to indemnify and to keep indemnified and held harmless on a continuing basis the Company against all and any liability to make any payment to or in connection with the Pension Scheme other than to pay contributions pursuant to paragraph 3(B)(1); and

(6) to procure that the Pension Scheme is maintained in full force and effect and does not cease to admit new members until after the Company ceases to participate in the Pension Scheme.[25]

(B) Purchaser's Undertaking

The Purchaser shall procure that the Company:

(1) pays or procures to be paid to the Pension Scheme the employer contributions which accrue to the Pension Scheme during the Interim Period in respect of the Pensionable Employees [and the Life Assurance Employees] from time to time, such contributions to be deemed to be payable at [the same rate as is in force at the date of this Agreement] [the same rate as is generally payable from time to time by other employers participating in the Pension Scheme] [an annual rate of:

(*a*) in relation to a Pensionable Employee, [ ] per cent of [ ] from time to time;

(*b*) in relation to a Life Assurance Employee, [ ] per cent of [ ] from time to time;]

plus the contributions (if any) payable during the Interim Period by the Pensionable Employees; and

(2) complies in all other respects with the provisions of the Pension Scheme during the Interim Period.[26]

[(C) Contracting-out in Interim Period

The Vendor and the Purchaser undertake to co-operate with each other with a view to procuring that the employment of the Pensionable Employees is contracted-out by reference to the Pension Scheme at all applicable times during the Interim Period under a contracting-out certificate in the name of the Company.]

[(D) Sex Equality

The Vendor undertakes to the Purchaser, for its own benefit and as trustee and agent for the Company and for the Purchaser's Scheme, to indemnify and to keep indemnified and held harmless on a continuing basis the Company and the Purchaser's Scheme against all and any liabilities, actions, claims and costs (including legal expenses) which may be brought or made against or incurred by the Company and/or the Purchaser's Scheme of any nature relating to

discrimination on grounds of sex arising out of or in connection with
the provisions or former provisions of the Pension Scheme
applicable to all or any of the Relevant Employees and/or the terms
of their employment or former employment prior to Completion
with the Company and/or any member of the Vendor's Group
relating to relevant benefits (within the meaning of the Income and
Corporation Taxes Act 1988, s 612) and/or any transfer payment to
the Purchaser's Scheme from the Pension Scheme and/or the
benefits granted under the Purchaser's Scheme in respect of any such
transfer.][27]

4   THE PURCHASER'S SCHEME

(A)   Purchaser to Provide Scheme
The Purchaser shall nominate or procure the nomination of a
retirement benefits scheme for the purposes of this schedule which is,
or which is designed to be capable of being, an exempt approved
scheme (within the meaning of the Income and Corporation Taxes
Act 1988, s 592).

(B)   Purchaser to Offer Membership[28]
The Purchaser shall procure that those of the employees of the
Company on the Membership Transfer Date who are Pensionable
Employees immediately prior to that date are offered membership of
the Purchaser's Scheme with effect from the Membership Transfer
Date [on terms in respect of service before that date which, when
considered as a whole, are substantially no less favourable than those
currently applicable to the Pensionable Employees under the
Pension Scheme having due regard to whether a transfer is to be
made to the Purchaser's Scheme in respect of the accrued rights (if
any) of the Transferring Employees under the Pension Scheme to
guaranteed minimum pensions (such terms being subject to the
transfer or payment being made in full in accordance with paragraph
5(B) or 5(C) and to the powers of amendment and discontinuance
under the Purchaser's Scheme).] [. The Purchaser's Scheme shall (at
the Purchaser's option) be of either the final salary or money
purchase type and the Purchaser shall procure that in respect of
service before the Membership Transfer Date benefits are provided
under the Purchaser's Scheme as stated in (1) or (2) below (as
applicable), subject to the transfer or payment being made in full in
accordance with paragraph 5(B) or 5(C) and to the powers of
amendment and discontinuance under the Purchaser's Scheme.

(1)   Final Salary Scheme
The Transferring Employees are credited under the
Purchaser's Scheme in respect of pensionable service up to

the Membership Transfer Date with benefits which would (if the credit had been made on the Membership Transfer Date) have had on that date a capital value which in the joint opinion of the Vendor's Actuary and of the Purchaser's Actuary (or, as the case may be, in the opinion of the independent Actuary appointed under paragraph 7) equals (or as nearly as may be) the Transfer Value and for this purpose the Actuarial Assumptions shall apply *mutatis mutandis.*

(2) Money Purchase Scheme
The benefits are such that the Vendor's Actuary and the Purchaser's Actuary (or, as the case may be, the independent Actuary appointed under paragraph 7) shall certify the apportioned amount of the Adjusted Transfer Value to be credited to each Transferring Employee and that amount will be credited to an account in the Purchaser's Scheme designated for that Transferring Employee and that amount adjusted for investment return (positive or negative) less relevant expenses after the Payment Date shall (subject to the requirements for approval of the Purchaser's Scheme by the Board of the Inland Revenue) be applied exclusively for the benefit of that Transferring Employee in respect of his service before the Membership Transfer Date.

5 PAYMENT OF TRANSFER VALUE

(A) Calculation
Immediately following the Membership Transfer Date the Vendor shall procure that the Vendor's Actuary calculates the amount of the Transfer Value and submits his findings in writing to the Purchaser's Actuary. If the Purchaser's Actuary agrees the amount of the Transfer Value, the Vendor shall procure that the Vendor's Actuary and the Purchaser shall procure that the Purchaser's Actuary jointly certify that amount as the Transfer Value. If, however, the Vendor's Actuary and the Purchaser's Actuary fail to agree within two months from the date upon which the Vendor's Actuary first submits his findings to the Purchaser's Actuary as aforesaid, the matter may, at the option of either the Vendor or the Purchaser, be referred to an independent Actuary pursuant to paragraph 7.

(B) Payment
The Vendor shall use all reasonable endeavours to procure that the Pension Scheme transfers to the Purchaser's Scheme on the Payment Date the Adjusted Transfer Value in cash (or if the Vendor and the

Purchaser so agree transfers assets equal in value to the Adjusted Transfer Value).

(C)   Shortfall

If the sum actually transferred from the Pension Scheme to the Purchaser's Scheme in respect of the Transferring Employees on the Payment Date is less than the Adjusted Transfer Value (the amount of the difference being referred to in this paragraph as the 'Shortfall'), the Vendor shall forthwith pay, by way of adjustment to the consideration for the Sale Shares,[29] to the Purchaser (or to a third party, as the Purchaser may direct) an amount in cash equal to the Shortfall together with interest thereon (accruing daily and compounded monthly) from and including the Payment Date to but excluding the date upon which final payment is made in accordance with this paragraph, such interest to be at the base rate from time to time of [   ] Bank PLC plus [   ] per cent.[30]

[(D)   Payment on Account

If the Purchaser so requests at any time on or after the Membership Transfer Date, the Vendor shall use its best endeavours to procure that as soon as practicable after receiving such request a payment on account of the amount payable pursuant to paragraph 5(B) is made to the Purchaser's Scheme. Such payment shall be equal to [   ] per cent of the amount which the Vendor's Actuary, in consultation with the Purchaser's Actuary, reasonably estimates to be the amount of the Adjusted Transfer Value. In the event of a payment on account being made in accordance with this paragraph, the Pension Scheme shall be deemed to have transferred on the Payment Date to the Purchaser's Scheme (in addition to the amount (if any) actually transferred on the Payment Date) an amount equal to the payment made in accordance with this paragraph [multiplied by the Investment Adjustment for the period from and including the date upon which that payment is made to and including the Payment Date.]

6   ADDITIONAL VOLUNTARY CONTRIBUTIONS

For the purpose of the foregoing provisions of this schedule there shall be disregarded:
  (1)   any benefits under the Pension Scheme which are attributable to additional voluntary contributions made to it by the members of the Pension Scheme and in respect of which the members are not entitled to benefits based on their final pensionable earnings (however defined);
  (2)   any such contributions; and

(3) any transfer in respect of any such benefits or contributions.

The Vendor shall, nevertheless, procure that the Pension Scheme transfers to the Purchaser's Scheme on the Payment Date for the benefit of the Transferring Employees all such funds and assets of the Pension Scheme which represent any such contributions made by the Transferring Employees and the investment return on them.

7 DISPUTES

Any dispute between the Vendor's Actuary and the Purchaser's Actuary concerning the amount of the Transfer Value or any other matter to be agreed between them in accordance with this schedule may, at the option of either the Vendor or the Purchaser, be referred to an independent Actuary to be appointed by agreement between the Vendor and the Purchaser or, in default of agreement within 14 days from the first nomination of an Actuary by one party to the other, by the President for the time being of the Institute of Actuaries on the application of either the Vendor or the Purchaser. The independent Actuary shall act as an expert and not as an arbitrator.[31] His decision shall, save in the event of manifest error, be final and binding on the parties and his costs shall be paid as he directs.

8 WARRANTIES AND REPRESENTATIONS[32]

The Vendor hereby warrants and represents to and for the benefit of the Purchaser in the following terms:

(1) No Other Arrangements

Save for the Pension Scheme the Company is not a party to nor participates in nor contributes to any scheme, arrangement or agreement (whether legally enforceable or not) for the provision of any pension, retirement, death, incapacity, sickness, disability, accident or other like benefits (including the payment of medical expenses) for any Relevant Employee or for the widow, widower, child or dependant of any Relevant Employee.

(2) No Assurances etc

Neither the Company nor any member of the Vendor's Group:

(a) has given any undertaking or assurance (whether legally enforceable or not) to any Relevant Employee or to any widow, widower, child or dependant of any Relevant Employee as to the continuance, introduction, improvement or increase of any benefit of a kind described in (1) above; or (*b*)   is paying or has in the last two years paid any benefit of a kind described in (1) above to any Relevant Employee or to any widow, widower, child or dependant of any Relevant Employee.

(3)   All Details Disclosed

All material details relating to the Pension Scheme are contained in or annexed to the Disclosure Letter including (without limitation) the following:

(*a*)   a true and complete copy of the documentation containing the current provisions governing the Pension Scheme;

(*b*)   a true and complete copy of all announcements, explanatory literature and the like of current effect which have been issued to any Relevant Employee in connection with the Pension Scheme;

(*c*)   a true and complete copy of the report on the last actuarial valuation of the Pension Scheme to be completed prior to the date of this Agreement and of any subsequent written recommendations of an actuarial nature;

(*d*)   a true and complete copy of the last audited accounts of the Pension Scheme to be completed prior to the date of this Agreement;

(*e*)   details of all amendments (if any) to the Pension Scheme which have been announced or are proposed but which have not yet been formally made;

(*f*)   details of all discretionary increases (if any) to pensions in payment or in deferment under the Pension Scheme which have been granted in the ten years prior to the date of this Agreement or which are under consideration;

(*g*)   details of all discretionary practices (if any) which may have led any person to expect additional benefits in a given set of circumstances (by way of example, but without limitation, on retirement at the behest of the Company or in the event of redundancy); and

(*h*)   details of the rate at which and basis upon which the Company currently contributes to the Pension Scheme, any change to that rate and/or basis which is proposed or which is under consideration and all contributions paid to the Pension Scheme by the Company in the three years prior to the date of this Agreement.

(4) Augmentation

No power under the Pension Scheme has been exercised in relation to any employee or officer of the Company:

    (*a*)   to provide terms of membership of the Pension Scheme (whether as to benefits or contributions) which are different from those generally applicable to members of the Pension Scheme;

    (*b*)   to provide any benefits which would not but for the exercise of that power have been payable under the Pension Scheme; or

    (*c*)   to augment any benefits under the Pension Scheme.

(5) Death Benefits Insured

All benefits (other than any refund of members' contributions with interest where appropriate) payable under the Pension Scheme on the death of any person while in employment to which the Pension Scheme relates are insured fully under a policy with an insurance company of good repute and there are no grounds on which that company might avoid liability under that policy.

(6) Contributions

Contributions to the Pension Scheme are not paid in arrear and all contributions and other amounts which have fallen due for payment by the Company have been paid. The Company has (to the extent that it will be required to do) discharged its liability (if any) to pay or reimburse (whether wholly or in part) anyone who has paid any costs, charges or expenses which have been incurred by or in connection with the Pension Scheme.

(7) Company's Obligations

The Company:

    (*a*)   has been admitted to participation in the Pension Scheme on the same terms as apply generally to other employers participating in the Pension Scheme;

    (*b*)   has observed and performed those provisions of the Pension Scheme which apply to it;

    (*c*)   is not indebted to the Pension Scheme by virtue of s 58B of the Social Security Pensions Act 1975;[33] [and]

    (*d*)   may (without the consent of any person or further payment) terminate its liability to contribute to the Pension Scheme at any time subject only to giving such notice (if any) as is expressly provided for in the documentation containing the current provisions governing the Pension Scheme[34][.] [and (*e*)   has at all material times held or been named in a contracting-out certificate referable to the Pension Scheme.]

(8) Compliance
The Pension Scheme:
(*a*)   is an exempt approved scheme (within the meaning of s 592 of the Income and Corporation Taxes Act 1988; and
(*b*)   complies with and has at all times been administered in accordance with all applicable laws, regulations and requirements (including those of the Board of Inland Revenue and of trust law).

(9) Actuarial[35]
[The report dated [   ] of [   ] on the actuarial valuation of the Pension Scheme as at [   ] (the 'Valuation Date') (a true copy of the report being annexed to the Disclosure Letter) shows a true and fair view of the respective actuarial values of the assets and liabilities of the Pension Scheme at the Valuation Date on the basis of the actuarial assumptions and method detailed in that report. Since the Valuation Date nothing has occurred, been done or omitted to be done which may affect materially the level of funding of the benefits under the Pension Scheme.]
[The data used for the purposes of the last actuarial valuation of the Pension Scheme to be completed prior to the date of this Agreement was complete and accurate in all material respects and since the date as at which that valuation was undertaken nothing has occurred, been done or omitted to be done which may affect materially the level of funding of the benefits under the Pension Scheme.]

(10) Litigation
Neither the Pension Scheme nor the Company or any member of the Vendor's Group is engaged or involved in any proceedings which relate to or are in connection with the Pension Scheme or the benefits thereunder and no such proceedings are pending or threatened and so far as the Vendor is aware there are no facts likely to give rise to any such proceedings. In this Sub-paragraph 'proceedings' included any litigation or arbitration and also includes any investigation or determination by the Pensions Ombudsman.

9 DAMAGES FOR BREACH OF PENSION WARRANTIES

In determining the damages flowing from any breach of Warranties contained in paragraph 8, the Company shall be deemed to be under a liability:

(1) to provide and to continue to provide any benefits of a kind referred to in that paragraph which are now provided or have been announced or are proposed; and

(2) to procure and to continue to procure the provision of benefits (without any reduction) which are now payable (whether immediately, prospectively or contingently) under the Pension Scheme and under any other arrangements of a kind described in that paragraph which are now in existence or are proposed and to maintain and to continue to maintain any discretionary practices of a kind referred to in that paragraph which have hitherto been carried on.[36]

SIXTH SCHEDULE

Pensions [Company has own money purchase scheme][37]

1   INTERPRETATION

In this schedule, where the context admits:

    (1)   'Company' means the Company and the Subsidiaries or such one or more of them as the context requires;

    (2)   'Pension Scheme' means [the retirement benefits scheme known as [   ] which was established by a deed dated [   ] (or the trustees from time to time of that scheme, as the context requires);] [Scheme A [, Scheme B] and Scheme C (or such one or [other] [more] of them as the context requires;]

    (3)   'Relevant Employee' means any past or present employee or officer of the Company or of any predecessor to all or part of its business;

  [(4) 'Scheme A' means the retirement benefits scheme known as [   ] which was established by a trust deed dated [   ] (or the trustees from time to time of that scheme, as the context requires);] [and]

    (5)   'Scheme B' means the retirement benefits scheme known as [   ] which was established by a trust deed dated [   ] (or the trustees from time to time of that scheme, as the context requires) [.] [; and]

    (6)   'Scheme C' means the retirement benefits scheme known as [   ] which was established by a trust deed dated [   ] (or the trustees from time to time of that scheme, as the context requires).]

2   WARRANTIES AND REPRESENTATIONS[38]

The Vendor hereby warrants and represents to and for the benefit of the Purchaser in the following terms:

(1)   No Other Pension Arrangements

Save for the Pension Scheme the Company is not a party to nor participates in nor contributes to any scheme, arrangement or agreement (whether legally enforceable or not) for the provision of any pension, retirement, death, incapacity, sickness, disability, accident or other like benefits (including the payment of medical expenses) for any Relevant Employee or for the widow, widower, child or dependant of any Relevant Employee.

(2)   No Assurances etc

Neither the Company nor any member of the Vendor's Group:

    (a)   has given any undertaking or assurance (whether legally enforceable or not) to any Relevant Employee or to any widow, widower, child or dependant of any Relevant Employee as to the continuance, introduction, improvement or increase of any benefit of a kind described in (1) above; or

(b) is paying or has in the last two years paid any benefit of a kind described in (1) above to any Relevant Employee or to any widow, widower, child or dependant of any Relevant Employee.

(3) All Details Disclosed

All material details relating to the Pension Scheme are contained in or annexed to the Disclosure Letter including (without limitation) the following:

(a) a true and complete copy of the deed or other instrument by which the Pension Scheme was established and all deeds and other instruments supplemental thereto;

(b) a true and complete copy of all announcements, explanatory literature and the like of current effect which have been issued to any Relevant Employee in connection with the Pension Scheme;

(c) a true and complete copy of the report on the last actuarial valuation of the Pension Scheme to be completed prior to the date of this Agreement and of any subsequent written recommendations of an actuarial nature;[39]

(d) a true and complete copy of the last audited accounts of the Pension Scheme to be completed prior to the date of this Agreement and details of any material change in the investment policy of the Pension Scheme since the date as at which those accounts were made up;

(e) a true and complete copy of all insurance policies (if any) and annuity contracts (if any) held for the purposes of the Pension Scheme and details of any such policies and contracts (if any) which the Pension Scheme has agreed to effect;

(f) a true and complete copy of the memorandum and articles of association of any company which is a trustee of the Pension Scheme and the names and addresses of the directors and secretary of that company;

(g) the names and addresses of the trustees of the Pension Scheme;

(h) details of all amendments (if any) to the Pension Scheme which have been announced or are proposed but which have not yet been formally made;

(i) details of all discretionary increases (if any) to pensions in payment or in deferment under the Pension Scheme which

> > have been granted in the ten years prior to the date of this Agreement or which are under consideration;
> >
> > (*j*)   details of all discretionary practices (if any) which may have led any person to expect additional benefits in a given set of circumstances (by way of example, but without limitation, on retirement at the behest of the Company or in the event of redundancy); and
> >
> > (*k*)   details of the rate at which and basis upon which the Company currently contributes to the Pension Scheme, any change to that rate and/or basis which is proposed or which is under consideration and all contributions paid to the Pension Scheme by the Company in the three years prior to the date of this Agreement.

(4)   <u>Benefits</u>

All benefits which are not money purchase benefits and which are payable under the Pension Scheme on the death of any person while in employment to which the Pension Scheme relates are insured fully under a policy with an insurance company of good repute and there are no grounds on which that company might avoid liability under that policy. All other benefits payable under the Pension Scheme are money purchase benefits. In this sub-paragraph 'money purchase benefits' has the same meaning as in the Social Security Act 1986, s 84(1).

(5)   <u>Contributions and Expenses</u>

Contributions to the Pension Scheme are not paid in arrear and all contributions and other amounts which have fallen due for payment have been paid punctually. No fee, charge or expense relating to or in connection with the Pension Scheme has been incurred but not paid. If any such fee, charge or expense has been paid by any person other than the Pension Scheme the Pension Scheme has reimbursed that person if and to the extent that the Pension Scheme is or may become liable so to do.

(6)   <u>Company's Obligations</u>

The Company:

> > (*a*)   has observed and performed those provisions of the Pension Scheme which apply to it; [and]
> >
> > (*b*)   may (without the consent of any person or further payment) terminate its liability to contribute to the Pension Scheme at any time subject only to giving such notice (if any) as is expressly provided for in the documentation containing the current provisions governing the Pension Scheme[40] [.] [; and
> >
> > (*c*)   has at all material times held or been named in a contracting-out certificate (within the meaning of the

Social Security Pensions Act 1975) referable to the Pension Scheme.]

(7) <u>No Other Employer</u>
The Company is the only employer for the time being participating in the Pension Scheme. No employer which has previously participated in the Pension Scheme has any claim under the Pension Scheme and in respect of any such employer the period of participation has been terminated and benefits have been provided in accordance with the provisions of the Pension Scheme.

(8) <u>Administration</u>
All documentation and records in respect of the Pension Scheme are up to date and so far as the Vendor is aware complete and accurate in all respects.

(9) <u>Investments</u>
Save for any deposit with a bank or building society the only assets which the Pension Scheme has held are insurance policies and annuity contracts with insurance companies of good repute.

(10) <u>Compliance</u>
The Pension Scheme:

(*a*) is an exempt approved scheme (within the meaning of the Income and Corporation Taxes Act 1988, s 592);

(*b*) has properly and punctually accounted to the Inland Revenue for all and any tax for which the Pension Scheme is liable or accountable; and

(*c*) complies with and has at all times been administered in accordance with all applicable laws, regulations and requirements (including those of the Board of Inland Revenue and of trust law).

(11) <u>Litigation</u>
None of the Pension Scheme, the Company or any member of the Vendor's Group is engaged or involved in any proceedings which relate to or are in connection with the Pension Scheme or the benefits thereunder and no such proceedings are pending or threatened and so far as the Vendor is aware there are no facts likely to give rise to any such proceedings. In this Sub-paragraph 'proceedings' includes any litigation or arbitration and also includes any investigation or determination by the Pensions Ombudsman.

3   DAMAGES FOR BREACH OF PENSION WARRANTIES

In determining the damages flowing from any breach of Warranties contained in paragraph 2, the Company shall be deemed to be under a liability:

(1)   to provide and to continue to provide any benefit of a kind

referred to in that paragraph which is now provided or has been announced or is proposed; and

(2)   to maintain and to continue to maintain (without benefits being reduced) the Pension Scheme and any other arrangements of a kind described in that paragraph which are now in existence or are proposed and any discretionary practices of a kind referred to in that paragraph which have hitherto been carried on.[41]

[4   SEX EQUALITY

The Vendor undertakes to the Purchaser, for its own benefit and as trustee and agent for the Company and for the Pension Scheme, to indemnify and to keep indemnified and held harmless on a continuing basis the Company and the Pension Scheme against all and any liabilities, actions, claims and costs (including legal expenses) which may be brought or made against or incurred by the Company and/or the Pension Scheme of any nature relating to discrimination on grounds of sex arising out of or in connection with the provisions or former provisions of the Pension Scheme applicable to all or any of the Relevant Employees and/or the terms of their employment or former employment with the Company and/or any member of the Vendor's Group relating to relevant benefits (within the meaning of s 612 of the Income and Corporation Taxes Act 1988).][42]

SIXTH SCHEDULE
Pensions [Company participates in group money purchase scheme][43]

1 INTERPRETATION

(A) Definitions
In this schedule, where the context admits:
(1) 'Company' means the Company and the Subsidiaries or such one or more of them as the context requires;
(2) 'Interim Period' means the period from and including the day next following the date of Completion to and including [   ] (or such earlier date as the Purchaser may by not less than one month's notice in writing to the Vendor specify or such later date as the Vendor and the Purchaser may agree in writing) except that if for any reason the Company is unable to participate in the Pension Scheme in accordance with paragraph 2(A) until the date which would (apart from this exception) be the last day of the Interim Period the Interim Period shall end on the last day the Company participates in the Pension Scheme;
[(3) 'Life Assurance Employee' at any time means a person who at that time is both an employee or officer of the Company and covered by the Pension Scheme for certain death-in-service benefits but is not a Pensionable Employee;]
(4) 'Pension Scheme' means [the retirement benefits scheme known as [   ] which was established by a deed dated [   ] (or the trustees from time to time of that scheme, as the context requires);] [Scheme A [, Scheme B] and Scheme C (or such one or [other] [more] of them as the context requires)];
(5) 'Pensionable Employee' at any time means a person who at that time is both an employee or officer of the Company and is, or but for being absent from work would be, in pensionable service under the Pension Scheme;
(6) 'Relevant Employee' means any present or past employee or officer of the Company or of any predecessor to all or any part of its business;
(7) 'Schedule 1A' means Schedule 1A of the Social Security Pensions Act 1975;
[(8) 'Scheme A' means the retirement benefits scheme known as [   ] which was established by a trust deed dated [   ] (or the trustees from time to time of that scheme, as the context requires);]

(9) 'Scheme B' means the retirement benefits scheme known as [   ] which was established by a trust deed dated [   ] (or the trustees from time to time of that scheme, as the context requires);]

(10) 'Scheme C' means the retirement benefits scheme known as [   ] (or the trustees from time to time of that scheme, as the context requires);]

(11) 'Scheme Member' means a person who is or has been after Completion both an employee or officer of the Company and a Pensionable Employee.

2   THE PENSION SCHEME

(A)   Vendor's Undertakings

The Vendor undertakes to the Purchaser for its own benefit and as trustee and agent for the Company:

(1) to procure that subject to the consent of the Board of Inland Revenue being obtained (which consent the Vendor shall use all reasonable endeavours to procure), the Company is permitted to participate in the Pension Scheme throughout the period which would (apart from the exception to the definition of 'Interim Period') be the Interim Period;

(2) to procure that no power or discretion under the Pension Scheme is exercised in a way which would or might affect the Company and/or all or any of its employees or officers save with the consent of the Purchaser; and

(3) to indemnify and to keep indemnified and held harmless on a continuing basis the Company against all and any liability to make any payment to or in connection with the Pension Scheme other than to pay contributions pursuant to paragraph 2(B)(1).

(B)   Purchaser's Undertaking

The Purchaser shall procure that the Company:

(1) pays or procures to be paid to the Pension Scheme the employer contributions which accrue under the terms of the Pension Scheme during the Interim Period in respect of the Pensionable Employees [and the Life Assurance Employees] from time to time, such contributions to be deemed to be payable at [the same rate as is in force at the date of this Agreement] [an annual rate of:

(*a*) in relation to a Pensionable Employee, [   ] per cent of [   ] from time to time;

    (*b*)   in relation to a Life Assurance Employee, [   ]
           per cent of [   ] from time to time;]
    plus the contributions (if any) payable during the Interim
    Period by the Pensionable Employees; and
  (2) complies in all other respects with the provisions of the
      Pension Scheme during the Interim Period.[44]

[(C) Contracting-out in Interim Period
The Vendor and the Purchaser undertake to co-operate with each other with a view to procuring that the employment of the Pensionable Employees is contracted-out of the state earnings related pension scheme by reference to the Pension Scheme at all applicable times during the Interim Period under a contracting-out certificate in the name of the Company.]

[(D) Sex Equality
The Vendor undertakes to the Purchaser, for its own benefit and as trustee and agent for the Company and for the Purchaser's Scheme, to indemnify and to keep indemnified and held harmless on a continuing basis the Company and the Purchaser's Scheme against all and any liabilities, actions, claims and costs (including legal expenses) which may be brought or made against or incurred by the Company and/or the Purchaser's Scheme of any nature relating to discrimination on grounds of sex arising out of or in connection with the provisions or former provisions of the Pension Scheme applicable to all or any of the Relevant Employees and/or the terms of their employment or former employment prior to Completion with the Company and/or any member of the Vendor's Group relating to relevant benefits (within the meaning of s 612 of the Income and Corporation Taxes Act 1988) and/or any transfer payment to the Purchaser's Scheme from the Pension Scheme and/or the benefit granted under the Purchaser's Scheme in respect of any such transfer.][45]

3 Benefits and Options

The Vendor undertakes to the Purchaser for its own benefit and as trustee and agent for the Company and the Scheme Members to procure that:
  (1) benefits will be provided under the Pension Scheme for each Scheme Member who on ceasing to be in pensionable service under the Pension Scheme does not qualify for short service benefits (within the meaning of the Social Security Act 1973, Sched 16) as if he had qualified for such benefits unless the Scheme Member elects to take a refund of his contributions;[46]

(2) the Pension Scheme notifies each Scheme Member in writing as soon as practicable after he ceases to be in pensionable service under the Pension Scheme and in any event within 30 days thereafter of the options available to him under the Pension Scheme and the funds accumulated for his benefit under the Pension Scheme and all other information concerning the Pension Scheme and those options which the Scheme Member may reasonably require in order to decide which (if any) option to exercise;[47]

(3) any Scheme Member who on ceasing to be in pensionable service under the Pension Scheme does not acquire a right to a transfer value under Schedule 1A is given the option under the Pension Scheme of a transfer value as if he had acquired such a right;[48]

(4) the transfer value paid in respect of any Scheme Member shall not be less than it would have been had Schedule 1A required the amount of the transfer value to be the value of the funds accumulated for the benefit of the Scheme Member adjusted (upwards or downwards) for the investment return obtained on those funds up to the date the transfer value is paid;[49]

(5) subject to (4) above the amount of any transfer value for a Scheme Member is the cash equivalent (within the meaning of Schedule 1A);

(6) if a Scheme Member requests in writing that a transfer value be paid in respect of him in a manner permitted under Schedule 1A the Pension Scheme gives effect to that request as soon as practicable and in any event within 60 days of that request being made; and

(7) the Purchaser is forthwith on request advised in writing of the respective amounts of the transfer values for the Scheme Members and is supplied with such information and evidence as the Purchaser may request to enable the Purchaser to verify those amounts.

4   WARRANTIES AND REPRESENTATIONS[50]

The Vendor hereby warrants and represents to and for the benefit of the Purchaser in the following terms:

(1) No Other Arrangements

Save for the Pension Scheme the Company is not a party to nor participates in nor contributes to any scheme, arrangement or agreement (whether legally enforceable or not) for the provision of any pension, retirement, death, incapacity, sickness, disability, accident or other like benefits (including the payment of medical expenses) for any Relevant Employee or for the widow, widower, child or dependant of any Relevant Employee.

(2) <u>No Assurances etc</u>

Neither the Company nor any member of the Vendor's Group:

- (*a*) has given any undertaking or assurance (whether legally enforceable or not) to any Relevant Employee or to any widow, widower, child or dependant of any Relevant Employee as to the continuance, introduction, improvement or increase of any benefit of a kind described in (1) above; or
- (*b*) is paying or has in the last two years paid any benefit of a kind described in (1) above to any Relevant Employee or to any widow, widower, child or dependant of any Relevant Employee.

(3) <u>All Details Disclosed</u>

All material details relating to the Pension Scheme are contained in or annexed to the Disclosure Letter including (without limitation) the following:

- (*a*) a true and complete copy of the documentation containing the current provisions governing the Pension Scheme;
- (*b*) a true and complete copy of all announcements, explanatory literature and the like of current effect which have been issued to any Relevant Employee in connection with the Pension Scheme;
- (*c*) a true and complete copy of the report on the last actuarial valuation of the Pension Scheme to be completed prior to the date of this Agreement and of any subsequent written recommendations of an actuarial nature;
- (*d*) a true and complete copy of the last audited accounts of the Pension Scheme to be completed prior to the date of this Agreement and details of any material change in the investment policy of the Pension Scheme since the date as at which those accounts were made up;
- (*e*) details of all amendments (if any) to the Pension Scheme which have been announced or are proposed but which have not yet been formally made;
- (*f*) details of all discretionary increases (if any) to pensions in payment or in deferment under the

Pension Scheme which have been granted in the five
years prior to the date of this Agreement or which are
under consideration;

(g)　details of all discretionary practices (if any) which
may have led any person to expect additional
benefits in a given set of circumstances (by way of
example, but without limitation, on retirement at the
behest of the Company or in the event of
redundancy); and

(h)　details of the rate at which and basis upon which the
Company currently contributes to the Pension
Scheme, any change to that rate and/or basis which
is proposed or which is under consideration and all
contributions paid to the Pension Scheme by the
Company in the three years prior to the date of this
Agreement.

(4)　Benefits

All benefits (other than money purchase benefits) which
are payable under the Pension Scheme on the death of any
person while in employment to which the Pension Scheme
relates are insured fully under a policy with an insurance
company of good repute and there are no grounds on
which that company might avoid liability under that
policy. All other benefits payable under the Pension
Scheme are money purchase benefits. In this sub-
paragraph 'money purchase benefits' has the same
meaning as in the Social Security Act 1986, s 84(1).[49]

(5)　Contributions

Contributions to the Pension Scheme are not paid in arrear
and all contributions and other amounts which have fallen
due for payment have been paid punctually. The Company
has (to the extent that it will be required to do) discharged
its liability (if any) to pay or reimburse (whether wholly or
in part) anyone who has paid any costs, charges or
expenses which have been incurred by or in connection
with the Pension Scheme.

(6)　Company's Obligations

The Company:

(a)　has been admitted to participation in the Pension
Scheme on the same terms as apply generally to other
employers participating in the Scheme;

(b)　has observed and performed those provisions of the
Pension Scheme which apply to it;

(c)　may (without the consent of any person or further

payment) terminate its liability to contribute to the Pension Scheme at any time subject only to giving such notice (if any) as is expressly provided for in the documentation containing the current provisions governing the Pension Scheme[51][.][; and

(d)   has at all material times held or been named in a contracting-out certificate (within the meaning of the Social Security Pensions Act 1975) referable to the Pension Scheme.]

(7)   <u>Compliance</u>
The Pension Scheme:

(a)   is an exempt approved scheme (within the meaning of s 592 of the Income and Corporation Taxes Act 1988); and

(b)   complies with and has at all times been administered in accordance with all applicable laws, regulations and requirements (including those of the Board of Inland Revenue and of trust law).

(8)   <u>Litigation</u>
Neither of the Pension Scheme nor the Company or any member of the Vendor's Group is engaged or involved in any proceedings which relate to or are in connection with the Pension Scheme and no such proceedings are pending or threatened and so far as the Vendor is aware there are no facts likely to give rise to any such proceedings. In this Sub-paragraph 'proceedings' includes any litigation or arbitration and also includes any investigation or determination by the Pensions Ombudsman.

5   DAMAGES FOR BREACH OF PENSION WARRANTIES[52]

In determining the damages flowing from any breach of Warranties contained in paragraph 4, the Company shall be deemed to be under a liability:

(1)   to provide and to continue to provide any benefits of a kind referred to in that paragraph which are now provided or have been announced or are proposed; and

(2)   procure and to continue to procure the provision of benefits (without any reduction) which are now payable (whether immediately, prospectively or contingently) under the Pension Scheme and any other arrangements of a kind described in that paragraph which are now in existence or are proposed and to maintain and to continue to maintain any discretionary practices of a kind referred to in that paragraph which have hitherto been carried on.

SEVENTH SCHEDULE
Vendor's Protection

1   NO OTHER REPRESENTATIONS

The Purchaser admits that it has not entered into this Agreement in reliance upon any representation or promise other than those incorporated in the Disclosure Letter or this Agreement.

2   GUARANTEES

The Purchaser shall use its best endeavours to secure the release of the Vendor from the guarantees and other contingent liabilities listed in the Disclosure Letter for the purpose of this paragraph (offering its own covenant in substitution if requested by the Vendor) and shall in the meantime indemnify the Vendor and keep the Vendor indemnified against any liability (including costs, damages and expenses) thereunder or which may be incurred in relation thereto.

3   LOAN ACCOUNTS

At Completion the Purchaser shall procure that the Company and the Subsidiaries shall repay to the Vendor [and its subsidiaries] the amounts owing to [them] as specified in the Disclosure Letter.

4   LIMITATION OF LIABILITY

The provisions of this paragraph shall operate to limit the liability of the Vendor under or in connection with the Warranties and the Disclosure Letter and references to 'such liabilities' shall be construed accordingly. The parties agree as follows:

(1)   no such liabilities shall attach to the Vendor unless the aggregate amount of such liabilities shall exceed the total sum of £[   ] but if such liabilities shall exceed that sum the Vendor shall (subject to the other provisions hereof) be liable for the whole of such liabilities and not merely for the excess;

(2)   the aggregate amount of such liabilities shall not exceed £[   ];

(3)   claims against the Vendor shall be wholly barred and unenforceable unless written particulars thereof (giving reasonable details of the specific matter or claim in respect of which such claim is made so far as then known to the Purchaser) shall have been given to the Vendor:

(a)   in relation to the Warranties (other than those contained in the fourth schedule) within a period of [   ] years from the date hereof; and (*b*)   in relation to paragraph 2 of the fourth schedule and the Warranties contained in the fourth schedule, within a period of [   ] years from the date hereof,

but this item (3) shall not apply to claims which (or delay in the discovery of which) are the consequence of fraud, wilful misconduct or wilful concealment by the Vendor or any officer or employee, or former officer or employee of the Vendor;

(4)   if the Vendor makes any payment by way of damages for breach of the Warranties and within twelve months of the making of the relevant payment the Company, the Subsidiaries or the Purchaser receives any benefit otherwise than from the Vendor which would not have been received but for the circumstances giving rise to the claim in respect of which the damages payment was made the Purchaser shall, once it or the relevant company has received such benefit, forthwith repay to the Vendor an amount equal to the lesser of (*a*) the amount of such benefit and (*b*) the damages payment in question.

5   AVOIDANCE OF DOUBLE CLAIMS

In the event that the Purchaser is entitled to claim under paragraph 2(A) of the fourth schedule or under the Warranties in respect of the same subject matter the Purchaser may choose to claim under either or both but payments under paragraph 2(A) of the fourth schedule shall *pro tanto* satisfy and discharge any claim which is capable of being made under the Warranties in respect of the same subject matter and *vice versa*.

SIGNED by [   ])
duly authorised for and on   )
behalf of [   ] PLC)

SIGNED by [   ])
duly authorised for and on   )
behalf of [   ] PLC)

NOTES

Clause 1

1   Retain the definition of 'Completion' even if completion is to be simultaneous with the signature of the agreement.

2   The disclosure letter qualifies the warranties given in Sched 3 (see cl 7(A)). Schedule 3 provides for the following to be included in (or annexed to) the disclosure letter: audited accounts (para 1(1)); intellectual property (para 1(8)); intellectual property agreement (para 1(9)); management accounts (para 1(10)); memorandum and articles of association (para 2(5)); particulars of grants (para 2(26)); particulars of insurances (para 2(27)); particulars of trade names (para 2(28)); particulars of trade associations (para 2(29)); terms of business (para 2(30)); particulars of properties (para 2(39)); particulars of permissions and licences (para 2(42)); particulars of waste disposal agreements (para 2(45)(b)); statement of bank accounts (para 2(61)); schedule of employees (para 2(63)) and sale memorandum (para 2(69)). Schedule 4 requires the following: elections for group income (para 4(7)); agreements relating to the surrender of ACT (para 4(8)); agreements relating to group relief (para 4(12)); base values (para 2(18)), details of roll-over relief claims (para 4(19)) and VAT elections and other details (para 4(43)). Sched 6 requires particulars of pension schemes to be included. The accuracy of the disclosure letter is warranted by Sched 3, para 2(70), and Sched 7, para 2, refers to guarantees and other contingent liabilities of the vendors to be listed in the disclosure letter for the purpose of indemnity. The scheme of the agreement is to oblige the vendors to make all disclosures by way of the disclosure letter (see p 125). A precedent disclosure letter will be found on p 475.

3   See precedent on p 489. See also p 153.

4   Vendors will bear this in mind when considering the warranties and in some cases (eg Sched 3, para 2(71)) they may resist it. If time is short or if secrecy must be maintained during the negotiations vendors will wish to delete or qualify the statement, eg by saying they have enquired only of named individuals.

5   See p 133 as to joint and several liability.

Clause 3

1   Sub-clause (B) provides for a vendor placing (see p 153). It seems best to specify the consideration as shares, rather than as a sum of money to be satisfied by the issue of shares, as it may be argued on the authority of *Spargo's Case* (1873) 8 LR Ch App 407 that the latter amounts to an issue for cash requiring the authority of a special resolution under the Companies Act 1985, s 95, but see *Stanton (Inspector of Taxes)* v *Drayton Commercial Investment Co Ltd* [1982] STC 585 where the consideration was stated as a price to be satisfied by the issue of shares at an agreed value and it was held that the consideration was shares, and their value, for tax purposes, was the value agreed between the parties. See also the Companies Act 1985, s 738(2). The purchaser may wish to include a provision restricting the disposal of any of the consideration shares which are not to be placed. The sub-clause contemplates that the vendors have stipulated a fixed cash sum to be realised by a placing as opposed to a fixed number of shares or a number of shares to be ascertained by eg reference to the quoted price. For a precedent vendor placing agreement, see p 489. It is normal

for the vendors to enter into an agency agreement to confer authority to sell the shares on their behalf — see p 500.

2   See, for instance, Table A, reg 104, relating to the apportionment of dividends. The purchaser's articles should be checked.

Clause 4

1   For a discussion of the location of the beneficial ownership see *Sainsbury v O'Connor* [1991] STC 318 and the cases there cited. Vendors may insist that the purchaser undertakes to convene the necessary meeting and to apply for, and use its best endeavours to obtain, a listing for the consideration shares.

2   Amend if an increase of capital or authorisation of allotment under the Companies Act 1985, s 80, is unnecessary. If the acquisition requires shareholder approval by the purchaser insert this as a condition (this may apply even though the consideration is cash: see p 20). The purchaser will resist a commitment to recommend the acquisition to shareholders as changing circumstances may mean that directors cannot recommend the transaction, bearing in mind their fiduciary duties — see *John Crowther Group v Carpets International* [1990] BCLC 460 and see p 7.

3   If there is a placing the brokers will insist that their obligations are conditional upon the listing of the consideration shares so that the inclusion of this condition in the acquisition agreement itself becomes vital. In any event, the vendors are likely to insist upon it if they are retaining consideration shares. See p 160 as to the implications of including a condition in this form. It is not considered necessary to refer to 'The International Stock Exchange of the United Kingdom and the Republic of Ireland Limited'.

4   Whether or not the vendors will agree to this is a matter of negotiation. They may insist that the purchaser remains bound to pay cash if the placing agreement is rescinded or fails to become unconditional.

5   Other conditions might include 'the Office of Fair Trading indicating, in terms satisfactory to the [vendor and] purchaser that it is not the intention of the Secretary of State for Trade and Industry to refer the proposed acquisition of the Company [or the Subsidiaries] or any matter arising therefrom to the Monopolies and Mergers Commission' (see Chapter 4). Such a condition should be waivable by the Purchaser to deal with the case where a merger notice expires without a reference.

6   See p 260.

7   Even where completion is simultaneous with signing this clause should be retained as a checklist.

8   Item (*b*) may be necessary if the vendors have granted pre-emption rights to third parties. Pre-emption rights under the target's articles will not be relevant in the case of a single corporate vendor.

9   Delays in stamping the transfers where adjudication is required will often mean that the purchaser will not be registered for some time after completion and in such a case it is a useful precaution to take a power of attorney. Inclusion of the power of attorney in the agreement would require the agreement to be executed as a deed and, in any event, the power should be granted by the registered holder(s) who are not necessarily the vendor(s). For a precedent power of attorney see p 487.

10   Notwithstanding delays in registration it is good practice for the board of the target to approve the transfers at completion so as to perfect the purchaser's title as far as possible.

11   See precedent letter of resignation on p 485. Note that the acknowledgement that the director has no claim for compensation does not necessarily bar a claim for redundancy pay or for unfair dismissal (Employment Protection (Consolidation) Act 1978, s 140); hence the concluding words of the sub-clause. In a case where there is any real possibility of a director claiming compensation the conciliation officer procedure should be used (see p 66).

12   Vendors agreeing to this should be aware of the provisions of the Companies Act 1985, s 394, which provides for the form of notices of resignation and their filing at the Companies Registration Office.

13   See p 116. The property warranties are contained in Sched 3, para 2(39) to (41). If time permits, the certificate can be given on exchange (in which case the vendors should refer to it in the disclosure letter so as to qualify the warranties).

14   This may not be possible if the properties are mortgaged.

15   A purchaser may wish the books (other than the register of members which should be checked on completion) to be handed over at the target's offices rather than at completion.

16   The purchaser will certainly wish to change nominees if they are directors who are retiring.

17   Unless it is the vendors themselves who are to enter into the service agreements it will be appropriate to obtain commitments from the executive concerned.

18   If this sub-clause is not included and time is not made of the essence, the party not in default will have to make it so by giving reasonable notice if it wishes to rescind by reason of failure to complete. The sub-clause is obviously unnecessary if completion is simultaneous with exchange. Note cl 8(D) with regard to the right of rescission.

Clause 5

1   Any accountants' investigation should have been concluded before exchange of contracts, but it is always useful for a purchaser to have access to the target's books. Vendors may object to this while the agreement remains conditional.

Clause 6

1   Purchasers sometimes feel that the inclusion of this sub-clause casts doubt upon the reasonableness of the restrictions and prefer a firm statement that they are reasonable for the preservation of the target's goodwill. See p 27.

2   See p 29.

Clause 7

1   This is unlikely to work — see p 125.

2   See p 127.

3   This is sometimes drafted as a restatement of the warranties at completion, with an exception for breaches outside the vendor's control.

4   As to the right to rescind, see p 125, and note cl 8(D). Sub-clauses (D), (E) and (F) are not necessary if completion is simultaneous with exchange. Vendors sometimes ask for a provision that rescission is not possible after completion.

5   It is difficult to draft these provisions satisfactorily. If the period referred to in subcl (I) is not co-terminous with the limitation period (as reduced, if applicable: see eg Sched 7, para 4) and if the purchaser notifies a claim and withholds a larger amount than that eventually due, any excess will be available against another claim notified after the end of the period stipulated in sub-cl (I). If any of the vendors is a company, it is open to question whether these sub-clauses evidence a charge registrable under the Companies Act 1985, s 395 et seq. It is suggested that they do not, but nothing is lost by registration.

Clause 8

1   See p 122. It will be appreciated that the concluding words of the first sentence will not be effective in all circumstances.

2   See p 133. Although this clause should enable the purchaser to release any one of the vendors without thereby releasing the others, it may not release the vendor in question from his liability to make a contribution if he has accepted joint liability (see the Civil Liability (Contribution) Act 1978, s 1(3)). This is, of course, not the concern of the purchaser.

3   If any of the parties is foreign, consider the appointment of a process agent.

Third Schedule

Para 1

1   For a general note on warranties, see p 125. The warranties contained in the schedule are extensive and it is most unlikely that they would all be appropriate in any particular transaction.

2   The definition of connected persons is wide-ranging and, in relation to an individual, includes relatives, partners, trustees of settlements of which the individual is a settlor and companies controlled by the individual; it also includes companies under common control.

The Company's Constitution

3   The Companies Act 1985, s 380, applies to special resolutions; extraordinary resolutions; elective resolutions or a resolution revoking an elective resolution; resolutions which have been agreed to by all the members of the company, but which, if not so agreed to, would not have been effective for the purpose unless, as the case may be, they have been passed as special resolutions or as extraordinary resolutions; similar resolutions or agreements which have been agreed to by all the members or some class of shareholders; a resolution passed by the directors of a company in compliance with a direction under s 31(2) (change of name on Secretary of State's direction); a resolution of a company to give, vary, revoke or renew an authority to the directors passed under s 147(2) (alteration of memorandum on ceasing to be a public company, following acquisition of its own shares); a resolution conferring, varying, revoking or renewing authority under s 166 (market purchase of company's own shares); a resolution for voluntary winding-up, passed under s 572(1)(*a*);

and a resolution passed by the directors of an old public company under the Companies Consolidation (Consequential Provisions) Act 1985, s 2(1), that the company should be re-registered as a public company.

The Company and the Law

4   See Chapter 15.

The Company's Accounts and Records

5   The vendors will object to warranting that the accounts are 'true and accurate in all material respects' preferring to restrict their warranty to the wording of the auditors' report on the accounts (which, of course, may vary depending upon the type of target).

6   Changes in stock valuation or in the bases and policies of accounting can, of course, affect the recorded profits of the target. Such policies should be stated by way of note to the accounts (see Statement of Standard Accounting Practice No 2: 'Disclosure of Accounting Policies').

7   The wording of this warranty will frequently be the subject of negotiation. Vendors will be alert to ensure, by appropriate words in the disclosure letter, that they do not indirectly warrant the 'accuracy' of management accounts under warranty (70/71). This is a point which may also apply to other annexures to the disclosure letter.

The Company's Business

8   Note cl 7(D).

9   The vendors may object to giving warranties as to the 'prospects' of the company and may wish this to be qualified, eg to the best of their knowledge and belief.

10   See p 20.

11   Vendors who themselves seek insurance against liability under warranties will find insurers wary of this warranty.

The Company's Assets

12   See p 130.

13   Vendors may regard this as an indemnity rather than a warranty. Insurers of warranty liabilities will normally exclude it from cover.

The Company and the Environment

14   See p 110. These warranties are quite full and can be shortened considerably in a normal case.

The Company and its Employees

15   It is envisaged that the schedule of employees will show not only remuneration but also length of service, age, position held etc. In the case of a target with a large number of employees, the purchaser may waive the requirement except in respect of employees earning more than a specified amount.

Material Disclosure

16   Vendors who dishonestly conceal material facts may be liable under the Financial Services Act 1986, s 47 (see p 99).

Fourth Schedule

Para 1

1 For a general discussion of this see Chapter 13.

2 'Audited Accounts' and 'Balance Sheet Date' may be supplemented or replaced by 'Completion Accounts' and 'Completion Accounts Date' where the fifth schedule applies and if there is a pound for pound adjustment where there is no limitation to its application. If this refers to the completion accounts, change 'this Agreement' to 'the Warranties' in Sched 5, para 5.

3 For example, the target or a subsidiary ceasing to be a member of a group (see also note 6) or another former group company (ie a member of the Vendor's group) deciding not to surrender group relief but to disclaim capital allowances instead. It also covers secondary liabilities.

4 This covers liabilities under the Inheritance Tax Act 1984.

5 This covers close company apportionment (for accounting periods beginning before 1 April 1989) and also controlled foreign companies (where the target's interest could be as low as 10 per cent).

6 See Income and Corporation Taxes Act 1988, s 410 (group relief), s 240 (ACT carry forward) and Taxation of Chargeable Gains Act 1992, s 178.

7 The 'combined events' clause. An acceptable limitation is that pre-completion events are outside the ordinary course and post completion events are within it. May catch the triggering of roll-over relief claims, hold-over relief claims (eg TCGA 1992, s 165), *Zim* liabilities (in the absence of a grossing-up clause), or TCGA 1992, s 178 when a subsidiary is sold post-completion and the Purchaser did not know of any previous TCGA 1992, s 171 transfer.

8 Includes foreign tax credit for which unilateral double tax relief available.

9 'Taxation claim' includes claims made against the purchaser to cover any potential liability levied on the purchaser under the Taxes Act 1988, s 347 or the VAT Act 1983, s 29. This is sometimes inappropriate — eg non-UK resident purchaser. See also clause 1(6)(*d*) and note 14.

10 A satisfied claim is included to prevent the Vendor from avoiding liability by paying off the claim before completion but after the Balance Sheet Date and thereby reducing the net assets of the target.

11 This allows the purchaser to make a claim where a loss or relief (most commonly trading losses) available to the target is lost. If the purchaser is not paying for the losses, then the vendor may seek to limit the purchaser's rights to recover. If the purchaser is buying on the basis of profit projections which take into account the availability of tax losses as a tax shelter, then he may require the Vendor to indemnify the purchaser for the loss of any losses (and perhaps warrant the existence of the losses). If the purchaser is buying at a price calculated by reference to net asset value, the vendor may wish to exclude any loss save to the extent that it has been taken into account in computing (and so reducing or eliminating) any provision for taxation or deferred taxation.

12 This will assume greater importance and FA 1989, s 102 (surrender of company tax refund — pay and file) comes into force.

13 Capital gains that have accrued, but have not been realised, and perhaps for which no deferred tax provision has been made may also be included in the

scope of the indemnity. Vendors may wish to make an amendment to cover this point.

14   A grossing up mechanism.

15   If there is a liability which is unsatisfied, there should be a provision; if it has been satisfied, such satisfaction (ie payment or discharge) will have been taken into account as net assets (ie cash) will be reduced.

16   Vendors may seek to include change in practice. This should be limited to published practice only.

17   Business is wider than trading and may be more appropriate if a holding company is being purchased (although of course it is more favourable to the vendor).

18   There is often long debate over this last phrase. A common qualification is that the purchaser was aware, or ought reasonably to have been aware. Those acting for the purchaser will resist deletion of the phrase as it then makes the exclusion absolute — ie any act of the purchaser whether he knew of the consequences or not.

19   The definition of taxation includes stamp duty; however, the schedule is not an indemnity for stamp duty but an adjustment to the price, so the Stamp Act 1891, s 117 should not apply.

20   Any problems which it is agreed will be for the vendor's account should be referred to here, particularly if they could be said to have arisen in the ordinary course of business since the Balance Sheet Date (see para 1(6)(*c*)).

Para 2

21   Some vendors insist, particularly if there are other parties to the Agreement, that the purchaser applies the monies to satisfy the relevant taxation claim (usually a liability of the target) so as to ensure the relevant taxation claim is extinguished. This is acceptable provided the target has no enforceable right to the monies paid as this can result in the company having a *Zim* right (see p 230).

22   The reference to rates of taxation current at the date of the loss of the relief in cl 2(A)(2)(*b*) is arbitrary but to specify or even ascertain when the economic loss is suffered by the target is, in practice, impossible.

23   This excludes (*a*) relief from the purchaser's group or (*b*) relief the economic burden of which has been borne by the purchaser (ie which arises after completion) but if a corporate vendor satisfies a relevant taxation claim by using group relief or surrendering ACT this will extinguish a relevant taxation claim.

24   This is again arbitrary; although it is possible to set out a clause which would specify the date when the economic loss is suffered, in practice the date may not be ascertainable. Further, if the purchaser has previously acquired the share capital of another company, and the acquisition agreement contained such a provision, then he may find that he cannot fulfil his obligation to mitigate his loss by deferring the date tax becomes due by using reliefs available to him, in respect of both agreements.

25   This merely states what TCGA 1992, s 49 already states. Where the sale is 'share for share' then no disposal takes place (TCGA 1992, ss 127 and 135) and as s 49 only applies for the purposes of computing a liability under TCGA 1992, Chapter III, Part II ie when there is a disposal, then it will not apply.

However, the author understands that the Inland Revenue do not take the point and will allow the amount of a payment as deductible expenditure for the purposes of TCGA 1992, s 38(1)(*b*) on a subsequent disposal of the shares or debentures obtained.

26   Disclosure should not apply to paras 1 and 2 of the fourth schedule. If there is any matter which the vendor wishes to exclude, then it should be dealt with by express exclusion in para 1(6) referring specifically to the tax liability, ie to the type of tax involved and the amount in question, rather than the circumstances giving rise to the claim. For example, the vendor discloses that it has made an interest free loan to a director and has not reported it on form P11D as a benefit in kind (Taxes Act 1988, s 160). The director is also a shareholder and the target is close. There is therefore a liability on the target to account for tax pursuant to the Taxes Act 1988, s 419 (loans to participators).

27   If the relevant taxation claim is for ACT not paid, then the vendor must make payment notwithstanding that the Company will eventually receive credit for the ACT against its corporation tax liability. When credit is received, the vendor is repaid.

28   Neither the vendor nor the purchaser have had the use of such monies — the relevant taxation authority has. Therefore the vendor, who is supposed to be providing a full indemnity, should not be entitled to interest.

29   This does not cover an over-provision for deferred taxation as this is not an over-provision in the amount of taxation that is due, only an over-estimate of the amount which may become due in the opinion of the directors as applied in accordance with SSAP 15.

30   The words from 'but no failure . . . ' to the end are often deleted by the vendor. A suggested compromise would be to add 'save to the extent the vendor is prejudiced thereby'.

31   This is never to be increased beyond 21 days as time limits for appeal are 30 days. It does ensure that the purchaser is prompt in passing on notices of assessment etc.

32   This is a compromise to resolve the conflict between the purchaser's management time and the vendor's ethical right to fight a claim to the death. Given that certain first instance decisions can be perverse, you may end up negotiating a provision to the effect that the decision to appeal further shall depend upon the opinion of tax counsel of at least ten years' standing.

33   Certain taxes, eg ACT and VAT, cannot be postponed, and with other taxes, the amount not in dispute must be paid.

34   For example, one may wish to bring proceedings against a tax authority in another jurisdiction.

35   This rate should be so penal that the vendor will pay because the interest cost to the vendor is greater than his cost of funds.

36   As in the case of interest.

37   If the target has no subsidiaries and is not being sold by a UK resident company, delete warranties (7), (8), (12), (28) and (43)(*d*) ((44)(*d*) in the individual vendor form) consider deleting the definition of group relief in the corporate vendor form and delete in the individual vendor form, and para 1(11).

38   If the target is not and has not been a close company, omit the remainder of this warranty.

39   If there is no interest in a controlled foreign company, delete the remainder of this warranty.

Fifth Schedule

1   These provisions must be discussed with the purchaser's accountants and amplified where necessary. The key question is whether the 'net tangible assets' will be clearly shown. See *Shorrock v Thegitt plc* [1991] BCC 471 and the paper entitled 'The Involvement of Accountants in Commercial Agreements' issued in November 1991 by the Institute of Chartered Accountants.

2   For authority on the words 'act as expert and not as arbitrator', see *Arenson* v *Arenson* [1977] AC 405; *Campbell* v *Edwards* [1976] 1 WLR 403; *Barber* v *Kenwood Manufacturing Co Ltd* [1978] 1 Lloyd's Rep 1975; and *Burgess* v *Purchase & Sons (Farms) Ltd* [1983] 2 WLR 361.

3   The drafting attempts to ensure that the purchaser is not precluded from claiming damages is a result of a breach of warranty because the matter concerned is taken into account in the completion accounts. However, the amount taken into account is deducted from the claim.

Sixth Schedule (Pensions [Company has own final salary scheme])

1   The valuation of the assets of the pension scheme requires careful consideration in conjunction with the actuary. With an insured scheme, it would be normal to refer to the face (as distinct from the surrender) value of the policy.

2   The exclusion of debts of the target may be inappropriate if there are to be completion accounts.

3   If pensionable pay is increased only annually under the pension scheme the purchaser should ensure that the assumed increases in pensionable pay apply from the last annual review date and not from completion. Alternatively, the purchaser may require the past service liabilities to be based on actual earnings at completion. Check that there have been no unusual increases in earnings which count for pension, eg consolidation of bonuses.

4   Until the law has been clarified, sex equality is likely to be a major issue. From the vendor's point of view it may be better to give an indemnity rather than assume all benefits must be equalised. See p 85.

5   The vendor may wish to aggregate if the surplus in one scheme can be used to offset a deficit in another.

6   For authority on the words 'act as expert and not as arbitrator', see *Arenson* v *Arenson* [1977] AC 405; *Campbell* v *Edwards* [1976] 1 WLR 403; *Barber* v *Kenwood Manufacturing Co Ltd* [1978] 1 Lloyds Rep 175; and *Burgess* v *Purchase & Sons (Farms) Ltd* [1983] 2 WLR 361.

7   Where the consideration for the acquisition is small, consider wording such as that contained in Sched 4, para 2(C) in place of 'by way of adjustment to the consideration for the Sale Shares'.

8   If exchange and completion are not to be simultaneous, the purchaser should ensure that it is adequately protected during the intervening period. The schedule relies on clause 7(D). The purchaser should ensure that all matters

against which it requires protection are referred to in the warranties. Conversely, the vendor should bear in mind the limited control which it has over the pension scheme.

9   To guard against, eg, the company having given a covenant to the trustees to pay contributions over a number of years (eg for a benefit augmentation).

10   See p 67.

11   Only material if the purchaser is relying on the actuarial valuation report. Also, see p 70.

12   See p 85.

13   See p 85. If the principle of an indemnity is conceded, the vendor should seek the conduct of any litigation and protection against the purchaser or target promoting claims against it.

Sixth Schedule (Pensions [Company participates in group final salary scheme])

14   Whether a 'share of fund' is justifiable commercially depends on how the purchase price is determined (eg does it assume that the target will be able to continue after completion any contribution holiday/reduction which it currently enjoys). If the purchaser's scheme is in surplus, then the effect of transferring the target's employees without transferring any surplus may affect adversely the purchaser's group accounts (SSAP 24) and part of the surplus in the purchaser's scheme may have to be applied to provide limited price indexation (see p 72).

15   See note 1 above.

16   See note 2 above.

17   See note 3 above.

18   See note 4 above. Also, the wording is slightly different from the corresponding provision in the schedule for use where the target has its own scheme as the purchaser is not concerned with the funding of the pensioners' benefits in the vendor's group scheme.

19   The appropriate method of investment adjustment will depend upon how the pension scheme is invested and the number of employees involved. There is no particular justification for either side trying to make a profit out of the transitional arrangements and so the adjustment should be one which can reasonably be obtained by the pension scheme.

20   If pensionable pay is increased annually under the pension scheme the vendor may wish to provide for the Membership Transfer Date to fall before the next annual review date so as to immunise the scheme from pay increases granted after completion.

21   The Investment Adjustment should stop on the transfer value being paid. The last four lines cater for the possibility of the transfer value being paid before the final date for payment (see the definition of 'Adjusted Transfer Value').

22   It may be possible to dispense with the need for consents (see p 81). If consents are to be obtained, the vendor may wish to approve the form in which they are given.

23   The vendor may seek to aggregate the transfer values if a deficit in one scheme can be made good by transferring surplus from another.

24   See (e) on p 79.

25   All employees participating in a scheme when it ceases to admit new members are liable for any deficiency in the scheme even if that deficiency does not arise until after the target ceased to participate (Social Security Pensions Act 1975, s 58B).

26   The vendor may require the purchaser to contribute to the administration expenses either by making a direct payment to the vendor or by an additional deduction being made in (*b*) of the definition of 'Transfer Value'. The vendor may also wish to include protective provisions preventing the target from increasing the liabilities under the pension scheme during the transitional period (see p 77).

27   The purchaser should bear in mind that the target will be liable for any sex discrimination under the pension scheme against the target's employees and former employees unless art 119 of the Treaty of Rome applies directly to the pension scheme trustees. See p 85 and note 13 above.

28   The vendor should consider in conjunction with the pension scheme trustees whether any additional provisions are required to ensure that the transfer value is applied for the benefit of the transferring employees. See p 80.

29   See note 7 above.

30   The purchaser should ensure that the shortfall provisions do not constitute a penalty (see *Export Credits Guarantee Dept v Universal Oil Products Company* [1983] 2 All ER 205 and *Alder v Moore* [1961] 1 All ER 1). The vendor may require certain deductions to be made in calculating the shortfall (see p 76).

31   See note 6 above.

32   See note 8 above.

33   See (d) on p 78.

34   See note 9 above.

35   See note 11 above.

36   See p 85.

Sixth Schedule (Pensions [Company has own money purchase scheme])

37   The schedule is drafted on the assumption that the scheme is insured. If it is self-administered, more extensive warranties may be required, as in the schedule for final salary schemes.

38   See note 8 above.

39   There may not be an actuarial valuation report (see IR 12 (1991), paras 13.3 and 16.6).

40   See note 9 above.

41   See p 85.

42   See note 13 above.

Sixth Schedule (Pensions [Company participates in group money purchase scheme])

43   See note 37 above.

44   The vendor may require the target to contribute towards the administration expenses.

45   Consider whether the indemnity should be expanded to cover the trustees of any purchaser's scheme. See note 27 above.

46   See p 84.

47   Expands on the statutory requirements. See p 80.

48   As to when the statutory transfer option is available, see p 84.

49   It is not particularly satisfactory to rely on the statutory requirements. They impose a duty on the trustees to pay the transfer value within 12 months of the application. Penal interest is payable if payment is delayed, without reasonable excuse, for more than six months but otherwise no interest need be paid (Social Security Pensions Act 1975, Sched 1A, para 16(3) and The Occupational Pension Schemes (Transfer Value) Regulations 1985, reg 4(4) — SI No 1931).

50   See note 8 above.

51   See note 9 above.

52   See p 85.

Seventh Schedule

1   See p 123.

2   See p 131. Other limitations on liability are often included, for example: individual limits on small claims; a provision that proceedings have to be commenced within a certain time after a claim; deduction for insurance recoveries; deduction for compensation from other sources etc. It would seem, however, that recoveries by the target should be taken into account in assessing damages without the need for express provision to that effect — see p 131.

Chapter 17

Other Documents

The following precedents and specimens are given in this chapter:
(*a*) Disclosure Letter (p 475);
(*b*) Completion Board Minutes (p 482);
(*c*) Letter of Resignation by director/secretary and by auditors of the target (p 485);
(*d*) Power of Attorney (p 487);
(*e*) Vendor Placing Agreement (p 489);
(*f*) Vendor Placing Agency Agreement (p 500);
(*g*) Placing Letter (p 503);
(*h*) Offer Circular complying with the terms of the Financial Services Act 1986 (Investment Advertisements) (Exemptions) (No 2) Order 1988 (p 505);
(*i*) Acquisition Circular to shareholders (p 523); and
(*j*) Outline Checklist (p 537).

DISCLOSURE LETTER

[On letterhead of the Vendor or Vendor's solicitor]

The Directors
[Purchaser PLC]

[Registered office]

Dated [   ] 19[   ]

Dear Sirs

[Target] Limited

(1) Interpretation

(*a*) This letter, together with schedules A and B hereto and all documents expressed to be annexed hereto or delivered herewith or deemed to be incorporated herein, constitutes the Disclosure Letter as referred to in clauses [(1) Interpretation] and [(7) Warranties] of the agreement (the 'Agreement') proposed to be entered into today between [Vendor] and [Purchaser] relating to the sale and purchase of shares in [Target] Limited.

(*b*) Unless otherwise defined herein, or unless the context otherwise requires, words and expressions used in this Disclosure Letter shall bear the same meanings as are assigned to them in the Agreement and subject thereto the provisions of clause [(1) Interpretation] of the Agreement shall apply to this Disclosure Letter, mutatis mutandis, as they apply to the Agreement.

(*c*) Documents in schedule A and disclosures in schedule B are listed by reference to clauses or to sub-paragraphs of paragraph [2 of the third schedule, paragraph [3/4] of the fourth schedule and paragraph [2/4] of the sixth schedule] to the Agreement for ease of reference only. All disclosures shall be deemed to be made for all purposes of the Agreement and not merely in relation to any sub-paragraph specifically referred to.

(2) General Disclosures

(*a*) This Disclosure Letter shall be deemed to include, and there are hereby incorporated into it by reference and generally disclosed, the following:
(i) the contents of all documents listed in schedule A [and of all other documents referred to herein as being incorporated by reference];
(ii) all matters contained or referred to in the Agreement and any documents in, or expressed in the Agreement to be in, [agreed

terms] (whether or not the same are in fact signed by or on behalf of the parties for identification);

(iii) [all information and all documents available from a search of the public files maintained by the Registrar of Companies in respect of [the Vendor and] the Company and the Subsidiaries at [   ] 19[   ];]

(iv) [the statutory registers and books of the Company and the Subsidiaries]; and

(v) [the documents of title in respect of the [Properties]];

(vi) [all matters which are or would be revealed by searches in relation to the [Properties] at the Land Registry, Land Charges Registry, or any appropriate local authority];

(vii) [all matters which are or would be revealed by a physical inspection of the Properties by a prudent purchaser and his professional advisers;]

(viii) [all matters contained or referred to in the [valuation reports and certificates of title] relating to [certain of] the [Properties] from [   ] to the Purchaser dated [   ]];

(ix) [all information and all documents available to public inspection or in respect of which a search may be made at the Trade Marks Registry];

(x) [all information contained in the report ('the Accountants' Report') on the Company prepared for the Purchaser by [   ] ('the Accountants');]

(xi) [all information, and the contents of all documents, made available to [   ] (as actuaries acting for the Purchaser) by the Vendor or [the Vendor's solicitors/actuaries] in connection with the actuarial review of [the Pension Scheme(s)]]; and

(xii) [the contents of all correspondence passing between the Vendor's solicitors and the Purchaser's solicitors in connection with the negotiation of the Agreement and the acquisition contemplated thereby];

[The provisions and contents of all such documents shall in the event of inconsistency prevail over the provisions and contents of any summary of any document(s) contained in this Disclosure Letter unless otherwise expressly stated in the summary.]

(3)   Specific Disclosures

Without prejudice to the generality of the foregoing we disclose the matters set out in Schedule B hereto.

(4)   Acknowledgement

Signature by you of the enclosed copy of this letter constitutes an acknowledgement of receipt of this letter (including Schedules A and B hereto) and of copies of the documents specified in Schedule A hereto as annexed hereto, and your acceptance of the terms hereof. Please sign and return the enclosed copy of this letter.

[if on the Vendor's solicitors' letterhead:

(5) Disclaimer

This letter is written on behalf of the Vendor and is given without liability on the part of this firm or any of its partners or employees.]

Yours faithfully,

....
[For and on behalf of [Vendor]]

[ON COPY:
We acknowledge receipt of the letter (including Schedules A and B thereto), a copy of which is set out above, and of copies of the documents specified in Schedule A, and accept the terms thereof.

....
For and on behalf of [Purchaser]]

SCHEDULE A

Part I Documents copies of which are annexed hereto

A Documents by reference to particular Clauses and Warranties
Clause/Schedule/Paragraph   Document

1(A)(7)   List of Properties.

Third Schedule (General)
1(1)   Audited Accounts.
1(9)   List of Intellectual Property.
1(10)   List of Intellectual Property Agreements.
1(11)   Copies of Management Accounts.
2(5)   Copy of the memorandum and articles of
                                association of the Company and its
                                Subsidiaries.

2(27)	Particulars of all the Company's and the Subsidiaries' insurances.
2(28)	Details of trading names.
2(29)	Details of trade associations.
2(30)	Standard terms of business.
2(42)	Environmental authorisations.
2(45)(*b*)	Environmental contracts.
2(48)(*b*)	Environmental audits.
2(59)	Details of overdrafts, loans and other financial facilities with copies of documents relating thereto.
2(61)	Statement of all the bank accounts of the Company and the Subsidiaries and of the credit or debit balances on such accounts.
2(63)	Schedule of employees.
2(69)	Sale memorandum.

Fourth Schedule (Taxation)
[Paragraph references are to Corporate Vendor precedent agreement]

4(7)	Particulars of all elections made by the Company and the Subsidiaries under Income and Corporation Taxes Act 1988, s 247.
4(8)	Particulars of all arrangements and agreements to which the Company and the Subsidiaries is or has been a party relating to the surrender of advance corporation tax made or received by the Company and the Subsidiaries under Income and Corporation Taxes Act 1988, s 240.
4(12)	Particulars of all arrangements and agreements relating to group relief to which the Company or one of the Subsidiaries is or has been a party.
4(16)	Details of controlled foreign companies.
4(18)(*a*) and (*c*)	Details of base values and assets in respect of which relief would be available under Taxation of Chargeable Gains Act 1992, Sched 4.
4(19)	Details of roll-over relief.
4(30)	Details of elections under the Income and Corporation Taxes Act 1988, ss 524 and 534 (lump sum receipts for patents and copyright) and the Finance Act 1985, s 57 (short life assets).
4(31)	Copies of clearance applications.
4(36)	Details of PAYE dispensations and audits.

4(44)(*i*)	Details and copy VAT elections.
4(44)(*k*)	Copies of VAT certificates issued pursuant to Finance Act 1989, Sched 3, para 13(4)(*f*).
4(44)(*m*)	Details of assets to which Value Added Tax (General) Regulations 1985, Part VA apply.

Sixth Schedule (Pensions)

	All material details relating to the Pension Scheme including:
2/4(3)(*a*)	Copy documentation governing the Pension Scheme.
2/4(3)(*b*)	Copy announcements and explanatory literature issued to any Relevant Employee.
2/4(3)(*c*)	Copy report on last actuarial valuation of the Pension Scheme.
2/4(3)(*d*)	Copy last audited accounts for the Pension Scheme.
2/4(3)(*e*)	Copy investment management, nominee and custodian agreements to which Pension Scheme is a party.
2/4(3)(*f*)	Copy insurance policies and annuity contracts held for the purpose of the Pension Scheme.
2/4(3)(*g*),(*h*)	Memorandum and articles of association and directors details of any corporate trustee; names and addresses of individual trustees.
2/4(3)(*i*)	Proposed amendments to the Pension Scheme.
2/4(3)(*j*)	Discretionary increases to pensions in payment or in deferment under the Pension Scheme granted in the five years prior to the date of the Agreement.
2/4(3)(*k*)	Discretionary practices which may have led any person to expect additional benefits in a given set of circumstances.
2/4(3)(*l*)	Contributions paid to the Pension Scheme by the Company and the Subsidiaries in the five years prior to the date of the Agreement.

Seventh Schedule

2	List of guarantees and other contingent liabilities.

3   Details of amounts owed to the Vendor
by the Company and the Subsidiaries.

B   *Other documents*

No	*Date*	*Parties*	*Document*

Initials

For Vendor..................   For Purchaser ....

Part II   **[Documents copies of which have been delivered to the Purchaser or its financial adviser, solicitors or accountants]**

No	*Date*	*Parties*	*Document*

Initials

For Vendor..................   For Purchaser ....

SCHEDULE B

Disclosures by reference to particular Warranties (for ease of reference only)

Schedule/Paragraph   *Warranty*   *Disclosure*
[*Third Schedule*]

[*Fourth Schedule*]

[*Sixth Schedule*]

Initials

For Vendor...................   For Purchaser ....

COMPLETION BOARD MINUTES

[These minutes may be reproduced and adapted in relation to Subsidiaries.]

[TARGET] LIMITED

MINUTES of a Meeting of the Board of Directors of the Company held on
[   ] 19[   ] at [   ] am/pm at [   ].

PRESENT

being a quorum.

IN ATTENDANCE

1 Transfers
There were produced to the meeting duly executed transfer forms, together
with the relative share certificates, in respect of the following transfers:

Transferor	*Transferee*	*Class of Shares*	*No of Shares*

IT WAS RESOLVED that the transfers be and they are hereby approved
and (subject to the transfer documents being duly stamped) that the names of
the transferees be entered in the register of members of the Company in
respect of the shares represented by the respective transfer forms and that the
common seal of the Company be affixed to certificates issued in respect of
the shareholdings of the transferees in accordance with the Articles of
Association of the Company and that such certificates be issued to the
transferees accordingly.

2 Appointment of Additional Directors
IT WAS RESOLVED that, upon conclusion of the meeting, the following
persons who have consented to so act be appointed new directors of the
Company with immediate effect:

There were produced to the meeting forms 288 duly signed by the above
consenting to act as directors.

3 Resignation of Directors
There was produced to the meeting letters of resignation from
as directors of the Company and it was resolved that such
resignations be and are hereby accepted with effect from the conclusion of
the meeting.

4   Appointment of New Secretary
There was produced to the meeting a letter of resignation from
as Secretary of the Company and IT WAS RESOLVED that such
resignation be and it is hereby accepted with effect from the conclusion of the
meeting and that, with effect from the conclusion of the meeting
be appointed as Secretary of the Company in his place.

There was produced to the Meeting a form 288 duly signed by the above
consenting to act as Secretary of the Company.

5   Registered Office
IT WAS RESOLVED that the registered office of the Company be changed
to   and that a form 287 be completed in respect thereof.

6   Bankers
IT WAS RESOLVED that the authority of the Company's bankers,
            Bank PLC,   Branch, be revoked and such branch
be notified accordingly forthwith and that the Company open a bank
account with   Bank PLC,   Branch and that the
resolutions contained in the Bank's standard form and mandate, a copy of
which is attached to these minutes, be and are hereby passed and that [any
Director or the Secretary] be and are hereby authorised to sign cheques and
all other documents relating to such account in accordance with such
resolutions.

7   Auditors
There was produced to the Meeting written resignation of   with
effect from [   ] 19[   ] together with their statement as auditors of
the Company pursuant to Companies Act 1985, s 394(1). IT WAS
RESOLVED that such resignation be accepted with effect from the
conclusion of the meeting and that   of   be
appointed Auditors of the Company with effect from the conclusion of the
meeting.

8   Filings
IT WAS RESOLVED that the Secretary be instructed to submit all forms
and documents to the Registrar of Companies as necessary.

9 Conclusion
There being no further business, the meeting concluded.

Chairman

LETTERS OF RESIGNATION

The Directors,
[TARGET] LIMITED

[Registered office]

Dated [   ] 19[   ]

Dear Sirs

[TARGET] LIMITED ('the Company')

I hereby resign from the office of [Director/Secretary [of], and as an employee of,] the Company with effect from the conclusion of the board meeting at which this letter is presented, and I acknowledge and confirm that [, save in respect of any statutory rights,][1] I have no claim of whatsoever kind outstanding for compensation or otherwise against the Company, its servants, officers, agents or employees in respect of the termination of my appointment or otherwise whatsoever.

Yours faithfully,

SIGNED and DELIVERED as a   )
DEED by the said [   ]   )
in the presence of:)

[1] See the Agreement for Sale, clause 4(C), and the notes thereon (p 280).

The Directors,
[TARGET] LIMITED

[Registered office]

Dated [   ] 19[   ]

Dear Sirs

<u>[TARGET] LIMITED ('the Company')</u>

We hereby resign as auditors of the Company and, in accordance with Companies Act 1985, s 394, we confirm that there are no circumstances connected with our resignation which we consider should be brought to the notice of the members or creditors of the Company.

We further confirm that there are no sums owing to us by the Company at the date hereof on any account.

Yours faithfully,

[Auditors]

POWER OF ATTORNEY

To whom it may concern:

[Vendor or nominee of registered holder] [Limited] (the 'Member') of [address] being the registered holder of [ ] ordinary shares (the 'Shares') in [TARGET] Limited (the 'Company'), having by an agreement (the 'Agreement') dated [ ] 19[ ] between [Vendor] and [Purchaser] PLC (the 'Attorney') sold the Shares to the Attorney, together with all rights now and hereafter attaching thereto, hereby as the deed of the Member:

(*a*) irrevocably appoints the Attorney as the Member's attorney to exercise in the absolute discretion of the Attorney all rights attaching to the Shares or exercisable by the Member in his capacity as a member of the Company, and without prejudice to the generality of the foregoing the powers exercisable by the Attorney shall include the power to execute, deliver and do all deeds, instruments and acts in the Member's name and on his behalf in pursuance of the foregoing, and shall include the power to sub-delegate this power;

(*b*) undertakes and agrees not, save upon the written request of the Attorney, to exercise any rights attaching to the Shares or exercisable by the Member in his capacity as a member of the Company or to appoint any other person to exercise such rights;

(*c*) undertakes and agrees, save as may be provided to the contrary in the Agreement, that any moneys, securities or other benefits, or notices, documents or other communications which may be received after the date hereof by the Member (including any officer, employee, banker or other agent thereof) from the Company or any third party in respect of the Shares or in the Member's capacity as a member of the Company shall be received by the Member (including as aforesaid) and held in trust for the Attorney and, without prejudice to the generality of the obligations imposed by the foregoing, promptly to procure the forwarding to the Attorney for the attention of [the Secretary] all such benefits or communications and to account to the Attorney for all benefits arising therefrom;

(*d*) agrees and undertakes upon written request by the Attorney to ratify all deeds, instruments and acts exercised by the Attorney in pursuance of this power;

(*e*) agrees that in acting hereunder the Attorney may act by its secretary or any director or person acting pursuant to authority conferred by its board of directors or any director; and

(*f*) declares that such power, undertaking and agreement shall cease and determine upon the Member ceasing to be a member of the Company, but without prejudice to any power exercised prior to such date and shall not, save as may be required by law, terminate on [the commencement of any winding up of the Member or appointment of any administrator or receiver] OR [the Member's previous death, bankruptcy or mental disorder], and shall, save as aforesaid, in connection with the Shares be accordingly binding upon [any liquidator, administrator or receiver] OR [any personal representative, trustee in bankruptcy or trustee in respect of any mental disorder].

This deed shall be governed by and construed in accordance with English law.

Dated [   ] 19[   ]

THE COMMON SEAL of [   )
          ] LIMITED was   )
affixed to this deed in the   )
presence of:)

    Director

    Secretary

OR

SIGNED and DELIVERED as a   )
DEED by the said [   ]   )
)
in the presence of:)

VENDOR PLACING AGREEMENT

THIS AGREEMENT is made on   19   .

BETWEEN:

(1) [   ] PLC a company registered in England under number
[   ] whose registered office is at [
        ] (the 'Company'); and
(2) [   ] a company registered in England under number
[   ] whose registered office is at [
        ] (the 'Bank').

WHEREAS:

(A) By an Agreement dated [   ] 19[   ] between the Company
and [the Vendors], the Company has agreed to acquire the entire issued
share capital of [Target] Limited in consideration for the allotment by the
Company of the Consideration Shares to the Vendors.

(B) The Bank has agreed to use reasonable endeavours to procure
purchasers of the Placing Shares and to the extent that purchasers cannot be
found, itself to purchase the Placing Shares on the terms and subject to the
conditions of this Agreement.

(C) The Company is proposing, in connection with the Placing, to
despatch the Circular giving details of the Placing.[1]

NOW IT IS HEREBY AGREED as follows:

1 INTERPRETATION

(A) Definitions

In this Agreement, where the context admits:

'Admission' means the time at which the admission of the Consideration
Shares to the Official List of the London Stock Exchange becomes effective
by the announcement of the decision of the London Stock Exchange to
admit the Consideration Shares to listing in accordance with Rule 520 of the
Rules of the London Stock Exchange;

'Agency Agreements' means, together, the agreements of even date herewith
in the agreed form for the irrevocable appointment by each of the Vendors of
the Bank as its agent for the purpose of making the Placing;[2]

'Balance Sheet Date' means [   ] 19;

'Circular' means the circular letter to the shareholders of the Company in
agreed form comprising letters by the Company and the Bank;

'Completion' means completion of the Placing in accordance with clause 6;

'Consideration Shares' means the [   ] Ordinary Shares to be allotted and
issued to the Vendors pursuant to clause [   ] of the Share Acquisition
Agreement;[3]

'Issue Documents' means the Press Announcement, and the Circular;

'Listing Rules' means the listing rules made by the London Stock Exchange
pursuant to Part IV of the Financial Services Act 1986;

'the London Stock Exchange' means the International Stock Exchange of the United Kingdom and the Republic of Ireland Limited;

'Ordinary Shares' means ordinary shares of [   ] each in the capital of the Company;

'Placees' means persons procured by the Bank to purchase Placing Shares pursuant to this Agreement;

'Placing' means the arrangements for sale of the Placing Shares made by the Bank pursuant to this Agreement;

'Placing Letter' means the placing letter in the agreed form to be delivered or sent to Placees by [   ] 19[   ] on behalf of the Bank;

'Placing Price' means the price of £[   ] per Placing Share;

'Placing Shares' means [   ] of the Consideration Shares;[3]

'Press Announcement' means the press announcement in the agreed form containing, inter alia, details of the Placing;

'Share Acquisition Agreement' means the agreement dated [   ] 19[   ] between the Company and the Vendors in the agreed form;

'Specified Event' means an event occurring, or matter arising, on or after the date hereof and before Admission which, if it had occurred or arisen on or before the date hereof, would have rendered any of the warranties, representations or undertakings contained in clause 10 incorrect; and[4]

'the Vendors' means [   ]

(B) Construction of Certain References

In this Agreement, where the context admits:

(1) references to clauses are references to clauses hereof, references to sub-clauses are, unless otherwise stated, references to sub-clauses of the clause in which the reference appears;

(2) references to any document being in the agreed form are to that document in the form signed by or on behalf of the Company and the Bank for identification with such alterations (if any) as may be agreed between the Company and the Bank. A complete list of documents in agreed form is set out in the schedule to this Agreement; and

(3) words and phrases the definitions of which are contained or referred to in Part XXVI Companies Act 1985 shall be construed as having the meanings thereby attributed to them.

(C) Headings

The headings and sub-headings are inserted for convenience only and shall not affect the construction of this Agreement.

2 CONDITIONS

(A) List of Conditions[5]

The obligations of the Bank under this Agreement are conditional upon:

(1) the Press Announcement being released to the London Stock Exchange by not later than [   ] am on [   ] 19[   ] (or such later time as the Bank may agree);

(2) application for listing of the Placing Shares on the London Stock Exchange having been made;

(3) the Circular having been approved by the London Stock Exchange;[1]

(4) the posting of the Circular to shareholders of the Company not later than [   ] am on [   ] 19[   ] (or such later time as the Bank may agree);[1]
(5) the Agency Agreements remaining in full force and effect;
(6) the Share Acquisition Agreement having been completed in accordance with its terms (subject to such amendments as the Bank may agree and save for the condition set out in clause [   ] thereof relating to this Agreement and the Company's obligations under clause [   ] thereof relating to payment);[6]
(7) Admission occurring on or before [   ] am on [   ] 19[   ] (or such later time as the Bank may agree).

(B) Company to Procure Fulfilment of Conditions
The Company will use all reasonable endeavours to procure (so far as is within its power) the fulfilment of each of the conditions set out in clause 2(A) and do all such acts and things as may reasonably be required to enable the admission of the Consideration Shares to the Official List to become effective and to comply with the Listing Rules. In the event that any such condition is not or becomes incapable of being fulfilled, the Company shall forthwith give to the Bank in writing notice of the circumstances thereof.

(C) Bank to Assist
The Bank undertakes to the Company that it will take all reasonable steps to assist the Company's application for listing within the meaning of, and for the purposes of, the Listing Rules.

(D) Non-fulfilment
If any of the conditions set out in clause 2(A) is not or shall have become incapable of being fulfilled by [   ] pm on [   ] 19[   ], and such condition or conditions have not by then been waived by the Bank, this Agreement shall cease and no party will have any claim against any other for costs, damages, compensation or otherwise under this Agreement except in respect of any antecedent breach or under clauses 7 or 11.

3 CIRCULAR

Subject to approval of the Circular by the London Stock Exchange the Company will procure that the Circular is dispatched to Shareholders of the Company not later than [   ] 19[   ].

4 BANK'S OBLIGATION IN RESPECT OF THE PLACING

The Bank shall, pursuant to the Agency Agreements, as agent of the Vendors, use all reasonable endeavours to procure purchasers for the Placing Shares at the Placing Price, and otherwise on the terms of the Placing Letter and on the basis of the information contained in the Press Announcement. The Bank shall consult with the Company as to the identity of the Placees. Any Placing Shares for which purchasers cannot be found by the Bank shall, subject to the terms of this Agreement, be purchased by the Bank at the Placing Price.

5 ALLOTMENT OF THE PLACING SHARES

(A) Allotment

On [   ] 19[   ] (or such later date as the Company and the Bank shall agree), and upon completion of the Share Acquisition Agreement, the Company shall allot the Consideration Shares to the Vendors in accordance with the provisions of the Share Acquisition Agreement, conditional only upon Admission.

(B) *Delivery of Documents*

Upon such allotment, the Company shall deliver to the Bank:

(1)   on behalf of the Vendors, duly executed renounceable allotment letters in respect of the Placing Shares duly renounced by the Vendors; and

(2)   a certified copy of the resolution of the board of directors (or a duly constituted committee thereof) conditionally allotting the Consideration Shares[7]

which shall be held to the order of the Company pending satisfaction of the conditions set out in clause 2(A).

6 COMPLETION

(A) Events at Completion

Completion shall take place promptly following satisfaction of the conditions set out in clause 2(A) and performance by the Company of its obligations under clauses 3 and 5 when the Bank will deliver on behalf of the Vendors the renounceable allotment letters in respect of the Placing Shares to the registrar of the Company, together with a list of Placees (which may include the Bank) who are entitled to be registered as holders of the Placing Shares.

(B) Registration of Placing Shares

As soon as practicable following delivery of the renounceable allotment letters in accordance with sub-clause (A), the Company shall procure the registration of the persons in whose favour the Placing Shares are renounced as the registered holders of the Placing Shares. The Company shall procure that definitive certificates in respect of the Placing Shares will be prepared and, by not later than [   ] pm on [   ] 19[   ] delivered to the Bank for onward delivery to the persons entitled thereto.

(C) Proceeds of Issue

Following satisfaction of the conditions set out in clause 2(A) and performance by the Company of its obligations under clauses 3 and 5 the Bank will pay or cause to be paid in accordance with the Agency Agreements the aggregate sum of £[   ] payable to the Vendors thereunder being the aggregate amount payable for the Placing Shares at the Placing Price, such sum being paid or caused to be paid on [   ] 19[   ].

(D) Discharge for Bank

The payments made by the Bank under sub-clause (C) shall constitute a complete discharge by the Bank and the Placees of their obligations and neither the Bank nor any Placee shall be concerned as to the division of such monies between the Vendors or any of them.

7 FEES, COMMISSIONS AND EXPENSES

(A) Amounts payable
In consideration of the Bank's services in connection with the Placing, the Company will pay to the Bank (together with VAT where applicable):
 (1) [agreed fee and/or commission (which may include a 'success' element)];
 (2) the Bank's legal advisers' fees and expenses and the Bank's out-of-pocket expenses incurred in connection with the Placing (including an amount equal to any VAT thereon).

(B) Commissions payable in certain circumstances
Payment of the amounts referred to in sub-clauses (A)(1) [minimum commission] and (2) shall be made whether or not the Bank's obligations under this Agreement become unconditional or are terminated pursuant to clause 13(B). Payment of the [additional] amount referred to in sub-clause (A)(1) [if there is any 'success' element] shall be made only in the event of Completion.

(C) Time for payment
The amounts payable pursuant to sub-clause (A)(1) shall be paid in town clearing funds upon any payment being made or caused to be made by the Bank under clause 6(C) or, if applicable, within two business days of an announcement that the Placing has not become unconditional or has been terminated. Any amount payable pursuant to sub-clause (A)(2) shall be paid within five business days of the Bank submitting a written claim therefor.

(D) Company to bear expenses
The Company will bear all expenses of, or incidental to, the issue of the Placing Shares and the Placing including, without limitation, the fees of its professional advisers, the cost of printing and distribution of the Issue Documents, registrar's fees and the London Stock Exchange listing fees and, where applicable, VAT. The Company will forthwith, upon request by the Bank, reimburse the Bank the amount of any such expenses which the Bank may have paid on behalf of the Company. The Company shall further pay any stamp duty or stamp duty reserve tax or other duty or tax imposed under the laws of the United Kingdom which is paid or payable by the Bank or by Placees or purchasers of the Placing Shares procured by the Bank pursuant to, or as a result of, the arrangements contemplated by this Agreement.[8]

8 CAPACITY OF THE BANK

(A) Agency
The Bank agrees with the Company (and the Company confirms the appointment of the Bank in such capacity) that (notwithstanding its appointment pursuant to the Agency Agreements) it shall act as the agent of the Company, subject to this Agreement to arrange the Placing.

(B) Release of Press Announcement
The Company hereby authorises and requests the Bank to release the Press Announcement immediately after the execution of this Agreement.

(C) Information to be produced to Bank

The Company undertakes to deliver to the Bank all such information and documents as the Bank shall reasonably require in connection with this Agreement and the implementation of the Placing.

9 ANNOUNCEMENTS

Save for the Issue Documents, no public announcement or communication concerning the Company or its subsidiaries or in connection with the Share Acquisition Agreement which is or may be material in relation to the Placing or the issue of the Placing Shares may be made or despatched between the date hereof and Admission (inclusive) without the consent of the Bank as to the content, timing and manner of making or despatch thereof, save for any such public announcement or communication as expressly required by law or the London Stock Exchange, in which case the Company shall consult with the Bank and take into account its reasonable requirements in respect thereof.

10 WARRANTIES AND UNDERTAKINGS

(A) Warranties[9]

The Company warrants, represents and undertakes to the Bank that:

(1) all statements of fact contained in the Issue Documents are true and accurate in all material respects, are in all material respects in accordance with the facts and are not misleading and do not omit any fact which is material in the context of the Placing, and all forecasts, expressions of opinion, intention and expectation contained therein are made on reasonable grounds, are fair and honestly held and have been made after due and careful consideration;

(2) the audited consolidated balance sheet of the Company and its subsidiaries as at the Balance Sheet Date and the audited consolidated profit and loss account of the Company and its subsidiaries for the financial year ended on that date (including the notes thereto) (together, the 'Latest Accounts') have been prepared in accordance with the requirements of all relevant statutes and statements of standard accounting practice and generally accepted accounting principles consistently applied and give a true and fair view of the state of affairs of the Company and its subsidiaries as at the Balance Sheet Date and the profit and loss of the Company and its subsidiaries as at the Balance Sheet Date and the profit and loss of the Company and its subsidiaries for the financial year to the Balance Sheet Date;

(3) neither the Company nor any of its subsidiaries is engaged in any litigation, arbitration, prosecution or other legal proceeding which may have or has had during the twelve months preceding the date hereof a material effect on the financial position of the Company and its subsidiaries, nor, so far as the directors are aware, (i) is any such proceeding pending or threatened against the Company or any of its

subsidiaries or any such person as aforesaid or (ii) is there any claim or any fact likely to give rise to any such proceeding;

(4) since the Balance Sheet Date the Company and its subsidiaries have carried on business in the ordinary and usual course without entering into any contract or commitment which is unusual, onerous or otherwise material for disclosure in the context of the Placing and there has been no material adverse change in the financial or trading position of the Company and its subsidiaries;

(5) no outstanding borrowed money of the Company or any of its subsidiaries in an aggregate amount which is material in the context of the Company and its subsidiaries has become payable or capable of being demanded by reason of default or otherwise before its stated maturity by the Company or any of its subsidiaries and no event has occurred or is impending which, with the lapse of time or the fulfilment of any condition or the giving of notice of the compliance with any other formality, may result in any such amount of borrowed money becoming payable;

(6) the Company has power under its Memorandum and Articles of Association and otherwise to enter into and perform each of this Agreement and the Share Acquisition Agreement and to allot and issue the Placing Shares without any further sanction or consent and each of this Agreement and the Share Acquisition Agreement is duly authorised and constitutes legally binding obligations of the Company and the completion of the Share Acquisition Agreement, and the issue of the Placing Shares will not, together or separately, result in any breach of any restrictions on borrowing binding on the Company contained in its Articles of Association or any trust deed or other agreement to which the Company or any of its subsidiaries is a party or by which the Company or any of its subsidiaries is bound; and

(7) the allotment and issue of the Placing Shares and the issue or publication of the Issue Documents will comply in all respects with the Financial Services Act 1986, the Companies Act 1985, the rules and regulations of the Board of Directors of the London Stock Exchange, and all other relevant laws and regulations of the United Kingdom and will not breach any agreement binding on the Company or any of its subsidiaries which is material in the context of the Placing or the issue of the Placing Shares.

(B) Effect of Completion

The representations, warranties and undertakings given in sub-clause (A) and the provisions of clauses 7 and 11 shall remain in full force and effect notwithstanding Completion.

(C) Company's Undertaking

The Company undertakes not to cause and to use all reasonable endeavours not to permit any Specified Event to occur.

(D) Notice to Bank

The Company shall procure that if any breach of any of the warranties, representations or undertakings in sub-clause (A) or any other provision of this Agreement or if any Specified Event shall occur and come to the knowledge of the Company or any director prior to Admission, it or he will promptly give notice to the Bank of the same.

(E) <u>No Material Commitments</u>

Notwithstanding any other provision of this Agreement the Company will not and will procure that none of its subsidiaries will, without the prior approval of the Bank, between the date hereof and Admission enter into any commitment or agreement (including for this purpose allot or issue any Ordinary Shares or commit or agree to do the same) which is material in the context of the business or affairs of the Company and its subsidiaries and is not in the ordinary course of business of the Company or its subsidiaries and which could materially and adversely affect the Placing or the issue of the Placing Shares.

11 INDEMNITY

The Company will indemnify the Bank (which expression for the purpose of this clause shall include the Bank, its holding company, all subsidiaries of its holding company and, unless the context otherwise requires, each of their officers and employees) against all losses, liabilities, claims, costs, charges and expenses which are suffered or incurred directly or indirectly by the Bank in connection with or arising out of the issue of the Issue Documents (or any of them) or of the Placing Shares or any breach or alleged breach of the laws or regulations of the United Kingdom resulting from the Placing or the performance of this Agreement or any breach by the Company of any provision thereof save for such losses, liabilities, claims, costs, charges and expenses which arise as a result of the negligence or wilful default of the Bank.

12 THE SHARE ACQUISITION AGREEMENT

The Company undertakes with the Bank not to alter or amend or agree to any alteration or amendment of the Share Acquisition Agreement or waive any condition thereof or right thereunder or grant any time for performance thereof or exercise any right of rescission or termination thereof, except with the consent in writing of the Bank.

13 TERMINATION

(A) <u>Notice by Bank</u>

If, before Admission, it shall come to the notice of the Bank that:

(*a*) there has been a breach of any of the warranties, representations or undertakings contained in clause 10 or a breach of any other provision of this Agreement; or

(*b*) a Specified Event has occurred,

the Bank shall forthwith give notice thereof to the Company and sub-clause (B) shall apply.

(B) Effect of clause
Where this sub-clause applies then the Bank may in its absolute discretion:
(1) allow the Placing and the issue of Placing Shares to proceed on the basis of the Issue Documents; or
(2) give notice to the Company at any time thereafter, but not later than Admission, to the effect that this Agreement shall terminate and cease to have any effect, whereupon this Agreement and the Bank's obligations under this Agreement shall forthwith terminate and cease to have effect in any such case without prejudice to any accrued rights of, or claims by, the Bank pursuant to clauses 7, 10 and 11.

14 GENERAL

(A) Time of Essence
Any time, date or period mentioned in any provision of this Agreement may be extended by mutual agreement between the Bank and the Company but, as regards any time, date or period originally fixed or any time, date or period so extended as aforesaid, time shall be of the essence.

(B) No Assignment
This Agreement shall be binding upon and enure for the benefit of the successors of the parties but shall not be assignable.

(C) Whole Agreement
This Agreement (together with any documents referred to herein) constitutes the whole agreement between the parties relating to its subject matter and no variation hereof shall be effective unless made in writing.

(D) No Waiver
No neglect, delay or indulgence on the part of the Bank in enforcing any term or condition of this Agreement or any of its rights or remedies under this Agreement shall be construed as a waiver of any term or condition of this Agreement or any of its rights or remedies under this Agreement.

15 NOTICES

Any notice or other communication shall be in writing and shall be communicated to the following addresses:

If to the Company: [   ]

Attention: [   ]

If to the Bank: [   ]

Attention: [   ]

16 GOVERNING LAW

This Agreement is governed by and shall be construed in accordance with English law.

IN WITNESS the hands of the parties or their duly authorised representatives the day and year first before written.

SCHEDULE

Documents in the agreed form

Agency Agreement
Circular
Placing Letter
Press Announcement
Share Acquisition Agreement

Notes

1   If the acquisition for any reason requires shareholder consent, or if there is any Open Offer (which this Agreement does not contemplate), then a Circular will need to be issued in connection with the Vendor Placing. There is no need to refer to its publication if the Circular is to be issued solely for Stock Exchange Class 1 requirements, although it will be preferable to do so if it is to be published at the same time as the Placing.

2   Although not strictly necessary, it is preferable for there to exist a direct contractual relationship between the Bank engaged in the Placing, and the vendors. There will usually be a separate agency agreement outlining this appointment, and a precedent can be found on page 500. The relationship could be created by the vendors becoming a party to the Vendor Placing Agreement, but negotiations are often simplest when they are not.

3   The Placing Shares will be all of the Consideration Shares allotted to the vendors under the Share Acquisition Agreement, unless the vendors elect to retain some of the shares. Particularly where a substantial number are to be retained by the vendors, the Purchaser should consider imposing restrictions on the timing of disposals so as to prevent immediate sales which could upset the Placing.

4   The Bank may require the right to rescind the Placing Agreement at any time prior to admission of the Placing Shares, if the warranties given by the purchaser become untrue by reason of post-contractual events. This will be particularly significant if the period between contract and completion is lengthy. This agreement does not include the right to terminate in the event of *force majeure*, which in exceptional circumstances will be a matter for negotiation.

5   It will be noted that items which are included as conditions are elsewhere repeated as obligations of the Company. Although not strictly necessary, it is thought helpful to produce a shopping list of the important obligations in this form.

6   It will be a matter for negotiation whether the Share Acquisition Agreement is also conditional upon the Vendor Placing Agreement becoming unconditional. If it is not and the purchaser has an obligation to pay cash if the Placing is terminated, then this condition will be straightforward. If the Placing and Acquisition are dependent upon each other, however, care will need to be taken with this condition and the equivalent condition in the Share Acquisition Agreement to ensure that the conditions are not circular.

7   The Bank may require, in relation to the Placing Shares, a certificate from the secretary of the Company setting out the available and uncommitted share capital, and also that the certificate and resolutions be produced as a condition of completion.

8   It is usual for the purchaser to bear the stamp duty/SDRT costs in respect of the Placing Shares, although where the Placing has been arranged at the request of the Vendors, this is a matter which may be open to negotiation. The purchaser should be reminded of this additional stamp duty cost of a vendor placing.

9   The warranties set out in this precedent are conventional, although the Bank and the purchaser should consider whether they are appropriate, and the extent to which any additional warranties (for example in respect of an interim report published since the Balance Sheet Date) are appropriate.

10   The purchaser's adviser should consider the financial assistance implications of giving such an indemnity (see p 56). It may be appropriate to negotiate limitations on its liability under the indemnity (and indeed the warranties), including the time limit for bringing claims, and a claims handling procedure.

VENDOR PLACING AGENCY AGREEMENT

THIS AGREEMENT is made on [   ] 19[   ].

BETWEEN:

(1) [VENDOR] of [address   ] (the 'Vendor');
(2) [THE BANK] a company registered in England under number
[   ] whose registered office is at [
                            ] ('the Bank')

NOW IT IS HEREBY AGREED as follows:

1 This Agreement is made pursuant to an Agreement (the 'Placing Agreement') of even date herewith made between [
                        ]. Words and expressions defined in the Placing Agreement shall bear the same respective meanings herein.
2 The Vendor hereby irrevocably appoints the Bank as its agent (with full power of sub-delegation) for the purpose of the Placing in relation to the number of Placing Shares set out in the Schedule on the terms and subject to the conditions set out in the Placing Agreement and the Issue Documents and the Bank hereby accepts such appointment.
3 The Vendor undertakes with the Bank to perform such acts, and execute and deliver such documents as may reasonably be required by the Bank to complete the sale and purchase of the Placing Shares contemplated by the Placing Agreement, this Agreement and the Issue Documents upon the terms thereof and for the purpose of securing the performance of such obligation, the Vendor hereby irrevocably and by way of security for its obligations hereunder appoints any officer of the Bank as its agent and attorney (with full power of sub-delegation) in its name and on its behalf and as its act and deed to take delivery of the renounceable allotment letter(s) in respect of the Placing Shares allotted to the Vendor, to renounce the same in favour of such persons as the Bank may nominate (including the Bank), to do all acts and things as the Bank may reasonably require (including, without limitation, bring proceedings) to enable the Bank to be fully subrogated to the position of the Vendor with respect to any rights the Vendor may have against any Placee or other person who may acquire Placing Shares for non-payment of any moneys agreed to be paid by them pursuant to the Placing and to do all other acts and things as the Bank may reasonably require in connection with or incidental to the Placing and the Vendor hereby agrees to ratify and confirm everything which any such officer of the Bank shall do or purport to do in its name and on its behalf in his capacity as the Vendor's agent and attorney pursuant to this clause.
4 The Vendor hereby undertakes, warrants and agrees to and with the Bank that:
(*a*) it shall not give any instructions to the Company or the directors of

the Company or take any action which is inconsistent with its obligations or authorities under this Agreement or which prevents the registration of the Placing Shares in such names as the Bank may specify and shall hold the Bank harmless accordingly.

(*b*) subject to the allotment of the Placing Shares to the Vendor in accordance with the Placing Agreement and the Share Acquisition Agreement, the Placing Shares shall be sold by the Vendor free from all claims, equities, liens, charges and encumbrances and together with all rights attaching thereto and, otherwise than in connection with the Placing, the Vendor has not granted, or agreed to grant, to any other person any conflicting right, contingent or otherwise, to purchase or to be offered the right to purchase the Placing Shares or any of them.

(*c*) the Vendor has full power and authority to sell the Placing Shares through the agency of the Bank as envisaged by the terms of this Agreement and the Placing Agreement and to perform the Vendor's other obligations hereunder and the terms of this Agreement will not result in any breach of the terms of, or constitute a default under, any instrument or agreement to which the Vendor is a party.

5 The Vendor agrees and acknowledges that it is not, and will not be, in respect of the Placing, a customer of the Bank or of a connected company of the Bank and that the Bank is not responsible for providing the Vendor with the protections afforded to its customers or advising the Vendor on the sale of the Placing Shares pursuant to this Agreement.[1]

6 The Bank hereby agrees that on the terms and subject to the conditions set out in the Placing Agreement it will pay or cause to be paid to the Vendor on [   ] 19   , the sum set out in the schedule being the aggregate amount payable for the Consideration Shares to be sold on behalf of the Vendor pursuant to the Placing Agreement and this Agreement at the Placing Price.

7 If the Placing Agreement shall not become unconditional in all respects on or before [   ] or the obligations of the Bank thereunder shall terminate or be terminated prior thereto this Agreement shall lapse and thereupon become null and void in all respects and neither the Bank nor the Vendor shall have any obligation under this Agreement, save for antecedent breach.

8 This Agreement shall be governed by and construed in accordance with English law.

IN WITNESS WHEREOF this Agreement has been executed as a deed by or on behalf of the Vendor and signed by the duly authorised representative of the Bank the day and year first before written.

SCHEDULE

No of Ordinary Shares
of Purchaser to be placed: [   ]

Amount payable to Vendor: £[   ]

Note

1   The Bank will usually be authorised under the Financial Services Act 1986, s 7 to carry on investment business, by membership of a self-regulating organisation whose rules may impose duties (for example, of best execution) in respect of the Vendor. The rules of the relevant SRO should be checked.

PLACING LETTER[1]
MERCHANT BANK LIMITED
(Registered in England No 987654)

To: [The Placees]

Dear Sirs

Purchaser plc ('Purchaser')
Conditional Placing of   new Ordinary Shares
('the Placing Shares') at [   ]p per share ('the Offer Price')

Further to our telephone conversation earlier today concerning the proposed acquisition of Target Limited, we confirm your conditional commitment to purchase Placing Shares at a price of [   ]p per share.

The Placing Shares will be free of stamp duty, stamp duty reserve tax and commission.

The Placing Shares will rank *pari passu* in all respects with the existing issued Ordinary Shares of Purchaser and will carry the right to receive in full all dividends and other distributions declared, made or paid hereafter, save that they will not rank for the [interim/final] dividend in respect of the financial year ending [   ] 19[   ].

The Bank has entered into a placing agreement (the 'Placing Agreement') whereby it has agreed as agent for the Vendors of Target Limited, to purchase or procure purchasers for the Placing Shares.

The Placing Agreement and your commitment are conditional[2] upon, *inter alia*, the following conditions being fulfilled on or prior to [   ] (or such later time or date as the Bank may agree):

(i) Admission of the Consideration Shares to the Official List of the London Stock Exchange and such Admission becoming effective;

(ii) completion of the Share Acquisition Agreement between Purchaser and the Vendors, save in respect of certain matters relating to the Placing Agreement and payment; and

(iii) the Placing Agreement having become unconditional in all respects and not having been terminated in accordance with its terms.

In consideration of your commitment to purchase Vendor Placing Shares, we confirm that the following commissions[3] will be paid:

[minimum commission, and any additional 'success' element]

Payment for the Placing Shares will be required in full not later than [   ] (or such later date as may be notified to you). Share certificates are expected to be despatched on [   ]. Dealings in the Placing Shares are expected to commence on [   ] for normal account settlement.

You will be sent a cheque for the amount of the commissions due to you within five business days of the Placing Agreement becoming unconditional in all respects or, in the event that any of the above conditions are not satisfied by [   ] within five business days of such date.

By agreeing to purchase the Placing Shares, on the terms and subject to the conditions of this letter, you confirm and represent that you are not a US person or a resident of Canada[4] and that you are not applying for the Placing Shares on behalf of or with a view to resale of such shares to a US person or a resident of Canada and that you undertake to advise any purchaser of the Placing Shares from you of the restrictions on resales of such shares to such persons.

Yours faithfully

for and on behalf of
MERCHANT BANK LIMITED

Notes

1   The Bank will usually have a preferred form of Placing Letter and this specimen is included by way of example.
2   Clearly, the conditions and the end date by which they are to be satisfied should be tailored to fit the Placing Agreement.
3   Commissions are generally paid out of (and not in addition to) commissions payable by the Company under the Placing Agreement.
4   It is common for the Placing Letter to contain wording of this nature which is intended as a protection against breaking the securities laws of the USA and Canada. Consideration should be given to seeking local advice on these matters.

OFFER CIRCULAR

If you are in any doubt about this offer you should consult a person authorised under the Financial Services Act 1986, who specialises in advising on the sale of shares and debentures.[1]

RECOMMENDED OFFER

by

PURCHASER PLC[2]

to acquire the whole[3] of the share capital of

TARGET LIMITED

The terms of the offer contained

in this document are recommended by all

the directors of

Target Limited[4]

Acceptances should be received by 3.00 pm on Tuesday 5 January 1993. The procedure for acceptance is set out on page [   ].

---

[1] Schedule to The Financial Services Act 1986 (Investment Advertisements) (Exemptions) (No 2) Order 1988 (SI No 716), para 8.

[2] Schedule, para 6. Schedule, para 7. Note that the offer must be recommended by all the directors.

[3] The offer must be for all of the shares of the relevant class in the target, other than those held by or on behalf of the offeror. Schedule, para 2.

[4] There is no provision for cases in which some directors are unable to participate.

TARGET LIMITED

(Registered in England No 7654321)

Directors: Registered Office:
A Feather   The Glade
R Bow   Oakdene
J Quiver   Nottingham NX4 8MB

15 December 1992

To the shareholders

Dear Sir or Madam

Recommended cash offer for your shares

Your board and the board of Purchaser PLC ('Purchaser') reached
agreement on the terms of an offer to be made by Purchaser for the whole of
the share capital of Target Limited ('Target'). Details of this offer are set out
in the accompanying letter from Purchaser. As you will see, you are being
offered 200p in cash for each ordinary share of £1 of Target. Your directors
and their financial advisers, Merchant Bank Limited, consider that the offer
is fair and reasonable, having regard to the net asset value of Target and its
profit record.

The financial effects of accepting the offer are set out in paragraph 5 of the
letter from Purchaser and your attention is also drawn to paragraph 6
headed 'Taxation on Capital Gains'.

Your directors have received assurances from Purchaser that the rights of all
employees of Target will be fully safeguarded.

Your directors unanimously recommend shareholders to accept the offer.
Your directors, and certain other shareholders, who together hold 2,629,800
shares (representing 43.83 per cent of the issued share capital of Target) have
irrevocably undertaken to accept the offer in respect of their entire holdings.

Copies of the accounts of Target for the year ended 30 September 1992[1] and
of Purchaser for the year ended 31 December 1991 and the letter from
Merchant Bank Limited dated 15 December 1992 addressed to the board of
Target containing their advice on the financial implications of the offer are
enclosed with this letter.[2] A statement by your board is set out in paragraph 2
of Appendix IV of the accompanying letter from Purchaser.[3]

Yours faithfully

A Feather
Chairman

[1] Schedule, para 12(*a*).
[2] Schedule, para 12(*b*).
[3] Schedule, para 12(*c*).

PURCHASER PLC
(Registered in England No 123456789)

Directors: Registered office:
R Hood (Chairman)   Grove House
L John   Sherwood Gardens
A A Dale   Nottingham NX2 3LZ
M Marion
F Tuck MA
W Scarlett

15 December 1992

To the shareholders of Target Limited

Dear Sir or Madam

RECOMMENDED OFFER BY PURCHASER PLC

1 Introduction

As stated in the accompanying letter from your chairman, agreement has
been reached between your directors and Purchaser PLC ('Purchaser') for
Purchaser to make an offer ('the offer') to acquire, at a price of 200p in cash
per share,[1] all the issued ordinary shares of Target Limited ('Target').

This document sets out the terms of the offer.

[1] The consideration must be cash, shares or debentures—Schedule, para 2(*f*).

2 The Offer

Purchaser, as principal, hereby offers to acquire, on and subject to the terms
and conditions set out herein, all the 6,000,000 ordinary shares of £1 each of
Target ('Target shares') now in issue on the basis of 200p in cash for each
Target share.

The Target shares will be acquired free from all liens, charges, equities and
encumbrances and together with all rights and advantages now or hereafter
attaching thereto, including rights to all dividends and other distributions
declared, made or paid hereafter. Signature of the enclosed form of
acceptance will constitute a warranty by the accepting shareholder to that
effect in respect of the Target shares for which the offer is accepted.

Your directors have agreed to accept the offer in respect of their
shareholdings[1] and, as stated in your chairman's letter, unanimously
recommend all shareholders to accept the offer. Save pursuant to its
agreement with Target directors and certain other shareholders who have
together irrevocably undertaken to accept the offer in respect of 2,629,800

Target shares, Purchaser does not own or have any interest in, any Target shares.[2]

[1] Schedule, para 12(*d*).
[2] Schedule, para 11(*a*).

3 Conditions of the Offer

The offer is subject to the following conditions and the further conditions and terms set out in Appendix I:

(*a*) valid acceptances being received by 3.00 pm on 5 January 1993 (or such later date(s) as Purchaser may from time to time decide and notify shareholders subject to paragraph 2(*c*) of Appendix I) in respect of 90 per cent of the shares comprised in the offer or such lesser percentage as Purchaser may decide, provided that the offer will not become unconditional unless Purchaser shall have acquired or agreed to acquire pursuant to or during the offer:

    (i) shares carrying more than 50 per cent of the voting rights then exercisable in general meetings of Target; and

    (ii) shares carrying more than 50 per cent of the votes attributable to the equity share capital of Target;[1]

(*b*) approval by the shareholders of Purchaser (for which purpose an extraordinary general meeting has been convened for 31 December 1992); and

(*c*) notification being received that the Board of Inland Revenue are satisfied that the exchange to be effected under the share election referred to in paragraph 4 will be effected for bona fide commercial reasons and will not form part of any such scheme or arrangements as are mentioned in the Taxation of Chargeable Gains Act 1992, s 137(1).[2]

The offer will be open for acceptance by every shareholder for at least 21 days from the date of this document.[3] In the event that the conditions set out above have not been fulfilled by the later of the dates referred to in paragraph 1 of Appendix I, the offer will lapse.

The offer is not conditional upon shareholders of Target approving or consenting to any payment or other benefit being made or given to any director or former director of Target in connection with, or as compensation or consideration for, his ceasing to be a director, or loss of any office held in conjunction with any directorship or, in the case of a former director, loss of any office which he held in conjunction with his former directorship and which he continued to hold after ceasing to be a director.[4]

The directors of Target have the right to decline to register any transfer of Target shares but have resolved to sanction any transfer of Target shares to Purchaser made pursuant to the offer. Save as aforesaid there are no restrictions on the transfer of Target shares other than those imposed by law.[5]

¹ This follows the wording of para 2(*c*) of the Schedule. The Purchaser will usually include a 90 per cent acceptance condition in similar form so as to enable operation of the Companies Act 1985, s 428 *et seq.*
² See p 176.
³ Schedule, para 2(*d*).
⁴ Schedule, para 2(*e*). This is required by para 9 of the Schedule to be stated 'clearly' and is accordingly contained in the letter itself rather than relegated to an appendix.
⁵ Schedule, para 11(*h*).

4 Share Election

Holders of Target shares who validly accept the offer by 3.00 pm on 5 January 1993 may irrevocably elect ('the share election') to receive, subject to the limitation set out below, ordinary shares of £1 each in Purchaser ('Purchaser shares') instead of all or part of the cash consideration which they would otherwise receive under the offer. For the purpose of the share election, the value of each Purchaser share will be taken to be 130p, which is based on the middle market quotation of 130p at the close of business on 14 December 1992 (the latest practicable date for the purposes of finalising the terms of the offer).

The maximum number of Purchaser shares which may be issued under the share election will be limited to a total of 900,000 Purchaser shares, representing in value approximately 9.75 per cent of the total consideration. If share elections cannot be satisfied in full, such elections will be scaled down pro rata and the unsatisfied balance of the consideration will be paid in cash.

No fractions of a Purchaser share will be issued to Target shareholders accepting the offer. Such fractions will be aggregated and sold and the net proceeds will be distributed to the Target shareholders entitled thereto, but so that no individual amount of less than £2.50 will be distributed.

The Purchaser shares to be issued pursuant to the share election will rank pari passu in all respects with the existing Purchaser shares and will rank in full for all dividends declared, made or paid after the date of their allotment. The first dividend to which Target shareholders accepting the offer and making the share election will be entitled will be the final dividend in respect of Purchaser's financial year ending 31 December 1992 which would normally be paid in June 1993. There are no restrictions on the transfer of fully paid Purchaser shares save those imposed by law.¹

¹ Schedule, para 11(*g*)(iii).

5 Financial Effects of Acceptance¹

The effects of acceptance as shown below do not take account of the incidence of taxation. Your attention is drawn to paragraph 6.

(a) Capital Value
Target shares have not been quoted on any stock exchange and no meaningful comparison of capital values may therefore be made. On the basis of the statement of the net tangible assets of Target set out in Appendix II, derived from the most recent audited accounts, the net assets attributable to each Target share at 30 September 1992 were 34.2p.

(b) Income
The income available to shareholders of Target who accept the offer is dependent on individual circumstances and the manner in which the cash proceeds are reinvested.

A holder of 100 existing Target shares who accepts the offer and makes the share election would, if the election were satisfied in full, receive 153 Purchaser shares. On the assumptions:

   (i) that the cash consideration is reinvested to yield 10 per cent gross (which could be achieved by reinvesting the cash consideration in government securities); and
   (ii) of gross annual dividends for Purchaser at the rate announced in respect of its latest financial year ended 31 December 1991;

an accepting shareholder who received consideration *(a)* wholly in cash and *(b)* wholly in Purchaser shares, will benefit from an increase in income as follows:

	All cash consideration £	All share consideration £
Income from 100 Target shares	2.67	2.67
Income from £200 cash reinvested	20.00	–
Income from 153 Purchaser shares	–	13.26
Increase in income	£17.33	£10.59

¹ Schedule, para 11(*g*)(iv).

6   Taxation on Capital Gains

To the extent that they receive and retain their consideration in Purchaser shares Target shareholders will not, under present legislation, be deemed to have made a disposal for the purposes of United Kingdom capital gains tax. To the extent that shareholders receive their consideration in cash, they will be treated for capital gains tax purposes as making a disposal, or part disposal, as the case may be and may, therefore, depending on their circumstances, incur a liability to tax.

If you are in any doubt as to your tax position, you should consult your professional adviser.

7 Business of Target

Target was incorporated in 1894 to acquire a business which had been manufacturing archery targets since shortly before the battle of Agincourt in 1415. It now carries on business from a freehold factory, having a floor area of approximately 12,000 square feet, at Nuthall near Nottingham and its European operations are conducted from Poitiers, France. Target is also engaged in fast food retailing through its 'Bullseye' franchise. 'Bullseye' has outlets throughout the United Kingdom and United States of America.

Purchaser expects, following acquisition, to realise certain of Target's non-care operations, notably 'Bullseye'.

Further information relating to Target is set out in Appendix II.

8 Management and Employees

Purchaser has given assurances that it will have regard to the interests of employees of Target and that the rights of such employees, including existing pension entitlements, will be fully safeguarded.

9 Business of Purchaser

The Purchaser group is an international group with widespread interests in leisure industries. Companies in the Purchaser group are engaged in toxophily, windsurfing and other trivial pursuits. The turnover of the Purchaser group in the year ended 31 December 1991 amounted to some £32.5 million and profits before tax amounted to some £2.6 million. The Purchaser group has approximately 2,000 employees world-wide. Further information on Purchaser is set out in Appendix III.

During the current economic climate conditions in the leisure industry continue to be difficult. Despite this, the Purchaser group has experienced a significant increase in sales in 1992 and the directors of Purchaser believe that prospects are excellent. They intend to continue their policy of expansion of the group's core business.[1]

[1] Schedule, para 11(g)(i).

10 Procedure for Acceptance

To accept the offer you should complete and sign part A of the enclosed form of acceptance and transfer in accordance with the instructions thereon.

To exercise the share election you should complete and sign part A and part B of the enclosed form of acceptance and transfer in accordance with the instructions thereon.

You should return the completed form together with your share certificates and any other documents of title for the number of shares for which you wish to accept the offer in the enclosed pre-paid, pre-addressed envelope to Purchaser PLC, Grove House, Sherwood Gardens, Nottingham NX2 3LZ (ref Target Offer) so as to arrive as soon as possible and in any event not later than 3.00 pm on 5 January 1993. The share election ceases to be available thereafter.

Even if any document of title is not readily available, the form should nevertheless be completed and returned so as to arrive by the time and date stated and the document of title forwarded to Purchaser as soon as possible thereafter. Purchaser reserves the right to treat as valid any acceptance which is not entirely in order or not accompanied by the relevant documents of title, but in any case the consideration due will not be despatched until the acceptance is completely in order and the remaining documents or satisfactory indemnities have been received.

11 Settlement

No acknowledgement of receipt of documents will be issued but in the event of the offer becoming unconditional in all respects and provided the form of acceptance and transfer and your share certificates and other documents of title (if any) are in order, a cheque and, where applicable, definitive share certificates in respect of Purchaser shares will be posted in accordance with the authority contained in the form within seven days of the offer becoming unconditional in all respects or of the receipt of a valid acceptance (including all necessary documents of title or satisfactory indemnities therefor) whichever is the later.[1]

Application will be made to the London Stock Exchange for the Purchaser shares to be issued pursuant to the offer to be admitted to the Official List. It is expected that dealings in such shares will commence on the first dealing day following that on which the offer becomes or is declared unconditional in all respects. Pending despatch of definitive certificates, transfers will be certified against the register.

If the offer lapses the completed form and share certificates and other documents of title (if any) will be returned to accepting shareholders by first class post not later than seven days thereafter.

All documents and payments sent by or to shareholders or their agents are sent at shareholders' risk.

Settlement of the consideration to which any shareholder is entitled under the terms of the offer will be implemented in full in accordance with the terms of the offer without regard to any lien, right of set-off, counter-claim or other analogous right to which Purchaser may otherwise be or claim to be entitled as against such shareholder.

---

[1] Schedule, para 11(*f*).

12 Additional Information

The Appendices to this letter contain:

I   Further conditions and terms of the offer.
II   Further information relating to Target.
III   Further information relating to Purchaser.
IV   General information.

13 Documents Available for Inspection

Paragraph 7 of Appendix IV lists certain documents relating to Target and Purchaser which will be available for inspection free of charge at the place and at the time specified therein.[1]

[1] Schedule, para 10.

Yours faithfully

R Hood
Chairman

APPENDIX I
FURTHER CONDITIONS AND TERMS OF THE OFFER

1 Lapse

If conditions (*b*) and (*c*) set out in paragraph 3 on page [508] of this document are not fulfilled prior to whichever is the later of 14 February 1993 and the expiration of 21 days after the offer becomes unconditional as to acceptances by fulfilment of condition (*a*), then the offer will lapse.

2 Acceptance Period

(*a*) If the offer becomes unconditional as to acceptances, it will remain open until further notice and Purchaser will give not less than fourteen days' notice in writing to shareholders before it is closed.[1]
(*b*) The offer will not be revised or increased.
(*c*) The offer will not be capable of becoming unconditional as to acceptances after 3.00 pm on 14 February 1993 nor will it be kept open after that time unless it has previously become unconditional as to acceptances.[2]

[1] Schedule, para 11(*d*).
[2] Schedule, para 11(*c*).

3 Announcements

On the business day next following the day on which the offer is due to expire, or the day on which the offer becomes unconditional as to acceptances, Purchaser will notify shareholders by letter of the total number of shares (as nearly as practicable) for which acceptances of the offer have been received.

In any announcement of an extension of the offer the next expiry date will be stated. In computing the number of shares represented by acceptances, there may be included for the above purposes acceptances not in all respects in order or subject to verification.

4 Rights of Withdrawal

An acceptance shall be irrevocable.

5 General

(*a*) If circumstances arise in which an offeror is able compulsorily to acquire shares of any dissenting minority under Part XIIIA of the Companies Act 1985, Purchaser intends so to acquire those shares.[1]

(*b*) The form of acceptance and transfer (including the instructions and notes thereon) shall be deemed to be an integral part of this document.

[1] Schedule, para 11(*e*).

APPENDIX II
FURTHER INFORMATION RELATING TO TARGET[1]

1 Secretary and Registered Office

A Quiver
The Glade, Oakdene, Nottingham NX4 8MB

2 Share Capital

The present called up share capital of Target is as follows:

	Authorised	Allotted and fully paid
Ordinary Shares of £1 each	6,500,000	6,000,000

3 Results Summary[1]

The following is a summary of certain results of Target based on the published audited accounts for the five years ended 30 September 1992:

Year ended 30 September

	1988 £000s	1989 £000s	1990 £000s	1991 £000s	1992 £000s
Turnover	2,370	2,710	3,051	3,751	4,310
Profit before taxation	555	605	772	938	990
Profit after taxation	333	363	421	450	462
Total amount of dividends paid	90	100	110	120	120
Earnings per share	5.6p	6.1p	7.0p	7.5p	7.7p
Rate per cent of dividends paid (net)	1.5%	1.7%	1.8%	2.0%	2.0%

4 Net Assets

The following is a summary of the net assets of Target at 30 September 1992 based on the published audited balance sheet at that date:

	£000s	£000s
Fixed assets		
Tangible assets		1705
Current assets		
Stocks	475	
Debtors	845	
Cash at bank and in hand	342	
	1662	
Current liabilities — Amounts falling due within one year	(815)	
Net current assets		847
Total assets less current liabilities		2552

Creditors — amounts falling due after more than one year	150	
Provisions for liabilities and charges	352	
		502
Net assets attributable to shareholders		2050

5 Abridged Accounts

The financial information set out above does not constitute statutory accounts of Target within the meaning of the Companies Act 1985. Statutory accounts of Target for the five years ended 30 September 1992 have been delivered to the Registrar of Companies. The auditors of Target have made unqualified reports under the Companies Act 1985, s 235 in respect of all such accounts.[2]

[1] Schedule, para 11(*g*)(ii).
[2] Companies Act 1985, s 240(3).

APPENDIX III
FURTHER INFORMATION RELATING TO PURCHASER[1]

1 Secretary and Registered Office

M Marion
Grove House, Sherwood Gardens, Nottingham NX2 3LZ

2 Share Capital

The present called up share capital of Purchaser is as follows:

	Authorised	Allotted and fully paid
Ordinary Shares of £1 each	12,500,000	10,000,000

Purchaser has not issued any share capital since 31 December 1991, the date of the latest audited accounts of Purchaser and Purchaser has no securities in the nature of loan notes or debenture stock in issue at the date of the offer.

3 Results Summary[1]

The following is a summary of certain results of Purchaser based on its published audited consolidated accounts for the five years ended on 31 December 1991.

Year ended on 31 December

	1987 £000s	1988 £000s	1989 £000s	1990 £000s	1991 £000s
Turnover	18,243	20,656	25,755	29,336	32,453
Profit before taxation	2,857	2,861	2,432	2,305	2,593
Profit after taxation	2,097	1,902	1,621	1,202	1,379
Total amount of dividends paid	300	300	337	450	650
Earnings per share	28.0p	25.4p	21.6p	12.0p	13.8p
Rate per cent of dividends paid (net)	4.0%	4.0%	4.5%	4.5%	6.5%

4 Summary of Consolidated Audited Balance Sheet of Purchaser as at 31 December 1991[2]

	£000s	£000s
Fixed assets		
Tangible assets	18,309	
Investments	1,441	
		19,750
Current assets		
Stocks	2,290	
Debtors	4,826	
Investments	613	
Cash at bank and in hand	302	
	8,031	
Creditors—amounts falling due within one year		
Finance debt	1,185	
Other creditors	4,113	
	5,298	
Net current assets		2,733
Total assets less current liabilities		22,483
Creditors—amounts falling due after more than one year		
Finance debt	4,283	
Other creditors	1,777	
		6,060
Provisions for liabilities and charges		657
		15,766

Represented by:
  Capital and reserves
    Called-up share capital   10,000
    Share premium account   906
    Reserves   4,860
                                            15,766

5 Half-year Results to 30 June 1992

The following information has been extracted from the announcement on 16
September 1992 regarding the unaudited consolidated results of the
Purchaser group for the six months ended 30 June 1992:

	Six months ended 30 June		Year ended 31 December
	1992 £000s	*1991* £000s	*1991* £000s
Turnover	22,175	15,260	32,453
Profit before taxation	1,967	1,240	2,593
Profit after taxation	1,102	678	1,379
Earnings per share	11.0p	6.8p	13.8p
Dividends per share			
Interim	2.5p	2.0p	2.0p
Final			4.5p

In his accompanying remarks the chairman of Purchaser, Mr R Hood,
commented on the improved profitability following the acquisition in 1991
of F Tuck & Sons Limited and M Marion & Sons Limited, both of which
were now starting to make useful contributions to the group's results. As a
consequence of these better prospects for the group, a higher interim
dividend had been paid and it is hoped to match this increase again when the
final dividend is declared.

6 Abridged Accounts

The financial information set out above does not constitute statutory
accounts of Purchaser within the meaning of the Companies Act 1985.
Statutory accounts of Purchaser for the five years ended 31 December 1991
have been delivered to the Registrar of Companies. The auditors of

Purchaser have made unqualified reports under the Companies Act 1985, s 235 in respect of all such accounts.[3]

[1] Schedule, para 11(g)(ii).
[2] Schedule, para 11(n).
[3] Companies Act 1985, s 240(3).

APPENDIX IV
GENERAL INFORMATION

1 Responsibility

(a) The directors of Purchaser and Target are responsible for the information contained in this document and those accompanying it insofar as it relates to their respective companies and to themselves and to the best of their respective knowledge and belief (having taken all reasonable care to ensure that such is the case) the information is in accordance with the facts and does not omit any material fact, and each of them accepts responsibility accordingly.[1]

(b) The directors of Purchaser hereby state that the information in relation to Purchaser and to Purchaser shares contained in this document by virtue of sub-paragraph 12(e) of the Schedule to The Financial Services Act 1986 (Investment Advertisements) (Exemptions) (No 2) Order 1988, is correct.[2]

[1] Schedule, para 12(g).
[2] Schedule, para 12(e).

2 Statement of Directors of Target[1]

The directors of Target, acting as a board, hereby state that:

(a) There has not been any material change in the financial position or prospects of Target since 30 September 1992, the date to which the latest available accounts of Target are made up.

(b) The interests which the directors of Target have in the securities of Target which are required to be entered in the register kept by Target under the Companies Act 1985, s 325 are as follows:

Director	Ordinary shares held beneficially		
	Held Personally	Family Interests	Percentage
A Feather	1,080,000	195,000	21.25
R Bow	588,000	76,500	11.07
J Quiver	24,000	–	0.4

   (*c*) None of the directors of Target has any interests in the securities of Purchaser which would be required to be entered in the register kept by Purchaser under the Companies Act 1985, s 325, if any such director were a director of Purchaser.

   (*d*) Save for the undertaking referred to in paragraph 3 below none of the directors of Target has any material interest in any contract entered into by Purchaser or in any contract entered into by any member of the group of which Purchaser is a member.

¹ Schedule, para 12(*c*). It is convenient, although slightly odd, to include this in the offer circular. The Schedule only requires the circular to be 'accompanied' by such a statement. It could be included in the letter from the chairman of the target set out at the front of the circular but would look even odder there.

3 Acceptance by Directors of Target[1]

The directors of Target have undertaken to accept the offer in respect of their beneficial shareholders and to procure acceptance in respect of their family shareholdings as set out in paragraph 2(*b*) above. These shareholdings represent in total 32.72 per cent of the Target shares.

¹ Schedule, para 12(*d*).

4 Disclosure of Interests[1]

   (*a*) The following dealings in Target shares by the directors of Target and their families have taken place since 15 December 1991:

Director	Date of Transaction	Nature of Transaction	Number of Shares	Price per Share
A Feather	20 Dec 1991	Sale	3,000	£1.50
	14 Feb 1992	Purchase	1,200	£1.60
R Bow	3 March 1992	Purchase	3,000	£1.50

Save as aforesaid, none of the directors of Target nor any person who has been a director of Target since 15 December 1991 has dealt in the share capitals of Target or Purchaser since 15 December 1991.

   (*b*) Neither Purchaser nor any person acting on behalf of Purchaser holds any securities of Target.

   (*c*) None of the directors of Purchaser has dealt in the share capital of Purchaser or Target since 15 December 1991.

¹ Schedule, para 11(*m*).

5 General

(a) It is not proposed in connection with the offer that any payment or other benefit shall be made or given to any director or former director of Target in connection with or as compensation or consideration for his ceasing to be a director or loss of any office held in conjunction with a directorship or, in the case of a former director, loss of any office which he held in conjunction with his former directorship and which he continued to hold after ceasing to be director.[1]

(b) Following the acquisition of Target, Mr A Feather is to be appointed a director of Purchaser. Save as aforesaid there is no arrangement made between Purchaser or any person with whom Purchaser has an agreement of the type described in the Companies Act 1985, s 204, and any of the directors or shareholders of Target or any persons who have been such directors or shareholders in the period since 15 December 1991 having any connection with or dependence on the offer.[2]

(c) There is no agreement or arrangement whereby any of the shares in Target acquired by Purchaser pursuant to the offer will or may be transferred to any other person. However, Purchaser reserves the right to transfer any of such shares to a nominee on its behalf or any company from time to time being a member of the Purchaser group of companies.[3]

(d) All expenses of and incidental to the preparation and circulation of this document and any stamp duty payable on transfers of Target shares pursuant to the offer will be paid by Purchaser.

(e) There has not been, within the knowledge of Purchaser, any material change in the financial position or prospects of Target since 30 September 1992, the date of the latest available accounts of Target.[4]

(f) Merchant Bank Limited has given (and has not withdrawn) its consent to the issue of this document with the reference to its name in the form and context in which it appears.

[1] Schedule, para 11(*i*).
[2] Schedule, para 11(*j*).
[3] Schedule, para 11(*l*).
[4] Schedule, para 11(*k*).

6 Material Contracts[1]

The following contracts entered into by the Purchaser in the period of two years immediately preceding the date of the offer (not being contracts entered into in the ordinary course of business) are, or may be, material:

(i) agreement dated 1 April 1991 for the acquisition by Purchaser of F Tuck & Sons Limited from Mr F Tuck and members of his family for £1,185,000; and

(ii) agreement dated 17 July 1991 for the acquisition by Purchaser of M Marion & Sons Limited from Miss M Marion for £3,200,000.

There are no such agreements by Target which are considered to be material.

[1] Schedule, para 11(*g*)(*v*).

7   Documents Available for Inspection[1]

Copies of the following documents will be available for inspection free of charge at the offices of Coke & Littleton, 1 Moor Alley, London EC3Z 2FL between 10.00 am and 4.00 pm on weekdays (Saturdays and public holidays excepted) so long as the offer remains open for acceptance:

(i) the memorandum and articles of association of each of Target and Purchaser;

(ii) the audited accounts of Target for the two years ended 30 September 1991 and 1992;

(iii) the audited consolidated accounts of Purchaser for the two years ended 31 December 1990 and 1991 and Purchaser's announcement dated 15 September 1992 in respect of its Half-year Results to 30 June 1992;

(iv) the letter dated 15 December 1992 from Merchant Bank Limited to the Board of Target;

(v) the consent of Merchant Bank Limited referred to in paragraph 5 (*f*) above;

(vi) the contracts referred to in paragraph 6 above; and

(vii) the existing contracts of service between Target and its directors and between Purchaser and its directors, each of which has been entered into for a period of more than a year.

---

[1] Schedule, paras 2(*g*) and 10.

ACQUISITION CIRCULAR[1]

PURCHASER PLC
(Registered in England under No 123456789)

Directors: Registered Office:
R Hood (Chairman)   Grove House
L John   Sherwood Gardens
A A Dale   Nottingham NX2 3LZ
M Marion
F Tuck, MA
W Scarlett

                                                    15 December 1992
To the shareholders

Dear Sir or Madam

Acquisition of Target Limited

It was announced today that Purchaser PLC ('Purchaser') has conditionally agreed to acquire from Mr A Feather and Mr R Bow the whole of the issued share capital of Target Limited ('Target') at the price of £12,000,000 payable in cash on completion.

In view of its size, the acquisition is conditional, *inter alia*, on the approval of shareholders.

Business of Target

Target was incorporated in 1894 to acquire a business which had been manufacturing archery targets shortly before the Battle of Agincourt in 1415. It now carries on business from a freehold factory, having a floor area of approximately 12,000 square feet, at Nuthall near Nottingham and its European operations are conducted from Poitiers, France. Target is also engaged in fast food retailing through its 'Bullseye' franchise. The 'Bullseye' business has outlets throughout the United Kingdom and United States of America.

A report by Messrs Profit and Loss, Purchaser's auditors, on the financial position of Target at 30 September 1990 to 30 September 1992 and of its results and cash flows for the three years ended 30 September 1992 is set out in Appendix I. The report shows that the net tangible assets of Target on 30 September 1992 amounted to £2.05 million and Target's profit before tax for the year ended 30 September 1992 was £0.99 million.

Purchaser sees this acquisition as a logical step in its programme of expansion in the toxophily industry in an area not so far covered by its operations. Purchaser has funded this acquisition from existing bank facilities. Purchaser expects to reduce its borrowings following acquisition by realising certain of Target's non-core operations, notably 'Bullseye'. The effect on the group's cash balances will be offset by the increasing profit contribution which Target is expected to make following acquisition.

Management and Staff

Mr Albert Feather (aged 61) has been an executive director of Target since 1966 and is responsible for overall policy and management. Mr Robert Bow (aged 37) joined Target in 1983 and was appointed a director of Target in 1987. He is responsible for export sales and for overseas operations. It is intended that both will enter into service agreements with Target for a term of two years from completion, as directors of Target. The Board of Target now comprises Mr R Hood, Mr L John, Mr F Tuck, Mr A Feather and Mr R Bow. There are some 200 employees of Target and Purchaser intends that their interests will be respected.

General

During the current economic climate conditions in the leisure industry continue to be difficult. Despite this, the Purchaser's group has experienced a significant increase in sales in 1992, and prospects for the current financial year are considered excellent. Your directors intend to continue their policy of expansion of the group's core business. Although no further acquisitions are currently in contemplation, your directors are alert for opportunities to acquire companies active in the more dangerous leisure activities.

Extraordinary General Meeting

Due to its size, the acquisition of Target is subject to the approval of shareholders of Purchaser. Set out at the end of this circular is a notice convening an EGM of Purchaser to be held on 31 December 1992. A form of proxy is enclosed for use in connection with that meeting.

Recommendation

The directors of Purchaser, who have been advised by Merchant Bank Limited, consider the acquisition of Target to be in the best interests of Purchaser and its shareholders. They unanimously recommend you to vote in favour of the resolution at the EGM as they intend to do in respect of their own shareholdings.

A pro forma statement of net assets of the enlarged group is contained in Appendix II and information with regard to Purchaser and further information with regard to the acquisition is set out in Appendix III.

Yours faithfully

R Hood
Chairman

¹ The Circular has been prepared on the assumption of a Super Class 1 transaction for the London Stock Exchange purposes. At the time of publication, however, Stock Exchange requirements are under review and a new Yellow Book is due for publication which may affect the content requirements of such a circular. In particular, requirements regarding an accountants' report on Target are believed likely to change.

APPENDIX I

The following is a copy of a report received from Profit & Loss, Chartered Accountants, the auditors of Purchaser.

The Directors	Calculator House
Purchaser PLC	Strand
Grove House	London WC1 4LF
Sherwood Gardens	
Nottingham NX2 3LZ	15 December 1992

Gentlemen

A Introduction

On 15 December 1992, Purchaser PLC ('Purchaser') conditionally agreed to acquire the whole of the issued share capital of Target Limited ('Target') for a consideration of £12 million to be satisfied in cash.

We have examined the audited accounts of Target for the three years ended 30 September 1992. These accounts were audited by Jones & Co, Chartered Accountants. The financial information set out below has been derived from the audited accounts of Target after making such adjustments as we consider necessary. Our work in connection with this report has been carried out in accordance with the Auditing Guideline: Prospectuses and the reporting accountant.

In our opinion the financial information set out below gives a true and fair view of the results and cash flows of Target for the three years ended 30 September 1992 and of its state of affairs at 30 September 1990 to 30 September 1992.

No audited accounts have been prepared for Target subsequent to 30 September 1992.

B Accounting policies

The significant accounting policies which have been consistently applied in arriving at the financial information set out in this report are as follows:

1 *Basis of preparation*
The financial information presented in this report has been prepared under the historical cost convention.

2 *Turnover*
Turnover represents sales invoiced to customers, exclusive of value added tax.

3 *Stocks*
Stock and work in progress are valued at the lower of cost and net realisable value. Cost represents materials, direct labour and an appropriate proportion of production overheads.

4 *Depreciation*
Fixed assets are depreciated to write-off their cost, which in the case of freehold buildings excludes an estimate by the Directors of the cost of land, by equal annual instalments over their expected useful lives as follows:

Freehold buildings	50 years
Plant and equipment	15 years
Motor vehicles	4 years

5 *Deferred taxation*
Deferred taxation is provided, using the liability method, on all material timing differences which are not expected to continue for the foreseeable future.

6 *Foreign currencies*
Transactions denominated in foreign currencies are recorded at the rate of exchange ruling at the date of the transaction.
Assets and liabilities denominated in foreign currencies are translated into sterling at the rate of exchange ruling at the balance sheet date.
All foreign exchange differences are included in the profit and loss account.

7 *Leasing*
Rentals paid under operating leases are charged to income on a straight line basis over the lease term.

8 *Pension costs*
Target operates a defined contribution pension scheme. Contributions are charged to the profit and loss account in the period in which they are incurred.

C Profit and loss accounts

The results of Target for the three years ended 30 September 1992 are as follows:

| | Notes | *Year ended 30 September* | | |
		1990 *£000s*	*1991* *£000s*	*1992* *£000s*
Turnover	1	3,051	3,751	4,310
Cost of sales		(1,678)	(2,026)	(2,392)
Gross profit		1,373	1,725	1,918
Selling and distribution costs		(301)	(468)	(571)
Administrative expenses		(265)	(309)	(355)
Operating profit	2	807	948	992
Other income		5	8	5
Net interest payable	3	(40)	(18)	(7)
Profit before taxation		772	938	990
Taxation	4	(351)	(488)	(528)
Profit after taxation		421	450	462
Extraordinary items	5	(51)		
Dividends		(110)	(120)	(120)
Retained profit		260	330	(342.5)

Notes
1 Segmental analysis

	1990 *£000s*	*1991* *£000s*	*1992* *£000s*
(a) By class of business:			
Turnover:			
Archery targets	2,598	2,963	3,448
Fast food retailing	453	788	862
	3,051	3,751	4,310
Profit on ordinary activities before tax:			
Archery targets	587	682	797
Fast food retailing	185	256	193
	772	938	990
Net assets:			
Archery targets	968	1,140	1,288
Fast food retailing	409	567	762
	1,377	1,707	2,050
(b) By geographical origin:			
Turnover:			
United Kingdom	1,987	2,250	2,500
Europe	863	1,127	1,408
North America	201	374	402
	3,051	3,751	4,310

Profit on ordinary activities before tax:			
United Kingdom	588	692	749
Europe	107	145	139
North America	77	101	102
	772	938	990

Turnover by geographical destination is not materially different from turnover by geographical origin.

2   Operating profit is stated after charging:

	Year ended 30 September		
	1990 £000s	1991 £000s	1992 £000s
Depreciation	157	168	211
Directors' remuneration	87	100	125
Staff costs	938	972	1,007
Auditors' remuneration	8	9	13
Hire and leasing charges	4	5	5

3   Net interest payable comprises:

	Year ended 30 September		
	1990 £000s	1991 £000s	1992 £000s
Bank loans and overdrafts repayable within five years	42	20	10
Interest receivable	(2)	(2)	(3)
Net interest payable	40	18	7

4   Taxation charge comprises:

	Year ended 30 September		
	1990 £000s	1991 £000s	1992 £000s
UK corporation tax	320	475	530
Deferred taxation	31	13	(2)
	351	488	528

5   The extraordinary item in the year ended 30 September 1990 related to the loss on disposal of an investment property.

D Balance sheets

The balance sheets of Target at 30 September 1990 to 1992 are as follows:

	Notes	1990 £000s	1991 £000s	1992 £000s
FIXED ASSETS				
Tangible assets	1	1,616	1,576	1,705
CURRENT ASSETS				
Stocks	2	432	452	475
Debtors	3	671	791	845
Cash at bank and in hand		–	107	342
		1,103	1,350	1,662
CREDITORS: amounts falling due within one year	4	850	714	815
Net current assets		253	636	847
Total assets less current liabilities		1,869	2,212	2,552
CREDITORS: amounts falling due after more than one year	5	150	150	150
PROVISIONS FOR LIABILITIES AND CHARGES	6	342	355	352
Total assets less liabilities		1,377	1,707	2,050
CAPITAL AND RESERVES				
Called-up share capital		125	125	125
Profit and loss account		1,252	1,582	1,925
		1,377	1,707	2,050

At 30 September

Notes

1 Tangible assets comprise:

	Cost £000s	Depreciation £000s	Net Book amount £000s
Freehold property	1,040	190	850
Plant, equipment and motor vehicles	1,995	1,140	855
At 30 September 1992	3,035	1,330	1,705
At 30 September 1991	2,694	1,118	1,576

2 Stocks comprise:

	1991 £000s	1992 £000s
Raw materials	68	54
Work in progress	73	79
Finished goods	311	342
	452	475

3 Debtors are analysed as follows:

	1991 £000s	1992 £000s
Trade debtors	757	819
Other debtors	15	7
Prepayments	19	19
	791	845

4 Creditors falling due within one year are analysed as follows:

	1991 £000s	1992 £000s
Trade creditors	98	104
Sundry creditors	33	59
Bank loan	42	40
Corporation tax	421	492
Proposed dividend	120	120
	714	815

5 Creditors falling due after one year comprise a secured bank loan repayable in 1995 on which interest is payable at 12 per cent per annum.

6 Provisions for liabilities and charges comprised:

	Amount provided £000s	Full potential liability £000s
Taxation deferred by capital allowances:		
At 30 September 1992	353	400
At 30 September 1991	354	380

7 The called up share capital at 30 September 1992 comprises:

	Authorised	Allotted and fully paid
Ordinary shares of £1 each	£125,000	£125,000

8 Target had contractual commitments for capital expenditure at 30 September 1992 of £325,000, of which £215,000 is in respect of leased plant, equipment and motor vehicles. The directors had authorised further capital expenditure of £60,000.

9 Contingent liabilities

An overseas customer has commenced an action against Target in respect of goods claimed to be faulty. It is estimated that the maximum liability, should the action be successful, is £75,000.

The directors of Target have received legal advice that the action is unlikely to succeed and accordingly no provision for any liability has been made.

10 Post balance sheet events

Since 30 September 1992, Target has opened a factory in Crécy, France.

E Statements of cash flows

The cash flow statements for each of the three years ended 30 September 1992 are as follows:

	Notes	*Year ended 30 September*		
		1990 £000s	*1991 £000s*	*1992 £000s*
OPERATING ACTIVITIES:				
Net cash inflow from operating activities	1	601	907	1,164
RETURNS ON INVESTMENT AND SERVICING OF FINANCE:				
Interest received		2	2	3
Interest paid		(42)	(20)	(10)
Dividends paid		(100)	(110)	(120)
Net cash (outflow) from returns on investment and servicing of finance		(140)	(128)	(127)
TAX:				
UK corporation tax paid		(285)	(506)	(459)
INVESTING ACTIVITIES:				
Purchase of tangible fixed assets		(587)	(128)	(341)
Sale of investment property		(151)	–	–
Net cash outflow from investing activities		(436)	(128)	(341)

NET CASH INFLOW/ (OUTFLOW) BEFORE FINANCING		(260)	145	237
FINANCING				
Repayment of loan		(20)	(38)	(2)
Long term loan		150	–	–
Net cash inflow/(outflow) from financing		130	(38)	(2)
INCREASE (DECREASE) IN CASH AND CASH EQUIVALENTS	2	(130)	107	235

Notes

1   Reconciliation of operating profit to net cash flow from operating activities:

	Year ended 30 September		
	1990 £000s	1991 £000s	1992 £000s
Operating profit	807	949	993
Other income	5	7	5
Depreciation	157	168	212
(Increase) in stocks	(207)	(20)	(23)
(Increase) in debtors	(148)	(120)	(55)
Increase/(Decrease) in creditors	(13)	(77)	32
Net cash flow from operating activities	601	907	1,164

2   Analysis of changes in cash and cash equivalents

Cash balance at beginning of year	130	–	107
Net cash (outflow)/inflow	(130)	107	235
Cash balance at end of year	–	107	342

Yours faithfully

Profit & Loss
Chartered Accountants

APPENDIX II

Pro forma statement of net assets of the enlarged group

An illustrative pro forma consolidated statement of net assets of the enlarged group is set out below. The figures are extracted from the audited consolidated balance sheet of Purchaser PLC and its subsidiaries at 31 December 1991 and the balance sheet of Target at 30 September 1992 as shown in the Accountants' Report in Appendix I of this document.

	Purchaser PLC £000	Target £000	Adjustment £000	Enlarged group pro forma £000
Fixed assets				
Tangible assets	18,309	1,705	—	20,014
Investments	1,441	—	—	1,441
	19,750	1,705	—	21,455
Current assets				
Stocks	2,290	475	—	2,765
Debtors	4,826	845	—	5,671
Investments	613	—	—	613
Cash at bank and in hand	302	342	—	644
	8,031	1,662	—	9,693
Creditors—amounts falling due within one year				
Finance debt	1,185	40	12,000	13,225
Other creditors	4,113	775	—	4,888
	5,298	815	12,000	18,113
Net current assets (liabilities)	2,733	847	(12,000)	(8,420)
Total assets less current liabilities	22,483	3,552	(12,000)	13,035
Creditors—amounts falling due after more than one year				
Finance debt	4,283	150	—	4,433
Other creditors	1,777	—	—	1,777
Provisions for liabilities and charges	657	352	—	1,009
Net assets	15,766	2050	(12,000)	5,816

Notes

1 No adjustment has been made for profits earned by either Purchaser PLC or Target since the respective dates of the above balance sheets.

2 The pro forma statement of net assets excludes any provision for the expenses of the acquisition.

3 The pro forma assumes that the purchase consideration of £12,000,000 was satisfied in cash.

4 No adjustment has been made to reflect the fair value of Target's net assets acquired. Any goodwill arising on pro forma consolidation has been written off against reserves.

APPENDIX III

General Information

1 As at 30 November 1992 Purchaser and its subsidiaries (including for this purpose Target) had outstanding secured bank indebtedness of £44,500, other secured indebtedness amounting to £48,800 and unsecured indebtedness amounting to £7,320. Save as aforesaid and apart from intra group indebtedness neither Purchaser nor any of its subsidiaries had outstanding any borrowings or indebtedness in the nature of borrowing including loan capital issued or unissued bank loans, bank overdrafts, liabilities under acceptances (other than normal trade bills) or acceptance credits, mortgages, charges, hire purchase or finance lease commitments or guarantees or other material contingent liabilities.

2 Shareholders of Target have given to Purchaser the usual indemnities in respect of liabilities for income tax, corporation tax and inheritance tax.

3 The directors of Purchaser are of the opinion that, taking into account existing facilities (including those available to Target), Purchaser and its subsidiaries (including Target) have adequate working capital for their present requirements.

4 Save as mentioned in this letter, there has been no significant change in the financial or trading position of the Purchaser group since 31 December 1991, being the date to which the last audited accounts of Purchaser were prepared.

5 Neither Purchaser nor any of its subsidiaries is engaged in any litigation or arbitration proceedings which may have or have had during the twelve months preceding the date of this circular a significant effect on the financial position of the Purchaser's group nor are there any such proceedings known to the directors of Purchaser to be pending or threatened against any of such companies.

6 The financial information given in this document in respect of profits for the three years ended 30 September 1992 and assets and liabilities at that date does not constitute statutory accounts of Target within the meaning of the

Companies Act 1985. Statutory accounts of Target for the three years ended 30 September 1992 have been delivered to the Registrar of Companies and unqualified audit reports under s 235 were made in respect of those statutory accounts.

7 Messrs Profit & Loss have given and have not withdrawn their written consent to the inclusion in this circular of their report and references thereto in the form and context in which they are included.

8 Merchant Bank Limited has given and not withdrawn its consent to the inclusion in this circular of its name in the form and context in which it appears.

Directors' and Other Interests

9 The directors of Purchaser have the following interests in the share capital of Purchaser as shown in the register of directors' interests as required to be entered in the register referred to in the Companies Act 1985, s 325 (or which have been notified to Purchaser pursuant to the Companies Act 1985, ss 324 or 328).

	Shares	
	Beneficial	*Non-Beneficial*
R Hood	28,500	4,000
F Tuck	10,000	–
W Scarlett	–	12,500

The directors of Purchaser are not aware of any interest in the share capital of Purchaser of any person connected with them, within the meaning of the Companies Act 1985, s 346.

Save for the interest in 3.8 per cent of the issued share capital of Purchaser notified by Richard King PLC, the directors of Purchaser are not aware of any interests, direct or indirect, in 3 per cent or more of the issued share capital of Purchaser.

10 There will be no variation in the emoluments of any of the directors of Purchaser arising from the acquisition of Target other than such as may arise under Mr R Hood's service contract with Purchaser dated 12 January 1990 under which he receives an annual commission of 0.5 per cent of the pre-tax profits of Purchaser and its subsidiaries.

11 Apart from the acquisition of M Marion & Sons Limited (details of which were sent to shareholders on 17 August 1991) none of the directors of Purchaser has had any interest in transactions which are or were unusual in their nature or conditions or significant to the business of the Purchaser group and which were effected since 1 January 1991 or which were effected during an earlier period and remain in any respect outstanding or unperformed.

12 There has been no variation in the service contracts of the directors of

Purchaser with Purchaser or any of its subsidiaries since 1 April 1992 (the date of the notice convening Purchaser's last annual general meeting).

Material Contracts

13 Save as mentioned in this letter, no material contracts other than the following have been entered into by Purchaser or its subsidiaries (including Target) otherwise than in the ordinary course of business during the two years preceding the date of this letter:

(i) an agreement dated 1 April 1991 for the acquisition of F Tuck & Sons Limited from Mr F Tuck and members of his family for £1,185,000; and

(ii) an agreement dated 17 July 1991 for the acquisition of M Marion & Sons Limited from Miss M Marion for £3,200,000 in cash.

Details of these contracts were sent to shareholders on 1 May 1991 and 17 August 1991 respectively.

Documents for Inspection

14 Copies of the following documents will be available for inspection at the offices of Coke & Littleton, 1 Moor Alley, London, EC3L 2FL, and the registered office of Purchaser on weekdays (Saturdays and public holidays excepted) during usual business hours up to and including 31 December 1992:

(i) memorandum and articles of association of each of Purchaser and Target;

(ii) the audited consolidated accounts of the Purchaser's group for the two years ended 31 December 1991;

(iii) the audited accounts of Target for the two years ended 30 September 1992;

(iv) the agreement for the acquisition of Target;

(v) the report of Messrs Profit & Loss set out in Appendix I together with the Statement of adjustments relating thereto, and their written consent to the inclusion of their report in this circular;

(vi) the written consent of Merchant Bank Limited;

(vii) the contracts referred to in paragraph 11 above together with the circulars from Purchaser to shareholders giving information relating to those contracts; and

(viii) the service agreements of the directors of Purchaser and the service agreements of Mr Feather and Mr Bow referred to above.

PURCHASER PLC

Notice of Extraordinary General Meeting

Notice is hereby given that an extraordinary general meeting of Purchaser PLC will be held at Grove House, Sherwood Gardens, Nottingham NX2

3LZ on Thursday, 31 December 1992 at 10.00am for the purpose of considering and, if thought fit, passing the following resolution:

THAT the acquisition by the company of the entire issued share capital of Target Limited substantially upon the terms and subject to the conditions set out or referred to in the circular dated 15 December 1992 from the chairman to the shareholders of the company be and is hereby approved and the directors be and they are hereby authorised to take all such actions as they consider necessary or appropriate to implement such acquisition and to waive, amend, vary, revise or extend any of such terms and conditions as they shall think fit.

15 December 1992   By order of the Board

Registered Office
Grove House
Sherwood Gardens   M Marion
Nottingham NX2 3LZ   Secretary

Note
A member entitled to attend and vote at the meeting is entitled to appoint one or more proxies to attend and, on a poll, vote instead to him. A proxy need not be a member of the company. The appointment of a proxy does not preclude a member from attending and voting at the meeting.

OUTLINE CHECKLIST

1 Consents and Approvals

1.1 Does the acquisition require any consent from creditors or vendors of target (p 20)?
1.2 If consideration is shares, is it necessary to increase purchaser's capital and is any consent needed to issue shares (eg under purchaser's articles, loan stock trust deeds, etc) (p 20)?
1.3 Is consent of purchaser's, or vendor's shareholders required (p 20)?
1.4 If vendor or purchaser (or the holding company of either) is listed, what are the London Stock Exchange requirements (p 138)? Does the transaction involve a sale to or by a director or former director such that there may be a requirement for shareholder approval under Class 4 or Companies Act 1985, s 320?
1.5 Does the target have any special qualification requiring third party consent to a change in control (p 22)?
1.6 If target is technically public (or has had its shares listed or issued on prospectus within the last ten years), can dispensation from the City Panel be obtained (p 2)?
1.7 Is clearance required under the Taxation of Chargeable Gains Act 1992, s 138 (p 175), or under the Income and Corporation Taxes Act 1988, ss 707 (p 182) s 765 (p 187) or 776 (p 186)?.

1.8   Are there any European or restrictive trade practices implications (p 26)?
1.9   Does the acquisition fall within the criteria of the Fair Trading Act 1973, s 64 (p 32)?
1.10   Are there any overseas subsidiaries where local consents may be required? Is advice on overseas laws required?
1.11   Is any shareholders' meeting of the target necessary, to approve any matter or to modify any pre-emption provision in its articles?

2 Information

2.1   Full company search against vendor, target and target's subsidiaries (p 100). Winding up search against target and corporate vendors; bankruptcy only search of Land Charges Register against individual vendors (p 261).
2.2   Particulars of share capital, names of registered holders and beneficial owners and details of any option scheme or arrangement relating to shares.
2.3   Memorandum and Articles.
2.4   List of directors.
2.5   Latest report and accounts.
2.6   Accountants' Report.
2.7   Details of all borrowing and charges.
2.8   Details of properties.
2.9   Details of guarantees given by or on behalf of the target.
2.10   Details of any intellectual property owned by the target.
2.11   Copies of material contracts.
2.12   Pensions questionnaire (p 89).
2.13   Other information regarded as important by purchaser.

3 Taxation

3.1   Are there any special reliefs available to the vendors (eg roll-over relief, retirement relief, etc) or are they liable to be subject to any special charge (p 166)?
3.2   Is the target a close company (p 213)?
3.3   Is the target a member of a group (p 193)?
3.4   Does the target have allowable losses (p 208)?
3.5   Are there any inheritance tax implications (p 220)?
3.6   How much stamp duty/stamp duty reserve tax will be payable (p 189)?

4 Preparation of the Agreement

4.1   If the target's shares are widely held, should the acquisition be by way of offer under the Financial Services Act 1986 (Investment Advertisements) (Exemptions) (No 2) Order 1988 (SI No 716) (p 505)? Will that order apply?
4.2   If the consideration for the acquisition is shares in the purchaser, what

are the rights attached to the consideration shares in particular with regard to entitlement to dividend? What are the provisions in the purchaser's articles with regard eg to apportionment of dividends?

4.3 If the purchaser's shares are listed, will listing particulars need to be prepared (p 138)? Will ABI guidelines require clawback to be available to existing shareholders (p 6)?

4.4 Will all the target's directors retire? Are there to be any service agreements?

4.5 Will the target's auditors change at completion?

4.6 Is the target's title to its property to be investigated or is a certificate to be obtained (p 116)?

4.7 Should completion be conditional upon the obtaining of any necessary consent or approval?

4.8 What special warranties are required?

4.9 Are there any specific matters with regard to taxation (eg continuation of group relief arrangements) which ought to be incorporated in the sale agreement?

4.10 Are there loans by the vendors to the target to be repaid on completion? Are any guarantees given by the vendors on behalf of the target to be released?

4.11 Is the target entering into any transaction as part of the sale arrangements? Are there financial assistance implications under the Companies Act 1985, s 151 (p 37)?

4.12 If the purchaser's shares form part of the consideration, should there be restrictions on their disposal?

4.13 Are completion accounts required?

4.14 Are any limitations on the vendor's liability under warranties appropriate?

4.15 Do the vendors have any special characteristics which require consideration (are they trustees, liquidators or receivers?) (p 244)?

5 Accounting

5.1 Does any accountants' report recommend special warranties be taken? Are there disclosed contingencies which should be excluded from the transaction?

5.2 What will be the accounting treatment of the acquisition?

5.3 If shares are to be issued as consideration, will merger relief be available under the Companies Act 1985, s 131 (p 95)?

6 Procedure

6.1 Title investigation (p 116).

6.2 Investigation of funding of pension scheme (Chapter 7).

6.3 Preparation and agreement of contracts.

6.4 Preparation and agreement of disclosure letter.

6.5 Submission of proof circular and any temporary documents of title to consideration shares for London Stock Exchange approval (if applicable).

6.6 Exchange of contracts (with press release if desired or required by the London Stock Exchange) (p 141).
6.7 Despatch of circular (if shareholder consent required).
6.8 Preparation and agreement of ancillary documents for completion.
6.9 Application for listing of consideration shares (if applicable).
6.10 Completion.
6.11 Despatch of circular (if Class 1).
6.12 Filing at Companies Registration Office.
6.13 Stamp transfers.

Index